Logical Reasoning

Logical Reasoning

Bradley H. Dowden

California State University
Sacramento

Wadsworth Publishing Company

Belmont, California
A Division of Wadsworth, Inc.

Philosophy Editor: Kenneth King
Editorial Assistant: Gay Meixel
Production: Del Mar Associates
Text and Cover Designer: Stuart Paterson/Image House
Print Buyer: Karen Hunt
Copy Editor: Jackie Estrada
Technical Illustrator: Kristi Mendola
Cover: The Image Bank/West/Antonio © 1992
Signing Representative: Robin O'Neill
Compositor: Thompson Type, Inc.
Printer: Arcata Graphics/Fairfield

Credits continue on page A-89.

1 2 3 4 5 6 7 8 9 10—97 96 95 94 93

Library of Congress Cataloging in Publication Data
Dowden, Bradley Harris.
    Logical reasoning/by Bradley H. Dowden.
        p.   cm.
    Includes bibliographical references and index.
    ISBN 0-534-17688-7 (alk. paper)
    1. Critical thinking.   2. Logic.   I. Title.
BC177.D64   1993
160—dc20   92-8349
                                        CIP

Preface

There are more cells in one person's brain than there are people on Earth. Putting more of our students' cells to work thinking critically is our goal, but we are often less than happy with the textbooks available for doing so. Some books overemphasize formal logic; others are weak on improving writing skills; still others are dry, turning off students who sign up for a critical thinking course only because it meets a requirement. This textbook tries to overcome these and other problems. The book was designed to improve an undergraduate's ability to penetrate right to the heart of other people's ideas — to follow their reasoning and detect any errors. It is also designed to help students generate their own ideas — to argue, to explain, and to communicate effectively, patching up any flaws in advance. It tries to teach students to write so their readers don't need seatbelts to follow the hairpin turns in their reasoning processes. Other books are designed to do this, too, so what is special about this one?

Unique Features

Active Reading Approach. The book's focus is not solely on critical thinking as a passive, skeptical eye applied to someone else's argument. It requires students to be active. First, it requires active reading. Within each chapter the students are stopped about a dozen times and asked a question, called a Concept Check, about what they've just read. Students are encouraged to consider the question, then to look at the answer and its accompanying explanation, and only then to read on. The book also requires more active participation in answering the end-of-chapter exercises. For example, in addition to the usual exercises along the lines of "Spot the straw man in this passage," the book recommends unusual exercises such as "Create an example of the straw man fallacy in reaction to this passage."

Adequate Emphasis on Rigor. Some critical thinking courses offer a heavy dose of Venn diagrams, truth tables, and simple proofs in propositional logic. Newer courses may teach electronic circuit diagrams and some computer programming. This book is written by an ex-programmer whose Ph.D. dissertation was on symbolic logic but who then converted to the other side — the side that says students in critical thinking courses do need to appreciate rigor, but they have a greater need to learn to summarize an argument contained within a newspaper editorial, to detect where vagueness is an obstacle to communication, to uncover hidden assumptions, to create a counterargument, and to write a coherent and convincing argumentative essay. Too much attention to rigor will lead to rigor mortis. This book reflects that philosophy.

Focus on Writing Skills. High school writing instructors have enough of a problem teaching the basics of writing. They have little time left either for teaching critical thinking or for testing whether students' critical thinking skills transfer to their writing. This book was designed from the beginning to teach critical thinking directly while promoting its transference to writing. Training about writing skills is integrated throughout the book and is not stuffed into one chapter. There are many innovative writing assignments, which are indicated by a special symbol in the end-of-chapter exercises. The book provides opportunities for improving writing while permitting instructors to spend as much or as little time on this task as they desire.

Emphasis on Special Topics. This book gives special emphasis to the following topics: Who has the burden of proof at a particular point during a controversy? How do a contradiction, a counterexample, and a refutation differ? Is this particular appeal to authority sufficient to make that particular point? What are the successful techniques used by advertisers and politicians to encourage us to reason illogically? How does a logical reasoner decide whom to vote for? What do you look for to determine whether a scientific experiment is well designed? In this book students are frequently required to create an argument for the opposite side of an argument they agree with. Also, students must evaluate arguments whose conclusions they definitely will agree with but whose reasons do not make a good case for that conclusion.

Strong Student Interest. The book introduces the reader to the more entertaining material early on. The difficult details of argument anatomy are placed in later chapters, while the early chapters discuss con games, propaganda, and easy-to-recognize fallacies. The notion of a simple argument is defined to be a set of reasons presented with the intention of promoting belief in a conclusion, but the arguments used in the early chapters contain ample premise indicators and conclusion indicators and few significant implicit premises so that the reader's attention can be drawn to other topics. Also, this book is more careful than most to explain how being logical makes a helpful difference in the real world; and, for most of the major points, the book provides more examples than do other books. Another technique used to arouse the students' interest is to explore what logical techniques, and violations of techniques, are used to create jokes. Finally, the book does not take the reader to a wondrous land "where troubles melt like lemon drops away above the chimney tops." Instead, the reasoning situations used in the book are interesting enough for students to care about them, and the book sticks to examples that the students will consider to be relevant to their education, if not to their immediate personal lives.

Light-Hearted Tone. The book tries to improve on the somber tone of informal logic and critical thinking books. Too many of the ones I've read are as lively as a slug on Valium.

Unique Instructor's Manual

In addition to answering the exercises that are unanswered in this book, the accompanying instructor's manual offers hundreds of new exercises, plus suggestions for in-class projects requiring students to work in small groups, background information about topics and persons mentioned in each chapter, and a considerable amount of new material that can be added to lectures — related topics that could be introduced, alternative methods and orders of presenting topics, and techniques to spark classroom discussion. Multiple-choice test items are at the end of each chapter and are also available on disk for IBM and Macintosh computers.

If you have suggestions, large or small, for how to improve the next edition, I'd be happy to hear from you.

Acknowledgments

The following friends and colleagues deserve thanks for their help and encouragement with this project: Clifford Anderson, Hellan Roth Dowden, Louise Dowden, Robert Foreman, Richard Gould, Kenneth King, Marjorie Lee, Elizabeth Perry, Heidi Wackerli, Perry Weddle, Tiffany Whetstone, and the following reviewers: David Adams, California State Polytechnic University; Stanley Baronett, Jr., University of Nevada–Las Vegas; Shirley J. Bell, University of Arkansas at Monticello; Phyllis Berger, Diablo Valley College; Kevin Galvin, East Los Angeles College; Jacquelyn Ann Kegley, California State University–Bakersfield; Darryl Mehring, University of Colorado at Denver; Dean J. Nelson, Dutchess Community College; James E. Parejko, Chicago State University; Robert Sessions, Kirkwood Community College; and Stephanie Tucker, California State University — Sacramento. Thinking and writing about logical reasoning has been enjoyable for me, but special thanks go to my children, Joshua, 8, and Justine, 3, for comic relief during the months of writing. This book is dedicated to them.

Brad Dowden
California State University
Sacramento, California

Contents

CHAPTER 1

Making Reasonable Choices 1

Facing a Decision 2
Advice for Reasoning Logically 4
Examples of Good Reasoning 11
What Is an Argument? 13
Review and Writing Exercises 18

CHAPTER 2

Defending Against
Deception 20

Deception Is All Around Us 20
Exaggeration and Lying 21
Telling Only Half the Truth 25
Telling the Truth, While Still
   Misleading 30
Saying Little with Lots of Words 31
Persuading Without Reasons 32
Deceiving with Loaded
   Language 33
Review and Writing Exercises 38

CHAPTER 3

Obstacles to Better
Communication 41

Not Realizing What You Are
   Saying 41
Abusing Rules of Grammar and
   Semantics 43
Using Euphemisms 46
Making Unintended Innuendos 48
Disobeying Rules of Discourse 50
Review and Writing Exercises 52

CHAPTER 4

Writing with the Appropriate
Precision 55

Being Ambiguous 55
*Context and Background
   Knowledge 56*
Translation by Machine 59
Semantic Disagreements 61
Equivocation 62
Being Too Vague 63

Being Too General 65
Being Pseudoprecise 66
Improper Operationalization 70
Review and Writing Exercises 76

CHAPTER 5

Sticking to the Issue and Treating It Fairly 85

Who Has the Burden of Proof? 85
Diverting Attention from
    the Issue 87
Covering Up the Reasons That Favor
    Your Opponent's Position 91
Relating the Argument to
    the Issue 92
Review and Writing Exercises 97

CHAPTER 6

Detecting Fallacies 107

Ad Hominem (Attack on the
    Reasoner) 107
Straw Man Fallacy 108
The False Dilemma Fallacy 110
The Fallacy of Faulty
    Comparison 113
Fallacious Appeal to Authority 115
*Assessing the Credibility of Sources
    and Experts 116*
Spotting an Authority's Bias 120
The Genetic Fallacy 122
Non Sequitur 123
Review and Writing Exercises 128

CHAPTER 7

Argumentative Writing 135

Describing, Explaining, and
    Arguing 135

How Arguments Differ from
    Explanations 137
Writing with Precision and to Your
    Audience 140
Improving the Structure of Your
    Writing 141
The Introduction 142
The Middle 143
The Ending 144
Digressions 144
Improving the Style of Your
    Writing 149
Creating an Argument to Prove Your
    Conclusion 151
Creating Counterarguments 154
Criticism, Counterargument, and
    Revision 156
Review and Writing Exercises 165

CHAPTER 8

Evaluating Unusual Statements and Creating Good Explanations 173

The Principle of Fidelity 173
When Should We Accept Unusual
    Statements? 175
Assessing a Source's Credibility 176
Seeking Second Opinions 178
Suspending Belief 179
Getting Solid Information About
    Whom to Vote For 181
Criteria for Creating Good
    Explanations 185
Review and Writing Exercises 191

CHAPTER 9

Consistency and Inconsistency 198

Recognizing Inconsistency and
    Contradiction 198

Identifying Self-Contradiction and
 Oxymorons 200
Noting Inconsistency with
 Presuppositions 203
Refuting General Statements by
 Finding Counterexamples 205
Resolving Inconsistencies 208
Review and Writing Exercises 213

CHAPTER 10

Does the Conclusion Follow from the Premises? 222

Implying with Certainty Versus with
 Probability 222
Distinguishing Deduction from
 Induction 227
Drawing Conclusions from Large
 Passages and Texts 232
Review and Writing Exercises 235

CHAPTER 11

Implicit Premises, Argument Structure, and Diagrams 245

Premise Indicators and Conclusion
 Indicators 245
Rewriting Arguments in Standard
 Form 248
Conditionals and the Logic of the
 Word *If* 249
Locating Unstated Conclusions 251
Uncovering Implicit Premises 252
Detecting Obscure
 Argumentation 255
Multiple Arguments and
 Subarguments 258
Diagraming Argumentation 260
Review and Writing Exercises 269

CHAPTER 12

Induction: Analogies and Statistical Reasoning 284

Varieties of Inductive
 Arguments 284
Arguments from Authority 285
Induction by Analogy 287
Appealing to a Typical Example 291
Induction from the Past to the
 Future 292
Generalizing from a Sample 295
Random Sample 297
Sample Size 301
Sample Diversity 302
Stratified Samples 303
Statistical Significance 305
Designing a Test 307
*Obstacles to Collecting Reliable
 Data* 309
Induction from the General to the
 Specific 310
Review and Writing Exercises 315

CHAPTER 13

Reasoning About Causes and Their Effects 327

Correlations 327
*Correlations Among
 Characteristics* 330
Significant Correlations 332
Causal Claims 333
Inference from Correlation to
 Causation 335
Diagraming Causal Relationships 337
*Criteria for Assessing
 Correlations* 338
Creating and Assessing Alternative
 Explanations 340

*The Scientific Method for Uncovering the
    Truth 341*
Some Case Studies and Examples 342
Review and Writing Exercises 350

CHAPTER 14
. . . .

Logical Reasoning in
Science 360

. . . .

Reviewing the Principles of Scientific
    Reasoning 360
Testability, Accuracy, and Precision 362
Reliability of Scientific Reporting 363
*Descriptions, Explanations, and
    Arguments 365*
Good Evidence 366
*A Cautious Approach with an Open
    Mind 366*
*Discovering Causes, Creating Explanations,
    and Solving Problems 368*
Confirming by Testing 369
Aiming to Disconfirm 370
Superstition 371
Alternative Explanations 379
Creating and Testing Scientific
    Explanations 382
*Probabilistic and Deterministic
    Explanations 382*
*Fruitful and Unfruitful
    Explanations 384*
Designing a Scientific Test 385
*Retaining Hypotheses Despite Negative Test
    Results 386*
*Three Conditions for a Well-Designed
    Test 388*
Deducing Predictions to Be Tested 389
Detecting Pseudoscience 391
Paradigms and Possible Causes 393
Review and Writing Exercises 399

APPENDIX A
. . . .

A List of Fallacies with
Examples A-1

APPENDIX B
. . . .

Creating Helpful
Definitions A-11

. . . .

Different Definitions for Different
    Purposes A-11
How to Avoid Errors in Creating
    Definitions A-12
Review and Writing Exercises A-16

APPENDIX C
. . . .

Logical Form and Sentential
Logic A-19

. . . .

Logical Equivalence A-19
Logical Forms of Statements and
    Arguments A-21
The Logic of *Not* A-23
The Logic of *And* A-24
The Logic of *Or* A-25
The Logic of *If-Then* A-26
Necessary and Sufficient
    Conditions A-31
The Logic of *Only, Only If,* and
    Unless A-32
Review Exercises A-35

APPENDIX D
. . . .
Aristotelian Logic and Venn
Diagrams   A-42

. . . .

Aristotle's Logic of Classes   A-42
Using Venn Diagrams to Test for
    Invalidity   A-45
The Logic of *Only* in Class
    Logic   A-54
Review Exercises   A-57

. . . .
Answers to Selected Exercises   A-63
Endnotes   A-77
Index   A-82
Credits   A-89

Logical Reasoning

Making Reasonable Choices

The goal of this book is to improve your logical-reasoning abilities. You are reasoning whenever you are solving problems, making decisions, evaluating whether a statement is true, assessing the quality of information, or arguing about issues. Good-quality reasoning is called *logical reasoning*. Logical reasoning is a skill that can be learned and improved. It is not a case of "Either you're naturally good at logical reasoning, or you'll never be any good." Rather, everyone is capable of reasoning well and everyone is capable of improvement. Logical reasoning is also called *critical thinking*. The opposite of logical reasoning is uncritical thinking, examples of which are fuzzy thinking, confused thinking, acquiring beliefs that have no good reasons to back them up, and narrowly thinking about a problem without bringing in the most relevant information. For example, uncritical thinkers seeking gorilla suits first look under "Gorillas" in the Yellow Pages.

Your logical-reasoning skills are a complex weave of abilities that help you get someone's point, explain a complicated idea, generate reasons for your viewpoints, evaluate the reasons given by others, decide what or what not to do, decide what information to accept or reject, see the pros as well as the cons, and so forth.

This chapter explains what it means to be logical—that is, to use logical reasoning. It demonstrates the usefulness of logical reasoning as a means to making more effective decisions about your own life—decisions about what to believe and decisions about what to do. This chapter begins a systematic program of study of all the major topics regarding logical reasoning. Along the way, the book focuses on developing the following five skills: (1) writing logically, (2) detecting inconsistency and lack of clarity in a group of statements, (3) spotting issues and arguments, (4) detecting and avoiding fallacies (reasoning errors), and (5) generating and improving arguments and explanations.

Facing a Decision

Imagine this situation. You are on a four-day backpacking trip in a national wilderness area with your friends Juanita and Emilio. The summer weather's great, the scenery is exotic, and you've been having a good time. Yesterday you drove several hours into the area and parked in the main parking lot. Then you hiked six hours to your present campsite. The three of you carried all your food, water, sleeping bags, and tents. Last night you discovered that somebody had accidentally cracked the large water container. Now you are stuck with no water. Although there is a small stream nearby, you remember that the packets of water-sterilization tablets are in the pocket of your other coat — the one you left at home at the last minute. The three of you are thirsty and have only dehydrated food left, except for four apples. You wish you had bothered to haul in that twelve-pack of Dr. Pepper you decided to leave in the trunk.

What do you do? You could yell, but that is unlikely to help; you haven't seen any other hikers since the trip began. You try it, but all you get is an echo. You briefly think about snow, but realize there isn't any. Then Emilio has an idea: Boil the water from the stream. When it cools, you could drink it and make breakfast and continue with your good times. Juanita mentions seeing a sign back in the parking lot: "Warning, *Giardia* has been found in some streams in the area. Sorry, we are out of sterilization tablets." "*Giardia* is a microorganism that causes a disease," she says. You and Emilio have never heard of it. Emilio says he's willing to bet that boiling the water will kill the critters. "Besides," he says, "our stream might not have giardia. I'll take the first drink." Juanita winces. "No way," she says. "Let's just pack up and go home." When you ask her why, she explains that a friend of hers got giardiasis and had a bad experience with it. She doesn't want to risk having the same experience. When you hear the details, you understand why. The symptoms are chronic diarrhea, abdominal cramps, bloating, fatigue, and loss of weight. "Also," she says, "the signs about *Giardia* are probably posted because the organisms cannot be killed by boiling." However, she admits that she isn't sure of her interpretation, and she agrees with Emilio that the nearby stream might not even contain *Giardia*, so she agrees to do whatever the majority wants. She adds that the three of you might get lucky while you are hiking out and meet someone who can help, maybe a hiker who knows more about *Giardia* or has extra water-sterilization tablets. Then again, you might not be so lucky; you didn't pass anybody on the way in.

Emilio agrees to go along with the majority decision, too. He wants to stay, but not by himself. Still, he isn't convinced by Juanita's reasons. "Look," he says, "if the stream were poisonous, everything in it would look dead. There are water spiders and plants in the stream. It's no death trap."

At this point you are faced with one of life's little decisions: What do you do about the water situation? Go or stay? Someone else might make this decision by flipping a coin. A logical reasoner is more rational.

A first step in logical reasoning is often to get some good advice. You already have some advice, but how do you decide whether it's any good? There is one best way to identify good advice: It can be backed up with good reasons. Juanita's advice to go back home is backed up by various reasons: (1) the consequences of getting giardiasis are pretty bad, and (2) the posted signs probably indicate that boiling won't work. Unfortunately, she is not sure about the boiling. So the burden falls on your shoulders. Can *you* back up her reasoning even if she can't? Or can you show that her reasoning isn't any good?

One way to back up a statement is to point out that the person making it is an expert. So you think about Juanita's and Emilio's credentials. Let's see—Juanita is a student majoring in psychology, and Emilio is a communications major and works at a pet store. Does that make them authorities on *Giardia* and the safety of drinking water? No. So if you need an expert, you will have to search elsewhere.

But is it worth your trouble to search for more information from an expert? The search will probably require a hike back to the ranger station near the parking lot. Besides, if the expert's advice is to avoid drinking the boiled water unless you have sterilization tablets, then you'll have to hike all the way back to camp to tell the others and then start the process of packing up and hiking out. It would be a lot easier just to follow Juanita's advice to pack up and leave.

So what do you decide to do? Let's say you decide not to search for more advice and to boil the water. You now owe it to Juanita and Emilio to give them the reasons behind your decision. First, you discounted Emilio's remark that if the stream were poisonous then everything in it would look dead. If the stream were poisonous, everything in it could be dying without *looking* dead. Also, you are certain that there are microbes that harm humans but not plants and fish. (Do crabgrass and catfish catch cholera?) Your second reason comes from reconsidering that sign at the ranger station. If nothing works to kill *Giardia*, then you wouldn't even have been allowed into the park or would have been warned in person. The sign said the station is out of sterilization tablets, implying that sterilizing the water will make it safe. Safe in what sense? Sterilizing means to kill or remove all the living organisms, but not necessarily all the harmful chemicals. (If you were to sterilize water containing gasoline, that wouldn't make it safe to drink.) So the problem is definitely the microorganisms. Now surely the rangers know that hikers are apt to try to sterilize water by boiling it. You reason that if boiling wouldn't work, the sign would have said so. Therefore, it is quite likely that boiling *will* do the trick. So the danger of getting a bad disease such as giardiasis is more than offset by the low probability of actually getting the disease.

That's how you have made your decision. Is it a reasonable one? Yes, because it is based on good reasons. Is it the best decision—the one an expert would have made in your place? Yes, the experts do say that stream water will be safe if you boil it. The reason people use water-purification tablets is for convenience; it takes a lot of time for the water to boil and then cool to drinking temperature.[1]

Now let's turn to the principles of logical reasoning that have been used in the situation. The principles, which are the focus of the next section, are neither rules nor recipes; they are simply pieces of advice that must be applied flexibly. They are called "principles" only because it sounds odd to call something "piece of advice eleven" or "thing to do seven."

Advice for Reasoning Logically

All of us use these principles every day, so the following short introduction is just a reminder of what you already know. First, *ask for reasons before accepting a conclusion*, unless you already have good enough reasons. You applied this principle when you asked Juanita why she thought it best to leave. Similarly, if you expect people to accept your own conclusion, then it's your responsibility to give them reasons they can appreciate. Let's examine that last remark. A conclusion backed up by one or more reasons is called an **argument**, even when the reasoner is not being argumentative or disagreeable. So, being logical means that you should *give an argument to support your conclusion* if you expect other people to accept it. In addition, give people arguments they can understand. Don't get overly technical. Otherwise, you might as well be talking gobbledygook. In other words, *tailor your reasons to your audience*. Your goal in giving an argument is to *design your reasons to imply the conclusion*; that is, the conclusion should follow from the reasons given to support it.

■ ············ Concept Check 1* ············ ■

Which of the following three paragraphs contains an argument, as we've just defined that term?

a. *David*: Look what I'm smashing under my foot.
   Sarah: You're worthless. You're a disease.
b. I'm sure Martin Luther King Jr. didn't die during the 1960s, because it says right here in the encyclopedia that he was assassinated in Memphis in 1990.
c. The Republican party began back in the 1850s as a U.S. political party. Abraham Lincoln was the first Republican candidate to win the presidency.

Let's continue with our introduction to the principles of logical reasoning. (There are quite a few more to be uncovered.) For example, in the camping-trip story, you paid attention both to what Juanita said and to what Emilio said, and you wished there was a park ranger nearby to ask about *Giardia*. The underlying principle you applied is to *recognize the value of having more relevant information*. In the camping

---

*Each Concept Check has an answer and an explanation at the end of the chapter. Try to discipline yourself to read and answer these sample exercises before looking up the answer or before reading on. You need not write out the answer; try to answer mentally. The exercises are designed to test your understanding of concepts in the material you've just read. If you can answer the Concept Checks, then you will be ready to tackle the more difficult Review and Writing Exercises at the end of each chapter.

situation, it would not have been irrational to choose to pack up and go home. The point is to make your decision on the basis of a serious attempt to assess the relevant evidence. You did this when you paid attention to probabilities and consequences—you weighed the pros and cons—of going or staying. In short, logical reasoners *weigh the pros and cons*, which means (1) *considering the possible courses of action* (pack up and hike home, stay and boil the water, or hike for help), (2) *looking at the consequences of those various courses of action* (being thirsty, continuing the camping trip, getting a disease), (3) *evaluating the consequences* (being thirsty is a negative, continuing the camping trip is a positive, getting giardiasis would be terrible), and (4) *considering the probabilities that those various consequences will actually occur* (it is 100 percent probable that you won't be thirsty after you drink from the stream, but it is only slightly probable that you'll catch giardiasis if you drink boiled water).

It can be helpful to *delay making important decisions when that is practical*. During the extra time, you will have an opportunity to think through the problem more carefully. You could discover consequences of your decision that you might not have thought of at first. For example, in the camping situation with Emilio and Juanita, you might have quickly agreed to let Emilio taste the water first to see whether it had *Giardia*. Perhaps only later would you have thought about the consequence of his becoming too sick to hike back out of the forest. Would you have been able to carry him?

Here is a second example of logical reasoning that weighs the pros and cons. Imagine that you are in the following situation. A few days ago you promised Emilio you would go to the movies with him this Friday evening. You have every intention of going, but you are considering going with Juanita instead, and telling Emilio you are sick. Doing so would be an *alternative course of action*. Let's weigh the pros and cons of taking the original action or this alternative course of action. (We won't consider other alternative actions, such as asking Emilio whether Juanita can go with the two of you.)

One possible consequence of going only with Juanita is that you would have more fun. It's not that you would have no fun with Emilio; it's just that you believe it would be more fun to go only with Juanita, all other things being equal. Another possible consequence of going with Juanita is that you would *not* have more fun. You estimate that the odds are about 60–40 in favor of more fun if you go with Juanita instead of Emilio. Another possible consequence is that Juanita will at first be flattered that you asked her to go with you.

There is still another possible consequence to consider: You will be breaking your promise to Emilio, which would be morally wrong and thus have a negative value. It wouldn't be as negative as murdering Emilio, but it is clearly negative, and the probability of this consequence is 100 percent; that is, it is certain to occur if you tell Emilio you are sick. In addition, if Emilio finds out, your friendship with him might end. This is also a negative, and one that is likely to occur, although it is not certain. Finally, there is one more consequence worth considering: If Juanita finds out, she will consider you less trustworthy than she originally thought. This is a negative, too. At this point, you cannot think of any other consequences that should be taken into account.

After pondering all this, you realize that it is quite likely that most of the negative consequences will actually occur if you do go with Juanita and that it's only 60 percent likely that you will have more fun with Juanita than with Emilio. So the negatives swamp the positives. You weigh the pros and cons of the two alternatives and decide to keep your promise to Emilio. This is logical reasoning in action.

Reasoning in a logical way means applying the principles of logical reasoning. However, different situations require different applications of the various principles. For example, in a situation where you're playing baseball and a friend yells "Duck!" it is illogical to spend much time searching around for good reasons. The logical thing to do is to duck *right away*. Nevertheless, even in this situation you don't duck without a good reason. You know from previous experience that "Duck" said in a certain tone of voice means that there is a danger to your head that requires lowering it fast and protecting it from a sudden impact. You don't stick your head up and say "Where's the duck?" Similarly, if someone were to run out of Wells Fargo shouting, "Look out, the bank is being robbed," it wouldn't be logical to spend much time wondering what river bank the person is talking about. The point is that logical reasoners *assess what is said in light of the situation*. Be sensitive to the situation. If you happen to know what time it is when someone passes you on the street and asks "Do you know the time?" it is illogical to answer only "Yes." Logical reasoners *don't take people too literally*. This principle of good reasoning is violated in the accompanying cartoon.

FRANK & ERNEST reprinted by permission of NEA, Inc.

Concept Check 2

Ramone's friend says, "Ramone, spy those two white guys on the other side of the street. They look friendly. The blond guy with him looks like he would rip your lungs out just to see what would happen. The other one is just as fierce, and he's carrying the radio I lost yesterday; it's got my sticker on the side."

If Ramone leaves believing that the two guys are friendly because his friend said, "They look friendly," he has violated some advice about logical reasoning. What advice?

a. Reasons should be tailored to the audience.

b. Don't take people too literally.

c. Consider the possible courses of action.

d. Weigh the pros and cons.

You, like everyone else, are curious, so you continually add new beliefs to your old beliefs. There are logical — that is, appropriate — ways of doing this, as well as illogical ones. The goal is to add truths, not falsehoods. For example, you are waiting in the grocery store checkout line and notice the front-page headline "World War II Bomber Discovered Intact on Surface of Moon." You didn't know that, did you? Well, it wouldn't be logical to believe it. Why not? Here are three reasons: (1) Bomber's can't fly to the moon, (2) no one is going to bust the national budget to send one there by rocketship, and (3) there aren't any alien-piloted UFOs that snatch military antiques. The principle behind this logical reasoning is: *Use your background knowledge and common sense in drawing conclusions*. The Calvin and Hobbes cartoon makes this same point.

CALVIN AND HOBBES (1988) Watterson. Dist. by UNIVERSAL PRESS SYNDICATE. Reprinted with permission. All rights reserved.

This cartoon also demonstrates another principle of logical reasoning: *Extraordinary statements require extraordinarily good evidence to back them up*. A bit of charcoal is not extraordinarily good evidence of a UFO landing. Similarly, if I were to say to you, "I met my friend Tiffany Whetstone at the Co-op Grocery yesterday afternoon," you would demand little evidence that this is so. Perhaps the confirming word of a mutual friend would settle any doubts you might have. However, if I were to say to you, "I met my friend Tiffany Whetstone, who has been dead for the last ten years, at the Co-op Grocery yesterday afternoon," you would probably think I was lying or crazy. You certainly would demand extraordinarily good evidence before accepting what I said as true. In this case, even a confirmation by our mutual friend would be insufficient evidence. However, suppose I said, "I met my friend Tiffany Whetstone at the Co-op Grocery yesterday afternoon. She has a wooden leg and had just won two sets yesterday in her doubles tennis match. She is the best player on her tennis team in Antarctica." This statement is not as weird as the one about her being dead for ten years, and it wouldn't take as much to convince you of this truth, if it were true. But confirmation by our mutual friend would still not be good enough evidence.

By not relying on the principles of logical reasoning, some people are apt to make the mistake of believing too easily that there are antique airplanes on the moon, that UFOs have landed in someone's backyard, and that dead friends have come back to life. All these things *might* have happened, but currently available evidence is weak. The only reason to believe these things is that a few people have said they've happened. Since you cannot be confident about their reports, you cannot be confident about concluding that these things have actually happened.

It is a sign of being logical if the degree of confidence you have in your reasons directly affects the degree of confidence you place in the conclusion drawn from those reasons. A person who believes strongly even though the reasons are flimsy is being stubborn or dogmatic. Logical reasoners, on the other hand, follow the principle that *firmer conclusions require better reasons*.

■ ⋯⋯⋯⋯⋯ **Concept Check 3** ⋯⋯⋯⋯⋯ ■

Here are three arguments concerning the death of David's uncle. All three are arguing for the same conclusion — that David's uncle died of a drug overdose. Which of these arguments should be considered the most convincing?

a. David said that his uncle died of a drug overdose, so his uncle must have died of a drug overdose.

b. David's uncle died of a drug overdose because David predicted two years ago that this is how his uncle would die and David has a good track record of making correct predictions.

c. Look, the cororner's report specifically says that David's uncle is dead. Also, everybody in the neighborhood knows that the uncle did drugs every day. Therefore, David's uncle died of a drug overdose.

■ ⋯⋯⋯⋯⋯ **Concept Check 4** ⋯⋯⋯⋯⋯ ■

Suppose that you are considering some major decisions about what direction to take in your life: whether to drop out of college, adopt a new religion, and so on. When, if ever, is the following Jules Feiffer comic strip offering good advice and when, if ever, is it offering bad advice?

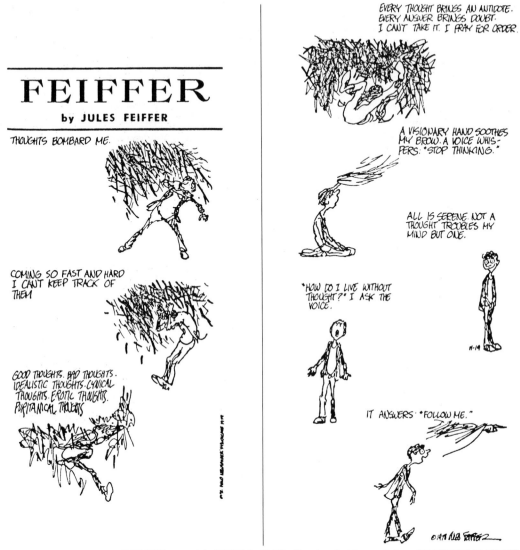

FEIFFER
by JULES FEIFFER

THOUGHTS BOMBARD ME.

COMING SO FAST AND HARD I CAN'T KEEP TRACK OF THEM

GOOD THOUGHTS. BAD THOUGHTS. IDEALISTIC THOUGHTS. CYNICAL THOUGHTS. EROTIC THOUGHTS. PURITANICAL THOUGHTS

EVERY THOUGHT BRINGS AN ANTIDOTE. EVERY ANSWER BRINGS DOUBT. I CAN'T TAKE IT. I PRAY FOR ORDER.

A VISIONARY HAND SOOTHES MY BROW. A VOICE WHIS-PERS: "STOP THINKING."

ALL IS SERENE. NOT A THOUGHT TROUBLES MY MIND BUT ONE.

"HOW DO I LIVE WITHOUT THOUGHT?" I ASK THE VOICE.

IT ANSWERS: "FOLLOW ME."

Following the rules of logical reasoning comes more easily to some people than to others. All of us, however, are capable of improvement, and we all should want to improve, because improvement has a yield, a payoff. Being logical isn't the only way to make good decisions. Sometimes good decisions are made by accident; sometimes they are made in illogical ways, such as by following a horoscope. In the long run, however, statistics show that the smart money is on logical reasoners. Logical reasoning pays. When the expert says, "Hey, don't drink that stuff; it could kill you," the logical reasoner will *defer to the expert* and put down the cup. The irrational thinker will think, "Experts have been wrong in the past; I'm drinking anyway."

Everyone knows that the best decisions are based on facts, but how do we go about distinguishing facts from everything else that is said to us? This book provides many helpful hints on this topic. One hint is to avoid accepting inconsistencies; they are a sign of error. We made use of this logical-reasoning principle when we noticed that Juanita's advice to end the camping trip was inconsistent with Emilio's advice to continue it. Simply detecting an inconsistency doesn't reveal whose advice is faulty, but it does tell us that somebody's is. For example, if Dwight Gooden says that the surface of Neptune on average is colder than 200 degrees below zero, and his sister says that it's not that cold, one of the two must be wrong about the facts. We know this even if we don't know the facts about Neptune. So one of the cardinal principles of logical reasoning is: *Be consistent in your own reasoning, and be on the lookout for inconsistency in the reasoning of others*. Here is a definition of inconsistency:

Definition   A group of statements is **inconsistent** if it requires, that is, implies, that some statement be both so and *not* so. Similarly, a group of instructions is inconsistent if together the instructions imply that somebody must both do some one thing and *not* do it. A group of statements is **consistent** if it's not inconsistent.

Statements are inconsistent with each other if you can tell just from their meaning that they can't all be true.

Which of the following, if any, are most likely *not* principles of logical reasoning?

a. Don't accept inconsistent beliefs.
b. You ought to give an argument in defense of what you want another person to believe.
c. The degree of confidence you have in your reasons should affect the degree of confidence you have in your conclusion.

Create two statements about basketball that are inconsistent with each other.

A contradiction is almost, but not quite, the same thing as an inconsistency. The difference isn't important for our purposes, so if you want to call statements "contradictory" instead of "inconsistent," no one will misunderstand you.[2]

Examples of Good Reasoning

So far we've explored the importance of reasoning logically in situations that require a decision—either a decision about what to do or a decision about what to believe. Along the way we've introduced a variety of rules of thumb for good reasoning, which we've called *principles of logical reasoning*. We have examined short examples of good, or logical, reasoning and short examples of bad, or illogical, reasoning. The *Giardia* example was the only long example of good reasoning. What follows is a second long example—one that is slightly more complicated and uses some other especially interesting principles of good reasoning. The scene is a jury room in which jurors are discussing whether Jesse Mayfield is guilty of armed robbery. The State of Alabama, represented by the prosecutor, has charged Mayfield with using a handgun to hold up the All-Night Grocery in downtown Birmingham. Juror Washington Jones begins the dialogue by reasoning about the case presented by the prosecuting district attorney against Mayfield. Another juror, Dr. White, disagrees with what Jones says. Each speaker offers his own argument about which explanation of the defendant's actions is best.

Jones: OK, let's consider what the prosecutor's got here. We know there was a crime, since we can believe the grocery owner's testimony that all the night's receipts are missing. The grocery clerk confirmed his story. She is the lone eyewitness to the crime; there were no others in the store at 2 A.M., when she said the crime was committed. The grocery's videotaping system had been broken all week. The prosecutor has also proved that Mayfield arrived at the grocery that night at about that time. The evidence for that is that the time was on the grocery receipt found in the wastebasket when the police arrested Mayfield at his house that morning. Mayfield matches the general description of the robber given by the clerk at 2:30 A.M., when she talked to the police. So we've got to conclude that Mayfield was in the store at 2 A.M. and that the robbery occurred before 2:30 A.M., probably at 2 A.M. The clerk also stated that the robber ran out of the store and headed into a nearby apartment complex. Mayfield lives in an apartment in the direction she pointed to. A neighbor told the police that Mayfield ran up his apartment's steps some time around 2 or 3 A.M. that night. What else do we know that can be considered as evidence against Mayfield? Let's see. Mayfield has no record of robbery, but he was convicted of minor assault against a neighbor six years ago. Well, that's about it. Does that make the case for the prosecution?

Dr. White: Yes, he's guilty; there's no other explanation for the evidence. I say we vote right now.

Jones: Hold it, Doc. There sure is another explanation, and Mayfield's defense attorney gave it to us. Maybe Mayfield was there all right, just to buy a bottle, but the clerk ripped off her boss after Mayfield left. She could have stashed the cash and called the cops. The whole case against Mayfield hangs on what she alone says. Mayfield says he is innocent but admits being in the store in the early morning to buy whiskey. The prosecutor admitted that none of the stolen money was found, and no gun was found. So all the facts fit that other explanation as well as the prosecution's explanation. Besides, there is an additional reason to suspect the clerk: The defense has shown that she was thrown out of her college sorority for stealing their petty cash. I say the defense attorney has shown that Mayfield could have been framed. Sure, there's some evidence against Mayfield, but not enough.

Dr. White: Mayfield is as guilty as sin. He won't even look the judge or the prosecutor in the eye when they talk to him. Very suspicious. You left that out of the story, Jones. Mayfield's an alcoholic, too. Think of the number of crimes committed by alcoholics. They need that next drink, right? Also, even though he now admits being in the All-Night Grocery that morning, Mayfield lied about being there when he was first arrested, didn't he?

Jones: Yes, but what does that prove? He was arrested with his wife present, which is why he lied about being at the grocery that night. He said she wouldn't let him buy whiskey with her money. Now, about that guilty look. Guilty looks don't make you guilty. I can think of ten reasons why he looks that way. The case against Mayfield isn't proven, at least not beyond a shadow of a doubt. Better that five robbers go free than one innocent person get locked up. What do the rest of you think?

Dr. White: That's just crap! He's guilty. Jones, you can't call that nice young white clerk a liar. It's Mayfield who's the liar!

If this is supposed to be an example of good reasoning, what is so good about it? First, Jones uses the following principle of logical reasoning when he is explaining the facts of the robbery case: *Explanations should fit all the relevant facts.* Second, Jones demonstrates good reasoning in that he understands his responsibility to back up his conclusion: that the case against Mayfield isn't proven. Jones backs it up by showing that a second explanation, the frame-up story, fits the facts. In doing so, he listens to the opposition, tries to consider all the evidence, and weighs the pros and cons. By pointing to the defense attorney's explanation of the facts and cautioning his fellow jurors that the DA has not presented enough evidence, Jones uses a key principle of logical reasoning: *Your opponent's explanation is less believable if you can show that there are alternative explanations that haven't been ruled out.* Jones demonstrates an understanding of the fact that weaker reasons require a more cautious conclusion; he doesn't rush to judgment. He is careful to follow this principle: *Don't draw a conclusion until you've gotten enough evidence.* Jones obeys another principle of logical reasoning: *Stick to the subject.* White goes off on a tangent, talking about alcoholism and whether Mayfield looked the judge and DA in the eye. The comment about the clerk being white is also irrelevant, as well as racist. On the other hand, all of Jones's remarks are relevant.

What Is an Argument?

There is much more that could be said regarding the reasoning in this robbery case, and we will return to the principles in later chapters. But for now, let's return to the important notion of argumentation. As previously mentioned, the word *argument* has more than one meaning. In this book it will normally mean "to support a conclusion by giving one or more reasons." Accordingly, it takes only one person to have an argument, not two. Saying that two people are "in an argument" means that there are at least two arguments, not one. Each person has his or her own argument — namely, the person's own reasons plus the conclusion those reasons are meant to support. In short, *our* word *argument* is a technical term with a more precise meaning than it has in ordinary conversation.

■ .... Concept Check 7 .... ■

Describe the following numbered passages by placing the appropriate letter to the left of each passage number.

a. Simply a claim with no reasons given to back it up.
b. An argument using bad reasons.
c. An argument using good reasons (assuming that the arguer is being truthful).
d. None of the above.

　1. What time does the movie start?
　2. This card can save you a lot of money.
　3. Vote Democratic in the next election. Doing so will solve almost all the world's problems.
　4. John Adams was the second president of the United States. My history professor said so, and I checked it in the encyclopedia.

■ .... Concept Check 8 .... ■

Pick the one best choice for the conclusion of Sanderson's argument in the following disagreement.

Sanderson: Do you realize just what sort of news you get on a half-hour American TV news program?
Harris: Yes, newsy news. What do you mean?
Sanderson: Brief news, that's what.

Harris: Brief news? Are you talking boxer shorts?

Sanderson: Ha! Look at a time breakdown of the average half-hour news program broadcast on American TV. It is nine minutes of news!

Harris: What's the rest?

Sanderson: Eleven minutes of commercials, six of sports, and four of weather. You can't do much in nine minutes. I say nine is not enough if you are going to call it the "news." What do you think?

Harris: It is enough for me. News can be boring. Besides, if the American public didn't like it, they wouldn't watch it.

Sanderson: Now that's an interesting but ridiculous comment. But I've got to go now; let's talk again after lunch.

a. If the American public didn't like brief TV news, they wouldn't watch it.

b. Do you realize just what sort of news you get in a half-hour American TV news program?

c. That's an interesting but ridiculous comment [about the American public's taste].

d. There is not enough news on a thirty-minute TV news program in America.

e. An average half-hour American TV news program is eleven minutes of commercials, nine of news, six of sports, and four of weather.

After choosing Sanderson's conclusion from the above list, comment on the quality of his argument for that conclusion.

Arguments are usually given to help settle an issue. The issue is whatever is in dispute. The issue is what is being argued for or against. When two people are "in an argument," they are divided on the issue.

It is important to be able to detect arguments when they do occur, but this is not always easy to do. Sometimes the start of a conclusion is indicated by the word *therefore*, *so*, or *thus*. In addition to these *conclusion indicators*, the terms *because* and *suppose that* signal that a reason is coming. They are two *reason indicators*. Often, however, arguers are not so helpful, and we readers and listeners have to recognize an argument without these **indicator terms**.

Reasoners often leave parts of their reasoning unstated. For example, Emilio left something unsaid when he argued that "if the stream were poisonous, everything in it would look dead. There are water spiders and plants in the stream. It's no death trap." Emilio meant for Juanita and you to assume that the water spiders and plants in the stream are not dead; he just didn't say so explicitly. What is the unstated conclusion you are supposed to draw from the following piece of reasoning about white people and government funding of the space program?

I can't feed my kids, and whitey's on the moon. Rats bit my little sister. Her leg is swelling, and whitey's on the moon. The rent is going up. Drug addicts are moving in, and whitey's on the moon.

The unstated conclusion is that the government's spending priorities need revision; there should be less emphasis on funding the space program and more on doing something about poverty, health, and drug addicts.

Another difficulty in spotting arguments is that they can differ greatly in their structure. Instead of backing up a conclusion by only one package of reasons, an arguer might give a variety of lines of argument for the conclusion. That is, the arguer could produce two or more sets of reasons in support of the conclusion, and might even add why the opposition's argument contains errors. Jones did this. He gave a set of reasons for acquittal by arguing that there is an alternative explanation of all the facts. In addition, he argued that the prosecution's strong reliance on the clerk's testimony is no good because the clerk stole from her sorority. Arguments can have other complexities, too. Often arguers defend one or more of their reasons with reasons for those reasons, and even reasons for those reasons, and so forth. In addition, an arguer may simultaneously argue for several conclusions, or draw a second conclusion from a first conclusion. So the structure of an argument can become quite complex. However, just as molecules are composed of atoms, so complex arguments are composed of "atomic" arguments, each with its own single conclusion and reasons to back it up. Breaking down complex arguments into their simpler elements in this way can make the complicated understandable. Chapter 11 pursues the topic of analyzing complex arguments, but the next chapter explores con games, propaganda, and misleading advertising.

Review of Major Points

Logical reasoning is your guide to good decisions. It is also a guide to sorting out truth from falsehood. This chapter began with several case studies of logical reasoning. It also pointed out some common errors in reasoning. From these examples we were able to extract the following principles of logical reasoning: (1) ask for reasons before accepting a conclusion, (2) give an argument to support your conclusion, (3) tailor reasons to your audience, (4) design your reasons to imply the conclusion, (5) recognize the value of having more relevant information, (6) weigh the pros and cons, (7) consider the possible courses of action, (8) look at the consequences of these various courses of action, (9) evaluate the consequences, (10) consider the probabilities that those various consequences will actually occur, (11) delay making important decisions when practical, (12) assess what is said in light of the situation, (13) don't take people too literally, (14) use your background knowledge and common sense in drawing conclusions, (15) remember that extraordinary statements require extraordinarily good evidence, (16) defer to the expert, (17) remember that firmer conclusions require better reasons, (18) be consistent in your own reasoning, (19) be on the lookout for inconsistency in the reasoning of others, (20) check to see whether explanations fit all the relevant facts, (21) make your opponent's explanation less believable by showing that there are alternative explanations that haven't been ruled out, (22) stick to the subject, and (23) don't draw a conclusion until you've gotten enough evidence.

These principles are merely pieces of advice; they are not rules or recipes. All the points, principles, and problems discussed in this chapter will receive more detailed treatment in later chapters. Those chapters will continue to systematically explore the intricacies of being logical. Although not *all* the logical principles in the world will be introduced in this book, all the most important ones will be. Regarding the problem of whether some are more important than others: not to worry; the relative importance of the principles will become clear as we go along.

Glossary

argument   An argument is a conclusion backed up by one or more reasons.

consistent   Not inconsistent.

indicator term   A conclusion indicator term is a word or phrase in an argument that signals the occurrence of the conclusion; a reason indicator signals a reason.

inconsistent   A group of statements is inconsistent if they require something both to have some characteristic and also not to have it, or if you can tell just from their meaning that they can not all be true.

Answers to Concept Checks

1. Answer (b) is the only argument. The argument's conclusion, that Martin Luther King Jr. didn't die during the 1960s, follows from the reason, even though the reason is based on wrong information. (King actually died in 1968.) One moral to draw from this is that an argument based on wrong information is still an argument. A second moral is that an argument can have just one reason. A third moral is that even though this argument does satisfy the principle that an argument's reasons should imply its conclusion, if those reasons are faulty the argument fails to establish its conclusion. Answer (a) does show two people having a disagreement, but neither one is arguing, because neither is giving reasons for what is said. Answer (c), on the other hand, merely describes the Republican Party.

2. Answer (b) is correct. From what else the friend says, he wasn't serious about the two guys being friendly. He didn't mean for his statements to be taken literally.

3. Answer (a) provides the best reason to believe that David's uncle died of a drug overdose. Although the world has lots of liars in it, we generally take people at their word unless we have a reason to be suspicious. Answers (b) and (c) give worse reasons. Answer (b) asks us to believe David's prediction from two years

earlier. It makes more sense to trust what David is saying today (which is what we have in answer [a]) than what he said two years ago about the future. Answer (c) gives us good reason to believe that the uncle is dead but gives us no information about the cause of death. Maybe the uncle did drugs but got hit by a truck. So, answer (a) is best. (The best answer would be the coroner's report on what caused the death.)

4. The comic strip is tongue-in-cheek and is not meant to be taken literally. Taken literally, it offers bad advice for most decision making. If you stop thinking, you are likely to be led into trouble and away from the path you should take. There may be situations in your life in which consciously analyzing the available evidence doesn't clearly indicate one choice over another. In that situation, if you cannot hold off making the decision, perhaps you should follow your "inner voice" in making your choice. Usually, however, deferring to an inner voice is not a convincing method of arguing.

5. All are principles of good reasoning. The word *contradictory* means almost the same thing as *inconsistent*; the difference between the two will be explained in a later chapter.

6. Michael Jordan is a basketball player. No, he's not.

7. (1) d, (2) a, (3) b, (4) c
(1) is a question, not a claim. A claim is simply an assertion that something is true and is usually made with a declarative sentence.

8. Answer (d) is correct. Sanderson's conclusion is that more time should be spent on the news during a thirty-minute TV news program. Answer (e) is wrong because it is simply a fact that Sanderson uses in his argument. It is something he wants the reader to believe, but it is not something he is arguing for.

Regarding the quality of Sanderson's argument, saying only "I don't like his argument" is insufficient; it doesn't go deep enough. This kind of answer is just opinion. To go deeper, the opinion should be backed up by reasons. The weakest part of Sanderson's argument is that he isn't giving us good enough reasons to believe his conclusion. He makes the relevant comment that news occupies only nine minutes out of thirty. He then suggests that you cannot "do much in nine minutes," and he evidently thinks this comment is a reason to believe his conclusion, but by itself it is quite weak. He probably believes it is obvious that nine is brief, but he ought to argue for this. It's not obvious to his opponent, Harris. Harris could respond by saying, "You can do nine minutes' worth of news in nine minutes. What do you want instead, ten minutes?" Sanderson should have mentioned that too much important news is left out in nine minutes and then tried to back up this remark.

Because you were asked to comment on the quality of the argument rather than on the quality of the argument's conclusion, you need not have mentioned your opinion about whether nine minutes is or is not too brief. Maybe you think that sports news is also news. Maybe you think the nine minutes should be shrunk to three minutes. It is OK to mention your own beliefs about the conclusion, but you should explicitly recognize that such comments are about the truth or false-hood of Sanderson's conclusion and not about the issue in the question, which is whether Sanderson's own reasons are convincing enough to accept that conclusion.

To argue convincingly that nine minutes is too short, Sanderson should have focused on nine minutes being too short for some purpose or other. It could well be that nine minutes is just the right amount for the purpose of maximizing TV station income. Shortening the news by eight more minutes and selling the eight minutes to advertisers would lead to loss of viewing audience and loss of advertising income in the long run. The station manager might well be able to show that lengthening the news from nine to nineteen minutes would have the same bad effect on income. Sanderson is probably thinking about the news serving some other purpose than station revenue, don't you suppose?

Review and Writing Exercises*

- 1. Select some decision you made this week and write a short essay (under two pages, typed double-spaced) in which you explicitly weigh the pros and cons of making the choice you made as opposed to alternative choices you might have made.

- 2. Suppose that your family has decided it needs a new car. Also, suppose that your family has enough money to buy a car, although cost is a factor. You have been asked to make all the other decisions, such as which car to buy, how and where to buy it, what financing to use, and so forth. You should create — that is, make up — the primary reasons for buying the car: to use in the family business, as a second car that is always available to take your live-in Aunt Mary to the doctor twice a week, or simply to be the family's primary car. Make your situation realistic; don't, for example, have your primary reason be to have a getaway car for a bank robbery. Once you've created the situation, make recommendations to your family. Describe how you went about making your decision. Include details, starting with what sources of information you used to help you with your decision. Concentrate on being clear in expressing yourself and on trying to make a logical (that is, rational) decision.

- 3. During the rest of the school term, collect examples of reasoning that you find in your own experience. Sources might be newspaper or TV ads, magazine articles, conversations, books, and so on. Cut out, photocopy, or write up each example on a regular-size page (8.5 × 11 inches). Below each example (or on an accompanying page) identify where it came from, including page number and the date of publication or broadcast. Then identify the reasoning that occurs, and defend your identification. Your goal should be twenty examples. Staple them together in the upper left corner, adding a cover page containing your name and class hour.

*Exercises preceded by a ● are writing exercises rather than multiple-choice or short-answer exercises.

The best journals will be those that contain a wide variety of examples from this chapter and future chapters, such as (a) examples of deceptive techniques by advertisers, salespersons, and propagandists, (b) examples of reasoning errors discussed in later chapters, (c) examples of violations of several principles of good reasoning or good criticism, and (d) examples of good reasoning.

- 4. For the following hypothetical situation, state what decision you recommend and why you recommend it. Weigh the pros and cons.

  A West Virginia radio telescope recently detected an unusual signal beamed in our direction from somewhere across the Milky Way galaxy. After six months of study by the world's best scientists, it is agreed that the signal comes from an intelligent source and contains the message "Can you hear us? Describe yourself and where you are located." The continuously repeating message also includes a brief description of the other civilization, indicating that they are a hydrocarbon-based life form that lives on two planets around a central star. Their signal gave no indication they know we exist. You, a leading government official, have been asked by your president for your opinion about how or whether Earth should respond to the message.

5. Describe the following numbered passages by placing the appropriate letter to the left of each passage number.

  a. Simply a claim with no reasons given to back it up.

  b. An argument using bad reasons.

  c. An argument using good reasons (assuming that the arguer is being truthful).

  d. None of the above.

  1. You said that all deliveries from your firm would be made on Mondays or Tuesdays and that you would be making a delivery here one day this week. Since it is Tuesday morning and we've had no deliveries this week, your firm should make a delivery today.

  2. That night, over icy roads and through howling winds, Paul Revere rode the 60 miles, and even before the British got into their transports, word had come back to Boston that the King's fort at Portsmouth had been seized and His Majesty's military stores stolen by the rebellious Americans.

  3. Will you or won't you take me and Johnny Tremain across the Charles River?

  4. Not a word to the old gentleman, now; not a word.

Defending Against Deception

2

Chapter 1 mentioned several of the most important principles of logical reasoning, and it briefly analyzed examples of good reasoning. Learning from examples of good reasoning and applying the principles of logic are defenses against the forces of irrationality. However, the path to the truth and to the best decision is easier to follow if you've been there before. That is why this chapter explores deceptive techniques used to get people off the path. You'll learn about the techniques of deception used by those who are after your mind or your money. The more you know about the techniques of deception, the better you'll be able to defend yourself.

Deception Is All Around Us

Deception has been practiced in so many ways, and new ways are being created so fast by so many creative people, that we readers, consumers, voters, and potential converts have a tough time keeping our defenses up. Nevertheless, we can do it. Once we've studied some of the known techniques, it becomes much easier to spot new ones. Sometimes deception takes the form of outright lying; at other times it is practiced by telling only part of the truth; and sometimes the whole truth is presented but the problem is in how it is presented. We will explore obvious and subtle examples of each.

This chapter's first piece of advice about deception is the reminder that

> The primary purpose of ads and sales presentations is not to
> pass on helpful information but to cause you to buy a product.

"How much would you pay for all the secrets of the universe? Wait, don't answer yet. You also get this six-quart covered combination spaghetti pot and clam steamer. _Now_ how much would you pay?"

•   •

Drawing by Maslin; © 1981 The New Yorker Magazine, Inc.

When you are considering whether or not to buy a product, you usually want solid information. You want to know the product's features, what is wrong with the competition's product, new ways to use the product, the real cost of it for you, and so forth. Not always, though. For example, don't you already have enough information about Pepsi? If you have to watch a Pepsi commercial, wouldn't you rather be entertained than informed? Do you want to know Pepsi's ratio of corn syrup to sucrose, or would you rather have music, humor, and dancing? However, except for such special cases where you already know enough, what you do want is solid, objective, significant information. This chapter focuses on techniques of deception that are obstacles to your obtaining this information.

Exaggeration and Lying

A **lie** is a false statement made with the intent to deceive. What are salespersons doing when they say that "$15,000 is absolutely the best price" they can sell you the car for, and then after ten more minutes of negotiating drop the price another $500? The statement about the $15,000 was false — just another sales pitch. We consumers are so used to this sort of behavior that we hardly notice that it's an outright lie.

> ## Sales pitches: The lies have it
>
> Have I got a deal for you. A steal, really. Act now and you can have this little beauty for a song. Trust me, you'll love it.
>
> You've heard it before—the siren song of a salesperson on the prowl. And you can tell, by an arch of the seller's eyebrows, a stammer, a nervous shuffle, when you are being lied to, right? Not quite.
>
> In sales situations, the seller is unlikely to give away deceptive intentions with nonverbal cues, report psychologists Peter J. DePaulo of the University of Missouri in St. Louis and Bella M. DePaulo of the University of Virginia in Charlottesville. The researchers videotaped simulated sales pitches by 14 people — 10 experienced retail salespersons and four automobile customers who had bargained over the price of at least three trade-ins. Sellers made pitches for products and cars they liked and disliked. Videotapes were then judged by 107 college students, some of whom were told to pay attention to body movements and speech patterns linked to deception in nonsales situations.
>
> Judges, even those given special instructions, could not tell when sellers were being truthful or deceptive, report the investigators. Nonverbal cues associated with lying were picked up by the judges, they explain, but these cues did not correlate with sellers' lies. Their conclusion: Experienced sellers, confident in their ability to deceive and with no qualms about doing so, may not inadvertently give away their lies with nonverbal cues.

Reprinted with permission from *Science News*, the weekly news-magazine of science, copyright 1988 by Science Service, Inc.

Ditto for exaggerations. Here is a short ad: "Wiler's Whiskey; it's on everyone's lips." If it is, then you won't be safe driving on any road. But it isn't. The ad's exaggerated claim is literally a lie.[1]

People at home, hoping to make some money in their spare time, are often exploited by scams. **Scams** are systematic techniques of deception. They are also called *cons*. Here is an example: the craft con. In a magazine ad, a company agrees to sell you instructions and materials for making some specialty items at home, such as baby booties, aprons, table decorations, and so on. You're told you will get paid if your work is up to the company's standards. After you've bought their package deal, knitted a few hundred baby booties, and mailed them, you may be surprised to learn that your work is not up to company standards. No work ever is; the company is only in the business of selling instructions and materials.[2]

What can you do in self-defense? If you are considering buying a product or service from a local person, you can first check with your local Better Business Bureau about the company's reliability. If you have already been victimized, and if the ad came to you through the U.S. mail, you can send the ad plus your story to U.S. postal inspectors.

Here's another example of the craft con. If you have ever written a humorous story, you might be attracted by this advertisement in a daily newspaper:

Mail me your personal funny story and $5 — perhaps win $10 if I use. Write Howard, 601 Willow Glen, Apt. 14, Westbury, N.D.[3]

If your good buddy Howard were just keeping the $5 bills and throwing all the stories in the wastebasket without even reading them, would you be the wiser? Hardly anyone will take the trouble to call the Better Business Bureau before sending in a mere $5. And once victimized with this scam, few will take the trouble to alert the postmaster or the newspaper that carried the ad. After all, it's only $5, and it takes your valuable time and effort to contact the postmaster. Then there is the possibility that even if you do complain, the government won't do anything about it; it has bigger problems. Besides, maybe Howard hasn't run off with your $5; maybe he is just slow in answering his mail. Howard is probably counting on you to reason just this way.

The moral to be drawn is not that most advertisers are dishonest; they are not. The moral is that it is far riskier to send money through the mail to an advertiser than it is to deal with a salesperson face to face.

■ ············ Concept Check 1 ············ ■

This is a multiple-choice question. What conclusion about deception can be drawn from the following newspaper article?

LOS ANGELES — Evangelist Peter Popoff, who admitted 16 months ago to relying on a radio receiver in his ear to identify people and their ailments at his faith-healing rallies, is off television and recently filed bankruptcy petitions for himself and his evangelistic association.

Popoff's attorney, William J. Simon of San Bernardino, in an interview last week attributed the collapse of his ministry to financial mismanagement more than to disclosures about Popoff.

Popoff and other Pentecostal faith healers have described the purported ability of an evangelist to call out people and illnesses as made possible by a "word of knowledge" from the Holy Spirit.

But a group headed by magician/debunker James Randi, struck by Popoff's remarkable recall of information provided on cards filled out by audiences, surreptitiously set up a radio receiver at several healing rallies and recorded transmissions from Popoff's wife, Elizabeth.

The next month, Popoff told the *Los Angeles Times* that he used the device about half the time. But he also denied that it was kept secret from his followers. His business manager said Popoff's ministry was receiving an average of $550,000 a month in contributions.

The evangelist's attorney said Popoff filed both petitions for protection from creditors under Chapter 7 of the federal bankruptcy code.[4]

a. When in financial crisis, the best legal advice is to file under Chapter 7 of the federal bankruptcy code.

b. Politicians sometimes lie to their electorate.

c. If a faith healer admits to sometimes using secret radio transmissions in order to read minds, then the healer's admission makes it likely that he or she did not cheat during the other times.

d. Some faith healers use electronic tricks in order to make money from the public.

Have you ever seen ads suggesting that if you don't buy a certain brand of tire you will be endangering your family? This is a **scare tactic**, and it is unethical if it exaggerates the danger of not buying those particular tires. Here is an especially sleazy use of the tactic. It is the first page of a booklet advertising something. Are you detective enough to spot what it is advertising?

This Is an Important Notification
Regarding Your ZIP Code

OFFICIAL NOTICE: Contact us at once regarding checks being delivered to your ZIP code.

WARNING: This ZIP Code Notification may not be legally delivered by anyone except U.S. Government employees.

Attention Postmaster

Postal customer shown below is the only person eligible to receive this mailing.

from: Auditing Department
     Box 22341
     Washington, DC 11821

                to: John Doe
                   11 Elm Street
                   Columbus, OH 43210

Did you figure out that this is a perfume ad? You weren't supposed to. The page is supposed to intimidate you — make you fear that your ZIP code is about to change, that checks are being delivered incorrectly, that you are being audited, or that you are about to receive vital government information. When you open the booklet you find out that everyone in your ZIP code is being offered the chance to buy a new brand of perfume. The sentence "This ZIP Code Notification may not be legally delivered by anyone except U.S. Government employees" simply means that only postal workers may deliver the mail.

Telling Only Half the Truth

Although some advertisements contain lies and exaggerations, the more sophisticated ones walk the narrow line between truth and falsehood. You get a little truth, but not enough. A sophisticated ad doesn't lie outright and say, "Our toothpaste is 25 percent more effective than all other brands." Instead, it says "Our toothpaste is 25 percent more effective." When we see this ad, we should ask ourselves: "More effective than what?" The advertiser counts on the fact that we will believe it is more effective than all the competing toothpastes. Yet when the Federal Trade Commission demands to know what the company means by "more effective," the answer will perhaps be that it is 25 percent more effective than no brushing at all. When ads make comparisons, we readers need to be sensitive about what is being compared to what.

Besides watching out for comparisons, we should ask ourselves how the claimed effectiveness is measured and just who has determined that it is 25 percent. Are we supposed to take the advertisers' word for it, or can they instead cite a better authority? Suppose the ad had said, "Our toothpaste is 25 percent more effective, doctors say." That is better, we think. Doctors should know, right? But *which* doctors are doing the saying? Let's hope it's not witch doctors. Were the doctors offered money to agree to a company statement prepared in advance for them to sign? Unless we can rule out these possibilities, we should be cautious about believing that this toothpaste ad is giving us a *good reason* to buy a product.

Before you say that you know ads cannot be trusted and that you aren't fooled by ads that fail to give good reasons to buy a product, ask yourself why advertisers bother to spend millions of dollars each year using the same advertising techniques in ad after ad. Advertisers know that the techniques *do* work on many people.

"Lozengine fights bad breath," says an ad. So it does, but do not jump to the conclusion that it *eliminates* bad breath, or that it is *more effective* in fighting bad breath than Coke. In fact, Lozengine and Coke both "kill germs on contact." The ad has told you only part of the truth. That's not enough.

Using select information to sway someone's opinion is called the technique of *selective representation*. It is also called telling a **half-truth**. Logical reasoners should look for the full story, not just the select information in an ad. A logical reasoner's duty is to consider both sides, not merely the good side. It is the propagandist who pushes one side no matter what.

Newspapers often use the technique of selective representation. Here is a rather subtle example, a carefully selected headline that pushes a stereotype on the readers:

Former Mental Patients Suspected in 14 Killings in County

In the middle of the article, the newspaper chose to emphasize this sentence: "At least five people with a history of mental illness have been accused of killing up to 14 people and injuring 12 in the County." Without any other information, many readers will go on to the next page with the thought embedded in their minds that mental patients are especially violent. However, the logical reasoner will ask the crucial question, "Are the former mental patients killing more than their 'fair share'?" That is, if former mental patients constitute 1 percent of the population, are they guilty of more than 1 percent of the murders? Neither the headline nor the article contains an answer to this crucial question, so the reasonable thing to do is to suspend judgment about whether mental patients are "getting out of hand." The more general conclusion we should draw here about logical reasoning is to *suspend judgment rather than leap to a conclusion with insufficient evidence*.

The **stereotype** (general image) of the crazed mental patient lunging with a bloody knife is an inaccurate characterization of the class of mental patients. Even severely ill mental patients are no more violent than the general population.[5]

Below is an example of selective presentation of information in two newspapers. Both newspaper editors printed the same column—with one difference. The paper on the right removed one phrase. The paper on the left used the column as originally written by the columnist. The key phrase is italicized. Can you guess which candidate for mayor was favored by the editor of the paper on the right?

Street People

HOUSTON—"Get the street people out of our sight," the voters said yesterday.

Mayor Anthony Burgess was defeated last Tuesday, *despite, just two years ago, having been generally considered to be one of the most popular mayors in the United States.* Exit polls clearly said why. The voters cared primarily about one issue: removing the homeless and the panhandlers from the streets and parks. The newly elected mayor, Heinz Pagels, promised to remove them; Burgess didn't . . .

Street People

HOUSTON—"Get the street people out of our sight," the voters said yesterday.

Mayor Anthony Burgess was defeated last Tuesday. Exit polls clearly said why. The voters cared primarily about one issue: removing the homeless and the panhandlers from the streets and parks. The newly elected mayor, Heinz Pagels, promised to remove them; Burgess didn't . . .

Clever editing, isn't it?

The **hedge**, another common but devious tactic, is based on selectively presenting information so that what one appears to be saying can later be denied. An ad might say, "You could make $1 million this year if you . . ." The word "could" is the hedge. Whether you can reasonably *expect* to make $1 million is something else again. At first the ad appears to be saying you *will* make a million, but on careful reading you realize that the advertiser could claim "Hey, we never actually promised a million." The logical reasoner will always apply this principle: *Be alert to hedges.*

■ ·········· Concept Check 2 ··········· ■

Identify the hedge in the following passage, from Jerry Mander, *Four Arguments for the Elimination of Television* :

> If you have ever participated in a public event of any sort and then watched the news report of it, you are already aware that the news report barely resembles what you experienced. You are aware of this because you were there. Other viewers are not aware. When television describes events that happened at some other historical time, no one can know what is true.
>
> The best article I ever read on the inevitable distortions resulting from television's inherent need to condense time was written in *TV Guide* by Bill Davidson (March 20, 1976). Writing about the new spurt of "docudramas," which represent themselves as true versions of historical events, he said, "Truth may be the first victim when television 'docudramas' rewrite history."

Advertisers also use the technique of **selectively emphasizing the trivial**. Their goal is to take advantage of your ignorance about what is trivial. For example, a Freedom shampoo advertisement might say that the shampoo "adjusts precisely to your hair, taking away the oil and dirt just where it needs to." Great, but so does any shampoo. When it needs to, it cleans; when it doesn't need to, it doesn't clean. So what? If you didn't know this about shampoos, you might believe the ad is giving you a good reason to buy Freedom shampoo. The moral: advertisers and politicians love to make a big deal out of no big deal.

Product advertisers face the problem of promoting their product over that of the competition. Often, as is the case with shampoos, shaving cream, and toothpaste, there are many competitors but not much of a difference among the products. Thus the advertiser's goal is to create the illusion of important differences among brands when in fact the most significant difference for the consumer is price.

The logical reasoner's best defense against the tactic of selective presentation of information is to become well informed. Well-informed persons know what is trivial and what is not and know what is likely to be left out or covered up. All other things being equal, the more you know, the less apt you are to be convinced by bad reasoning.

Advertisers have more influence on the content of magazines and TV programs than most of us realize. In women's magazines, for example, almost every issue contains ads that glamorize smoking. Ironically, these ads are sprinkled among articles about women's health and fitness. Yet the magazines never carry articles mentioning that cigarette smoking is a growing problem among women and that it is known to cause lung cancer, heart disease, and miscarriages. Every year since 1985, over 100,000 American women have died from the effects of smoking. These deaths are preventable, and the U.S. government has been trying to publicize this fact. You'd expect women's magazines to take a leading role in alerting women. Yet an analysis of articles that appeared during a five-year period in the 1980s in *Cosmopolitan*, *Good Housekeeping*, *Mademoiselle*, *McCall's*, *Woman's Day*, and *Ms.* magazines by a University of Oregon researcher in *Journalism Quarterly* showed just the opposite. Not a single article, review, or editorial on any aspect of the dangers of smoking was published. The researcher found thirty-four articles about breast cancer, but none about lung cancer.[6] Cigarette makers normally cancel ads in magazines that do run articles on the health hazards of smoking, but the financial risks for the magazines are even greater. Tobacco companies have invested their profits by buying up other large corporations, such as Nabisco and General Foods. Thus, when the tobacco ads are withdrawn, so are many of the ads for the food products. It is understandable why magazine publishers don't want to offend tobacco advertisers.

This example of the high frequency of cigarette ads in women's magazines, coupled with the low frequency of articles attacking cigarettes, is meant to be suggestive. It does not make a definitive case for the influence of advertisers on magazines, newspapers, and TV programs. Maybe women's magazines don't run articles on lung cancer for the same reason they don't run articles on the dangers of fast driving; neither lung cancer nor fast driving is a danger specific to women. Breast cancer is specific to women; so perhaps that is why the women's magazines have articles on breast cancer but not lung cancer. However, cigarette smoking during pregnancy does cause low infant birth weights, which can be considered a problem of special interest to women, so it is odd that the women's magazines carry no articles about the dangers of smoking. Nevertheless, one research paper is not enough to make the case against women's magazines. To make a better case about the influence of advertisers, it would help to have testimonials from editors and publishers saying that they were in fact intimidated by the advertisers. Until you get that evidence, you should suspend belief about the influence of advertisers.

Hey duck hunter, here is an attractive offer. Or is it?

Why Are We Giving Away Hand-Carved Mallard Decoys for Only $10?

Hard to believe, *but true*. As part of a nationwide advertising publicity campaign, a leading New York firm will give away its best-selling (and most expensive) duck decoys — genuine hand-carved Mallards (*Anas Platyrhynchos*) — for the astonishing publicity price of only $10 each to every person who writes to the company address (below)....Fully 14 inches long, with astonishingly alert amber eyes and the brilliant green head that unmistakably characterizes adult male Mallards....Our version of decoys nationally advertised at $135, they are the best-selling decoys ever sold by this multimillion-dollar New York firm....Collectors should know that each decoy is not only covered by a full one-year money-back guarantee, but also by a 50-year Repurchase Guarantee. Should you ever wish to sell or redeem your Mallard Decoy, the company pledges to repurchase it from you, any time you wish within the next 50 years, for the full cash price you paid....

To order, mail $10 for each decoy. Add $3 shipping per decoy. Add sales tax. *Make check payable to Acme Co.* Mail to: Acme Mallard Decoy, Box 113, Eastwitch, CT 21595.[7]

Well, fellow duck hunters, to determine whether or not this is a deal, there are some specific questions that need answers. Who made the duck? You don't know. You only know who is advertising the duck. What is the difference between a money-back guarantee and a repurchase guarantee? The 50-year guarantee is suspiciously long, too. Forty-nine years from now, when you are tired of staring into your duck's astonishingly alert amber eyes, will you be able to get your money back with no penalty? Doesn't this guarantee look too good to be true? You should feel lucky to actually receive the duck after sending in your $13 plus tax. Does the ad contain lies? You can't tell for sure. Is there selective representation, or is the reader being given the whole story? It is difficult to say. What you can be sure of is that you should be suspicious. Quack, quack.

■ .... Concept Check 3 .... ■

Evaluate the reasons this ad gives for buying the product.

Recommended by doctors

Wackerli's Hair Spray

The choice of Hollywood's stars

The only hair spray with Formycin

Telling the Truth, While Still Misleading

Even when you get all the relevant facts, there can be serious problems. It depends on how the facts are presented. For example, consider Grandpa's Granola Bars — pressed bars of breakfast cereal. The primary ingredient in Grandpa's Granola Bars is sugar. The manufacturer of this "health food bar" does not want to broadcast this fact, yet he must obey federal law and list the ingredients in the order of their weight. (The U.S. Food and Drug Administration requires the main ingredient to be listed first.) The corporate management that is pushing Grandpa's Granola Bars has found a clever way to tell the sugar story: List each of the seven kinds of sugar separately. In this case, at the top of the list goes "rolled oats," followed by "sucrose, dextrose, fructose, honey, chocolate chips, invert sugar, and corn syrup." Many consumers won't recognize some of these as sugars. Clever of the manufacturer, but deceitful. The unwary reader thinks "Ah, the bar is mostly rolled oats."[8]

■ ············   Concept Check 4   ············ ■

Analyze the following offer to determine whether you should join. This ad exploits people whose minds fog over when they see numbers.

BINGO! We've finally uncovered the secret, and we will share it with you for a small part of your profits. Here's how to claim your winnings from Las Vegas. The entry fee is only $19.95. The secret is that you play as a group. We arrange for you to play with 99 other players. That way, you can buy so many more bingo cards, and your chances of winning go up astronomically. In fact, we guarantee that your group will win at least $1,000, or double your money back. Act now. Send your entry fee to Dr. Dardanelles, 3381 Magdalen Ave., New York, NY 10009. Add $2 for our expenses.

This guy is going to give you $1,000. Guaranteed. How could any logical reasoner walk away from such a good deal?

Saying Little with Lots of Words

When a politician pounds her fist on the podium and yells, "A tax is a tax!" she tells us she does not want more taxes, but literally what she is saying is trivial. We know to look beyond the literal triviality. Unfortunately, some speakers and writers have no depth; there is nothing beyond the triviality. This newspaper headline is an example:

Heat Wave Blamed for Record High Temperatures Across U.S.

What else would you blame? This headline has a low information content. It contains no information that isn't already known by everybody. Similarly, you receive little information when you hear a politician mention that she supports her country, that she wants schools to teach the children better, that she believes it is now time to cut the fat from government, that she believes it is the government's responsibility to protect the people, and so on. The problem with what the politician says is not that the speech selectively emphasizes the trivial; it wouldn't be trivial to create better schools or cut the fat from government. But it *is* trivial to say you want to do these things, because so does everyone else — what's new?

Concept Check 5

What is wrong with the following comment?

> If we don't change direction soon, we'll end up where we're going.
> — Professor Irwin Corey.

Persuading Without Reasons

Suppose you see a billboard with a picture of a smiling doughnut and the phrase "Mmmmm, DOUBLE DONUTS." The advertiser hopes to trigger a gut-level response so you will buy the product. What information are you getting from that billboard? You are *not* being given a reason to buy those donuts. This ad is trying to *motivate* you; it's not trying to give you a reason. Ads such as this are designed only to create moods or to provide name recognition for a product.

If I'm trying to sell my house and I bake chocolate chip cookies one hour before prospective buyers will arrive for an open house, is the aroma a *reason* for them to buy the house? No, but it might *cause* them to buy it, or it might help a little. If they stop and think about it, they will realize I won't be baking those cookies for them after I move out, and they will realize they should worry that the cookie aroma might be covering up some problem, perhaps the odor of cat urine in the carpets.

We open a magazine and notice a beautiful woman wearing Gentleman Jim jeans saying, "I like to be close to my Gentleman Jims." The advertiser is hoping we readers will identify with the woman and will want to do what she would like us to do. The ad lures us unconsciously into buying Gentleman Jims for this "reason," but the ad is giving us *no good reason* to buy Gentleman Jim jeans.

People who are out to persuade often have style without content. A used-car salesperson with a dynamic, evangelical style is more effective than one with a snarling style or a "blah" style. When the enthusiastic salesperson conveys real excitement about the car, the listener often unconsciously assumes that this is a good reason to buy; however, it's not a good reason at all.

The point of these examples is to show that causes are different from reasons. Propagandists use reasons only if they believe they will help cause you to do what they want. You, on the other hand, should be on the lookout for solid reasons. You don't want to be pushed around by causes.

■ ············   Concept Check 6   ············ ■

What technique of deception is used in the following beer commercial?

"Schultz Beer: It's as real as it gets!"

Most commercials are aimed at your emotions, not your intellect. The goal of the commercial is to give you a feeling, not to pass on useful data. Your goal is to see past the fluff and extract the information, if it's there. Too often it isn't. Most ads take the time only to reinforce the product's name and make you feel good. The advertiser hopes you will unthinkingly associate the product with your good feelings. Market research probably tells the advertiser that doing this is more effective than broadcasting facts about the product's merits.

Deceiving with Loaded Language

Early one morning in April of 1986, the Libyans were yawning when United States bombers streaked out of the clouds and bombed President Khadafy's palace. The next day, Soviet newspapers objected to this attack by the United States. In reporting that fact, one U.S. news story said "As expected, the Soviet Bear kicked up a fuss about Libya." The use of the phrase "kicked up a fuss" is a propagandistic slap at the Soviets; it is an example of **loaded language**. So is the phrase "as expected," which tends to discount the complaint in advance. An unloaded way to present the information would have been for the newspaper to say, "The Soviets strongly objected to the Libyan incident." Saying it that way is sticking to the facts.

Loaded language is a major way of persuading you without giving you good reasons. Look for loaded language in the following headline:

Big Oil Asks Senator Roberts for a "No" Vote

Calling the major oil companies "Big Oil" evokes negative images for most people. Can't you just see the fat-cat oil executive in the smoke-filled room with his cigar and pinky ring? Most people root for the little guy and against the big guy. If you were the newspaper editor, you could have written an unloaded headline this way:

Major Oil Companies Ask Senator Roberts to Vote "No"

The term *major oil companies* is associated with more neutral images in people's minds. The mental images and evaluations that people associate with a word or phrase are called **connotations**. The negative connotation of "Big Oil" slants the headline against the major oil companies.

The news story complaining about the Soviet response to the American bombing of Libya exploited the connotations of the phrase "Soviet Bear." A bear is an aggressive animal, so labeling the Soviets as "bears" connotes aggressiveness rather than fairness. Slanting a description by using loaded words is not giving an *objective* description. Using loaded language is a way for writers and speakers to slip their opinions into what would otherwise be an objective description. With slanting, the author doesn't give just the factual description; instead, the author adds his or her *values*. Thus he or she indicates whether the thing described is to be valued positively or negatively.

Logical reasoners must be on the alert to *sort out the facts from the values*. For example, if I tell you that I like La Toya Jackson, I've given her a positive evaluation. I've not stated a single descriptive fact about her. But if I say I like La Toya Jackson's singing, or say that she is the world's greatest singer, then I've described her by calling her a "singer," and I've also evaluated her singing. On the other hand, if I tell you that La Toya Jackson is short and has a high-paying job, then I've stated two descriptive facts about her but have not offered any evaluation of her. Some readers might read the description and respond with a negative evaluation because they dislike short persons, but my original statement did not express this evaluation.

Selectively choosing the facts is an even more subtle way to deceive another person. Republicans complain that when Democrats describe a Republican program, they usually choose to mention the unpleasant consequences of the program and never the positive consequences. Republicans are probably right to complain, although Democrats can probably make the same complaint about Republicans.

■ ············ Concept Check 7 ············ ■

In the following passage, replace the loaded expressions with wording that slants in the *opposite* direction. That is, replace a positively loaded term with a negatively loaded term (not with an unloaded term).

> During the most recent artillery and tank battles, the freedom fighters have been able to liberate one more square mile of the Beirut suburbs.

Political campaigns do not target politically aware voters; they target undecided voters, especially those who pay little attention to politics and know little about the issues. Most campaign material is aimed at the target person's emotions. Being remarkably candid when asked about this topic, Joel Bradshaw, a political consultant from Washington, D.C., answered that in the 1980 presidential election one candidate "talked about issues," whereas the other candidate addressed the voters differently and "made them feel good. It is always more powerful to be emotional in a campaign message." Ideas about how to do this come mostly from campaign consultants, not from the candidate. The consultant's relationship to the candidate boils down to "We fool 'em and you rule 'em."[9]

Calling that piece of cloth "Old Glory" instead of "the national flag" can make a difference. People don't think straight when their emotions are all charged up, and it takes just a little emotional arousal to affect the brain. It can alter the chemical balances and reduce logical reasoning ability. Nobody can or should live without emotion. Nevertheless,

> People reason better when they are in control of their emotions.

Your aunt Mary is grieving over her husband's accidental death when in steps her lawyer saying, "I know this is an especially hard time for you, and we all want to help you, so if you'll just sign these papers giving me the power to make all the financial decisions, your life will be so much easier." The lawyer's terminology is not loaded, but the whole remark is.

One of the more effective ways to use loaded language is in conjunction with body language: a subtle smile here, an awkward glance there. Loaded language isn't all bad; it can be effectively used to enliven dull discourse. But employing it to slant a supposedly objective description is a technique of deception.

■ ············ Concept Check 8 ············ ■

Locate the loaded language in the following newspaper report and indicate how to rewrite the report so that it is more objective.

SHARON PRATT DIXON has been inaugurated as mayor of Washington, D.C., becoming the first black woman to lead a large U.S. city. Her inauguration formally ended the twelve-year rule of Marion Barry, who is appealing against a six-month prison sentence for cocaine possession.

Guardian Weekly

The following quotation reveals how some campaign aides viewed their candidate:

> At one point, Spencer [a long-time Reagan adviser] said that Reagan, wounded in a 1981 assassination attempt, might attract more sympathy if he were shot again. "If he got a bullet in the toe, it would help the election," he said, then quickly added: "Turn that tape off."

On a loftier plane, Spencer, who ran Reagan's successful gubernatorial campaigns in California, said the president might give some "sophisticated" speeches that would sound good but contain little content — "talk about things like sound money, constitutional reform, education; . . . people will think he sure as hell knows something — without really saying something."[10]

No doubt the campaign aides and political consultants for both Democrats and Republicans feed us their candidates prepackaged and weak on specifics.

You, as the potential customer or voter, normally want solid information that is not obscured by body language, snide remarks, loaded language, or unasked-for evaluations and opinions.

Review of Major Points

To defend yourself against the bombardment of propaganda, con games, political hype, and sales pitches, you should demand good reasons before you act and before you change your beliefs. This is easier said than done. One problem is to get a reason, any reason. A second problem is to determine whether an offered reason is good or bad. In this chapter, we examined deceptive techniques that rely on lying, exaggerating, and selectively withholding information. We also considered how we can be manipulated even when all the relevant information is available to us; the problem in this case is in how that information is presented. Finally, we examined loaded language and the difference between facts and values. Loaded language isn't all bad; it can be effectively used to enliven dull discourse. But using it to slant a supposedly objective description is a technique of deception.

The chapter presented three more principles of logical reasoning: (1) Suspend judgment rather than leap to a conclusion with insufficient evidence, (2) be alert to hedges, and (3) sort out the facts from the values. The following concepts played an important role in our discussion: scam, scare tactic, half-truth, stereotype, reason versus cause, connotation, slanting, value, and objective description. We aren't yet done exploring the means of deception. Almost every chapter to follow will add to what we've already discussed.

Glossary

connotations The mental images and evaluations that many people associate with a word or phrase. The negative connotation of "Big Oil" in a headline slants the piece against the major oil companies.

half-truth A deceptive technique that uses half or some other portion of the available information in order to sway your opinion. It is also called the *technique of selective representation.*

hedge A deceptive technique based on carefully selecting the information to be able to later deny what one at first appeared to have said. For example, you could hedge on saying "You will make $20 per hour" by instead saying, "You will make up to $20 per hour."

lie A false statement made with the intent to deceive.

loaded language Language that unnecessarily uses a word that has emotional overtones or evaluative connotations. It is language that masquerades as objective description but in fact is slanted to introduce the speaker's own values.

scam Systematic techniques of deception usually aimed at making money off the unwary. They are also called *cons*.

scare tactic A technique of deception that uses fear to cause a particular action. An example would be an ad suggesting that you will be endangering your family if you don't buy a certain brand of tires.

selectively emphasizing the trivial Making a big deal of no big deal. The point would be to target a group who did not realize that it was no big deal. For example, you would be using this technique if you advertised that your shampoo contains hydrogen hydroxide and didn't mention that this is just a fancy name for water.

stereotype A mistaken but commonly held mental image of some group. For example, many U.S. citizens uncritically hold a stereotype of Mexicans as being lazy and untrustworthy.

Answers to Concept Checks

1. Choice (d) is correct. Answer (b) is wrong because the article is not about politicians. Answer (c) is an example of illogical reasoning. Answer (a) is wrong because the bankruptcy advice is a minor point. The major point of the article is whether fraud occurred. Randi was mentioned to back up the claim that it did. The moral, then, is to watch out for this kind of fraud.

2. The hedge is capitalized in the following sentence:

    Truth MAY be the first victim when television 'docudramas' rewrite history.

3. The careless reader could leave this ad believing that the hair spray is somehow medically better and that it is the hair spray used by most of the people in Hollywood, who especially care about the beauty and health of their hair and who have made their decision on the basis of careful examination. However, the reader is reading all this in; the information is not really there in the ad. How many Hollywood stars actually chose Wackerli's hair spray out of the many who were sent free samples? On what basis did the stars choose the hair spray? The doctor part sounds good, but on careful reading we see that the ad does not say how many doctors recommended the hair spray or what kinds of doctors they are. The

appeal to Formycin would be a good reason if you happened to know that Formycin is really good for hair or for holding hair in place. However, you don't know
that; Formycin might be an inert ingredient. Maybe it's what we call "H_2O."
Besides, Wackerli hair spray is probably the only hair spray containing Formycin
simply because the Wackerli Company has a copyright on the name so that no
other company is allowed to use it.

4. Your group is going to give this guy approximately $2,000, and he is guaranteeing
your group will get half of it back. What a ripoff.

5. Too obviously true. Low information content. But a great joke from the notorious
professor.

6. What does this comment have to do with the quality of the beer or with why you
should buy it? Does an *unreal* beer exist? All beers could make the same claim.
Thus, this ad uses the technique of selectively emphasizing the trivial.

7. The loaded term *freedom fighters* (positive) can be replaced with *terrorists* (negative). Also, *liberate* (positive) can be replaced with *extend their grip on* (negative).
Replacing *freedom fighters* with *soldiers* would remove the positive emotional
charge but would not add negative charge.

   Do not replace words that do not need replacing. In particular, the phrase
artillery and tank battles is not a positive way of saying "war."

8. The loaded term is *rule*. That term implies the mayor acted like a king or dictator.
An unloaded replacement is *administration*.

Review and Writing Exercises

Note: A color square indicates questions that are answered at the end of the book

General Exercises

- 1. Examine some ads, commercials, and so on, and find examples of three techniques
of deception mentioned in this chapter. Clip, copy, or describe each one, and then
say what it is an example of and how you made this determination.

2. You receive a letter that says, "You've just won a free vacation for two in Hawaii or
Puerto Rico. Four days, three nights, in a lovely island paradise. Call 666-7733 to
claim your prize." Sounds pretty good, no? If you were to call, you would eventually learn the rest of the story. Yes, you will be given three nights for free in a
hotel, but you have to agree to attend a three-hour lecture about purchasing land
on the island. Near the end of the lecture, you will learn that there are certain
strings attached to the trip. You must agree to pay for a high-priced flight on the
advertiser's chartered planes. You must also stay in their hotel and pay for at least
two meals a day in the hotel restaurant.

This deceptive advertising technique can best be described as

a. failing to appreciate that extraordinary statements require extraordinarily good evidence to back them up.

b. inconsistency in the reasoning.

c. using a half-truth.

d. stereotyping.

- 3. In the following story, a young woman makes some choices about what to do and what to believe. Ask yourself whether she made the right choices. What do you think? Why? Are the reasons that convinced you good enough to convince someone who doesn't agree with you?

> A young woman was in need of guidance — her father had been diagnosed with inoperable cancer, she was in legal trouble because of an exboyfriend, and she had just lost her job. One day she saw a sign that said "Fortune-Teller, Money-Back Guarantee." She felt she had nothing to lose and went in. The fortune-teller collected $40 and told her to come back in three days because her life was in danger. The next visit cost her $80, and she was told she had been cursed. The cure: Bring the fortune-teller a box with blue velvet, something made of gold, something made of silver, and, by the way, $100 cash.
>
> The woman borrowed money to do this. Finally the fortune-teller requested one more thing: a handful of dirt from Jamaica. The woman couldn't afford the trip, but she was told that if she didn't go she'd die in a car crash in the next two years. She was so afraid that she actually went to Jamaica, put a handful of dirt in a box, and returned to the fortune-teller within forty-eight hours.
>
> However, when she got there the fortune-teller had moved with no forwarding address.[11]

- 4. Prepare a six-minute debate between yourself and someone in your class who disagrees with you about whether the woman did the right thing.

- 5. Create a 5-second radio commercial that advertises some product. Use the technique of persuading without giving any reasons. Make the commercial seem realistic, not silly.

- 6. Choose a recent news story and compare the pros and cons of how it is treated on the nightly TV news with how it is treated the next day in the newspaper.

7. Compose an original paragraph that uses some means of deceiving the reader yet still gives the whole truth.

8. When you receive a chain letter, you receive a letter with a message you are likely to agree with plus a short list of people and their addresses. You are asked to (a) send money to the person at the top of the list, (b) copy the letter, placing your own name and address at the bottom of the list and removing the name and address of the person at the top of the list, and (c) send copies of the revised letter

on to several new people you know. Why does a chain letter qualify as being a technique of deception?

Loaded-Language Exercises

■ 1. Here is a news report that is not objective in that it contains loaded terminology. Rewrite it to be more objective.

> The spokeswoman for the pro-abortion group blatantly admitted today that the mother of the unborn child can murder the child if she "chooses."

■ 2. Here is a news report that is not objective in that it contains loaded terminology. Edit it to be more objective.

> The "female" leader of the anti-choice group said today that a pregnant woman is "guilty of murder" if she exercises her right to control her own body by aborting the fetus.

3. Find the loaded language, if any, that is used to slant the following description positively or negatively. The speaker is Jewish writer Annette Rubenstein, author of the two-volume work *The Great Tradition in English Literature: From Shakespeare to Shaw*. She is describing an event that occurred right after her graduation.

> When I left Columbia [University] with a doctorate in philosophy I graduated into the Depression [of the 1930s]. I wanted very badly to teach philosophy, but it was difficult for a woman to find such employment. The head of the philosophy department got me an offer at Bryn Mawr University on condition I would change my name. At that time there were very few Jewish professors and those that were there were teaching German and foreign languages mostly. Of course I wouldn't change my name and he said, "Well, they know it; it's not deceiving anybody. It's just that they thought it wouldn't look good in the catalogue. Why don't you translate it to Redstone?"

Which word is loaded?

a. Jewish   d. Redstone

b. offer   e. none of the above

c. foreign

Exaggeration Exercises

■ 1. Find and document an example of exaggeration that has occurred in print, on the radio, or on TV. (a) State the exaggerated claim, (b) explain why it is correct to call it "exaggerated," and (c) give the source of the claim (date, page number, program, channel, or other information needed to pinpoint the source).

2. Explain why the following claim is or is not exaggerated: "Voilà perfume. It was used by Cleopatra of ancient Egypt; it's one of the secrets of her success."

Obstacles to Better Communication

3

This chapter is designed to reveal some of the major pitfalls in normal communication. Usually your goal is to communicate well. You want to be clear, to be precise, and to get the message across with the proper tone. But not always. There are many reasons for not wanting to directly say what you mean. That birthday present from Aunt Bessie deserves a thank you, but you don't want to tell her that the present itself is useless to you. And when you insert into your history essay the famous remark "History is a pack of tricks played on the dead," you don't intend to be taken literally. However, this chapter explores the logical aspects of good communication when you *do* want to say what you mean and mean what you say. This goal is not always easy to achieve, as we will see in this chapter.

Not Realizing What You Are Saying

All of us sometimes say things that aren't quite what we mean, but those whose native language is not English have special troubles in this regard. Here are some examples of items written in English by non-native speakers[1]:

> Sign outside a doctor's office in Rome: "Specialist in women and other diseases."

> Bucharest hotel lobby: "The lift is being fixed for the next day. During that time we regret that you will be unbearable."

> In a Yugoslav hotel: "The flattening of underwear with pleasure is the job of the chambermaid."

> On the menu of a Swiss restaurant: "Our wines leave you nothing to hope for."

"Congratulations, Dave! I don't think I've read a more beautifully evasive and subtly misleading public statement in all my years in government."

•   •

Drawing by Stevenson; © 1987 The New Yorker Magazine, Inc.

In a Norwegian cocktail lounge: "Ladies are requested not to have babies at the bar."

In an Acapulco hotel: "The manager has personally passed all the water served here."

On the door of a Moscow hotel room: "If this is your first visit to the USSR, you are welcome to it."

You wouldn't make errors like these, but you might be apt to make less blatant ones associated with inappropriate use of language. One logical principle about communication to be drawn from all this is: *Be sensitive to the subtleties of language use.*

> ■ ....   Concept Check 1   .... ■

You've been hired by a Tokyo car rental firm to revise the following paragraph of its brochure in order to improve the English. How would you rewrite it?

When passenger of foot heave in sight, tootle the horn. Trumpet him melodiously at first, but if he still obstacles your passage then tootle him with vigor.[2]

Abusing Rules of Grammar and Semantics

Bad spelling is a source of communication problems, though not an especially subtle one. The great individualist from Tennessee, Davy Crockett (1786–1836), was a frontiersman who had little respect for book learning; he spelled words any way he wanted and said that the rules of English spelling are "contrary to nature." He had a point, because English spelling isn't designed for easy learning — ask a foreigner. But none of us can change that situation. Crockett couldn't, and you can't. So if we're to communicate effectively, we've all got to spell words the way most everybody else does.

One of the first rules of good communication is to use *grammar* correctly. Here are some of the more common errors of grammar:

> Errors of numbers ("Everybody must turn in *their* own list" should be "Everybody must turn in *his or her* own list").
>
> Misplaced modifiers and dangling participles ("*Turning cartwheels and yelling frantically*, the mother appeared with her youngest daughter," which would be clearer as "The mother appeared with her youngest daughter who was turning cartwheels and yelling frantically").
>
> Lack of parallel structure ("The horses were expected *to plow, to haul, and deliver* lumber," which should be rephrased as ". . . to plow, haul, and deliver . . .").
>
> Gerund errors ("Do you want Yolanda *playing* soccer?" which should be rephrased as ". . . to play . . .").
>
> Possession errors ("Did you care for *Yolanda* scoring an illegal goal?" which should be rephrased as ". . . Yolanda's . . .").

Abusing the principles of *semantics* also interferes with communication. Semantic principles have more to do with meaning than grammar principles do. For example, the sentence "She is a person lovely" is bad grammar, but the grammatical sentence "She is a negative square root" is good grammar but bad semantics. Your goal as a communicator is to avoid nonsense. Easier said than done, no?

A common semantical error is to make phrases modify unintended parts of a sentence. The reader can get the wrong idea. The "turning cartwheels" sentence was an example. Here is another from a newspaper article:

Coach Pucci offered his resignation effective at the end of the current school year, on Christmas.

This report puzzles the reader because the school year ends in the spring, not at Christmastime. It would have been better to put the words *on Christmas* closer to the part of the sentence they relate to, as in the following rewrite:

Coach Pucci offered his resignation on Christmas, to be effective at the end of the current school year.

The original sentence was odd — odd enough that the reader had to stop and try to be charitable toward the writer by looking for the intended meaning.

> The reader applies the **principle of charity** by taking the writer to mean something sensible when the writer has said something silly or obviously false.

According to the principle of charity, you should give the benefit of the doubt to writers or speakers whose odd statements you are trying to understand; if the statements appear to be silly, then look for a less silly, but still likely, interpretation. The lesson the principle of charity offers to speakers and writers is that you should clearly say what you mean so that your listeners or readers won't be put through unnecessary mental gymnastics trying to figure out what you really intended to say.

Communication is often hampered when people are sloppy and don't realize what they are saying. Here are some humorous but authentic examples. Imagine being a teacher at an elementary school and receiving these excuses from Anne's parents[3]:

Anne didn't come to school. She was in bed under the doctor and could not get up.

Please excuse Anne. She was sick and I had her shot.

With a little charity and empathy, you can figure out what the parent meant.

What would you think if you were a welfare department employee and you received this letter from a woman applying for financial assistance?

I am forwarding my marriage certificate and six children. I had seven, but one died which was baptized on a half sheet of paper.[4]

If you take her literally, you might wonder when the six kids will be arriving. Can you imagine the scene as that seventh child was baptized while it sat balanced on a half sheet of soggy paper? There are effective ways to clear up such writing problems. Here is one way:

I am mailing you my marriage certificate and the birth certificates of my six children. I had a seventh child, but he died. That child's baptismal certificate is on the enclosed half sheet of paper.

Writers need to take some care in expressing themselves or run the risk of saying something they don't mean; conversely, readers must be continually aware of not taking writers too literally.

■ .... **Concept Check 2** .... ■

The person receiving the following letter at the welfare department knew not to take it too literally:

> "I want money quick as I can get it. I have been in bed with the doctor for two weeks, and he doesn't do me any good."

Select one of the following choices as the better rewrite of the welfare letter:

a. "I am in urgent need of funds. For two weeks I have been in bed with the doctor, but I am still ill."

b. "I want money quick as I can get it. At my doctor's request, I have been in bed for the last two weeks, but I am still ill."

■ .... **Concept Check 3** .... ■

One day the people of Los Angeles looked up and saw this sky-writing message: "Pray for Death: Baby-Killer Brennan." What is going on? What does it mean? The message is unclear. It could have been said better. The following passage will provide the background information you need to make sense of the sky writing.

> Springing up across the nation are even more extreme extremists who, of all things, *pray for your death* if you disagree with their political views. Instead of charging you're siding with Satan, they want you to join him — now. . . .
>
> In Los Angeles, Robert Hymers, pastor of the Fundamentalist Baptist Tabernacle, has launched his own death-prayer campaign against the "Hitler-like" Supreme Court. He ordered a [sky-writing] banner reading "Pray for Death: Baby-Killer Brennan" be flown over Loyola Marymount University, where Justice William Brennan was delivering the commencement address. Later, he led his congregation in prayer under another banner, "Pray for the Death of Pro-Death Court."
>
> [According to] John Buchanan, ". . . there is [a] danger associated with these death-prayer campaigns: that someone may take this extremism one step further and kill a public official, in an effort to do God's will.
>
> "Frankly, I doubt very seriously that God answers death prayers. But will someone else?"[5]

Pick one best way to clarify the sky-writing message "Pray for Death: Baby-Killer Brennan."

a. "Brennan, Pray for the Death of Other Baby Killers"
b. "Brennan, You are a Baby Killer"
c. "Death to Baby Brennan and his Killer"
d. "Pray for the Death of Baby-Killer Brennan"
e. "Brennan Prays for the Death of a Baby-Killer"

Using Euphemisms

When you replace a harsh-sounding phrase with one that means more or less the same but is more gentle, you are using a **euphemism**. Taking a brick from King Tut's tomb during a visit to the Egyptian pyramids is really stealing, but the person who does so is likely to cover it up with the euphemism "souvenir hunting." If the mortician mentions your "dearly departed" grandmother, that's a euphemism for your dead grandmother. The term *dead* is a more accurate though harsher one. If you're the type of person who tells it like it is, you will have a hard time being a successful mortician or politician.

As was mentioned in the previous chapter, the connotations of a term are what it suggests to the reader or hearer. Euphemisms have fewer negative connotations; that is, they have fewer associations that are unpleasant to think about or that offend the hearer's morality or sensitivities. Euphemisms include genteelisms such as "disrobed" for naked and "bosom" for you know what. A "Rocky Mountain oyster" is not an oyster at all, is it? The Bowlers' Association has resolved to use euphemisms to make bowling a more upscale sport. They plan to get bowling out of the bowling "alleys" and into the bowling "centers." They also plan to get the balls out of the "gutters" and into the "channels."

■ ············ Concept Check 4 ············ ■

What is a euphemism for "armpit sweat-stopper"?

Using a euphemism in place of a negatively charged term can keep a discussion going past sensitive points that might otherwise end the discussion or escalate hostilities. However, euphemisms have their down side. They can be used for very serious deception. In the 1930s and 1940s, the German bureaucratic memos called their Nazi mass murder of the Jews "the final solution to the Jewish problem."

■ ············ Concept Check 5 ············ ■

Which term is a euphemism for "American"?

a. Yankee   d. all of the above

b. capitalist pig   e. none of the above

c. imperialist

Sometimes we pay insufficient attention to the connotations of what we say. Suppose you were asked one of the following questions.

1. Is the government spending too much for welfare?
2. Is the government spending too much for assistance to the poor?

In a recent public opinion poll, it was found that twice as many Americans said "yes" to question 1 than to question 2. Can you see how connotations accounted for the difference? Pollsters, poets, and advertisers are the three groups in our society who need to be the most sensitive to connotations.

Two words that are synonymous according to a dictionary or a thesaurus can often have radically different connotations. Some public relations people make their fortunes by trading on their appreciation of these subtleties. Others achieve success by finding synonyms that disguise what is meant. Let's suppose you are designing a product for the U.S. Department of Defense. You discover that the D.O.D. purchasers will pay your company a lot more money for a tool if you call it a "manually powered fastener-driving impact device"[6] than if you simply call it a "hammer." The phrase isn't a euphemism for hammer, but it does serve to obscure what is really meant. Such phrases are called *doubletalk*. One D.O.D. purchase order called a steel nut a "hexiform rotatable surface compression unit." Can you imagine a guy with sunglasses and a trenchcoat walking into the local hardware store and whispering a request for a hexiform rotatable surface compression unit? During the 1991 U.S. war in Kuwait and Iraq, the Navy reported a 90 percent success rate for its Tomahawk missiles. By "success rate" the Navy meant the rate of successfully leaving the launch pad when the fire button was pressed. An even worse coverup term was "collateral damage," which was what the military called damage to ordinary citizens and their homes and vehicles.

"*Damn it with faint praise.*"
•   •

Drawing by Ross; © 1988 The New Yorker Magazine, Inc.

Making Unintended Innuendos

Here is another letter from Anne's parents to her elementary school teacher:

> Anne was late because she was not early. . . . She is too slow to be quick.

If you were Anne's teacher, you would notice the implication that Anne is dimwitted, but you'd discount it as sloppy communication because you would apply the principle of charity and figure out what the parent probably meant instead.

An **innuendo** is a negative suggestion made by disguised references or veiled comments about a person. If your teacher or school counselor were to write a letter of recommendation for you that said, "This student always managed to spell his name correctly," you would be upset by the innuendo. The writer is suggesting that you have few talents; being able to spell one's own name correctly is such a minor positive feature that the reader is likely to believe the writer cannot find anything more positive to say. This letter is an example of damning with faint praise, even if the counselor was sincerely trying to say something positive about you.

■ . . . .   **Concept Check 6**   . . . . ■

Identify the innuendo in the following passage.

The vice-president is a man who projects the image of being honest.

Not all innuendo is unintended. If you call your opponent a "possible liar," you are insinuating something. You aren't specifically charging that he is a liar, but you aren't exactly withholding the charge either.

Imagine that you are a university professor who has been asked to write a short letter of recommendation for a student, Juanita Barrena, who wants to be admitted to social work graduate school. Here are two recommendation letters. Notice that they both state the same facts, yet one is positive and one is negative. How could that be?

> To whom it concerns:
>
> Ms. Juanita Barrena, one of my ex-students, surprise me by asking that I write a letter of recommendation to you. Although she got an A- instead of an A, she was friendly and, if I remember correctly, organized a study group for the texts. Occasionally she spoke in class. I recommend her.
>
> Yours truly,
>
> Washington Carver

> To the Graduate School of Social Work:
>
> I am delighted to have been asked by my student Juanita Barrena to write a letter of recommendation to your graduate school of social work. Juanita excelled in my European history course, capturing an A-. In addition to her good grade, she stands out in my mind as being quite exceptional. Not only did her insightful comments capture the attention of the entire class while demonstrating an excellent grasp of the material, but she also showed special initiative by organizing a study group for my tests. Organizing this group demonstrated her special talent for using her social skills to achieve a specific goal that contributed to the group as a whole. Regarding her personality, I am again happy to be able to add more favorable comments; she is very friendly, an especially appropriate asset for a future career in social work. I am convinced that Juanita has demonstrated a high level of academic and social skills and shows promise of succeeding in her graduate work. Again I am happy to recommend her wholeheartedly for admission to your graduate program.
>
> Yours truly,
>
> Prof. Washington Carver
> History Department
> phone: (415) 278-6424

The emotional tone of the second letter is more animated and positive. For example, the second says "capturing an A −," which is more positive than "getting an A − instead of an A." In the second letter, Carver says he is "delighted to have been asked" to write the letter, but in the first letter he says he is "surprised" to have been asked, raising the possibility that the request was an unpleasant surprise. The second letter is longer, showing that the professor gave more attention to the student's request. The typos in the first letter are at best a sign of Carver's inattention. In the second letter, Carver added his phone number, demonstrating his willingness to talk further if the admissions committee desires; doing so is evidence he believes Barrena is worthy of some extra effort on his part.

Disobeying Rules of Discourse

A cardinal rule of good communication is to *imagine yourself in the shoes of the person you are trying to communicate with.* Here is another rule: If you don't like what someone has to say, don't let him say it again. This rule is not, however, a rule of good communication. This one is, though: *Obey the rules of discourse.* The rules of discourse are the rules that guide communicators in normal writing and conversation. These rules are the guidelines most everyone follows and expects others to follow. We try, for example, to interpret other people's speech the way they intend it to be interpreted. We try not to be long winded or roundabout. We try to be courteous. We violate a rule of discourse when we praise faintly. If you are going to praise something, you are normally expected not to praise it at a lower level than it deserves.

Some of the rules of discourse are rules of logical reasoning, and some are not. Interpreting someone's speech the right way is a rule of logical reasoning, but being courteous is not.

It's a rule of discourse not to ask someone to do the impossible, and it's a rule not to say something unless you believe it. That is why it is so odd to say, "That is true, but I don't really believe it." It is also a rule not to give too little information, too much information, or irrelevant information.

These rules are for normal situations. You don't follow the rules when you want to keep information secret or when you want to distract people by providing them with so much information that they won't think to ask you the questions you don't want asked.

■ ⋯⋯⋯⋯ Concept Check 7 ⋯⋯⋯⋯ ■

What rule of discourse are you violating if, when there is a knock on your door, you open it smiling and say, "You're not unwelcome to come in"?

Using sarcasm is a technique that intentionally violates the rules. Saying in a sarcastic tone "Yes, I believe you" conveys just the opposite. It is an interesting way to say, "No, I do not believe you." We occasionally violate conversational rules in order to achieve some special effects. However, such violations are unusual.

Review of Major Points

This chapter examined a variety of ways that writers and speakers communicate less well than they expect. Sometimes a writer will unwittingly make statements with low information content, will mask the true meaning with euphemism, doubletalk, or innuendo, will use sloppy sentence construction, or will violate the rules of discourse. The chapter also introduced the principle of charity, which readers use to help interpret materials by writers who do not say what they mean or mean what they say.

Glossary

euphemism A more gentle word or phrase used to replace a harsh-sounding one.

innuendo A negative suggestion made by disguised references or veiled comments about a person.

principle of charity Giving the benefit of the doubt to writers and speakers who have said something silly or obviously false, and not taking them too literally.

Answers to Concept Checks

1. You *did* get rid of "tootle," didn't you? There are many ways to rewrite the statement more clearly. Here is one: "Lightly honk your horn if a pedestrian blocks your path. If he continues to block your path, honk more vigorously."

2. Answer (b). The point is to eliminate the sexual allusion.

3. Answer (d). Brennan is accused of being a baby-killer, and the speaker wants you to pray for Brennan's death. Answer (b) is not as good as (d) because it contains much less information. The pastor would have done better to have paid attention to the following rule of discourse: Imagine yourself in the shoes of the person you are trying to communicate with.

4. Underarm antiperspirant.

5. Answer (e). Answers (b) and (c) are more negative than "American." Answer (a) is not more negative than "American" in some regions of the world. New Englanders have no problem with being called "Yankee" as long as they aren't called "Yankee dogs." But "Yankee" is not *less* negative for anybody, so cannot be a euphemism.

6. The innuendo is that the vice-president is not as honest as his public relations image would suggest.

7. Don't be roundabout.

Review and Writing Exercises

1. What is wrong with the following headline, which appeared in an American daily newspaper?

Religion Plays Major Part in the Message of Easter

2. Write a realistic 10-second TV commercial for Goldstar perfume in which you say too little with too many words.

3. Match the harsh words in the left column with their euphemisms on the right:

retreat   mentally deranged

mad   adjust downward

drop   neutralize

murder   strategic movement to the rear

son of a bitch   pass away

bite the dust   s.o.b.

4. Find a more euphemistic equivalent of these terms:

disaster   spying

fired (from a job)   old person

false teeth   tell a lie

5. Give a euphemism for urination, and use it in a sentence.

6. The best euphemism for his "death" is his

   a. being butchered   d. inspiration to us all

   b. living   e. treachery

   c. passing away

7. A boy named Stephen gets the nickname "Steve" and a girl named Susan gets the nickname "Sue," but a girl named Helen has a connotation problem. Explain.

8. Which one of these synonyms has the greatest negative connotation?

   a. inform   c. apprise

   b. squeal   d. notify

9. Rewrite these excuses more clearly[7]:

   a. Stanley had to miss some school. He had an attack of whooping cranes in his chest.

    b. Please excuse Jane on Monday, Tuesday, and Wednesday. She had an absent tooth.

    c. Please excuse Jim Friday. He had loose vowels.

    d. The basement of our house got flooded where the children slept so they had to be evaporated.

    e. Please excuse Connie from gym class today, as she has difficulty breeding.

    f. Anne did not do her homework because I couldn't understand it.

■ 10. Edit the following passage, concentrating on removing abuses of the rules of grammar:

> In these early times, as communication by sea became easier, piracy become a common profession both among the Hellenes and the barbarian who lived along the Greek coast and on the islands. The leading pirates were powerful men, both acting out of self-interest and in order to support the weak among their own people. They would descend upon unprotected settlements and cities to kill, rape, and to plunder. Everyone was afraid for their lives when the pirates landed. Nobody wanted a pirate knocking at their front door.

● 11. Imagine that Susan Waltham is a receptionist in the laser printer division of your corporation, and you are her direct supervisor. Write two letters of recommendation for her, one very positive and the other much less so, although it is still a recommendation, not an attack. Both your letters should contain the same facts: (a) she gets to work on time, (b) she is courteous and helpful both on the phone and with employees and clients who contact her, and (c) she is as good a receptionist as the last three you've employed. Don't add other significant facts.

12. Doubletalk is not a euphemism, but it is a way of disguising what you mean. Create some doubletalk for the term "pencil."[8]

13. For each of the following sentences, guess what the author meant to say, then rewrite it more clearly.[9]

    a. I had been driving for forty-five years when I fell asleep at the wheel and had an accident.

    b. The guy was all over the road. I had to swerve a number of times before I hit him.

    c. The telephone pole was approaching. I was attempting to swerve out of its way, when it struck my front end.

    d. An invisible car came out of nowhere, struck my vehicle, and vanished.

    e. I saw a slow-moving, sad-faced, old gentleman as he bounced off the hood of my car.

    f. I was thrown from my car as it left the road. I was later found in a ditch by some stray cows.

● 14. Select some controversial topic about which you have an opinion (i.e., a belief). Write a one- or two-page argument giving reasons to support your opinion. The reasons should not merely be a history of your thinking in arriving at your opinion but instead should be reasons that are likely to convince other people to adopt it. That is, deemphasize the genesis of your opinion and emphasize the justification of your opinion. Your argument must contain no loaded language whatsoever. Hand it in typed and double-spaced, if possible.

■ 15. What did Mrs. Malaprop probably mean in Sheridan's play *The Rivals* when she said, "He is the very pineapple of politeness"?

CHAPTER

4

Writing with the Appropriate Precision

Good communication requires that we be precise enough for the purpose at hand. Writers can fail to achieve this goal of precision when they create passages that are ambiguous, vague, overly general, or pseudoprecise, as we shall see in this chapter.

Being Ambiguous

Newspaper headlines are a notorious place where the rules of grammar get bent, and we readers have to make the best of it. The following headline is about retaliation for the trade barriers between the U.S. and Japan:

More Sanctions Coming, Japan Warned

This headline is difficult to interpret. Is Japan doing the warning, or is Japan being warned? There is no way to tell; the headline has more than one reasonable interpretation. Because there is more than one interpretation, the headline is said to be *ambiguous*. Ambiguity is one way of the many ways writers can be imprecise.

Here is another imprecise headline that can be taken in two ways:[1]

Air Force Considers Dropping Some New Bombs

Are officials going to delete a weapons program, or are planes going to drop some new bombs on the enemy? Half the readership will go away believing something different from what was intended by the headline writer.

In the Japan headline, ambiguity occurs in the grammar and thus in the meaning of the whole sentence; in the Air Force headline ambiguity occurs in the meaning of a single word. In the first case, the problem is ambiguity of syntax; in the second it is ambiguity of semantics.[2] It is not especially important to be able to distinguish the two kinds; the main point is that both kinds are sources of imprecision that block effective communication.

Definition   If a word, phrase, or sentence is too imprecise (for the needs of the audience) because it has two or more distinct interpretations, it is **ambiguous**.

Ambiguity is a kind of imprecision; it's a way of being unclear. So, one principle of good communication is to *avoid ambiguity*.

Concept Check 1

The grammar of the following headline is ambiguous. How?

Egyptians Are More Like Italians Than Canadians

Context and Background Knowledge

The sentence "Revolutionary War Admiral John Paul Jones is at the bank" doesn't contain enough clues for you to tell whether he is at a river bank or a financial bank. Therefore, the term *bank* occurs ambiguously in the sentence.[3] However, that same word doesn't occur ambiguously in the following sentence:

> Leroy is at the bank frantically trying to withdraw his savings before the financial system collapses.

The river bank interpretation would now be too strange, so the word *bank* here means financial bank. The other words that occur in the sentence give strong clues as to which sense is meant. These surrounding words are part of the **context** of the sentence. The context can also include surrounding sentences and paragraphs. In addition, the context includes the situation in which the sentences are used, the time, the identity of the speaker, and the speaker's body language. In the above example, the word *bank* is unambiguous not only because of the context but because of our background knowledge that people withdraw savings from financial banks and not river banks. That is, we can **disambiguate** in favor of financial bank and against river bank. The conclusion to be drawn from this example is that the principle "Avoid ambiguity" requires not that you completely avoid using words that have multiple meanings but that you avoid them when they interfere with communication. The corresponding principle for the listener or reader is to *use the context of the sentence and your background knowledge to identify what statement is being made with the sentence.*

Definition A **statement** is what a speaker or writer states.

The one sentence "Leroy is at the bank" can be used to make two statements: in one context, a statement about a river bank; in another context, a statement about a financial bank.

The failure to properly disambiguate using context is the key to the effectiveness of the following joke, about the President and the First Lady eating out in a restaurant:

Waiter: Madame, what would you like to drink?

First Lady: A glass of your house white wine will be fine.

Waiter: And for an appetizer?

First Lady: Tonight, I'll skip the appetizer.

Waiter: And for the main dish, madame?

First Lady: I'll have the T-bone steak.

Waiter: And for the vegetable?

First Lady: Oh, he'll have the same thing.

■ ············ Concept Check 2 ············ ■

Consider this ambiguous sentence construction: "I saw the man on the hill with a telescope." Which one of the following is *not* a legitimate disambiguation?

a. The hill with a telescope was where I saw the man.

b. I was on the hill with a telescope, and the man saw me.

c. The man with a telescope, who was on the hill, was seen by me.

d. I was on the hill and I used a telescope to see the man.

The word *inconsistent* has multiple meanings that can produce difficulties. A person is said to be "inconsistent" if he or she changes his or her mind more often than you'd expect. That sense of the word is synonymous with *inconstant*. However, in this book the word *inconsistent* is normally used in the sense of saying that something is both so and not so, as in this inconsistency from Woody Allen: "I don't believe in the afterlife, but I'm going to take a change of underwear."[4]

Concept Check 3

For the last month, sometimes Beth has loved Mark on weekdays and Todd on weekends, but at other times she has loved Todd on weekdays and Mark on weekends. Is she being inconsistent? What does the word *inconsistent* mean in this question?

The word *some* also has multiple meanings. It can mean "at least one and possibly all" or "at least one but not all." Only the context can reveal which. Suppose three people corner me in an alley at night. After a brief but futile attempt to solve the problem with words, I pull a knife and say, "Get out of here, or some of you are going to die." Here, I am using the word *some* to suggest at least one and possibly all will die. I don't mean some will and some won't. For a second example using this sense of the word *some*, suppose I bring back rock samples from a mountain. I do a chemical analysis of one rock and discover that it contains sulfur. Then I say, "OK, now we know that *some* of those rocks contain sulfur." Here *some* also means at least one and possibly all. On the other hand, if I say, "I grade on a curve, and some of you are going to flunk," I mean at least one but not all. Your sensitivity to context and background knowledge enables you to pick the intended sense of *some*.

Concept Check 4

Which of the two meanings of *some* is intended in the following sentence, or can't the reader tell?

> The survey of major corporate executives indicates that 60 percent of those sampled believe that some American graduates are not trainable for any entry-level management position in their corporations.

The principle "Avoid ambiguity" can now be clarified. Multiple meanings are not necessarily a sign of ambiguity. If you say, "I don't want to fish on that muddy bank. Let's stay in the boat," you won't cause a communication problem. Speakers and writers who use phrases that have multiple meanings can legitimately count on the audience or readers to pay attention to context and to rely on their background knowledge to remove potential ambiguity. Good writers do not make their readers struggle hard to do so, though.

If I say, "I climbed a tall mountain last year," I am not saying something ambiguous simply because I did not state the name of the mountain. The point here regarding the uncertainty about the name of the mountain is that, although ambiguity is a cause of uncertainty, not every kind of uncertainty produces ambiguity. Ambiguity is a kind of uncertainty about meaning, but it's not an uncertainty about reference. What is to be avoided with ambiguity is multiple meaning, not multiple reference. The name *George Washington* is not ambiguous; you just don't know what specific person is being referred to. Similarly, the word *bank* is not ambiguous in "Leroy is at a financial bank," but you are uncertain as to which specific financial bank is being referred to. Uncertainty of reference is not ambiguity, although some other writers do prefer to call it so.

■ .... Concept Check 5 .... ■

Explain why the following statement is humorous.

> Elasas and other researchers say they believe that aspartame can do more damage over a long period of time than federal health officials.[5]

Ambiguity causes trouble for arguments as well as for individual sentences. Suppose, for example, someone argues as follows:

> Shipments of our tools to Toronto take place on Mondays.
> Today is Monday.
> So, there is a shipment of our tools to Toronto today.

This is a sloppy argument because the first reason is ambiguous. Is the first reason saying that we ship every Monday or only that, whenever we do ship, it is on a Monday (but not necessarily every Monday)? This example demonstrates that ambiguity can affect argument quality.

Translation by Machine

What do you tell a computer when you want it to disambiguate by being sensitive to context and to use its background knowledge — that is, its database? For example, suppose you want to build a computer to understand English and to translate English into another language. How would the computer handle these two sentences?

Time flies like an arrow in the sky.

Fruit flies like an apple on the tree.

When you read these two sentences, you figured out unconsciously that *flies* is a verb in the first sentence but not in the second.[6] Much of our understanding of English requires a great amount of unconscious disambiguation of this sort. A computer probably cannot be told everything it needs to "know" to do this kind of processing for all possible English sentences.

To explore this problem further, try to make sense of the following statement:

The chickens are ready to eat.

Are the chickens ready to do something, or are they about to be eaten? No ambiguity problem occurs with this grammatically similar statement:

The steaks are ready to eat.

When you read this statement, you unconsciously searched your background knowledge for whether steak is the kind of thing that eats other things, and you were then able to rule out that interpretation of the statement.

If there is ever going to be an *artificially intelligent* computer program that uses background knowledge to disambiguate, someone is going to have to instruct it to do all the information processing that is done unconsciously by us humans, who are *naturally intelligent*.

In the 1950s, when the field of computer science was beginning, many computer designers and programmers made radically optimistic claims about how they were on the verge of automating language understanding and language translation. The U.S. government was convinced, and it invested a great amount of money in attempts to automate language translation. For example, it funded a project to develop a computer program that could readily translate from English to Russian and also from Russian to English. After years of heavy investment, one of the researchers tested the main product of all these efforts by feeding in the following English sentence:

The spirit is willing, but the flesh is weak.

The researcher then took the Russian output and fed it into the machine to be translated back into English, expecting to get something close to the original sentence. Here was the result:

The vodka is strong, but the meat is rotten.

As a consequence, the government drastically reduced funds for the machine translation studies. Machine understanding of natural language is still a distant goal. Machines seem to need special, artificial languages so that what an instruction means is in no way dependent on context and background knowledge. To talk to a computer, you have to be unambiguous.

The examples of the failure of machine translation show us that ambiguity is a serious obstacle to any mechanical treatment of language understanding. We humans, who are naturally intelligent, have an unmechanical method, or at least a highly sophisticated mechanism, that we use in the art of disambiguation. This art requires our developing a subtle sensitivity to the context of what is said and requires an impressive ability to detect what in our background knowledge is relevant to removing any potential ambiguity.

Semantic Disagreements

When two people disagree, the source of their disagreement might be that they are using the same term in two different senses. If they could clear up the ambiguity, their disagreement might end. Here is an example:

1st speaker: Since you're from Brazil and speak Portuguese, you are not an American.

2nd speaker: We South Americans are as American as you North Americans, and I say you are an ignorant Yankee who will someday choke on your own conceit.

The first speaker is probably a U.S. citizen who believes that only U.S. citizens are "Americans." The second speaker uses "American" more broadly to refer to anybody from North, Central, or South America. Their disagreement is a **semantic disagreement**; they are disagreeing about the meaning of a word. A semantic disagreement is also called a *verbal disagreement*. Semantic disagreements are disagreements about meanings, but *substantial disagreements* are disagreements about how the world is or about what should be done. Ambiguity is one cause of semantic disagreements, and clarifying of terms will often resolve the disagreement.

Nevertheless, people sometimes have substantial disagreements in addition to mere semantic disagreements, and clearing up their disagreements about word meanings won't settle their conflict.

■ .... Concept Check 6 .... ■

Identify the term below that is the cause of the semantic dispute:

Look what it says here on page 14. The *National Enquirer* reports that the average American family with at least one Filipino ancestor has 1.3 family members who speak the language called Tagalog. That is both correct and incorrect. I agree with the newspaper that a lot of American families do speak some Tagalog, because I have a friend from Hawaii whose grandmother was Filipino, and she taught him to speak Tagalog. Now he is the only one who can. His family is average, too. So, the newspaper is correct about all that, but it is incorrect when it says every typical family has 1.3 members who speak Tagalog. Only one family member can speak Tagalog, not 1.3. There can't be 1.3 family members in any family, even a typical one like my friend's, can there? The newspaper is being silly.

Equivocation

If you went to an electronics store to buy a stereo on sale only to discover that the store didn't have the advertised item and tried to sell you a higher-priced one instead, you'd be upset. The store's technique is called *bait and switch*. In reasoning, too, it is unfair to begin an argument using a word with one sense and then later use it in a different sense. That's equivocating. **Equivocation** is the illegitimate switching of the meaning of a term during the reasoning. For example, the word *discrimination* changes meaning without warning in the following passage:

> Those noisy people object to racism because they believe it is discrimination. Yet, discrimination is hard to define, and even *they* agree that it's okay to choose carefully which tomatoes to buy in the supermarket. They discriminate between the overripe, the underripe, and the just right. They discriminate between the TV shows they don't want to watch and those they do. Everybody discriminates about something, so what's all this fuss about racism?

The passage begins talking about discrimination in the sense of denying people's rights but then switches to talking about discrimination in the sense of noticing a difference. The conclusion that racism doesn't deserve so much attention doesn't follow at all. Because of the switch in meanings, the reasons for the conclusion are ultimately irrelevant.

For a second example of equivocation, watch the word *critical* in the following passage:

> Professor Weddle praises critical thinkers, especially for their ability to look closely and not be conned by sloppy reasoning. However, critical thinkers are critical, aren't they? They will attack something even if it doesn't deserve to be attacked. Isn't it irritating to meet someone who is always knocking down everything you say, for no good reason? These critical people sure don't deserve to be praised, do they? Evidently, then, Professor Weddle praises people who do not deserve to be praised. What a confused person he is. He should take a course in critical thinking himself.[7]

Many people are apt to confuse the two meanings of *critical thinker*; does it refer to a picky person or to a perceptive thinker on the lookout for good reasons? The title of this book was changed from *Critical Thinking* to *Logical Reasoning* for that very reason.

■ ·········· Concept Check 7 ·········· ■

Fill in the blank: "Dolores has more money than Barbara, and Barbara has more money than Terri, so Dolores _____ more money than Terri."

a. does not have

b. might have

c. most probably has

d. has

Isn't the answer (d)? This question will seem trivial to you if you have properly used your background knowledge about how test questions work, thus discounting the possibility that the two *Barbara* words might refer to different Barbaras. Wouldn't you have been upset if this were a real test question and the answer was (c) because you were supposed to worry that maybe two different Barbaras were being talked about? Your experience in test taking tells you to assume that *Barbara* refers to the same person unless there is some reason to believe otherwise, which there isn't in this example. Because we readers do properly make such assumptions, we would accuse a test maker of equivocating if the correct answer were supposed to be (c).

Being Too Vague

> In this business a little vagueness goes a long way. — Jerry Brown, politician

In the statement "Jane Austen is a poor person," the term *poor* is ambiguous. The ambiguity can be removed by expanding the context of the statement and saying, "Jane Austen is a poor person to choose for such a complicated job." Suppose, instead, the ambiguity is removed by saying, "Jane Austen is a financially poor person." Still, you might well ask, "How financially poor?" You recognize that financial poverty is a *matter of degree*. When there is a matter of degree about whether something is an *x*, then the word *x* is *vague* in that context. In the sentence "Jane Austen is a financially poor person" the word *poor* occurs vaguely, but not ambiguously. Although it is quite common for vagueness and ambiguity to occur together in one statement, *vagueness is different from ambiguity*.

When somebody uses the word *bald*, it can be reasonable to ask about the degree of baldness by saying, "Just how bald do you mean?" But when someone uses the word *seven* it would *not* be reasonable to ask, "Just how seven do you mean?" Nor would it make sense to ask, "Seven to what degree?" *Seven* is one of those rare words that is not vague at all in any context.

Imagine a man having just enough hair that you have a tough time telling whether he is bald. Perhaps he is on the fuzzy borderline between bald and balding. You may want to say that he is "bald, by and large" or perhaps that he is "not exactly bald but surely doesn't have much hair." In the first case you are saying he is bald, but in the second case you are saying he is not bald. The existence of this borderline case of being bald makes the word *bald* vague. Vagueness is fuzziness of meaning. The line between bald and not bald is not sharp; it is fuzzy.

Definition An expression *x* is **vague** when it is imprecise either because there are borderline cases of being an *x* or because there are degrees of being an *x*.

Fuzzy phrases are vague, but fuzzy heads are not. Language and thought can be vague; the physical world cannot be.

Judges often tear their hair out trying to deal with fuzzy language. They must decide what counts as "stealing," for example, and they don't like borderline cases. They are always trying to make language be more precise than it is for ordinary speakers. Suppose a prosecutor charges a delivery person with stealing, because she used snow from a homeowner's yard to resupply the ice in her van's ice chest. This taking of snow is a borderline example of "stealing," but the judge has to make a decision; either she is innocent, or she is not. The judge cannot say she is "sort of innocent." If the judge of an appellate court decides that the action is not stealing, that very decision helps redefine the term *stealing* for future cases. It sets a precedent. This example shows that *redefinition is a way to remove vagueness.*

To find language that is free of ambiguity and vagueness, look to the terminology of mathematics, computer programming, and symbolic logic. Computers cannot tolerate imprecision; we have to be precise about everything to communicate with a computer. For just this reason computers are hard for us to talk to. In ordinary conversations with human beings we don't need to be as precise. Saying "I'll probably go to see that film with you soon" is good enough for a human. Saying "The probability is 72 percent that I'll go to the film with you within the next forty-two to forty-six hours" would be strange because it is too precise. It's a social convention that we usually don't go to the trouble of being precise unless we need to be.

Scientists do need to be precise. They speak of "volt," not "jolt." They use "species" instead of "kind of critter." Scientists define their terms more precisely than the rest of us do, and this precision is one key to their success. Our ordinary word *bug* is vague and not as useful in accurately describing our world as are the scientific words *insect* and *arachnid*, which have fairly sharp definitions. For example, a creature must have six legs to be an insect and eight to be an arachnid (e.g., a spider). Count the legs on a cockroach sometime. The definition of *insect* is sharp because there is a way to determine whether something is an insect; it is clear which objects in the world count as being insects and which do not. The definition of *bug* is not precise. The term has many borderline cases. Retaining the familiar but vague term *bug* in communications among biologists would be an obstacle to the growth of the science.

Precision is helpful not only in scientific classification but with measurement as well. If scientists measured feet using a notion of feet that varied with each scientist's own foot, can you imagine the difficulties?

Concept Check 8

Following are four choices for completing the sentence. They vary in their vagueness. Rank them, beginning with the least vague (i.e., the most precise).

I'll meet you . . .

a. outside Sears' north entrance next to where the Salvation Army lady usually stands.
b. nearby.
c. at the north entrance of the Sears store.
d. at Sears.

Being Too General

What, then, is generality, as opposed to vagueness? A statement is called a **generalization** if it uses a general term. **General terms** refer to a class of objects. The general term *metal* refers to the class of metals. Classes are sets or groups. The bigger the class, the more general the term. Classes are more general than their subclasses and usually are more general than any of the members of the class. For example, the term *detective* is more general than *English detective*, which in turn is more general than *Sherlock Holmes*. The latter term is not general at all; it is **specific**.

Vagueness is not the same as generality. In fact, being more general can in some cases make a term even less vague. For example, *even numbers* is more general but less vague than *lucky even numbers*.

Overgenerality can cause imprecision. Suppose you are asked, "Who would you like to see run for your state's attorney general in next year's election?" You would be answering at too general of a level if you responded with "Oh, a citizen."[8] The term *citizen* is neither ambiguous nor vague. It is too general. The questioner was expecting a more specific answer.

Often we state generalizations with **quantity terms**, such as *17, all, many,* or *some*. For example, the statement "All metals conduct electricity" is a generalization about metals. So is "Many metals are magnetic." The former is called a **universal generalization** because of the quantity term *all*, whereas the latter is a **nonuniversal generalization** because of the quantity term *many*. By using the word *many*, the speaker hedges and implies that the property of being magnetic need not be as universal (pervasive) for metals as the property of conducting electricity. Saying that "33 percent of all metals are magnetic" is also a generalization. It is a nonuniversal, **statistical generalization**. Universal generalizations are sometimes called *categorical generalizations*, although we won't use this term.

When someone says, "Generally speaking, adults prefer chocolate ice cream to vanilla ice cream," the word *generally* also indicates a nonuniversal generalization. *Generally* means "most of the time but not necessarily all the time." Ditto for *in general* and *usually*.

Generalizations aren't always easy to detect. "A shark can be dangerous" is a generalization about the class of sharks. Generalizations about time are even more difficult to spot. "This grain of salt is water soluble" is a universal generalization about the class of all times, because the speaker is essentially saying that if this specific grain of salt were put in water at *any* time, it would dissolve.

■ ⋯⋯⋯⋯ Concept Check 9 ⋯⋯⋯⋯ ■

When the babysitter says, "I caught your baby almost every time I threw him in the air," she is generalizing about her ability. Her generalization is

a. universal

b. nonuniversal

Suppose you know Jane Austen's street address and you know that your friend Susan needs to get in touch with her. You and Susan are citizens of the U.S. and are in Iowa. If Susan asks you if you know where Jane Austen lives and you say, "I think she lives in the United States," Susan will think you are weird. Your answer is too general. You are violating the rule of discourse that a person should answer with the appropriate precision for the situation and not be overly general.

Being Pseudoprecise

Vagueness, ambiguity, and overgenerality are three forms of imprecision. Imprecision, in turn, is intimately connected to lack of sufficient information. For example, when a salesperson describes a stereo receiver as "powerful," "having twice the clarity of the competition," and "being well designed," you are getting a bunch of vague descriptions and hardly any information at all.

There is a certain safety in imprecision. It's the kind of safety enjoyed by writers of fortunes for Chinese fortune cookies. These fortunes are always sufficiently imprecise that anyone can find a way of making them apply to his or her own life. A cookie says, "You will have success tomorrow." This is surely true, because almost everyone will have *some* success at something, even if it's only the success of tying one's shoelaces in the morning before getting hit by that truck. Here is an astrological example of safety via imprecision:

> Astrologer Judi sees a good year for all Zodiac signs, except that those born under the signs of Scorpio, Taurus, Aquarius, and Leo will remain in a continuing state of transformation — a period of intensity. "My advice to people with these signs is to do what has to be done and do it the very best you can. This will be very important."[9]

How could you test whether this astrological forecast turned out as predicted?

The value of a precise claim, as opposed to an imprecise one, is that you learn so much more when you learn that it is true. Saying that Latonya is twenty-three years old is more informative than saying she isn't a teenager any more. Putting a number on her age makes the claim more precise and thus more informative. Nevertheless, making a precise claim is riskier than making an imprecise one. If her twenty-third birthday is still a week away, then calling her twenty-three is incorrect but saying she's not a teenager any more is correct.

> The more precise a claim, the more informative it is if it does turn out to be true.

Another value of precise claims is that they are easier to check out. If someone says that the city of Vacaville has ghosts, the person is not being very precise about where or when or how the ghosts appear. As a result, scientists won't pay much attention. However, if someone reports that two ghosts in blue gowns appear at midnight in front of the Vacaville City Hall whenever there is a full moon, this claim is more worthy of scientific attention, provided reasonable eyewitness testimony exists to support it. The scientist now has a better idea of how to test this ghost story as opposed to the original, imprecise one. In short, the precise claim is more readily testable, and testability is a scientific virtue.

> Untestable claims are unscientific.

Concept Check 10

It's Monday and you are a factory manager who has just sampled some of the resistors manufactured in your electronics factory today. All of them are defective. However, you believe you have detected the cause of the problem, and you have some good ideas about how to fix things for tomorrow. After making those changes, you have to forecast the quality of tomorrow's production of resistors. Which one of the following statements would be most likely to be true?

a. All of Tuesday's total output of resistors will work OK.

b. Many of Tuesday's total output of resistors will work OK.

c. Some of Tuesday's total output of resistors will work OK.

Concept Check 11

Suppose the following were your choices for the previous exercise. Which one is most likely to be true?

a. Over 90 percent of Tuesday's total output of resistors will work OK.

b. Exactly 95 percent of Tuesday's total output of resistors will work OK.

c. At least 95 percent of Tuesday's total output of resistors will work OK.

d. 94 to 96 percent of Tuesday's total output of resistors will work OK.

Saying "exactly 95 percent," if it were true, would be much more informative than hedging with "over 90 percent." Normally, when you improve the precision of a number, you are being more informative. But there are exceptions. Here is one. The nineteenth-century American writer Mark Twain once said he was surprised to learn that the Mississippi River was 1,000,003 years old. He hadn't realized that rivers were that old. When asked about the "3," he answered with a straight face that three years earlier a geologist had told him the Mississippi River was a million years old. In this case, "1,000,003" is not precise; it is silly. Technically, "1,000,003" is called *pseudoprecise*. Pseudoprecision is an important cause of fallacious reasoning when quantifying something—that is, putting a number on it. A claim is pseudoprecise if it assigns a higher degree of precision than makes sense.

Definition A number used by a person to quantify some property that an object has is **pseudoprecise** if (1) the property cannot *be* quantified, (2) the object cannot have the property to *that* degree of precision, or (3) the object could have the property to that degree of precision but the person is not justified in claiming that much precision.

The Mississippi River story is an example of type 3. A number (1,000,003) is used by a person (Mark Twain) to **quantify** (measure with a number) some property (age) that an object (the Mississippi River) has. The river could be precisely old, but Twain was not justified in claiming that much precision.

Here is an example of pseudoprecision of type 1. If you heard that Mark Twain admired Andrew Jackson 2.3 times as much as he admired the previous president, John Quincy Adams, you would be hearing something pseudoprecise, because the precision is a sham. All you can sensibly say about admiration is that some is strong, some is weak, and some is stronger than others.

Although quantifying can often improve precision, there is a limit to how precise you can get. For example, if you were to read that Napoleon Bonaparte was 5 foot 1.4748801 inches tall, you shouldn't believe it. Measuring people's height doesn't make sense to this many decimal places. Inhaling can raise a person's measured height by tenths of an inch, while taking a bath can lower it by a hundredth. Too precise a height for Napoleon is an example of pseudoprecision of type 2.

If a statistical report mentions that the average size nuclear family in your community has 2.3 children, is this number pseudoprecise? No. The 2.3 statistic is the result of dividing the whole number of children in nuclear families by the whole number of nuclear families. It doesn't imply that any real family has 2.3 children, which would be silly.[10]

Concept Check 12

Which one statement below probably suffers the most from pseudoprecision?

a. There are an average of 1.5 guns in each household in Dallas, Texas.

b. Our company's computer can store 64,432,698 characters simultaneously.

c. The first flowering plant appeared on earth nearly 100 million years ago.

d. Today, David used his new precision laser distance-measuring tool and discovered the diameter of the cloud overhead to be 0.4331 times the diameter of the cloud that was overhead yesterday at the same time.

e. The reading head of the computer's magnetic disk is 0.4331 inches from the disk itself.

Improper Operationalization

In the following newspaper article, ask yourself how the researchers are counting Christians.

Number of Christians in the World Reported Up

A religious statistician says the number of Christians in the world rose last year from 1.57 billion to 1.64 billion, up from 32.4 percent of the total world population to 32.9 percent.

The Rev. David Barrett, editor of the *World Christian Encyclopedia*, says the trend indicates that a previous decline has been "dramatically halted and reversed."

Barrett, an Anglican priest now serving as consultant to the Southern Baptist Foreign Mission Board, said the most surprising growth has been in China, where there now are more than 52 million Christians.

Of the world's total, he says there are 907 million Roman Catholics, 322 million Protestants, 51.6 million Anglicans, and 273 million Eastern Orthodox Christians.[11]

The article does not tell you how the researchers decided whom to count as a Christian. You have to guess. Did the researchers mail a questionnaire to all the Christian churches in the world asking for membership totals? This way of counting would miss everyone who considers himself or herself a Christian but who isn't affiliated with a specific church, and it would overcount those persons who belong to more than one church. Did the researchers instead do a small poll of New Orleans and then assume that the rest of the world is like New Orleans as far as religion is concerned? There are many other operations they could have used to count Christians. The *operation* or method the researchers used could make a difference to their count. That is, the operationalization of the term *Christian* would make a difference in what the study says is the total number of Christians.

Definition The **operationalization** of a term is the operation or method used to tell whether the term applies.

When you question the operationalization of a term, you are essentially asking, "How did they measure *that*?" The word *Christian* and other imprecise terms need good operationalizations if accurate claims are going to be made using them. Without good operationalization, a claim using the term will suffer from inaccuracy, pseudo-precision, or both.

> Pseudoprecise numbers are produced by bad
> operationalization.

■ .... Concept Check 13 .... ■

What operationalization problem occurs here?

> Lying by politicians is up 10 percent in New York this year.

How intelligent are polar bears? Does South America have more political instability than Central America? It is more difficult to establish claims that use imprecise terms such as *intelligence* and *political instability* than it is to establish claims that use precise terms such as *voltage* or *mile*. That's one reason why social scientists have a tougher job than physical scientists in making scientific advances.

Let's consider the special problem of the social scientist. Suppose the newspaper reports on a scientist's finding that rich females are more intelligent on the average than poor males. The logical reasoner will ask, "How did the researcher figure out who is rich and who is intelligent?" Let's focus on the term *rich*. If the researcher merely *asked* each person whether he or she was rich, the answers are unreliable. But perhaps the researcher operationalized the concept of *rich* in some other way. Did she check each individual's finances and decide that anybody making over $100,000 per year was rich and anybody under that was poor? Even one cent under? If so, then the researcher does not mean what you and I do by the term *rich*.

Finding the best way to operationalize the vague term *intelligent* to decide whether rich females are more intelligent than poor males is also difficult. Yet some ways are better than others. Which among the following is the best?

a. Intelligent people are smarter than unintelligent people.

b. See whether the word *intelligent* has positive connotations.

c. Use an IQ test.

d. Ask the people involved whether they are intelligent.

e. Ask a large random sample of people whether they believe rich females are more intelligent than poor males.

Only (c) and (d) are operationalizations, so (a), (b), and (e) can be ruled out. Method (e) is a way to answer the question of whether rich women are more intelligent, but it's not a way to measure intelligence. Method (d) can be ruled out because of the subjectivity; people can be expected not to give honest assessments of themselves. That leaves the IQ test as the best of the lot.

Typically, an IQ test measures the ability to answer written questions. So, a typical IQ test is not an ideal measure of human intelligence. For example, if a person were to do poorly on an IQ test yet have been the primary inventor of an automobile engine that is 20 percent more energy efficient than all other automobile engines, that person should still be called "intelligent." In short, intelligence can show itself in many ways that aren't measured on an IQ test.

When you do read a headline such as "Biologists Report That Dolphins Are More Intelligent Than Polar Bears" or "Political Scientists Report That South America Is More Stable Politically Than Central America," you should probably give the reporter the benefit of the doubt that the scientists used some sort of decent operationalization for the key terms. If you can actually discover what operationalization was used, and you have no problem with it, you can believe the scientists' report more firmly. And if you learn that the scientists published their results in a mainstream scientific journal and not the proceedings of the Conference on Star Trek Reruns, you can be even more confident in the report. It is safe to assume that the editors of the scientific journal checked to see that there were no significant problems with the operationalization of the key terms, nor any other problems with the scientific study. That wouldn't be as safe an assumption to make about either editors of daily newspapers or TV reporters.

■ ············ **Concept Check 14** ············ ■

When a Gallup poll reports that Americans are 5 percent happier with America now that the U.S. has completed negotiations on an international fishing treaty designed to say who can fish for which fish, critical thinkers know that the most difficult term for the pollster to operationalize was

a. reports   b. that   c. 5 percent   d. poll   e. happier

■ ············ **Concept Check 15** ············ ■

"Social scientists from the University of Michigan report that over a quarter of all Canadian citizens they tested who had driven into Detroit from Canada on Saturday night had blood alcohol levels of .05 percent or greater." This sentence probably

a. contains pseudoprecision.

b. is exaggerating.

c. needs operationalization of the evaluative term "Saturday night."

d. is relying too heavily on a euphemism.

e. none of the above.

Review of Major Points

Ambiguity, vagueness, overgeneralization, and pseudoprecision are sources of imprecision and obstacles to communication. Vagueness can almost never be entirely eliminated from our statements, but excessive vagueness should be, as should overgeneralization and excessive multiple meaning (ambiguity). Vagueness is not the same as ambiguity. For example, the word *purple* is vague because there is no sharp boundary between purple and not purple, but it wouldn't be proper to call the word ambiguous, since there are not a small number of *distinct* interpretations. With vagueness, the uncertain interpretations form a continuum.

To stay on track, the logical reasoner must be sensitive to inadequate precision that occurs in semantic disagreements, equivocation, and faulty operationalization. The logical reasoner must also be aware of the effects of interpretation, context, background knowledge, universal and nonuniversal generalizations, and quantifying a concept.

Glossary

ambiguity A type of imprecision; a term is ambiguous if the context cannot be used to sufficiently rule out all the term's possible meanings but one.

context The sentence that a word or phrase occurs in, plus the surrounding sentences, the situation in which the sentences are used, the time, the identity of the speaker, and even the speaker's body language.

disambiguation Using context and one's background knowledge to detect the intended interpretation of a phrase and thereby remove the potential ambiguity.

equivocation Illegitimately switching the meaning of a term during some reasoning with the term.

general terms Terms that refer to a class of objects. For example, *Sherlock Holmes* is a specific term; *detective* is a general term.

generalization A general statement that attributes some property to a class. For example, the statement "Politicians have aggressive personalities" is a generalization about the class of politicians. Generalizations use quantity terms to attribute properties. In our example, the quantity term *all* is unstated.

nonuniversal generalization A generalization that does not require the property to apply to every member of the class. For example, saying "Most stars are not surrounded by life-sustaining planets" is a general statement about stars, but it is nonuniversal because the quantity term *most* does not apply the property of being surrounded by life-sustaining planets to the entire class of stars; it applies the property only to most of the class.

operationalization The operation or method used to tell whether a term applies in a particular context.

psuedoprecision Using a number to quantify some property that an object has when (1) the property cannot *be* quantified, (2) the object cannot have the property to *that* degree of precision, or (3) the object could have the property to that degree of precision but the person is not justified in claiming that much precision. For example, it would be pseudoprecise to say that apples taste 2.65 times better than oranges.

quantify To put a number on something. You can quantify a computer printer's maximum output by saying that it can print 100 characters per second. You cannot quantify the value of a human life.

quantity term A term assigning a quantity to a class, such as *17, each, every, most, all, some,* and *zero*.

semantic disagreement A disagreement about meaning; also called a verbal disagreement. Clarifying terms can resolve a semantic disagreement.

specific term A word or phrase that refers to a single object rather than to a class of objects. For example, *Madonna* is specific, but *singer* is general.

statement What a speaker or writer states. Uttering a declarative sentence is the usual way to make a statement.

statistical generalization A generalization whose quantity term is a percentage or statistic. Here is a true generalization about California women: one out of five California women smoke.

universal generalization A generalization that applies a property to every member of the class that is being generalized about. For example, saying "All Americans are rich" applies the property of being rich to every member of the class "Americans." Universal generalizations are sometimes called categorical generalizations.

vagueness Fuzziness of meaning. For example, the word *closer* is vague (but not ambiguous) in the sentence "Step closer." Vagueness need not be an obstacle to good communication if the command is precise enough for the situation — for example, the statement is made in response to the question "Did you say to step back or step closer?"

Answers to Concept Checks

1. The headline could mean "Egyptians are more like Italians than Canadians *are*," or "Egyptians are more like Italians than *like* Canadians."

2. Answer (b). The problem is with "the man saw me," because the original says I did the seeing; I was not seen.

3. Well, she *has* changed her mind and is being inconsistent in the sense of being inconstant or fickle, but she is not being *logically* inconsistent in the way that it is inconsistent to say "*x* is greater than 11 and also less than 11." The first sense of *inconsistent* concerns time, but logical inconsistency does not.

4. At least one but not all. Choosing the other interpretation of *some* would require the speaker to believe that maybe *every* graduate is untrainable; but surely the speaker isn't that pessimistic.

5. Personally, I believe federal officials can do more damage than aspartame, not less, don't you? The passage takes a shot at the federal health officials. To remove the disambiguation difficulties, the sentence should end with the word *believe*.

6. The reasoner has misinterpreted what the newspaper meant by the word *average*. The paper meant arithmetical average, the result of taking the mean value of several numbers. Yet when speaking of the average family that he knew from Hawaii, the reasoner used the word *average* in the sense of "typical." The reasoner is merely having a semantical dispute with the newspaper.

7. The answer is in the next paragraph of the text.

8. The appropriate order would be (a) (c) (d) (b).

9. Answer (b). It is nonuniversal because it permits exceptions.

10. The least precise answer is (c).

11. The least precise answer is (a). There is more room for success in "90 to 100" than in "at least 95" or in "94 to 96." Notice that answer (a) is not especially vague or ambiguous; the problem is just imprecision.

12. Answer (d). Can a cloud be given a width to an accuracy of a ten thousandth of an inch?

13. The main problem is to measure lies. One subproblem is that liars will cover up their lying. A second subproblem is that even if you can uncover the lies, you must still find a way to count them. The problems here are that one big lie might contain many small lies and that there is a fuzzy border between lying and stretching the truth.

14. Answer (e). How do you quantify (put a number on) happiness? Notice that *happier* is the *evaluative* term. The term *5 percent* is not hard to operationalize. What is hard to operationalize is "5 percent happier," but that is not one of the answer choices.

15. Answer (e). The .05 percent level can be accurately measured, so answers (a) and (b) are not correct. The word *Saturday* is not evaluative. There are no euphemisms here. Thus, by elimination, the answer is (e).

Review and Writing Exercises

1. Newspaper headline writers are notorious for creating headlines that are ambiguous or have a funny alternative interpretation that can be removed by the reader by using the principle of charity. Try your hand on these headlines. Rewrite them so that they are unambiguous and don't have a humorous interpretation:[12]

    a.   Red Tape Holds Up New Bridge

    b.   Prison Warden Says Inmates May Have 3 Guns

    c.   19 Feet Broken in Pole Vault

    d.   Babies Are What the Mother Eats

    e.   Police Discover Crack in Australia

    f.   Sharon to Press His Suit in Israel

    g.   Buildings Sway from San Francisco to L.A.

    h.   Cause of AIDS Found — Scientists

    i.   Potential Witness to Murder Drunk

    j.   Jerk Injures Neck, Wins Award

    k.   Terminal Smog Not Lethal

2. Add a comma to disambiguate the following headline and remove the humor. Make no other changes in the headline. Why is the headline humorous?

Honduran Military Chief Quits Saying He Is Fatigued[13]

3. Suppose a menu states, "You can have eggs and juice or cereal." Replace this ambiguous statement with one of the following statements. The replacement must be a legitimate interpretation of the sentence in the menu, yet it must disambiguate the sentence to make it clear that the customer cannot have both eggs and cereal. The best replacement is:

    a.   You cannot have both eggs and cereal.

    b.   You can have eggs, but not juice or cereal.

    c.   You can have (eggs or juice) and cereal.

    d.   You can have either eggs and juice, or else cereal.

    e.   You can have eggs, and you can also have your choice of either juice or else cereal.

■ 4. If Mario says, "Some of these grapes have seeds in them," can you be sure he also means that some of them don't, assuming that he intends to make a true statement?

5. The following statement might appear in a recommendation letter:

> In my opinion, you will be very fortunate to get this person to work for you.

How does this statement send two messages?

6. Which of the following are not ambiguous recommendations that both support and attack the job candidate? Assume that the sentences occur among many other sentences describing the candidate.

   a. I simply cannot recommend this person highly enough.
   b. I most enthusiastically recommend this candidate with no qualifications whatsoever.
   c. In my opinion you will be very fortunate to get this person to work for you.
   d. The recommendation that I can offer for this candidate is that she works hard and is productive.
   e. I would urge you to waste no time in making this candidate an offer.

7. If a headline were to say "New Pill Controls Birth Twice a Month," it would be unintentionally funny. Which one rewriting of it says only what was most probably intended?

   a. New Pill Works Twice a Month to Control Pregnancy
   b. Twice a Month New Birth Control Pill Taken
   c. Taking New Pill Twice a Month Controls Pregnancy
   d. Taking New Pill Controls Pregnancy Two Times a Month

8. Explain why there is a problem with what the will means:

> David Chavez died, leaving an estate worth $15,000. His lawyer, upon reading Chavez's will, noted that it said, "I hereby leave $5,000 to my friends John Smith and William Jones."

9. What could be deviously ambiguous about an ad stating that "Laramie margarine is made from 100 percent corn oil"?

10. What are the greatest obstacles facing the AI program of natural language processing? Give examples of the obstacles. Begin your answer by defining *AI* and *natural language*.

■ 11. Suppose a hunter walks all the way around a tree trying to get a shot at a squirrel. Meanwhile, the squirrel never leaves the tree but keeps crawling away from the hunter so that he can never can get a clear shot at the squirrel. In other words, the squirrel keeps the tree between the hunter and itself. When John and Susan discuss this hunting situation, John says the hunter circled the squirrel because the squirrel never left the tree and the hunter got to the north, east, south, and west of the tree. Susan disagrees, saying the hunter never circled the squirrel because he never got round to the back of the squirrel. The disagreement between John and Susan centers on what issue?

   a.   Whether John is being honest.

   b.   Whether the squirrel could have been shot.

   c.   Whether the hunter would agree with John.

   d.   Whether the squirrel was circled by the hunter.

   e.   Whether circling really brings you back to the place where you started.

■ 12. The disagreement between John and Susan mentioned in question 11:

   a.   is not merely a semantic dispute.

   b.   turns on the ambiguity of "circled the squirrel."

   c.   turns on the difference between a hunter and a killer.

   d.   is one that a logical reasoner would have no trouble in adjudicating in favor of John.

13. Explain why the following passage contains a semantic disagreement.

Emilio: When you think about American foreign policy, you've got to admit that Andre is a real American. He is always first to fly the flag. He supports America when other Americans are bad-mouthing it.

Juanita: Andre is a citizen of Argentina who is living here and hoping to become a citizen. So, he's not a real American. He just happens to support American foreign policy.

14. The following four choices for completing the sentence vary in their precision. Rank them, beginning with the most precise.

Starting with the new budget, our country will be

   a.   focusing more on the unemployment problem.

   b.   making changes for the better.

   c.   changing the definition of *unemployment* as far as statistics are concerned for computing the percentage of workers who are unemployed.

   d.   reconsidering the unemployment calculations.

■ 15. Rewrite the following statement in a way (your choice) that makes it less vague:

You have to get more centered and in touch with yourself.

■ 16. Rewrite the following statement in a way (your choice) that makes it vaguer:

You have to get more centered and in touch with yourself.

17. Rewrite the following sentence to make it vaguer.

Pele died of asphyxiation during the Brazil-Argentina soccer championship in 1987.

18. As far as logical reasoning is concerned, spot the most significant difficulty with the following astrological forecast:

    May 20 is an unusually bad time for a Leo or a Scorpio to make major decisions.

    a. Some astrologers might not like either a Leo or a Scorpio.
    b. A bad time for a Leo is usually a good time for a Scorpio.
    c. Ambiguity occurs with *time* because it could mean time of day or time of week or time in music.
    d. The difficulty is with not specifying which major decisions.
    e. There have been some bad times at Ridgemont High School, says Madonna.

19. Use a vague term in two contexts. Make it clear, without saying so directly, that vagueness is not a problem in the first but is a problem in the second.

20. Find a vague word or phrase in a recent daily newspaper. Clip the article, paste it to a regular-size page, and write on the page why the statement is vague. Say whether the vagueness interferes with the communication, and why.

21. Create an original sentence that is too imprecise for the context because it is too general. Say why it is too general.

■ 22. Rewrite the following sentence to make it less precise:

    Patrick McEnroe was defeated by Jimmy Connors in the 1991 U.S. Open tennis tournament in five sets.

23. Take your answer to the previous question and rewrite it to make it even less precise.

■ 24. Rewrite the imprecise sentence "It is raining fairly hard over there right now" to make it less precise. Explain why it is less precise.

25. The following statement is from an astrology forecast. It is imprecise. Why? What are the sources of imprecision?

    Soon, you will be involved in an unusual relationship.

26. Following this passage are four answers given in response to the request "Identify any argumentation in the passage." Which of the four answers is best?

    China is not a sexually permissive society. There is no sex in advertising, and movie couples rarely get beyond hugging. Indeed, to avoid official disfavor, [the Italian filmmaker] Bertolucci had to go back to Rome to shoot nude scenes for his movie. The Chinese are, as Wong puts it, "into their puritanical period."
    "There are over a billion Chinese and the government wants the Chinese to forget about sex for a few decades or so," notes Wong.
    Still, the Chinese are more permissive than us in at least one respect. On the dance floor, not only is it acceptable for women to dance with

women, but it is also acceptable for two men to form a couple, even for slow dances.

Smith describes one such scene: "I saw two men dancing the tango, facing the same direction, wearing the classic tango expression, each having a cigarette dangling from his lips." . . .

On one occasion, Smith recalls seeing two Peoples Liberation Army soldiers crossing the street, holding hands.

"At the movies I frequently assumed I was sitting behind two lovers, one's head resting on the shoulder of the other, only to discover when the lights came up that it was two men," Smith recalls.[14]

a. The fact that two Chinese men dance together or show their friendship more freely than those in our culture has nothing to do with sex in advertising and movies.

b. One argument concluded that China is not a sexually permissive society. The reasons were that China downplays sex in its advertising and movies. In addition, moviegoers show less affection, and we are asked to consider comments by Wong [whoever he is] about China being in a puritanical period. The second argument (or explanation) concluded that the Chinese are more sexually permissive than us in respect to people of the same sex touching each other in public, which was defended (or illustrated) by examples.

c. It is too vague because it doesn't describe what is sexually permissive. It gives an example of sexual permissiveness that is too vague.

d. First, Smith is very vague in his definition of sexually permissive. What is his definition of sexually permissive, and does it apply to the Chinese in China? "Sexually permissive" may mean different characteristics in the two countries. Second, Smith's argument is inconsistent. He first states that "China is not a sexually permissive society." Then he goes on to say, "Still, the Chinese are more permissive than *us* in at least one respect."

27. Explain why the three incorrect answers to question 26 are incorrect.

28. What is odd, logically speaking, about the following report from the planning commission?

> If traffic density continues to grow as predicted, then the flow at Howe Avenue and Marconi Boulevard should become congested in two years from next December 2.

29. The treasurer of the State of California died in office in 1988, and the governor nominated a replacement, his friend Dan Lungren. Lungren was voted on by the two houses of the state legislature, the Senate and the Assembly. The vote occurred within 90 days of the governor's submission of the nomination, and the senate approved the nominee but the assembly disapproved. The problem is whether Dan Lungren can go ahead and take office. Following is the relevant part of the Constitution of the State of California, Article V, Section 5:

(a) . . . the Governor may fill a vacancy in office by appointment until a successor qualifies.

(b) Whenever there is a vacancy in the office of the Superintendent of Public Instruction, the Lieutenant Governor, Secretary of State, Controller, Treasurer, or Attorney General, or the State Board of Equalization, the Governor shall nominate a person to fill the vacancy who shall take office upon confirmation by a majority of the membership of the Senate and a majority of the membership of the Assembly and who shall hold office for the balance of the unexpired term.

(c) In the event the nominee is neither confirmed nor refused confirmation by both the Senate and the Assembly within 90 days of the submission of the nomination, the nominee shall take office as if he or she had been confirmed by a majority of the Senate and Assembly; provided, that if such 90-day period ends during a recess of the Legislature, the period shall be extended until the sixth day following the day on which the legislature reconvenes.

Provided the two houses do vote on a nominee, the trouble is that for a person to take office, (b) suggests he needs to be approved by *both* houses but (c) suggests he needs to be approved by *only one* house. If the intent is really as (b) suggests, the constitution should be amended to clear up the ambiguity. Assuming the intent is also to leave intact the notion that the nominee may take office if neither house actually votes on the nomination, the best amendment would say to

a. replace "shall take office upon confirmation by a majority of the membership of the Senate and a majority of the membership of the Assembly" with "shall not take office upon confirmation by a majority of the membership of the Senate and a majority of the membership of the Assembly unless voted upon."

b. replace "neither confirmed nor refused confirmation" with "not confirmed."

c. replace "is neither confirmed nor refused confirmation by both the Senate and the Assembly" with "is not refused confirmation by the Senate nor the Assembly."

d. replace "neither confirmed nor refused confirmation" with "not refused confirmation."

■ 30. "Some women volleyball players are taller than some men volleyball players of the same age." This sentence expresses

   a. no generalization.

   b. a universal generalization.

   c. a nonuniversal generalization.

31. Create a true, explicitly universal generalization about racism that explicitly uses the word *racism*.

32. Create a true, explicitly nonuniversal generalization about racism that explicitly uses the word *racism*.

■ 33. Give one original example of a true universal generalization about the class of fish and one example of a true nonuniversal generalization about fish.

34. Suppose Napoleon's height is determined to be 5.114748 feet. It was, let's say, measured by using the following operation. Scientists placed a horizontal bar on Napoleon's head while he stood next to a vertical beam. They marked on the vertical beam where the floor was and then marked on the beam how high the bottom of the horizontal bar reached. Using very precise instruments, the scientists then measured the distance between the marks.

    Did you notice something unusual, from a logical reasoning perspective, in the previous paragraph?

35. Comment on the most significant operationalization problem of the following statement from a scientific report: "People who lie are more likely to be born in May than people who don't." Say *why* it is a problem.

36. For the following disagreement, answer these questions. (a) Is the disagreement factual or merely verbal? (b) If it is factual, state the fact in dispute and then state what observation, test, or discovery would settle the dispute. If it is verbal, identify the key term in the dispute and state the different senses in which the two persons are using it.

    Leonard: I visited Elvis Presley's grave in Tennessee last summer. I know the King is dead, but it is hard to believe.

    Angela: The King isn't dead. He is still influencing music. He is alive and well and living in London where he works as a ghost writer.

    Leonard: Ha! A ghost maybe, but not a ghost writer. Elvis departed this world in Las Vegas and was buried at Graceland in Tennessee. Why do you say he's ghost writing?

    Angela: A music magazine I read said he is. Everyone in the article said he is still active musically.

■ 37. Read the following dialogue:

    Samantha: Didn't you hear that Andrea is in Kaiser Hospital with brain injuries from that motorcycle accident? She is alive but so lifeless lying there, so pitiful, no brain activity, just a slowly beating heart and a faint breath. David, you've really got to visit her before she dies.

    David: No, she has already died, because she has no brain activity. I heard this from Susan, who talked to the doctor. I'll go to the funeral instead.

    This is a verbal dispute, not a factual dispute.

    a. true   b. false

■ 38. The dialogue in question 37 is a dispute about either the brain or the meaning of the word *brain*.

    a.   true   b.   false

■ 39. The dispute in question 37 could be cleared up if the two persons would agree that *death* means having no heartbeat.

    a.   true   b.   false

40. Create an original example of equivocation. Underline the term that changes meaning.

41. "When a liquid turns to vapor, it loses heat and gets colder," says the book *The Way Things Work*.[15] What is the antecedent of the word *it*? Is the word *it* referring to the liquid or the vapor or both? The sentence isn't clear to a reader who doesn't have scientific background knowledge about the principle behind the refrigerator. Rewrite the sentence to make it clearer.

● 42. (a) Your instructor will supply you with a blank sheet of paper. Use it to list six statements that you believe to be true about your state or its government. Put your name on the paper. You won't be graded on the quality of your answers but only on your participation. (b) When asked by the instructor, exchange your paper with someone else. On the other person's paper, place an asterisk next to the statement that you believe is the least precise or most vague. (c) On the paper, place a question mark next to any statement that you believe to be questionable because it is either false or susceptible to a false interpretation. (d) Your instructor will ask the class to provide examples of statements from the papers that are imprecise and that are questionable. (e) When asked by the instructor, get together with the person whose paper you have and explain why you made the assessments you did in parts (b) and (c). (f) When asked by the instructor, hand in the paper with your assessments.

43. From a logical reasoning perspective, the following passage provides an example of what?

> Because of the influx of Hispanics and Asians, only about 16 percent of the United States will be white (and non-Hispanic) by the year 2020, according to statistics produced by the scientific research firm.

    a.   The term *United States* is pseudoprecise.

    b.   The term *Asian* cannot be operationalized.

    c.   The year is vague.

    d.   The term *statistics* is ambiguous.

    e.   None of the above.

■ 44. Occasionally in disputes about the theory of evolution, someone will say it is a theory and someone else will disagree, saying that evolution is, instead, a fact. This could be an example of a semantic disagreement. Explain why.

45. What is the first and what is the last general claim made in the U.S. Declaration of Independence? Defend or explain your choices.

46. A reporter who is accused of quoting a politician "out of context" is being accused of taking a phrase one way when the context indicates it should be taken another way. Create an original example of this.

47. The italicized phrases in the following items are vague. Are they too vague, given the likely context in which they are expressed?

    a. The government wastes *millions* of dollars every week. I can think of a lot better things to do with that money. Let's use those *millions* for education and health care instead.

    b. Stop right there! Put your hands *up* slowly, or I'll shoot you in the back.

    c. Nurse, please give the patient *some* of that pain killer.

    d. *Add* milk even though the recipe doesn't call for it. Go ahead. Do it now.

    e. Mom, I know you've already given me $500, but I still don't have enough money to buy the car. Can I have *more*?

    f. Letter to the editor of a medical journal: Medicare payment limits for out-patient prescriptions need to be raised by 10 percent because our study indicates that the elderly use a *sizeable* percent of all outpatient prescriptions.

    g. Letter to the editor of a medical journal: Last year, our state's poison control centers *handled* 338,304 telephone calls at an average cost of $18.24 per call. The state's health department has rigorously evaluated and analyzed the state poison center system by conducting onsite visits to each local poison center operation. They confirm the $18.24 figure, and have recommended continued funding for another five years. The legislature should take the health department's advice.

48. All creationists agree that the universe was created during six days by God's design. After a careful reading of the Bible in 1658, one creationist, Irish Anglican Archbishop James Ussher, calculated the origin of the world to be at 9 am, Sunday, October 23, 4004 B.C., Greenwich Mean Time. Referring to the chapter's definition of pseudoprecision, did the Archbishop probably make a mistake of type 1, 2, or 3?

CHAPTER

5

Sticking to the Issue and Treating It Fairly

I n this chapter we explore the notions of accepting the burden of proof, identifying the issue in a disagreement, sticking to the issue, and altering the issue. The goal is to get a better understanding of what counts as fair play in argumentation.

Who Has the Burden of Proof?

If a neighbor says, "Jeff slit the tires on my son Jeremy's bike," he is expressing his *opinion*. An opinion is a belief. But is his opinion also a *fact*? Maybe. He can show it is a fact if he can prove it to be true. If he expects to convince other people of his opinion, it is his duty to prove it. A **proof** of a statement is a convincing argument for that statement; it doesn't need to be the sort of thing you would find in a math book. You prove a statement to other persons if you give them reasons that *ought* to convince them, even if those reasons don't actually convince them. You know whatever you can prove, and what you can prove is what you know.

Definition Your **knowledge** is your true beliefs that you can verify — that is, back up with solid evidence, a proof.

I noted that if the neighbor expects others to adopt his belief, it's his duty to show it to be true. The point about whose duty it is to create the proof is usually expressed by saying that the **burden of proof** is on the person's shoulders. There is a burden on his or her shoulders — the burden of proving the case.

Sometimes, however, it isn't so obvious who has the burden of proof. If two people each make a statement disagreeing with the other, who has the heavier burden of proof? You can't tell by asking, "Who spoke first?" Usually the burden is on the shoulders of the person who makes the strangest statement. A statement is considered strange if it would be likely not to be accepted by the majority of experts in the area under discussion. *People who make controversial statements have the burden of proving their statements.*

The claim that an alleged mass murderer is innocent may be extremely controversial to most people in the community because they have been convinced of his guilt by media coverage. Nevertheless, the burden of proof does not rest with those who make the controversial claim of his innocence; it still rests with those who assert his guilt. The legal experts would say that the controversial claim is the claim that he is guilty before the trial has concluded.

There are other problems in determining where the burden lies. A few years ago an English researcher discovered a poem inserted between two pages of an obscure book in the Bodleian Library of Oxford University in England.[1] The poem was handwritten by a seventeenth-century scribe who attributed it to William Shakespeare. Surprisingly, however, this poem was not part of the currently known works of Shakespeare. Was it really by Shakespeare? That's the question. Examination of the paper and ink verified that the poem was indeed copied in the seventeenth century. Shakespeare himself died in the early seventeenth century. The poem is clearly written in the style of a Shakespearean poem, although it is not an especially good poem. The researcher is convinced the poem is Shakespeare's. At this point, does the researcher have the burden of providing more proof, or does the skeptic have the burden of proving the poem is not Shakespeare's?

■ ············ Concept Check 1 ············ ■

Jeremy says, "My goldfish are dumb, dumb, dumb. They don't know one-tenth as much about the world as I do." David responds, "That's bull. You can't say that. Maybe we just can't communicate with the fish to find out." Who has the burden of proof in this dispute?

Regarding that seventeenth-century poem, the burden of proof is on the skeptic, not on the person who said it was written by Shakespeare. Unfortunately, it takes expertise to know this. Because of how the poem was discovered, when it was copied, and the style it is written in, experts on English poetry generally concede that the case has been made in favor of Shakespeare, as author, and the burden is on somebody to show he was not. Many skeptical researchers have analyzed the poem, looking at such things as the number of words that aren't in any of Shakespeare's other works, but they have failed to prove their case.

Diverting Attention from the Issue

Besides shouldering one's share of the burden of proof, an equally important duty for a logical reasoner is to *stick to the issue* during an argument. The **issue** in a particular piece of reasoning is what the reasoning is all about; it's the topic, subject, or central question under discussion. In the example of the neighbor accusing Jeff of slitting the bicycle's tires, suppose another neighbor says, "Quit picking on Jeff. He didn't do it." Now the second neighbor is taking a different **position on the issue**. The issue is whether Jeff did it. The first neighbor's position is that Jeff did do it; the second neighbor's position is that Jeff didn't.

A good reasoner follows the principles of sticking to the issue and treating it fairly. The goal is to *pursue the truth about the issue, not to sidetrack, confuse, or con one's opponent*. Logical reasoners argue in good faith. The purpose is not to win, but to discover the truth. However, political debaters usually don't pursue such a high ideal. Similarly, lawyers fight for their client; they don't try to convince the jury their client is guilty, even when they believe that the client is indeed guilty.

It is possible to learn a lot about good reasoning by examining the major errors in faulty reasoning. Errors in reasoning are called **fallacies**; in this chapter we will explore some of the major fallacies having to do with getting off the issue. These are often called the *fallacies of irrelevance*, because when you stray off the issue you make irrelevant remarks.

When trying to spot the issue in an argument, one technique you can use is to search for some conclusion that is being defended. Then try to spot which side of a controversy the conclusion takes. That controversy will be the issue. Figuratively, the technique works like this. Imagine that you are walking along the top of a fence, and someone is giving you reasons to come down on one side. The issue in the argument is *whether* to come down on one side or the other. The arguer is not arguing in good faith if he is pulling you off the fence onto his side by some means other than giving good reasons.

■ ············ **Concept Check 2** ············ ■

Identify the specific issue in the following discussion.

Jennifer: You are worrying too much. You should spend less time thinking about the consequences for police officers and more about the consequences for the mayor's office. If the mayor or vice mayor were injured, there would be an outpouring of grief throughout the city.

James: Police put their lives on the line for us every day. Each police officer's life is valuable, as valuable as the life of the mayor. Our police deserve our respect.

Jennifer: You are thinking of TV shows. Being a farmer is a lot more dangerous than being a cop, but that's a side issue. Look, if some of the police guarding the mayor and her staff get shot during the event we are planning, well, that's life. They know the risk. That's why we politicians pay them so much money.

James: That sounds pretty callous to me. I don't think you should write off police lives the way you write off the latest 2 percent budget cut.

Jennifer: Wake up to the realities. I'm talking political power, and you're just talking sentiment and morality.

The issue is:

a. that police lives are valuable.

b. whether political power is more important than morality.

c. that Jennifer is being callous about police lives and James is being sensitive and showing respect for them.

d. whether the lives of the police are as valuable as those of the mayor and vice mayor.

e. that if the mayor or vice mayor were injured, there would be an outpouring of grief all through the city.

■ ············   **Concept Check 3**   ············ ■

What is the specific issue about minority politics referred to in the headline of the following newspaper article? The article's author isn't taking a position on either side of the issue.

Minority Politics at Issue in Merger

If Johnson County voters approve the merger of city and county governments into one mega-government in the November election, how minorities exercise political power could be dramatically transformed.

At least two current elected officials — both minorities — contend that the transformation means that minority communities will lose what little influence they now have.

Those minorities who helped write the proposal insist, however, that the local community councils formed under the merger will offer an unprecedented opportunity for minorities to hold office and to sway the debates on issues vital to their communities. There will be no loss of adequate representation, they contend.[2]

a. The issue is the election in Johnson County.

b. The issue is minority politics in Johnson County.

c. The issue is that the local community councils formed under the merger will offer an unprecedented opportunity for minorities to hold office and to sway the debates on issues vital to their communities.

d. The issue is whether the merger in Johnson County will weaken minority influence in government.

e. The issue is whether the result of the election for a merger in Johnson County will hurt minorities.

A discussion is easier to follow if everybody stays on the topic and doesn't stray off on tangents. The duty of the logical reasoner is to avoid getting lost and diverting the attention of others from the topic at hand. Stacey doesn't do her duty in the following conversation:

Susan: Would the Oakland A's be in first place if they were to win tomorrow's baseball game?

Stacey: What makes you think they'll ever win tomorrow's game?

Stacey has committed the **fallacy of avoiding the question**. Her answer does not answer the question; it avoids it. This fallacy is one kind of **fallacy of avoiding the issue**, because answering the question is the issue here. Answering a question with a question is a common way of avoiding the issue.

Like magicians, most politicians are experts at steering our attention away from the real issue. For example, a politician was asked, "Do you think either the U.S. National Security Council or the Pentagon is actively involved in covert activities in this region of Central America?" The politician responded with, "I think the fact that the president has sent troops into Central America in the past is not necessarily a reason to expect that he will do so now in this region of the world. There has been a lot of pressure by the U.S. banking community to upset the economic situation, but I seriously doubt that we can expect anything as overt as the sending of U.S. troops into the region. On the other hand, neighboring countries may be upset, so there is always a threat of invasion from that direction."

Did the politician's fallacious reasoning succeed? It did if you read the last paragraph and reacted with "OK," or "So what?" or "Change the channel." The issue was whether the government was involved in *covert* (secret) activities in Central America. The politician avoided that issue by directing attention toward *overt* (public) activities. The politician cleverly and intentionally committed the fallacy of avoiding the issue. Because politicians are so likely to use this avoidance technique, reporters at

"And here with us this evening, to skirt the issues, are Senator Tom Kirkland and Congressman Alan Sullivan."

Drawing by H. Martin; © 1988 The New Yorker Magazine, Inc.

press conferences are often permitted a follow-up question. A good follow-up here would be, "Thank you, sir, but I asked about the likelihood of covert operations, not overt ones. Can you speak to that issue?"

■ ....   Concept Check 4   .... ■

In the following interview, does Pee-Wee Herman answer the question put to him, or does he avoid it?[3]

Interviewer: Did you include the romance in your film as a response to people labeling you as asexual or of indeterminate gender?

Pee-Wee: It's just something I wanted to do. I never understand why people say that, though. A lot of the reviews of the show mentioned stuff like "His gender is confusing to children." To me it's clearly male on my TV show. I don't see the confusion. I don't wear wigs or cross-dress. My name is Pee-Wee. There aren't a lot of women named Pee-Wee. Probably from this interview a lot of them will write to me, [gruffly] "Mah name is Pee-Wee and ah'm a woman."

A final note about avoiding the question. If somebody asks you a question, you wouldn't automatically be committing the fallacy by refusing to answer the question. Only if you should answer but don't do you commit the fallacy.

An arguer might suggest several issues while addressing another issue. The distinction is important. Take this conversation, for example:

Sanderson: These Korean video cassettes are a lot cheaper than the ones Sony makes.

Tamanaka: Yeah, it's a shame. It's time Congress quit contemplating its navel and created tariffs against Korean electronic imports.

Sanderson: I don't see any reason for tariffs. Tariffs just restrict free trade.

Tamanaka: There should be more U.S. tariffs against Korean electronic imports because Koreans are getting unfair assistance from their government to subsidize their electronics manufacturing and because Koreans already have too much influence in the American economy.

The issue in the conversation is whether there should be more tariffs against Korean electronic imports. The argument in Tamanaka's last remarks addresses this issue. However, his remarks also suggest other issues, such as: Is there anything wrong with having Korean influence on the American economy? If it depends on how much Korean influence, then how much is too much? Are Korean electronics manufacturers really getting a government subsidy? If so, is that unfair? These side issues get suggested, but they don't get addressed in Tamanaka's argument. An argument will normally address one issue at a time. If you create an argument, your reasoning will be easier to follow if you take the issues one at a time and not try to handle everything at once.

Covering Up the Reasons That Favor Your Opponent's Position

The reasoner who is trying to be fair and seek the truth not only stays on the issue but also avoids misrepresenting the views of the opposition. In addition, the logical reasoner doesn't hide the opponent's reasons under the carpet. The reasoner who does so is guilty of a "cover-up." Take this passage, for instance:

When you are considering which kind of apartment to live in you should prefer wood to brick buildings. Brick buildings are more dangerous during earthquakes because wood will bend during the quake, but brick will crack and crash down on you. Also, and even more important, brick has been discovered to be radioactive. If you put a sensitive Geiger Counter up to a brick, any brick, it will click; and it won't with wood. We already have enough sources of radiation in our lives without living surrounded by hundreds of brick sources. So, next time you are apartment hunting, remember to look for wood.

Did you spot the cover-up? This little passage uses the scare tactic. It sounds well reasoned, but it is covering up the bad aspects of wood while scaring you away from bricks. Although it is true that earthquakes are more of a danger for brick apartments than for wood apartments, earthquakes are rare, while fire is a much greater danger everywhere, and bricks don't burn. Second, although it is true that bricks are radioactive, the radioactivity is so trivial that it is not worth bothering about. The danger of wood fires is far more serious. The moral is:

> Give opponents a fair hearing, and don't misrepresent their argument.

Relating the Argument to the Issue

Arguments are usually created to settle an issue. The arguer gives reasons to conclude that the issue should be settled her way. Often the issue is controversial, and a second person hearing the argument might be motivated to create a counterargument, or to "get into an argument" with the first person. A **counterargument** is an argument for the opposite conclusion. The conclusion of either person's argument is the person's position on the issue.

The relationship between the issue and the argument is interesting, but before going on to explore it, let's take a moment to review some points about argumentation. Arguments have structure. Some arguments can be fairly complicated, but every argument must meet a minimum requirement: *it must contain at least a conclusion plus the reason or reasons intended to back it up*. In this technical sense of the word *argument*, it takes only one person to have an argument. That is, there can be arguments without explicit disagreements—there need be no one else offering a counterargument.

More complex arguments might have subarguments that make smaller points used in drawing the main conclusion. There are other types of complex argumentation, but we won't pursue the details here; the anatomy of complex argumentation will be the topic of a later chapter. The main point for now is that the normal goal of an arguer is to provide convincing reasons for a conclusion that takes a position on the issue at hand. Arguments that do not achieve that goal are said to be bad, illogical, or fallacious.

If the issue is whether a particular Toyota will start in the morning, the following argument doesn't speak to the issue:

> The Toyota is owned by a citizen of the state of Hawaii, and aren't Hawaiians Americans? So, the car is owned by an American citizen.

The argument is fallacious. Yet the same argument would be fine if the issue were the nationality of the car's owner. In fact, this particular argument would be good enough to **shift the burden of proof** to anybody who doesn't agree that the car is American owned.

It is one thing to argue about an issue but another to agree on what the issue is that you are arguing about. For example, on the twenty-fifth anniversary of the first U.S. government report on smoking, the Surgeon General said that cigarette smoking was responsible for more than one out of every six deaths in the United States. Noting that nearly 30 percent of American adults still smoke, despite the Government's warnings, the Surgeon General said that many publications that carry cigarette advertisements also refuse to run articles on the danger of smoking. In addition, the Surgeon General defended taxes on cigarettes. The issue, said the Surgeon General, is health. Not so, said the cigarette companies; the issue is individual freedom — whether our society should have more or less government interference in private enterprise. The issue is whether the government should be involved, by taxation and by requiring warnings on cigarette packs, in an unconstitutional attempt at censorship. It's time for more people, including the Surgeon General, to wake up to the fact that "smokers and the tobacco industry are productive forces in the economy," said the director of media relations for the Tobacco Institute, which is the lobbying organization for the industry.[4]

Notice that both parties in this argument are trying to redefine the issue for their own benefit. It is probably a mistake to say that one party has identified the right issue and the other has not. All these issues should be addressed. Bringing them all out into the open gives the public a better appreciation of the situation and the ability to make more informed choices. The moral is that progress can occur when issues are identified or are identified more clearly.

Suppose Otis has been trying to convince his sister that doctors and nurses working in federally funded family counseling centers should not be allowed to tell pregnant women about the option of getting an abortion. His reasons are that abortion is immoral and that the federal government should not be in the business of promoting immorality. Suppose Otis's sister reacts to his argument by saying that nurses and doctors should be able to give any medical advice they believe to be in the best interests of their patients, so the federal government should not be interfering in the doctor-patient or nurse-patient relationship by outlawing counseling about abortion. This argument will miss its target because it does not address Otis's point about the morality of abortion. Their dialogue will be especially frustrating for both of them until they realize that they are talking about different issues.

Progress can also be made in some disagreements by focusing on the issue in other ways: by defining the issue more precisely, by narrowing the issue, and by noticing when one issue must be settled before another can be fully addressed. For an example of the dependence of issues, consider the lobbyist for San Francisco who is deciding whether the city should take a position to support or oppose a proposed state law to redefine the formula for distributing state monies to county hospitals. The lobbyist will probably not be able to decide whether to recommend support for or opposition to the bill until another issue is settled — whether the bill will give more or less money to San Francisco County Hospital. Local governments usually don't take a stand for or against a bill based solely on fiscal impact, but they always keep fiscal impact in mind.

For a second example of making progress in argumentation, consider narrowing the issue. Suppose a student in a government or political science class is asked to write a four-page essay on a topic of his or her choice. Choosing the issue of whether capitalism is better than communism would be inadvisable. Because this issue is so large and the essay is supposed to be so short, the issue would not be manageable. The essay would have to discuss every country in the world and its economics, political freedom, military, lifestyles, and so forth. The essay would be improved if the student narrowed the issue to, let us say, whether race relations were better under American capitalism or under Soviet communism during World War II.

■ ·········· Concept Check 5 ·········· ■

Suppose two people are having a disagreement over whether *The Simpsons* TV programs are better than programs showing pro football games. As it is stated, the issue concerns a matter of personal opinion, and you can imagine the dispute continuing endlessly. Changing to which one of the following issues would be a way to narrow the issue to one that can be settled more easily?

a. Whether comedy programs are better than sports programs.
b. Whether a poll of viewers would show that more of them prefer watching *The Simpsons* than watching a pro football game.
c. Whether *The Simpsons* is better in the sense of being more entertaining than airings of football or basketball games.

■ ·········· Concept Check 6 ·········· ■

State the issue in the following letter to the editor. Then sketch the argument for the other side of the issue — that is, the side that the letter writer is *opposed* to.

> Regarding "Driver dies after chase on I-5," Oct. 28: The article seemed to be really confused. It stated, "The death was the fifth this year in the Sacramento area resulting from high-speed police chases." In fact it resulted, as most if not all of them do, from some low-life scumbag fleeing officers attempting to apprehend him, in this case for auto theft.
>
> What would you suggest officers do, wave good-bye as soon as someone's speed exceeds the limit? Or would you prefer that police just never arrest anyone who travels at high speeds? I'm sure suspects would like that, but I'm also sure decent, law-abiding citizens wouldn't.

■ ········· ■

Review of Major Points

People who make statements have the burden of proving their statements. Their goals should be to stick to the issue, to pursue the truth about the issue, and not to sidetrack, confuse, or con the opponent. Progress can sometimes be made when issues are identified, or are identified more clearly. It is important to distinguish between the issue that is addressed and the side issues that are suggested when someone does argue for one side of an issue. Progress can also be made in some disagreements by focusing on the issue in other ways: by more precisely defining the issue, by narrowing the issue, and by noticing when one issue must be settled before another one can be fully addressed.

In this chapter we also briefly distinguished fact from opinion, introduced the minimum requirements for an argument, and defined counterargument, position on an issue, shifting the burden of proof, and fallacy. The next chapter will concentrate on fallacies created by arguers who do not accept the burden of proof and stick to the issue.

Glossary

burden of proof The duty to prove some statement. The burden is usually on the shoulders of the person who wants others to accept his or her statement. When two people make statements that disagree, the burden falls on the shoulders of the person making the more controversial statement.

counterargument An argument for the conclusion opposite to that taken by another arguer.

fallacies Reasoning errors.

fallacy of avoiding the issue Failing to address the issue at hand by going off on tangents. However, the fallacy isn't committed by a reasoner who says that some other issue must first be settled before the original issue can be adequately addressed.

fallacy of avoiding the question A type of fallacy of avoiding the issue that occurs when the issue is how to answer some question. The fallacy would be committed if someone's answer were to avoid the question rather than answer it.

issue The topic, subject, or central question under discussion.

knowledge Your true beliefs that you can prove.

position on an issue Your belief about how an issue should be settled.

proof A convincing argument for a statement. It doesn't need to be the sort of thing you would find in a math book. You prove a statement to other persons if you give them reasons that *ought* to convince them, even if those reasons don't actually convince them.

shift the burden of proof Making a reasonable case for your position on an issue, thereby switching the responsibility of proof to the shoulders of your opponent who disagrees with your position.

Answers to Concept Checks

1. Jeremy doesn't. He is simply making a claim that agrees with common sense. David is challenging common sense, so he has the burden of proving his claim.

2. Answer (d). (a) is not the answer because it makes a statement on James's side of the issue. (b) is not the answer because, although it does give an approximate statement of the general issue, the more specific issue is better stated by answer (d). Answer (c) states James's position on the issue, but it does not state the issue itself. (e) states something that James and Jennifer might agree to, but it is not the subject of their controversy.

3. Answer (d). The issue is whether the merger of the city and county governments of Johnson County will result in loss of adequate political representation for minorities. Answer (e) is not as good because it doesn't say what minorities might lose. Answers (a) and (b) are too imprecise, though they say nothing false. Answer (c) is the worst answer because it comes down on one side of the real issue by using the word *that* instead of *whether*.

4. Pee-Wee's comments do answer the question that was asked; they don't sidestep it. When asked whether he included the romance in order to overcome accusations about his sexuality, he directly answered the question by saying he included it just

because he wanted to and not because he wanted to overcome accusations about his sexuality. He then went on to address the accusations about his sexuality. You may believe he has a weak answer, or you may believe he didn't say enough. However, a weak answer is still an answer to the question, so Pee-Wee doesn't commit the fallacy of avoiding the question.

5. Answer (b). This issue is narrower because the wide-open notion of *better* is replaced by the narrower, more specific notion of *prefer watching*. The issue in (b) can be settled relatively easily by taking the poll and seeing whether more people choose *The Simpsons*. This is not the case for (a) and (c). Answer (a) is wrong because its issue is not narrower.

6. The issue is *whether* police should chase criminal suspects at high speed (or at least whether the police should do it as often as they do).

It is important to say that the issue is *whether* police should chase suspects and not *that* police should chase suspects. Stating the issue with the word *that* is stating one side of the issue, not the issue itself. Also, answering that the issue is deaths from high-speed police chases is almost right but might be taken as a disagreement over how many deaths occurred. The better and more specific answer should convey the point that the issue is whether the chasing should continue.

In the first paragraph, the letter writer suggests that the issue is who's to blame for deaths during high-speed chases, but in the second paragraph the true issue is revealed—namely, whether the police are justified in chasing. Also, although the letter writer's first paragraph mentions only criminals who steal cars, the tone of the letter and the information in the second paragraph clearly indicate that the issue is about any speeding criminals, not just those who are suspected of car theft.

The letter writer's side (i.e., position on the issue) is that the police are justified. The writer's argument is that they should engage in chases because, if they don't, the suspects will get away, and the suspects shouldn't get away.

The argument for the other side would probably go like this:

The police should not chase criminal suspects at high speed (or they shouldn't do it as often as they do) because such chases lead to too many serious problems, including five deaths this year in one city.

Review and Writing Exercises

■ 1. Suppose you are only trying to make a case for your position. You don't want to create some knock-down, drag-out, absolute proof; you just want to persuade the person you are talking to. Do you have the burden of *proof* in such a situation?

2. What is the main issue in the following argument?

Several lines of biological evidence have now fixed the time at which humans and chimpanzees descended from a common, primitive African apelike species. It must have been less than 20 million but more than

5 million years ago. This is because *Homo sapiens* (humans) and *Pan troglodytes* (chimpanzees) are so similar in details of anatomy, physiology, chromosome structure, and enzyme chemistry. Admittedly the clocks of anatomy, physiology, chromosome structure, and enzyme chemistry do disagree slightly, but they all agree that the evolutionary tree must have branched during this time.

3. Where in the following dialogue does one of the participants not accept his burden of proof? Justify your answer. The scene: Mr. Harris is walking up to a group of people that includes you, several of your neighbors, Jeremy (the twelve-year-old son of Mr. Harris), and Jeff (a fifteen-year-old son of one of the neighbors who isn't present).

Mr. Harris: There you are! Jeff, did you slit the tires on my son Jeremy's bike?

Jeff: What? What are you talking about?

Mr. Harris: Thursday afternoon. (Pointing to the bike) Look at those slits, one in the front tire, one in the back.

Jeff: I didn't do it.

Mr. Harris: Maria saw you on Thursday showing somebody a red knife.

Jeff: It was new so I showed people. I'm sorry about the tires, but I didn't cut them.

Mr. Harris: Maria said you were arguing with Jeremy. Jeremy's spray paint cans are missing from our garage. So are some boards. I hear that boards in your garage have new spray paint all over them. Black and green. Jeremy's black and green cans are missing.

Jeff: I was just taking back some boards that were mine. Jeremy owed me boards. He said he would pay me back, but he never did. I didn't take any more than what was due me. I didn't do the tires.

Mr. Harris: Are you denying you had a knife on Thursday afternoon?

Jeff: My grandfather gave me his Swiss army knife. I showed it to everybody. Jeremy was jealous. He wanted the knife. Those tires could have been slit with any knife.

Mr. Harris: OK, you're right that any knife could have been used, but the person who used the knife was probably mad at Jeremy, mad enough to steal his paint cans and boards, too. Where'd you get the paint for those boards you took?

Jeff: Why did you talk to Maria?

Mr. Harris: Where did you get the paint? Let's see those cans.

Jeff: Maria had no business butting in.

Mr. Harris: She didn't do anything wrong. You did.

Jeff: I was going to pay Jeremy for his paint cans. Jeremy, what do you want for the paint? Here's two dollars. The cans were practically empty. You were done with them. You said so.

- 4. Write a 200–400 word essay defending your own rational belief about how likely it is that Jeff (Exercise 3) is guilty.

- 5. Write a paragraph (on any topic of your choosing) that clearly shows that the speaker has misunderstood where the burden of proof lies.

- 6. State the issue of the following argument:

    I know you are thinking of not going to the film with Emilio, but remember that you promised him you would go with him. You now seem to be saying to me that you might go with Juanita instead and might tell Emilio you are sick and won't be going with him. Don't. One consequence of doing this is that you will be breaking your promise to Emilio. That would be morally wrong, wouldn't it? In addition, if Emilio finds out the truth, you could lose your friend. Aren't those reasons enough?

- 7. Create a dialogue in which (a) one speaker shows insight when he or she says, "That's fine, but the real issue is . . . ," (b) the second speaker disagrees, and (c) the first speaker makes a convincing case for being correct.

- 8. What is the issue being described in the following newspaper article? What is Rabbi Goren's position on the issue?

Holy City Sculpture Stirs War of Words

JERUSALEM (AP)—A Holocaust memorial erected without a permit by a prominent rabbi near Judaism's sacred Western Wall has sparked a controversy between Orthodox Jews and conservationists who demand it be taken down.

A compromise is unlikely in the conflict, which reflects the ongoing tug of war between the religious and the secular in Israeli society.

Rabbi Shlomo Goren, an Orthodox religious leader, said the monument was built to honor the memory of 6 million Jews killed by the Nazis in World War II and vowed it will "remain until the Messiah comes." Those who don't like it "can put a handkerchief over their eyes," he said in an interview.

Daniella Shamir, director of the Jerusalem branch of the Council for a Beautiful Israel, an environmental lobbying group, calls it "terrible kitsch" and says she will not rest until the city takes it down.

Goren dismissed those opposing the monument as "leftists and atheists allergic to Rabbi Goren."

Shamir, in turn, said the case is typical of the "chutzpah" (audacity) of religious groups. "People take the law into their own hands," she said. "It's especially true of religious people.

They think they have the right to do whatever they want."

The monument, created by Israeli sculptor Jacob Agam, consists of six 8-foot-high glass towers symbolizing the Holocaust victims.

Each is shaped like the Star of David, the six-pointed emblem that appears on the Israeli flag. Flames burn inside the towers, and water runs down their sides.

Hebrew letters attached to the towers spell out the word "Remember."

The monument stands on the roof of Goren's yeshiva, or Jewish seminary, which abuts the square and is about 225 feet from the 2,000-year-old Western Wall of the Second Temple, in the heart of Jerusalem's Old City.

Hundreds of people flock to the wall every day for prayer and contemplation, and critics say the monument is too flashy and disturbs the atmosphere of serenity.

"It (the monument) dominates the square," said Shamir. "You can see it from everywhere in the (Western Wall) area. It goes very much against the grain of all the monuments in the area."

The Polish-born Goren, who lost many relatives in the Holocaust, said he was not concerned with aesthetics but wanted to commemorate Holocaust victims by lighting eternal flames.

The municipal government, which strictly controls all building in Jerusalem because the city is holy to Judaism, Christianity, and Islam, got involved in the argument because Goren erected the monument two months ago without first getting a permit.

City Engineer Amnon Niv said any structure in the Old City must be approved by the local planning board and then be submitted for public comment before getting final permission.

After consulting with his lawyers, Goren refused to get the necessary permits, saying the monument is not a structure but a group of large candles.

"I put candles on top of my building to commemorate the souls of the martyrs," he said in a recent interview. "Do you need permission to light Hanukkah candles?"

Niv suggested some compromises, such as moving the monument from the yeshiva roof into a niche in the courtyard where it would be less obtrusive, but Goren refused.

Another option would be to erect the monument at the Yad Vashem Holocaust Memorial several miles away, but Goren said he wants to keep it on yeshiva property.

Niv said he is now waiting for a ruling from Attorney General Yosef Harish on whether the city should go to court to either force Goren to apply for a permit or dismantle the monument.

The conservationists, meanwhile, accuse the city of treating Goren, a former chief rabbi of Israel, with kid gloves, saying the monument should have been taken down right away.

Shamir said city officials have not responded to letters of protest by her council and similar organizations.

Sivannah Maryn, spokeswoman for Mayor Teddy Kollek, said the decision on the monument's fate won't be easy. "It is a sensitive issue because it is a memorial to the Holocaust," she said.[5]

● 9. Find an editorial or letter to the editor in one of your local newspapers and create a short (75–100 words) argument for why the author is mistaken about something. Begin by stating the issue. Assume that your audience is the other students in your class. In your answer, include a copy of the editorial or letter.

● 10. Create a dialogue between two people in which progress is made in their dispute because they agree to redefine the issue.

■ 11. What is the central issue of the following dialogue?

Mother: My fifteen-year-old daughter failed two courses at school. The worst part is, she didn't even try. She just said, "Oh well, it's not important." If she had *tried* and failed, that wouldn't be so bad.

Friend: Are you sure it wouldn't be so bad? Maybe it would be *worse* if she tried and failed.

Mother: No, it wouldn't, because if she tried she wouldn't fail the courses.

Friend: Oh, I think I see what you mean. Do you mean that anybody who tries will succeed at least in the sense that they did try and didn't just give up?

Mother: No, I just mean that if my daughter tries, she will get a grade higher than an F.

12. What is the issue or question that the author is concerned with in the following letter to the editor? Choose from the options listed.

No one says that the death penalty is the only answer to brutal murder. But it is a sure way to stop repeat offenses, and it's far cheaper than keeping a killer in jail 30 or 40 years. While it may not deter a hard-core killer or a psychotic, it probably would deter the Bernard Goetzes and the kind of youths accused of assaulting the jogger in Central Park.[6]

    a.   What will stop repeat cases of crime?

    b.   Whether brutal murders will increase or decrease.

    c.   Should brutal murderers be killed by the government?

    d.   Whether the death penalty deters hard-core killers or psychotic killers.

13. Consider the issue in the following conversation:

Saghit: Take a look at Jane Fonda and her ex-husband Tom Hayden from Santa Monica, California. There's a couple of typical Democrats for you. Those two radicals are self-admitted organizers of anti-war protests against our sons who were laying down their lives during the Vietnam war. Nowadays, Democratic State Assemblyman Hayden is corrupting the California Legislature. That's the story with the whole party. The California Democratic party has done a few good things now and then, but basically it is corrupt. It's even corrupt financially. You know the saying, "California has the best legislature that money can buy."

Jorgen: Ja. Ja. Funny joke, but get serious. Not everybody in the California Legislature is a Democrat. Just most of them.

Saghit: You are making my case. The leaders of the State Assembly and the State Senate are Democrats, and everyone knows that these two men are interested only in getting enough money for their reelection campaigns; whether their votes help or hurt the citizens is not their major concern.

Jorgen: Look. The ex-Imperial Wizard of the Ku Klux Klan was elected as a Republican to the Louisiana Legislature. Can the Republicans be proud of that? Are you going to stand there and defend the Ku Klux Klan and the rest of those bigots? So, let's not hear so much from you about Democrats in California.

What is the *principal* issue in the above conversation?

a. Are California Democrats corrupt?

b. Are Jane Fonda and Tom Hayden corrupting the legislature?

c. Are the majority of Democrats too interested in getting money for their reelection campaigns?

d. Whether a member of the Klan was ever elected to the Louisiana Legislature.

14. Regarding the previous question, comment on all the other possible answers that you did not pick. Do the possible answers contain some subissues or smaller issues surrounding the main issues? Do the answers speak of points that were never at issue in the dialogue?

15. If we analyze Saghit's argument in question 13, we see that one of the following statements is *not* a reason he uses to back up his conclusion. That one statement is

a. Tom Hayden is a California Democrat who is corrupting the California Legislature.

b. Jane Fonda and Tom Hayden are typical of California Democrats.

c. At least two, and maybe a lot more, California Democrats are too interested in getting enough money for their reelection campaigns.

d. California has the best legislature that money can buy.

e. Corruption is bad for America.

• 16. Consider the following newspaper article:

... If we take just four days of the world's military spending and apply that money toward food, not one person in the world will have to go hungry.

That's women's logic. It's the kind of thinking that leads to slogans like "No more (war) toys for (big) boys."

Nationally, the connections are simple. The government's budget allocates $1.5 trillion dollars for the military. That's equivalent of $14,000 for every household. The money for the military is taken away from programs that feed, shelter, educate, and provide for the health care of people. "People" in this case basically means women and children. 80 percent of the poor in this country are women and children. 10,000 children die each year in the United States from poverty. Which will it be, bigger bombers or school lunch programs? Maternal health programs or Star Wars?

For women it's a simple choice. . . . No longer ridiculed into submission and silence for their aversion to the top priority given to gang-murder by male governments, great numbers of women are organizing to change the priority to programs that help people.[7]

    a. What is the main issue addressed in this newspaper article?

    b. Which side of that issue does the author's conclusion advocate?

    c. Create an argument for the other side of the issue.

17. Create a multiple-choice question, with answer, about fairness in argumentation.

18. During the next week, pay attention to the occurrence of any argumentation that you find outside your school—argumentation you take part in or observe. Describe one of those arguments. More specifically, describe one person's argument by restating the reasons and the conclusion as full, declarative sentences. Label each sentence as being a reason or a conclusion. State the issue that is in dispute. Remember that when we say informally that two people are in *an* argument, from a logical perspective there are at least two arguments, not one. Each person in "the" argument has his or her own argument. When answering the question, give only the argument of one person for one side of one issue.

19. (i) Create a list of three beliefs you have. Each belief must be sufficiently controversial that you can imagine there being reasonable people who hold the opposite opinion and disagree with you. Hand the list in to your instructor. (ii) Create arguments in defense of your beliefs, but do not yet hand them in unless requested to do so by your instructor. From your list, your instructor later will arbitrarily pick one of your three beliefs and ask you to give a convincing argument for why other people should accept your belief. (iii) Create arguments against your beliefs. Your instructor will also pick one belief from your list and ask you to give an argument against it. Each argument should be a short essay of a page or two, typed double-spaced, if possible.

20. Tom Haypole is a member of a state legislature. His ex-lawyer, William Kunsinger, has complained that Tom Haypole is no longer in favor of banning the death penalty in all situations. Kunsinger says Haypole used to be against the death penalty with no exceptions. Here is a newspaper report of Haypole's response to Kunsinger's charge. Explain why the stated issue by Haypole is not the real issue.

After Kunsinger's charge that Haypole switched positions on the death penalty in order to advance his career, Haypole replied that Kunsinger "should start looking at some of his own clients before he criticizes other people. The issue is whether Kunsinger has a record of honesty. A good look at the record will reveal a forked tongue."

Labeling Kunsinger's criticism of him "very offensive," Haypole added a charge of his own as to why his former defender spoke out. "I think he's just trying to promote a book."

21. Read this passage, written by Rose Bird, a former Chief Justice of the Supreme Court of the State of California. Then respond to the exercises that follow.

> U.S. Supreme Court Justice William J. Brennan Jr. has articulated that promise [of an inclusive society] well. [Brennan said] "The Constitution embodies the aspiration to social justice, brotherhood, and human dignity that brought this nation into being." However, he hastened to add that "part of this egalitarianism in America has been more pretension than realized fact." . . . Over the years, the courts have [pointed to] both the "delicacy" and the "toughness" of women as a basis for the denial of many rights and privileges accorded to men. In 1872, the asserted frailty and inequality of women compared with men were used by the Supreme Court as a rationale for denying a woman a license to practice law in *Bradwell v. Illinois*. The alleged strength and equality of women vis-à-vis men served as the high court's rationale for denying women a guaranteed minimum wage in *Adkins v. Children's Hospital* in 1923. . . . [Currently (in March, 1987) the court is changed, and it now] does not prohibit an affirmative action plan that (1) "is designed to break down old patterns of [sexual] segregation and hierarchy"; (2) "does not unnecessarily trammel the interests of the [male] employee"; (3) "does not require the discharge of [male] workers and their replacement with new [female] hirees"; (4) "does [not] create an absolute bar to the advancement of [male] employees"; and (5) "is a temporary measure . . . not intended to maintain [sexual] balance, but simply to eliminate a manifest [sexual] imbalance."[8]

i. What reasons, if any, does Bird give for why Brennan can say part of this egalitarianism in America has been more pretension than realized fact"?

  a. The court does not prohibit an affirmative action plan that (1) "is designed to break down old patterns of [sexual] segregation and hierarchy"; (2) "does not unnecessarily trammel the interests of the [male] employees"; (3) "does not require the discharge of [male] workers and their replacement with new [female] hirees"; (4) "does [not] create an absolute bar to the advancement of [male] employees"; and (5) "is a temporary measure . . . not intended to maintain [sexual] balance, but simply to eliminate a manifest [sexual] imbalance."

  b. The Constitution embodies the aspiration to social justice, brotherhood, and human dignity that brought this nation into being.

  c. "Over the years, the courts have [pointed to] both the 'delicacy' and the 'toughness' of women as a basis for the denial of many rights and privileges accorded to men."

  d. No reasons are given by Bird.

ii. What is the issue that Justice Bird is dealing with in the above passage?

  a. Whether or not the Constitution of the United States embodies the aspiration to social justice, brotherhood, and human dignity that brought this nation into being.

  b. Whether or not the Constitution of the United States bars women from equal access to a guaranteed minimum wage and denies them a license to practice law.

  c. Whether or not the Constitutional ideal of egalitarianism for men and women is supported by past actions of the Supreme Court.

  d. Whether or not to implement an affirmative action plan that will break down old patterns of sexual segregation and hierarchy.

  e. Whether or not an affirmative action plan will trammel the interests of the male employees.

iii. Bird's position on the issue is:

  a. That an affirmative action plan will indeed trammel the interests of the male employees.

  b. That, as evidenced by previous rulings, the Supreme Court has not fully supported the ideal of equal rights for women and men.

  c. That an affirmative action plan is OK if it (1) "is designed to break down old patterns of [sexual] segregation and hierarchy"; (2) "does not unnecessarily trammel the interests of the [male] employees"; (3) "does not require the discharge of [male] workers and their replacement with new [female] hirees"; (4) "does [not] create an absolute bar to the advancement of [male] employees"; and (5) "is a temporary measure . . . not intended to maintain [sexual] balance, but simply to eliminate a manifest [sexual] imbalance."

  d. That the Constitution of the United States has always embodied the aspiration to social justice, brotherhood, and human dignity that brought this nation into being.

  e. That the Constitution of the United States does not support the ideal of egalitarianism in the U.S. because it uses the term "brotherhood" to represent the population of the U.S. instead of using a more inclusive term like "personhood."

22. Suppose someone argues that since murder is wrong, and since capital punishment is murder by the state, it follows that capital punishment is wrong, too. The issue here is

  a. that murder is wrong.

  b. whether murder is wrong.

  c. that capital punishment is murder.

  d. whether capital punishment is murder.

  e. is capital punishment wrong?

  f. why capital punishment is wrong.

23. What is the issue in the following passage?

   The inside of this portable computer's box is not the standard fare. Mounted on the system board are a 33-Mhz 80386SX chip, a socket for an 80387SX math coprocessor, a VGA video chip set, and an AMI BIOS. As tested, the system had 2MB of 33-nanosecond DIP RAM, using 1-megabite chips. Do you find these items as standard fare on a portable?

24. For each of the following disagreements, explain why it is or isn't merely a semantic disagreement.

   a. **José:** Scientists have proved that there is no such thing as telepathy. Apparent cases of direct mind-to-mind communication, when investigated and tested, cannot be repeated under carefully controlled conditions required for scientific experiments.

   Susan: They may have done good science, but they proved no such thing. A proof that there is no telepathy requires axioms and inferences from axioms, but no scientist has yet produced the axioms of telepathy. So they surely have not established the theorem that telepathy does not exist.

   b. **Leon:** Christopher Columbus was a Jew. I read it in the *Jewish Chronicle*.

   Washington: He was no Jew. If he had been a Jew I would have heard about it. I'm a Jew.

   c. **Munitions expert:** Fifty percent of the Polaris missiles in the U.S. arsenal would fail if they were fired. Maintenance is too haphazard.

   Missile expert: Ninety percent of those missiles will work perfectly fine. I have looked at ten of them, and nine worked during a simulated firing.

   d. **Daryl:** My candidate is no fool. She is well educated because she has lots of common sense and is well read and could carry on a coherent, interesting conversation on any of a wide variety of subjects from politics to science to sports.

   Mary: Your candidate is not well educated. She doesn't even have a college degree.

Detecting Fallacies

I n Chapter 2 we examined several techniques of deception: exaggeration, telling only half the truth, using loaded language, and so forth. Fallacies, too, can be used to deceive, as we saw in the previous chapter's discussion of the fallacy of avoiding the issue. In this chapter, we explore other important fallacies, such as the straw man fallacy, in which our opponent distorts what we have said, or the ad hominem fallacy, in which our opponents divert our attention with irrelevant attacks on our character. Other fallacies, such as the false dilemma, are designed to divert our attention not by making irrelevant remarks but by selectively withholding important information. Knowing the main ways that people are lured into these errors will improve your chances for logical self-defense in the future.

Ad Hominem (Attack on the Reasoner)

If you venture to disagree with some people about any matter of religion or politics, they will be on your back like a rooster on a tater bug. They'll scratch at you any way they can; call you names; humiliate you. Suppose a soccer player is trying to convince somebody that black-and-white soccer balls are easier to see at dusk than red-and-yellow balls, when a third person butts in and says, "Who are you to talk about good and bad soccer balls? You've been thrown out of more soccer games for rules violations than anyone else on the team, and you still owe me five bucks for last season's team trophy." The person butting in commits the **ad hominem fallacy**: attacking an argument by pointing out some irrelevant characteristic of the reasoner rather than by pointing out some error in the reasoning itself. Purposefully using the ad hominem fallacy is a kind of *smear tactic*. The way to avoid committing this fallacy is to concentrate on the reasons, not on the reasoner.

■ ·········· Concept Check 1 ·········· ■

How many of the following brief arguments are examples of the ad hominem fallacy? Which ones are they?

a. Buy Cheerios; it's the breakfast of champions.

b. Don't buy Cheerios. They're too expensive.

c. Don't listen to Andy's argument for buying Cheerios. He's admitted the reasons behind his concluding that they aren't worth buying or eating, and those reasons really do not support his conclusion.

d. I believe that Cheerios cost less, and all Emilio's numbers and figures about how relatively expensive the cereal is are not convincing, because he's some sort of politician.

Frustrated by a doctor's warnings against smoking, a patient might strike back by saying, "Who are you to talk? You smoke." Has the patient committed an ad hominem fallacy? This is a difficult question. At first sight, you might be apt to say something like this: "Yes, the doctor might be a hypocrite, or a victim of weakness of the will, but the patient's complaint is *irrelevant* to whether or not the doctor's reasons against smoking are good reasons. 'Do as I say, not as I do,' is what the doctor is suggesting. Therefore, the patient has committed an ad hominem fallacy." But on second thought, the patient has a point. It is well known that you can learn a lot more about what people *really* believe by observing how they act than by listening to what they spout off about. It could be argued reasonably that if the doctor really believed what he says about smoking, he would follow his own advice. Because he doesn't follow his own advice, it is reasonable to conclude that the advice should not be followed unless other authorities can be found to back up the advice. If the patient had never heard anything negative about smoking except for what this doctor has said, the patient would be acting properly in hesitating to follow the advice. So, the reasoning does not commit the ad hominem fallacy.

Straw Man Fallacy

When you are arguing with someone, your goal is usually to create an argument that successfully shows the other person's position to be false. Your argument is then called a **refutation** of your opponent's position. From a logical reasoning perspective, which is one of fairness to the opposition, you ought not mistreat your opponent, nor should you misrepresent your opponent's position. Here is an example of someone misrepresenting a position:

Lobbyist for the logging company: I'm asking you to help encourage Congress to pass that bill to provide subsidies to western logging companies for selective cutting of 10,000 acres of federal timber land.

Environmentalist: I don't see how you can seriously ask any of us for our help. You are asking our grandchildren to live in a world in which they will never see a tree, never spot a deer, never smell the sweet scent of pine needles. Do you have any idea how bad it would be to live this way? No trees means bad air. No trees means muddy rivers. No trees means no wildlife. How can you defend the rape of the land? Land is precious; forests are precious; our grandchildren are precious. I don't understand how you can ask us to pick up the banner of desolation.

What an exaggeration! The environmentalist offers all sorts of reasons why there shouldn't be land rape or deforestation of the planet. That's easy to attack, but the lobbyist wasn't asking for that. The lobbyist was asking for logging subsidies, not land rape. The environmentalist has misrepresented the lobbyist's position and then begun to beat up on the misrepresentation. This unfair approach is called the **straw man fallacy**.

A speaker commits the straw man fallacy whenever she falsely attributes an especially weak position to her opponent that he wouldn't have proposed himself and then proceeds to attack the weak position. The opponent is a *real* man with a real argument; the weak position is an artificial one held by an artificial person — the "straw man" or scarecrow the speaker has created. It's easier to attack a straw man; nevertheless, the attack is irrelevant. It is a diversion from the main issue.

You are not committing the straw man fallacy simply by drawing a consequence from what the man says that is not what he himself would draw. It must be clear that you are also misinterpreting what he did say. In the accompanying cartoon the remarks about the manicurist commit the straw man fallacy. Here is another example of the straw man fallacy, committed by Bob:

Andy: We should liberalize the laws on crack.

Bob: No way. Any society with unrestricted access to drugs loses its work ethic and goes only for immediate gratification. We don't want that, do we?

Andy: Hey, I didn't say anything about unrestricted access to drugs. That's not the liberalization I want.

Bob has attacked a position that Andy doesn't hold. So, Bob's attack is an irrelevant smokescreen, and it commits the straw man fallacy. Bob's argument is ineffective logically, although it may still be effective psychologically, especially when Bob goes on to make other points against Andy and doesn't give him time to come back and defend himself.

© 1988 Washington Post Writers Group. Reprinted by permission.

To avoid committing the fallacy, Bob could, instead, have said to Andy something like the following:

Bob: What do you mean by liberalize? If you mean unrestricted access to drugs, then society will lose its work ethic and go only for immediate gratification, which we don't want, do we? But if you mean some other kind of liberalization, let's hear it. However, what we need is more crackdown on crack, not more liberalization, because . . .

When someone criticizes you by using the straw man fallacy, your natural reaction is to say, "Hey, wait a minute, I didn't say that." Unfortunately, you usually receive the criticism at the last second. Your opponent misrepresents your position while you are not around to defend yourself. In politics, this fallacy frequently occurs in leaflets and ads on the day before the election.

The False Dilemma Fallacy

Reflect on your own work experience, then respond to this item from a questionnaire:

> On average, each week your present employer (or your previous employer if you are not now employed) is drunk on the job

a. occasionally
b. usually
c. always

Suppose your employer is never drunk on the job. What answer could you choose? You don't have one to pick, so you are in a dilemma. Because it is false to say that the three given choices are all that exist, the dilemma is a false one, and the error of reasoning committed by the creator of the question is called the **false dilemma fallacy**. To remove the fallacy, the question could be revised to add a fourth choice, "never." False dilemma reasoning is an example of *slanting* by unfairly presenting too few choices. It *loads* the set of choices unfairly by not offering a fair range of choices.

The **black-white fallacy** is a false dilemma fallacy that limits you to two choices that are opposites. Real life is often not so black and white. What about part black and part white? What about the gray? Saying "You are either for our proposal or you are against it" is the most common example of the fallacy. Dick Gregory put it this way: "Either you are part of the solution or you are part of the problem." If you rightly complain that the dilemma you face is unfair and that there is another choice you should be offered, you are finding a way to **escape between the horns of the dilemma**. That is, you escape being gored by the choices offered. For three-horned false dilemmas you may escape *among* the horns instead of *between* the horns.

Not all dilemmas are false ones. If your employer's drinking problem does occasionally interfere with the quality of his (or her) work, you have to consider whether you will ignore it or instead report it to someone. Now you face a *true dilemma*. If you do nothing, the problem may not get solved. But if you blow the whistle by reporting the problem to another superior, you might have to deal with your employer's reaction when he finds out. He could start assigning you the more unpleasant assignments, and you may suddenly find letters in your personnel file describing your poor work performance.

■ ‥‥‥‥‥ Concept Check 2 ‥‥‥‥‥ ■

Which of the following passages, if any, contain a false dilemma fallacy?

a. Would you vote for the president if he were to run again, provided that code section D of article 20 were repealed, and supposing that under provision 60B the president were to declare his assets and swear not to have been involved in lobbying for a foreign power in the interim?
b. How many alcoholic beverages have you drunk in the last 24 hours?
c. Is the president doing about the same quality job as he was doing last year or is he doing better this year?

d. Please suggest improvements, if any, you would make in Einstein's theory of relativity.

e. Is Einstein's theory of relativity better than Isaac Newton's for predicting orbits of planets?

Here is a false dilemma fallacy you can commit on purpose if you want to trick a toddler into doing something:

Do you want to go to bed now or after you've had a glass of apple juice?

The child who doesn't want to go to bed at all might be tricked into choosing the apple juice. After the child is done with the juice you can say, "OK, remember you agreed to go to bed after the juice." The child who can see his or her way through the horns of this petty manipulation has reached a definite step up in logical reasoning ability.

A politically significant example of the false dilemma fallacy occurs in a resolution recently adopted by a major political party in Arizona. It states that the United States is "a republic based on the absolute laws of the Bible, not a democracy based on the changing whims of people."[1] A logical reasoner should ask, "Must it be one or the other?" One of the two choices offered by the resolution is that democracy is based on whims; the readers are offered no choice of a democracy based on something else, such as on reasoned opinion hammered out in the marketplace of competing ideas. By slanting the list of acceptable choices, the resolution guides the reader to making the favored choice. Successful stacking of the deck has to be somewhat subtle. If the resolution had said "a republic based on the Bible, not a democracy based on the changing whims of the stupid voters," it would not have passed because it would have been too heavy handed.

Does the sign at the top of the next page commit the false dilemma fallacy? Whether it commits the fallacy depends on whether there are really only two choices. Are there? How you answer this question may depend on your ideology or worldview. People with certain ideologies would say that ultimately there are just these two choices—Jesus Christ or Satan. Those with a different ideology—Christian Scientists or Moslems or atheists, for example—will say that there are other choices. So, to decide whether the fallacy has been committed here, we first need to settle the issue of the correctness of the religious ideology holding that there are just these two choices. That is a large task, not one well suited to this book. However, it would be incorrect to answer the question of whether the sign commits the false dilemma fallacy by saying, "Yes, it's a false dilemma if you have one ideology; but it's not a false dilemma if you have another ideology." This would be incorrect because the sign either does or doesn't commit the fallacy. Whether it does depends on whether the religious assumption behind the sign is correct. Thus, what it would be correct to say is that people who hold one sort of ideology will say, "Yes, it's a false dilemma,"

> **Jesus Christ OR the Devil?**
>
> **Eternal life in heaven OR Eternal pain in hell?**
>
> **THE CHOICE IS YOURS**

whereas those who hold another ideology are apt to say, "No, it's not a false dilemma." In short, the issue of whether the sign commits a false dilemma fallacy depends in turn on resolving another issue, the correctness of the religious assumptions behind it.

To summarize, by using the false dilemma fallacy, a speaker withholds important choices. The choices presented divert the reader's or hearer's attention away from the other choices. Pointing out one of those other choices is called escaping between the horns of the dilemma.

The Fallacy of Faulty Comparison

A TV commercial shows a woman wearing Jones & Jones gardening gloves. She is finishing her Saturday rose gardening without scratched hands, while her neighbor who gardens without gloves eventually quits because of the wear and tear on her hands. The commercial ends with the comment, "Don't you wish *you* had Jones & Jones gardening gloves?" This commercial tries to lure you into doing some faulty reasoning. The commercial creator wants you to compare having no gloves with having Jones & Jones gloves and then to conclude that you should buy Jones & Jones gloves rather than other brands. The logical reasoner will draw another conclusion. The commercial gives some reason to believe that, for gardening, wearing gloves is better than not wearing gloves, but it gives no reason to believe that Jones & Jones gloves are better than any other brand of gloves. This commercial offers a faulty comparison. The comparison should have been between Jones & Jones gloves and competing brands of gloves, not between Jones & Jones gloves and no gloves at all. The advertising agency that created the commercial intentionally used the **fallacy of**

faulty comparison to deceive viewers. What was compared wasn't what should have been compared.

Explain why the fallacy of faulty comparison occurs in the following advertisement for Flox mouthwash, and explain how to revise the ad to remove the problem:

> When compared with brushing alone, Flox removes 300 percent more plaque. Isn't that reason enough for *your* family to buy Flox?

Consider this ad: "Enzine detergent motor oil causes less exhaust emission than the leading seller. Buy Enzine." The faulty comparison problem can be useful for understanding this ad. Even if the ad is correct in what it says, you still need to worry about other things before you decide to buy Enzine. For consumers to make an informed decision about which product to buy, shouldn't the Enzine oil be compared with *all* the other motor oils, not merely the leading seller? The best seller might be so simply because it is the most highly advertised or least expensive, not because it is a high-quality product. The second major difficulty with the ad is that Enzine might be better than all the other products in terms of exhaust emission, but what about *other* considerations, such as price and constancy of viscosity, that are important for motor oils? When all these factors are considered, the leading seller might be better for your engine than Enzine, even if what the ad says is true. By selectively presenting the comparison information and by not giving you the other relevant information, the ad is presenting a half-truth, as discussed in Chapter 2.

Concept Check 4

What is the key to the humor in the sign on page 115?

a. The city is not called by its real name.

b. The mathematical sum is incorrect.

c. 4663 what?

d. We know the population number cannot be trusted.

e. The altitude must be incorrect.

Photo by David Middlecamp/Telegram-Tribune.

Fallacious Appeal to Authority

You know that the moon is a big, hard rock, don't you? But wait! How do you know? How do you know it's not made out of soft plastic? *You've* never been to the moon. You could be wrong, couldn't you?

Don't let that argument intimidate you. You don't have to *go* to the moon to know about it. You know that the moon is a big, hard rock because you have probably read that fact in a science book or have heard it from a science teacher. Science teachers can *speak with authority* on this matter. If you believe that the moon is a big rock for a reason like this, then you know it. Much of what you know you have learned this way. You don't find out for yourself; you believe what authorities say, at least when you can be reasonably sure they are in agreement with each other. You are right to do so. It is not firsthand knowledge, but it is still knowledge.

Suppose you came to believe that the moon is a rock only on the basis of what your sister told you. Then you wouldn't *know* the truth about the moon, assuming that she is no authority. You would *believe* the truth about the moon, but you wouldn't *know* the truth. To have knowledge you need more than true belief. To know something you have to have solid justification for it. *Knowledge is justified true belief; your knowledge is your true beliefs that you could back up by good reasons.* The reasons are crucial; without them you just have opinion, not knowledge.

Truth is also an important ingredient of knowledge. If you were to learn that some person's supposed knowledge turned out not to be true, then you would say the person never really knew it after all. For example, in Medieval times most people thought they knew the Earth to be flat, but they were mistaken and didn't really know it. They did have a justification for believing what they believed: they could climb a hill, look out, and see that the world appeared to be flat. That was good evidence for the time. Yet their belief was not knowledge, even though it was reasonable for them to hold the belief. They had a good reason to believe something false, but because it was false it was not knowledge.

■ ············ **Concept Check 5** ············ ■

Without having a justification, a person's claim to have knowledge is unsuccessful, but with the justification the person

a. will never be mistaken and will really know.

b. might be mistaken.

c. will always be mistaken, and thus the person will not know.

■ ············ **Concept Check 6** ············ ■

Explain the error in the following sentence, then rewrite it to make the point correctly:

> In Medieval times, people knew that the world is flat, but we now know that it's not.

Assessing the Credibility of Sources and Experts

Suppose your next-door neighbor says you shouldn't marry your sweetheart. When you ask her why, she says it's because her older brother thinks so. "So what?" you say. She responds by pointing out that he is an expert psychologist. At this point are you going to call up your true love and say it's all over? No. Being an expert on psychology doesn't make your neighbor's brother an expert on your love life. You know that your neighbor picked an *inappropriate authority* to back up her claim. The neighbor has made a famous error of reasoning, the **fallacious appeal to authority**. When it comes to your love life, there probably isn't any authority. Newspaper columnist Ann Landers might have helpful advice, but she isn't an authority on your love life. Ditto for a psychologist. It's usually good reasoning to appeal to authorities to support beliefs, but there are several ways to make fallacious appeals to authority, as we shall see.

There is an appeal to authority in this article from a college newspaper. Does it commit the fallacy?

The Lottery — The Odds to Beat

Just what are the chances of winning the state lottery? Statistician Peter Bennett says there is one chance in 25 million of winning the $2 million grand prize.... The odds are pretty slim, but remember, a $1 ticket could turn into $2 million!

Did the newspaper reporter commit a fallacious appeal to authority when he cited statistician Peter Bennett? No. Statisticians are just the right sort of people to appeal to about such a matter. So, unless you have a good reason to doubt Bennett's statistics, you should accept them. This acceptance is based on the following principle of logical reasoning: If a person is especially knowledgeable about a subject, then that person's views on the subject should be trusted more.

A fallacious appeal to authority can occur when an appeal is to someone who really is not an authority in the area. Don't ask a chemist when you want an expert opinion about hockey rules. The fallacy can also occur when a claim is backed up by an appeal to an authority in the appropriate area yet the authorities themselves are in significant disagreement with each other. When authorities disagree, none of them can "speak with authority." If I find ten authorities who say to vote Republican in the next U.S. presidential election, you can probably find ten authorities who say to vote Democratic. So if I appeal to my ten authorities as the reason why you should vote Republican, I've committed a fallacious appeal to authority. Sometimes, however, political experts should be trusted. If they say who won last year's election, you should trust what they say unless you have a good reason not to. You have background knowledge that the experts won't disagree on this topic.

Here is a more difficult question along this line. Does the following passage commit a fallacious appeal to authority?

According to psychologists, telepathy (mind reading) occurs more often between friends. The closer the friend, the more frequent the telepathy. Only the most gifted of people can read the thoughts of total strangers.

What should you think about all this? First, ask yourself whether psychologists are the right authorities. Shouldn't the speaker appeal instead to brain surgeons? No, psychologists are the appropriate authorities. The fallacy occurs because the speaker has twisted what the authorities really do say about telepathy. Only a small percentage of psychologists believe in telepathy, and they are not experimental psychologists (the scientists). Almost all scientific experts agree that telepathy is impossible. Therefore, the rest of us are justified in saying so, too.

How could the position of the psychological authorities be changed to favor telepathy? Here is one way. Have a purported mind reader pass a test. The mind reader could agree in advance to tell some of those psychologists what they are thinking about — say, at 2 P.M. each day for the next three days. If the mind reader is correct in even only two out of the three days, I'm sure the psychologists would kneel down and kiss the mind reader's feet. Claims to be able to read minds on demand are at least testable, and passing the tests should make the case in favor of the existence of telepathic powers. Unfortunately, nobody has ever been able to pass such a test.

You should critically examine such phrases as "According to psychologists . . ." and "Science has shown that . . ." These phrases are occasionally misleading. When people cite an authority, you have to worry that they might not understand what the authorities do say, might not realize that the authorities disagree with each other, or, worse yet, might not be telling the truth about what an authority says.

Most of us, not being scientists ourselves, cannot evaluate the scientific details. We have to rely on what others tell us the scientists say. Those others are usually reporters for newspapers, magazines, radio, and TV. Sometimes in their rush to get the story done, reporters will not bother to examine the quality of the science they are reporting on. They won't be careful to evaluate the reputation of the scientist or to check whether other scientists dispute the quality of that scientist's work. For example, suppose the issue is whether the state legislature should pass a bill favoring cloth diapers over disposable diapers. The relevant scientific issue is the impact of both kinds of diapers on the environment. One reporter may incorporate into his news article some paragraphs from a press release crafted by the cloth diaper company that financed the research. The press statements might say, "Independent research shows cloth diapers to be environmentally sound, while disposable diapers clog our nations landfills without decomposing." The reporter won't bother to determine whether the scientific research really was done by an "independent" researcher. Perhaps it was done by a scientist specifically paid to do the research because the company suspected he or she would come up with the "right" results about the product. Meanwhile, perhaps unknown to the first reporter, some other reporter is incorporating into her own article the key paragraphs from the press release of the disposable diaper company. It has financed its own scientific research showing that "disposable diapers are environment-friendly while cloth diapers must be washed with suds that foul our rivers." We consumers need to be wary of these possibilities of sloppy reporting.

One thing you can do as a reader is to be alert for a sentence saying that the scientist was not financed by the company whose product is being reported on. We should also be alert for a sentence indicating that other researchers support the scientist's work. When such helpful sentences are absent, do we conclude that the reporter didn't check all this out, or do we conclude that he or she did but just didn't bother to tell us? We really are stuck in a dilemma. And there is a second dilemma.

Do we accept the reported conclusion of the scientific research, or do we remain skeptical? We are too busy to check up on the report ourselves — we barely have enough time to read the entire article from just one reporter. Most reports we receive are not personally important enough for us to engage in a massive reading project to determine just what to believe. Ideally, we might want to withhold our judgment about cloth versus disposable diapers until we get better information, but realistically we will probably never get that information. Nor will we get definitive information about the thousands of other large and small issues facing us throughout our life, and we cannot go through life never having an opinion on anything. George Santayana may have been correct when he said that skepticism is the chastity of the intellect, but our intellects can't be skeptical all the time; we have to embrace most of the beliefs of the reporters. It is for this very reason that the information media are so powerful; they inevitably shape our minds even when we are trying to be logical reasoners and careful about what beliefs we adopt.

■ .... Concept Check 7 .... ■

Identify the appeal to authority in the following piece of reasoning. Why aren't you convinced by the speaker's reasoning?

> Our government is standing in the way of progress. What the government should be doing is solving our problems. Yet the government is not doing this because it is not funding a request for what it needs most of all, a universal answering machine. This machine would give an answer to nearly all factual questions that were fed into it. For example, if you want to know if a piece of reasoning is fallacious, you input the reasoning into the machine and then check the output for an answer. If you want to know the cure for AIDS or for some other disease that has no known cure, then just feed in the question, and the universal answering machine will give the answer. The machine would do all this without the programmer first feeding it the answers. We don't have such a machine yet, but we should get one right away because having it would be so helpful. Scientific reports show that its creation is not far off; there just needs to be a major increase in funding. There should be a lot of money offered for the best grant applications. That will draw in the best scientific minds to work on this most important project.
>
> The government knows about the universal answering machine project. I wrote Congress and the president two years ago about it. Their inaction shows that the government is standing in the way of progress. Either they are stupid, or there is a cover-up.

■ ...... ■

Spotting an Authority's Bias

There is an additional element you have to worry about when someone appeals to authority: bias on the authority's part. Suppose a British politician claims that there is no significant corruption in Venezuela's oil ministry. The politician's evidence is that the chief oil minister of Venezuela was quoted in last week's *Newsweek* as saying his ministry is free of corruption. Should you accept the British politician's argument? Well, since you probably don't know anything about Venezuelan oil, isn't the oil minister in a better position to know whether there is corruption in his oil ministry? Yes, and he is the right authority on the matter. Also, you don't have any reason to believe that he was misquoted. So shouldn't you accept the British politician's claim that there is no corruption? No. It is doubtful that this particular authority will tell the truth. Wouldn't he be likely to cover up corruption if it existed?

When someone wants you to accept a claim because a certain authority says it is so, you should ask yourself a few questions:

1. Is the authority an authority on *this* subject?
2. Do the authorities agree with each other (except for the occasional lone wolf)?

Reprinted by permission of Tom Tomorrow.

3. Can the person who appeals to the authority be trusted to report honestly and accurately what the authority said?

4. Can the authority be trusted to tell the truth on this topic?

If any of the answers are negative, the speaker has made a fallacious appeal to authority. If the answers are satisfactory, you should probably go ahead and believe the claim. Still, look before you leap. For example, all of us trust doctors to be authorities. They have expert knowledge that we do not have. What would you do, though, if you ventured into a doctor's office with symptoms of flu and the doctor said, "I'm sorry, but your leg has to come off right away; sign this release form, and we will get you straight into the hospital"? The principle of logical reasoning that you apply at this moment is the following: *When the stakes are higher, it is more important to get better evidence before making the decision.*

   Appeals to expert opinion will sometimes lead you to error. Even experts make mistakes. However, occasional slip-ups by the experts are no reason to quit using authorities as sources of knowledge.

■ ············ Concept Check 8 ············ ■

You've been asked to research living conditions in two large American cities, Kansas City and Baltimore. The specific problem you face is how to find out whether the cost of living of the average person is greater in one city or the other. The cost of living encompasses the cost of food, housing, car insurance, and other regular expenses. Which person would be most likely to give you the best answer or the best suggestion on where to go to get the answer?

a. A local building contractor who owns land in Baltimore and who has recently built homes and apartments in both Baltimore and Kansas City.

b. Your college's urban studies professor.

CALVIN AND HOBBES (1990) Watterson. Dist. by UNIVERSAL PRESS SYNDICATE.
Reprinted by permission.

c. Your uncle who lived in Baltimore for five years before moving to Kansas City last year.

d. The personnel director of the company that offered you a new job this week in Kansas City.

■ ············ Concept Check 9 ············ ■

Here is a brief biography of a person, followed by a list of topics. Rank the topics according to her expertise in them, beginning with those on which she would be able to speak with the most authority.

> Judy Wilson is currently the director of government documents for the Library of Congress in Washington, D.C. Ten years ago she took a three-year leave from the library to co-direct the census for the Chinese government in Beijing. In 1979 she received a Ph.D. from the Food Research Institute at Stanford University, where she wrote her dissertation on current food consumption patterns throughout China. She has published a book on mathematical methods in geography and has published several scholarly articles on the wages and working conditions of women in Asia and Africa.

a. How can interested members of the public obtain classified research documents as they are declassified and released by the Pentagon and the National Archives?

b. Are Chinese and Indian foods as popular in the U.S. as they were five years ago?

c. Are more women raped in Japan than in China?

d. Are the disabled people in China currently as well fed as those elsewhere in Eastern Asia?

e. Would an accurate census be more difficult to carry out in Ecuador or in Egypt?

The Genetic Fallacy

A critic commits the **genetic fallacy** if he or she attempts to discredit a claim because of its origin (genesis) when such a criticism is irrelevant to the claim. For example, suppose a friend of yours is reading the newspaper and mentions a report about Senator Friedman's bill to redraw the boundaries of the political districts in your state. Your friend is describing the senator's reasons for the new boundaries when he mentions that, according to the article, the senator got the idea for the new boundaries from a dream she had one night. You say to your friend, "Hey, stop right there. There's got to be something wrong with Senator Friedman's reasons, because she got the idea from a dream." When you say this, you are committing the genetic fallacy because you are paying too much attention to the genesis of the idea rather than to the content of the idea and the justification offered for it.

Similarly, if Sigmund Freud, the father of psychiatry, had said that a patient's reasons for believing in God must be faulty because she arrived at her belief as a product of needing a strong father figure who would protect her and answer her prayers, Freud would have been committing the fallacy.

Sometimes more than one fallacy can be assigned to the same error in reasoning. For example, suppose you were asked to evaluate the reasoning in the following passage:

> In a recent American presidential campaign, a U.S. senator was running against the president for the party's nomination. The senator argued in a speech that the president should be held responsible for an international crisis that hurt American influence in the world because the president had advance signals of the coming crisis but had not acted effectively to prevent the crisis. How did the president reply? By dismissing the senator's argument on the grounds that it was "politically motivated."

Clearly the president, and not the senator, made the error in reasoning here. What error, though? There are several ways to correctly label the mistake:

1. Ad hominem, because the president attacked the senator's character as being that of a politically motivated person.
2. Fallacy of avoiding the issue, because the president did not address the senator's question of who is responsible for the crisis but instead chose to change the issue to whether the senator's charges were politically motivated.
3. Genetic fallacy, because the president attacked the genesis or origin of the senator's complaint rather than the complaint itself.

Non Sequitur

Suppose you've been shopping for a TV set and I tell you not to buy a television set today because it is Tuesday. "Why Tuesday?" you might ask. "Because Tuesdays are so boring," I answer. I have a reason for your not buying the TV set, so I have an argument. But what sort of argument? The reason is so weak that many people are apt to say, "That's no reason at all." My reason may not be totally irrelevant to the issue, but it does not provide significant support for my position on the issue. It would only convince somebody who already was anti-Tuesday or opposed to your purchase. When a conclusion is supported only by weak reasons or by irrelevant reasons, the argument is fallacious and is said to be a **non sequitur**. This Latin term means "does not follow." Any fallacious argument is one whose conclusion doesn't follow from its supporting reasons, so any fallacious argument is appropriately called a "non sequitur." However, we usually apply the term only when we cannot think of how to label the argument with a more specific fallacy name and when it is fairly easy to show that the reasons are weak.

Sometimes when we say, "That's no reason at all," we do expect to be taken literally, because there really is no reason there. If so, there is no argument, and thus no non sequitur either. Although there is a fuzzy line between a radically weak argument and no argument at all, there is a difference between the two. The weak one has at least some reasons. Here is an example of a disagreement in which a person thinks he is giving an argument but in fact is giving no argument at all:

> NONARGUMENT: Jim, you really ought to vote for the Democrat. I just don't understand how you can think of voting for that Republican. I mean, where's your head? The Democrat is so obviously the one to vote for, you should do it and get it over with. Don't sit there and even think about that Republican.

If there were an argument here, the conclusion would be for Jim to vote for the Democrat. But there is no argument because there is no reason given for the conclusion. Sometimes the term *non sequitur* is defined more broadly to include a nonargument that is mistakenly put forward as an argument. On that definition, the above nonargument would count as a non sequitur.

Here is another example of a passage that you are apt to react to by saying, "That's no argument at all":

> NON SEQUITUR ARGUMENT: Nuclear disarmament is a risk, but everything in life involves a risk. Every time you drive in a car you are taking a risk. If you're willing to drive in a car, you should be willing to have disarmament.

At this point you might think, "Hey, that's no reason for disarmament." All it is saying is that the risks of disarmament are OK because some other risks are OK. Well, some other risks are OK, but some are not OK. So the reason given is extremely weak. If the advocate of nuclear disarmament wants to revise his remarks and avoid the fallacy, he should try saying something like this: "Nuclear disarmament is a risk, but it's not as great a risk as continued nuclear escalation, because the political situation is such and such . . ."

In summary, whenever you react to a piece of reasoning with a comment such as "Hey, that's no reason for that," you've probably detected a non sequitur fallacy.

■ ·········· Concept Check 10 ·········· ■

Is the following argument a non sequitur? If it is, explain why.

> Your information proves that part of Canada is south of part of California. Therefore, we can be sure that John was right when he said, "Some of Canada is south of part of either California or Oklahoma."

■ ··········· Concept Check 11 ··········· ■

Which description(s) apply to the following piece of reasoning?

> None of the senator's friends owns a horse racing track. Susan Mauring owns Scioto Downs, and Scioto Downs is a horse racing track in Columbus, Ohio. So, you shouldn't expect to find her on a list of the Senator's friends, should you?

a. avoiding the issue
b. genetic fallacy
c. straw man
d. fallacious appeal to authority
e. the reasoning is OK
f. faulty comparison

Review of Major Points

The logical reasoner sticks to the issue, makes only relevant remarks, doesn't withhold relevant information, and accurately represents the position of the opposition. Failing to do some of these things is the source of the following fallacies: ad hominem, straw man, false dilemma, faulty comparison, fallacious appeal to authority, genetic fallacy, and non sequitur. In this chapter we saw how to identify these fallacies and how to revise passages containing them. There are many more fallacies, although these are some of the most important and common ones. A more comprehensive list of the fallacies is presented in Appendix A.

The world is full of con artists, many of whom are out there right now thinking of new ways to con you into doing things for the wrong reasons. You, the logical reasoner, need eternal vigilance.

Glossary

ad hominem fallacy Attacking an argument by pointing out some irrelevant characteristic of the reasoner rather than by pointing out some error in the reasoning itself.

black-white fallacy A false dilemma fallacy that limits you to only two choices.

escape between the horns of a dilemma Rightly complaining that the dilemma you face is unfair and that there is another choice that you should be offered. For three-horned false dilemmas you may escape *among* the horns instead of *between* the horns.

fallacious appeal to authority An appeal to authority in which the authority is not really an expert in this subject or cannot be trusted to tell the truth, in which authorities disagree on this subject (except for the occasional lone wolf), or in which the reasoner misquotes the authority.

fallacy of faulty comparison Arguing by comparison but using inappropriate items or aspects.

false dilemma fallacy Unfairly presenting too few choices and implying that a choice must be made only between the offered choices.

genetic fallacy Attempting to discredit a claim because of its origin (genesis) when such a criticism is irrelevant to the claim.

non sequitur "Does not follow"; an argument in which the reasons given are irrelevant or very weak.

refutation A disproof. A refutation of another person's position is an argument that successfully shows the other person's position to be false.

straw man fallacy Falsely attributing an easily refuted position to one's opponent that the opponent wouldn't have proposed himself and then proceeding to attack the easily refuted position. The opponent is a *real* man (or woman) with a real argument; the easily refuted position is an artificial position held by an artificial person — the "straw man" the speaker has created. It's easier to attack a straw man; nevertheless, the attack is irrelevant. It is a diversion from the main issue.

Answers to Concept Checks

1. Answer (d). Only in this argument does the reasoner reject someone's argument by pointing out irrelevant characteristics of the arguer. Answer (c) gives an argument that might appear to attack the arguer, but notice that the attack is on the arguer's reasons and really not on the arguer.

2. Answer (c). Maybe the president is doing worse.

3. The advertisement encourages you to buy Flox instead of competing mouthwashes by luring you into comparing Flox with brushing alone. To remove the fallacy and make the point the advertiser wants to make, the Flox mouthwash should be compared with other mouthwashes. For example, the ad could say, "When compared to all other mouthwashes, Flox removes 15 percent more plaque. Isn't that reason enough for *your* family to buy Flox?"

4. Answer (c). The sign is comparing apples and oranges. This is a faulty comparison

because these items cannot be added together. Imagine what the units should be on the answer.

5. Answer (b). With the justification, the claim could still fail to be knowledge; it must also be true.

6. It is mistaken to say that the people know the world is flat. People never knew this because people cannot know something that is false. Here is a way to make the point correctly:

> In Medieval times, people believed they knew that the world is flat, but we now know that the world is not.

Here is another way to make the point correctly:

> In Medieval times, people claimed to know the world is flat, but we now know that their belief was false.

7. The speaker is wrong when he appeals to authorities by saying "Scientific reports show." The reports show no such thing, as we all know. The reasoning is based on the assumption that such a machine is feasible. There is good evidence that it isn't feasible; the government recognizes this, which is why it has not acted. In short, the speaker is a crackpot.

8. Answer (b). Who is going to know more about the cost of living in a city — somebody who lives there or somebody who studies the city? The urban studies professor is supposed to be an expert who studies cities in all their aspects, and the professor would not have a reason to give a biased answer. If the professor didn't know the answer, he or she would definitely know how to get it. The personnel director might well be biased. Your uncle can speak only from personal experience, as far as you know, and doesn't know the statistics; yet the statistics would be a more reliable source of information than firsthand stories even from someone you trust. The building contractor could well know about the cost of housing, but there is little reason to suspect he would know about the cost of other aspects of living in the two cities.

9. She could speak with the most authority on (a) and the least on (b). She must know when and where classified documents get released by government agencies because her section of the library would most probably be the first to get them of any library in the country. There is no reason to suppose she knows anything special about rape. She might know how to count the disabled people in China, if this were a question on the Chinese census that the government wanted answered (and you don't know whether it is), but there is little reason to suppose she would be interested in how well they eat today, even though she did study food consumption patterns back in the 1970s. Regarding (e), she has expert knowledge about how to do a census, but there is no good reason to suppose she could give a decent answer about the problems of conducting one in Egypt versus Ecuador. Regarding (b), she is unlikely to have solid information about the popularity of Chinese and Indian food with U.S. consumers. There is no

reason to suspect her degree in food research would provide her with expertise on the current popularity of such foods. So, on this topic she is likely to speak from her own experiences rather than from reliable statistical data. Therefore, the ranking should have (a) on top; then (c), (d), and (e) ranked equally in the middle; and (b) at the bottom.

10. It is not a non sequitur because the information, whether true or false, does give a good reason to believe the conclusion. As a matter of fact, the information is true.

11. Answer (e). The reasoning commits no fallacies; if the reasons are OK, the conclusion follows. That is, on the basis of the information given, it would be a good bet that her name would not be on that list.

Review and Writing Exercises

■ 1. Label the fallacy committed by the district attorney in the following passage, and rewrite it to remove the fallacy.

Will you tell the jury where you bought the gun used to shoot the liquor store clerk? Just a simple "yes" or "no" please.

■ 2. Create an ad hominem fallacy in your response to the following:

I don't think it's appropriate at all to celebrate Columbus Day. The holiday honors a man who was responsible for the destruction of millions of Indians. People think Christopher Columbus was a good man, but he wasn't. We opened our arms to welcome him, but he took the land from us.

● 3. Create a believable dialogue between two people in which the first person uses a non sequitur. Make the non sequitur be a serious argument, not a silly one. Have the second person point out the fallacy, and have the first person agree and correct the error in a way that now does make the point that was originally intended. Begin with a helpful description of the situation by giving background information to aid the reader in understanding the issue involved.

4. Suppose I decide not to buy a television set today because my horoscope says it is a bad day for buying anything. I have a reason for not buying the TV set, so I have an argument. Is the argument a non sequitur?

■ 5. The fallacious appeal to authority is so named because it's always inappropriate to appeal to authority in support of a conclusion.

a. true   b. false

6. Does the following argument use a fallacious appeal to authority? Why?

Glass is mostly silicon atoms that slow the speed of light down to 122,000 miles per second. I know this because I overheard one of the employees at the science museum say so.

7. Is a fallacious appeal to authority committed in the following argument for the conclusion that men are naturally better at basketball and weightlifting?

John: Men make better basketball players than women do. I would say the same about weightlifting, too.

Susan: Yes, I agree. You rarely see women competing in these sports. However, someday, when interests change, women will be as good as men.

John: Oh, no, I wasn't clear. I mean that men will always be better, because men are just naturally better at these sports. Average men will be better than average women, and the best men will be better than the best women.

Susan: What makes you say this?

John: I've consulted an expert, that's why.

Susan: Oh yeah, who?

John: My mother.

Susan: Ha! Your mother. Who's your mother?

John: She was a coach.

Susan: So?

John: She's athletic director at a women's college; she once was hired by a state university to scout high school basketball players, men and women, for potential athletic scholarships; she is a specialist in sports physiology; and she has carefully followed basketball and weightlifting at all levels of the sports. She even wrote an article about all this for *Sports Illustrated*.

Susan: Well, that may be true about her, but I still think that women could be as good as men if they just had an equal chance.

John: No way. Women are hopeless. They should not even be allowed to try out.

8. Create an original paragraph that uses a believable but fallacious appeal to authority.

9. Create an original example of the straw man fallacy that occurs in response to the following argument:

I urge you to join the campaign for the proposal. This initiative proposal is in circulation under the title "Law Invalidation." It is an initiative constitutional amendment, sponsored by two private citizens, that seeks to abolish the California State Bar Association and prohibit its members from holding public office or practicing law in California courts. Among other things, the initiative would also prevent judges from interpreting the law in courts and repeal all laws enacted by the legislature since 1926.

10. Suppose Jones argues for some point *x*. Suppose *x* is attacked by Smith for two reasons: *x* implies *y*, and *y* is incorrect. If Smith is correct about both reasons, his argument is

    a. a straw man

    b. an ad hominem

    c. avoiding the question

    d. not fallacious

    e. irrelevant to the issue of whether *x* is so.

11. State how to go between the horns of the following dilemma. Ignore the loaded language.

    > I understand what you are saying about business ethics, but you've got to see it from the businessperson's perspective. The choice in business is simple: either I adopt a vow of poverty and go for sainthood, or I take the more sensible path of maximizing personal income no matter what.

12. Create a straw man fallacy in your response to the passage in Exercise 2, and then explain why your response deserves to be called an example of that fallacy.

■ 13. Which choice below is a *single* horn of the false dilemma created by the speaker?

    > There are no black women conductors of major American symphony orchestras. I can guess why. Either black women aren't musical, or else God wanted no black women conducting those orchestras. But we all know there are some black women who are musical, so I guess it's all part of God's plan.

    a. God wanted there to be no black women conductors of major American symphony orchestras.

    b. There are no black women conductors of major American symphony orchestras.

    c. Black women are musical.

    d. Either black women aren't musical, or else God wanted no black women conducting those orchestras.

14. You will commit the fallacy of faulty comparison if you

    a. compare apples with tangerines and then say that the cost per pound of one is outrageously high in comparison with the cost per pound of the other.

    b. fail to compare apples that you are offering for sale with apples that are rotten.

    c. compare apples with oranges and fail to consider that at current prices, two apples equal one orange in California but not in New York.

    d. promote the health value of your own apples over the competition's apples by comparing the health of eaters of your apples with people who eat no fruit at all.

e. say that Jones & Jones gloves are best for protecting gardener's hands on the basis of a comparison between those gloves and other means of hand protection, including the competition's gloves.

15. Is the fallacy of faulty comparison committed in the text of this 1950s magazine advertisement?

MORE DOCTORS SMOKE OUR CIGARETTE. Check for yourself—smoke our cigarette and see if you don't get less throat irritation.

---

16. What fallacy, if any, is committed here?

Physicist Jones won the Nobel prize for his advances in astronomy.
Physicist Jones says Republicans are ruining the economy.
So, Republicans are ruining the economy.

17. Which fallacy, if any, occurs in the following piece of reasoning?

I left my car keys in the house. I've looked carefully all over the bedroom for my car keys and failed to find them. Therefore, I left them in some other room.

a. fallacious appeal to authority

b. ad hominem

c. avoiding the question

d. straw man

e. false dilemma

f. none of the above

18. What is the best characterization of the following passage?

As of January 23, 1977, 88 percent of all U.S. homes had at least one TV set. As of January 23, 1987, 77 percent of all U.S. homes had at least one color TV set. So, as of January 23, 1998 nearly 66 percent of all U.S. homes will have a video cassette player.

a. straw man

b. fallacious appeal to authority

c. ad hominem

d. non sequitur

e. no fallacy occurs here; it's fine reasoning

19. During a heated battle in an earlier century, a Prussian emperor, whose troops were displaying fear, urged his men forward with "Onward! What do you want? Do you want to live forever?" Identify a false dilemma here. What is a reasonable way for a Prussian soldier to escape between the horns of this dilemma? First, explicitly define the dilemma. (*Hint:* The dilemma is not between living and dying, nor between obeying and disobeying.)

■ 20. The verb *go* is conjugated in the present tense as *I go, you go, he goes*. Bertrand Russell once said that something can be learned from the correct conjugation of words. For example, he conjugates the word *firm* this way: *I am firm; you are obstinate; he is a pig-headed fool*. What point is Russell really making?

■ 21. Comment on the quality of this argument:

> Microorganisms are small living creatures that can be seen only through a microscope. Bacteria, yeast, and molds are the three most important microorganisms in food fermentation. Therefore, the most important microorganisms in food fermentation are bacteria, yeast, and molds.

22. Comment on the quality of the following reasoning and give a justification for your comment.

> Listen, Jerry. You've been convicted twice of molesting children, so your reasons for why the new child-care center should be built near your house aren't going to be acceptable to this committee.

23. What fallacy or fallacies, if any, are committed in the following passage?[2]

> The scientific method simply sets a rigorous yet easily communicated standard for communicating information. . . .
>
> Before a scientist can accept a phenomenon as conclusively proven, several things must happen:
>
> First, the experiment must be designed so that *no other factors can account for the result*. A psychic may correctly identify all the cards in a Zener deck [a set of symbols used for testing telepathy] — but if the cards were so thin they could be read through their backs (as has happened), the experiment doesn't prove anything.
>
> The scientist also demands that findings should be repeatable by other scientists in other locations following the same methods. If not repeatable, the result is not conclusive.
>
> Now apply these standards to the case of the paranormal.
>
> Scientific tests going back more than a century have shown a resounding inability to provide solid evidence for the existence of telepathy, clairvoyance, psychokinesis [moving things by mindpower], precognition [seeing the future], levitation, reincarnation, transmigration [of souls], or miraculous healing.

■ 24. In the following letter to a newspaper, where is the loaded language? When the author says that Thurow "issued his absurd suggestion," is she committing a fallacy? Explain your answer.

To the Editor:

  Though I can hardly claim the credentials of Lester Thurow (Op-Ed May 3), I would like to respond (albeit with an admittedly imperfect understanding of inelastic demand curves) to his proposals for change in United States drug laws and policies.
  Mr. Thurow has a gift for simplifying economics so lucidly that an average person (myself) can understand today's most complex issues. Now he has gone one step further, oversimplifying the American drug scene to conform to his academic, economic theories.
  Perhaps what he says is so: legalization will bring down the street price of drugs, thereby cutting into the profits that have made drug dealers powerful kingpins. There will no longer be a criminal element connected with the drug trade. Organized crime will have to find some other illegal industry to control. The violence will end, the prisons will be empty, and we can concentrate on educating our children to stay away from drugs. That is a very pretty picture. It is also incredibly naive.
  And dangerous. The much-publicized death of the athlete Len Bias proved that even occasional or one-time drug use can be fatal. Do we want our children making such dangerous experiments? And what about the addicted? Will the easily affordable, uncontaminated drugs provide them any incentive to quit? Or are those people expendable?
  Moving to economic issues, who will be allowed to produce drugs in the United States? Will any farmer with a spare plot be eligible in Mr. Thurow's market-based society? Should demand fall, would the government provide subsidies as it has for the wheat producers? And what about the distribution network? Will there be drug salesmen? Will they be held liable for overdoses? Will drug users be allowed to function as teachers? Airline pilots? Senators? Will minors have access to drugs? The questions are endless.
  The basic question is, Do we want to expose the next generation to legalized drugs? Now that we know the colossal risk, do we really want to hand another generation a line of cocaine, or even a marijuana joint, and hope that supply-and-demand economics will take care of everything?
  These are not questions Mr. Thurow addressed, nor is there evidence that he even considered them before he issued his absurd suggestion. Perhaps the dean of the Sloan School of Management at the Massachusetts Institute of Technology should set aside his graphs and theories and concentrate on the misery that his prescription for a drug-free America would cause.[3]

- 25. Imagine what somebody might say who sincerely disagrees with one of your own beliefs. Construct a one- or two-page argument that gives reasons for why your belief is incorrect. That is, argue for the other side of the issue. Begin by stating the issue. The new argument must contain no fallacies and no loaded language and should be typed, double-spaced, if possible.

26. Revise the sentence below to correct the errors:

> In the Dark Ages, people lived on a flat world because everyone knew that the world was flat.

- 27. Examine the following conversation and look for a fallacy in the reasoning:

Mother: My fifteen-year-old daughter failed two courses at school. The worst part is, she didn't even try. She just said, "Oh well, it's not important." If she had *tried* and failed, that wouldn't be so bad.

Friend: Are you sure it wouldn't be so bad? Maybe it would be *worse* if she tried and failed.

Mother: No, it wouldn't, because if she tried she probably wouldn't fail the two courses.

Friend: Oh, I think I see what you mean. Do you mean that anybody who tries will succeed at least in the sense that they did try and didn't just give up?

Mother: No, I just mean that if my daughter tries, she most likely will get a grade higher than an F.

Who made the error, the mother or the friend? What error?

28. Revise the dialogue between the mother and her friend so that it no longer commits the fallacy.

29. Create an ad hominem fallacy in your response to the following argument:

> Our department could use the new MouseMan mouse. Since it doesn't use a wire connected to the computer, buying it won't cause more desk clutter. Also, it doesn't have the annoying electrical interference problems that plague other infrared cordless mice. And new MouseMan "sleeps" when you're not working, so a common battery lasts up to a year inside of it. Sounds perfect to me. Let's order a batch of these mice.

30. For the passage in Exercise 13, write a response that goes between the horns of the dilemma and briefly explain the social issues involved.

Argumentative Writing

7

Writing logically is the usual goal when composing a written product, but that's not always the goal. Sometimes you may want to stand your language on its head to shock or amuse your readers. However, you should be logical when you are writing to describe, explain, or argue. The writing in a term paper, an essay, a business report, a newspaper editorial, or a position paper normally needs to be logical to be effective. "Be logical" means more than that the reasoning be free of fallacies; it also means that the writing should be clear and exact. Writing logically requires paying attention to both the structure and the style of the written piece. This chapter offers suggestions about how to improve structure and style; these suggestions are rules of thumb, not rules to be obeyed to the letter. The chapter begins by exploring the differences among descriptions, explanations, and arguments. It ends with an elaborate discussion of argumentation. Explanation is the focus of Chapter 8.

Describing, Explaining, and Arguing

Language is a tool we can use for many purposes. We use language to state facts, explain events, and argue that our statements should be believed. But we also use it to intimidate, to promise, to perform marriages, to forgive, to apologize, and to insult. However, most of our reasoning occurs when we use language to describe, explain, or argue, which is why this book concentrates on descriptions, explanations, and arguments.

Explanations of events often indicate the forces or causes that made the event occur. A forest fire might be explained as having been caused by the action of lightning. In the case of events that are human actions, such as Dwayne's unscrewing the lid on a jar of peanut butter, the explanation might appeal to his intentions, such as that he wanted to satisfy his hunger. Intentions are mental causes, not physical causes.

A **description** of the same event wouldn't focus on what caused what; instead, it would just state the facts. A description might be "Dwayne used his greasy hands to unscrew the sticky peanut butter jar in the dark kitchen." **Arguments**, on the other hand, try to convince you that the something is so. The argument might be "Dwayne unscrewed the lid because Loretta saw him do it." The argument wouldn't need to mention that he was hungry. Conversely, the explanation of Dwayne's behavior would mention the hunger but wouldn't mention Loretta's witnessing the event. Her presence would be irrelevant to the explanation. So, descriptions, explanations, and arguments can be, and usually are, quite different.

To appreciate the difference between a description and an explanation, consider one of the current limits of medical science. Scientists do not know what causes pimples, but they do have a clear understanding of what pimples are. That is, they can provide a detailed description of pimples, but they can offer no explanation of why some people get them and others do not. Scientists can describe pimples but not explain them.

Normally, explanations apply to events, not persons or objects. Historians don't explain Napoleon. Instead, they explain events such as Napoleon's becoming emperor of France after the French Revolution. Their explanation would point out the forces at work and the conditions that made it possible for Napoleon to succeed where no one else did. On the other hand, a description of the same event would be a special sort of listing of the facts about the event, such as that it occurred in 1804, that Napoleon crowned himself, and so forth. If the "description" were to add that the event was made possible by Napoleon's successfully engineering a coup d'etat in 1799, then strictly speaking this "description" would now be offering an explanation as well. A pure description of an event should not say *why* it occurred. That is what an explanation is supposed to do. When we ask for a description of an event, we might be happy to learn why the event happened, but in this case we would be getting more than we asked for—an explanation in addition to the description.

Arguments are different still. An argument is designed to convince someone to do something or to believe something, which it does by giving specific reasons. For example, we could argue that Napoleon became emperor of France because history professors say so. Notice that this argument doesn't describe the event (of Napoleon's becoming emperor of France) or explain it. The argument simply gives a reason to believe that it occurred.

> The main goal in a good argument is that the conclusion follow from the reasons given—that is, that the reasons imply the conclusion.

Although we have demonstrated here that describing, explaining, and arguing are very different things, in real life they get jumbled together. This is fine; we don't often need them to occur in their pure form. However, it's hard to appreciate all that is going on in a jumbled whole unless we appreciate the parts.

So let's consider a few more examples. If Betsy Ross says, "The new flag I designed has red and white stripes with thirteen stars," is she explaining the flag? No, she is just describing it. She is not explaining where the flag came from or what motivated her to make it. Nor is she arguing about it. However, if Betsy Ross says something a little more elaborate, such as "The new flag I designed has red and white stripes with thirteen stars for the thirteen new states," she is describing the flag and also explaining why it has thirteen stars instead of some other number. So it is possible to describe and to explain in the same sentence.

If Betsy Ross says, "I designed the flag because I wanted to help our new nation," she is only explaining why she designed it; she is not describing it or arguing that she designed it.

Couldn't you say that when Betsy Ross says, "The new flag I designed has red and white stripes with thirteen stars" she is explaining what the flag is like? Well, people do say this, but they are being sloppy. To "explain what something is like" is really to describe it, not explain it.

■ ·········· Concept Check 1 ·········· ■

Is the following passage most probably an argument, an explanation, or a description?

> The most striking thing about Beijing, indeed about all of China, is that there are people everywhere. You need to imagine yourself in a never-ending Macy's sale. There are lines to everything. You have to get in a line to find out which line to be in.[1]

How Arguments Differ from Explanations

There are several good reasons to learn to distinguish arguments from explanations. You would be wasting your time explaining what caused some event if the person you were speaking to did not believe the event ever occurred. Instead, you should be directing your comments to arguing that the event did occur. Or, suppose you take an author to be arguing when in fact she is explaining. If you complain to yourself about the quality of her argument and dismiss her passage as unconvincing, you will have failed to get the explanation that is successfully communicated to other readers of the same passage.

A passage might be either an explanation or an argument, yet nothing within that passage may give a clue as to which it is. The difference may be only in the head of the speaker or writer. In many cases, the same sentences can be given with the intention to argue or to explain. For example, "Don't touch that snake — it might bite you" could be either.

An argument and an explanation are different because speakers present them with different intentions. If you see me close a door, you don't need an *argument* to convince you of the fact that I closed it, but you might desire an *explanation* of that fact. That is, you might want to know *why* I closed it. Arguments are intended to establish their conclusion. Explanations aren't. They are intended to provide the motivation of the actor or the cause of whatever it is that is being explained.

An argument concluding that it is raining is intended to convince you that it is raining, whereas the explanation of the fact that it is raining presumes you already agree to that fact. Instead, the explanation shows what caused this rain.

Often the only way to tell for sure whether a passage is a description, an argument, or an explanation is to look for clues in the context. When Betsy says, "I'm hungry," she could simply be describing her state of mind. However, she is also explaining her actions if she says it in response to being asked, "Why are you looking so intently at that apple pie?" She is explaining her actions by describing her state of mind. This is an example of explaining *A* by describing *B*.

Concept Check 2

Indicate whether each of the following passages is most probably an argument, an explanation, or a description.

a. The apple fell because the drying stem was no longer strong enough to resist the weight of the apple.

b. You should eat an apple a day because doing so will keep the doctor away.

Concept Check 3

What is the explanation of the price increase mentioned below?

> Need Gas? Too bad. It costs a nickel a gallon more today — and don't blame the Persian Gulf crisis. Federal taxes on gasoline increase today, from 9 cents a gallon to 14 cents.
>
> According to an AAA Michigan survey, the increase will take the price of gasoline in the Detroit area to an average $1.35 a gallon for self-serve regular unleaded, $1.50 for unleaded premium.[2]

■ .... Concept Check 4 .... ■

Characterize the following passage.

Africa: Then Came the Locusts

After being plagued by a 20-year parching drought, Africa got some temporary relief this year. But the rains that came also made conditions ripe for a return of the Senegalese grasshopper; by March its swarms were reaching plague proportions. With help from the United Nations' Food and Agricultural Organization, the grasshoppers were recently brought under control. Then came the locusts [which fly farther than grasshoppers]. For the first time in 50 years, all four of Africa's main locust pests are swarming at once, attacking crops down the entire length of the continent.[3]

a. It is an argument trying to convince the reader that after being plagued by a 20-year parching drought, Africa got some temporary relief.

b. It is an explanation of how Africa got some rain after the drought.

c. It is an argument trying to convince the reader that for the first time in 50 years all four of Africa's main locust pests are swarming at once, attacking crops down the entire length of the continent.

d. It is primarily only a description of Africa's troubles with drought and pests.

Suppose you and your friend Edward are standing in an apple orchard looking at an apple that just fell to the ground in front of you. Edward, who is a scientist, explains that the apple fell because the force of gravity pulling down on the apple caused tension in the apple stem and eventually broke it once the stem had dried out and got brittle; gravity then pulled the apple toward the center of the Earth until the resistance of the ground stopped the fall. His explanation is *not* an argument that the apple fell. It is taken for granted that the event occurred; what's in doubt is why it occurred. When Edward appeals to the existence of gravitational force and to the structural weakness of the apple's stem to explain why the apple fell, he is giving a *possible* explanation of why it happened, perhaps even the right explanation. Nevertheless, he doesn't defend his explanation. He doesn't argue that his is the right explanation. He doesn't give any reasons why the apple's falling should be explained this way instead of by saying that "It was the apple's time" or by appealing to magnetic attraction between the apple and the nickel core at the center of the earth.

However, explanations often *are* accompanied by arguments. A person creates both when he explains why event *E* occurred and then argues for why this explanation of E is better than alternative explanations. For example, articles in science journals are often devoted to arguing that one explanation of a phenomenon is better than a previously suggested explanation. Sometimes arguments are offered as to why some-one's explanation of an event is the right one, and sometimes the argument is inter-mixed with the explanation. Nevertheless, the argument and the explanation are distinct, not identical. Even if an argument does not accompany the explanation, every scientist who claims to offer *the* explanation of some event has the burden of proving this claim by providing that argument if challenged.

■ ············ Concept Check 5 ············ ■

Construct an argument, but not an explanation, for the fact that dinosaurs became extinct 65 million years ago. (Don't worry too much about the quality of the argu-ment; just make sure that it is an argument and not an explanation.)

■ ············ Concept Check 6 ············ ■

Construct an explanation, but not an argument, for the fact that dinosaurs became extinct 65 million years ago. According to the theory of evolution, this is approxi-mately the time that the Rocky Mountains and European Alps were created. And it was at about this time that the world got its first plants with flowers. (Don't worry too much about the quality of the explanation; just make sure that it is an explanation and not an argument.

Writing with Precision and to Your Audience

One suggestion for promoting effective writing is to *be precise*. But how do you follow a suggestion like that? *When* should you be precise? *Where* should you be precise? *How* precise? These are tough questions. Unfortunately, there is no recipe to follow. About all that can be said is that you should be precise "where appropriate," but you should not be pseudoprecise. Nevertheless, after seeing an example or two of how to be precise and comparing it with examples of failing to be precise, you should immediately get the point.

Here is a question that is answered precisely and then imprecisely. "How do you get to Bill's house from here?"

PRECISE ANSWER: Go six blocks up this street to the first traffic light. Turn right, and it will be the red house about in the middle of the next block on your left. Or maybe it's on your right; I can't remember.

IMPRECISE ANSWER: You can't miss it. He lives in the house next to my friend Ted. Ted lives on Braithwaite Street. Ted's is the most bodacious house on the block; Bill and Ted practice their electric guitars there in the garage every night. Keep an eye on their phone booth when you're there.

Even though it contains the imprecise terms *about* and *maybe*, the first answer is relatively more precise.

Another suggestion is to *write to your audience*. How do you do so? Well, first you have to decide who your audience is. Don't write as if you might be read by any human being either now or in the future. That's too big an audience. For example, if you are writing a description of Theodore Roosevelt and your audience is all professional historians, you wouldn't bother to mention that he was president before that other Roosevelt, Franklin D. However, if your audience is junior high school students, you would make a mistake if you failed to mention this fact. When you write a college term paper, assume that your audience is your instructor. With that in mind, you do not need to make elementary points that you might need to make if your audience were your fellow students. You can assume that the instructor is aware of the topic you are writing about but may not have had the specific new ideas you have had. Only by writing for a specific audience can you answer the question "Should I argue [explain, describe] this point, or can I presume it or leave it unsaid?" Ask yourself this: "If my audience were right here in front of me and I were talking to them, should I say this now in order to get my idea across?" There is no formula for tailoring your writing product to your audience. Good tailoring is affected by the subject matter, by the characteristics of the audience, and by the purpose of the writing. It's hard to be more precise than this.

Improving the Structure of Your Writing

Part of what makes writing precise is helpful structure. The structure provides a framework. In the example of directions to Bill's house, the structure in the precise answer is a sequence of steps the reader can follow to get there. The only helpful direction offered in the imprecise answer is to go to somewhere on Braithwaite Street.

Writing should have a specific structure, an overall plan of development, a method of organization. Although there are many acceptable structures, not everything is acceptable. Good readers can readily tell the difference between good and bad structure. They can distinguish an ice sculpture from a puddle.

One usually effective rule of thumb is to mentally *divide the piece of writing into three parts — an introduction, a middle, and an ending.* In the introduction you announce your intentions or briefly describe what you are going to say; in the middle you provide the details; and in the ending you summarize what you've said and perhaps speculate about its implications. This common structure can be thought of this way: you tell them what you're going to say, then you say it, then you tell them what you've said. This rule gets to be more important with the length of your piece.

The Introduction

The title or headline is often the first element of an introduction. It gives the audience some idea of what the writing is about and perhaps suggests the main point. The book title *The Chocolate Bible* immediately tells the reader that what is inside will probably have nothing to do with religion but a lot to do with eating or preparing chocolate. If the same book had been given an overly cute but less precise title such as *Your Face or Mine?* the reader wouldn't have gotten as much information. That information would have to come later, such as in the first sentence of the book:

> Almost all of us love chocolate, but how much do you really know about this elixir of the gods?

Such a simple introductory sentence sets the stage by outlining the rough boundaries of the discussion to follow.

Usually a title alone or a single introductory sentence is not sufficient to introduce the reader to the material that will follow. For example, if we want to make clear that *The Chocolate Bible* is a book for manufacturers and marketers of chocolate, not consumers, the following additional sentences can go a long way toward introducing the book:

> You know the subtleties of its taste, and how to manufacture and market it in your area, but what about southern Japan? Northern Japan? What manufacturing techniques and marketing strategies would you change if you wanted to reach the Egyptian market with a similar chocolate product? There is considerable room around the world to create or expand the chocolate market. Will you profit in these new markets, or will your competitor? This book will show you how to successfully produce medium-quality and high-quality cost-effective chocolate for the mass market in a variety of countries around the world.

Thanks to this introduction we readers now know this is a book about the chocolate business, with emphasis on international marketing and manufacturing. It is not a book intended for consumers.

The introduction limits the scope of the discussion to follow. That is, it provides a context for the writing. It should also give some hint of why it's worth reading. Unless the writer has a captive audience, it is his or her duty to capture the reader's interest and indicate why the writing should not be ignored. The chocolate book's introduction captures the reader's attention by suggesting that there is money to be made by reading on.

The type of introduction appropriate for one kind of writing might not be appropriate for another. If you are writing a newspaper article, you need to provide a summary of the whole article in the introduction: the who, what, where, when, and how. That way, if the ending of the piece is snipped off, the article won't be hurt substantially; it will still make sense and communicate a lot of information. This same structure is appropriate for many business reports, in which the summary of the costs and the recommendations for changes in the business are made up front for the busy manager who wants to know the bottom line first and the details later.

So, one helpful rule in writing is to *give the reader the overall picture of the article by clearly announcing your intentions*. Here is another example:

> This report will make the case that it is time to divest our interests in peripherals for large computers and concentrate on developing peripherals for desktop and laptop computers.

This sentence sets up the reader's expectations for what is to follow. When facts and figures are presented later, the reader will have a context to fit them into. Imagine yourself as the reader of a similar report with the same content but without this introduction; the facts and figures are just thrown at you without any explanation of why you should know them. Such an illogical structure would destroy the effectiveness of the report.

In scholarly writing, as opposed to, say, propagandistic writing, the introduction should also refer to what other scholars have said on the issue you are writing about. Give credit where credit is due, so that the reader can more readily evaluate how your own work fits in or how it challenges other work in the field.

The Middle

The body of the text is where you provide the details and do what you said you would be doing. If you were planning to describe, this is where you place the details of the description. If you were planning to argue, this is where you provide convincing reasons for your claim and perhaps clarify just what the claim is that you are trying to establish. However, when arguing logically, you should concentrate on what *ought* to convince, not what *will* convince. Even if you know your audience's prejudices and how to exploit them to get them to do what you want, don't follow this path if you want to be a logical reasoner rather than a propagandist or con artist.

Suppose your goal is to create an essay that argues for a conclusion. How should you structure the essay? The first thing to keep in mind is that you need a fairly clear idea of the content before you can bother with the structure. Once you have a clear idea, you must still choose from a number of effective ways to structure the essay. However, one helpful rule of thumb is that *the middle can be structured so the reader is moved by understandable steps from the more obvious to the less obvious*. You can establish your essay's important reasons by carefully taking the reader from points of ready agreement to your more controversial points. At the same time, *the flow of argument should usually be from the simple points to the complex points*. Without this structure, many of your readers will fall by the side of your road. Your structure is your road, and if readers cannot see where they are going, they will become confused and lose interest in what you have to say. In long pieces or writing that can be complicated to follow, it doesn't hurt to occasionally remind readers of what the road is, how far you've gone, and what lies ahead.

Although it is important for your writing to have a clear structure, remember to do first things first: *Write first, organize later*. Brainstorm first; get your ideas onto paper. Later you can go back and tie them together effectively by adding the proper organization.

The Ending

Although it is almost always helpful for *you* to divide your writing into an introduction, a middle, and an ending, you don't need to tell the reader, "The introduction is over; here comes the middle." Doing so would look awkward. However, it is best to be clear when you are done with the middle, especially if you are creating an argumentative essay. By beginning a paragraph with a phrase such as "To summarize, . . ." you signal that all the main points you intended to make have now been made. At this point you should review those main ideas, especially if the piece is longer than two pages, so that the reader can stop looking at the trees and refocus on the forest — that is, on whether you've succeeded with the grand program you promised in your introduction. But to repeat a point, there is no formula for good writing. An argumentative essay isn't necessarily imperfect if it lacks a summary.

Digressions

To make a final point about the structure of a piece of writing, consider what a digression does. If you are writing a business letter to a supplier explaining how the five generators the company sent were not the quality that you had agreed to purchase, you shouldn't take a weird turn in the middle of the letter to tell a story about how you were fascinated with generators when you were fourteen years old and how you took one apart and got your first electrical shock. That would be an unreasonable digression because it would be irrelevant. It doesn't speak to the issue.

Digressions take you down some side road and away from the main road. *Normally, a digression is a fault in any writing*. The reader's mental response to a digression that doesn't give strong hints of its relevance is usually something like "Enough already; now let's get back on track and make some progress."

■ ⋯⋯⋯⋯ Concept Check 7 ⋯⋯⋯⋯ ■

If you were going to remove the digression in the following business letter, what would you take out?

Dear Mr. Harris,

You recently wrote our company regarding a problem with the transistors we supplied to you for your FC-70 circuit boards. I am sure we can solve your problem.

Referring to your purchase order #334-88-09, dated October 12, you requested 77,000 transistors meeting the specifications in your bid #33-92, dated July 7 of this year. Our quality control engineer certified that your order met those specifications, and the first half of your order was shipped to you on November 1. The second half was shipped on November 27. According to the records you supplied to us, the first shipment arrived on November 7, and the second on December 3. Your purchasing department indicates that all the 77,000 transistors did arrive safely. Initial checks by you, according to the documents you sent us on December 20, indicate that there was some trouble with the transistors, although you do not know whether the problems were with the transistors in the first shipment or the transistors in the second shipment.

Our quality control engineers do try to fill orders correctly. Not only do we use the familiar testing via the Z-bar procedure, but we also have added the Z-bar supplement procedure which is recommendation by the American Association of Quality Control Engineers. Our quality control engineers are not new employees, and they have a great deal of experience in filling orders such as yours.

We were quite surprised to learn that your own checking of our transistors indicates there is a 10 percent failure rate in our transistors. We will be happy to refill your order at no expense to you. Today we have begun the procedure of sending you another 77,000 transistors meeting the specifications as indicated in your purchase order #334-88-09. Meanwhile, it would be helpful for us if you would return the remaining transistors that we sent to you. Please feel free to call me at (916) 443-0455 or fax me at (916) 443-0492 if you have any further questions.

Very truly yours,

Dwayne W. Edwards
Assistant Manager

Occasionally, though, a digression can enrich a piece of writing. The key is to set up the reader so that he or she expects to profit from taking the side trip. Here is a successful example from John Steinbeck's *The Grapes of Wrath*. The novel is about poor white farmers from Oklahoma, Texas, and Arkansas who migrated to California in the 1930s during the Depression. The story begins by following the travels of an Oklahoma City trucker and a hitchhiker, Tom Joad, the lead character. Here is how

Steinbeck spins his tale in Chapter 2, before the digression begins. Notice how well Steinbeck describes the situation.

> The hitchhiker stood up and looked across through the windows. "Could ya give me a lift, mister?"
>
> The driver looked quickly back at the restaurant for a second. "Didn't you see the *No Riders* sticker on the win'shield?"
>
> "Sure — I seen it. But sometimes a guy'll be a good guy even if some rich bastard makes him carry a sticker."
>
> The driver, getting slowly into the truck, considered the parts of this answer. If he refused now, not only was he not a good guy, but he was forced to carry a sticker, was not allowed to have company. If he took in the hitchhiker he was automatically a good guy and also he was not one whom any rich bastard could kick around. He knew he was being trapped, but he couldn't see a way out. And he wanted to be a good guy. He glanced again at the restaurant. "Scrunch down on the running board till we get around the bend," he said.[4]

Steinbeck's narrative contains an example of successful description. Didn't these paragraphs help you create a vivid image of the situation? The story continues. The hitchhiker is mad at the driver for being so curious:

> "The hell you ain't," said Joad. "That big old nose of yours been stickin' out eight miles ahead of your face. You had that big nose goin' over me like a sheep in a vegetable patch."
>
> The driver's face tightened. "You got me all wrong — " he began weakly.
>
> . . ."Well, hell! I done time. So what! You want to know what I done time for, don't you?"
>
> "That ain't none of my affair."
>
> "Nothin' ain't none of your affair except skinnin' this here bull-bitch [truck] along, an' that's the least thing you work at. Now look. See that road up ahead?"
>
> "Yeah."
>
> "Well, I get off there. Sure, I know you're wettin' your pants to know what I done. I ain't a guy to let you down." The high hum of the motor dulled and the song of the tires dropped in pitch. Joad got out his pint and took another short drink. The truck drifted to a stop where a dirt road opened at right angles to the highway. Joad got out and stood beside the cab window. The vertical exhaust pipe puttered up its barely visible blue smoke. Joad leaned toward the driver. "Homicide," he said quickly.[5]

Steinbeck's strategy is to follow the Joad character in the book. The reader senses this, and the reader's interest is piqued, yet the whole next chapter describes a turtle beside the road. That's the digression. Afterward, the story continues, describing Joad and his family's struggle to make a living by going west to California. Why do you suppose the digression was not cut? What's the payoff for the reader's bothering with a turtle?

An exercise at the end of the chapter reasks this question. The point, of course, is that this digression effectively develops the story. Here is all of Chapter 3 of *The Grapes of Wrath,* devoted to describing a few moments in a turtle's life:

> The concrete highway was edged with a mat of tangled, broken, dry grass, and the grass heads were heavy with oat beards to catch on a dog's coat, and foxtails to tangle in a horse's fetlocks, and clover burrs to fasten in sheep's wool; sleeping life waiting to be spread and dispersed, every seed armed with an appliance of dispersal, twisting darts and parachutes for the wind, little spears and balls of tiny thorns, and all waiting for animals and for the wind, for a man's trouser cuff or the hem of a woman's skirt, all passive but armed with appliances of activity, still, but each possessed of an anlage* of movement.
>
> The sun lay on the grass and warmed it, and in the shade under the grass the insects moved, ants and ant lions to set traps for them, grasshoppers to jump into the air and flick their yellow wings for a second, sow bugs like little armadillos, plodding restlessly on many tender feet. And over the grass at the roadside a land turtle crawled, turning aside for nothing, dragging his high-domed shell over the grass: His hard legs and yellow-nailed feet threshed slowly through the grass, not really walking, but boosting and dragging his shell along. The barley beards slid off his shell, and the clover burrs fell on him and rolled to the ground. His horny beak was partly open, and his fierce, humorous eyes, under brows like fingernails, stared straight ahead. He came over the grass leaving a beaten trail behind him, and the hill, which was the highway embankment, reared up ahead of him. For a moment he stopped, his head held high. He blinked and looked up and down. At last he started to climb the embankment. Front clawed feet reached forward but did not touch. The hind feet kicked his shell along, and it scraped on the grass, and on the gravel. As the embankment grew steeper and steeper, the more frantic were the efforts of the land turtle. Pushing hind legs strained and slipped, boosting the shell along, and the horny head protruded as far as the neck could stretch. Little by little the shell slid up the embankment until at last a parapet cut straight across its line of march, the shoulder of the road, a concrete wall four inches high. As though they worked independently, the hind legs pushed the shell against the wall. The head upraised and peered over the wall to the broad smooth plain of cement. Now the hands, braced on top of the wall, strained and lifted, and the shell came slowly up and rested its front end on the wall. For a moment the turtle rested. A red ant ran into the shell, into the soft skin inside the shell, and suddenly head and legs snapped in, and the armored tail clamped in sideways. The red ant was crushed between body and legs. And one head of wild oats was clamped into the shell by a front leg. For a long moment the turtle

*A start of growth of some part of an embryo.

lay still, and then the neck crept out and the old humorous frowning eyes looked about and the legs and tail came out. The back legs went to work, straining like elephant legs, and the shell tipped to an angle so that the front legs could not reach the level cement plain. But higher and higher the hind legs boosted it, until at last the center of balance was reached, the front tipped down, the front legs scratched at the pavement, and it was up. But the head of wild oats was held by its stem around the front legs.

Now the going was easy, and all the legs worked, and the shell boosted along, waggling from side to side. A sedan driven by a forty-year-old woman approached. She saw the turtle and swung to the right, off the highway, the wheels screamed and a cloud of dust boiled up. Two wheels lifted for a moment and then settled. The car skidded back onto the road, and went on, but more slowly. The turtle had jerked into its shell, but now it hurried on, for the highway was burning hot.

And now a light truck approached, and as it came near, the driver saw the turtle and swerved to hit it. His front wheel struck the edge of the shell, flipped the turtle like a tiddly-wink, spun it like a coin, and rolled it off the highway. The truck went back to its course along the right side. Lying on its back, the turtle was tight in its shell for a long time. But at last its legs waved in the air, reaching for something to pull it over. Its front foot caught a piece of quartz and little by little the shell pulled over and flopped upright. The wild oat head fell out and three of the spearhead seeds stuck in the ground. And as the turtle crawled on down the embankment, its shell dragged dirt over the seeds. The turtle entered a dust road and jerked itself along, drawing a wavy shallow trench in the dust with its shell. The old humorous eyes looked ahead, and the horny beak opened a little. His yellow toe nails slipped a fraction in the dust.[6]

You can see why this sort of digression enriches the story, whereas the same digression within a letter from a pet store owner to a pet wholesaler placing an order for 50 turtles would be ridiculous. It would upset the logical structure of the letter. The moral for your own writing is either to not digress or else to take special care to do it well, because normally a digression is a fault.

Concept Check 8

Assuming the turtle in Chapter 3 of *The Grapes of Wrath* is supposed to represent a human being instead of a turtle, give a short description of that person's life experiences.

Let's summarize this section's points about structure. A piece of writing without structure is chaotic. Every piece of writing needs some sort of method of organization, even though different kinds of writing can use different methods. Write the piece first — get your meaning out onto the paper. Then go back and organize. When doing so, mentally consider how you are going to introduce the topic. What way will you organize the main body? How do you intend to end your piece? Can the reader always see the road you are on? Will making a particular point just cause a detour from the main road?

Improving the Style of Your Writing

The manner of presentation of a piece of writing is its style. However, the phrase "writing with style" doesn't mean writing with just any style. It means writing with an effective style. How do you write with style? Here are some suggestions.

Be brief. One mark of good writing style is brevity. There are exceptions, however. Brevity is not a virtue when writing letters appealing for contributions to your organization. Fund raisers have learned that a simple, clear, and concise request doesn't bring in the money. What works is a long letter that provides more information about the organization and that goes into great detail about how the money will be spent. The letter makes the recipient feel like he or she is part of the inner workings of the organization. Another exception to the rule of brevity is that a complicated point sometimes requires repeating. Just don't repeat it with the same words, and don't do it more than once.

Be straightforward. Another mark of good style is "saying it straight," as Emily Dickinson would say. You should say that Mary had a little lamb whose fleece was white as snow. Only a lawyer could get away with "Mary was the legal owner of a diminutive, potential sheep, whose fleece was as innocent of coloring as congealed atmospheric vapor." Avoid jargon. Also, remember that it is easier to follow a group of sentences, each expressing one idea, than a single sentence that strings several ideas together. Break up those long, rambling strings. And don't use elevated language that you aren't familiar with. Sounding like a politician or a bureaucrat isn't a sign of intelligence. The computer may be the world's most complicated machine, but writing about computers need not be the world's most complicated writing.

When you are writing to argue a point or to convey information, you should be as brief and as straightforward as possible, given the level of sophistication expected by the intended audience. However, it can be a mistake to be too brief and straightforward when your audience is reading for entertainment. The following passage from a short story by William Faulkner illustrates this point:

> Five miles farther down the river from Major de Spain's camp, and in an
> even wilder part of the river's jungle of cane and gum and pin oak, there
> is an Indian mound. Aboriginal, it rises profoundly and darkly enigmatic,
> the only elevation of any kind in the wild, flat jungle of river bottom.
> Even to some of us — children though we were, yet we were descended of

literate, town-bred people — it possessed inferences of secret and violent blood, of savage and sudden destruction, as though the yells and hatchets which we associated with Indians through the hidden and secret dime novels which we passed among ourselves were but trivial and momentary manifestations of what dark power still dwelled or lurked there, sinister, a little sardonic, like a dark and nameless beast lightly and lazily slumbering with bloody jaws — this, perhaps, due to the fact that a remnant of a once powerful clan of the Chickasaw tribe still lived beside it under Government protection.[7]

Faulkner could have made his point briefly and simply by saying

Five miles farther down the river from Major de Spain's camp there is an Indian mound, which we children fear. A small Chickasaw Indian reservation is nearby.

But saying it that way is obviously less interesting and less memorable than the way Faulkner wrote it.

Yes, you usually want to rid your writing of excess vegetation, but a tree can be pruned so much that it dies. There are five-page plot summaries of Faulkner novels, but the only people who buy them are students in English courses. The people who read for their own pleasure and interest prefer less brevity and more complexity.

Avoid being general and abstract when you can just as well be specific and concrete. It takes more intellectual energy to think abstractly than concretely, so try to make word choices that shy away from the abstract. For example, the general phrase *news media* has its uses, but if you can talk specifically about TV and newspapers instead, do so. A student who misunderstands Heidegger may say too abstractly, "IBM faces Microsoft, not with the nothingness of Being, but with the nothingness of dread." You should say, more concretely, "IBM executives fear their stock will be less valuable if they merge with the Microsoft Corporation."

Give examples; get to the point. This advice is good, but it is a little superficial. By giving examples, you may be deviating from your main goal, such as to state a general claim. So the suggestion should be modified to state: Give examples when doing so is appropriate for the audience. If the audience will immediately catch on to your general claim, skip the examples; but if they need the examples to appreciate the general claim, don't skip them. Some of your textbooks have no doubt moved too quickly through the subject matter and have not given enough examples, while other textbooks have plodded along wasting your time by giving example after example of a simple idea that you caught on to right away.

■ ············ Concept Check 9 ············ ■

Which response below is the best answer to the request "Give a specific description of the Indian mound in Faulkner's short story"?

a. The mound rises significantly above the plain of the surrounding river bottom.

b. Even to some of us — children though we were, yet we were descended of literate, town-bred people — the mound possessed inferences of secret and violent blood, of savage and sudden destruction, as though the yells and hatchets which we associated with Indians through the hidden and secret dime novels which we passed among ourselves were but trivial and momentary manifestations of what dark power still dwelled or lurked there, sinister, a little sardonic, like a dark and nameless beast lightly and lazily slumbering with bloody jaws — this, perhaps, due to the fact that a remnant of a once powerful clan of the Chickasaw tribe still lived beside it under Government protection.

c. The mound is an earthen cone with a base of about 100 feet and an altitude of 30 feet. The mound sits on a plain that contains a river bottom.

Here is a final suggestion that is perhaps the most important of all in producing logical writing: *Reread what you've written.* After you've written what you set out to write, let it cool. Forget about it for a while; the longer the better. Then go back and reread it with an open mind, as if you were a member of your intended audience seeing it for the first time. Ask a helpful friend to read it and give you a reaction. You are likely to gain valuable information about what you may need to clarify.

Chapter 8 will focus on writing intended to explain some fact or event. The rest of this chapter explores the process of creating arguments.

Creating an Argument to Prove Your Conclusion

I've already said a great deal in this book about what counts as giving good reasons for believing something. A package of reasons plus the conclusion constitute the "argument" for that conclusion. When the reasons do establish the conclusion, the argument is called a **proof**. We also say we have a proof if we simply *believe* that our reasons do establish the conclusion; whether they actually do or not is another question. So, the word *proof* can be ambiguous, and some proposed proofs may not really be successful proofs; that is, some proofs are not really proofs.

Even for the successful proofs, some are more successful than others, because proof is a matter of degree. That is, even though two proofs imply their conclusions, one might establish its conclusion more firmly. Because the line between when a conclusion gets established and when it doesn't is a fuzzy one, the term *proof* is vague, in addition to being potentially ambiguous. Mathematical proofs are not a matter of degree; they are either correct or incorrect. But the kind of proofs we have in ordinary life and in science are a matter of degree; they make their case more or less strongly.

Some things are harder to prove than others, as we all know. You may have heard someone say, "It's impossible to prove a negative." This statement is an exaggeration, but it contains a valuable kernel of truth. It is an exaggeration, because it is easy to prove the following negative statement:

(1) My car keys are not in the desk drawer.

This statement is easily proved because the place to be searched is well defined and accessible. Here is a successful argument that, if the reasons given are true, would prove this fact to yourself or to anyone else:

If my car keys were in the desk drawer, then I would find them if I searched carefully in all parts of the drawer under normal lighting conditions (including my not being blindfolded, and so forth).

I did search carefully in all parts of the drawer under normal lighting conditions, but I did not find the car keys.

So, my car keys are not in the desk drawer.

But some negative statements are indeed much harder to prove. It is very difficult to prove the following negative statement:

(2) There is no telepathy.

In this case the place to be searched is not well defined and there is uncertainty about what counts as being an actual case of telepathy; for example, a psychic says that some event is a sign of telepathy, but a skeptic says the psychic is jumping to conclusions. Even though statement 2 cannot be directly proved, there are still good reasons to believe it. The reasons in favor of this statement are the following:

Given what else we know about nature, especially what else we know about brain physiology, telepathy is highly improbable, so not only is the burden of proof on anyone who says telepathy *does* exist, but the burden is a heavy one in the sense that it will have to be an extraordinarily good proof.

Systematic searches for telepathy by qualified scientists have turned up no solid evidence.

These two reasons prove there is no telepathy. But notice that saying (2) isn't the same as saying

(2′) There can't be telepathy.

The reasons don't prove (2′) as well as they prove (2). The case for (2′) is much more difficult to make. However, even if there were no proof of (2′), the difference between (2) and (2′) shouldn't serve as a foot in the door for someone to say, "I believe in telepathy because no one has proved there can't be telepathy." Our knowledge of science implies, instead, holding off believing that something exists until you get the evidence in favor of it. Science is both a body of knowledge and a way of getting knowledge. In the latter sense, which is the sense we will be concerned with, science is just an extension of common sense. It is not something radically different from what we do every day. Science involves a skeptical attitude that says, "I won't believe you until you show me the solid evidence."

When is evidence solid evidence? For most of us, the most solid form of evidence we have are the reports of experts we trust plus the knowledge that the experts agree. But among the experts themselves, it often does take an expert to decide what counts as solid evidence. Usually, though, solid evidence must be reproducible. For example, if one researcher says, "I tested the subject and found her to be a psychic," other researchers will need to be satisfied that she can actually perform as well when the testing is repeated by themselves or by some other researcher they trust. The truth will be able to stand up to repeated tests, but falsehood will eventually be exposed.

People sometimes ask, "Why can't scientists give poorly supported suggestions the benefit of the doubt and simply accept them? Why the obsessional preoccupation with matters of validation?" The answer is that this liberal attitude leads to a contradiction. Suppose you have poor support for some suggestion *S,* and you also have poor support for its negation, Not-*S.* For example, let *S* = "The number of inches between the end of your nose and the center of the sun is an even number." The liberal attitude above would have us accept both *S* and Not-*S,* which is absurd. Besides, the track record of accepting unsupported hypotheses is quite poor; they turn out to be unhelpful for creating good explanations and making accurate predictions, which are the two main goals of science.

When you argue that some conclusion should be drawn from the evidence you present, be careful not to defend a stronger conclusion than what the evidence justifies. Here is an example that illustrates the point. Two Italian-speaking men suffered strokes that damaged their brains, but not in the usual ways. According to a report in the British science journal *Nature,* examination of the first man two weeks after his stroke revealed that he omitted all vowels when writing about himself, his town, or common objects. He would leave blank spaces for the vowels. For example, he spelled the name of his town, Bologna, as "B l gn ." He was aware of the fact that he had misspelled the words, but he could not correct his errors. The second man also had a vowel-specific disturbance. He could write vowels, but he misspelled many words, and most of the misspellings involved errors with vowels rather than with consonants. Both men had no such difficulties before their strokes. The experimental psychologist who reported these two astonishing cases said that they may indicate the brain contains two different mechanisms, one for identifying and generating vowels and one for identifying and generating consonants. The evidence of these two cases does no more than "indicate" this, as the researcher was careful to note. If, instead, the researcher had said that the evidence of these two cases "proves" there is a cerebral vowel organizer, he would have drawn too strong a conclusion and likely would have been told by the journal editor to tone down or hedge his conclusion before the article would be printed.

Further research may someday more strongly support the claim that there is a cerebral vowel organizer separate from the cerebral consonant organizer. If so, then at that time it would be proper to say that the claim has been "proved."

Concept Check 10

"In good scientific reasoning, the scientific reasoner should be cautious and never claim that something is known or proved unless it can be shown that from the evidence acquired that it would be absolutely impossible for the claim to be false." What is the error in this sentence?

Creating Counterarguments

When we argue, we must be alert to our own errors. We need to become competent critics-in-advance of our own argument, spot any errors, and patch up the argument before asserting it. In creating our own argument we need to make sure that it can stand on its own two feet.

Sometimes we argue to make a simple point. At other times we argue for the purpose of finding fault in another person's argument. At still other times, we argue for the opposite point that someone else has argued for. In this latter case we are involved in **counterargument**. All those things happen in this dialogue about what caused armored knights to disappear from the scene of battle:

Diana: You know that in Medieval Europe the knights wore armor all over their body, but do you know why European armies stopped using these armored knights? It was because of the Battle of Agincourt in France.

Antonio: How do you know?

Diana: Well, the battle was in 1415 during the Hundred Years War. It was a really big battle between the French and English. The French were defeated by the English, who were led by King Henry V. Both sides' knights wore thick metal all over their bodies; they even put it on their horses. The horses had to be powerful enough to hold up the heavy knights. The French lost about 7,000 soldiers, but the English lost only a few hundred. The English used their new weapons, the big, powerful Welsh longbows; the French knights were slaughtered. After that the European armies began phasing out armored knights.

Antonio: That is very interesting. I suppose you are probably right about what caused armored knights to go out of fashion in warfare, but when I asked you for an argument, I thought you were going to convince me that this battle caused armies to stop using armored knights. You've said nothing to convince me if I weren't already convinced. That is, you've presented a possible, even plausible explanation, but you have not argued for why your explanation is the correct one. Where is the historical evidence that the battle caused a change? You've mostly just described the battle and explained what happened rather than argued that the battle was decisive. Your argument is a non sequitur.

Diana: Oh, I see what you mean. OK. Well, the evidence is here in my world history book. It says right here on this page that the English army's use of the Welsh longbow was what really defeated the armored French knights, and after other armies learned what happened, they stopped using the armored knights in battles.

Antonio: Okay, I'm convinced.

Ed: Hey, I'm not. I read a book about warfare. They had knights in Spain at the time of Christopher Columbus. I remember the book saying that armies stopped using armored knights in 1600 when some Italian general — I think it was Galileo — convinced everyone that guns could penetrate the knights' armor. That made the heavy armor a disadvantage, not an advantage. Armored knights went out when guns replaced bows and arrows. Tougher armor could stop bullets, but the knights weren't strong enough to carry that kind of armor. So, bullets stopped the armored knights; the Battle of Agincourt didn't.

Laura: No, I disagree with all three of you. What caused the European armies to stop using armor was the fact that all the iron ore mines were in the Near East and were seized by the Muslims. They refused to sell the iron to the Christians, and without the iron, the knights couldn't have armor.

Let's analyze this dialogue. These three people are arguing about the correct explanation of the disappearance of armored knights. Diana starts off by claiming, and then weakly arguing, that the Battle of Agincourt caused their disappearance. Antonio attacks her argument, saying that it didn't make the case. Notice that Antonio does *not* offer a counterargument. In fact, he does not disagree with Diana about her conclusion; he merely doesn't like how she tried to prove it. Then Diana revises her argument to make her case to Antonio's satisfaction. Ed, on the other hand, does create a counterargument. He attempts to prove that the Battle of Agincourt did not cause the cessation of armored knights. He offers an elaborate explanation, but the argument part is simply his appeal to "a book about warfare." He gives a long explanation, but a short argument. Laura, on the other hand, gives an explanation, but no argument in defense of her explanation.

■ .... Concept Check 11 .... ■

A counterargument to argument *S* is always an argument for why the conclusion of *S* is not true.

a. true   b. false

■ .... ■

When it comes to issues that cannot be settled by scientific investigation, the proofs or arguments take on a different character from the sort we've been examining. The reasons for you to favor a social policy, for example, will more often appeal to the values you hold than to the facts about the world. Values cannot be detected with voltmeters, nor measured with meter sticks. The rest of this chapter will consider arguments that appeal to the values held by the participants in the argument.

Criticism, Counterargument, and Revision

Sometimes when we respond to an argument that attacks our own position we try to expose weaknesses; for example, we might point out that the reasons given are not true, or that the reasons don't make the case even if they are true, and so forth. At other times we don't directly attack the argument but rather create a new argument for the opposite conclusion. This indirect response is called "creating a counterargument." Successfully using the techniques of argument criticism or of creating a counterargument, our position lives on to bury its undertaker. In courts of law, these techniques are called *rebuttal*. The point of rebuttal is to turn our vaguely felt objections into convincing arguments.

What follows in the next few pages is an example of the give-and-take in argumentation. The exchange contains arguments, counterarguments, criticisms of arguments, criticisms of criticisms, and revisions of criticisms. The issue is whether utilitarianism is the proper way to decide right from wrong. Utilitarianism is the ethical viewpoint based on the following claim:

> UTILITARIAN CLAIM: Among the possible actions a person can take in a situation, the right action is that which produces the most overall happiness for everyone affected by the action.

John Stuart Mill, a nineteenth-century English philosopher, argued for utilitarianism. He wanted an antidote to the practice of English judges and legislators making social and ethical decisions on the basis of how the decision "felt" to them. Mill wanted the decision method to be more scientific. He hoped that in principle the decision could be the result of a process of calculation of the positive and negative consequences for each possible choice. The alternative that produced the maximum number would be the one to choose. His utilitarianism is a kind of cost-benefit analysis that focuses not on the benefits to a company or special group but to society as a whole, to all people.

> ARGUMENT FOR UTILITARIANISM: We all have or should have feelings of generalized benevolence, of caring in general for our fellow human beings. Utilitarianism expresses these feelings. In addition, most all of the actions that utilitarianism says are immoral are in fact believed to be immoral by most people; and most of the actions that utilitarianism says are moral are generally believed to be moral, so utilitarianism coincides with most of what we already believe. In fact, utilitarianism agrees

so well that it provides the most coherence to our chaotic ethical beliefs. Because we want this coherence, we should adopt utilitarianism and accept the consequences of adopting it — namely, that if utilitarian reasoning declares some action to be immoral, then even though we intuitively believe the action to be moral, we must revise our intuitions to be in agreement with what utilitarianism says.

The American philosopher William James did not accept this line of reasoning. He argued against utilitarianism. James's objection arose from his belief that it would be immoral to demand that a single individual suffer even if that suffering were to promote the overall happiness of everyone else. He based his reason on the immediate moral feeling of revulsion we'd have if we thought about the special situation he had in mind. He said:

> COUNTERARGUMENT: If the hypothesis were offered us of . . . millions kept permanently happy on the one simple condition that a certain lost soul on the far-off edge of things should lead a life of lonely torture, . . . [would we not] immediately feel, even though an impulse arose within us to clutch at the happiness so offered, how hideous a thing would be its enjoyment when deliberately accepted as the fruit of such a bargain?

The operative word is *feel*. According to James, utilitarianism implies that trading off someone's pain to achieve the greater good of everyone else is acceptable. Yet it is really unacceptable, he says, because of our moral feelings of revulsion at running roughshod over the dignity of that one individual.

Here is a simpler version of James's counterargument. Imagine yourself on a wagon train of settlers moving westward in 1850. You are attacked by a gang of outlaws. Circling your wagons, you prepare to defend yourself against an overwhelming force. You count your few guns and bullets and realize you are in a desperate situation. Just then the outlaw leader makes an offer. He promises to let the wagon train pass through to Oregon provided you will hand over the daughter of your wagon master. Otherwise, he says, his gang will attack and kill you all. You happen to know that this gang of outlaws has a tradition of keeping its promises. So if they get the daughter, the rest of you will likely make it through unharmed. You also know that the daughter will likely face unspeakable horrors. What do you do? The utilitarian will say to give her up. She has just one life, but the rest of the wagon train has many more lives to be saved; it's a matter of cost-benefit analysis. Surely in this imaginary scenario, William James would say that trading the girl for the greater good of the wagon train would be morally abhorrent. It wouldn't be right to do this to her, regardless of the consequences to the wagon train. Therefore, utilitarianism leads to immorality, and it cannot be the proper basis of moral reasoning. End of counterargument.

When faced with an argument against one's own position, a person often strikes back, getting defensive. Thus, John Stuart Mill might have responded with, "Well, it's easy for *you* to criticize; you don't have to face the consequences of these important decisions on a day-to-day basis." This remark is the kind of thing we say when we want to discount the force of someone else's argument. Empress Catherine the Great used the same tactic against eighteenth-century Enlightenment philosophers who were criticizing her social policies toward the Russian peasants; she said, "It's easy for you to talk. You write on paper, but I write on human flesh." In the following passage, the defender doesn't get defensive; instead the utilitarian offers a more substantial criticism that tries to undermine the main points made in James's counterargument. This new argument is based on two reasons: (1) there is no need for us to pay much attention to James's feelings of revulsion, and (2) we do make trade-offs of people's lives all the time without calling it immoral.

> CRITICISM OF THE COUNTERARGUMENT: Moral feelings are very strong, but this does not prevent them from appearing as irrational taboos to those who do not share our conventions. This should warn us against the tendency to make ethical philosophy an apology or justification of the conventional customs that happen to be established. Suppose that someone were to offer our country a wonderfully convenient mechanism, but demand in return the privilege of killing thousands of our people every year. How many of those who would indignantly refuse such a request will condemn the use of the automobile now that it is already with us?[8]

The point of the criticism is to say that if you accept the trade-off for the automobile, then you should accept the trade-off of a lonely soul's pain for the greater good of everyone else. Thus, utilitarianism has not been shown to lead to absurdity, as James mistakenly supposed. So the counterargument fails, and the argument for utilitarianism stands.

Let's review the flow of the discussion so far. The issue is the truth or falsity of utilitarianism. James's position is that utilitarianism is incorrect. His counterargument depends on his evaluation of the example of the lost soul on the far-off edge of things. The criticism of James's counterargument goes like this. James's situation with the lost soul is analogous to the situation of people being killed by the automobile, and just as it would have been OK to proceed with automobile construction, so it would be okay to send that lost soul to the far-off edge of things. James is being unrealistic. We often consider it moral to trade off some people's pain against the greater good of the rest of us. So, utilitarianism is correct.

At this point, James could counterattack by criticizing the analogy between torturing individuals and killing them in car accidents.

> CRITICISM OF THE CRITICISM OF THE COUNTERARGU-MENT: The analogy between the torture and the automobile situation isn't any good. The two situations differ in a crucial respect. My situation with the far-off lost soul requires *intentional* harm. The lost soul did not voluntarily give up his right not to be tortured; if he did, that would have been praiseworthy on his part, but he didn't. Instead he was seized against

his will. But automobiles were introduced into our society voluntarily with *no intention to harm* anybody. The car manufacturers didn't build cars with the goal of "killing thousands of our people every year." They set out to make money and provide society with efficient transportation. In my situation one person is singled out for harm. In the automobile situation each person runs an approximately equal risk of accidental harm. The lost soul is not free to refuse, and his pain is foreseen. Any particular driver is free not to drive, and his pain is unpredictable. But if we could predict that you would die in an auto accident this week if you took a certain route, and if you were still forced to drive this route this week as part of the auto manufacturers' deal with society, then wouldn't we feel revulsion about just such a deal? So the analogy breaks down. My point stands.

The person who originally criticized the counterargument now makes a change in light of the criticism of his criticism.

REVISION OF THE CRITICISM OF THE COUNTERARGUMENT: Maybe the analogy with automobiles does break down, but the motivation behind it is still correct and can show what is wrong with James's counterargument against utilitarianism. We often consider it moral to trade off some people's pain against the greater good of everyone else even when the pain is intentionally inflicted and even when those who receive it are not free to refuse it. U.S. Immigration and Naturalization requires people coming into this country to suffer the pain of certain vaccinations for the good of the rest of us who don't want to catch foreign diseases. There is no universal sense of revulsion about such situations. Most people think it is the right thing to do, being the lesser of two evils. It is understandable why individuals look out for themselves and don't choose to do what is in the interest of all society, but that doesn't make what they do morally right, does it? So, utilitarianism is the proper viewpoint on ethics after all.

Well, we won't decide here who has won in this dispute about utilitarianism. There are many more moves and countermoves that might occur before the issue is settled. However, the discussion does demonstrate the give-and-take that occurs in a serious dispute.

■ ·········· Concept Check 12 ·········· ■

Briefly state a counterargument to the following argument:

Communism is better than capitalism because communism is designed to promote cooperation among equals whereas capitalism is designed to promote competition, greed, and the domination of one person by another.

■ ············ **Concept Check 13** ············ ■

Consider the following debate, which contains a series of arguments, criticisms of arguments, counterarguments, revisions, clarifications, arguments in defense of previous assumptions, and so forth. The main issue is whether robots could someday think. (a) Where does the first clarification occur? (b) Where does the first criticism occur? (c) Where is the first counterargument? (d) Which side should win this debate? (e) What is the most convincing point made for the winning side?

A. First Person: A robot could never think. You can tell that right away, just by thinking about what the terms mean.

Second Person: Are you suggesting that a robot cannot think because *thinking* and *robot* are conflicting terms the way *round* and *triangular* are?

B. First Person: No, I mean even if some future robot appeared to think, the real thinking would belong to its programmer. A robot couldn't think on its own.

Second Person: When the robot walks, you don't say it's really the programmer who is doing the walking, do you?

C. First Person: No, of course not.

Second Person: Robots can think because they do all sorts of things that we used to say required thinking. They play chess, for example, though not the way we do.

D. First Person: They play chess, but they don't think when they play it. Robots cannot think on their own because robots can only do what they are programmed to do.

Second Person: OK, program it to think.

E. First Person: But you can't do that.

Second Person: Why not? I hope you don't answer by saying, "because robots can only do what they are programmed to do." That would be circular reasoning.

F. First Person: Thinking requires flexibility in the sense that one can change one's thoughts. But since robots can't change the thoughts that are programmed into them, they cannot really think either.

Second Person: A robot could change its thought without changing its programming, just as a chess-playing computer changes its moves without changing its programming.

G. First Person: My point about change is that a thinking being must be capable of original thought, but a robot can do only what it is programmed to do.

Second Person: Couldn't a chess-playing computer come up with a chess move that had never been played before and that would surprise even its programmer? That move would be as original for it as our thoughts are for us. Besides, isn't an original human thought just a surprising thought that is actually only the product of the person's genetic code plus his or her life's conditioning?

H. First Person: No, an original thought is uncaused.

Second Person: If it's uncaused, then it is just random. Surely, good thinking isn't just random mumbling, is it? If you tell me it is uncaused physically but instead caused by our intent, I don't understand that.

I. First Person: I wouldn't be so quick to write off intentions, but look, a thinking being must be able to handle itself in new situations. There are too many new situations for them to be explicitly handled in advance by the programmer; the task is just too large. So a robot couldn't ever really think.

Second Person: There are an endless number of new addition and multiplication problems, yet a small machine can handle them, can't it?

J. First Person: Because of individual growth as well as the growth of our species itself, we're all the end products of our entire history, but human history cannot be written down and programmed into a computer. We all know a lot that we can't say, or can't write down in notation. We know it implicitly in our flesh and blood, so to speak. A computer knows only what can be written down.

Second Person: I disagree. Ok, so you know something you can't write down. You know how to ride a bicycle but can't write down the details. It doesn't follow that the details can't be written down just because you can't write them down. Someone else can write them down and use them to permit a robot to ride a bicycle, too. Besides, why are you making such a big point about being made of flesh and blood? You can add, and you are made of hydrocarbon; a calculator can add, and it's made of copper and silicon. The stuff can't be that important.[9]

K. First Person: We carbon-based beings really know what we are doing when we add; the calculator doesn't.

Second Person: I agree, but you're overestimating "stuff." If living organisms are composed of molecules that are intrinsically inanimate and unintelligent, why is it that living, conscious matter differs so radically from unconscious nonliving matter? They both are made of molecules. The answer must be the ways those molecules are put together, because the essence of life and thinking is not substance but instead complex patterns of information. Life and thinking are properties of the way stuff is organized. If you organized the stuff correctly, then life and thought might exist in most any substance, whether it be flesh or silicon chips.

L. First Person: It isn't really a question of "stuff" nor of programming. It is more a question of essence. We are essentially of a different nature. Thinking beings have souls, but robot computers do not.

Second Person: If a machine were built with sufficient ingenuity, couldn't God give it a soul?

M. First Person: Yes, God could, but God wouldn't.

Second Person: How do you know what God would do?

Review of Major Points

In this chapter we explored the differences among descriptions, arguments, and explanations. Descriptions state the facts, report on states of mind, and so forth. Arguments aim at convincing you that something is so or that something should be done. Explanations don't. They assume you are already convinced and instead try to show the cause, the motivation, or the sequence of events that led up to it.

Whether writing to describe, argue, or explain, providing a clear and precise structure can dramatically improve the writing's effectiveness. Longer pieces are more effective when they are divided into three parts: an introduction, a body, and an ending, each with its own purpose. Getting the main points down on paper should come before worrying about the organizational details. Write first; then worry about how to structure the ideas effectively. In creating arguments, the body of evidence plus the conclusion being argued for is called the *proof* of the conclusion. Purported proofs are not necessarily successful proofs, and proofs are generally a matter of degree; they are not wholly successful or wholly unsuccessful. Sometimes when we respond to an argument we try to expose weaknesses in it, such as that the reasons given are not true, the reasons don't make the case even if they are true, and so forth. At other times we don't directly attack the argument but rather create a new argument for the opposite conclusion. This indirect response is called creating a counterargument. The next chapter explores the process of creating and evaluating explanations rather than arguments.

Glossary

argument An argument is a conclusion backed up by one or more reasons.

counterargument An argument for the conclusion opposite to that taken by another arguer.

description A statement or sequence of statements that characterize what is described. Descriptions state the facts, report on states of mind, and so forth. A pure description does not explain or argue.

explanation A statement designed to show the cause, the motivation, or the sequence of events leading up to the event that is being explained. Pure explanations do not describe. Nor are they designed to convince you that something is so or that something should be done.

proof A convincing argument for a statement. It doesn't need to be the sort of thing you would find in a math book. You prove a statement to other persons if you give them reasons that *ought* to convince them, even if those reasons don't actually convince them.

Answers to Concept Checks

1. It is most probably only a description. It is at least a description because it describes Beijing as being a crowded city containing many lines. Nothing is explained. There is no explanation of Beijing itself, whatever that would mean. There is no explanation of why Beijing has so many people, or why it has so many lines. You might try to conceive of the passage as being an argument for the conclusion that Beijing is crowded and has lines, but no reasons are given in defense of this claim. It probably would be a mistake to say the passage uses the reason that Beijing has many lines to conclude that it is crowded. This would probably be a mistake, because the comments about lines seem to be there to illustrate or describe in more detail the crowded nature of the city, not to make a case for the claim that the city is crowded.

2. (a) This is an explanation of the apple's falling. (b) This is an argument concluding that you should eat an apple a day.

3. The increase is explained as being caused by the jump in federal taxes on gasoline from 9 cents to 14 cents a gallon. Suppose this question had instead asked you to give the *reason* for the rise in the cost of gasoline. Wouldn't the answer have been the same — namely, the rise in federal taxes on gasoline? Yes, but this use of the word *reason* would obscure the distinction between an explanation and an argument. The intent in the newspaper article is to give the reader a fact — that gasoline prices are high — and then to provide the cause — the rise in gasoline taxes. The intent is not to use the fact that there is a rise in taxes to convince the reader that there is a rise in prices. Consequently, if the question had been "What is the reason for the rise in gasoline prices?" it would not have been using the word *reason* as we use it in this book, which is as a statement intended to be used to convince someone of a conclusion.

4. Answer (d). The passage definitely describes Africa's troubles with drought and pests, because it offers descriptive details (the drought has lasted twenty years, the pests were Senegalese grasshoppers, and so forth). The passage gives no reasons to believe that Africa got some temporary relief after the twenty-year parching drought, beyond the assertion in the passage that this is so; therefore

answer (a) is incorrect. There is no indication of the cause of the rain, so answer (b) is incorrect. Regarding (c), the passage says all this but cites no authority's statement as a reason to believe it, nor does it give any other reason; so (c) is incorrect as well.

5. A plausible argument would be this: The experts in geology and biology confirm this, and they generally agree among themselves, except for a few lone wolves such as the creationists.

6. An asteroid crashed into our planet 65 million years ago, knocking up so much dust that the Earth was dark for about a month. During this month the weather turned very cold, and the dinosaurs' main food plants died. This so disrupted the dinosaurs' life that they couldn't adapt to the new conditions, and they died. (The air sure must have smelled bad that month!)

7. Delete the two paragraphs in the middle of the letter.

8. He (or she) persisted on his life's path (continued across the road), despite occasional, near tragic events caused by forces (speeding cars) that he could not control and that he probably assumed were random, if in fact he ever thought about their cause at all. Although oblivious to the effects of his own actions, he in fact helped promote the life of others very different from himself (the oat seeds).

9. Answer (a). Answer (b) is not correct because it is not a description of the mound but instead is a description of the children's reaction to the mound. Answer (c) is not correct because there is no basis for claiming that the mound had the specific measurements mentioned in the answer. Answer (c) would be a better answer than (a), however, *if* (c) were true.

10. This statement is making it too difficult for scientific reasoning to establish its claims. A proof of a claim is simply a strong, convincing argument; it need not be an argument so strong that "it would be absolutely impossible for the claim to be false."

11. Answer (a).

12. An answer to this question might distinguish goals from actual practice and point out the specific results of twentieth-century communist economies and capitalist economies.

13. (a) B (by first person). (b) B (by the second person). (c) C (by the second person). (d) It is not at all clear who has won this debate, (e) nor even who has made the best point. The points made in this debate have appeared in the literature of philosophy and computer science from some of the greatest minds of the second half of the twentieth century. The debate occurs at a high intellectual level; it does not degenerate into name calling or confused circles. The main problem, however, is that many of the excellent points are not developed in enough detail but instead are drifted away from as the debaters continue to launch the missiles stored in their intellectual arsenals.

Review and Writing Exercises

The Argumentative Essay

- 1. Create a four-page argumentative essay, typed double-spaced, that analyzes the following argument and that creates a counterargument in response to it.

> Animals may appear to have minds, but in fact they don't. Do you seriously believe that a one-celled animal has a mind? Besides, to have a mind it has to have a soul. Yet if every gnat had a soul, there would be a population explosion in the domains of the spirit, i.e., in heaven. Heaven surely has no such room. So, gnats and other beasts are mindless.
>
> There are several other reasons I can offer in defense of my point. I have recently been reading the works of Louis Racine, who wrote in 1700 in France. Here is Louis's convincing argument. He is commenting on René Descartes's claim that animals are automata. "If beasts had souls and were capable of feelings, would they show themselves insensible to the affront and injustice done them by Descartes? Would they not rather have risen up in wrath against [Descartes who] so degraded them?"
>
> God is good, and we can see "how much more humane is the doctrine that animals suffer no pain." What Cardinal Melchior de Polignac meant by saying this is that it takes a mind to feel pain, but animals feel no pain — they just flinch when pricked — and this attitude that animals feel no pain is correct because the attitude is the most humane approach to animals. I agree.
>
> Everyone knows animals are just creatures of instinct. Essentially all animal behavior is unsophisticated by our standards; a lion sees an antelope and lunges after it. The antelope sees the lion, and lurches away.

  You will be graded on the clarity and organization of your essay, on the lack of incorrect and silly comments, and on the depth of your insight into the topic.

- 2. Write an essay in which you weigh the pros and cons involved in hiring either Roth or Toomey as a legislative advocate for the City of Newark, New Jersey. In this fictitious case, you are an independent consultant, making a recommendation to the city council, and you have interviewed and eliminated all other candidates except these two. The council is voting on this personnel matter at its next meeting in three days. Your essay should be written as a confidential letter to the council. Begin with your recommendation, then give an argument justifying your recommendation by weighing the pros and cons. Here is the description of the job that the two candidates are applying for.

> The Legislative Advocate, i.e., lobbyist, will represent the interests of the City of Newark before the state government of New Jersey, including but

not limited to the legislature, the office of the governor, and the state's various departments, staff, offices, and committees. This position requires writing legislation, recommending legislation, providing information to the city and its staff about the activities of the state government, representing the city before the state government, providing testimony at hearings, lobbying for passage or defeat of bills before the legislature, encouraging the governor to sign or veto bills that have passed the legislature, and other related activities.

The Legislative Advocate reports directly to the president of the city council and supplies monthly reports to the entire council. Salary $62,000 per year plus medical, dental, and optical benefits. The city will supply one full-time secretary, office space, two telephone lines, two telephones, a desktop computer, fax machine, copy machine, and office supplies.

Background on the City Council: 3 Republicans, 6 Democrats; president is a Republican; 6 men, 3 women; 5 white, 3 black; 1 Hispanic.

Background on New Jersey: Democratic governor. Republicans hold a two-thirds majority in the two houses of the Legislature.

CONFIDENTIAL analysis of personnel matters:

ROTH: Has previously been a legislative advocate for an Illinois public employee labor union and also for Planned Parenthood in Illinois. Eighteen years ago she and another black female were fired from their positions as county social workers for continuing to picket the county during a strike in violation of a court injunction declaring the strike illegal. The case reached the Illinois Supreme Court and was overturned, winning public employees in Illinois the right to strike. She is currently one of two lobbyists for the City of Chicago, representing the city before the Illinois state government. Her specialties are lobbying for issues concerning health care, labor relations, and urban planning. Holds a master's degree in public health from the University of Pennsylvania. Has letters of support from two Democratic and two Republican city council members in Chicago. Has never lived in New Jersey. No convictions. Age 43. Registered Democrat. Main new idea offered during interview: Lobby for a state bill enabling Newark to legally offer free hypodermic needles to drug addicts in exchange for their used needles.

TOOMEY: Lawyer. Served for two years as a researcher on a taxation committee in the New York legislature. Toomey was an administrative aide for the current lieutenant governor of New Jersey, a Republican, but was fired from that position after serving four months. Ran for city council of Princeton eight years ago, receiving 27 percent of the vote. Presently is a legislative advocate representing the U.S. Steel Corporation and the Association of Airports of New Jersey before the state. Has worked actively on the election campaign of the speaker of the state senate of New Jersey, who is a personal friend of two Republican members of the Newark city council. Recently convicted of drunken driving and then of driving while his driver's license was suspended; driver's license is still suspended. White. Age 63. Registered Republican. Main new idea offered during interview: Newark should make the homeless and the panhandlers less visible to other citizens.

- 3. This is a three-week assignment. Your instructor will give you a description of a controversial issue. Pick one side of the issue and write an essay defending your opinion. Make it about four pages long, typed double-spaced. It is due one week after it is assigned. Don't put your name on your essay, only your social security number. The class's essays will then be randomly redistributed to the class. Make sure you don't get your own essay back. For the essay you receive, write a three-page analysis of the quality of the essay. Can you think of better points the writer could have made? Can you think of counterarguments the writer failed to notice? This analysis is due in one week. Put your social security number on it, not your name, and staple it to the back of the first essay. The essay-analysis pairs will then be randomly redistributed to the class. Make sure you don't get any of your own work back. For the pair that you receive, write a three-page critique of both the original essay and the analysis given of it. Put your social security number on your critique, and staple it to the back of the pair. Turn in the trio within one week.

- 4. Write a short essay explaining to a sixth-grade science class the similarities and differences between a shadow and a reflection.

- 5. *Common Sense* was published anonymously on January 10, 1776. The American radical Thomas Paine wrote this fifty-page argumentative essay for a variety of reasons, the main one being to convince readers that the colonies should pursue revolution rather than reconciliation. In 400 to 700 words, summarize the argument against reconciliation. To get some flavor of the arguing, consider Paine's reaction below to the assertion that Great Britain is America's parent, the implication being that after some bad times the child should reconcile with the parent rather than revolt and drive away the parent:

    Even brutes do not devour their young, nor savages make war upon their families; wherefore, the assertion, if true, turns to her reproach; but it happens not to be true, or only partly so, and the phrase *parent* or *mother country* hath been jesuitically adopted by the king and his parasites, with a low papistical design of gaining an unfair bias on the credulous weakness of our minds. Europe, and not England, is the parent country of America.

- 6. After the quotations given in the chapter, *The Grapes of Wrath* continues to follow the adventures of Tom Joad and his family. In a later chapter, Tom's mother encounters a policeman:

Ma's face blackened with anger. She got slowly to her feet. She stooped to the utensil box and picked out the iron skillet. "Mister," she said, "you got a tin button an' a gun. Where I come from, you keep your voice down." She advanced on him with the skillet. He loosened the gun in the holster. "Go ahead," said Ma. "Scarin' women. I'm thankful the men folks ain't here. They'd tear ya to pieces. In my country you watch your tongue."

The man took two steps backward. "Well, you ain't in your country now. You're in California, an' we don't want you goddamn Okies settlin' down."[10]

Research the history of California in the 1930s, then create an argumentative essay making the police officer's case for Okies not settling there.

- 7. John Steinbeck and his editor both knew that irrelevant digressions hurt a story. Why then do you suppose that the turtle chapter was not cut from the book? Defend your answer to somebody who gives the opposite answer.

- 8. View the film *The Grapes of Wrath* in your college library, then write an essay speculating on why the film treated Chapter 3 the way it did.

- 9. Write an argumentative essay about utilitarianism in which you conclude either for or against it. Predict the criticisms that might be offered by your opponent and deal with them in your essay.

- 10. Create an argumentative essay on one of the following topics.

    A. Should Columbus Day celebrations be promoted or downplayed?

    B. Is a fetus a person with rights?

    C. Should our country's defense budget be increased, decreased, or kept the same?

    D. If you drop your new toothbrush in the toilet, should you throw it away, should you wash it in hot water and continue using it, or should you do something else?

    E. How sure can you be that you are not now dreaming?

    F. What is wrong with the following reasoning?

    It is impossible for the instructor to leave this room through the door. In order to get out, he (or she) must move from where he is now and walk across the room to the door. But before that, he must reach the halfway point from where he is to the door. But before that, he must reach the one-quarter point from where he is to the door. But before that, he must reach the one-eighth point, and so forth. He has an infinite number of places to go before leaving the room, and nobody has enough time to visit an infinite number of places.

    G. Is the punishment for using crack cocaine too lenient?

    H. Are numbers real objects, or are they just in our heads?

I. In what ways is the system of taxes unfair — that is, who or what is not taxed the proper amount?

J. Should a judge ever be able to require a reporter to reveal the identity of her sources (informants)?

K. When is it ever proper to steal?

L. Should there be a death penalty for any crimes?

M. Should flag burning ever be illegal?

N. Should it be legal to copy a computer program if you don't use the copy to make money?

O. Assess the following statement and the issue behind it:

Environmentalists do not work from facts. They use tainted theory to scare Americans into believing their lies. Trust me. The Earth will be here for our great-grandchildren to enjoy, even if you do use disposable diapers.

P. Is it OK to pay a worker below the minimum wage if the worker voluntarily agrees to work for less?

Q. Should the federal and state governments create more regulations and red tape for companies involved in producing or selling the food we all eat?

R. Who was the best U.S. president?

S. What country has the worst foreign policy?

T. Are college sports programs overfunded or underfunded?

U. Should county health departments have the right to give out free, clean needles to drug addicts as a means of curbing the spread of AIDS?

V. Should employers be able to refuse to hire people who have AIDS, and should insurers be able to refuse to sell them insurance for this reason?

W. If (you believe) the amount spent on public welfare is too high, where should the money be spent instead? If (you believe) the amount spent on public welfare is too low, where should the government get the money for the increase?

X. Is it OK for the federal government to use our tax monies to bail out failed businesses such as savings and loans?

Y. Who will probably do more to improve the United States in the future, the Republicans or the Democrats?

Z. Property owned by organized religions or by insurance companies does not and should not pay property taxes, right?

AA. Should the border between the U.S. and Mexico be made more open like that between the U.S. and Canada, or should it be made more difficult to cross?

Descriptions, Explanations, and Arguments

■ 1. Are the following passages most probably expressing arguments, explanations, descriptions, or what?

    a. A quartz crystal oscillator is very small and contains a crystal of the mineral silicon dioxide that can be made to vibrate when stimulated electrically.

    b. A clock's quartz crystal oscillator is a fascinating device that is not as complicated as it may seem to be. Here is how it works. Power from a small battery makes the crystal vibrate, and when this happens the crystal gives out pulses of current at a very precise rate, i.e., a fixed electrical frequency. A microchip reduces this rate to one pulse per second, and this signal activates the time display mechanism — for example, the second hand.

    c. Many clocks and watches contain a quartz crystal oscillator that controls the hands or the time display. Power from a small battery makes the crystal vibrate, and it gives out pulses of current at a very precise rate — that is, a definite frequency. A microchip reduces this rate to one pulse per second, and this signal activates the time display mechanism.

2. Suppose you asked someone to explain why tigers eat meat but not plants, and you got the answer, "Because a zookeeper once told me that's what they eat." You should consider this to be an incorrect answer. Why?

    a. You asked for some sort of explanation of why tigers eat meat but not plants, yet the answer mentioned nothing about plants.

    b. You requested an explanation but got an argument instead.

    c. The argument that a zookeeper said so commits a fallacious appeal to authority.

3. Given only what is said about Tom Joad in this chapter:

    a. Create a description of him.

    b. Write a description of Tom Joad as might be given by the truck driver in a letter to his wife.

    c. For extra credit, read part of the book or view the film, then write more about Tom Joad's character.

4. Suppose you ask your English teacher why Ernest Hemingway won the 1954 Nobel prize for literature, and suppose she answers, "He won because the Swedish Nobel Committee liked his short stories and novels about his own experiences in World War I and in the Spanish Civil War of the late 1930s." She is

    a. explaining but not arguing.

    b. explaining and arguing.

    c. only describing.

    d. describing and arguing.

    e. only arguing.

■ 5. When Betsy says "I'm angry," she is reporting information about her state of mind, not arguing for a conclusion. But is she explaining or not explaining? Why?

■ 6. The following passage is primarily

    a. a description   b. an argument   c. a request

About two-thirds of the salt in sea water is sodium chloride. Other substances present are magnesium chloride, sodium sulfate, potassium chloride, and calcium chloride. In the remaining 1 percent of salts are tiny traces of about forty different elements, including iron, uranium, silver, and gold. The percentage of gold is so small that you would have to process tons of seawater to get even a tiny amount. If the salt were taken out of all the seawater in the world, it could cover all the land areas on Earth with a layer 500 feet thick.

7. The following passage is primarily

    a. a description   b. an argument   c. a request

The sun's rays do not fall vertically outside the tropics, even at noontime. June 21 in the northern hemisphere is the day of the year with the longest daytime. On this day, the perfectly vertical fall of the sun's rays is farther north than on any other day of the year. This farthest north place, which is actually a line of places around the earth, is the 23.5° north latitude and is called the Tropic of Cancer. The day when the sun reaches the Tropic of Cancer is called the solstice, and it begins the summer. Hawaii is the only part of the U.S. that is south of the Tropic of Cancer.

8. Is this passage primarily an argument or an explanation?

Mayfield is guilty because the FBI report says that his fingerprints match those on the countertop beside the cash register.

9. Is this passage primarily an argument or an explanation?

The passenger died because the driver was drunk and speeding on the freeway.

10. Take the following sentences and work them into an argument and a counterargument on the issue of which computer your office should purchase. Create your own conclusion to each argument in which you say to buy one computer and not the other. Be obvious that one argument is a counterargument against the other. (*Hint:* You wouldn't want to place *every* sentence below into your argument.)

    a. The Apple clone is cheaper than the Cray-Sinclair, although both are within our budget.

    b. The Cray-Sinclair computer is faster than the Apple clone.

    c. The Cray-Sinclair won't run WordPerfect, and the Apple clone runs all the software we want right now.

    d. The Cray-Sinclair has a better service contract than the Apple clone.

- 11. Discuss the following argument. At the very least, describe it and evaluate it. Are some reasons better than others?

    Drinking alcohol causes kidney disease, traffic accidents, and other serious problems. In addition, the singer Michael Jackson says drinking is an undesirable habit. Your older brother says no one will kiss a person whose breath smells like alcohol. Therefore, no sensible, intelligent person should ever drink.

  12. Why do you suppose Steinbeck made such a big deal about the wild oats in his chapter about the turtle?

Evaluating Unusual Statements and Creating Good Explanations

Suppose that a friend of yours says she just read that several soldiers who were lost in action during the U.S. invasion of Iraq in 1991 have been discovered in graves in Antarctica. What would it take to convince you that her statement is true? More generally, what methods should you use to evaluate unusual, improbable statements? Reasoning well requires having a good sense of what is improbable and what would count as sufficient evidence to believe it. This chapter begins by examining these issues. The lessons learned can be applied in creating your own explanations, which is the focus of the second half of the chapter.

The Principle of Fidelity

When someone says something that is obviously false, the logical reasoner will look deeper and not be too quick to find fault. Maybe the person meant something true but simply slipped up. "I collided with a stationary truck coming the other way," a driver wrote in an insurance statement, attempting to summarize the details of an accident. Because a truck cannot be simultaneously moving and stationary, you note the inconsistency but are charitable and assume that the person didn't literally mean what he wrote. Maybe he meant that he collided with a truck carrying stationery and other paper products, or maybe he meant that the truck was stationary but that he, himself, was coming the other way.

By trying to make sense of apparent inconsistencies, and by trying to make sense of false statements that are too obviously false, we are again applying the principle of charity or the principle of charitable interpretation. This principle, which was introduced in an earlier chapter, is really a request to be kind and to try to make reasonable sense of odd statements.

Besides applying the principle of charity, we want to respect the *principle of fidelity*. That is, we should preserve the intended meaning of the speaker's original statements when analyzing them or reacting to them. We don't want to twist the original so that the speaker would react with "Hey, I didn't mean that." Nor should we be so charitable that we are blind to real falsehoods and real inconsistencies.

> The **principle of fidelity** requires you to preserve the intended meaning of the speaker's original statements when analyzing them.

Concept Check 1

Suppose you are trying to interpret what someone meant by saying "You will have some good luck." Which of the following interpretations would violate the principle of fidelity?

a. You will have some good luck today, or soon.
b. You will have something positive happen to you.
c. You will cause somebody to have some good luck.
d. Eventually good luck will happen to you, but it won't be that far off.

It is important to accurately represent what people are intending to say. If they intend to say something that turns out to be false or inconsistent, they are being false or inconsistent, and that is that. It's their confusion, not yours. But what do you do when faced with a statement that is blatantly inconsistent? For example, suppose a friend of yours says, "I don't believe in God's existence; nevertheless, God exists." Perhaps your friend intended to say something consistent, so you ask yourself, "What else could the sentence mean?" Maybe (but just maybe) it means "I find it hard to believe in God's existence; nevertheless, I actually do believe in God's existence." That would not be inconsistent. When you are in doubt about apparent inconsistencies or weirdness, ask the speaker to clarify if you can. The burden is on the speaker not to confuse you. Tension may occur between the principles of fidelity and charity. To maintain fidelity, the analyst will say that a sentence that appears to make a false statement is in fact false, yet to be charitable the analyst will try to find a way to interpret the sentence so that it doesn't make a false statement. Consequently, applying the principles is an art that requires a delicate sensitivity.

■ ·········· Concept Check 2 ··········· ■

Applying the principles of charity and fidelity to the sentence "The musician Tommy Tutone is dead, but alive," it would be best to say what?

a. Tommy Tutone is probably not a musician but a detergent.
b. "Dead" means "not alive."
c. "Alive" means "his music is still listened to."
d. There are some people who are biologically both dead and alive.
e. If a person is dead, then the person cannot be a musician.

When Should We Accept Unusual Statements?

In ancient Egypt at the time of the pharaohs and their pyramids, a group of magicians would walk into the marketplace and begin displaying their powers. The lead magician would hold up a walking stick that had been carved in the shape of a snake and pass it around the audience. Soon after getting it back, the magician would hold up the stick, call on the supernatural powers of the Egyptian gods, and throw the stick on the ground. There the stick would turn into a live snake and crawl away into the crowd, leaving the audience stunned and even more in awe of the power of the pharaoh and his magicians.

Did the stick really turn into a snake? "No, that's impossible," you are apt to say, "it's got to be a trick." In fact, you are right. Unknown to most people, there is a certain Egyptian snake that can be temporarily paralyzed by applying well-placed pressure to the back of its neck. A physical shock to its head can unparalyze it. The lead magician's stick looked like this snake. After the stick had been passed around and while other magicians were performing other tricks, the lead magician switched sticks with a magician who had been carrying the paralyzed snake. When the lead magician threw the snake down head first, it woke up and crawled away—naturally, not supernaturally.

The magician's audience accepted the performance as a straightforward demonstration of the powers of magic and the supernatural. The typical Egyptian did not approach the demonstration with the critical attitude of the modern logical reasoner.

Instead, he or she was gullible and already predisposed to accept supernatural explanations for surprising phenomena. A logical reasoner such as yourself would demand better evidence before accepting the magician's explanations, because you have a better feeling for what is a likely explanation and what is not. You know that it's more probable that sleight of hand is behind the snake trick or that some natural but little-known phenomenon is the secret.

Being logical requires the ability to identify strange events and a knowledge of the best way to go about explaining why the events appear to be happening. A strange event is an improbable one, and probability is always assessed against a base of background knowledge and available evidence. Strange events or statements are improbable because they conflict with what else you believe; they appear to be weird or surprising.

The core of background knowledge that you use in making judgments of improbability is called *common sense*. It is the knowledge that most of us acquire in the normal process of growing up in our society. The common sense of today's logical reasoner is quite different from the common sense of the ancient Egyptian.

Because of your common sense, you probably won't believe the following headline from the *Weekly World News* without a great deal more evidence:

DYING MAN'S BRAIN
PUT IN COMA WOMAN

You probably know a few people who could use a good brain transplant — for one, the author of the headline. The gullible person will buy the newspaper to learn more details about the world's first successful brain snatch. However, you as a logical reasoner will first ask yourself, "Why am I finding out about this in the supermarket checkout line?" If it is true, why haven't you heard about it in your daily newspaper, on the TV news, or from your friends? This headline is inconsistent with your background knowledge about the state of medicine today. You don't have to be a doctor to know that brain transplants have yet to be attempted. At most, small bits of brain tissue have been transplanted. If a brain transplant were even going to be attempted, there would have been a lot of advance publicity. A person who did not know these facts of medicine could easily be conned by the headline. For the rest of us, the most it should do is sensitize us to noticing whether other newspapers or the TV news mention any recent brain transplant attempts. Reading the article in the tabloid would be unlikely to provide any good reason to believe the original headline.

Assessing a Source's Credibility

The *Weekly World News, The Star, The National Enquirer,* and other popular tabloids whose headlines shout out from the checkout racks of grocery and drug stores are a much less reliable source of information than *The New York Times, The Christian Science Monitor,* and your local daily newspaper. The grocery store tabloids often

TOT FALLS 5,000 FEET — AND LIVES!
Baby boy sucked through door of plane — & lands in a tree

WEEKLY WORLD 50¢
NEWS

November 5, 1985

SWEET REVENGE!
Cashier fired because of
her big bust wins back pay!

30587   VOL. 7, Issue 4

THE MOST INCREDIBLE TRANSPLANT IN MEDICAL HISTORY!

DYING MAN'S BRAIN PUT IN COMA WOMAN

From *Weekly World News*, November 5, 1985.

exaggerate their stories and will print almost anything anybody says. They will portray the stories as being true without checking them out. The editor of the *Weekly World News*, when asked about the reliability of the stories he prints, admitted this when he said, "Of course we are skeptical about some of the stories, but we wouldn't question ourselves out of a story, particularly when it has no health-related ramifications." The editor added, "If we got a fellow who said he was taken aboard a UFO, for instance, we would really see no reason to check it out if it was entertaining, a good story. If we did some probing, we could find out that he'd been in a mental hospital for the past 60 days and then [have to] kill the story." When the reporters locate somebody who calls himself an "expert on UFOs," they aren't apt to question the credentials and will simply report that "experts on these matters have said . . ."[1]

Tabloids are notorious for trying to convince readers by appeal to anecdotes. **Anecdotes** are reports of individuals' own experiences. There is nothing wrong with gathering information from individuals, but a few unsystematically acquired anecdotes do not constitute a scientific proof. For example, Lupe says to you, "Forget about seatbelts. They do more harm than good. I was in a car accident once, and the doctor said it was lucky that I wasn't wearing one. If I had been wearing one I would have been burned up with the car. Instead I was thrown through the windshield and only broke my neck and back." This anecdote may support the generalization that car seatbelts shouldn't be used, but it cannot stand up to statistics showing that overall, people with seatbelts suffer fewer injuries. It is understandable that you might want to pay more attention to your friend Lupe than to some statistical report from people you do not know, but it is more reasonable to pay attention to the statistics. By the same token, if Lupe had asked her doctor, he no doubt would have said she was lucky not to have had the seatbelt buckled but that in the future she should buckle up. The doctor's own views about seatbelts will probably have been acquired by paying attention to the statistics, not to the anecdotes of his own few patients.

Although the "coma woman" headline in the *Weekly World News* isn't a good enough reason for you to change your beliefs about brain transplanting, the same headline in more reputable publications *should* cause you to change your beliefs. The same information in a medical journal, or backed up by a "Yes, it's true" comment from your doctor, would be a good reason to believe the story. Some of our most valuable knowledge is simply knowledge about which sources are credible sources and which are not.

Concept Check 3

If you wanted to know whether electricity will flow through certain kinds of plastic, who would be the most credible source of information?

a. A friend of yours who has invented and patented three kinds of plastic toys.

b. The county librarian who specializes in government documents.

c. A professional proofreader who has just worked on a new textbook about plastics and electronics.

d. Your neighbor who is an electrical engineer.

e. The sales representative of the largest plastics manufacturer in your state.

Above the "coma woman" headline was a smaller headline: "Tot Falls 5,000 Feet and Lives!" Should you believe this surprising claim? Well, that depends on what it means. Does it mean that the tot fell without a parachute? If so, you'd expect this stunt tot to be a flat tot, wouldn't you? But maybe the tot did have a parachute. If so, the story could well be true. When you see such a headline, you are sensitized to wonder whether some crucial information has been left out.

Seeking Second Opinions

Even if you were to read the story and find out that the tot did not have a parachute but still lived, you should be cautious about believing it, because your common sense says this feat is highly improbable. So, *before you put much faith in a story like this, you should get some independent verification.* You should get a reliable second opinion that supports the story. The newpaper that reported on the tot's fall might just be repeating someone's unjustified opinion.

What *is* an authoritative second opinion? The opinion of an eyewitness interviewed by your local newspaper's reporter, not by the tabloid's reporter, should be a good enough second opinion for you to believe the story, and the burden falls on your shoulders either to show that the story is false or to undermine the evidence by, say, showing that other experts disagree with the witness. A videotape would also serve the purpose of providing independent verification. Remember, though, that the more improbable the belief you are considering adopting, the better the evidence has to be. A videotape can be doctored; even ten eyewitnesses can suffer a mass hallucination.

Verifying the falling tot story is much easier than verifying whether St. Matthew wrote down the Gospel while visiting Mt. Ararat. Verifying current events is easier than verifying most historical events, because the trail isn't so cold. There are more traces of current events, more eyewitnesses, more available data, more evidence to find.

Here's another headline from the same issue of *Weekly World News:*

Cashier Fired Because of Her Big Bust Wins Back Pay

Is this headline inconsistent with anything you know? No, and it is not especially improbable, only mildly surprising. So you should believe the headline. It is unlikely that the newspaper is wrong about everything. Still, the *Weekly World News* is not a sufficiently reliable source for you to believe anything of importance without first checking elsewhere. If it were important to you to get the facts right about the big bust story, you should not rely solely on this paper's report. Try harder to verify it. Get more information from more reliable sources. Would six more copies of the same issue of *Weekly World News* make the story six times as probable?

Suspending Belief

It is not easy to decide whether to believe what you read. When it comes to improbable claims, the first principle is that the burden of proof in producing the good evidence is on the shoulders of whoever makes the claim or adopts the belief. If you decide to adopt a belief—that is, to believe something you have read—you should have found enough evidence to justify your doing so. It is not good enough to say, "Well, it's never been proved false, so I believe it." Instead, you should *suspend your belief.* That is, if you are in a situation in which somebody makes an improbable claim but doesn't supply good evidence to back it up, don't believe it until somebody gives you enough evidence or until you get it for yourself. Don't believe it even if you might *like* to believe it. I'd like to believe that my sweet Aunt Emma is telling me the truth when she introduces her new friends as aliens from beyond our galaxy, but rationally I should not believe her until they show me some ID.

Logical reasoners discriminate among sources of information. They trust information from a reputable scientific journal over information from a daily paper. Regarding news about events outside their own city, they would expect to get the most reliable information from *The New York Times, The Wall Street Journal,* and perhaps *Newsweek,* followed by network TV news, the local daily paper, and then local TV stations. They are suspicious of TV docudramas, and they don't trust grocery store tabloids.

■ .... Concept Check 4 .... ■

Here are three reports from a friend, Ramone, who is no expert in these matters. All are bizarre, but some are more improbable than others. Which report is the most improbable, and why? The focus of these questions is not on whether Ramone is being truthful but on whether what he says is actually true.

a. I saw my uncle die because he threw salt on the ground. He did it when he and I were camping. My grandmother told us never to throw salt away or else something bad would happen soon. The very next day after the camping trip he was hit by that truck on the freeway.

b. Hey, you won't believe this. Less than ten minutes ago, I saw Mary, the one who moved away to Germany last year. Remember she went to be a gymnastics coach in Berlin? Well, she was running into the grocery store as I drove past on the freeway. She's changed a lot. She looks tens years older, and she has a plastic, prosthetic leg.

c. I swear it's true. The president of the United States called at 3 A.M. this morning. He asked me to join the Defense Intelligence Agency and spy on Bulgarian businessmen visiting Toronto. What a surprise; I've never done any spying in my life, and I don't even know where Bulgaria is. I'm just a shoe salesman, but today is my special day. My brother Bill was home when he called. Ask him.

■ .... Concept Check 5 .... ■

To someone who has not made up his or her mind about which religion is correct, or whether any is, what are the improbable statements made or suggested in these classified advertisements, and why are they improbable?[2]

Getting Solid Information About Whom to Vote For

Suppose an election is coming up and you want to make an informed choice about the ballot measures and candidates. How do you do so? You might simply ask your parents or friends for advice, then follow their recommendations, especially if they agree. But if you want to think things through for yourself, you should seek out other sources of information. Would it help to reserve one evening before the election and sit down with all the campaign leaflets you have collected during the previous month? If you use these leaflets to figure out who stands where on the issues, you will get frustrated. All candidates sound good, too good, in their own literature. You won't even be able to figure out what the important issues are this way, although you may get some inkling when one candidate's literature attacks the opposition. The government's voter pamphlets can be more helpful. They let the candidates speak to whatever issues they desire, and the issue statements are fairly informative, given their short length.

Are there better sources of information? Consider television. It is definitely easier to watch TV than to read a newspaper or a leaflet. The advantage of TV is that you can see the candidate in action and get some emotional connection. TV information comes in two forms: paid ads and news. The paid TV advertisement is mostly junk food for the eye and mind — fast and appealing, but nutritionally barren. In fact, the techniques used to sell senators are practically the same as those used to sell soft drinks. Any political advertiser worth a sound bite is aiming for your heart strings.

TV news is a better source of political information. Which is not to say it is a good source. It's more nutritional, but still junk food. A study by Harvard fellow Kiku Adatta produced a surprising statistic: the average bloc of uninterrupted speech by presidential candidates on TV shrunk from 42 seconds in 1968 to 10 seconds twenty years later.[3] Ten seconds is enough time for a slogan, but not thoughtful argumentation. Today, TV commentators use these 10-second "sound bites" of the candidate to provide flavor, not information. Commentators believe they can say it better than the candidate; they give themselves a good 20 seconds, and the candidate 10. Their fear is that the public, with its short attention span, will click the channel changer once the candidate starts going on and on.

> The primary commandment of most TV news directors is that the news has to entertain but doesn't have to inform.

The big-budget campaign managers know the territory. For example, they have crafted an excellent strategy for getting their candidate on TV without the candidate having to answer tough questions. Suppose a TV station has a well-informed reporter who knows just what to ask, given the chance. When that reporter is out in the field covering some event, the campaign manager calls the station manager to say that the candidate is nearby and can be at the station in 15 minutes. The manager cannot resist the opportunity. He calls over to his news staff and says, "Andy, get ready; you're on in 15 minutes in a one-on-one with the senator." This reporter will be more apt to treat the senator as a visiting dignitary and will throw fewer of the hardball questions than the well-informed reporter would have. In the next news broadcast an hour or so later, the senator will look great during those crucial 10 seconds.

TV news is dangerous for the public in other ways. After having watched nightly news stories about a candidate, too many viewers falsely believe they know enough to make a decent choice.

> "People think they are informed, but they are not. They see this very shallow picture of what a race is about, but they actually get very little view of the real candidate. That leaves people worse off because they don't know that they are uninformed. They are less cautious about their judgments of candidates."
>
> — John McManus, communcations professor

TV does provide some high-quality reporting. "Ted Koppel," the "McNeil-Lehrer Report," and similar lengthy news programs occasionally offer in-depth interviews with candidates. A candidate debate is another valuable source of information. But watch out for the ordinary TV news.

OK, if you can't rely on the ordinary TV news you are most apt to watch, how about the newspaper? There you go. But what part of the newspaper? How about the list of recommendations in the newpaper's editorial page? This list usually appears a day or two before the election. To be safe in adopting your paper's recommendations, you need to know the political ideology of the publisher that drives the recommendation process. Is your ideology the same as his or hers?

Columns written with a columnist's byline are another source of information in the newspaper. The writer of a newspaper column is like an editorial writer — opinions can be mixed in with the facts. Libel laws are looser for columnists; often they can get away with saying what a regular news story cannot. Columns can be helpful sources of information if the columnist is careful to give reasons for his or her opinions and is careful to distinguish the reasons from the opinions. The problem with editorials and columns that offer advice is that even if they give you reasons for the advice, you always have to worry that they are covering up the reasons that weigh against their advice.

New stories, on the other hand, are supposed to be more sanitized, cleansed of opinions, full of facts, and more reliable. Very often they are. The best news stories are usually the ones that appear early in the campaign. In these, the writers interview the candidates and probe for positions on the important campaign issues. Writers of the early stories are the best informed of all the reporters on a newspaper's staff. Early on, the candidate isn't slinging so much mud and is trying to show the highly politicized voters, especially those who give campaign contributions or volunteer in campaigns, that he or she has significant positions on key issues and is a credible candidate. Later in the campaign, the atmosphere changes. The least politicized voters, those who are undecided as the election nears and those whose decision to vote for a candidate or ballot measure could be easily changed, are the primary target of the bulk of the campaign's media blitz. To these voters, the campaign offers short, memorable slogans plus blasts at the opposition. The newspapers react and give primary attention to these slogans, to the mud slinging, and to the rise and fall of the polls.

When Arkansas Governor Bill Clinton was campaigning for the presidency, the vast majority of the coverage of his campaign was about whether he had slept with a woman who had been paid for her story that appeared on the front page of a supermarket tabloid. The average voter kept saying, "I want to hear about the issues," but the news reporters kept covering the sex angle. "This is all inane, stupid and insulting, and I hope the American people jam it down you-all's throat," said Bob Slagle, the chairman of the Democratic Party in Texas. "The national press corps is acting like a common street gossip in a small town." Meanwhile, the nation's top newspapers were trying to set things straight. On the same day, *The Boston Globe*'s front page headline said, "Poll Shows Clinton's Lead Undiminished," while across town *The Boston Herald*'s main headline said, "Clinton on the Run." We voters have a tough time, don't we?

The searching reader will have to look back on page 14 for any in-depth reporting of the issues, and even then readers need to be aware that story placement can be affected by the paper's editorial policy. Busy readers usually read only the headlines, and a story's favorable treatment of a candidate can be torpedoed by an editor's unfavorable headline.

Other significant barriers block the sincere, interested reader who tries to use news stories as a source of information. Reporters too often fail to write stories that take the trouble to explain the issues, and it's not just that those stories aren't viewed by readers and editors as sufficiently entertaining. Explaining the news is harder work than simply stating what is new. Also, there is little reward for writing in-depth reports. The reporter rarely gets a pat on the back from his fellow reporters with the accompanying remark, "Beautiful piece of writing." There is no glamour in this part of the business.

In addition, a different factor obscures the public's vision of what is going on. The reporter's notion of objectivity gets in the way. When there are two candidates in an election, reporters believe they must give equal weight and equal column space to both sides. The idea is to present the facts, then back off and let the voters decide for themselves. Unfortunately, this notion of fairness gets in the way when a campaign gets dirty and one candidate starts making false accusations about the opponent. The reporter sees what is going on but rarely will tell the public directly. Instead, when the attacked candidate tries to respond and say that the accusations are not true, the reporter will treat this reaction on a par with the smears themselves and will run the story with a headline "Mud flies," falsely suggesting to the public that both sides are engaging in negative campaigning. The reporters are reluctant to tell what is really going on because they believe doing so would be putting their own judgment into a story, which it would be. However, the reporters really are the only experts in touch with the readers, so if the experts won't tell them what is really going on, who will? Perhaps that is where the columnists and editors come in.

All in all, though, more good information is available than we are likely to take the trouble to use. The five best sources of information, not ranked in order of importance, are the newspaper stories and magazine articles that profile the candidates and discuss the issues long before election day; government voter pamphlets; extended TV news programs; public debates (but not the 60-second TV summary of the debates); and the arguments of editors, columnists, and well-informed friends. All these are better than TV ads, campaign leaflets, and sound bites on the ordinary TV news.

To underline my warnings about TV news, read this excerpt from a book by Jerry Marnder:

> Do you remember the Howard Johnson's shootout in New Orleans a few years ago? I watched it all on television.
>
> The regular programming was interrupted to take me to New Orleans where a wildly murderous band of black revolutionaries had taken over the upper floors of a Howard Johnson's hotel. They were systematically murdering the white guests. This was a truly frightening story. Images of race war ran through my mind.

The announcer said that a massive police assault was underway, and I saw helicopters, police with drawn guns, and a lot of tense faces.

I didn't see any murderous black revolutionaries, although I certainly imagined them, and they were described for me by the police on the scene. The death toll was uncertain.

A few hours later, the news reported that the siege was continuing but that the police had reduced their estimate of murderous black revolutionaries to two or three and that the death of only one white guest had been thus far confirmed. However, a number of policemen had been killed by the murderers. The death toll was still uncertain but it could be as high as a dozen.

Back to the regular programming.

By the morning, the siege was over, and the police were able to find only one of the revolutionaries, who apparently had been dead for quite a while, long before the assault was halted. There was still only one dead white guest but there were eight dead police, killed by the band. Police were baffled as to how the other members of the murderous group had eluded them.

A week later, after an investigation, the New Orleans police department reported that they had found that only one white guest had been killed, only one black man had been involved in the killing, and that this one man was not a black revolutionary but a crazy person. He had been dead for several hours while the invasion of the hotel continued, and all of the dead police had been killed by each other's ricocheting bullets. The story was carried in the back pages of the newspaper; I wasn't able to find it in any television news reports.

It turned out that virtually all of the facts as reported on television were totally wrong. Ignoring for the moment that television did not correct its own report, newspapers did, I was given the opportunity to straighten it all out in my mind. There were no murderous revolutionaries; there was only a crazy man. The police had all shot each other. But even now, several years later, I can recall the images of the police assault. Brave men acting in my behalf. The images of the murderous band. I can recall them now even though the information was completely false.[4]

Criteria for Creating Good Explanations

We create explanations to show our listeners or readers how something works or how things got to be the way they are. If you're creating an explanation for why China has so many more people than Siberia, you may want to talk about history and the social, political, and geographical forces shaping those two areas of the world. In doing so, you take it for granted that your audience accepts the fact that China really does have more people than Siberia. If you have to get your audience to first accept this fact, you need to argue for it, not explain it.

To create a good explanation of something is not easy. Here we examine some of the faults in explanation construction and criteria for constructing good explanations. Explanations have many features in common with arguments, so many of these criteria apply to constructing good arguments as well.

The explanation should fit the facts to be explained and should not conflict with other facts. When you are explaining an event, you must show why the event should have occurred, and your explanation should not be inconsistent with any facts. For example, suppose you want to explain why your friend recovered from the flu after only four days of being ill. Here is an explanation of this event: Your friend drank five glasses of orange juice every day he was sick, and drinking orange juice in such heavy doses will knock out anybody's flu virus within four to six days. This explanation does imply that your friend's recovery is to be expected. That's a plus for the explanation. Unfortunately, a doctor can tell you that many, many flu victims who have been tested with orange juice this way have not recovered for several weeks. So your explanation is in conflict with the facts about these other people. Consequently, the explanation violates our rule and should be rejected.

An explanation should do more than simply describe the situation to be explained. For example, suppose we ask a psychic, "How do you successfully locate oil and gold with your mental powers?" and he answers, "Geologists conduct an initial survey of the area for me. Afterward I fly over it, extend my hand, and sense the location of the underground deposit. Or I run my finger over a map and point out where to drill." This answer describes the sequence of events leading up to the event to be explained, but it is intellectually unsatisfying, since we wanted to find out more details about the cause of the psychic's supposed success. We hoped for a causal explanation that would show what makes the psychic's actions work for him when they won't work for us.

Good explanations are not circular. A good explanation doesn't just rephrase what it is trying to explain. A biologist makes this mistake if she tries to explain why humans have two feet by saying it is because they are bipeds. It is true that humans are bipeds, but the definition of *biped* is "two-footed animal," so the biologist's "explanation" simply names the phenomenon; it does not explain it. It does not give us what we want—either the causal mechanism that makes humans have two legs instead of some other number, or some story of the genesis of two legs in humans. What would a noncircular explanation look like? Well, the causal explanation might say that our genes control growth and force humans to have two legs as they develop. A second kind of explanation could point out how, through evolution, a gradual change occurred in hip structure as our ancestors adapted to situations that favored walking on two legs. Whether either of these two explanations is correct is another matter; however, neither of them is circular.

Supernatural explanations should be avoided unless it is clear that more ordinary, natural explanations won't work. For example, suppose Inge says, "I got skin cancer because my number came up; evidently it was my *time*." She is explaining her cancer as being the consequence of some supernatural force that intervenes into the natural causal order of things and makes events happen; this is the supernatural force we call "fate." It's not impossible that she is correct, but her explanation is very weak. Here is a better explanation: Inge works in a manufacturing plant where she comes in daily contact with benzene fumes, and benzene is a well-known cause of skin cancer, so the benzene caused Inge's skin cancer. Until we rule out benzene, let's not pay much attention to fate.

Good explanations explain something in terms of something else that we can understand to be relevant. A Toyota is a Japanese car. If I explain why Julie has never owned a Toyota by saying that she hates German cars, I can be accused of violating the need for relevancy. Her hating German cars might explain why she doesn't own a BMW, but it's not clearly relevant to why she doesn't own a Toyota. If there is some connection, it should have been stated as part of the explanation.

Good explanations explain something unfamiliar in terms of something familiar. Most of us are unfamiliar with the principles of electricity, such as the relationship between current and voltage, but we are familiar with how water flows through a pipe. So, a good explanation of electricity might be based on an analogy between electrical current and water flow. The amount of water flowing through a pipe per second is analogous to the amount of electrical charge flowing through a wire per second, and this amount is called the electrical "current." If you want to increase water flow, you've got to increase the water pressure. Similarly, if you want to increase the electrical current in a wire, you have to turn up the voltage.

Explanations should be consistent with well-established results except in extraordinary cases. Suppose I explain why I have a headache almost everyday at noontime by pointing out that at noon I'm the closest I am to the sun all day; because the sun's gravitational pull on me is strongest at noon, its pull must be the cause of my headaches. This would be an odd explanation. It is a well-established scientific fact that the sun does exert a gravitational pull on us and that this pull is strongest at noon. However, it is also well established that our bodies are insensitive to these small gravitational changes. So, I should look elsewhere for the cause. The inconsistency of my explanation with well justified scientific theory detracts from the quality of my explanation. My explanation might still be correct, but for it to be convincing to the experts a revolution would have to occur in the field of biology. Extraordinary explanations are those that require big changes in the beliefs of the experts, and *extraordinary explanations require extraordinarily good evidence.* An ordinary explanation of the headaches, such as their being caused by my eating a half-pound of beets only on the days I get the headaches, would be a more promising one that could be established with just a little more evidence.

Explanations should be tailored to the audience whenever possible. Suppose we try to explain the red marks on Emilio's nose as being due to overexposure to sunlight. If our audience already knows that sunlight can cause skin cancer and that skin cancer can cause red marks, we may not need to add any more to the explanation beyond perhaps reminding the audience of these facts. However, if the audience doesn't know these facts, we are obliged to support the facts. Also, our explanation should be pitched at the proper level of difficulty for our audience; we cannot use technical terminology on an audience that won't understand the technical terms.

The more precise the explanation, the better. Excessive vagueness weakens an explanation. Don't say, "Lousy pitching explains why the Dodgers lost the game last Tuesday" when you could also justifiably say, "The Dodgers lost the game last Tuesday because their three best pitchers were out with injuries and because the pitchers they did use walked at least one batter in every inning." The more precise a claim, the easier it is to test and thus to refute. If someone claims that eating five medium-sized dill pickles will bring on a headache within twelve minutes, you can test it on someone, perhaps yourself. However, if the person is vaguer and instead claims only that eating pickles will produce headaches, you have a tougher time. What kind of pickles? What size? How many? Will eating them produce headaches in five minutes, five days, next year? This vague claim is too hard to test. The more precise claim is more easily refuted, if it is false. This is why precise claims are more "scientific" than vaguer ones.

Wherever possible, explanations should be testable. Saying "She wasted all her month's food money on lottery tickets because she was in the wrong place at the wrong time" would be an example of an untestable explanation. How do you check it out? A better explanation would be that she wasted her food money on lottery tickets because she is a cocaine addict and was desperate to get a lot of money fast. This may be the wrong explanation, but at least it suggests some idea of what to do to check out whether it is wrong.

■ ⋯⋯⋯⋯   Concept Check 6   ⋯⋯⋯⋯ ■

All the following statements are trying to explain why tigers eat meat but not plants. Which explanation is the best, and why?

a. Tigers are carnivores.

b. Professor DeMarco says so, and he is an expert on tigers.

c. Tigers are naturally meat eaters, because many years ago the most powerful witches on earth placed a spell on the tigers and forced them to be that way.

d. Tiger cells contain a gene that prevents their stomachs from digesting plant cells.

■ ⋯⋯⋯⋯   Concept Check 7   ⋯⋯⋯⋯ ■

In the following passage, (a) what is Frost explaining? (b) What is his explanation for it? (c) How should you evaluate the explanation? Why? (d) Are any reasons given by Frost or by the author of the passage to argue that the explanation is correct? Do not bother to assess the quality of any reasons you find.

Pave Your Path with Accurate Astrology

Honolulu's premier astrologer for the past 20 years has returned to Kauai, [he is] Rollin Frost, master astrologer of Accurate Astrology. Frost begins with a hand-drawn chart which maps out your strengths, talents, delays, and blind alleys. First he briefly examines the natal chart—the patterns of planets at the time of your birth. . . ."People are similar," he [says]. "The results of prior lifetimes impact the present one. That is why some of us have easier lives than others. The rewards and problems follow us from prior lifetimes."[5]

Chapters 13 and 14 will probe deeper into the problem of creating good explanations.

Review of Major Points

In this chapter we clarified the principles of charity and fidelity and explored the intricacies of assessing unusual claims. Our judgments of improbability depend on our background knowledge and the evidence available. When a claim is inconsistent with our background knowledge, we judge the claim to be improbable. Often we accept a claim based on the credibility of the sources suggesting that we accept the claim. The reliability and credibility of magazines and newspapers differ radically; with the less credible ones we should always get independent verification before accepting any of their unusual claims. The more knowledge we have, and thus the closer our body of background knowledge approaches that of the experts, the better will be our judgments. Anecdotes of people's experiences are not as good evidence as statistical reports.

Criteria for creating good explanations include the following: (1) The explanation should fit the facts to be explained and should not conflict with other facts. (2) An explanation should do more than simply describe the situation to be explained. (3) Good explanations are not circular. (4) Supernatural explanations should be avoided unless it is clear that more ordinary, natural explanations won't work. (5) Good explanations explain something in terms of something else that we can understand to be relevant. (6) Good explanations explain something unfamiliar in terms of something familiar. (7) Explanations should be consistent with well-established results except in extraordinary cases. (8) Extraordinary explanations require extraordinarily good evidence. (9) Explanations should be tailored to the audience whenever possible. (10) The more precise the explanation, the better. (11) Explanations should be testable.

Glossary

anecdote   A report of an individual's own experience, such as a firsthand report.

principle of fidelity   The principle requiring you to preserve the intended meaning of the speaker's original statements when you are analyzing them.

Answers to Concept Checks

1. Answer (c). It twists the original statement by changing who the good luck will happen to, whereas statements (a), (b), and (d) are all reasonable interpretations of what the original statement might have meant.

2. Answer (c). If you say that a person is physically dead but that his music is still listened to, you are not being inconsistent. Answer (a) also is consistent, but that answer violates the principle of fidelity.

3. Answer (d). The electrical engineer would be required to learn this sort of thing as part of his or her professional training. Proofreaders need not know anything about what they are reading. Librarians might be able to find the right book, but they themselves wouldn't necessarily be able to understand the book. The inventor would have no reason to be aware of the electrical properties of a plastic, even if he or she used plastic in an invention.

4. Answer (a) is the strangest. Although all three stories are unusual, the spy story and the plastic leg story are not as unusual as the salt story because the salt story violates our basic understanding about what can cause what in the world; the spy story and the plastic leg story are merely about unusual human actions. Answer (a) is unlikely because our background knowledge about what causes death tells us that throwing salt isn't the kind of thing that will easily hurt anybody. Regarding (b), Ramone probably didn't get a very good look at Mary if he was zipping by on the freeway and Mary was running, but this event is not as impossible as a death caused by salt thrown down on the ground the day before. Mary's return from Germany would not be that big of a deal; people do change their plans. Losing her leg could have caused her to lose the gymnastics coaching job. The remark about Mary running with a wooden leg is odd. Answer (c) is probably an unreliable report, too. If spy agencies want someone to spy for them, they don't usually call on the phone, they don't give the candidate a specific assignment without first making sure he (or she) can keep his mouth shut, and they don't have the president make the call. So this whole story is very unusual. Ramone is joking, or he takes you for a fool. His brother is probably in on the joke, or else he is naive.

5. The second ad says there is "Photographic evidence of a realm beyond the physical domain." How could a nonphysical realm be detected photographically? A camera is a physical object; it takes pictures of physical objects. Nevertheless, there is a slim possibility that the camera could do so indirectly. If the nonphysical Devil

exists, to pick one example of a nonphysical object, he might be able to intervene in the physical world and leave evidence of his existence by some evil deed or other. Suppose someone tells you that the Devil just spoke to him and told him, "In 60 seconds the ten commandments will appear in solid gold in front of you. They will be suspended in mid-air, with no strings attached, yet you can touch them. However, each of them will contain typos." Well, that might be a sign of the Devil's work. Oh those devilish typos! Still, this is a highly unlikely situation, isn't it? And even if it did occur, the camera would really be taking a picture of the Devil's work, not the Devil. Consequently, it is highly improbable that the author of this ad can provide photographic evidence of a realm beyond the physical realm. Save your $9.50.

6. Answer (d) is best. Although (d) is probably not a correct explanation of why tigers are carnivores, at least it is testable, consistent with well-justified biological theory, not circular, and doesn't appeal to the supernatural. Answer (a) is circular because *carnivore* just means "eater of flesh, not plants." Answer (b) is an argument, not an explanation; it provides a good argument for believing that tigers are meat eaters and not plant eaters, but it gives no explanation of why tigers are this way. Answer (c) is not acceptable because it violates the canon to be cautious about offering supernatural explanations until it is clear that more ordinary, natural explanations won't work.

7. (a) Frost is explaining why some of us have easier lives than others. (b) His explanation is that we are currently feeling the effects of our prior lifetimes. In other words, our lives before we were born presumably cause our present life to be easy or hard. (c) How can we test whether his explanation is correct? This explanation is not testable, and thus it should not be believed. Psychologists and sociologists can give a better explanation of why some of us have easier lives than others. (d) No reasons are given to defend the explanation; the explanation is only stated.

Review and Writing Exercises

The Principles of Fidelity and Charity

1. Create a single sentence that is a rewrite of the following sentence and that simultaneously applies both the principles of charity and fidelity:

   The criminal trial of Amy Boycott began yesterday in Illinois and Indiana, making headlines in both states.

2. Consider the following sentence: "I'm not alive today." The sentence is weird. Which of the following sentences would count as being an interpretation of that

sentence (i) that violates fidelity but applies charity, (ii) that applies fidelity but violates charity, and (iii) that applies both fidelity and charity.

   a. I'm not alive tomorrow.

   b. I'm alive today but not alive today.

   c. I'm not very animated today.

   d. I'm not under arrest today.

3. Which is the best example of interpreting the following sentence by applying the principle of charity while violating the principle of fidelity? Background: there will be a meeting between the heads of states of two countries to settle their border dispute.

   Tuesday's summit meeting begins at dawn in Switzerland and Italy.

   a. Wednesday's summit meeting begins at dawn in Switzerland and Italy.

   b. Tuesday's summit meeting begins at dawn in Switzerland.

   c. Tuesday's summit meeting begins at dawn on the border of Switzerland and Italy.

▪ 4. How does the principle of fidelity differ from the rule not to commit the straw man fallacy, and how is it similar to it?

5. The statement below is apparently contradictory because it suggests that a cheetah is faster than a dog but not faster than a dog. What is the best way to be charitable and rescue what the speaker probably intended?

   The cheetah is the fastest land animal, but the cheetah in our zoo is sick and cannot run as fast as a dog.

   a. All cheetahs run fast, but the cheetah in our zoo is sick and cannot run fast.

   b. Most cheetahs can run faster than any other kind of land animal, but the cheetah in our zoo is sick and cannot run as fast as a dog.

   c. The cheetah is the fastest land animal, but not the fastest water animal.

   d. The cheetah is not the fastest land animal, although some are very fast, and the cheetah in our zoo is sick and cannot run as fast as a dog.

   e. Some cheetahs are fast and some are not; for example, the cheetah in our zoo is sick and cannot run as fast as a dog.

6. Create a dialogue in which the speaker clearly fails to properly apply the principle of charity. Don't mention the principle during the dialogue, but at the end identify where the failure occurs and why it occurs.

Improbability

1. Visit a local supermarket's magazine rack, or a similar place, and find what you take to be the most preposterous claim you've read this week (outside of this class). State the claim, and identify the source.

■ 2. The more shocking or bizarre the claim, the more apt you should be to demand more and better evidence for it.

    a. true b. false

3. Discuss the quality of the reasoning in this cartoon, explicitly using the concept "more probable than."

CALVIN AND HOBBES 1988 copyright Watterson. Distributed by UNIVERSAL PRESS SYNDI-CATE. Reprinted with permission. All rights reserved.

4. Suppose the following paragraphs had appeared in two different local news stories in the *Washington Post,* the major daily newspaper of Washington, D.C. Do you have any comments? What reasons do you have for your comments? (No, you don't get any more precise directions than this. You will be graded on your depth of insight in regard to the course material as it applies here.)

    a. Senator David Brown was charged by a traffic patrolman last Tuesday for a moving violation. According to the patrolman, Brown crossed the intersection at 12th and Broadway without slowing to a complete stop, and, when stopped, he acted oddly. But after successfully passing a breath test for alcohol, the senator was not charged with drunken driving. The patrolman reported that the front seat of Brown's car contained multiple copies of a pamphlet that describes how to exorcise demons that have taken control of someone's body. According to Brown, the patrolman was the one who acted oddly because he recognized Brown as being a U.S. senator he didn't like.

    b. A man who had been in a coma for six weeks was saved by exorcism from a demon trying to kill him. A doctor and two psychics drove the demon out of the man and into a rat, which began shrieking until it was burned to death, at which point the man stood up and began to talk.

■ 5. As he was standing in the grocery store checkout line, your neighbor read in a magazine (he doesn't remember which one) that farmers in West Virginia reported encountering visitors from outer space. Your neighbor asks you where he can go to find out if anybody has ever really seen extraterrestrials. Which of the following would be the most reliable source of information to recommend to your neighbor?

    a. A bestseller called *Space Creatures Terrorized My Baby!*

b. Your uncle who has many friends in West Virginia who are farmers.

c. A U.S. army radar screen operator.

d. A catholic priest who recently wrote an article in *Scientific American* magazine titled "Is There Life Beyond Earth?"

e. A scriptwriter for the movie *E.T.*

6. Rank the following three headlines in order from most to least bizarre. Defend your ranking.

a. # DEAD CAPTAIN STEERS GHOST SHIP TO PORT!
She'd been missing since 1715

b. ## SCIENTIST FINDS EVIDENCE OF VISITOR FROM 2081 A.D.

We have found a coin with that date on it, a coin which is yet to be made — delivered here by a man who has yet to be born.

c. # U.S. MILITARY LANDS AND SEIZES MARS; U.S. BOUNDARIES ARE ENLARGED TO OUTER SPACE

■ 7. Explain the point of this famous quotation by the philosopher George Santayana: "Skepticism is the chastity of the intellect."

8. Rank the following sources of information in terms of their believability or credibility in regard to whether the U.S. banking system is becoming less stable. You may need to go to outside sources to learn more about them.

a. *Weekly World News* (newspaper)

b. Radio Baghdad (radio station in Iraq)

c. *The Christian Science Monitor* (newspaper)

d. *The Nation* (magazine)

Put the letter of the most credible source first or highest on your list.

● 9. Scientists generally believe that (i) there are no fire-breathing dragons or abominable snowmen and that (ii) there are no ghosts. Scientists believe this despite many reports by people claiming to have seen these unusual beings. Scientists believe one of the two much more strongly. Which one, i or ii? Why? Write a short essay explaining and defending your answer. (The terms can use some clarification. The abominable snowman is called "Bigfoot" or "Yeti" in other parts of the world. A dragon is an exotic flesh-and-blood animal that looks somewhat like a dinosaur but has special physical abilities such as the ability to fly and the ability to direct a stream of flame outward from its mouth. By the word *ghost* we mean the soul of a person that appears to the rest of us in bodily form except that it cannot be photographed and can be semitransparent.)

• 10. Perhaps you heard about the woman who had a space alien's baby. You didn't? Could this have been because of the conspiracy of silence by the media — TV and radio and other newspapers? The story appeared, to your best guess, only in the *Weekly World News.* How would you evaluate the following reasoning about the space alien's baby? How strongly should you believe the doctors, and why?

STUNNED EXPERTS CONFIRM MOM-TO-BE'S INCREDIBLE CLAIM! I'M GOING TO HAVE A SPACE ALIEN'S BABY!

Doctors have confirmed that a 32-year-old woman is pregnant — with a space alien's baby!

The child is due July 29. And barring unforeseen complications, it will be born.

"It's frightening and incredible but true," Dr. Rolf Ahlqvist told reporters in Hasselholm, Sweden. "The baby is half human, half extraterrestrial.

"It's totally unlike anything I have ever seen. Ultrasound testing has shown us that it is a being of unusual grace and beauty.

"The fetus of a human looks like a peanut. But this one is slender, long-armed and long-legged. The size of the head indicates it will have a brain at least one and a half times normal human size.

"It also has two hearts — and gills behind its ears."

The obstetrician refused to identify the mother or even say where she lives. He did confirm that she is happily married to a computer engineer.

She has two other children and claims to have no idea how she was impregnated by anyone other than her husband.

"The only clue is a mysterious blackout she suffered in late November," said Dr. Ahlqvist. "It is conceivable that she was somehow rendered unconscious by the alien father and impregnated at that time."

Eerily, authorities have logged an unprecedented number of UFO sightings near the woman's home since she blacked out last year, said the expert . . .

Dutch UFO researcher Jan van der Moer notes that hundreds of women claim to have been impregnated by space aliens over the past 40 years.

"Many of these women were suffering from delusions but some of them were quite sane," he said.

"Sources tell me that is the case with Dr. Ahlqvist's patient."[6]

Give a critical analysis of the reasoning in this story. (A *critical analysis* is a careful explanation of what the issues are, what statements have been made and defended, how well they have been defended, where the more controversial claims are, what critics of the claims have said or would be likely to say, and how the reasoning in the passage might be improved.) What does the specialist on un-identified flying objects mean by saying "that is the case with Dr. Ahlqvist's patient"? What is the case?

Creating and Evaluating Explanations

- 1. Write an essay explaining one of the following:

    A. How to torpedo a nonmoney bill in the state legislature before it reaches the floor for a vote. Audience: fellow lobbyists.

    B. How the game of basketball has changed since its creation. Audience: college physical education majors.

    C. How to build a fireplace in a new house. Audience: homeowners.

    D. Why World War I was not won by the Germans. Audience: high school seniors in a history class.

    E. How a refrigerator refrigerates. Audience: high school science class at the sophomore level.

    F. How to get shelf space in U.S. supermarkets for the new cereal your company is planning to manufacture. Audience: your manager.

  2. Which comment below most accurately characterizes this letter to the editor, adapted from the *Toronto Globe and Mail*?

    Dear Editor:

    You smeared the public relations trade in your editorial when you said, "If Ollie North is lying [to the U.S. Senate], he's lying very well, which would make him a highly excellent PR guy." This is a terrible indictment!

    In my 18 years as a public relations consultant, working on some very controversial issues, I have never found it necessary to lie on behalf of a client, nor have I ever been asked to. Lying is not an important criterion for becoming an "excellent PR guy."

    a. The writer believes most public relations people do lie to help their clients.

    b. The writer is appealing to anecdotal evidence.

    c. The writer believes that lying for one's client usually causes bad public relations for that client.

    d. The writer is committing the black-white fallacy.

    e. The writer is committing the straw man fallacy.

  3. What is the main principle of good explanation construction that is violated in this explanation?

    Reporter: Why do you suppose that National Football Conference teams always win the Super Bowl, and the American Football Conference teams always lose?

Coach: I think it has something to do with the caliber of the teams in each conference. The AFC teams such as the Buffalo Bills just aren't as good as the Redskins and Giants of the NFC.

a. The explanation is supposed to fit the facts to be explained and not conflict with other facts.

b. A good explanation doesn't just rephrase what it is trying to explain.

c. Good explanations will explain something in terms of something else that we can understand to be relevant.

d. Good explanations will explain something unfamiliar in terms of something familiar.

e. Explanations should be consistent with well-established results except in extraordinary cases.

4. Discuss the pros and cons of the explanation in this letter to the editor. Begin by clearly identifying the explanation — that is, by saying what is being used to explain what.

There is an evil current running throughout history. People simply haven't been nice to each other. Take a look most recently at Nazism in Germany and Stalinism in the Soviet Union. Look at all the cases of demon possession in the files of the Catholic church. It's time for your readers to wake up to the fact that the Devil is at work.

Consistency and Inconsistency

9

....

Chapter 8 focused on the process of distinguishing the probable from the improbable. As we saw, the process is intricate, with no neat formulas to follow, but one way to determine what is improbable is by detecting inconsistencies between what we are asked to believe and what we already believe. A goal of good reasoning is to maintain the consistency of our beliefs as we add new beliefs to our old ones. This chapter is devoted to exploring how to achieve this goal.

Recognizing Inconsistency and Contradiction

In Chapter 1 we introduced and defined the concept of inconsistency, which plays an important role in judgments of improbability. Here is an alternative definition that is helpful:

Definition A statement is **logically inconsistent** with other statements if it is not possible for them all to be true together.

For example, it is not possible for these two sentences to be true together, so they are inconsistent:

> Samantha is taller than Carlos.
> Carlos is taller than Samantha.

Using the definition of inconsistency from Chapter 1, we'd say instead that these two sentences are inconsistent because they imply that something is so and not so—namely, that Samantha is and is not taller than Carlos.

What does the definition mean by the term *possible*? It means something like conceivable or imaginable, although not quite. It's "not quite," because what a person is unable to imagine may nevertheless be so. The notion of possibility should not ultimately depend on some failing of human imagination. Nevertheless, for our purposes we can say that the two sentences about Samantha and Carlos are inconsistent because we cannot conceive how they could both be true. We cannot imagine a possible world, even very different from our actual world, in which the two sentences are used to make true statements.[1]

Sentence pairs that are not inconsistent are consistent. For example, the negations of the two sentences about Samantha and Carlos are consistent with each other:

> Samantha is not taller than Carlos.
>
> Carlos is not taller than Samantha.

This pair is consistent because it is *possible* that they are both true: Samantha and Carlos could be the same height.

Now, here is the subtle part. Suppose you happened to know that Samantha and Carlos are *not* the same height. Would that last pair of statements now be inconsistent? No. They are consistent with each other no matter what else you learn about the actual heights of Carlos and Samantha. That is why the word *possible* appears in the definition.

An inconsistency does exist somewhere, however. The pair is inconsistent with the statement that Samantha and Carlos are not the same height. Therefore, the following triplet of sentences is mutually inconsistent:

> Samantha is not taller than Carlos.
>
> Carlos is not taller than Samantha.
>
> Samantha and Carlos are not the same height.

Are the following two statements inconsistent?

> Samantha was running in the Boston Marathon at 8 A.M. today.
>
> Samantha was having breakfast at Bob's Restaurant at 8 A.M. today.

Yes and no. The two are consistent with each other because maybe Samantha had a brief, mobile breakfast at 8 A.M. Nevertheless, the two are inconsistent with the normal assumptions that the two events occurred in the same time zone and that a person cannot both run in a marathon and have breakfast in a restaurant at the same time.

■ ············   Concept Check 1   ············ ■

Consider this consistent list of statements:

  i. The president admires the first lady.

 ii. The first lady also admires the president.

iii. Everybody else admires the president, too.

These statements are consistent even though (iii) is definitely false. Label the following sentences as being consistent or inconsistent with the above list:

a. Everybody but the admiral admires the first lady.

b. The admiral admires the first lady but not the president.

c. The president admires other people besides the first lady.

d. The vice-president does not admire the first lady.

e. The first lady does not admire the vice-president.

■ ············   Concept Check 2   ············ ■

Are these two statements inconsistent?

       All real televisions are appliances.

       Some real televisions are appliances.

    Statements can even be made with body language. A man could say, "Sure, sure, I believe you" as he lifts his eyebrows and rolls his eyes. In doing so, *his actions contradict what he says.*

Identifying Self-Contradiction and Oxymorons

Self-contradiction is logical inconsistency within a single statement; one part of the statement is inconsistent with another part. An example would be "This replica of a coin manufactured by the Continental Congress in 1776 is authentic in every detail." Here is a slightly more complicated example: "Sharks were on Earth millions of years before any of the dinosaurs, but a few of the early, small dinosaurs lived before the first sharks." You can just look at that statement and see that the author is confused about sharks; you need not be an expert on sharks and dinosaurs.

Self-contradictory statements are false, but false statements need not be self-contradictory. Nevertheless, there is an intimate connection between falsehood and inconsistency: "False" is another way of saying "inconsistent with the facts."

Concept Check 3

The statement "All California corporations employ 100 or more employees" is false and is inconsistent with the facts about California corporations, but it is not self-contradictory.

a. true   b. false

When George Bush was campaigning for the presidency, he said the following about the resignation of eight campaign aides accused of anti-Semitism: "I hope I stand for anti-bigotry, anti-Semitism, anti-racism. This is what drives me . . ."[2] A slip-up. If you are for anti-Semitism, then you are thereby for bigotry, so Bush contradicted himself. Anti-Bush folks got a big laugh out of this one; many pro-Bush folks believed the press shouldn't have bothered to make such a fuss about it.

Concept Check 4

Explain the self-contradiction that occurs in this dialogue. If you take the colonel literally, his hormones are staging a coup d'état on his brain.

Colonel: (angry at the soldier he is speaking to): Are you on our side or theirs, soldier?

Private: On our side, sir.

Colonel: Soldier, I don't demand very much from my men . . . just that they obey me like they would the word of God.

Nobody has ever built a time machine that could take a person back to an earlier time. Nobody should be seriously trying to build one, either, because a good argument exists for why the machine can never be built. The argument goes like this. Suppose you did have a time machine right now, and you could step into it and travel back to some earlier time. Your actions in that time might then prevent your grandparents from ever having met each other. This would make you not born, and thus not here to step into the time machine. So, the claim that there could be a time machine is self-contradictory.

I wish I could show you a round square; I cannot because "round square" is a **contradiction in terms.** The very meanings of the terms *round* and *square* conflict, so there can be no round squares. "Jumbo shrimp" is not a contradiction in terms; it doesn't mean "large and not large"; it means "large for a shrimp." A contradiction in terms is also called an **oxymoron.** Debates are often started by asking whether a term is an oxymoron. For example, is *artificial intelligence* an oxymoron? Jokes are often based in oxymorons; is *military intelligence* an oxymoron?

When a communicator unintentionally uses a contradiction in terms, this mistake doesn't usually destroy the main point being made. It does, however, cause the audience to lose respect for the communicator. The mistake is a sign of carelessness or lack of sophistication.

A theologian once said that capital punishment is inconsistent with forgiveness. Evidently, he meant that if the government kills a criminal, then it cannot forgive the criminal for his crimes. Forgiveness is fundamental to this theologian's worldview. The inconsistency he noted can be expressed as an inconsistency among the following three statements:

> There should be capital punishment for people convicted of certain crimes.
>
> There should be forgiveness for people convicted of those crimes.
>
> If a person is given capital punishment for a crime, that person cannot be forgiven for that crime.

A more general conclusion can be drawn from this example of inconsistency: Whenever anything is logically inconsistent, it can be broken down into underlying inconsistent statements. Why *round square* is an oxymoron is that the following two statements are inconsistent: "It's round" and "It's square."

■ ············   Concept Check 5   ············ ■

The Health-o-meter personal scale says "100 percent electronic spring-free strain gauge technology. Consistent accuracy . . . up to 300 pounds or 136 kilograms." This ad

a. contains an oxymoron.

b. does not use *consistent* in the sense of logically consistent.

c. makes a mathematical error.

d. says the personal scale is logically consistent with its description.

Noting Inconsistency with Presuppositions

You may have seen cars bearing this threatening bumper sticker: "If you don't like the way I drive, then stay off the sidewalk." The statement *presupposes* that the driver drives on the sidewalk.

Definition The **presuppositions** of a statement are unsaid, relevant statements that would normally be taken for granted in order to make that statement.

Referring to U.S. arms shipments to Iran in exchange for the release of U.S. hostages, comedian Mark Russell, impersonating the president, said, "We sold no weapons to Iran, and we won't do it anymore." The joke here turns on inconsistency. A speaker probably wouldn't say "We won't do it anymore" unless he or she were presupposing that we did it once. But the first part of this joke explicitly says we didn't do it, making a claim that is *inconsistent with a presupposition* of the second part.

■ .... Concept Check 6 .... ■

Gandhi[3] led India to independence from Britain in 1947, a few years after World War II. British soldiers killed, injured, or jailed many Indians in an attempt to suppress the revolution. When asked by a reporter what he thought of Western civilization, Ghandi said, "I think it would be a good idea." Gandhi's joke turns on a presupposition. That presupposition is

a. The British are still there in spirit and were never expelled.

b. The Western world is not civilized.

c. Western civilization is a good idea.

d. He had a good idea.

e. It would be a good idea for the British to be expelled.

Concept Check 7

The United States and Iran were the two parties involved in the 1980s scandal about trading U.S. weapons in return for U.S. hostages who had been seized by Muslim fundamentalists. Impersonating the president, a comedian referred to the trade and said, "There was no third party involved, and we want to thank Israel for all their help." What is the presupposition that is being contradicted?

Well, we've been talking a lot about jokes. Now it's time to get serious. Let's examine astrology — the ancient science of how the stars and planets affect earthly events. My personal reason for not believing in astrology is that I'm a Scorpio. That completes our examination of astrology. It also demonstrates something about presuppositions, doesn't it?

You may enjoy trying to detect the inconsistency that makes you doubt Harpy's excuse in the following story.

> Harpy lived with his grandmother next to the freeway in Cleveland, Ohio. He and his grandmother, Mrs. Harker, were on welfare because his father had disappeared and his mother drank so much every day that she was in no condition to raise her children. Harpy didn't like going to middle school, but he did like model airplane glue. Fortunately, he wasn't old enough to buy it himself. In Ohio you have to be eighteen or have a note from your parents. One morning he asked his welfare worker to buy him some glue. A friend had promised to give him a kit for a small airplane, he said. He wanted to start with fifteen tubes.
>
> Although he never got the glue from her, Harpy did enjoy talking to the welfare worker whenever she came for a visit. A few months after the glue incident, between Christmas and New Year's, she arrived for one of her scheduled morning visits. She was surprised to find Harpy's grandmother alone and crying about the Christmas they had just had. Mrs. Harker was crying because her grandson had given her such wonderful presents for Christmas. She wasn't crying for joy. She was crying for another reason.
>
> The next time the welfare worker had a chance, she asked Harpy about those presents. He responded very seriously, "I talked to God in my dream just before Christmas. God said my grandmother loved me very much, and I hadn't done nothin' for her. She worked real hard all her life, and she deserved somethin' real good. We didn't have no money, so God said to me, 'Harpy, you go to Sears.' I went to Sears."

First, why was the grandmother crying? It was because Harpy had shoplifted the gifts. Do you believe Harpy's reason that he went to Sears? Isn't it inconsistent with something? Harpy was implying that God told him to shoplift the Christmas presents. He might even truly believe God said this, but God probably wouldn't say it. So, Harpy's claim that God told him to shoplift is inconsistent with most people's beliefs about what God would really say.

Refuting General Statements by Finding Counterexamples

Your opponent's statement has been *refuted* when you have made a totally convincing case that the statement is false. A **refutation** is a successful disproof. However, showing that your own belief is inconsistent with your opponent's isn't enough to refute his or her statement. An inconsistency merely shows that both of you cannot be correct. You also need to show that *your* belief is the true one.

A counterexample is one way to refute a general claim. If someone were to say that all mammals normally live on land, you could find many *examples*. A cow is a mammal that normally lives on the land, a squirrel is a mammal that normally lives on land, and so forth. Despite these many examples, the statement isn't true. It is false because it has at least one *counterexample:* the whale. Behind this notion of an *object* being a counterexample is the notion of a *statement* offering a counterexample to another statement. The whole statement "The whale doesn't normally live on land, but it's a mammal" serves as a counterexample to the original statement that all mammals normally live on land.

Definition Statement *B* offers a **counterexample** to statement *A* if (i) *B* is true, and (ii) *B* is inconsistent with *A*, and (iii) *B* is about some specific item in a category mentioned in *A*.

For some general statement *A*, a counterexample will show an example of how *A* has got it wrong. The counterexample will be an exception. A true statement cannot be refuted, so a true generalization will have no counterexamples. Clause (iii) in the definition is there to make sure that the counterexample to "All mammals normally live on land" is a mammal, not a fish. That is, clause (iii) prevents a swordfish from being a counterexample.

Here is a faulty generalization that can be refuted:

Generalization: All professional basketball players are tall.

Example: Michael Jordan is a tall professional basketball player.

Counterexample: Spud Webb is a short professional basketball player.

■ ············ **Concept Check 8** ············ ■

Suppose Chandra says every U.S. president has been a man, and Stephanie says the third president was female. Stephanie has ———— Chandra.

a. contradicted

b. refuted

c. given a counterexample to

d. done all of the above to

■ ············ **Concept Check 9** ············ ■

What statement, if any, would be a counterexample to the statement "All grapefruit are vegetables or fruit"?

a. Some grapefruit are vegetables or fruit.

b. All grapefruit are fruit.

c. No grapefruit are vegetables or fruit.

d. This grapefruit in my hand is not a vegetable.

e. None of the above.

If someone makes the general claim that all *A*'s are *B*'s, you know a good way to test whether this universal generalization is true. Sample some *A*'s and check to see whether they are also *B*'s. If you find even one exception, the universal generalization is refuted. This is the technique you'd mentally follow to challenge the general claim that all birds can fly or that all swans are white. Nonuniversal generalizations cannot be attacked with this technique because they are consistent with there being exceptions. For example, the nonuniversal generalization "Most birds can fly" is consistent with there being exceptions, such as penguins, that cannot fly.

Unfortunately, things are much more complicated in practice. Scientists believe the generalization that there are no ghosts—that all ghosts are nonexistent. Yet every alleged sighting of a ghost appears to be a counterexample to the generalization. Nevertheless, the generalization against ghosts continues to be held; it hasn't been refuted. The scientific community believes that the eyewitness evidence is more likely to be false than their accepted belief in the nonexistence of ghosts. The scientists use their belief to undermine anyone's claim to have found a ghost.

Do you suppose this example is typical of how science operates in general? That is, can this example be generalized to the claim that whenever scientists hold a belief, they will use that belief to undermine others' reasons for rejecting the belief? If so, it follows that scientists are too stubborn and never rationally change their minds.

Actually, scientists are not so stubborn. The scientists will use their well-confirmed belief that there are no ghosts to place a heavy burden of proof on anyone who claims to have refuted this belief. But the scientists' belief can be changed if the evidence for ghosts is strong enough.

Some people criticize science for being a closed club, not sufficiently open to change. Why can't scientists accept more hypotheses on less evidence? Take mind reading for example. The establishment scientists say that telepathy does not exist and that people who report that they have read minds or had their mind read were simply mistaken, perhaps overemphasizing a coincidence. In response, some critics of science point out that mind reading has not been refuted by any experiment, so why can't scientists be open-minded and accept it? The scientists' answer is this. First, as we saw in an earlier chapter, the case against mind reading does count as a disproof, or as a refutation. Second, suppose that there were no refutation; should mind reading then be accepted? No. Lots of **hypotheses** have not been refuted. In this situation there are two central hypotheses: that mind reading does exist and that mind reading doesn't exist. Would the critics of science have the scientists be open-minded and accept both?

Refutation is the engine driving science forward. Science progresses by trying to refute statements. That is, scientists attempt to refute predictions, conjectures, claims, hypotheses, laws, theories, and so on. To do so, they use experiments and observations. Claims that fail the tests or that are inconsistent with the observations and experimental results are declared to have been refuted. The scientific community holds on only to that which it has not yet refuted by experimenting and observing. The truth is what can stand up to this procedure of attempted refutation. For an everyday example of this procedure, suppose you flip the switch to turn on the light in your bedroom and nothing happens. Why did this event occur? That is, why did nothing happen? Can you think of any explanations? How about that the laws of electricity were just repealed? No, that is not a likely explanation. Here are four better ones:

The bulb is burned out.

A fuse is blown.

The switch is broken.

A wire in the circuit is broken.

Which one of the hypotheses is correct? Well, suppose you screw in a new light bulb and it lights up. That settles it. Your scientific experiment has supported the first hypothesis and refuted the others.[4]

Concept Check 10

The following passage describes a scientific test designed to confirm or refute some hypothesis. (i) State the hypothesis to be tested that had to do with both Uranus and something beyond Uranus. (ii) Describe the test — that is, state how the hypothesis was tested. (iii) What possible test result would have been consistent with the hypothesis? (iv) What possible test result would have been inconsistent with the hypothesis? (v) Were the actual test results consistent with the hypothesis or inconsistent with it?

> The success of the English astronomer Edmund Halley in using Newton's laws of mechanics and gravitation to predict the orbits of recurring comets and the success of other astronomers in predicting the positions of the planets convinced almost all astronomers in the Western world that the heavenly bodies are not supernatural beings but are in fact physical objects obeying Newton's laws. In the early 1800s, the outermost planet known to exist in our solar system was Uranus. Unfortunately the positions of Uranus that were predicted from using Newton's laws did not quite agree with the observed positions, and the deviation was too much to attribute to errors made with the astronomical instruments. Astronomers at the time offered two suggestions for the fact that the predicted positions did not agree with the observations. One conjecture was that Newton had made some mistake with his laws of mechanics and that the laws should be revised. The other conjecture was that Uranus wasn't the outermost planet after all — that some other unknown planet was attracting Uranus. To check this latter conjecture, the English astronomer J. C. Adams, in 1843, and the French astronomer Leverrier, in 1845, calculated that the positions of Uranus could be explained by Newton's laws if there were another planet nearby of a specific size and orbit. They suggested that astronomers begin looking in a certain place in the night sky for this planet, a place where the planet must be in order to account for Uranus's orbit. The planet was in fact observed there in 1846 by astronomers from several different observatories. The planet is now called Neptune.

Resolving Inconsistencies

In a Peanuts comic strip Charlie Brown says, "I tell you, Lucy, birds *do* fly south during the winter." Lucy responds with what she takes to be a counterexample: "Chickens are birds, aren't they? You never see a chicken flying south for the winter, do you?"

"Good grief," says Charlie Brown.[5] This exchange contains a good example of mis-interpretation resulting from ambiguity. Lucy takes Charlie Brown's claim one way, but he means it another way. The way Lucy takes it (*all* birds fly south) there is a counterexample; the way Charlie Brown means it (*many* birds fly south), there is no counterexample. Lucy doesn't have a counterexample for what Charlie Brown means. To avoid the misunderstanding, Charlie should *revise his statement* by saying what he means. He should show that he intends a nonuniversal generalization instead of a universal one. The moral is that clearing up ambiguity can *resolve* an inconsistency.

Sometimes a person has inconsistent moral principles that don't appear to be inconsistent. Suppose you believe the moral principle that

(1) People ought to keep their promises to their family.

and also the moral principle that

(2) You shouldn't do anything that is likely to hurt innocent persons.

Now suppose that your father insists you keep your promise to help him with his summer project. His project is, you later learn, to stop the burglaries on your family farm by booby-trapping the windows and doors of the barn. An infrared beam of light will pass by the inside of each window. If anyone forces open the window and sticks his head through, he will get a blast of birdshot in the side of the head. Then think of what could happen to the innocent but curious eight-year-old girl next door who finds the window unlocked on a day when the alarm is activated. She could be hurt, violating (2).

So (1) is incompatible with (2). This is so even if the neighbor girl never actually gets hurt; the problem arises simply because she *could* get hurt. Moral principles are supposed to cover possible situations as well as actual ones. Therefore, you are caught in an ethical dilemma. Which moral principle should be revised? One reasonable change would be to revise principle (1) in favor of (1'):

(1') People ought to keep their promises to their family unless doing so is likely to hurt innocent people.

Principles (1') and (2) are consistent. This process of resolving moral dilemmas by thinking in advance about potential situations is an important way to progress morally. Attention to logical inconsistency can promote moral growth.

■ ············ Concept Check 11 ············ ■

In the following table,[6] there is, on first glance, an inconsistency. After all, if you add up all the men and all the women, you should get 100 percent of all the people. Yet adding up each line gives *more* than 100 percent. Using the principles of charity and fidelity, rewrite the table's title to resolve the inconsistency and make sense of the statistics.

Percent of the U.S. Total Work Force of Each Sex

Year	Men	Women
1970	79.7%	43.4%
1977	77.6%	48.4%
1987	76.3%	55.9%

Source: Federal Reserve Bank of New York, *Quarterly Review* (Autumn 1987).

The notion of resolving contradictions also plays a central role in adding new information into your store of knowledge. Your goal in adding new information — that is, in adopting new beliefs — is always to add more while maintaining consistency. We all try to do this, but there are good ways and not so good ways to do so. Suppose, for example, that your problem is to decide whether George can swim well. If you knew that he was a lifeguard, that would be significant supporting evidence. Almost every lifeguard in the world is a good swimmer — let's say 99 out of a 100. Here is a good argument using that evidence:

> George is a lifeguard.
> 99 out of 100 of the world's lifeguards can swim well.
>
> So, George can swim well.

The two reasons for your conclusion are listed above the line. Your conclusion is below the line. You cannot be absolutely sure of the conclusion on the basis of those two pieces of information, but you can be about 99 percent sure. It would be unreasonable to conclude that he cannot swim well. Now, compare that argument with this one:

> Fred is a Frisian.
> 8 out of 10 Frisians cannot swim well.
>
> So, Fred cannot swim well.

You could be about 80 percent sure that Fred cannot swim well, given these two pieces of information. Both arguments are good arguments because they provide good reasons to believe their respective conclusions. You should add both conclusions into your store of information.

Now for the surprise. Suppose you acquire some new information: that Fred is in fact George. If you hold onto the conclusions from the two previous arguments, you will conclude that Fred can swim well and also can't. It is time to go back and revise your store of information. How are you going to resolve your contradiction?

You should retract your belief that Fred cannot swim well. The best conclusion on the total evidence is that he can swim well, but now you can no longer be 99 percent sure. You need to reduce your estimate of the probability. That is, you continue to believe that Fred can swim well, but you don't believe it as strongly as before.

An important moral can be drawn from this example: *Don't cover up counter evidence*. The more evidence you pay attention to, the better position you are in to draw the best conclusions.

Review of Major Points

In this chapter we examined the notion of inconsistency, which plays such an important role in judgments of improbability. We considered how one sentence can be inconsistent with another, as well as how a sentence can be self-contradictory and can be inconsistent with its presuppositions. A verbal statement can even be inconsistent with the speaker's body language or tone of voice. Finding an example that is inconsistent with a general claim will serve as a counterexample that refutes the claim. Finding a counterexample is not, however, the only way to refute a claim.

When you are given inconsistent information, you should reject some of the information to resolve the contradiction and achieve consistency among the remaining pieces of information. Because you also want to find the truth, you should always reject the information that is the least well supported or the most likely to be false. However, in cases where it isn't clear what to revise, you need to search for more information (and hope that in the meantime you will not have to act on the information you have). One important lesson from this discussion is that, when trying to assess a belief, you should not cover up counterevidence.

Glossary

contradiction in terms Applying two or more terms to give a logically inconsistent description. Calling a farmer's field a round square would be to use a contradiction in terms. Contradictions in terms are also called oxymorons.

counterexample A true statement that is inconsistent with a previous statement and that is about some specific item in a category mentioned in the previous statement. "Spud Webb is a short basketball player" is a counterexample to "All basketball players are tall."

hypothesis An hypothesis is a claim that is proposed. If someone were to offer a possible explanation of some phenomenon, then that explanation would be an hypothesis.

logically inconsistent statements A group of statements that could not all be true together.

oxymoron A contradiction in terms.

presuppositions Unsaid, relevant statements that would normally be taken for granted in order to make a particular statement.

refutation A successful disproof. Refuting a statement requires more than merely contradicting it.

self-contradiction Logical inconsistency within a single statement. Example: "Ahmed is taller than Steve, but Steve is not shorter than Ahmed."

Answers to Concept Checks

1. Answer (b) is inconsistent with the original list.

2. There might or might not be an inconsistency here. It all depends on the ambiguity of *some*. If *some* is supposed to mean "at least one but definitely not all," there is an inconsistency. But if *some* means "at least one and possibly more," there is no inconsistency. Because *some* could be meant either way here, you cannot tell whether an inconsistency exists. Speakers who intend to imply with their word *some* that some are and some aren't should stick in the word *only* and say "Only some of the real televisions are appliances."

3. Answer (a). It could be true in a world in which there were no small corporations.

4. In demanding that the private obey his word like the word of God, he *is* demanding very much—too much. This is inconsistent with his saying that he isn't demanding very much. What the colonel said implied (required) both "I do demand very much" and "I don't demand very much." He implied that something is so and also not so, which is the telltale sign of a logical inconsistency. What the colonel says is amusing because he is so obvious about being inconsistent. We in the audience are charitable and do not take him literally; instead we note the irony and reinterpret him to mean simply that he is *very* demanding. The dialogue is from the film *Full Metal Jacket*.

5. Answer (b). It means "unchanging" here.

6. Answer (b). He assumed that the Western world is not civilized and was remarking that it would be a good idea for it to become civilized. Because his assumption is not the questioner's assumption, the comment is funny.

7. If you thank Israel for their help, you presuppose that Israel did help and thus that there *was* a third party involved after all.

8. Answer (a). If you contradict someone, you don't have to be correct, but if you refute someone you *must* be correct. For this reason, Stephanie has contradicted Chandra but not refuted her. So (b) is the wrong answer. Stephanie has also not given a counterexample to Chandra's statement (Chandra gave no argument), because a counterexample must be correct, yet what Stephanie says is incorrect. So (c) is also the wrong answer.

9. Answer (e). True statements have no counterexamples. If something (e.g., grape-fruit) is a fruit, then it is a vegetable or a fruit. Similarly, if Abdul is an Egyptian, then he is either a vegetable or an Egyptian.

10. (i) Another planet beyond Uranus was attracting it sufficiently to account for the actually observed positions of Uranus in the sky according to an accounting using Newton's laws. (The hypothesis is not simply that there is another planet.) (ii) It was tested by using Newton's laws to predict where the new planet should be located. (iii) Test results consistent with the hypothesis: finding a new planet in the predicted location after a careful search. (iv) Test results inconsistent with the hypothesis: not finding a new planet in the predicted location after a careful search. (v) Yes.

11. "Percent of Each Sex That Are Members of the Total U.S. Work Force." In 1970, for example, 79.7 percent of all U.S. men were employed, while less than half of U.S. women were employed.

Review and Writing Exercises

Inconsistency

1. If somebody says to you that it is raining and it is not, by applying the principle of charity you can reasonably assume that the person intends to say something logically inconsistent — something that is really so and not so in the same sense at the same time.

   a. true   b. false

2. The principle of charity for inconsistency

   a. is a technique of thought for revealing or uncovering a contradiction in one's own thinking.

   b. says to be charitable to your principles regardless of the inconsistency in other people's principles.

   c. is applied to consistent sets of statements to turn them into inconsistent sets.

   d. says to try to find a consistent interpretation.

3. If Susan says, "Andre Agassi from Las Vegas once won the French Open Tennis Tournament," you can contradict her by saying "No, he didn't."

   a. true   b. false

4. Are these three statements logically consistent with each other?

   Only bears sleep in these woods.

   Squirrels sleep at night, but not in these woods.

   If a thing sleeps in these woods, then it's a bear.

5. Read the following newspaper editorial.

> Tfuneo Sakai won't be attending classes at the University of Rochester's William E. Simon School of Business this fall. He was admitted all right, but that was before the Eastman Kodak Company found out he worked for Fuji Photo Film in Japan and would actually be associating right there in the same classroom with some of its own employees in a two-year master's degree program for middle-level businessmen. Kodak doesn't approve of that kind of fraternization with its business rivals, and Sakai has been sent packing.
>
> When Kodak barks, Rochester jumps. The film and camera company isn't just the city's leading industry; it's also the reason why the university has one of the ten largest endowments in the country. Other American universities have run into criticism for undertaking research under proprietary contracts with private companies or for accepting funds from foreign countries or other sources of beneficence with strings attached specifying what's going to be taught with that money. But only in Rochester, so far as anyone knows, can a corporate benefactor actually reach right down into the admissions process to determine who's fit to be educated.
>
> Japanese companies like to send their employees to study here so that they can learn more about American business principles and practices. Sakai certainly obtained a terrific object lesson at the Simon school, which has heretofore loudly proclaimed its commitment to free markets and an absence of regulatory oversight. Kodak, for its part, says it was only concerned that some of its people might have felt constrained from talking in school while Sakai was around for fear that they might give away some company trade secrets. Meanwhile, Kodak has announced that it's giving the Simon school another $36,000 a year to train business executives in how to take creative risks. Obviously, there's no connection between the two events.[7]

The editorial writer reports that Kodak's contributions to the university are the real reason why the university has one of the ten largest endowments in the country, yet the article itself contradicts this claim by suggesting between the lines that this is *not* the real reason why the university has one of the ten largest endowments in the country.

a.   true   b.   false

6. The writer of the editorial in question 5 explicitly says there's no connection between the two events (requesting the student rejection and donating $36,000) but implies between the lines that there really is a connection, so the writer accuses Kodak of committing a contradiction between what they say is so and what is really so.

a.   true   b.   false

7. Given your common knowledge, and paying attention to the source of the information in question 5's editorial, it is reasonable to be skeptical and say it is fairly *improbable* that Kodak really intends to give $36,000 more a year to the University of Rochester.

   a. true   b. false

8. The writer of the editorial in question 5 says the Simon business school at the University of Rochester has publicly proclaimed a commitment to free markets and an absence of regulatory oversight, yet the writer suggests that the school's actions show they don't actually have that commitment, so the editor indirectly accuses the Simon school of an inconsistency between what they say and what they do.

   a. true   b. false

9. Notice in the following dialogue how Emilio slowly uncovers Washington's inconsistent set of moral beliefs.

   Emilio: Listen to what it says here in the paper. "David Jones was especially bitter after the experience. After commenting on the incident, he said 'I don't see why having sex with your mother is wrong. If it feels good, then it's OK. Of course, I would never do it; I wouldn't want to go to jail. Besides, in my own case I never really liked my mother, God rest her soul, but I don't believe it's unethical.'" Damn, Washington. Can you believe Jones really said that? I think these jerks ought to get what they deserve.

   Washington: What's that?

   Emilio: About twenty years making license plates in the prison factory.

   Washington: Do you mean Jones or the guy who would have sex with his mother?

   Emilio: Not Jones.

   Washington: Who's to judge?

   Emilio: What do you mean by that? I'm to judge, that's who!

   Washington: I doubt it. It's not your place. Are you planning on playing God here? It's for God to decide these things.

   Emilio: Are you saying that no ordinary person is supposed ever to make any moral judgments of right and wrong about anybody else's behavior?

   Washington: You got it.

   Emilio: You don't really believe that. I know what you've done.

   Washington: What are you talking about? Done what, when?

   Emilio: Remember the little boy you found in the psychology building when we were on our way to class?

   Washington: Yes.

Emilio: Well, you made a moral decision right there. You could tell he was lost, and you helped him find his way back to his family. He had gotten off the elevator on the wrong floor. You were fifteen minutes late to your psych class.

Washington: Just because I helped him doesn't mean I made any moral judgment of him.

Emilio: Right, you didn't judge him, but you did judge your own action. You acted to help, but you could have acted simply by doing nothing. A decision not to get involved is a moral decision. You chose. You weren't playing God. You just judged between the two ways for you to act.

Washington: OK, but I judged my own actions, I didn't judge anyone else's.

Emilio: Suppose I'd been alone and had found the same boy.

Washington: Then it would have been your problem.

Emilio: Wouldn't you have expected me to do the same thing you did?

Washington: Yeah, I'd have predicted that. I know you're apt to do that kind of thing just because you're you. It comes natural, Turkeyface.

Emilio: But wouldn't you have thought badly of me if I'd not done what you expected? You do believe I have the free will to do something you don't expect, right?

Washington: Uh, yes. OK, I'd approve if you did help the kid. Which reminds me, you never paid back the money I gave you when we both had turkey sandwiches at lunch the day before Thanksgiving.

Emilio: Oh. Well, Elephantface, your memory is as good as any elephant in your herd.

Washington: Why is it easier to remember who owes you money than who you owe money to?

Emilio: Maybe because it's easier to judge than to be judged.

Identify the inconsistent set of Washington's moral beliefs that Emilio uncovered with his questioning.

10. If a set of statements is inconsistent, then any addition to the set that doesn't revise the original statements will preserve inconsistency.

    a. true   b. false

11. State a sentence that uses a new example of an oxymoron.

■ 12. Is this group of three statements logically inconsistent? (In this problem, interpret the word *some* to mean "at least one and possibly all.")

    Every dog chases some cat.

    Some cats chase no dogs.

    Some dogs chase all the cats.

■ 13. The following statement is false:

    A rose is not a rose.

    a.   true   b.   false

■ 14. The following statement is self-contradictory:

    A rose is not a rose.

    a.   true   b.   false

■ 15. If a person is being inconsistent, as we have been using this term, then the person has irregular patterns of behavior or frequently changes his or her beliefs.

    a.   true   b.   false

16. Are these four statements logically consistent?

    Only bears sleep in this house.

    Goldilocks is not a bear.

    Smokey is a bear.

    Goldilocks and Smokey both sleep in this house although Smokey sleeps downstairs and Goldilocks sleeps upstairs.

17. Consider this list of statements:

    i. $x + 1 = 10$

    ii. x is unequal to 7

    iii. $x < 3$

If the following statement is added to the above three, will the resultant set of four statements be consistent?

$$x = 9$$

18. Consider this list of three statements:

    i. Modern works of art are not romantic.

    ii. But they are occasionally erotic.

    iii. However, an erotic work of art could be romantic.

Which statement(s) below, if added separately to the above list, would make an inconsistent list?

    a.   More than one romantic work of art is erotic.

    b.   Only one romantic work of art is erotic.

    c.   Two romantic works of art are modern works.

    d.   Romantic works of art are not modern.

    e.   All of the above.

■ 19. Is this set of statements inconsistent, provided there is no equivocation?

> The human body is totally a material thing.
>
> The human mind is totally a spiritual thing.
>
> Mind and body can interact.
>
> Spirit and matter cannot interact.

20. Which of the following statements, if added to the four statements in question 19, would make the new list of five statements be consistent?

   a.   Spirit and matter do interact.

   b.   The human body is both a material and a spiritual thing.

   c.   Sometimes the human body is a material thing and sometimes it is not.

   d.   None of the above.

■ 21. What logical inconsistency or improbability, if any, occurs in this hypothetical news story?

> The Soviet KGB says that it sold 150 bear missiles for $3 million to Central American freedom fighters. It says the USSR received full payment. The guerrillas say they paid $3 million to a representative of Soviet intelligence; they say they were promised they would receive 150 bear missiles, but only 50 missiles were ever delivered.

22. Defend your evaluation of the quality of the following explanation:

> Approximately two-thirds of the doctor's patients caught Barre's disease. This fact can be explained by pointing out that the doctor breathed directly on all his patients, that the doctor had Barre's disease, too, and that whenever a person with Barre's disease breathes directly on another person the other person will catch it, too.

23. Is the following sentence self-contradictory?

> Voters must be club members, but *some* club members are nonvoters.

24. Is the following sentence self-contradictory?

> Voters must be club members, but *no* club members are nonvoters.

■ 25. Are these two statements contradictory? (Assume the term *the senator* refers to the same person in both statements.)

   a.   The wife of the senator is an interesting person.

   b.   The senator has no wife.

■ 26. If two statements are consistent, then they've got to be true.

   a.   true   b.   false

27. If a group of two statements is consistent, then at least one of them must be true.

   a.   true   b.   false

■ 28. It is impossible for contradictory statements to accurately characterize the physical world, although people could hold contradictory beliefs about the world.

   a.   true   b.   false

29. My friend Stan told me that yesterday he had met my wife's friend Kate at a political meeting. He said they were going out to dinner this Saturday. My wife told me that she talked to Kate earlier today and Kate said she had met Stan at a political meeting; Kate told her that she and Stan were going to play tennis together on Saturday. What inconsistency, if any, is there here?

30. What inconsistency, if any, occurs in the following passage?

> [Bryn Mawr College's president] Martha Carrey Thomas, the second woman in the world to receive a doctorate of philosophy, . . . supervised a rigorous, classical education as free as possible from male distraction: "It is undesirable to have the problems of love and marriage presented for decision to a young girl during the four years when she ought to devote her energies to profiting by the only systematic intellectual training she is likely to receive during her life." Even if she were so ill-advised as to marry, the Bryn Mawr graduate should ideally be "both economically and psychologically independent" from her husband.[8]

   a.   One cannot both supervise and not supervise a rigorous, classical education as free as possible from male distraction.

   b.   Thomas suggests Bryn Mawr graduates should marry and not marry.

   c.   The author is advocating both that a woman be dependent and be independent.

   d.   There is no inconsistency in the passage.

31. Why is inconsistency at the heart of logical reasoning?

■ 32. Are these two statements logically inconsistent?

   Hell doesn't exist. Yet in a different sense it really does.

■ 33. Suppose Alex says, "Any oxide will melt if heated to at least 2000 degrees," and Linda says "Yttrium barium oxide melts only above 2300 degrees." Has Linda made a claim inconsistent with Alex's?

   a.   can't tell (briefly say why)   b.   yes   c.   no

34. Referring to the previous question, explain why you cannot tell whether Linda has refuted Alex.

35. If three statements are inconsistent (with each other), then at least one of them must be false.

   a.   true   b.   false

■ 36. If John says something that contradicts what Sandra says, does it follow that either John or Sandra is lying?

37. Is the following sentence, which contains three substatements, self-contradictory?

    An asterique is an emulator; all emulators can transverse-bilateralize, and an asterique cannot transverse-bilateralize.

38. What is the most significant inconsistency revealed in the Rose Bird passage about women and the courts in the end-of-chapter questions for Chapter 5?

    a. Delicacy in women is inconsistent with toughness in women.

    b. Rulings in the Supreme Court have been inconsistent with the prohibition of an affirmative action plan.

    c. Maintaining a sexual balance is inconsistent with eliminating a manifest sexual imbalance.

    d. Rulings of the Supreme Court have been inconsistent with the ideals of egalitarianism embodied in the Constitution of the United States.

    e. The frailty and inequality of women is inconsistent with the qualifications needed to practice law or earn a guaranteed minimum wage.

39. You are asked to find out if the following statement is true. What should a good critical thinker do? "A few dinosaurs lived on Earth before the first sharks, and some sharks were on Earth millions of years before any of the dinosaurs, but there are still some other sharks in today's oceans, although no dinosaurs that we've so far detected." Yes, the instructions are imprecise.

40. If I've contradicted what the manager of the New York Giants says, then I've thereby refuted what the manager says.

    a. true   b. false

■ 41. Are these four statements inconsistent?

    Either the U.S. or Russia will start a global thermonuclear war; nobody else can.

    If Russia starts it, then we will all die.

    Yet if the U.S. starts it, then we will all die, too.

    However, God has given us the knowledge that we won't all die, no matter what happens.

42. Create two graphs — one, a bar graph; the other, a pie chart. Make the two graphs be inconsistent with each other.

● 43. Write a short essay discussing whether the following two quotations are really inconsistent. Mention why somebody might say they are and why somebody else might say they aren't. Then try to resolve the issue of consistency. Stick to the issue; do not discuss the issue of whether slavery is morally wrong.

    "Slavery is morally wrong." (Abraham Lincoln for the Union)

    "Slavery is not morally wrong." (Jefferson Davis for the Confederacy)

Counterexamples

1. If statement *A* is a counterexample to *B*, then *B* is a counterexample to *A*.

   a. true   b. false

■ 2. (a) Create an original universal generalization about AIDS or about being HIV positive. (b) Give an example that is consistent with it and supports it, and (c) a successful counterexample that is inconsistent with it and refutes it.

■ 3. If it is possible, create an original statement that is easily recognized to be a universal generalization with no counterexamples.

4. If it is possible, create an original statement that is easily recognized to be a universal generalization that has a counterexample.

5. Create a *statement* (as opposed to merely a sentence) with nothing of significance left implicit that would be a counterexample to the claim that all things in the universe are cooler than a candle flame.

■ 6. Give a counterexample to the claim that all promises should be kept.

7. Identify the claim below that is a universal generalization that has no counterexamples.

   a. Most children know how to ride a bicycle.

   b. "There is no there there," said Gertrude Stein when she was talking about Oakland, California.

   c. All professional basketball players in the U.S. like to eat Cheerios.

   d. Every planet around the sun is held in orbit primarily by the force of gravity.

   e. In general, General Abrams has more clout than General Franklin.

8. Here is a refutation of the astrologers' claim that the stars determine every person's destiny. It is from the *Confessions* of St. Augustine, a Roman, who was a Catholic father born in North Africa and who wrote in about 400 A.D. First, briefly explain why his challenge is a successful refutation. Then revise and weaken the claim by making it less precise so that St. Augustine's remarks won't refute the revised claim.

> Firminus had heard from his father that when his mother had been pregnant with him a slave belonging to a friend of his father's was also about to bear. . . . It happened that since the two women had their babies at the same instant, the men were forced to cast exactly the same horoscope for each newborn child down to the last detail, one for his [father's] son, the other for the little slave. . . . Yet Firminus, born to wealth in his parents' house, had one of the more illustrious careers in life . . . whereas the slave had no alleviation of his life's burden.

Does the Conclusion Follow from the Premises?

I n any argument, the arguer intends the reasons to imply the conclusion. For example, if you want people to conclude that your product is the best buy for them, you ought to give them some good reasons. What makes the reasons good enough is that they *imply* that your product is the best buy. This chapter explores how the notion of implication lies at the heart of logical reasoning. The notion is ambiguous because, as we shall see, there are two kinds of argumentation that might be involved — deductive or inductive. The main question we'll address is "How do you tell whether the reasons really do imply the conclusion?" The notion of inconsistency that we explored in Chapter 9 is the key to understanding how a conclusion follows from the supporting reasons.

Implying with Certainty Versus with Probability

From the supposition that all moons, real and imaginary, are made of green cheese, does it follow that the Earth's real moon is made of green cheese? Yes, it **follows with certainty**. That is, you can be certain of it on the basis of the reason given. However, the reason is an odd one, isn't it? As you can see from this odd argument, the notion of *following from* is not about truth but only about what would be true if something else were true.

> In any good argument, the conclusion follows from the reasons given.

Try your hand at spotting what follows from the assumption that everything said in the following letter to the editor is correct:

Dear Editor:

It is no coincidence that society today is faced with a multitude of social problems that didn't exist forty years ago. We have reached a point when a school district reassigns fifty-six counselors whose primary responsibilities are in the area of abortion, drug addiction and suicide. Why? Because the family unit has been relegated to the backburner in our society through social changes, i.e., divorce is the way out of troubles, free love is OK, drugs in moderation are OK—in fact, everything is all right so long as it feels good and right.

The time has come, if it isn't too late already, for those citizens concerned with the preservation of moral values to shout loud and clear to Planned Parenthood, population control advocates, the ACLU, evolutionists, the scientific community and any other organization that is for the destruction of our society that we are not going to stand idly by even if we are relegated to being branded petty, zealous, and righteous religious fanatics.[1]

Does it follow for certain that the letter is saying that the scientific community is for the destruction of our society? Yes, because its last statement uses the phrase "and any other organization that is for the destruction of our society." In using this phrase, the writer presupposes that any group mentioned previously is also for the destruction of our society, and the scientific community is named previously.

Does it also follow for certain that the author of the letter believes God is good? No, this conclusion does not follow for sure. However, if you are familiar with the ideology, or worldview, of people who would write this sort of letter, it would be a very *good guess* that he does believe God is good. You are entitled to say that it **follows with probability**, or that it probably follows.

In a successful argument, the conclusion follows from the reasons given. The reasons used in an argument are called its **premises**.

Sometimes the inference can make an argument's conclusion follow with certainty, but in most arguments the premises are intended only to make the conclusion follow probably. For example, suppose you have talked to some baseball fans and they've all told you that the Baltimore Orioles won't win the next pennant. Suppose that on the basis of this information you conclude that the Orioles won't win the next pennant. You've just created an argument whose conclusion is probable, given the premises. Just *how* probable will be difficult to pin down precisely. If you talked only to fans who have biased views about the Orioles, your information makes your conclusion less probable than if you had talked to a wider variety of baseball fans, including perhaps some baseball experts.

Let's now consider an argument whose reasons, if true, *force* the conclusion to hold. Suppose that you were to hear that all vice-presidents of the United States since Martin Van Buren have secretly been the coordinators of U.S. intelligence operations during their terms of office. Also suppose you were to hear that Andrew Johnson was the vice-president of the United States under President Ulysses S. Grant, a president who served after Van Buren. What would this information imply with certainty? It would imply that Andrew Johnson was once the coordinator of U.S. intelligence operations. Another way of saying this is that if you wanted someone to conclude that Andrew Johnson was once the coordinator of U.S. Intelligence operations, you might consider giving the person the following two reasons: (1) All vice-presidents of the United States since Van Buren have secretly been the coordinators of U.S. intelligence operations during their terms of office, and (2) Andrew Johnson was the vice-president of the United States under President Ulysses Grant, a president who served after Van Buren. Reasons 1 and 2 *imply with certainty* that Johnson once coordinated U.S. intelligence operations.

However, there are other inferences you could make from 1 and 2. For example, you might offer them as reasons to conclude that Andrew Johnson once held secret discussions with President Grant about U.S. intelligence operations. This would be a reasonable conclusion to draw. The conclusion is very likely on the basis of the information at hand. However, it is not implied with certainty. Instead, it is *implied with probability*.

These new notions of implying with certainty and implying with probability can be defined in terms of the notions of inconsistency and improbability:

Definition A statement, or group of statements, *P* **implies** a statement *Q* **with certainty** if these two conditions hold: (1) it is logically inconsistent for *P* to be true without *Q* also being true, and (2) *Q* isn't irrelevant to *P*.

Definition A statement, or group of statements, *P* **implies** a statement *Q* **with probability** if these two conditions hold: (1) it is improbable for *P* to be true without *Q* also being true, and (2) *Q* isn't irrelevant to *P*.

Clause (2) appears in both definitions to rule out something such as this: "John Adams was the second U.S. president" implies "7 + 5 = 12." Without clause (2), we'd have to call this a good example of implication, but actually we want to say that American politics doesn't imply anything at all about arithmetic.

Implying with probability is the vaguer notion. Implying with probability admits of degrees. The probability cannot usually be measured with a number but instead is graded as high, low, very high, and so forth. However, in those rare cases when the probability can be measured with a number, the probability is always less than 100 percent; if the probability were exactly 100 percent, we'd say *P* implies *Q* with certainty, not probability.

When someone presents an argument intending to convince us of the conclusion, he or she tries to get us to see that an inconsistency or improbability is involved in accepting the premises but not the conclusion. If the arguer can show this, then the argument's premises really do imply their conclusion. The two definitions above try to codify these ideas. In criticizing an argument, as opposed to presenting it, the critic might try to show that there is no inconsistency or no improbability in accepting the premises while rejecting the conclusion. If the critic shows this, then the argument's premises do not really imply their conclusion.

To ask whether a statement *implies* another statement is to ask an ambiguous question. This question could mean implies with certainty or implies with probability. When *implies* occurs alone, it is best to assume that both senses might be intended. For example, suppose a person is arrested by the county sheriff. Does this action imply that the person is guilty of the crime he or she is arrested for? The best answer is "yes and no," depending on what is meant by the word *imply*. It doesn't follow with certainty that the arrested person is guilty, but it does follow with some probability. This is because it is much more probable that the arrested person is the guilty one than that a typical nonarrested person is.

Even if it is probable that the person is guilty, the mere fact that the person is arrested does not make the probability so high that you as a juror should vote for conviction on the basis of just this fact. You shouldn't vote for conviction until you have been shown that the probability of guilt is high enough to be called "beyond a reasonable doubt." District attorneys try to show that from the evidence of the case it follows with very high probability that the defendant is guilty. A D.A. could never hope to show that the guilt follows with certainty.

The following are different ways of saying that a statement P implies a statement Q with certainty:

> Q can be deduced validly from P.
>
> Q follows with certainty from P.
>
> Q follows necessarily from P.
>
> Q is logically implied by P.
>
> Q follows logically from P.
>
> Q can be deduced from P.
>
> P logically implies Q.
>
> P necessitates Q.
>
> P entails Q.

Let's look at some more examples of "following from" to get a better understanding of what follows from what and whether it certainly follows or just probably follows.

From the statement "The United States is more a Christian country than it is a Muslim country," does it follow that George Washington was the first president of the United States? No, this statement about Washington doesn't follow. It is *irrelevant* to the statement about religion, although it is consistent with the statement. Irrelevant statements never follow.

Does the statement "Everybody admires the first lady" imply with certainty that the current secretary of state admires the first lady? Yes, it does. Suppose you then learn that *not* everybody admires the first lady. Does the conclusion about the secretary of state admiring the first lady still follow with certainty from the statement

"Everybody admires the first lady"? Yes, it still does. The point can be stated more generally:

> If a statement *P* implies a statement *Q*, then it still does even when you learn that *P* is false.

Implying is a matter of "what if." We all do a lot of logical reasoning about false situations. Politicians, for example, will say, "This bill isn't law, but what if it were law? If it were law, then it would imply that things would be improved. So let's vote for the bill." The ability to do this kind of "what if" reasoning is valuable. At the beginning of this discussion, we did some "what if" reasoning from two statements: that Andrew Johnson was vice-president under Grant, who served after Van Buren, and that all vice-presidents of the United States since Van Buren have secretly been the coordinators of U.S. intelligence activities. Then we investigated what these statements implied. However, both statements are false. Vice-presidents have not actually been the coordinators of U.S. intelligence activities. Also, Andrew Johnson was not Grant's vice-president.[2]

Consider this argument: All happy people are rich, all beautiful people are happy, so all beautiful people are rich. Although the key terms *happy*, *beautiful*, and *rich* are vague, the conclusion nevertheless follows from the two premises with certainty. The moral is that you can have certainty in your reasoning even while using vague concepts.

If I feel certain that a particular person wouldn't have been arrested if he or she weren't guilty, that doesn't make it certain that the person *is* guilty. My psychological state of feeling certain doesn't make the person's being guilty follow with certainty from the fact about being arrested. *The certainty mentioned in the definition of "follows with certainty" is not a psychological notion; it is a logical notion.* That is, certainty is about the logical relationship of support among statements. Someone's feeling certain that *Q* follows from *P* is not what makes *Q* follow from *P* with certainty. *Q* follows from *P* with certainty only if it would be impossible for *P* to be true while *Q* is false. Another way of saying this is that *Q* follows from *P* with certainty only if *P* fully supports *Q* — that is, only if *P* entails *Q*.[3]

Julius Caesar did conquer Rome. If this point were in doubt, some historian might point out that it could be concluded with certainty from these two pieces of information:

> The general of the Roman Legions of Gaul crossed the Rubicon River and conquered Rome.
>
> Caesar was the general of the Roman Legions in Gaul at that time.

If "at that time" were missing from the second statement, it would *not* be clear whether it follows with certainty that Caesar conquered Rome. Here is why. Maybe Caesar was the general at one time but Tiberius was the general at the time of the river crossing. The more doubt you have that "at that time" is intended, the less sure you can be in concluding that Caesar conquered Rome.

Concept Check 1

If an advertisement promotes a sale of clothes that are 100 percent genuine simulated cotton, then it

a. follows with certainty
b. follows with probability
c. doesn't follow

that this is an offer to sell clothes that are essentially all cotton.

Concept Check 2

What follows with certainty from these three sentences?

> Only bears sleep in this house.
> Goldilocks is not a bear.
> Smokey is a bear.

a. Smokey does not sleep in this house.
b. Smokey does sleep in this house.
c. None of the above.

Distinguishing Deduction from Induction

When someone says to you, "That's a good argument," you need to figure out what the person means by "good." Arguments are properly evaluated as being good if they are deductively valid, deductively sound, or inductively strong.

Definition An argument is **deductively valid** if its conclusion follows with certainty from the premises.

Definition An argument is **deductively sound** if its conclusion follows with certainty from the premises and all the premises are actually true.

Definition An argument is **inductively strong** if its conclusion follows with high probability from the premises.

An argument can also be evaluated as to whether it is understandable for the audience intended to receive it, as to whether it addresses the issue under discussion, and so on. However, this section will focus only on validity, soundness, and inductive strength.

By definition, a **deductive argument** is an argument presented with the intention of being valid or sound. By definition, an **inductive argument** is one intended to be inductively strong. If the arguer's intentions aren't clear, then it's indeterminate whether the argument is deductive or inductive. It will be one or the other, though — there is no third kind. Here is an example that one speaker might give as a deductive argument but that another might give as an inductive argument:

> If she's Brazilian, then she speaks Portuguese. She does speak Portuguese.
> So, she is Brazilian.

This would be a deductive argument if its author intended for it to be deductively valid (which it isn't). The argument would be inductive if its author intended that speaking Portuguese be a "sign" or "positive evidence" making it probable that the person is Brazilian, in which case it would have some inductive strength. If you cannot guess the intentions of the arguer, you cannot tell whether you have been given an inductive argument or a deductive one, and you should assess the argument both ways. Then apply the principle of charity for arguments and suppose that the arguer intended the argument to be interpreted in the way in which it gets the best assessment.

Although inductive strength is a matter of degree, deductive validity and deductive soundness are not. In this sense, deductive reasoning is much more cut and dried than inductive reasoning. Nevertheless, inductive strength is not a matter of personal preference; it is a matter of whether the premise *ought* to promote a higher degree of belief in the conclusion.

The technical term *deductively valid* is for arguments only. A sentence shouldn't be called deductively valid unless it contains a whole argument. *Deductively valid* does not mean "legitimate." When somebody is said to have made a valid criticism of somebody's argument, the word *valid* is not being used in our sense.[4]

A comment about how to use the words *true* and *false* in regard to arguments is in order here. Declarative sentences are almost always true or false. For example, "It's noon" is a declarative sentence. "What time is it?" is not true or false, and it's not a declarative sentence. A command is neither true nor false; ditto for an argument.

Arguments can be good or poor, valid or invalid, sound or unsound, strong or weak; but it would be confusing to call them true or false.

Out on the street, people are not so careful with the use of our technical terminology. From the barest clues, the detective Sherlock Holmes cleverly "deduced" who murdered whom, but actually he made educated guesses and thus produced inductive arguments, not deductive ones. Charles Darwin, who discovered the process of evolution, is famous for his "deduction" that circular atolls in the oceans are actually coral growths on the top of barely submerged volcanoes, but to be precise he really performed an induction, not a deduction. He could not be sure.

Concept Check 3

Assess the quality of the following argument:

> Most all wolves are not white. King is a wolf you will soon be seeing at the zoo, so he is not going to be a white one.

a. inductively very weak
b. inductively strong
c. deductively valid

Concept Check 4

Is this argument deductively valid?

> The current president of Russia is an Asian, and all Asians are dope addicts, so the president of Russia is a dope addict.

Concept Check 5

Is the argument in Concept Check 4 deductively sound?

At the heart of the notion of deductive validity is the notion that, if an argument's conclusion follows with certainty from its premises, you would be violating the cardinal rule to avoid inconsistency if you were to assert the premises while denying the conclusion. So, for reasons of logical consistency,

> In deductively valid reasoning, true premises will never lead to a false conclusion.

Concept Check 6

If it can be done, give an example of a valid argument with a false conclusion. If it cannot be done, say why.

Valid reasoning will never lead you to a false conclusion, but the trouble is that invalid reasoning can lead you to a true conclusion and thereby trick you into thinking that the reasoning is really valid. Here is an example. You are already committed to believing the fact that a dog is not a cat. Therefore, if I argue as follows that a dog is not a cat, you will likely accept the argument:

> A lion is a cat.
> A dog is not a lion.
> ―――――――――――――
> So, a dog is not a cat.

This argument looks good at first, but it is a terrible one, giving absolutely no good reason to believe that a dog is not a cat. The argument is deductively invalid. What the arguer has done here is preach to the already converted. We have a psychological tendency to cheer for any argument that concludes with what we already agree with. We lower our standards of logical reasoning because we are happy with the conclusion. It's an unfortunate tendency that we all need to be careful to watch out for.

As we've seen in previous chapters and as we will explore in greater depth in later chapters, deciding whether a conclusion follows with probability from the premises is a matter of high art, deep science, and common sense. However, with deductive arguments, the following form is cut and dried. Consequently, if an argument is deductively valid and there is something wrong with the conclusion, we can be sure there is something wrong with one of the premises, although we still need to figure out which premise is the faulty one. For example, the following argument seems to be deductively valid:

> If something goes away, there has to be a place where it goes. In the morning, night is gone. So it must have gone somewhere and now be hidden someplace.

Do you agree that this is a deductively valid argument? It is. The conclusion is obviously false, though, isn't it? Would you agree that therefore the argument must have a faulty premise somewhere? The first premise looks OK, because when a horse runs away there is a place where it goes, even if you can't find it. The horse has to go somewhere, right? No. The first premise is not OK. When a wooden sculpture of a horse "goes away" by burning up, there is no place where the sculpture goes. It simply ceases to exist. A transformation of the molecules occurs. Similarly, in the morning the night just ceases to be; it doesn't go anywhere. So the whole trouble begins in the argument's first sentence.

You might think this explanation rather obvious, but it hasn't always been so obvious to people. Many ancient Greeks would have accepted the faulty first premise as common sense. Times change. A related, enduring philosophical debate concerns whether there is a place where you go when you die. Is death more like a horse's running away or more like a wooden sculpture's burning up? Well, we cannot settle this deep question here, but it is interesting to think about.

Sound deductive arguments are also called **proofs**, but so are strong inductive arguments, although in a different sense of the word *proof*. All mathematical proofs are deductively sound, but scientific proofs usually are not. Some scientific proofs meet the standards of mathematical proofs, but most do not. When science proves that dinosaurs are extinct, the evidence for this conclusion does not imply the conclusion with certainty, only with probability. The scientific proof that Jupiter revolves around the sun doesn't meet the high standard of the mathematical proof that $7 + 5 = 12$. Consequently, we can be more sure that $7 + 5 = 12$ than that Jupiter revolves. Nevertheless, the revolution is *almost* certain because the evidence is overwhelming. Ditto for the extinction of dinosaurs. Science accepts deductively sound arguments as proofs, as in mathematics; but, unlike mathematics, science also permits inductively strong arguments to be proofs.

Mathematical proofs that involve what mathematicians call "induction" are deductive and not inductive, by our standards. Similarly, in the field of mathematics called probability theory or statistics, the conclusions of mathematical proofs will be probability statements, but these proofs are deductively sound arguments whose conclusions about probability follow with certainty, not with probability. They are about probability, but they are deductive, not inductive.

When people say to you, "That may be a strong argument, but it's not really a proof," they are probably using *proof* in the sense of our "deductive proof" or "deductively sound argument." If this is what they are saying, they are making the good point that just because an argument is inductively strong, it need not be deductively sound.

Drawing Conclusions from Large Passages and Texts

So far we have been concentrating on arguments in which a conclusion has followed either from a single statement or from a small group of statements. However, the logical reasoner also has the ability to decide whether a conclusion follows from everything said in a book or in a long article. For example, does it follow from Herman Melville's book *Moby Dick* that the author believes each person has an inner nature that cannot be changed? Answering this question is much more difficult, and it won't be done here. An analogous question might be to ask whether, from Albert Einstein's 1916 physics paper introducing the general theory of relativity, it follows that there can be black holes in outer space. Black holes are places where gravity is so strong that a flashlight's light would go out into empty space and then be bent back toward the flashlight; light cannot escape from the hole. Because it takes special expertise to answer these sorts of questions, let's work instead on the following newspaper article. The concept checks after it will ask what follows from the information given in the article.

Jail Stun Gun Used to Abuse, Court Is Told

SAN JOSE—Amid claims that Santa Clara County Jail officers are misusing electric stun guns, a former jail nurse said she watched officers use a Taser gun to shock a cowering psychiatric inmate.

Superior Court Judge Henry Ramsey on Wednesday called a temporary halt to using the device in county jails as attorneys and county officials continued to debate the Taser, which allegedly led to the death of [the] inmate last week. Ramsey also ordered a broad review of jail officers' hiring and training.

Attorneys for the inmate in a class-action suit over jail conditions presented a sworn statement from a psychiatric nurse, identified as Kathy Vick, who formerly worked in the county jail's mental health ward.

Vick described an incident on March 9 in which an inmate identified as Michael R. refused to take a sedative prescribed by a jail psychiatrist.

When five officers arrived, she said, "Mr. R. was frightened and braced himself against the door. Mr. R. stepped back from the door against the sink or bed and cowered. I did not see him charge the officers."

Vick said the officers piled on top of the inmate. "Mr. R. could have been injected at this point. Instead, he was Tased." Vick said she left at that point and started to cry. She said she later quit her job.

Official reports give a different account, claiming the inmate refused to open the door of his cell for jail officers, who were summoned when he refused to take medication. When the officers managed to push the door open, the inmate charged at them with "tremendous strength," Lt. Wes Bowling said.

Officers also said the first shock did not subdue the inmate, who struggled with officers until they gave him a second shock, pinned his wrists, and handcuffed him.[5]

Concept Check 7

Does it follow from the newspaper story that someone alleged that a stun gun was used to kill a psychiatric inmate?

Concept Check 8

Does it follow from the information supplied in the newspaper story that Santa Clara County Jail officers are misusing their stun guns?

Concept Check 9

Does it follow from the newspaper story that a few Santa Clara County Jail officers would have nasty things to say about Kathy Vick behind her back if they were asked about her?

Review of Major Points

In exploring the notion of implication, which is at the heart of nearly all reasoning, we divided it into two types: implying with certainty and implying with probability. These two types are defined in terms of the notions of inconsistency and improbability, respectively. Arguments are evaluated as being deductively valid, deductively sound, and inductively strong. The strength of an inductive argument is a matter of degree but not of personal preference.

Glossary

deductive argument An argument presented with the intention of being deductively valid or deductively sound.

deductively sound An argument that is deductively valid and whose premises are all true.

deductively valid An argument whose conclusion follows from its premises with certainty.

follows with certainty Statement C follows from statement (or group of statements) P with certainty if P implies C with certainty.

follows with probability Statement C follows from statement (or group of statements) P with probability if P implies C with probability.

implies with certainty A statement (or group of statements) P implies a statement Q with certainty if these two conditions hold: (1) it is logically inconsistent for P to be true without Q also being true, and (2) Q isn't irrelevant to P.

implies with probability A statement (or group of statements) P implies a statement Q with probability if these two conditions hold: (1) it is improbable for P to be true without Q also being true, and (2) Q isn't irrelevant to P.

inductive argument An argument intended to be inductively strong.

inductively strong An argument whose conclusion follows from the premises with high probability. The strength of inductive arguments are a matter of degree; some are stronger than others.

premises An argument's reasons or assumptions.

proofs Sound deductive arguments or strong inductive arguments. Generally, mathematical proofs must be sound, and scientific proofs must be inductively strong.

Answers to Concept Checks

1. Answer (c). Simulated cotton is not cotton.

2. Answer (c). Answer (b) would be the answer if the first sentence had said "all bears" instead of "only bears."

3. Answer (b). If you had to bet on whether that next wolf was going to be white or not white, the best bet would be that it would not be white. Thus, the conclusion is made probable by the premises, which is a telltale sign of the inductive strength of the argument.

4. Yes, the two premises force the conclusion to be true.

5. It is unsound because it has a false premise.

6. Here is an example: George Washington is from Bangladesh, so he is from Asia.

7. Yes. Although death is mentioned only in the second paragraph, it is clear that the dead inmate is the one mentioned in the other paragraphs.

8. No, it would not be reasonable to conclude this. The facts are being disputed. The charge of misuse has been made, and the judge in the case has ordered a halt to

the gun's use pending further investigation, but that investigation might show that there has been no misuse. According to the information in the article, all you can conclude is that the misuse is a possibility that is being looked into.

9. Yes, it follows with some probability. Kathy Vick's testimony amounts to calling the "official reports" a lie, and it is reasonable to assume that people are psychologically disposed to say nasty things about anybody who attacks them by calling them a liar, especially if they don't have to say these things publicly.

Review and Writing Exercises

Following From and Implication

In answering the following questions, you should go light on applying the principle of charity or you will find yourself being so charitable that you can find no examples of bad reasoning. The concept checks and worked exercises can be helpful guides in deciding when to apply the principle.

 1. From the fact that all ice melts when placed in a pan above the lit burner of a gas stove, does it follow with *certainty* that if the president of France places some ice in a pan above the lit burner of a gas stove in Paris next Christmas, his ice will melt?

    a. yes   b. no

 2. Explain why "no" is an incorrect or less than adequate answer to the following question:

    Suppose a woman is arrested. Does it follow that she is guilty?

 3. If Senator Fairchild of New Mexico admits his guilt to the charge of breaking and entering, does it follow that he entered after breaking in? Why?

 4. Explain the error in this reasoning:

    According to this textbook, if Jeremy Irons says, "All U.S. presidents are American citizens" it follows that the current president is an American citizen. Surely that's a mistake. The current president is an American citizen not because Jeremy Irons says something but because of certain Constitutional requirements.

 5. Assuming (with the IRS) that all items from column C are to be listed in column F and that all items from column F are to be listed on form 1040 Schedule SA, then

    a. it follows with certainty   c. it does not follow

    b. it follows with probability

    that all items from column C should be listed on form 1040 Schedule SA.

6. Which of the following arguments are deductively valid?

 a.   Whales are mammals, but the biggest living thing in our sea is definitely not a mammal, so it's not a whale either.

 b.   Potatoes are a kind of produce, and not all of Bob's fattening foods are potatoes, so not all of his fattening foods are produce either.

 c.   That squirming thing has no backbone, but all fish have backbones. So it's not a fish.

 d.   All fat fish are good swimmers. No house cat is a fat fish. So no house cats are good swimmers.

7. To ask whether a statement implies another statement is usually to ask an ambiguous question, even if neither statement itself is ambiguous. Briefly explain why.

8. Find a real-life example of an argument that is not trivial and that doesn't deserve to be criticized because it is deductively sound.

9. Assuming that the following nursery rhyme is an accurate report, which are the only accurate headlines? That is, which can be deduced from the information in the song?

> Old MacDonald had a farm.
> Ee ii ee ii oh.
> And on this farm he had some pigs.
> Ee ii ee ii oh.
> With an oink! oink! here
> And an oink! oink! there.
> Here an oink! There an oink!
> Everywhere an oink! oink!
> Old MacDonald had a farm.
> Ee ii ee ii oh.

 a.   Old Man's Farm Overrun by Wild Pigs

 b.   Cries of Pigs Indicate Animal Abuse on MacDonald Farm

 c.   MacDonald Animal Farm Teaches Pigs Vowels

 d.   MacDonald Has Farm That Had Pigs

 e.   MacDonald Is Man Who Owned Farm That Had Pigs

 f.   MacDonald Had Farm That Had Animals

 g.   MacDonald Had Farm That Has Pigs

■ 10. Referring to the previous exercise, does statement (e) logically imply statement (f)?

 a.   yes   b.   no

11. Does statement (e) logically imply statement (g)?

 a.   yes   b.   no

■ 12. Do the statements in the Old MacDonald song imply statement (e)?

 a.   yes with certainty   b.   yes with probability   c.   not at all

13. Find three examples of reasoning in which the conclusion is intended to follow from the premises but does not. The sources must be from your own experience outside the college and its classrooms and textbooks. Sources might be newspaper or TV ads, magazine articles, conversations, books, and so on. Cut out, photocopy, or write up each example on a separate (8.5 × 11 inches) page. On that page, or on the next page if you need more room, identify where the example came from and the date of the publication or the broadcast. Then identify and explain the illogical reasoning that occurs. Staple together your examples in the upper left corner, after adding a cover page containing your name. Don't bother using a fancy binder or notebook. You will be graded on the accuracy and clarity of your identification of the illogical reasoning and on the variety of your examples.

14. Let B = "x is an even number" and let C = "x is 8/2." Then B logically follows from C.

   a.   true   b.   false

15. For question 14, if B is true, then C follows from B with certainty.

   a.   true   b.   false

16. Consider the following proposed argument:

   Every man is a potential killer. Everyone who went to the bank is a man. Therefore, everyone who went to the bank is a potential killer.

   As long as the ambiguous term *bank* is referring in both cases to the same financial bank or the same riverbank, does the ambiguity make any difference to whether the conclusion follows from the premises?

17. Assuming that a financial bank is intended in question 16, does the conclusion follow with certainty from the premises?

18. All cows are mammals and have lanthrobia. All squirrels are mammals and have lanthrobia. All humans are mammals and have lanthrobia. Therefore, all mammals have lanthrobia.

   In this argument the conclusion

   a.   follows with certainty from the premises.

   b.   follows with probability from the premises.

■ 19. All cows are mammals and have lanthrobia. All squirrels are mammals and have lanthrobia. All humans are mammals and have lanthrobia. Therefore, some mammals have lanthrobia.

   In this argument the conclusion

   a.   follows with certainty from the premises.

   b.   follows with probability from the premises.

20. The argument about lanthrobia in question 19 is deductively valid.

   a.   true   b.   false

21. If statement A follows from statement B, does statement B thereby follow from statement A?

- 22. Either you are no friend of Susan's or you will let me in to borrow your stereo for her. But since you obviously won't let me borrow your stereo for her, therefore you are no friend of hers. This argument is

    a. deductively valid.   c. none of the above.

    b. deductively invalid.

- 23. Write an essay of three pages (typed double-spaced, if possible) that answers the following question. (Background: Many liberals say "no" and many conservatives say "yes," so be sure to consider all sides of the issue.

    Does it follow from the Bill of Rights of the U.S. Constitution that individuals have the right to bear arms?

24. If the premises of an argument are true, and if their being true makes it improbable that the conclusion is false, then the argument is inductively strong.

    a. true   b. false (If so, what would you alter?)

25. If you knew that all fast swimmers have good lung capacity, and if you knew that some fast swimmers have bad politics, would it follow for certain that every student who has good politics and is a fast swimmer has good lung capacity?

- 26. Is it possible to have a deductively sound argument that is also deductively valid?

- 27. Is it possible to have an inductively strong argument that is deductively invalid?

28. "John isn't a good waiter because all good waiters have pleasant smiles, but John doesn't have a pleasant smile." If you were to learn that John really is a good waiter, then you could say that

    a. the argument is deductively invalid and unsound.

    b. the argument is deductively valid and sound.

    c. the argument is deductively invalid and sound.

    d. a premise is false.

29. Create an obviously deductively valid argument for the conclusion that the Bible is the word of God. One of your key premises must be that the Bible was written by the Christian prophets.

30. Create an obviously deductively invalid argument for the conclusion that the Bible is the word of God, using the following as one of your key premises: the Bible was written by the Christian prophets.

31. Suppose that a medical team has examined 21 randomly selected children of the Zambezi Desert and discovered that all of them have malaria or else once had it. It follows

    a. with certainty

    b. with probability

    c. neither with probability nor certainty

    that the next three randomly selected children of the Zambezi Desert will be found to have malaria or else to have once had it, if they are examined for malaria.

You may assume that there are approximately 8,000 children in the Zambezi Desert.

32. Premise: A survey of major corporate executives indicates that 60 percent believe that some American businesses often engage in price fixing.

    Conclusion: If you were to randomly pick five of the surveyed major corporate executives, you could reasonably expect that three of them would believe that all American businesses engage in some form of price fixing.

    The conclusion

    a. follows.

    b. does not follow.

33. President Kennedy was murdered. So if Oswald did not kill Kennedy, then someone else did.

    a. true   b. false

34. President Kennedy was murdered. So if Oswald had not killed Kennedy, then someone else would have.

    a. true   b. false

35. (a) If only great works of art are owned by the Crocker Gallery, does it follow that the only great works of art are owned by the Crocker Gallery? (b) How about vice versa? Assume that the gallery does own works of art.

■ 36. Bacteria use only an asexual form of reproduction. So, it

    a. follows with certainty

    b. follows with probability

    c. does not follow

    that bacteria do not use a sexual form of reproduction.

37. If the club members are not adults, and only adults have rights, then

    a. it follows with certainty

    b. it follows with probability

    c. it does not follow

    that the club members have no rights at all.

38. If a researcher *proved* that certain bacteria will cause pneumonia in any large animal because 100 percent of the tested animals given the bacteria caught pneumonia whereas none of the animals who weren't given the bacteria caught pneumonia, this proof would be

    a. a deductively sound argument

    b. an inductively strong argument

39. For the following argumentation, you may assume that the meaning of the words *tort* and *sequestration* are taught in every law school. (a) Identify any premise indicators and any conclusion indicators (these terms were defined in Chapter 1). (b) Is this argument deductively valid? (c) Discuss the question of the argument's

soundness. (d) How would you improve the argument if you believe it does need improvement?

> Any lawyer knows what the words *tort* and *sequestration* mean. Surprisingly, this so-called "friend" of yours doesn't know what the words mean. It follows that he's not a lawyer.

• 40. In a recent issue of your daily newspaper, find a letter to the editor that contains an argument. (a) What is the issue? (b) What conclusion is the writer arguing for? (c) Briefly list the main reasons offered, and number them. (d) Which of the reasons can the average reader tell are true? (e) Is the argument probably intended to be inductive or deductive, or isn't there enough information to tell? (f) Briefly discuss the quality of the argument. Are there weak spots in the argument? Where? Why? (g) Attach a copy of the letter to your answer.

Drawing Implications from Charts and Graphs

Refer to the charts as your only source of data for the questions that follow. Assume that the figures are current.

California's Thirstiest Crops[6]

This chart shows the crops that use the most water, indicating their cash value per acre and the amount of water, on average, needed to produce a dollar in crop sales to the California farmer.

Crop	Water use– gallons per acre (in millions)	Value per acre	Gallons needed to produce $1 of crop
Alfalfa	1.33	$ 520	2,564
Pasture	1.33	102	12,500
Almonds	1.17	1,210	971
Fruit trees	1.14	2,656	429
Rice	1.07	595	1,818
Grapes	.94	2,593	365
Sugar beets	.91	1,011	901
Cotton	.88	970	909
Tomatoes	.78	2,568	305
Corn	.72	480	1,493
Sorghum (grain)	.59	244	2,380
Small grains	.46	144	3,125

Water Per Serving[7]

Gallons of water needed to produce a single serving of:

Steak	2,607	Cherries	90	Wheat bread	15
Hamburger	1,303	Milk	65	Almonds	12
Pork	408	Corn	61	Cola	10
Chicken	408	Cantaloupe	51	Sugar (beet)	8
Eggs	136	Rice	36	Lettuce	6
Watermelon	100	Oranges	22	French fries	6
Margarine	92	Apples	16	Tomatoes	3

Answer the following questions or else mention why they cannot be answered based on the information in the two charts.

1. The primary food of cows is alfalfa and pasture. According to the chart, more land in California is planted in which of these two crops?

2. Given that you are a farmer with both an acre of alfalfa and an acre of pasture, which one will produce the most money (gross, not net)?

3. If, on your farm, the cost of water per dollar of crop value were the paramount factor to consider in which crops to farm (and you didn't have to worry that the market would be flooded with this crop), what should be your crop choice?

4. How would your answer to question 3 change if you were interested in the cost of water per *eight dollars* of crop value instead of one dollar?

■ 5. As a consumer, if your primary motivation is to eat a serving of food that required the least amount of water to produce, which of these would you choose?

    a. eggs

    b. lettuce

    c. apples

6. As a consumer, if your primary motivation is to eat a serving of food that required the least amount of water to produce, which two foods on the chart would you most avoid eating?

7. For the chart titled "California's Thirstiest Crops," would it be possible to devise a formula for computing the value in the first column, given that you know the values in the other two columns? If so, devise the formula. If not, say why not.

8. Assume that the information in the following chart is correct:

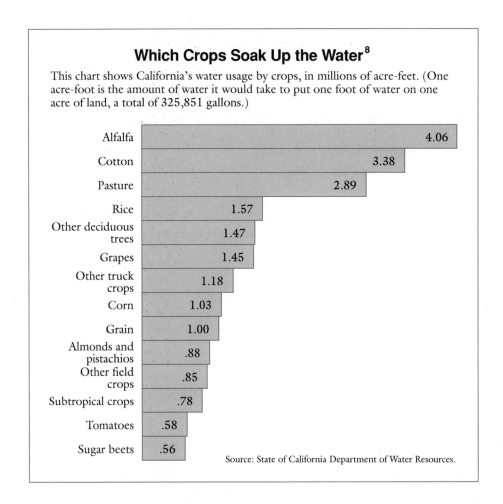

Discuss or answer the following using the chart as your only source of information.

a.   What California crop is more widely planted, i.e., planted in the greatest acreage?

b.   What crop planted in California uses more water (per total crop planted in California, not per plant) than any other crop?

c.   What crop planted in California uses the most water per acre?

9. Assume that the information in the following chart is correct:

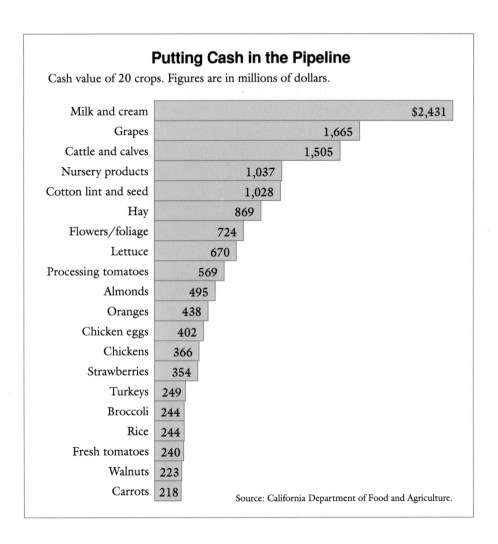

Putting Cash in the Pipeline

Cash value of 20 crops. Figures are in millions of dollars.

Milk and cream	$2,431
Grapes	1,665
Cattle and calves	1,505
Nursery products	1,037
Cotton lint and seed	1,028
Hay	869
Flowers/foliage	724
Lettuce	670
Processing tomatoes	569
Almonds	495
Oranges	438
Chicken eggs	402
Chickens	366
Strawberries	354
Turkeys	249
Broccoli	244
Rice	244
Fresh tomatoes	240
Walnuts	223
Carrots	218

Source: California Department of Food and Agriculture.

Is there enough information in the chart to name a crop whose value was greater than a billion dollars? If not, why not? If so, name a crop.

10. This is a chart of the ways poisons enter our body.

	Number	Percent
Ingestions	37,767	76.87
Inhalations	3,464	7.07
Ocular	3,068	6.26
Dermal	3,254	6.64
Bite/sting	1,059	2.16
Parenteral, other/unknown	488	1.00
Total	**49,009**	**100%**

Source: *San Francisco Regional Poison Control Center 1990 Annual Report.*

From this chart of the ways that poisoned people are exposed to their poison, it follows with certainty that snake bites and bee stings are more significant than poisoning by inhalation.

a.   true   b.   false

11. According to the chart in question 10,

   a.   it follows with certainty

   b.   it follows with probability

   c.   it doesn't follow

that poison control workers should spend more money educating the public about the dangers of what they eat than what they breathe.

Implicit Premises, Argument Structure, and Diagrams

Every argument contains at least one intended conclusion plus one or more supporting reasons, called premises. However, in some passages it is not easy to tell whether an argument occurs at all, what the premises and conclusion of an argument are, or how other arguments in the passage are related to that argument. This chapter explores such understatement. It begins with an introduction of special phrases that often indicate the presence of premises and conclusions. Then the chapter investigates the problems of identifying the unstated premises and conclusions of intended argumentation. For especially complex argumentation, the chapter introduces a diagraming technique that can display argument structure. Although most of the techniques discussed in this chapter have been presupposed in previous chapters or mentioned briefly, this chapter pursues them systematically and in greater detail.

Premise Indicators and Conclusion Indicators

Spotting an argument and assessing whether the argument is any good are two distinct abilities. Usually you use them both at the same time. You don't go looking for arguments without also evaluating them. However, before you can evaluate an argument, you have to identify its conclusion and premises. The special techniques you can use to do so are introduced in the following sections.

Concept Check 1

All good arguments have two or more premises plus at least one conclusion.

a. true   b. false

Arguments are produced in a variety of flavors; sometimes the conclusion is stated before the premises, sometimes after the premises, and sometimes embedded in the middle of the premises. Usually sentences are included that are neither premises nor conclusions; they are there for elaboration or for some other purpose, such as to entertain, to describe, to explain, and so forth. So that readers will understand what the actual argument is, helpful authors use *indicator phrases*. These are single words or phrases that indicate the presence of a premise or of a conclusion. When trying to determine which sentences are premises and which are conclusions, a logical reasoner looks for indicator words and phrases. **Premise indicators** highlight the presence of premises, but never of conclusions. **Conclusion indicators** are a sign of a conclusion, but not of a premise.

Here is an example of an argument from authority that contains both kinds of indicator phrases:

> *Because* the encyclopedia says that the whale shark is the biggest fish in the ocean, *it follows that* the whale shark really is the biggest fish on Earth.

Because indicates the one premise, and the phrase *it follows that* indicates the conclusion. Indicators normally come before what they indicate.

Here are more examples of indicator phrases:

Premise Indicators	Conclusion Indicators
since	therefore
because	consequently
for the reason that	thus
assuming	so
suppose	it follows that
as indicated by	shows that
is implied by	implies that
given that	proves that
in view of the fact that	leads me to believe that

These phrases are *not* indicator phrases:

if	on the contrary
yet	and
nevertheless	also

Unfortunately, indicator phrases do not always indicate a premise or a conclusion. For example,

> *Since* November when the inflationary spiral ended, state taxes have been high. State farm subsidies will therefore continue to rise.

This passage does contain an argument, and the conclusion indicator word *therefore* occurs within the conclusion, but the premise indicator word *since* isn't functioning to indicate a premise. It is working as a time indicator. Because *since* has multiple meanings, you need to determine whether it is functioning as a premise indicator in a particular situation. When it is a sign that some element of an argument is present, it always indicates a premise and never a conclusion.

■ ·········· Concept Check 2 ·········· ■

Find all the conclusion indicator phrases in the following argument and note whether they are actually indicating a conclusion. Do the same for premise indicators.

> I've been in love with you ever since you began going out with my friend Charles. So you shouldn't say no one loves you now that he doesn't love you anymore.

When you suspect that an argument is present, the best strategy is to ask yourself which statements would be reasonable premises for which other statements.

■ ·········· Concept Check 3 ·········· ■

Do these passages contain arguments? If so, locate the conclusion. Identify each indicator phrase as being either a conclusion indicator or a premise indicator.

a. Never pick up a recently killed rattlesnake, because its nerve reflexes enable it to bite for some time after death.

b. Never pick up a recently killed rattlesnake. Its nerve reflexes enable it to bite for some time after death.

c. In a country with a billion people, even if you're a one-in-a-million type guy, there are still a thousand just like you.

d. Though rare on Earth, plasmas are the most common form of matter in the universe, even more common than gases.

Rewriting Arguments in Standard Form

Here is another passage that contains an argument. Can you spot the conclusion?

> All machines have a finite working lifetime, and that big tree is really just a biological machine; therefore, I believe it will stop working someday, too.

The conclusion is that "That big tree will stop working someday," but this sentence does not occur explicitly in the passage. The conclusion is slightly hidden in the words that follow the indicator word *therefore*. The conclusion is "between the lines." We readers have to figure out that the word *it* is referring to "that big tree," and we must also mentally strip away the word *too* and the phrase *I believe*. After doing all this, we can give the following more explicit picture of the argument:

> All machines have a finite working lifetime.
> That big tree is really just a biological machine.
> _____
> That big tree will stop working someday.

Creating this picture is called (rewriting the argument in) **standard form**. In standard form, the premises are rewritten as full declarative sentences and are listed together above the line. Similarly, the conclusion is written out in full below the line. The order of the premises is not important. Indicator words and other fluff words are stripped away. When an argument is in standard form, it is supposed to stand alone, with everything significant stated explicitly so that the reader can view the whole argument and understand what it is, without needing additional information such as knowing that *it* refers to "that big tree." The argument was originally a single sentence, but this one sentence has been analyzed as being composed of three statements. The three make a deductively valid argument.

The process of transforming an argument into its standard form is quite like the subconscious mental process that occurs when a logical reasoner "sees the argument" in a passage. Explicitly writing down the standard form unpacks this "seeing." Normally, you would take the trouble to write down the standard form only when confronted with an especially complicated argument that you must figure out very carefully. Nobody is suggesting that from now on you sit down with the morning paper and rewrite all its arguments into standard form. However, trying your hand at rewriting a few simpler arguments will help build up your skill so you can succeed with more complicated arguments when the stakes are higher.

Rewrite the following explicit argument in standard form.

> Never pick up a recently killed rattlesnake, because its nerve reflexes enable it to bite for some time after death.

Conditionals and the Logic of the Word *If*

The word *if* is intentionally excluded from the list of premise indicator words. You cannot rely on *if* to indicate a premise and not a conclusion, because it may go with either. In argument A below *if* is followed by a premise, but in argument B it is in the conclusion.

A. If, as we know, all men are mortal and Jeremiah is a man, not a god, then he is mortal, too.

B. If a mercury thermometer is given prolonged heating, it will break. This is because prolonged heating will cause the mercury to expand a great deal. But the thermometer will break apart whenever the mercury expands this much.

Let's examine argument B more carefully. Does it assume that a mercury thermometer is actually given prolonged heating? No; doing so would break the thermometer. Notice also that the conclusion is not that the mercury thermometer will actually break, but only that it will break *if* heated. The conclusion is an if-then statement: *if* the thermometer is heated, *then* it will break. So, the *if* is not indicating a premise, nor is it indicating a conclusion; it is performing another function.

If-then statements are called **conditional statements**. Conditionals can be used either to make a statement or to encode an argument. Often only the context can disclose which is intended. However, if the conditional is being used as a whole argument rather than as a single statement within an argument, the *if* precedes the premises and the *then* precedes the conclusion. Only in this sense is the word *if* indicative of a premise. Nevertheless, *if* is not on our list of premise indicators because of the problem with arguments such as B above.

A statement can be conditional even if the word *then* is not explicit. For example, somebody might make the following conditional claim:

> If the Campbell's Soup Company puts less salt in its soup, sales of Campbell's soup will increase.

Does it follow from this conditional claim that Campbell's Soup Company puts less salt in its soup? No. Is the speaker committed to the claim that sales of Campbell's soup will increase? No, the commitment is only to an increase *on the condition that* the company does something about the salt. That is why conditionals are called "conditionals."

Can you conclude that if Campbell's sales do *not* increase, the company failed to put less salt in its soup? Yes, this conditional statement follows with certainty from the original conditional statement. Can you conclude that, if the company does not put less salt in its soup, then its sales will not increase? No.

Concept Check 5

Suppose you were to learn for certain that if a person is the governor of Alaska, then he or she is a U.S. citizen. If so, can you be *absolutely* sure that if somebody is not a U.S. citizen, then he or she is not the governor of Alaska?

Is the following conditional making a true statement about the real world?

> If President John F. Kennedy was born in Bangladesh, then he was born in Asia.

Yes it's true, and it is true even though both the if part and the then part are false. The truth of a conditional does not require the truth of its parts.

Concept Check 6

Answer "yes" or "no" to these conditional claims:

a. If it's an apple, then it's a fruit.

b. If it's a fruit, then it's an apple.

c. It's an apple if it's a fruit.

d It's a fruit if it's an apple.

e. It's not a fruit if it's not an apple.

f. It's not an apple if it's not a fruit.

g. If the current president of the United States were also the leader of Pakistan, then the president would be the leader of an Asian country.

h. If the tallest building in the U.S. is only 15 feet tall, then there is no building in the U.S. taller than 30 feet.

i. If Joshua Dicker or his dad, Stuart, are invited, then Joshua Dicker's dad is invited.

Locating Unstated Conclusions

The task of detecting arguments in passages is made more difficult when the arguer leaves the conclusion unstated, expecting that you, the detectives in the audience, will get the point anyway. For example, what is the implicit conclusion in the following argument?

> All insects have exactly six legs, but all spiders have exactly eight legs, so we can draw a conclusion about whether spiders are insects, namely that . . . well, you can see for yourself.

The conclusion is not "you can see for yourself." The conclusion indicator is *so*, which promises that a conclusion will be along soon. Unfortunately, the author never gets around to following the word *so* by the actual conclusion. The detective who is trying to figure out the conclusion needs to look back at the premises to see what sort of conclusion about spiders and insects will follow from the premises. In this example, the conclusion is that spiders are not insects.

People who are not sensitive to the implicit elements in argumentation can miss the point of a joke, as we will see in the following concept check.

■ ⋯⋯⋯ Concept Check 7 ⋯⋯⋯ ■

When an argument does not contain any indicator words, it takes greater logical skill to spot the argument. What is the implicit conclusion you are supposed to draw in the following joke?

> My father had a lot of patience with me when I was growing up. Whenever he got mad at me he would slowly count to twenty. Then he'd lift my head out of the water.

a. All people have fathers.

b. My father had a lot of patience with me when I was growing up.

c. My father was impatient with me when I was growing up.

d. My father would lift my head out of the water after a slow count to 20.

Is the first sentence in the joke in Concept Check 7 a premise or a conclusion?

Uncovering Implicit Premises

In addition to implicit conclusions, arguments can have implicit premises. These premises are the unstated assumptions of the argument. For instance, suppose a biologist argues that there is nothing ethically wrong in the fact that 100 animals per day are killed in her laboratory, because the deaths further her scientific research. In this argument, she uses the unstated assumption that animals don't have the same ethical rights that we humans do.

Definition An **implicit premise** of an argument is a statement that does not appear explicitly but that is intended by the arguer to be a premise to help make the conclusion follow from the premises.

The phrase *intended . . . to help* in this definition is important. It plays a crucial role in the problem of identifying the following argument's implicit premise:

> Tantalum can be melted, too, because *all* metals melt if you raise their temperature enough.

Choose the implicit premise from the following list:

a. Some metals melt.

b. Tantalum can be melted if all metals can.

c. Tantalum is not a metal.

d. Tantalum is a metal.

e. All metals melt.

Not everything the arguer believes at the time counts as a premise in the argument. For example, the arguer undoubtedly believes statement (a) — that some metals melt — but is not assuming this *in order to help* her argument. Instead, she needs to assume that tantalum is a metal. With this premise, her argument is deductively valid. That is, her conclusion follows with certainty from her premises. Without it, her argument is deductively invalid. So, the answer is (d), not (a). Here is her deductively valid argument:

> All metals melt if you raise their temperature enough.
> Tantalum is a metal. (implicit premise)
> _____
>
> Tantalum can be melted.

The argument is deductively valid; however, it is unsound because the implicit premise is false.

Concept Check 9

What is the missing premise in this passage?

> Most soft minerals will make a compound with tantalum, so baxalite probably will, too.

Not all the premises of an argument can be implicit; at least one premise must be present to clearly indicate that some arguing is going on. However, most arguments do have implicit premises. That's because speakers tend to present only the important parts of their argument, letting the listener fill in the rest. The helpful speaker usually gives enough premises so that the audience can follow the argumentation, yet doesn't give so many premises that the audience gets confused by all the details.

The most common implicit premises are definitions of words, principles of grammar and semantics, and rules of mathematics. For example, we might argue that because Dwayne loves Jesus, Jesus is loved by Dwayne. This deductively valid argument depends on some grammatical principles about passive voice transformations that we rarely need to spell out. Everybody who speaks English can follow the inference, even though few of us could actually write down the rules of our language. Also, the assumption that the word *Dwayne* in a premise names the same person as the word *Dwayne* referred to in the conclusion is a presupposition that encodes customs of language use. A writer who bothered to explicitly remind us of this fact would be cluttering up the argument with too many details.

A significant assumption, on the other hand, is an assumption that is essential or that would make the argument harder to understand if it were left out. In the following passage, the clause *all persons have DNA in their cells* is a significant assumption:

All persons have DNA in their cells, so the leader of Russia does too.

The argument *does* have an implicit assumption: that the leader of Russia is a person. Without this implicit assumption, the conclusion would not follow from the premises. Nevertheless, the clear writer wisely leaves this assumption implicit.

■ ·········· Concept Check 10 ·········· ■

In mathematical reasoning, it is customary to assume implicitly all the principles of mathematics. For example, if *y* is a positive integer less than 4, which of these necessarily follows?

a. *y* is even
b. *y* is not even
c. None of the above

Many jokes turn on who holds what assumption. For example, in the following joke, Suzanne says essentially that one of Jack's assumptions is mistaken:

Jack: Get those drugs out of this house; nobody is going to risk my daughter's sanity.
Suzanne: You can't risk what's not there, Jack.

■ ·········· Concept Check 11 ·········· ■

If you understood that joke, then you saw that (pick one):

a. Suzanne assumed that Jack is insane.
b. Jack assumed that Suzanne is insane.
c. Suzanne assumed that Jack's daughter is sane.
d. Jack assumed that Suzanne's daughter is insane.
e. Jack assumed that his daughter is sane.

Detecting Obscure Argumentation

The following newspaper article reports on an argument made by the Mexican arch-bishop, but it is a one-sentence argument. The rest of the argument must be mentally reconstructed by the reader. Do so as you read the article.

"Virgin Marilyn" Upsets Mexicans

MEXICO CITY — Marilyn Monroe may have been a goddess of sorts, but in Mexico she's no saint.

A painting depicting Mexico's revered Virgin of Guadalupe as the blonde movie goddess has touched off a battle over the sanctity of religious beliefs and freedom of expression.

The portrait of the Virgin as a green-and-gold-robed Marilyn Monroe so angered conservative Catholics that they were able to force Mexico City's Museum of Modern Art to remove it.

"Would you like it if they put Marilyn Monroe's face on your mother's picture?" Mexican Archbishop Ernesto Cardinal Corripio said in December when the painting was taken down.

After the exhibit was removed, about 200 of the country's most respected intellectuals signed an open letter saying the museum had set a dangerous precedent by allowing themselves to be censured by a small group of conservatives. Editorial cartoonists depicted the complaining group as white-hooded, Ku Klux Klan types[1]

Normally, the clues that an argument is being described are premise indicators or conclusion indicators. Those clues are not present here. Instead, the clue is that someone is angry regarding some issue. From what the archbishop says you can reconstruct his reasons for taking his side of the issue. In his argument, does he want you to conclude that you wouldn't like to have your mother's face covered up with Marilyn's? Yes, he does believe that, but that is not his conclusion. It's his premise. Evidently that premise was used by the archbishop and other conservative Catholics "to force Mexico City's Museum of Modern Art to remove" the Marilyn Monroe face. Here is his argument presented in standard form to make it clearer:

> You would not like Marilyn Monroe's face covering up your mother's picture. (explicit premise rewritten)

> If you wouldn't like Marilyn Monroe's face covering up your mother's picture, then you should support public censorship of any painting that covers up the face of someone considered by many people to be like their mother. (implicit premise)

> Many people consider the Virgin of Guadalupe to be like their mother. (implicit premise)

In the Virgin of Guadalupe painting in Mexico's Museum of Modern Art, the face of Marilyn Monroe covers up the face of the Virgin of Guadalupe. (indirectly said in the third and fourth sentences of the article)

You should support public censorship of the Virgin of Guadalupe painting in Mexico's Museum of Modern Art. (implicit conclusion)

But wait. Aren't we reading too much into what the archbishop says? Is he really giving an argument with all the implicit elements listed here? Isn't he giving no argument and merely stating one of his beliefs, which we then use to guess how he might argue *if* he were to argue? These are reasonable questions about how to apply the principle of fidelity. It's not clear whether this argument is implied in the passage. It is there more likely than not, but this is a judgment call. What is important to understand is the argument that the archbishop does or would give, which is indicated above in standard form.

The following example contains another argument that is deeply hidden but that can be brought to light by applying the tools we have acquired. Suppose a man has vital information for the president of the United States, information that could save the world from nuclear destruction, but he has to get the information to the president in the next few minutes. He is at a phone booth but doesn't have a coin to make the call. Only he and a soldier are in the vicinity. He asks the soldier to lend him money for the call, but the soldier cannot help. In desperation, he then asks the soldier to use his gun to smash open the box of money in the phone booth so that he can make the call. The soldier replies, "That would be stealing."

This reply expresses an argument, but an obscure one. Given the context, we can infer that the soldier's conclusion is "No, I won't shoot open the box of money." One unstated reason is "Stealing is wrong." If we put all this into standard form we have

Using my gun to shoot open the box of money would be stealing.
Stealing is wrong.

I won't use my gun to shoot open the box of money.

This is not a deductively valid argument. The conclusion does not follow with certainty from what is stated, yet the soldier probably intended it to. Therefore, some more premises are needed. The missing premise is "I won't do what is wrong." It is the premise for two reasons: It is the simplest premise that can be added that will produce deductive validity, and it is a premise that the arguer is likely to have believed. The premises conform to the principle of fidelity. So, the standard form of the soldier's argument is the following:

Using my gun to shoot open the box of money would be stealing.
Stealing is wrong.
I won't do what is wrong.

I won't use my gun to shoot open the box of money.

If a description is negative, that's a clue that between the lines may lie some unstated argument, with the unstated conclusion that the thing described is not supposed to be liked or done or purchased or whatever. Here is an example:

> The employee training manual for [the] restaurant just has to be titled "We Aim to Please."
>
> The help has digested the book well. One waitress smiled so persistently throughout a meal that it hurt just to look at her. Another asked so often and so emphatically whether everything was OK that I kept checking to make sure no one had collapsed and lay sprawled across the table. Hostesses were so bubbly they should have been tethered. . . . One of the restaurant's owners . . . circulated continually about the premises, like a teacher on recess duty, ever vigilant to respond promptly to trouble, stopping periodically to chit-chat.[2]

■ .... **Concept Check 12** .... ■

Explicitly, the above passage is only a description. Implicitly, there is an argument for what conclusion?

Math professors who create a proof rarely state every step in the proof. However, the reasoning from any one step to another is an argument that can be reconstructed and shown to be deductively valid; if it cannot, there is an error in the proof.

Here is an interesting dialogue that contains an obscure argument. Evidently this dialogue occurred several centuries ago.

King: I told you to bring me a head of a witch, and you've given me the head of a necromancer.

Executioner: The Inquisition has declared that all necromancers are witches.

King: Oh, all right then.

By saying, "Oh, all right then," the king infers that he has in fact been given the head of a witch. In that complicated piece of reasoning, he uses the following deductively valid subargument:

All necromancers are witches.
_____
All heads of necromancers are heads of witches.

Occasionally a speaker, often a politician or newsperson, will present all sorts of reasons for drawing an obvious conclusion but will never quite draw that conclusion for you. The speaker may just be disguising an argument. On the other hand, the speaker could get defensive and say, "I didn't make that argument, you did." Just such a problem occurs in the following excerpt from a newspaper article about a TV program on health care hosted by Walter Cronkite:

> In the end, whether we can afford to provide expensive medical care on demand for only some of our citizens is a question we Americans have yet to answer.
>
> "I would say," says economist Marmor, that "we're spending more and feeling worse."
>
> In sum, Cronkite says that every developed nation in the world except the United States and South Africa have agreed that health care is an inalienable right.
>
> "For an increasing number of Americans who are shut out, the American health care system is neither healthy, caring, nor a system," he says.[3]

Concept Check 13

Explain why the author of the newspaper article might be accused of arguing. Explain why Walter Cronkite might also be accused of arguing. Then explain why both persons might be able to defend themselves by saying that they were not really arguing.

When you are faced with some statements that could constitute an argument with an implicit conclusion, how do you tell whether you have an argument or simply a group of statements from which you are to draw your own conclusions and thus create your own argument? There is no simple answer to this question; it is a matter of the delicate application of the principle of fidelity. If it is clear what conclusion the writer hopes you will draw, then there is an argument; if not, there is no argument.

Multiple Arguments and Subarguments

Sometimes an argument contains several shorter arguments. For instance, an argument's conclusion can be used as a premise to draw yet another conclusion. Here is an example of such an argument chain:

> She's got the flu again, so she probably won't be here to chair the meeting. Therefore, I'll have to do it. Damn!

The word *so* is a conclusion indicator of the **subconclusion**, and the word *therefore* is a conclusion indicator of the **final conclusion**, or last conclusion. In standard form without the implicit premises, here are the two arguments:

> She's got the flu again.
> _____
> She probably won't be here to chair the meeting.
>> She probably won't be here to chair the meeting.
>> _____
>> I'll have to chair the meeting.

If you were asked whether the statement "she probably won't be here to chair the meeting" is a premise or a conclusion in the argument, the right response would be to go between the horns of this dilemma and say "Both."

The **multiple argumentation** in the following passage has a slightly more complex structure than the argumentation in the flu passage:

> The children's book *The Wizard of Oz* is objectionable because it portrays witches as good. [The evidence is that] the Witch of the North was called the "Good Witch Glinda" in an early chapter, and Witch Glinda helped Dorothy find her way back to Kansas.

The conclusion of the **main argument** — the most important subargument — is

> (C) The children's book *The Wizard of Oz* is objectionable.

The reason for this is that

> (A) The book *The Wizard of Oz* portrays witches as good.

The sentence about Glinda is not part of this argument from A to C. However, the sentence is part of another argument in which A is the conclusion rather than the premise.

■ ············ Concept Check 14 ············ ■

The word *so* is a conclusion indicator in the following passage. Is it an indicator of the final conclusion or only of another subconclusion?

> It's safe to conclude that all the patients given the AIDS antidote now have red hair. Remember, Jane had red hair before the experiment and there has been no change; Rudy has fairly red hair; and Sam's hair is red, isn't it? So, all three have red hair. But these three are the only patients that were given the AIDS antidote.

Diagraming Argumentation

Sometimes in analyzing a complicated argument that contains subarguments, it can be helpful to draw a diagram to represent which sentences support which other sentences. For example, here is a diagram of the chain of arguments about getting the flu and chairing the meeting:

The letters represent statements used in the argumentation:

> A = She's got the flu again.
>
> B = She probably won't be here to chair the meeting.
>
> C = I'll have to chair the meeting.

In this kind of diagram, which we will call a **tree diagram**, the line separates a premise from its immediate conclusion. The premise is always higher than the conclusion it is supporting. The angle of the line is irrelevant as long as it is not horizontal.

Let's try this diagraming technique on the argument about *The Wizard of Oz*, which has implicit parts. The structure of the explicit parts of the main argument is

with these definitions:

> C = The children's book *The Wizard of Oz* is objectionable.
>
> A = The book *The Wizard of Oz* portrays witches as good.

An implicit premise supports C because the author also assumes

> (B) Portraying witches as being good is objectionable.

So, the main argument has the following diagram:

In addition to the main argument, the author explicitly gives two reasons in favor of premise A. The two are

(D) The Witch of the North was called the "Good Witch Glinda" in an early chapter of the book.

(E) Witch Glinda helped Dorothy find her way back to Kansas.

A subargument from *D* and *E* to *A* occurs within the paragraph. Its structure is the following:

This subargument reads this way:

> The Witch of the North was called the "Good Witch Glinda" in an early chapter of the book. (*D*)
> Witch Glinda helped Dorothy find her way back to Kansas. (*E*)
>
> The book portrays witches as good. (*A*)

The structure of the subargument plus the structure of the principal argument together make up the overall structure of the whole two-sentence passage:

Because premise order is irrelevant, the following tree diagram would also be correct:

Notice how our analysis of the *two* sentences has revealed *five* statements linked together.

Concept Check 15

Draw the diagram of the following argument: E and J, so C. Don't worry about which statements the letters represent.

Let's diagram another example, an argument about whales:

> All whales have backbones; my biology teacher said so. Therefore, Humphrey has a backbone, too.

We first need to apply the principle of charity to spot the unstated assumption that Humphrey is a whale. Without that assumption, this would be a terrible argument, which it isn't. Now, let's number the key statements:

(1) All whales have backbones.

(2) My biology teacher said that all whales have backbones.

(3) Humphrey is a whale.

(4) Humphrey has a backbone.

The tree diagram for this argument is

The final argument that concludes 4 from 1 and 3 is deductive. However, the subargument from 2 to 1 is inductive; it's an argument from authority.

Now let's consider a more complicated example of multiple argumentation. Ultimately the diagram method should be used only in cases where the argument structure is so complicated that it cannot be held in our mind in one piece. The following is an excerpt from a longer *Newsweek* article; the excerpt reports on several arguments by a woman named Frost. How are these multiple arguments connected to each other? Are they all independent, or are some drawing conclusions that are then used as premises of another argument? Drawing the diagrams can display the answer to these questions, and the diagrams can be useful in settling disagreements about the arguments in the passage.

Magic Acts

As the trial opened in federal court in Greeneville last week, attorneys led Frost, Rachel Baker, and other plaintiffs through explanations of their beliefs. Frost said she objects to *The Wizard of Oz* because "it portrays witches as good" and to *King Arthur* and *Cinderella* because they contain magic and supernatural acts. Stories critical of the free enterprise system offend her, she said, because "capitalism is ordained by God." Her eyes brimming with tears, Frost also told the courtroom her daughter would never be a feminist, because God meant for women to be subservient to men. "I try to live by the word of God, and that governs everything I believe." She also objects to teachings about other religions. Even reading about Catholicism, she said, "could produce changes in my child's way of thinking—they could become confused." At one point, [the defense attorney] spread his hands in exasperation, saying, "There is no way this woman could attend public school and not be offended."[4]

The several arguments given by Frost are independent. That is, no argument here is a subargument of another argument. The first argument by Frost is this:

(1) *The Wizard of Oz* portrays witches as good.
(2) Portraying witches as good is objectionable. (implicit)
(3) *The Wizard of Oz* is objectionable.

Here is her second argument:

(4) *King Arthur* and *Cinderella* are stories that contain magic and supernatural acts.
(5) If a story contains magic and supernatural acts, then it is objectionable. (presupposition)
(6) *King Arthur* and *Cinderella* are objectionable.

The diagrams that represent the structure of Frost's two arguments look like this:

The independence of the two arguments is indicated by the fact that the two diagrams are not connected.

At a deeper level of analysis, you might want to connect the diagrams by noting that her implicit objection to portraying witches as good rests in turn on her belief that witches are magic or supernatural. Therefore, if you were asked to clarify the connection between her objection to *The Wizard of Oz* and her objections to the other two books, you could demonstrate this connection by explicitly connecting the tree diagrams.

■ .... Concept Check 16 .... ■

Draw a tree diagram of the premise-conclusion-support relationships for the following argument:

If defense spending were going to be significantly reduced, then the value of the dollar against the German mark would increase. The defense spending would have that effect because the U.S. balance of payments and national debt would be improved if defense spending were significantly reduced. Also, if the balance of payments and national debt were improved, the value of the dollar against the German mark would increase. However, we know that defense spending is not going to be significantly reduced, so the value of the dollar against the German mark won't increase.

In answering this question, use the following abbreviations:

REDUCED = Defense spending is significantly reduced.

INCREASE = The value of the dollar against the German mark increases.

IMPROVED = The U.S. balance of payments and national debt is improved.

Note the change to present tense in the abbreviated sentences.

So far we have taken arguments and produced the corresponding tree diagram. Now let's reverse the order.

Concept Check 17

Given the following tree diagram, rewrite the argumentation in decent English, being careful to add helpful indicator words.

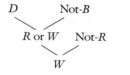

R = The prisoner has a red hat.

W = The prisoner has a white hat.

D = Samuelson says all prisoners have either a red, white, or black hat.

B = The prisoner has a black hat.

Some of that argumentation is deductively valid, and some is not. Which is which?

In other arguments, a premise might be used to draw more than one immediate conclusion, in which case there would be more than one line descending from that premise in the tree diagram.[5] For example, a weather report might say, "It is raining there," and from this statement you might draw these two conclusions: "It's cloudy there. Also, most of the trees' leaves are wet there." A correct tree diagram for this piece of reasoning would look like this:

A = It is raining there.

B = It is cloudy there.

C = Most of the trees' leaves are wet there.

Here is an incorrect tree diagram for the same piece of reasoning.

It is incorrect because it falsely suggests that B is stated as a reason to believe C. Instead, it represents "A, so B, and therefore C."

Let's examine a slightly more complicated example of reasoning that introduces a new kind of tree diagram. Suppose a fire inspector for an insurance company learns that (A) your apartment building burned down yesterday and that (B) a well-known arsonist, Jerry Lee, was arrested for speeding in a direction away from your apartment building about 15 minutes after the fire started. On the basis of this information, the fire inspector might say, "I'll bet (C) the building's landlord will soon be filing a claim against our company, and (D) Jerry Lee is the best suspect to question first." Notice that although C and D are two conclusions, C isn't the reason she gives for D, and D isn't the reason she gives for C. Instead, there are two arguments here:

$\begin{array}{c} A \\ / \\ C \end{array}$ $\begin{array}{c} A \quad B \\ \backslash / \\ D \end{array}$

The two could be combined as

Review of Major Points

Premise and conclusion indicator phrases serve as guideposts for detecting arguments. It is important to be alert to the role of conditional claims in arguments. Almost all arguments have some implicit elements. The most common implicit premises are definitions of words, principles of grammar and semantics, and rules of mathematics. Rewriting arguments in standard form is a helpful way to display their essential content. Arguments can have quite complex structure; for example, there are often subarguments within longer arguments. Drawing tree diagrams can help display the essential form of multiargument passages.

Glossary

conclusion indicators Words or phrases that signal the presence of conclusions but not premises. *Examples*: So, therefore, thus, it follows that.

conditional statement An if-then statement. The then clause holds on the condition that the if clause holds.

final conclusion In a chain of arguments, the last conclusion.

implicit premise A statement that does not appear explicitly in an argument but that is intended by the arguer to be a premise to help make the conclusion follow from the premises.

main argument In multiple argumentation, the most important subargument, the one that is the focus of attention. Its conclusion is the main conclusion even if not the final conclusion.

multiple argumentation More than one argument in a passage.

premise indicators Words or phrases that signal the presence of premises but not conclusions. *Examples*: Because, since, for the reason that.

standard form A single argument rewritten with its premises above the line and its conclusion below the line. The premises and conclusion should be expressed as declarative sentences. Pronouns should be replaced with their antecedents wherever possible. The order of the premises is not important. Indicator words and other fluff words are stripped away. When an argument is in standard form, it is supposed to stand alone with everything significant stated explicitly so that the reader can view the whole argument and understand what it is without needing additional information from the context.

subconclusion The conclusion of an argument that occurs among other arguments.

tree diagram A picture of an argument in which lines descend from premises to their immediate conclusion. A tree diagram is a tool intended to represent the details of complicated, multiple argumentation.

Answers to Concept Checks

1. Answer (b). Some good arguments have just one premise. For example, "Viruses are the simplest life forms on Earth, so that virus you are looking at under the microscope is simpler than other life forms."

2. *So* is a conclusion indicator, and it is indicating the conclusion. *Since* is a premise indicator that is not functioning here to indicate a premise.

3. (a) This is an argument. The conclusion is that (you should) never pick up a recently killed rattlesnake. *Because* is the premise indicator. (b) This is an argument with the same conclusion as in (a). Notice that the word *because* appeared in (a) but not in (b). Consequently, you have to work harder to locate the argument in (b). Good writers use indicator words to show their intentions to the reader. (c) This is not an argument. With a billion people, being one in a million is not very special, is it? (d) This is not an argument. This kind of plasma has nothing to do with blood plasma. Besides solids, liquids, and gases, matter also takes the form of plasmas. A plasma is super-ionized in the sense that every electron has been stripped away from the nucleus. There are no ordinary atoms in a plasma. All stars are made of plasma. So are electric sparks.

4. It is important to remove the first pronoun from the premise. Here is the standard form of the explicit argument:

The nerve reflexes of a recently killed rattlesnake enable it to bite for some time after death.

You should never pick up a recently killed rattlesnake.

5. Yes.

6. (a) yes (b) no (c) no (d) yes (e) no (f) yes (g) yes (h) yes (i) no. In (i), if the *or* were *and*, the answer would be *yes*.

7. Answer (c).

8. Consensus (c). The first sentence of the joke is neither a premise nor a conclusion, yet it contains essential information needed to locate the conclusion of the argument used in the joke. The sentence is an example of satire.

9. Baxalite is a soft mineral.

10. Answer (c).

11. Jack offered an argument for the conclusion that those drugs should not be in his house. Suzanne offered a criticism of Jack's argument; she saw a presupposition of Jack's argument—that Jack's daughter is sane—and implied that this presupposition is false. So the answer is (e).

12. The service at the restaurant is distracting.

13. The conclusion that both of them might want us to draw is that the American health care system needs to be improved. However, Cronkite could say, "I didn't say that in so many words; that was your conclusion from my facts; I just gave you the facts." The author of the article could also say that her quotes from Marmor and Cronkite were just giving us some information; she wasn't drawing any conclusion for us.

14. Subconclusion. The final and main conclusion is that all the patients given the AIDS antidote now have red hair.

15. $E \quad J$
$\quad \diagdown \diagup$
$\quad\quad C$

16. One important step in answering this question is to discover the *logical forms* of the component sentences of the argument. The statement

> If defense spending were going to be significantly reduced, then the value of the dollar against the German mark would increase.

has the logical form.

> If REDUCED, then INCREASE.

Therefore, the second sentence has this logical form:

> If REDUCED, then INCREASE
>   because
> IMPROVED, if REDUCED.

Note that the premise of this subargument is equivalent to

> If REDUCED, then IMPROVED.

The third sentence, "Also, if the balance of payments and national debt were improved, the value of the dollar against the German mark would increase," has this form:

> If IMPROVED, then INCREASE.

The fourth is

> NOT REDUCED, so NOT INCREASE.

In the complete diagram of the argument, the lines go down from premises to conclusion as follows:

> If REDUCED, then IMPROVED.   If IMPROVED, then INCREASE.
>
> NOT REDUCED.   If REDUCED, then INCREASE.
>
> NOT INCREASE.

Note that the main argument (whose conclusion is NOT INCREASE) is not deductively valid reasoning. However, the subargument (whose conclusion is If REDUCED, then INCREASE) is deductively valid.

    The notion of "logical form" is the central topic of Appendix C.

17. Here is why the prisoner must have a white hat. Samuelson says all prisoners have a red, white, or black hat. But we already know that the prisoner's hat isn't black. Therefore, the hat is red or white. However, we also know the prisoner's hat isn't red. So, it's got to be white.

The part that isn't deductively valid is the part that relies on what Samuelson says. The inference from "Samuelson says all prisoners have a red, white, or black hat" to "All prisoners have a red, white, or black hat" is inductive, not deductively valid. It's an argument from authority.

Review and Writing Exercises

Detecting Single, Explicit Arguments

■ 1. The sentence below is quite likely

    a. an argument   b. not an argument

    Dynamic Random Access Memory (DRAM) chips are the popular choice for memory storage on personal computers since, unlike the SRAM chip, they are less expensive per byte and the DRAM design essentially requires using only one transistor per bit.

2. The following passage contains

    a. an argument   b. a report of an argument   c. neither

    Through a process of trial and error, early people slowly learned that some contaminated food made them sick, while other contaminations improved the flavor, made an exhilarating fruit drink, or helped preserve the food for longer periods of time. In modern times, scientists learned that the contaminations are due to bacteria, yeast, and molds.

3. The sentence below is quite likely

    a. an argument   b. not an argument

    The life of a respected technical professional has few spare moments because there's all that work from running labs to teaching to speaking at colloquiums to writing grant proposals to selling research programs to administrating or managing to maybe even finding a few minutes to *think* about what to do.

■ 4. Which are the premise indicators in the following list?

    if, then, yet, nevertheless, on the contrary, but, thus, suppose that

■ 5. Which are the conclusion indicators in the following list?

    if, then, yet, nevertheless, on the contrary, but, thus, suppose that

■ 6. Does this argument contain any premise indicators that are working to indicate premises? If so, identify them.

President Kennedy was smart to have approved of the Bay of Pigs invasion of Cuba in 1961 since he could be reasonably certain the USSR wouldn't physically intervene to help Cuba, and since he wanted to do something that could overthrow the left-wing government that had replaced Cuba's right-wing dictatorship.

7. Is the word *since* working to indicate a premise or conclusion in the following?

   Since 5 P.M. I've been hungry.

8. Add a premise indicator, remove the conclusion indicator (without replacement), and rewrite the following argument as a single sentence.

   Ever since the inflationary spiral ended, state taxes have been high. State farm subsidies will therefore continue to rise.

9. Is the word *suppose* working as a premise indicator in the following?

   I suppose you're right that the New York Giants have a better passing game than the L.A. Rams.

10. Add a premise indicator, remove the conclusion indicator (without replacement), and rewrite the following argument as a single sentence.

    The average length of an ear of Iowa popcorn has been long ever since the 1991 planting regulations were adopted. State sales of popcorn will therefore continue to prosper.

■ 11. The following passage, in part, describes an argument. (a) State the issue. (b) Identify any premise or conclusion indicator phrases that are present and are actually functioning as signs of premises or conclusions. (c) Put the main argument into standard form. (d) Construct an argument for the other side of the issue — that is, a counterargument likely to be given by an elected school board member.

   The Illinois Supreme Court struck down Chicago's year-old school decentralization effort Friday. . . .

   The justices questioned the mechanics rather than the intent of the decentralization law. In a 6-1 decision, they ruled that the 5,400 parents, teachers, and residents chosen to run the city's 540 public schools had been elected illegally, because parents were given greater weight in selecting the board members than other citizens.

   City and school officials said they planned to ask the court to stay the order. . . .

   At issue is the way the councils got into office. In October 1989, six parents, two teachers, and two neighborhood representatives were chosen by their peers to sit on each school council. The principal chosen by the representatives is also a member of the council.

Parents whose children attended a given school could vote only for the six parent representatives — the majority of the council; teachers at the school could vote only for the two teacher representatives and neighborhood residents only for the two community representatives.[6]

■ 12. Consider the following argument:

All those containers contain petroleum since each one has a blue top, and since all petroleum containers have blue tops.

Let *A* = All those containers contain petroleum.
      B = Each of those containers has a blue top.
      C = All petroleum containers have blue tops.
      D = Everything with a blue top is a petroleum container.

Which one of the following would be the argument's standard form?

a.	*A*	b.	*D*	c.	*C*	d.	*C*	e.	*A*
	B		*C*		*A*		*B*		*D*
	C		*A*		*B*		*A*		*C*

13. Is the argument in question 12 deductively valid?

■ 14. Does the following contain an argument, and if so what are its conclusion and premises?

By the age of seven, Snow-White had grown more beautiful than her stepmother, the Queen. Then the Queen asked her mirror:

"Mirror, mirror on the wall,
Who is the fairest of us all?"

and it answered:

"Queen, thou art the fairest in this hall,
But Snow-White's fairer than us all."

Horrified, the envious Queen called a royal hunter and said:

"Take the child into the forest. Kill her, and bring me her lung and liver as a token."

15. Which of the following sentences contain explicit argumentation — that is, explicitly contain the two elements required to be an any argument (a conclusion plus one or more premises)?

a. Among all creatures, humans are distinguished by the extent to which they wonder about things that do not immediately affect their subsistence.

b. Every man is a potential killer, even if he believes otherwise. What I mean to say is, every man is capable of taking a life. And man is not the *only* creature on Earth who is a potential killer.

c. If you were to pick an apple at random from that basket, then you'd probably get one without a worm in it.

d. Stop right there, Jack; it's not raining today, so you won't need to take that umbrella. Put it back.

16. The following passage is most likely

a. an argument   b. not an argument

Although rattlesnakes are the most common poisonous snake in North America, there are four types of poisonous snakes on the continent: rattlesnakes, copperheads, moccasins, and coral snakes. The first three belong to the pit viper group, and the most reliable physical trait by which to identify them is the pair of pits between the eye and the nostril. These pits are heat sensitive and allow a snake to sense its prey. Keep in mind that a snake's venom is designed for catching food, not attacking people.

17. What is going on in the following passage from a 1986 newspaper article by Mark Grossman and Connie Matthiessen?

If a poultry slaughterhouse is to be technologically up-to-date, it must be equipped with steel-fingered evisceration machines. These gleaming metal contraptions scoop out entrails from chickens and turkeys through a cut below the breast bone. The rate can be 90 birds a minute.

During the past five years the machines have been introduced to almost every butchering assembly line in the United States. But for all their speed and efficiency, they are not as precise as a pair of human hands. Often the machines tear the intestines and spill fecal matter onto the meat.

In the fecal matter are salmonella, campylobacter, and *E. coli* bacteria, which are primary culprits in an alarming and increasing level of food poisoning in the United States.

In recent testing by the U.S. Department of Agriculture, 37 percent of supermarket-ready chickens were contaminated with salmonella, and the percentage has been even higher in privately conducted tests. "If the American public knew what garbage they were eating, they would revolt," said USDA inspector Hobart Bartley.

Critics like Bartley cite three major reasons for what they say is a serious decline in the quality of American poultry:

- The addition of high-speed, high-volume technology to the assembly line, particularly the evisceration machines, which accounted for an increase in production from 2.9 billion chickens in 1975 to 4.4 billion in 1985.

- Repeated reductions in the Food and Safety Inspection Service, which lost more than 400 of its inspectors to layoffs in February 1986.

- A shortcoming in federal meat inspection laws, which do not require slaughterhouses to clean off "invisible" amounts of bacteria.[7]

a. Critics like Bartley offer no argument, according to Grossman and Matthiessen, who themselves offer only a description of the poultry business.

b. Grossman and Matthiessen are arguing that a poultry slaughterhouse ought not be equipped with steel-fingered evisceration machines because 4.4 billion chickens disemboweled per year is too low a number.

c. Grossman and Matthiessen are trying to say that if the American public knew what garbage they were eating, they would revolt.

d. Critics like agriculture inspector Bartley argue for the conclusion that there has been a decline in the quality of American poultry, and they offer a few reasons in support of their conclusion.

e. Grossman and Matthiessen are making fun of Bartley and of his liberal views that there should be more big government and red tape and inspectors who interfere in the way slaughterhouses do business.

18. Locate the main point of this piece from a 1986 issue of the *New Yorker*.

Notes and Comment

You are the town and We are the clock.
We are the guardians of the gate in the rock.
     The Two.
On your left and on your right
In the day and in the night,
     We are watching you.

Wiser not to ask just what has occurred
To them who disobeyed our word;
     To those
We were the whirlpool, we were the reef,
We were the formal nightmare, grief
     And the unlucky rose.

   Thus Auden, speaking in the language of our day about what the Greeks used to call the Fates, who spun out the threads of human lives and severed them when their time was up. That time often came, the Greeks believed, when someone forgot his mortal limitations and started to act as if he thought he was a god. There was in the nature of things, the Greeks believed, a balance, or proportion, or moral harmony, that the overreaching, arrogant man upset, for he was forgetful of his human nature — meaning, above all, his moral nature, which was the basis of his common humanity with others. Death was the correction. Death was the reminder of the common humanity that the arrogant man had thought he could rise above.

Auden's Two came to mind with the news that Americans are boycotting Europe this summer. They are doing it, of course, because they don't want to be blown up at some airport or discotheque by the agents of Colonel Muammar Qaddafi, who has been presumed to have such plans since the United States's recent bombing attack on Libya, in which his adopted daughter was killed and two of his sons were injured. Afterward, President Reagan, when he was asked whether the raid, in which bombs had fallen at Qaddafi's living compound, had been intended to kill Qaddafi, answered that it hadn't but added that if Qaddafi had been killed no tears would have been shed — an only slightly circuitous manner of speaking, which can only leave the world thinking: They tried but missed. Secretary of State Shultz used more bluntly threatening language when, after the heads of Western states and Japan at the summit conference in Tokyo condemned Libya for supporting terrorism, he said, "You've had it, pal." Meanwhile, polls show, the public has continued to strongly support a belligerent policy. No one is obliged to volunteer to be the victim of terrorist attacks (though in this case it's possible that the fears of those canceling their plane reservations to Europe are out of proportion to the actual level of danger), but the combination of enthusiasm for military action and extreme personal caution when it comes to facing the consequences is not attractive. Having, as we believe, turned Europe into a danger zone, we now shun the place, leaving the Europeans to pay whatever price is to be paid. There is an itch in this country, evident in our cinematic and television fare as well as in our politics, to lash out violently at some enemy somewhere, but little readiness, it seems, to acknowledge the risks of being lashed back at that are inherent in such an operation. It's as if we wished to assert immunity to what, after all, are the laws of human existence — immunity to our mortal nature. We are ready to kill but not to die, as if we thought that the violence we visit on foreign countries really was a television program or a movie. That may be the modern form of the arrogance that the Greeks warned against: to forget that the world in the television news and the world of our lives are one and the same, and that the people dying on the screen are as real as those of us who sit in comfort watching them. And that could be our way of falling into the trap that The Two warn us against when they say, "But don't make the mistake of believing us dead." For then:

We're afraid in that case you'll have a fall;
We've been watching you over the garden wall
    For hours:
The sky is darkening like a stain;
Something is going to fall like rain,
    And it won't be flowers.[8]

The major point that the above piece is trying to convey is that:

a. Americans have mistakenly assumed that American foreign activities will have no disastrous consequences for Americans.

b. No American is obliged to volunteer to be the victim of terrorist attacks against America.

c. The Two Fates occasionally erupted into ancient Greek life, causing trouble for those Greeks who mistakenly began to believe they were invincible or beyond mortal limitations.

d. Colonel Qaddafi is an enemy of the United States and a target of its foreign policy initiatives.

■ 19. In the following paragraph, the second girl's response could be interpreted as a description of her reasons, as an explanation of her reasoning, or as an argument. Rewrite that argument in standard form and assess its strength.

> My question: "What percentage of American homes contain personal computers?" The first girl guessed 60 percent. The second girl thought about it a minute before saying that she thought the correct answer was "higher, more like 80 percent." Knowing that she was off by almost a factor of 10, I asked why she thought that there's a personal computer in nearly every American home. "Well, we have two computers at home and all of my friends have at least one." If her parents worked in the personal computer industry, she probably would have gone even higher.[9]

■ 20. Does the following passage contain an argument? If so, what is its conclusion and premises?

> Newton's predecessors, such as Galileo, Kepler, and Hooke, were moving away from the Aristotelian worldview, in which the behavior of objects is dictated by the "qualities" they possess; Aristotelians believed, for example, that a stone falls because its "nature" necessitates that it move toward the center of the universe, or that planets travel in circular orbits because the circle is a heavenly form.
>
> In contrast, the emerging view during the scientific revolution [of the seventeenth century] was more clearly rooted in the underlying forces or laws that can be expressed mathematically.[10]

21. Is this passage an argument, or not an argument, for the conclusion that Chinese women are not interested in sex?

> The Chinese women are not into sex. They do not fool around . . . The Chinese are into their puritanical period. There are over a billion Chinese and the government wants the Chinese to forget about sex for a few decades or so.[11]

22. Is the following passage an argument? Why or why not?

> If you get lost in the woods and no one responds to your calls, walk downhill until you come to a stream. Then walk downstream; you'll eventually come to a town.

23. The most likely main purpose of the following passage is to
    a.   explain why the Maya civilization wrote hieroglyphs.
    b.   describe characteristics of the Maya civilization.
    c.   argue for the conclusion that the Maya civilization was violent and barbaric.
    d.   argue for the conclusion that the Maya civilization wrote hieroglyphs.

> The recent interpretation of Maya hieroglyphs has given us the first written history of the New World as it existed before the European invasion. . . . At its height, Maya civilization flourished under great kings like Shield-Jaguar, who ruled for more than sixty years, expanding his kingdom and building some of the most impressive works of architecture in the ancient world. Long placed on a mist-shrouded pedestal as austere, peaceful stargazers, the Maya elites are now known to have been the rulers of populous, aggressive city-states. . . . The Maya were at once highly civilized, skilled in architecture and astronomy, and, to us, violent and barbaric, engaging in ritual bloodletting and many wars.[12]

Conditionals

1. Is the following statement a conditional?

> An ostrich is a bird; all birds can fly; and an ostrich cannot fly.

   a.   yes   b.   no   c.   can't tell

2. Is the following conditional true?

> If kids who are abused become abusive parents when they have children and John Drew is really being abused by his mother, then when he grows up he is likely to abuse his own children.

   a.   yes   b.   no   c.   need more information to tell

3. If the *if* part of a conditional claim is true, and if the conditional claim itself is true, will the *then* part *have* to be true?

4. Is the following statement an argument?

> If you had struck this match when it was dry, even though it's now wet, then it would have burst into flame.

Implicit Elements of Arguments

1. If there is an argument present, then there will always be a premise present.

    a. true   b. false

2. According to this textbook, if a premise or a conclusion is implicit, then it is:

    a. very probably true.

    b. always uncertain.

    c. unstated.

    d. none of the above.

3. Identify the implicit conclusion of the following argument, then indicate whether the argument is inductive or deductive.

    AIDS will kill everybody who gets it.
    Your mother has gotten AIDS.
    _____
    ?

4. What is the conclusion of this argument by analogy?

    To say that TEX, the scientific wordprocessor language, takes a little effort to learn is like saying that with a little effort you could build your own full-scale, working *Challenger* spacecraft and run your own space shuttle program. Surely you don't believe you can do this, do you?

5. Rewrite this deductively valid argument in standard form, adding any significant implicit premises.

    That animal is going to be one with stripes because *all* zebras have stripes.

6. Rewrite this argument in standard form so that it is deductively valid: "Joshua, quit that! Justine isn't bothering *you*!"

7. When the senator says, "Murder is wrong," and the reporter says, "Well, then you must think capital punishment is wrong, too," the reporter is making an argument, but she is leaving a lot unsaid. One of her significant implicit premises is that the senator thinks

    a. Murder is a kind of capital punishment.

    b. Capital punishment is a kind of murder.

    c. Capital punishment is neither right nor wrong.

    d. If capital punishment is wrong, then murder is wrong.

8. Identify the principal implicit element (and say whether it is a premise or a conclusion) in the following argument regarding the correctness of the theory of biological evolution.

According to the fossil record as it is interpreted by evolutionists, spiders have been on earth for 300 million years but have not changed. Yet, if evolution were really working, surely they would have changed by now, wouldn't they?

9. Identify the most significant implicit premise used in the following argument:

All good Americans hate communism and love the first lady. So, Roberto Salazar Rodriguez loves the first lady.

10. If any of these three passages below contain arguments, rewrite the arguments in standard form.

   a. Call me crazy. I just think Joe Montana can play well in big games. I don't know why, I just do.[13]

   b. When the Giants and 49ers both lost last week, their coaches told their teams, "Boys, we're still the best."

   c. Four researchers recently spent a few weeks in Sumatra swinging on lianas, the long woody vines that hang down from the jungle canopy. Their experimental procedure was simple: find a suitable liana, climb up on a footstool—one follows the call of the wild only so far—grab hold, and push free. Sometimes the researchers wore knapsacks full of rocks. And sometimes the lianas held.[14]

11. Give the standard form of this deductively valid argument, adding the significant implicit premises, if there are any:

If the moral thing to do is always whatever your society says, then Nazi brutality was ethically OK in Nazi Germany. Therefore, the moral thing to do is *not* always whatever your society says it is.

12. What premise is probably being assumed to make the following argument be deductively valid?

Tom New is running for state treasurer of Indiana, so he knows a lot about public finances.

   a. If a person knows a lot about public finances, then the person is running for state treasurer of Indiana.

   b. If a person is running for some public office, then the person probably knows a lot about public finances.

   c. Tom New is a candidate with financial savvy.

   d. Anybody who runs for state treasurer of Indiana is financially ambitious.

   e. All candidates for federal office know a lot about public finances.

   f. If a person is running for state treasurer of any state, then the person knows a lot about public finances.

    g.   People who know a lot about public finances often run for state treasurer in Indiana.

■ 13. The following statement is not an argument, but the reader most probably can assume that the speaker believes what?

    Stick your hands up or I'll blow your head off.

    a.   The hands of the person being spoken to are not up.

    b.   If you stick your hands up, I will blow your head off.

    c.   The two people have guns.

    d.   If I blow your head off, then your hands were up.

    e.   I will blow your head off.

14. In the following argument, the speaker is most probably assuming what in order for it to be deductively valid?

    He didn't stick his hands up, so he must have believed the gun was not loaded.

    a.   Whenever persons believe a gun is not loaded, they don't stick up their hands.

    b.   Whenever a man doesn't stick up his hands, he must believe this is the right thing to do.

    c.   Either he sticks his hands up, or he believes the gun is loaded.

    d.   A person believes the gun is not loaded if, in a situation like this, he doesn't stick up his hands.

    e.   Just because a person doesn't stick up his or her hands, it doesn't follow that he or she must believe anything about a gun being loaded or not loaded.

15. What is the most significant implicit premise used in the first subargument of the argument chain?

    She's got the flu again, so she probably won't be here to chair the meeting. Therefore, I'll have to do it. Damn!

16. In the article "Magic Acts" quoted in the chapter, the author describes several of Frost's arguments. Rewrite her Catholicism argument in standard form.

■ 17. In the article "Magic Acts" quoted in the chapter, the author describes several of Frost's arguments. Rewrite her capitalism argument in standard form, making it deductively valid.

18. Rewrite the conclusion of this argument as a declarative sentence.

    What do you mean "We should let a pregnant woman decide whether she has an abortion"? If you let them decide, then you are letting people commit murder. You can't let them do that, can you?

Multiple Arguments

■ 1. Write out the standard form of the first *sub*argument in the following argument. Then draw the tree of all the argumentation.

> Galileo said good science uses mathematics, yet Charles Darwin's work on evolution uses no mathematics. Therefore, Darwin's work on evolution is not good science.

2. Draw the tree diagram for the following deductively valid argument:

> (A) All birds we've ever found on this planet could fly or hop. (B) That thing you see over there is definitely a bird. (C) You can draw your own conclusion.

3. Draw the tree diagram for the following deductively valid argument:

> Everybody who tests HIV positive eventually will contract AIDS. Your mother evidently just tested HIV positive. You can draw your own conclusion.

4. Complete the tree diagram for the following complex argumentation. Assume that statement C is the final conclusion.

$$
\begin{array}{ccc}
P_1 & P_4 & \\
P_2 & P_5 & \\
\underline{P_3} & \underline{P_6} & \underline{P_7} \\
C & P_1 & P_3
\end{array}
$$

Answer:

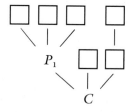

Does the complex argumentation in the following passage have the same structure as the preceding tree diagram? Defend your answer.

> Let's hike out of here. We'll get sick if we stay and drink the water from the stream. Also, we've been here so long that more camping will be boring, and aren't the mosquito bites worse than we expected? The water will make us sick because there was a sign back at the ranger station warning us about giardia and the dog we saw last night drinking from the stream is still vomiting. Besides, the water is murky.

5. Consider the following complex argument for the main conclusion C:

$$\frac{\begin{array}{l} P_1 \\ P_2 \\ P_3 \end{array}}{C} \quad \frac{\begin{array}{l} P_4 \\ P_5 \\ P_6 \end{array}}{P_1} \quad \frac{P_7}{P_3}$$

In this complex argumentation, P_2 serves as both a premise and a conclusion.

a. true b. false

6. In the complex argumentation in question 5, P_3 is the conclusion of a subargument.

a. true b. false

7. In the complex argumentation in question 5, P_4 is the conclusion of a subargument.

a. true b. false

8. Consider this argument:

> Either you are no friend of Susan's or you will let me in to borrow your stereo for her. But since you obviously won't let me in to borrow your stereo for her, you are no friend of hers, and I intend to tell her so.

Is the following a correct diagram of the premise-conclusion-support relationships? If not, why not?

B = You will let me in to borrow your stereo for Susan.

F = You are a friend of Susan's.

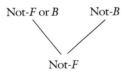

9. Draw the tree diagram of the multiple argumentation contained within the following passage:

> There is no way you are going to be able to convince David to go out with Yolanda on Saturday night. He is living with Cynthia. Besides, he doesn't really like Yolanda, does he? And don't try to talk to Michael, either. He and Yolanda haven't said much to each other ever since she got stuck holding the extra Kings tickets that she couldn't resell. And forget Steve, too. But those three guys are the only possible candidates for Yolanda, so there's no way that Yolanda is going out Saturday night with anyone from our class. If Yolanda goes out Saturday night, it will be with someone not in our class.

10. A juror is arguing that the defendant Mayfield is guilty of robbing the All-Night Grocery:

> No, he's as guilty as sin. Take a look at his face. He won't even look the district attorney in the eye. Besides, he refused to take the lie detector test. You failed to mention that the police report shows when he was first arrested he denied even being in the grocery store, but we've proved he was there, so he's a known liar.

Draw the tree diagram, and evaluate the quality of the argumentation.

11. Draw the tree diagram of the following multiple argumentation. You may ignore implicit premises and any explanations that are given in the passage. If you use any of the numbered statements below in your tree, use the numbers in the tree.

> (1) George recently filed a police complaint against his neighbor for making too much noise. So, (2) he will be contacted by the city after the investigation. It also follows that (3) he doesn't see much hope in solving his problem by talking to his neighbor any more. George filed not only because (4) there had been many incidents of loud noise, as far as he was concerned, but also because (5) his wife urged him to do so. (6) She was mad about his doing so badly in his job interview the morning after he was up several times complaining to her about the neighbor's noise.

Creating and Improving Arguments

- 1. Research the issue of whether the United States can afford to expand its space program. Take a side and create a 200- to 300-word argument in defense of your position. Give credit to your sources (i.e., use footnotes to say where your information came from).

2. Lesley and Rico say they've found a deductively valid, simple argument that, when rewritten in standard form, is a mixture of true and false sentences in which the premises are all true. Why is this unusual?

- 3. The following is an argument. Construct a new argument that defends the opposite conclusion but that devotes about half its attention to countering the points made in the first argument.

> America should have more alcoholics. Here is why. Drinking alcohol makes you feel good, and Americans deserve to feel good, if anybody does. Legislators who are alcoholics will be off playing golf or hanging out in bars; they will be preoccupied and therefore won't pass so much harmful legislation that rips off us taxpayers. Besides, if I want to be an alcoholic and don't do anything to harm you, then you shouldn't be telling me what I can do with my body; it's my body, not your body, right?

You will be graded on the clarity of your argument, your ability to foresee counters from your opponents, and the absence of silly, naive, or irrelevant comments. The upper limit on your new argument should be two pages, typed double-spaced.

- 4. Construct an argument defending your position on the issue of whether there ought to be a law permitting the county public health department to start a needle exchange program. Under this program, drug addicts would be given new or clean hypodermic needles in exchange for their old or used needles, no questions asked. The purpose of the program would be to slow the spread of AIDS.

    Background: Assume that it is a misdemeanor to possess a hypodermic needle that has not been prescribed by a doctor and that it is a misdemeanor for a doctor to prescribe or give away hypodermic needles and other drug addiction paraphernalia except for certain listed problems, such as diabetes and allergies.

    You will be graded not on what position you take but on the clarity of your argument, your ability to foresee counters from your opponents, and the absence of silly, naive, or irrelevant comments. Keep your argument to two pages, typed, double-spaced.

5. This is a voluntary exercise to be done by four students working as a group. The group chooses an issue to debate in front of the rest of the class, but the issue must be approved by the instructor. The group meets outside of class to research the issue. A typical issue might be whether the college should spend more money on athletic scholarships and less money on other projects. Another issue might be whether U.S. defense spending should be cut. Two students agree to argue for a yes position on the issue; the other two students agree to argue for the no position. During the class debate, all four students speak alternatively, each for five minutes or less. Speakers may use their time either to present arguments for their own position or to attack arguments presented by the opposition. When the four are done, the rest of the class get to ask them questions or otherwise enter into the debate. The goal of the exercise is to show a significant understanding of the issue and to carry out good logical reasoning on the issue.

6. Create an argument for why the following question was answered incorrectly.

   Question: Evaluate this explanation (without appealing to outside experts on mudslides): "The North Carolina coastal hills are especially prone to mudslides because of the loosely binding sandy soil, which has little clay, and because the coast's vegetation doesn't provide a stable root system."

   Answer: This explanation is circular because it states that there are mudslides in the first half, and then in the second half it states there is not stability, which is basically repeating the fact that the land is subject to mudslides.

CHAPTER

12

Induction: Analogies and Statistical Reasoning

I nductive argumentation establishes its conclusion with probability rather than certainty. Previous chapters explored arguments from authority and several other types of inductive arguments and examined ways to recognize, create, diagnose, and improve the arguments. This chapter focuses specifically on the nature of the inductive process because inductive arguments play such a central role in our lives. Almost every argument we create or encounter is inductive rather than deductive. After examining inductive arguments by analogy, by appeal to typical examples, and by inferring a prediction from past data, the chapter goes on to explore the techniques of effective sampling and polling.

Varieties of Inductive Arguments

> If it looks like a duck, walks like a duck, and quacks like a duck, then it's a duck.

This is usually good reasoning. Just don't assume that it *must* be a duck for these reasons. The line of reasoning is not surefire. Because it's in*duck*tive reasoning, the conclusion follows only with probability. The mark of good deductive reasoning, on the other hand, is that the conclusion follows with absolute certainty from the premises.

With inductive reasoning, there is always the risk that by drawing the conclusion from given premises we are being hasty and are committing the **fallacy of jumping to conclusions**. It's natural to want to draw a conclusion as soon as possible; if it walks like a duck and quacks like a duck, then how much more evidence do we need before calling it a duck? If we called it a duck right now, would we be jumping to conclusions? No, but if we want to be surer about our conclusion, we might go get some expert advice from a duck authority. If the expert says it's a duck, then we are more justified in calling it a duck. Still we could be wrong; we could have been tricked. In any given case, then, how do we tell when we are jumping to conclusions and when we aren't? Unfortunately, there is no formula, but we do have some rules of thumb. This chapter and the next will explore them.

Arguments from Authority

Inductive arguments are, in many ways, much more interesting than deductive arguments. Arguments in daily life are usually inductive. Here is one. It's an argument from authority. A high school science teacher is speaking to you:

> The scientists I've read agree that Neptune is a cold planet. So, Neptune is a cold planet.

This argument does not jump to conclusions. The high school teacher offers expert testimony although it is secondhand. It might be called hearsay in a courtroom, but it is reasonable grounds for accepting the conclusion. So, the conclusion follows with probability. But how *much* probability? Nobody knows, not even the scientists. Nobody can say authoritatively whether the conclusion is 85 percent probable or instead 90 percent probable. All we can say is that the appeal to authority makes the conclusion a safe bet because the proper authorities have been consulted, they have been quoted correctly, and they do not significantly disagree about this topic.

The conclusion of the following argument isn't such a safe bet:

> The scientists say astral travel is impossible. That is, our spiritual bodies can't temporarily leave our physical bodies and travel to other places. So *they* say. However, my neighbor and several of her friends told me they separately traveled to Egypt while their physical bodies were asleep last night. They visited the pyramids. These people are sincere and reliable. Therefore, the scientists are wrong about astral travel.

Is this a successful inductive argument? The arguer asks us to accept stories from his neighbor and her friends. These anecdotes are pitted against the claims of the scientists. Which should you believe? Scientists have been wrong many times before; couldn't they be wrong here, too? Yes, they could, but it wouldn't be a good bet. If you had some evidence that could convincingly show the scientists to be wrong, then you, yourself, would likely soon become a famous scientist. You should be cautious about jumping to the conclusion that the scientists are wrong because the stories are so extraordinary that you really need extraordinarily good evidence to believe them. The only evidence in favor of the stories is the fact that the neighbors and friends, who are presumed to be reasonable, agree on their stories and the fact that several times in history other persons also have claimed to be astral travelers.

The neighbor might say that she does have evidence that could convincingly show the scientists to be wrong but that she couldn't get a fair hearing from the scientists because their minds are closed to these possibilities of expanding their consciousness. Yes, the scientists probably would give her the brush-off, but by and large the scientific community *is* open to new ideas. She wouldn't get the scientists' attention because they are as busy as the rest of us, and they don't want to spend much time on unproductive projects. However, if the neighbor were to produce some knowledge about the Egyptian pyramids that she couldn't have gotten until she did her astral traveling, *then* the scientists would look more closely at what she is saying. Until then, she will continue to be ignored by the establishment.

This discussion illustrates that there is a significant difference between an argument that appeals to expert opinion and one that challenges it. Most of what we know we got from believing what the experts said either firsthand or, more likely, secondhand. Not being experts ourselves, our problem is to be careful about sorting out the claims of experts from the other claims that bombard us, while being aware of the possibility that experts are misinterpreted, that on some topics they disagree, and that occasionally they themselves cannot be trusted to speak straightforwardly. Sensitive to the possibility of misinterpreting experts, we prefer firsthand testimony to secondhand, and secondhand to thirdhand. Sensitive to disagreement among the experts, we prefer unanimity and believe that the greater the consensus, the stronger the argument from authority.

Also, we are sensitive to when the claim is made and to what else is known about the situation. For example, a man returning from a mountaintop might say to you, "Wow, from there the world looks basically flat." Twenty anecdotes from twenty such people who independently climbed the same mountain do not make it twenty times more likely that the world is flat. You can't trust the twenty stories because there is much better evidence to be had. However, in the days when the Egyptians were building their pyramids, the twenty anecdotes would actually have made it more reasonable to believe that the world is flat, although even then it wouldn't have been twenty times more. Consequently, what is reasonable to believe at any time depends on the evidence available at that time.

It's important to resist the temptation to conclude that in ancient times people lived on a flat world but that now they live on a round Earth. This is just mumbo jumbo; the world stayed the same — it was people's beliefs about the world that changed. This approach overemphasizes the power of the mind to shape the world.

So, inductions are more difficult than deductions, and they are connected to all sorts of problems that don't arise with those neat, clean deductions. Despite the difficulty with inductions, a great deal is known that can be useful in everyday reasoning, as we shall see as we explore these eight types of inductive arguments:

1. argument from authority
2. induction by analogy
3. appealing to a typical example
4. argument from the past to the future
5. generalizing from a sample
6. induction from the general to the specific

7. induction from correlation to cause

8. argument to the best explanation

To appreciate some of the fruits of the tree of inductive knowledge, the next sections will explore kinds 2 through 6. Although these categories of inductive arguments are helpful, keep in mind that an argument might fall into more than one; they aren't mutually exclusive.

Induction by Analogy

In an earlier chapter we explored the use of analogies to explain the unfamiliar in terms of the familiar. The unfamiliar world of electricity can be explained by showing how electricity in a wire behaves analogously to water flowing through a pipe. Analogies help with description, too. We envision a rolling ball when we hear that presidential candidate Roosevelt had momentum going into the New Hampshire primary. Analogies can also be used to argue. For instance, one could say that a woman without a man is like a fish without a bicycle. This joke would be making a radical feminist comment, because hidden between the lines is an argument for why women don't need men. The joke is intended to counter the conclusion of someone who would say that a woman without a man is like a fish out of water.

Here is a more serious example of an argument by analogy. Suppose that for several months a scientist gives experimental drug D to a variety of dogs confined to cages. A group of similar caged dogs do not receive the drug. The scientist then tests to see whether the dogs receiving drug D are more cardiovascularly fit than the ones not receiving the drug. The scientist checks blood pressure, stamina, and other physiological measures. The scientist's initial subconclusion is that dogs that get the drug are no more cardiovascularly fit than the other dogs. The scientist's final and main conclusion: For humans, taking drug D will be no substitute for getting lots of exercise, as far as cardiovascular fitness is concerned. This main argument uses what analogy? Here is the standard form of the argument:

> Dogs are like humans in many ways.
> Dogs cannot use drug D as a substitute for exercise.
>
> Humans cannot use drug D as a substitute for exercise.

The conclusion follows with probability; the argument is inductive. However, we could rewrite the first premise so that the conclusion follows with certainty:

> Dogs are like humans when it comes to deciding whether drugs can be a substitute for exercise.
> Dogs cannot use drug D as a substitute for exercise.
>
> Humans cannot use drug D as a substitute for exercise.

This argument is deductive. Which of the two ways of treating the argument is better? It is hard to tell and doesn't make much difference. The scientist is more likely to have intended inductive standards to apply; at least we shall assume this from now on. But what is more important to see is that both ways of analyzing the argument depend on accepting the analogy between people and dogs. If the analogy is unacceptable, the argument breaks down. Scientists get into serious disputes about whether testing drugs on rats, dogs, and rabbits gives reliable information about how these drugs will affect human beings. These disputes are about analogy.

To generalize, the simplest inductive arguments from analogy have the following form:

> A's are analogous to B's in several relevant respects.
> A's have characteristic C.
> _____
> B's have characteristic C.

A characteristic is a property or quality. In the drug-testing example, A = dogs, B = humans, and C = the characteristic of not being able to use drug D as a substitute for exercise. If A's have characteristic C but B's do not, the analogy between A and B is a **faulty analogy** as far as C is concerned.

Analogies are often stated without using the words *analogous to* and *like*. Can you find the analogy used in the following passage?

> Inside informers seldom appear of their own volition. They have to be consciously created, usually from among members of the terrorist organization who have been arrested. . . .
>
> Persuading a terrorist to defect is akin to a father's attempt to convert his child from watching TV after school to doing her homework — with persuasive arguments, hints of future rewards for compliance, and suggestions of punishment for noncompliance.
>
> There seem to be five reasons why suspects are induced to think that it is in their own interests to inform and defect: because they are tortured, because they are induced to do so by cash, because they are blackmailed into it as the lesser of two evils, because they lose their nerve, and because they are genuinely converted from their terrorist beliefs to supporting the Government cause.[1]

Persuading a terrorist to defect is supposed to be analogous to converting the child from watching TV to doing her homework. The key to seeing the analogy is in noting the word *akin*.

Is this a faulty analogy? The average reader is not in a position to tell. Only people who are familiar both with persuading a terrorist to defect and with raising children would be in a position to say. However, notice that in this passage the analogy is not used to draw some conclusion, as it is in the earlier analogies we have discussed. The analogy is used simply to explain the process of persuading a terrorist. The passage contains an explanatory analogy but not an argument by analogy. If it were to contain an argument by analogy, it would probably say that because the conversion of the child requires such and such, therefore persuading a terrorist does, too.

Concept Check 1

Arguments from analogy have the following logical form: *A* is analogous to *B* in important ways. *A* has property *C*. So, *B* has *C*, too. What would the letters *A*, *B*, and *C* represent in the following argument by analogy?

> I am a vegetarian, and I believe it's morally wrong to cook live shrimp. After all, it would be wrong for someone to toss you into a pan of boiling water, wouldn't it?

Advertising that uses testimonials often promotes an argument by analogy. Take the Hollywood beauty who testifies to the TV viewer: "I got a silicone breast implant from Dr. Wrigley, and I got the lead part in a commercial. His plastic surgery can help you, too."[2] You, the female viewer, are being asked implicitly to accept the analogy with your own situation and conclude that the surgery will get you what you want. But as a logical reasoner you will confront the analogy directly by thinking something like this: "That's fine for her, but I'm not trying to get a part in a commercial, so realistically what does her testimony have to do with me in my situation?"

By criticizing the analogy in the argument that the TV program encourages you to create, you are using the technique of pointing out the **disanalogies**. The disanalogies are the differences, the ways in which the two are not analogous. We point out disanalogies when we say, "Yes, they're alike, but not in the important ways." We are apt, also, to use this method in response to the analogy between people and shrimp by pointing out that we are not like shrimp in terms of sensitivity to pain, or intelligence, or moral worth.

A second method of attacking an argument by analogy is to **extend the analogy**. We do this when we find other ways the two things are similar and then draw obviously unacceptable conclusions from this similarity. For example, we can attack the argument that uses the analogy between people and dogs by saying, "Dogs are like people in other ways, too. For example, we both like to eat meat. Since dogs enjoy their meat raw, you won't mind eating your hamburger raw tonight, will you?" When the original advocate of the cardiovascular argument answers, "No, we aren't that much like dogs," you can respond with "I agree, so how can you be so sure we are like dogs when it comes to taking drug D?"

Let's now analyze a more complicated argument by analogy. You might have had the honor of getting involved in the following unpleasant discussion with Mario about white women marrying black men. During the conversation, Mario said:

> A dog breeder wouldn't think of mixing different breeds, so the human race should not be mongrelized by interracial breeding. You accept my argument, or aren't you logical? Of course you accept it; you aren't some kind of pervert. Besides, you are not a dog breeder, so you are in no position to doubt what I say.

Let's analyze this volcanic argument. Mario's statement "The human race should not be mongrelized by interracial breeding" is loaded language filled with negative connotations. A less loaded replacement would be, "The human race should not produce children of parents from different races." The argument is primarily based on an analogy. The analogy is between having puppies of different breeds and having children of different races. There are important disanalogies to notice. Our background knowledge tells us that the purpose of dog breeding is to retain the characteristics of the breed. The purpose of having children is not normally to retain the racial characteristics of each parent. Did your parents have you primarily for the purpose of improving the design of their race? A second difficulty with the analogy is that even if mixing breeds produces mongrels that are of lesser quality in terms of winning blue ribbons in dog shows, it doesn't follow that mixing races produces children who are of lesser quality. In most societies, the people do believe that races shouldn't mix and that when they do they produce children who are "inferior," but this belief is based only on custom; there is no biological reason to believe that such children are physically or mentally inferior to their parents.

Mario was also mistaken in saying that if you lack expert knowledge about dog breeding, you should not doubt his claim. Our criticism of his analogy was based on common sense, not on any expert knowledge. His threatening to label you a "pervert" and not "logical" if you reject his argument is itself just name calling or intimidation. From a logical-reasoning perspective these threats do nothing positive for his position. If Mario were your boss, his attacks might convince you not to *say* you disagree with him, but his reasons shouldn't actually convince you to agree with him.

■ ·········· Concept Check 2 ·········· ■

Evaluate this 1940 argument by analogy:

> Armies are like people. If you cut off the head, the body may thrash around a bit, but very soon it quits fighting. So, a good way to win this European war against the Nazis and Fascists would be to concentrate all our energies on killing Hitler and Mussolini.

Appealing to a Typical Example

If you like the first pineapple you eat, you don't have to eat forty-seven more pineapples to figure out whether you like pineapples. One example is enough. Similarly, if you are given a meal of lung fish and discover that it tastes awful, you might argue by analogy that you won't like eating any other lung fish if it is prepared the same way. This inference makes use of the assumption that one lung fish is like any other as far as taste is concerned, especially if the preparation is similar. You assume that your one lung fish is a **typical example** of lung fish. In doing so, do you commit the fallacy of jumping to conclusions? No, but you would do so if you did not implicitly rely on background information. You use your background information that kinds of food don't usually change their taste radically from one meal to another. Without this background information, you really ought to try some more examples of lung fish before concluding that you don't like this seafood.

This example about lung fish is a special kind of argument from analogy; the argument relies on the fact that nearly all the members of a group are analogous to some typical member of the group. We will call this kind of argument by analogy an induction by **appeal to a typical example**.

The following argument also tries to make its point by giving only one example, expecting the reader to accept the generalization from that example. What is typical of what here?

> Although it is true that intending to do something usually does not bring about the same consequences as doing it, morally it seems no different. Suppose I intend to kill my rich uncle for my inheritance. I am hiding in his house behind the door, with my axe in my hand, waiting for him to enter, but as he walks up the front porch steps, he has a heart attack and dies. Hey, it's my lucky day! I get the inheritance and I don't even have to clean the blood off my axe. Surely you will say that the fact that I did not carry out my intention to kill my uncle does not absolve me morally, for had he entered the house I would have killed him. Whether or not I actually killed him, I'm still immoral. It seems, therefore, that the intention is always as wrong as the action.[3]

The main generalization the author wants the reader to accept is that the intention to kill is as wrong as the action of killing. The strategy of the argument is to present a single case, show that it is an example in which the generalization applies, and then imply that the example is perfectly typical and thus that the generalization holds for all cases. The arguer is counting on the fact that the audience will be reminded from their own experience that the example is typical.

To evaluate the quality of this argument we need to ask ourselves whether this really is an example. Is the case of the potential axe murder really an example in which the person would be just as immoral whether he or she followed through with the crime or not? Second, even if it is an example, is it really typical of all other cases of intention to commit a crime?

■ ············ Concept Check 3 ············ ■

Which of the following arguments is an induction by analogy, using an appeal to a typical example?

a. John is a typical example of a farmer. He doesn't wear a suit to work. He understands about raising animals, planting crops, building fences, and so on. Yet all farmers are going to suffer with this new legislation, so John is, too.

b. We checked it out for ourselves. After drilling the right-size hole in the plastic, we poured the liquid hydrofluoric acid down the hole onto the steel and noticed that a perfectly circular hole in the steel appeared within a minute. So, hydrofluoric acid will always react with steel, at least if the acid is a liquid.

c. All boa constrictors are reptiles, and Matt Rasmussen's pet boa constrictor is a typical one, so it's a reptile, too.

Induction from the Past to the Future

As goes the past, so goes the future. That is a common style of inductive argument. Here is a specific example:

> The record book shows that the American track teams have won more meets than the Australian track teams. So, the Americans can be expected to dominate the Australians in future track meets.

This is an induction by analogy because it depends on the claim that the future will be analogous to the past in certain ways.

Not all past patterns can be justifiably projected to hold in the future. The chicken assumes that the hand that has fed it will continue to feed it in the future, but one day that hand will wring its neck. One of the principal problems of science is to discover which patterns are projectible into the future and which are not.

Arguments from past patterns to future patterns depend on a crucial premise: If we are ignorant of any reason that a past pattern should not continue, then it probably will continue.

Here is another problem about arguing from the past to the future. Suppose you are trying to decide whether the highway you plan to take to visit your grandparents on Christmas Eve will be covered with snow. You gather the relevant evidence from your memory:

> Every Christmas Eve in the past, the highway to my grandparents has been snow-covered.

Nobody has said anything that would imply that the highway conditions this Christmas Eve will be any different than in the past.

On the basis of these reasons, you conclude that

This Christmas Eve, the highway to my grandparents will be snow-covered.

This argument is deductively invalid. Nevertheless, it is a moderately strong inductive argument. The argument depends crucially on the premise that on every Christmas Eve in the past the highway has been snow-covered. Suppose you do not know this for a fact. Instead, you are relying on your memory. Now that you think about it, you can't be sure that you are right. If so, this doubt about your key premise should also cause some doubt about your conclusion. For that reason alone, you should put less faith in your conclusion. The principle of logical reasoning that this example illustrates is the following: *Apportion the strength of your belief in the conclusion to the strength of your belief in the premises.*

Let's take a closer look at revising potentially good inductive arguments that go from data about the past to a prediction about the future. Suppose you have collected the following data: the San Francisco 49ers football team has won five of its last six games. Here is a conclusion that could be drawn from that data: The San Francisco 49ers will win their next football game. This argument would be strengthened if the conclusion were to hedge a little and state that the 49ers "might win" their next football game. It would be worsened if the conclusion were that the 49ers will win their next *three* games.

Would the original argument be improved, weakened, or unaffected if you were to add the premise that the last six 49ers games were all against different teams? It would be improved because the premises would then show that the team has the ability to win against a variety of opponents, not just one or two. If you were to learn, however, that the price of rice in China was rising on days when the 49ers played their last six games but will be sinking on the day of their next game, the argument would be unaffected. If you were to learn that their last six games were played outdoors during warm, clear weather but that their next game will be played against the Chicago Bears outdoors in cold, snowy weather, the argument would be *weakened* because you know that playing conditions can affect the outcome of a game played outdoors.

Logical reasoners arguing from the past to the future need to be especially sensitive to the variety of the past data. For example, here are two inductions from past statistics to future performance, yet one is a better induction than the other. Why? Notice the variability in the scores.

Bob scored 10, 5, and 15 points in his three previous basketball games (an average of 10 points per game). So, he will score about 10 points next game.

Bob scored 10, 9, and 11 points in his three previous basketball games (an average of 10 points per game). So, he will score about 10 points next game.

The first argument is worse because of the variety of Bob's scores. The less variety in the past data, the better. On the other hand, the more variety in **the relevant past conditions** affecting the data, the better. That is, the more **diversity** among the relevant factors, the better. For example, regarding the second argument about Bob, if you learned that he had had a slight cold during the first game and that some of the games were on indoor courts but others were on outdoor courts, you could be surer of the conclusion than if you lacked this information. However, a relevant factor lacking in the past but existing in the future lowers the quality of the argument. For example, if you were to learn that Bob will play the next game with a sore ankle (and he didn't have a sore ankle during the previous games), you know that he is less likely to score about 10 points. Past diversity of conditions is a plus; future diversity is a minus.

■ ·············   Concept Check 4   ············ ■

Suppose you know the average heights of Japanese men and of American men. If you randomly pick a hundred Japanese businessmen, you can be more sure of their average height than you can be if you pick American businessmen. Use the concept of variety of the data to explain why.

■ ·············   Concept Check 5   ············ ■

Here is an argument from the past to the future:

> The Kings have played the Lakers in basketball three times this year, and each time the difference in their two scores has been under six points. So, their next game against each other should have a point spread of under six points.

The past performance of the Kings is analogous to their future performance. Following, various modifications of that argument are suggested or additional information is supplied. In each case, determine whether the alteration produces a stronger argument, produces a weaker argument, or has no effect on its strength. (All the modifications are to be considered separately. That is, modification b is in place of a, not in addition to a.)

a. Change "three times" to "thirteen times."

b. Their next game should have a point spread of exactly six points.

c. The Lakers lost to the Pistons yesterday but beat the Knicks last week.

d. Although there is a home court advantage, the three games were alternated between the two teams' home courts.

e. For the last three games against the Lakers, the starting center for the Kings has been Causewell, but he was hurt in a skiing accident today and won't be starting against the Lakers.

f. The Lakers have played the Kings only once.

g. In all previous games between the two, the announcer from the local TV station has drunk a beer during the game, but next time he won't drink.

h. In two of the three previous games between the Kings and the Lakers, the difference in their two scores was under six points, but in one it was over six.

i. In all previous games between the two, the Kings starting center was high on cocaine, but next time the center won't be.

The principles of reasoning that this section has applied to inductions from the past to the future also apply to inductions from the past to the present and to inductions from the present to the future.

Generalizing from a Sample

Scientists collect data. They do so not because they are in the business of gathering facts at random but because they hope to establish a generalization that goes beyond the individual facts. The scientist is in the business of sampling a part of nature and then looking for a pattern in the data that holds for nature as a whole. A sociologist, for example, collects data about murders, but the goal is to draw a general conclusion, such as "Most murders involve guns." A statistician would say that the scientist has sampled some cases of murder in order to draw a general conclusion about the whole population of murders. The terms *sample* and *population* are technical terms. The

Doonesbury Copyright 1980 G. B. Trudeau. Reprinted with permission of UNIVERSAL PRESS SYNDICATE. All rights reserved.

population need not be people; in our example it is the set of all murders. A **sample** is a subset taken from the set of things you are interested in, the **population**. The sample is examined to get a clue to what the whole population is like.

Whenever a generalization is produced by generalizing on a sample, the reasoning process (or the general conclusion itself) is said to be an **inductive generalization**. It is also called an induction by enumeration or an empirical generalization. Inductive generalizations are a kind of argument by analogy with the implicit assumption that the sample is analogous to the population. The more analogous the sample, the stronger the inductive argument.

Generalizations may be statistical or nonstatistical. "Most murders involve guns" contains no statistics. Replacing the term *most* with the statistic *80 percent* would make it a statistical generalization. The statement "80 percent of murders involve guns" is called a **simple statistical claim** because it has the form

> x percent of the group G has characteristic C.

In the example, $x = 80$, $G =$ murders, and $C =$ involving guns.

A general claim, whether statistical or not, is called an inductive generalization only if it is obtained by a process of generalizing from a sample. If the statistical claim about murders were obtained by looking at police records, it would be an inductive generalization, but if it were deduced from a more general principle of social psychology, then it would not be an inductive generalization.

■ ·········· Concept Check 6 ·········· ■

Is the generalization "Most emeralds are green" a statistical generalization? Is it an inductive generalization?

Back from the grocery store with your three cans of tomato sauce for tonight's spaghetti dinner, you open the cans and notice that the sauce in two of the cans is spoiled. You generalize and say that two-thirds of all the cans of that brand of tomato sauce on the shelf in the store are bad. Here is the pattern of your inductive generalization:

> x percent of sample S has characteristic C.
> ────────────────────────────────
> x percent of population P has characteristic C.

In this argument $x = 66.7$ (for two-thirds), $P =$ all the tomato sauce cans of a particular brand from the shelf of the grocery store, $S =$ three tomato sauce cans of that brand from the shelf of the grocery store, and $C =$ spoiled. Alternatively, this is the pattern:

> Sample *S* has characteristic *C*.
> _____
> Population *P* has characteristic *C*.

C is now not the property of being spoiled but instead is the property of being 66.7 percent spoiled.

> The goal of all sampling is for the sample to be representative of the population in regard to the characteristics that are being investigated.

The more the sample represents the population, the more likely the inductive generalization is to be correct. A representative sample is perfectly analogous to the whole population in regard to the characteristics that are being investigated. If a population of 888 jelly beans in a jar is 50 percent black and 50 percent white, a representative sample could be just two jelly beans, one black and one white. A method of sampling that is likely to produce a nonrepresentative sample is a **biased sampling method**. A **biased sample** is a nonrepresentative sample.

The **fallacy of hasty generalization** occurs whenever a generalization is made too quickly, on insufficient evidence. It occurs whenever an inductive generalization is made with a sample that is unlikely to be representative. For instance, suppose Jessica says that most Americans own an electric hair dryer because most of her friends do. This would be a hasty generalization, since Jessica's friends are unlikely to represent everybody when it comes to owning hair dryers. Her sampling method shows too much bias toward her friends.

A biased sample is not the same as a biased opinion, although the notions are related. A biased opinion is a belief that is held onto when the available evidence counts against it. Holding an opinion firmly is not necessarily a sign of being biased; what could make it biased is why it is held onto. A person would be biased if he knew that his generalization was based on a biased sampling method. If a person firmly believes some generalization from a sample, if the generalization is not the product of a hasty generalization, if there isn't convincing new evidence that the generalization should be rejected, and if the person is willing to reject the belief if such new evidence were to come to light, then the person's opinion isn't biased, even though the belief is firmly held.

Random Sample

Statisticians have discovered several techniques for avoiding bias. The first is to obtain a random sample. When you sample at random, you don't favor any one member of the population over another. For example, when sampling tomato sauce cans, you don't pick the first three cans you see.

Definition A **random sample** is any sample obtained by using a random sampling method.

Definition A **random sampling method** is taking a sample from a target population in such a way that any member of the population has an equal chance of being chosen.

It is easy to recognize the value of obtaining a random sample, but achieving this goal can be difficult. If you want to poll students for their views on canceling the school's intercollegiate athletics program in the face of the latest school budget crisis, how do you give everybody an equal chance to be polled? Some students are less apt to want to talk with you when you walk up to them with your clipboard. If you ask all your questions in three spots on campus, you may not be giving an equal chance to students who are never at those spots. Then there are problems with the poll questions themselves. The way the questions are constructed might influence the answers you get, and so you won't be getting a random sample of students' views even if you do get a random sample of students.

Purposely not using a random sample is perhaps the main way to lie with statistics. For one example, newspapers occasionally report that students in American middle schools and high schools are especially poor at math and science when compared to students in other countries. This surprising statistical generalization is probably based on a biased sample. It is quite true that those American students taking the international standardized tests of mathematics and science achievement do score worse than foreign students. The problem is that school administrators in other countries try hard to do well on these tests. "In many countries, to look good is very good for international prestige. Some restrict the students taking the test to elite schools," says Harold Hodgkinson, the director of the Center for Demographic Policy in Washington and a former director of the National Institute of Education. For example, whereas the United States tests almost all of its students, by the 12th grade Hong Kong has eliminated all but the top 3 percent of its students from taking mathematics and thus from taking the standardized tests. In Japan, only 12 percent of the 12th grade students take any mathematics. Canada has especially good test results for the same reason. According to Hodgkinson, the United States doesn't look so bad when you take a look at another statistic: the top 10 percent of American students are scoring 14 points higher on the Scholastic Aptitude Tests than they were 10 years ago.[4]

The following passage describes a nonstatistical generalization from a sample. Try to spot the conclusion, the population, the sample, and any bias.

> David went to the grocery store to get three cartons of strawberries. He briefly looked at the top layer of strawberries in each of the first three cartons in the strawberry section and noticed no fuzz on the berries. Confident that the berries in his three cartons were fuzz-free, he bought all three.

David's conclusion was that the strawberries in his cartons were not fuzzy. His conclusion was about the population of all the strawberries in the three cartons. His sample was the top layer of strawberries in each one. David is a trusting soul, isn't he? Some grocers will hide all the bad berries on the bottom. Because shoppers are aware of this potential deception, they prefer their strawberries in see-through, webbed cartons. If David had wanted to be surer of his conclusion, he should have looked more carefully at the cartons and sampled some bottom, middle, and side berries, too. Looking at the top strawberries is better than looking at none, and looking randomly is better than looking nonrandomly.

Those same four questions will be harder to answer about the following statistical generalization, and the problem won't be because of the statistics:

Quote, Misquote

News source (agitated, waving a copy of that day's paper): "Hey, you misquoted me. I didn't say what you said I said."

Reporter (calmly): "Wrong. You said it, and I quoted you correctly."

Source: "You did not."

Reporter (riffling through a spiral notebook): "It's right here in my notes." (Contentedly points to scrawls on the page.) "Here, see? You said it. My notes prove it."

Or do they?

There is now scholarly evidence revealing what one industry magazine writer called journalism's "darkest, deepest secret: Reporters are lousy quoters."

A study done in Canada by an eminent journalist showed that reporters using handwritten notes on the average got quotes wrong in some way, major or minor, as much as half the time.

The Canadian journalist is Peter Calamai, a national correspondent for the Southam News Agency who recently was a visiting journalism professor at the University of Regina in Saskatchewan.

He surveyed eight Canadian papers and two Canadian news wire services, comparing quotes they published against the official transcript for a sensational 1984 murder trial they covered.

The survey turned up an error rate among the papers ranging from 45 percent to 71 percent. That is, one of the surveyed papers made errors in 71 percent of all of the direct quotes it used from the trial.

The issues the study raises are serious. . . . Calamai put it like this in his study: ". . . Since many jurors and perhaps some judges also read newspaper accounts of trials in which they are participating, there is the potential for a far more serious distortion of justice."[5]

What is the inductive generalization's conclusion, population, sample, and sampling bias? The population P could be said to be either reporters' quotes or else reporters, provided characteristic C is appropriately chosen. The conclusion is that reporters are lousy quoters, but let's focus on the first inference. Just Canadian reporters? Probably not. Although the conclusion is imprecisely stated, it probably includes reporters from the United States. How about Egyptian reporters? Maybe, but less likely. How about reporters from the United States in 1802? No. So the conclusion should have the vague phrase "these days" tagged onto the end of it. Most likely the target population is the quotes from *all* reporters these days who use handwritten notes. The sample is a subset of this. It is the quotes by reporters of eight newspapers and two news wire services in Canada who covered a sensational 1984 murder trial.

Before you start believing that you cannot trust newspapers, consider the sampling process itself. It was biased. The procedure could have been improved by examining quotes in those Canadian newspapers and wire services from other trials and from other events besides trials. It would also have helped to have examined quotes from a wider variety of papers and wire services. With the revised sampling method, it is quite possible that different results would have been obtained. Perhaps a lot fewer errors on average would be found, or maybe more. Whatever the result, the revised sampling method would produce a more accurate inductive generalization than the original. There is no good reason to suppose that the reports of this one Canadian trial are somehow typical.

A different way to improve the argument without changing the sampling method would be to restrict the scope of the conclusion. Instead of the conclusion being about all reporters in all countries covering all kinds of events, we could draw a conclusion about only Canadian reporters who cover murder trials.

When we sample instances of news reporting in order to draw a conclusion about the accuracy of news reports, we want our sample to be representative in regard to the characteristic of "containing a reporting error." When we sample voters about how they will vote in the next election, we want our sample to be representative in regard to the characteristic of "voting for the candidates." Here is a formal definition of the goal, which is representativeness:

Definition A sample *S* is a **(perfectly) representative sample** from a population *P* with respect to characteristic *C* if the percentage of *S* that are *C* is exactly equal to the percentage of *P* that are *C*.

A sample *S* is less representative of *P* according to the degree to which the percentage of *S* that are *C* deviates from the percentage of *P* that are *C*.

If you are about to do some sampling, what can you do to improve your chances of getting a representative sample? The answer is to follow these four procedures, if you can:

1. Pick a random sample.   3. Pick a diverse sample.
2. Pick a large sample.   4. Pick a stratified sample.

We've already discussed how to obtain a random sample. After we explore the other procedures, we'll be in a better position to appreciate why some random samples are to be avoided.

Concept Check 7

Which is the strongest and which is the weakest argument? The four arguments differ only in their use of the words *random* and *about*.

a. Twenty percent of a random sample of our university's students want library fines to be lower; so, 20 percent of our university's students want library fines to be lower.

b. Twenty percent of a sample of our university's students want library fines to be lower; so, 20 percent of our university's students want library fines to be lower.

c. Twenty percent of a random sample of our university's students want library fines to be lower; so, about 20 percent of our university's students want library fines to be lower.

d. Twenty percent of a sample of our university's students want library fines to be lower; so, about 20 percent of our university's students want library fines to be lower.

Concept Check 8

For the following statistical report, (a) identify the sample, (b) identify the population, (c) discuss the quality of the sampling method, and (d) find other problems either with the study or with your knowledge of the study.

> Voluntary tests of 25,000 drivers throughout the United States showed that 25 percent of them use some drug and that 85 percent use no drugs at all while driving. The conclusion was that 25 percent of U.S. drivers do use drugs. A remarkable conclusion. The tests were taken at random times of the day at randomly selected freeway restaurants.

Sample Size

If you hear a TV commercial say that four out of five doctors recommend the pain reliever in the drug being advertised, you might be impressed with the drug. However, if you learn that only five doctors were interviewed, you would be much less impressed. Sample size is important.

Why is sample size so important? The answer has to do with the fact that estimations based on sampling are inductive and thus inherently risky. The larger the sample, the better its chance of being free of distortions from unusually bad luck during the selection of the sample.

To maximize the information you can get about the population, you will want to increase your sample size. Nevertheless, you usually face practical limits on the size; sampling might be expensive, difficult, or both. So when is your sample size big enough for your purposes? This is a fascinating and difficult question. For example, suppose you are interested in selling mechanical feeding systems to the farmers in your state. You would like to know what percentage of them do not already own a mechanical feeding system — they will be your potential customers. Knowing that this sort of information has never been collected, you might try to collect it yourself by contacting the farmers. Since it would be both difficult and expensive to contact every single farmer, you would be interested in getting your answer from a sample of small size. If you don't care whether your estimate of the percentage of farmers without a mechanical feeding system is off by plus or minus 10 percent, you can sample many fewer farmers than if you had to have an answer within 1 percent of the (unknown) correct answer. Statisticians would express this same point by saying that a 10 percent **margin of error** requires a smaller sample size than a 1 percent margin of error.

Let's suppose you can live with the 10 percent. Now, how sure do you need to be that your estimate will fall into that interval of plus or minus 10 percent? If you need only to be 90 percent sure, then you will need a much smaller sample size then if you need to be 97 percent sure. Statisticians would express this same point by saying that a 90 percent **confidence level** requires a smaller sample size than a 97 percent confidence level. Just exactly how much smaller is a matter of intricate statistical theory that we won't go into here, although we will explore some specific examples in later sections.

A margin of error is a margin of safety. Sometimes we can be specific and quantify this margin. We can say that our sampling showed that the percentage of farmers without a mechanical feeding system is 60 percent plus or minus 6 percent. Sometimes we simply express the idea vaguely by saying that the percentage is *about* 60 percent. At any rate, whether we can be specific or not, the greater the margin of error we can permit, the smaller the sample size we need. This result is an instance of our earlier principle that the less specific the conclusion of our argument, the stronger the argument.

This chapter will have more to say about sample size, but first we need to consider other ways of improving the sampling process.

Sample Diversity

In addition to selecting a random, large sample, you can also improve your chances of selecting a representative sample by sampling a wide variety of members of the population. Aim for *diversity*. If you are interested in how Ohio citizens will vote in the next election, will you be more apt to trust a pollster who spoke with 50 randomly picked white, female voters or 50 randomly picked voters of different races and sexes?

Even though those 50 white women were picked at random, you know you want to throw them out and pick 50 more. You want to force the sample to be diverse. The greater the diversity of relevant characteristics in your sample, the better the inductive generalization, all other things being equal.

One purpose of getting a large, random sample is to get one that is sufficiently diverse. If you already know that the population is homogeneous—that is, not especially diverse—you don't need a big sample, or a particularly random one. For example, in 1906 the Chicago physicist R. A. Millikan measured the electric charge on electrons in his newly invented oil-drop device. His measurements clustered around a precise value for the electron's charge. Referring to this experiment, science teachers tell students that *all* electrons have this same charge. Yet Millikan did not test *all* electrons; he tested only a few and then generalized from that sample. His sample was small and was not selected randomly. Is this grounds for worry about whether untested electrons might have a different charge? Did he commit the fallacy of hasty generalization? No, because physical theory at the time said that all electrons should have the same charge. There was absolutely no reason to worry that Tuesday's electrons would be different from Wednesday's, or that English electrons would be different from American ones. However, if this theoretical backup weren't there, Millikan's work with such a small, nonrandom sample would have committed the fallacy of hasty generalization. The moral: *Relying on background knowledge about a population's lack of diversity can reduce the sample size needed for the generalization, and it can reduce the need for a random sampling procedure.*

When you are sampling electrons, if you've seen one you've seen them all, so to speak. The diversity just isn't there, unlike with, say, Republican voters, who vary greatly from each other. If you want to sample Republican voters' opinions, you can't talk to one and assume that his or her opinions are those of all the other Republicans. Republicans are heterogeneous.

A group having considerable diversity in the relevant factors affecting the outcome of interest is said to be a **heterogeneous group**. A group with a relatively insignificant amount of diversity is said to be a **homogeneous group**. For example, Concept Check 4 discussed predicting the outcome of measuring the average height of two groups, Americans and Japanese. The diversity of American ethnicity makes Americans a heterogeneous group, while the relative absence of diversity among Japanese makes them more homogeneous. It is easier to make predictions for homogeneous groups than for heterogeneous groups.

Being homogeneous is relative, however. The Japanese might be more homogeneous than Americans relative to measurements about height, but the Japanese might be more heterogeneous than Americans when it comes to attitudes about socialism.

Stratified Samples

In addition to seeking a large, random, diverse sample, you can improve your chances of getting a representative sample by *stratifying* the sample. In the example in Concept Check 8, taking the drug tests at random times was a mistake, because many more drivers are on the road at, say, 5 P.M. than at 5 A.M. *Random sampling on times would be biased* in favor of the 5 A.M. drivers. To remove this bias, the sampling method should take advantage of this knowledge of who drives when by *stratifying* according to time of day. For example, if you know that 30 percent of drivers are on the road from 5 P.M. to 6 P.M., make sure that 30 percent of the sampled drivers are picked from 5 P.M. to 6 P.M. Do the same for the other driving times. Within each hour, do pick the drivers randomly, though.

The point about stratification can be clarified by considering this next example. Suppose you are planning a poll to learn how Ohio citizens will vote in the next presidential election. You can use your knowledge of politics to help pick the best sample. You already have specific political information that the race of a voter is apt to affect how he or she will vote. Suppose you also know that, even though Ohio citizens are 65 percent white and 30 percent black,* the expected voters will be 70 percent white and 25 percent black. You can use all this information about the voting population to take a better sample by making sure that your random sample contains exactly 70 percent white voters and exactly 25 percent black voters. If your poll actually were to contain 73 percent white voters, you would be well advised to randomly throw away some of the white voters' responses until you get the number down to 70 percent. The resulting *stratification on race* will improve the chances that your sample is representative. Stratification on the voters' soft drink preference would not help, however.

The following definition of stratification uses the helpful concept of a variable. Roughly speaking, a **variable** is anything that comes in various types or amounts. There are different types of races, so race is a variable; there are different amounts of salaries, so salary is a variable; and so forth. Each type or amount of the variable is called a possible **value of the variable**. White and black are two values of the race variable.

Definition   Suppose a population (say, of people) could be divided into different groups or strata, according to some variable characteristic (such as race). Suppose each group's members have the same value for that variable (for example, all the members of one group are black, all the members of another group are white, and so on). Suppose a sample is taken under the requirement that the percentage that has a given value (black) of the variable (race) must be the same as the known percentage of the value for the population as a whole. If so, then a **stratified sample** has been taken from that population, and the sample is said to be *stratified on that variable*.

Stratification is a key to reducing sample size, thereby saving time and money. If you want to know how people are going to vote for the Republican candidate in the next presidential election, talking to only one randomly selected voter would obviously be too small a sample. However, getting a big enough sample is usually less of a problem than you might expect. Most nonprofessionals believe that tens of thousands of people would need to be sampled. I asked my next-door neighbor how many he

---

*These figures are not reliable.

thought would be needed, and he said, "Oh, at least a hundred thousand." Surprisingly, 500 would be enough if the sample were stratified on race, income, employment type, political party, and other important variables. This 500 figure assumes the pollster need only be 95 percent sure that the results aren't off by more than 2 percent.

The most important variables affecting voting are the voters' party, race, sex, income, and age. The more such variables there are, the bigger the sample must be to make sure that enough voters representative of each value get polled. If the pollster has no idea what the variables are that will influence the results, he or she cannot know whether the sample is diverse in regard to these variables, so a very large sample will be needed. For example, if you wanted to know what percentage of jelly beans in an opaque jar are lime or licorice flavored, you wouldn't have any background information to use for stratification. All you could do is use simple random sampling, that is, shake up the jar and plunge in.

■ .... Concept Check 9 .... ■

Your quality control engineer conducts a weekly inspection of your company's new beverage. He gathers a random sample of 100 bottles produced on Mondays or Tuesdays. Over several weeks, at most he finds one or two sampled bottles each week to be faulty. So you conclude that your manufacturing process is doing well on an average every week, since your goal was to have at least 98 percent of the beverage be OK.

Suppose, however, that the quality control engineer knows that your plant produces an equal amount of the beverage on each weekday and that it produces beverages only on weekdays. Describe the best way for the quality control engineer to improve the sampling by paying attention to *stratification*.

a. Sample one beverage from each weekday.
b. Pick a larger and more random sample.
c. Take an equal number of samples on Saturdays and Sundays as well.
d. Make sure that 20 percent of the sample comes from each weekday.
e. Sample more of the bottles that will be delivered to your most valued customers.

Statistical Significance

Frequently, the conclusions of inductive generalizations are simple statistical claims. Our premise is "*x* percent of the sample is la-de-da." From this we conclude, "The same percent of the population is, too." When the argument is inductively strong, statisticians say the percent is **statistically significant**. A statistically significant statis-

© 1992 Tom Tomorrow. Reprinted by permission

tic is one that probably is not due to chance. The number need not be significant in the sense of important, the nontechnical sense of significant.

Suppose you are interested in determining the percentage of left-handers in the world. This target number is unknown, so you will have to guess by taking a sample of people and checking whether they are left-handed. You will use the fraction of people in your sample who are left-handed as your guess of the value of the target number. The target number is what statisticians call a **parameter**. The number you use to guess the parameter is called the **statistic**. Your statistic will have to meet higher standards the more confident you must be that it is a reliable estimate of the parameter.

I once told my seven-year-old son Joshua that he was unusual because he was left-handed. That surprised him, so he decided to check out whether I was correct. In the sophisticated terminology of mathematical statistics, we'd say Joshua's goal was to determine whether a certain parameter, the percentage of left-handers in the whole world, is much less than 50 percent. Here is what Joshua did to acquire a statistic to use to estimate the parameter. He said, "You're left-handed, Dad. Mom and my little sister aren't. That is two and two." What Joshua had just done, more or less, was to take a sample of four from the vast population of the Earth and calculate the statistic of 50 percent as his guess of the parameter. This statistic might seem to refute my claim that the parameter is much less than 50 percent, but a statistician would say that Joshua's statistic is not significant because the sample is too small. If Joshua were to take a larger sample, the resultant statistical claim would be more believable.

So Joshua set out to get a bigger sample. He asked all the children in his class at school whether they were left-handed. Two out of twenty-two. He also went around the neighborhood asking whomever he could. The new result from home, school, and neighborhood was seven left-handers out of thirty-seven. This statistic is more apt to be significant, and it is much less than 50 percent. The moral here is that the bigger the sample size, the more confident you can be that the calculated statistic is statistically significant. The more sampling, the less likely that the result is due to chance. Patterns that appear in small samples might disappear as the sample size grows; they might be shown to be **coincidental**. Significant patterns and significant statistics are those that are likely not to be accidental or coincidental; they are likely to be found to hold true on examination of more of the target population.

We still haven't answered the question of whether Joshua's statistic of 7/37 is statistically significant. Is it? It definitely is a better guess than 2/4, but to compute whether it is significant requires some sophisticated reasoning involving complex formulas about margins of error and levels of confidence, which we won't pursue here. We can, however, sketch three features of the answer.

First, the margin of error: We need to decide just how accurate we want our guess to be. Can we be satisfied with an accuracy of plus or minus 10 percent, or do we need a smaller margin, say plus or minus 1 percent? Second, the confidence level. Are we willing to be only 95 percent sure that we have the right answer, even allowing for the margin of error? Or must we be 99 percent sure? All other things being equal, the more confident we need to be, the less significant will be the statistics we have gathered. Third, how biased was the sampling? Was it random? Was the sample large and diverse? Population size is not normally something that needs to be taken into account, especially if the population is large compared to the sample size. The statistic for a relatively small sample will be statistically significant based on the size of the sample, not on the size of the population.

Designing a Test

Let's consider another example of acquiring statistics and deciding whether they are significant. Suppose you own a food business and you are considering marketing what your researcher/cook says is a better version of one of your old food products. The main factor in your decision will be whether your customers will like the taste of the new product better than the taste of the old one. You can make your marketing decision by guessing, by letting your cook choose, by asking advice from your friends, or by some other method. You decide to use another method: ask your customers. If the customers in your sample prefer the new product, you will believe that the whole population will, too, and you will replace the old product with the new one.

A good way to do this testing would be to use a procedure called *paired comparison*. In this kind of test, you remove the identifying labels from the old and new products and then give a few tasters the pairs of products in random orders. That is, some tasters get to taste the new one first; some, the old one first. In neither case are they told which product they are tasting. Then ask your taster/judges which product they like better. If a great many of them like the new one better than the old one, you can go with the new product. But how many tasters do you need? And if most of the tasters like the new product but some don't, how much disagreement can you accept and still be sure your customers will like the new product better? If three out of five tasters say the new product is better but two out of five disagree, would a conclusion that over half your customers would prefer the new product be a statistically significant result? These are difficult questions, but they have been studied extensively by statisticians, and the answers are clear.

Before your questions can be answered, you need to settle another issue. How sure do you have to be that your tasters' decision is correct, in the sense of representing the tastes of the general population of your customers? If you need to be 99 percent sure, you will need more tasters than if you need only to be 95 percent sure. Let's suppose you decide on 95 percent. Then, if you have, say, twenty tasters, how many of them would have to prefer the new product before you can be 95 percent sure that your customers will like the new product better, too? If your taster/judges are picked randomly from among your population of customers and aren't professionals in the tasting business, then statistical theory says you would need at least fifteen of your twenty judges (65 percent) to prefer the new product. However, if you had more judges, you wouldn't need this much agreement. For example, with sixty judges, you would need only thirty-nine positive responses (75 percent) to be confident that your customers will prefer the new product. What this statistic of thirty-nine out of sixty means is that even if twenty-one out of your sixty judges were to say that your new product is awful, you could be 95 percent sure that most consumers would disagree with them. Yet many business persons who are not versed in such statistical reasoning would probably worry unnecessarily about their new product if twenty-one of sixty testers disliked the product.

Statistical theory also indicates how much agreement among the judges would be required to raise your confidence level from 95 percent to 99 percent. To be 99 percent sure that your customers would prefer the new product to the old, you would need seventeen positive responses from your twenty judges, or forty-one positive responses from sixty judges.

■ ············ **Concept Check 10** ············ ■

You recently purchased a new gas station and have decided on an advertising campaign both to increase your visibility in the community and to encourage new customers to use the station. You plan to advertise a free gift to every customer purchasing $10 or more of gasoline any time during two weeks next month. The problem now is to select the gift. You have business connections enabling you to make an inexpensive purchase of a large supply of either six-packs of Pepsi or engraved ballpoint pens with the name of a local sports team. You could advertise that you will give away free Pepsi, or you could advertise that you will give away the pens. The cost to you would be the same, provided you offer just one of the gifts, not both. You decide to choose between the two on the basis of what you predict your potential customers would prefer. To do this, you use a paired comparison test. You decide you would like to be 95 percent sure of the result before you select the gift. You randomly choose twenty potential customers and offer them their choice of free Pepsi or a free ballpoint pen. Ten are told they can have the Pepsi or the pen; ten are told they can have the pen or the Pepsi. You analyze the results. Three customers say they don't care which gift they get. Five say that they strongly prefer Pepsi to the pen because they don't like the sports team. Six say they would be happy with either gift but would barely prefer the Pepsi. Four customers choose Pepsi because they have enough pens. The rest choose pens with no comment. From this result, can you be confident that it would be a mistake to go with the ballpoint pen?

Suppose you learn that your favorite TV program was canceled because the A. C. Neilsen Corporation reported to CBS that only 25 percent of the viewers were tuned to your program last week. CBS wanted a 30 percent program in that time slot. You then learn more about the Neilsen test. Neilsen polled 400 viewers, 100 of whom said they were watching your program. Knowing that the United States has 100 million TV sets, you might be shocked by CBS's making a major financial decision based on the simple statistical claim that 100 out of 400 viewers prefer your program. Can this statistic really tell CBS anything significant about your program? Yes, it can, provided CBS can live with a 2 percent error. Neilsen and CBS can be 95 percent confident that the statistics from a sample of 400 will have an error of only plus or minus 2 percent. A Neilsen rating of 25 percent from 4,000 sets out of 100 million will be significant with a margin of error of only plus or minus 1 percent.

Obstacles to Collecting Reliable Data

So far in our discussion of significant statistics, we have worried about how to make decisions using reliable information from a sample of our population. To obtain significant statistics we try to obtain a representative sample—one that is diverse, random, large, and stratified. However, how can we know, for example, whether the customers at our gas station are telling us truthfully whether they prefer Pepsi to ballpoint pens? More generally, a major obstacle to obtaining a representative sample is that unreliable data too easily creep into our sample.

There is the notorious problem of lying to pollsters. The percentage of polled people who say they've voted in the election is usually higher than the percentage of people who actually did vote in the election. More subtly, people may practice self-deception, honestly responding "yes" to questions such as "Are you sticking to your diet?" when they aren't. Another problem facing us is that even though we want diversity in our sample, the data from some groups in the population may be easier to obtain than from other groups, and we may be tempted to favor ease over diversity. For example, when counting Christians worldwide, it is easier to get data from churches of people who speak some languages rather than other languages. There are other obstacles to collecting reliable data. Busy and more private people won't find the time to answer our questions. Also, pollsters occasionally fail to notice the difference between asking "Do you favor Jones or Smith?" and "Do you favor Smith or Jones?" The moral is that natural obstacles and sloppy methodology combine to produce unreliable data and so to reduce the significance of our statistics.

Induction from the General to the Specific

Suppose you have acquired current, reliable statistical data that 80 percent of U.S. Republicans favor having the U.S. military budget increased. If you know that John Jones is a Republican, would it be a good bet to infer that he favors an increase in the military budget? Yes. The inference is inductively strong. The argument would be better if the statistic were 90 percent. The argument would be worse if "John Jones" were replaced by "John Jones and David Smith."

The style of this argument deserves consideration. The argument draws a specific conclusion from a general statistical premise. The fact that this kind of argument is inductive refutes the common misunderstanding (perpetuated in old textbooks) that all inductive arguments reason from the specific to the general.

Here is another argument from a general premise to a specific conclusion:

> Most swans are white.
> ——————————————
> The next swan I see will be white.

This is not a statistical argument. The strength of the inductive argument would be increased if the evidence permitted replacing *Most* with *Nearly all*. It would be reduced if *Most* were replaced by *Some*.

■ ·········· Concept Check 11 ·········· ■

Would the inductive argument about Republicans and the military budget be stronger or weaker if you were to learn that it is 90 to 95 percent probable that 80 percent of U.S. Republicans favor having the U.S. military budget increased?

Concept Check 12

Consider the following inductive argument from a general claim to a specific claim:

> Twenty-five percent of U.S. drivers use drugs. The drummer in the band is a U.S. driver. So, the drummer uses drugs.

(a) Assess the inductive strength of this argument. (b) Comment on how the strength would be affected if you were to learn that 70 percent of drummers use drugs. (c) Suppose you later learn that the drummer likes Lawrence Welk polka music and that such music fans rarely take drugs. Would this affect your previous assessment?

Review of Major Points

Inductive arguments are more common than deductive arguments, and they are more difficult to analyze. The quality of an inductive argument is always a matter of degree, unlike the quality of deductive arguments. In this chapter we considered the value of anecdotal evidence and reviewed some of the problems with arguments that appeal to the opinions of authorities. We focused on several types of inductive argumentation: reasoning by analogy, appealing to a typical example, arguing from the past to the future, generalizing from a sample, and drawing specific conclusions from general premises. Arguments by analogy are attacked by finding disanalogies and by extending the analogy in unexpected directions. Generalizing from a sample is also called inductive generalization. To improve your chances of obtaining a representative sample, you should get a random, large, diverse, and stratified sample when you can.

Glossary

appeal to a typical example Drawing a conclusion about a population from the characteristics of a single example believed to be typical.

biased sample A nonrepresentative sample.

biased sampling method A method of taking a sample that is likely to be nonrepresentative.

coincidental A pattern in data that appears by accident. A coincidental pattern would not persist if more data were acquired.

confidence level The percentage of confidence we need that the value of our statistic agrees with the target parameter, given the acceptable margin of error. For example, are we willing to be only 95 percent sure that we have the right answer, even allowing for the margin of error? Or must we be 99 percent sure?

disanalogies The ways in which two things are not analogous.

diversity Variety.

extend the analogy To point out additional ways in which two analogous things are alike.

fallacy of hasty generalization Jumping to conclusions when the conclusion is a generalization from the evidence.

fallacy of jumping to conclusions Drawing a conclusion prematurely or with insufficient evidence, even if the conclusion turns out to be true.

faulty analogy Claiming that two things are analogous with respect to some characteristic when in fact they aren't analogous.

heterogeneous group A group having considerable diversity in the relevant factors affecting the outcome of interest. For predicting the shape of a randomly picked snowflake, snowflakes are a heterogeneous group.

homogeneous group A group with an insignificant amount of diversity in the relevant factors affecting the outcome of interest. For predicting either the color or the melting point of a randomly picked snowflake, snowflakes are a homogeneous group.

inductive generalization Generalizing on a sample; also called induction by enumeration and empirical generalization.

margin of error A limitation on the accuracy of a measurement; it is the interval around the parameter that the statistic falls within.

parameter The target number in a measurement—that is, the true value of the characteristic being measured.

population The set or group whose characteristics are the focus of the measurement or inductive generalization. The population need not be a group of people; when a quality control engineer samples cereal boxes to measure their freshness, the population is the cereal boxes.

random sample Any sample obtained by using a random sampling method.

random sampling method Taking a sample from a target population in such a way that any member of the population has an equal chance of being chosen.

representative sample Less formally, a sample having the same characteristics as the population. More formally, a sample S is a perfectly representative sample from a population P with respect to characteristic C if the percentage of S that are C is exactly equal to the percentage of P that are C. A sample S is less representative of P according to the degree to which the percentage of S that are C deviates from the percentage of P that are C.

sample The subset of the population used to estimate the characteristics of the population, that is, used as the premises in the inductive generalization.

simple statistical claim A claim that has the form "x percent of the group G has characteristic C."

statistic The number used as the estimate of the parameter.

statistically significant A statistic that probably does not occur by chance.

stratified sample A sample that is divided into strata in the same way the population is. Suppose a population (say, of people) could be divided into different groups or strata, according to some variable characteristic (such as race). Suppose each group's members have the same value for that variable (for example, all the members of one group are black, all the members of another group are white, and so on). Suppose a sample is taken under the requirement that the percentage that has any given value (black) of the variable (race) must be the same as the known percentage of the value for the population as a whole. If so, then a stratified sample has been taken from that population, and the sample is said to be stratified on that variable.

typical example A single member that has the same characteristics as the population as a whole, in the sense that if it were the only member in a sample, the sample would be a representative sample of the population.

variable Anything that comes in various types or amounts. There are different types of races, so race is a variable; there are different amounts of salaries, so salary is a variable; and so forth.

value of a variable Each type or amount of a variable. For example, Caucasian is a possible value of the race variable; $30,000 would be the value of the salary variable for a person who makes $32,500 per year if the salary variable indicates annual salary to the nearest $10,000.

Answers to Concept Checks

1. A = people, B = shrimp, C = the characteristic of it being morally incorrect to cook them by tossing them alive into a pan of boiling water.

2. There is no doubt that if you cut off someone's head, the person will soon stop fighting. The problem is whether there is a message here for how to win World War II against the German and Italian armies led by Hitler and Mussolini, respectively. To some extent armies *are* like people. They eat, they sleep, they move, they fight. On the other hand, to some extent armies are not like people. They are composed of more than one person, they can be in many places at once, and so forth. The most important disanalogy, however, is that the person without a head *has* to stop fighting, but an army without a supreme leader *does not* have to stop fighting. Maybe the two armies *would* stop fighting if their supreme leaders were killed, but the argument by analogy does not provide a strong reason for this conclusion. In short, a person without a head has no brains; an army without a head still has the brains of its officer corps and individual soldiers. A much better case could be made for killing the supreme leader if it could be shown that, throughout history, armies have stopped fighting when their supreme leaders have been killed.

3. Answer (b). The phrase *typical example* in answer (a) isn't enough reason to say that the passage is an induction by analogy, using an appeal to a typical example.

Only (b) makes use of the example being typical. Arguments (a) and (c) would continue to be strong even if the example were atypical. Also, argument (b) is inductive, whereas arguments (a) and (c) are deductively valid.

4. The variety of the Japanese data is less than that of the American data because Japan is a more homogeneous society. The American people are more ethnically diverse and so are more genetically diverse, and genes affect human growth. Suppose the average Japanese man is 5′5″, and the average American man is 5′8″. Then the point the message is making is that the average of the 100 Japanese men you pick will be closer to 5′5″ than will the average of the 100 American men be to 5′8″.

5. a.   Stronger. A better track record makes for a more reliable prediction.

   b.   Weaker. A more precise conclusion is harder to defend.

   c.   No effect. Those games shouldn't affect how the Lakers will do against a different team, namely the Kings.

   d.   Stronger. The added diversity (variability) of the relevant conditions in the past makes it more likely that the pattern will hold into the future.

   e.   Weaker. A relevant condition that held in the past is now known not to be holding in the future, so the conclusion is now more chancy.

   f.   Weaker. There is not much of a pattern now.

   g.   No effect. The mental state of the announcer is not relevant.

   h.   Weaker. There is now more variety in the past data, so the inductive argument will be weaker.

   i.   Weaker. A relevant past condition no longer will hold, and thus the analogy between past and future is weakened.

6. It is not statistical, but you cannot tell whether it is an inductive generalization just by looking. It all depends on where it came from. If it was the product of sampling, it's an inductive generalization. If not, then it's not an inductive generalization. Either way, however, it is a generalization.

7. Answer (c) is strongest and (b) is the weakest. The word *about* in the conclusions of (c) and (d) make their conclusions less precise and thus more likely to be true, all other things being equal. For this reason, arguments (c) and (d) are better than arguments (a) and (b). Within each of these pairs, the argument whose premises speak about a random sample is better than the one whose premises don't speak about this. So (c) is better than (d), and (b) is worse than (a). Answers (d) and (b) are worse because you lack information about whether the samples are random; however, not being told whether they are random does not permit you to conclude that they are *not* random.

8. (a) The sample is 25,000 U.S. Drivers. (b) The population is U.S. drivers. (c) The sample size is large enough, but it is not random, for four reasons: (1) Drivers who do not stop at roadside restaurants did not have a chance of being sampled, (2) the study overemphasized freeway drivers, (3) it overempha-

sized volunteers, (4) it overemphasized drivers who drive at 4 A.M. (d) The most obvious error in the survey, or in the report of the survey, is that 25 percent plus 85 percent is greater than 100 percent. Even though the survey said these percentages are approximate, the 110 percent is still too high. Also, the reader would like more information in order to assess the quality of the study. In particular, how did the study operationalize the concept of a drug? That is, what counts as a drug? Aspirin? Caffeine? Alcohol? Only illegal drugs? Did the questionnaire ask whether the driver had ever used drugs while driving, or had ever used drugs period? Did the polster do the sampling on one day or over many days?

Lack of information about the survey is not necessarily a sign of error in the survey itself.

9. Answer (d). The suggestion in (b) would be good to do, but it has nothing to do with stratification.

10. Yes, you can be sure it would be a mistake. Your paired comparison test shows fifteen of twenty prefer Pepsi. At the 95 percent confidence level, you can be sure from this result that over 50 percent of your customers would prefer the Pepsi.

11. It would be worse, because the reliability of the key statistical premise dropped from 100 percent to somewhere between 90 percent and 95 percent.

12. (a) As it stands the argument is inductively weak because 25 percent is less than half. (b) This is a very difficult question. Notice that the 25 has not been replaced by 70, but rather a second piece of relevant data has now to be considered. Do you give equal weight to the 25 percent figure and the 70 percent figure? If you could be sure that all drummers are drivers, you should give zero weight to the 25 percent figure and pay attention only to the 70 percent figure; otherwise you would have to give some weight to both numbers. (c) This third factor complicates the situation even more. If you were to learn that the drummer is a fan of Lawrence Welk, and if you had statistical data telling you that only 5 percent of such fans use drugs, then you should pay attention to the 25, the 70, and the 5, and the answer to (c) should be less than the answer to (b). Exactly how much less is a complicated matter that won't be pursued here.

Review and Writing Exercises

Analogies, Typical Examples, and Inductions from the Past to the Future

■ 1. Suppose someone offers the following argument: Amassing a fortune is like winning an election because it takes hard work, new ideas, charisma, and so forth. Well, behind every great fortune there is a great crime. Explain the analogy by identifying the argument's conclusion and the *A*, *B*, and *C* that appear in the standard form of any argument by analogy.

■ 2. Create a short, serious argument by analogy for the following conclusion: "Bombing abortion clinics is the right thing to do."

3. Which one of the following three passages argues in a way that relies on an anecdote?

    a. Uncle Antonio told me, "Don't bother," but I didn't listen to him. Somehow I just didn't believe Sandra when she said Sacajawea was some president's wife. I really wanted to find out more about Sacajawea, so I asked the librarian. She said to check the encyclopedia. It said that Sacajawea was an Indian woman who guided Lewis and Clark's expedition in 1804. She didn't marry any president. But think about that expedition. Knowing what you know now about U.S. history since 1804, do you think things would have turned out better if Sacajawea would have refused to be the guide for Lewis and Clark?

    b. Mercy Otis Warren was a black activist who wrote political pamphlets during the American Revolution. I can still remember my grandmother saying to me, "When you grow up, you should read about that revolution. But don't read about it from your high school textbook. Read other books from big libraries." That's why I'm here. I want to know if you have any history books about Mercy Otis Warren. There is no listing for his name in the computerized catalog.

    c. Paula Abdul and Wynton Marsalis are better singers than Candy Chavez. I went to the same concert that you are talking about, but I was closer to the stage than you were. Trust me; Candy Chavez didn't sing those songs; she just moved her lips to make it look that way. Once, when she tripped while dancing across the stage, she closed her mouth, but the song kept right on going.

4. Identify the analogy that is used or mentioned in the following passage:

    Nobody likes to kill people. War is a messy, dirty, godforsaken business. Who wouldn't rather be home eating popcorn on the couch? But let's face it. You can't make an omelet without breaking eggs.

5. Create an argument about some aspect of warfare. Your argument must be reasonable and nontrivial, and it must rely on an appeal to an analogy.

■ 6. Discuss the strength of the following argument by analogy:

    Mercury is like water in that they are both liquids. Water seeks its own level, so the mercury in that thermometer will, too, if you break it open.

7. Discuss the quality of the reasoning in this argument:

    You have to be a lesbian to be a feminist, but the film *Still Killing Us Softly* doesn't promote lesbianism, so the film is antifeminist.

8. Which of the following passages contain arguments that are inductions by appeal to a typical example?

   a. This piece of copper is a typical example of copper. All copper conducts electricity. Therefore, this piece of copper does, too.

   b. Let me make this appeal one more time, but it's the last time. If you want to keep your roof from leaking next winter, you've got to buy our Number One roof treatment. It has worked for all our customers, so it will work for you, too.

   c. Woody Allen's *Annie Hall* was a funny film, so his films are probably all humorous, don't you think?

   d. Our polling indicates that very few black Canadians can name one famous black American who lived in the nineteenth century. Their best guess for an example of a black American was Huey Newton. Newton was black, but he was a Black Panther organizer in Oakland, California in the 1970s, not in the nineteenth century.

9. Do some independent research and then write a short essay explaining to what extent the flow of electricity in a wire is analogous to the flow of water in a pipe.

10. Write a short essay explaining to what extent running a family is and isn't analogous to running a country.

11. After receiving another student's answer to the previous question, write a short essay evaluating the student's answer.

12. State the implicit analogy used in the following argument:

    It's immoral for you to murder your neighbor, so it is immoral for any country to attack its neighbor.

13. State the implicit analogy used in the following argument:

    There's no challenge in defeating Princeton in baseball. Would you take candy from a baby for the challenge of it?

14. Choose the letter of the ranking that goes from best argument to worst:

    (1) Pele scored 10, 9, and 11 goals respectively in his last three games, so he will score 10 goals next game.

    (2) Pele scored 10, 9, and 11 goals respectively in his last three games, so he will score 9 to 11 goals next game.

    (3) Pele scored 10, 9, and 11 goals respectively in his last three games, so he scored an average of 10 goals in his last three games.

    a. 1 2 3   b. 3 2 1   c. 2 1 3   d. 3 1 2   e. 2 3 1

15. During this year's soccer season, our team has lost all three of its games against Princeton University. It's a good bet that tomorrow's game against them will also be one big tragedy.

Consider the following changes to the above argument. Would each change (separately) be likely to strengthen, weaken, or not affect the argument?

a. Meredith, who is Princeton's best player, played in all three of the previous games, but she won't be playing tomorrow.

b. Meredith, who is our team's best player, played in all three of the previous games, but she won't be playing tomorrow.

c. The last three games against Princeton were played on our field, and the next one will be, too.

d. The last three games against Princeton were played on our field, Princeton's, and the local community college's.

e. One of the games was played during a high wind, and the other two were played during a cold drizzle, but the weather prediction for tomorrow is warm, sunny, and calm.

f. During the past three games you have bet on the results and won, but this time you are not going to bet.

■ 16. Lady Theresa claims to be a psychic and to have perceptive abilities beyond those of most other people. She has been tested in a laboratory for her ability to guess which queen is missing from an ordinary deck of fifty-two playing cards with four different queens. You are a friend of Lady Theresa, and you were surprised to learn that she correctly identified the missing card only 50 percent of the time; you expected her to have a 100 percent success rate.

a. If in future card tests the experimenter were to have a professional magician specializing in card tricks observe Lady Theresa and help detect any cheating, should this make the test results more believable or less believable?

b. If not 50 percent, then what score should you expect the average, nonpsychic person to get on the card tests?

c. The experimenter says that Lady Theresa's 50 percent is not statistically significant. Why do you suppose it isn't significant, and what do you recommend doing to determine whether her ability on these card tests is significantly better than the average person's ability?

17. Is mathematical induction a particular kind of inductive argument?

18. Comment on the strength of these inductive arguments:

a. Our lunar module landed on Saturn's closest moon and found the surface everywhere to be powdery down to two inches. Therefore, the surface of Saturn itself is covered everywhere with two inches of powder.

b. The chemical 3,4,5-trimethoxylate benzaldehyde killed David and his son when they drank it, so it will kill anybody.

c. It's immoral for you to murder your neighbor, so it is immoral for any country to attack its neighbor.

19. Create a multiple-choice question, with answer, about induction by appeal to a typical example. Make the question realistic, unambiguous, and the appropriate level of difficulty for students in your own class.

● 20. Create an essay question, with answer, about induction by appeal to a typical example. Make the question realistic, unambiguous, and the appropriate level of difficulty for students in your own class.

21. For the problem of deciding whether a vaccine manufactured from chicken eggs will be effective against the common cold, would you say that a healthy sixty-two-year-old female designer of antitank weapons for the Boeing Corporation in Seattle, Washington would be a sufficiently typical member of the target population such that if the vaccine works on her it would work on anybody? Why? Mention any relevant background knowledge you have about diversity.

■ 22. State the conclusion of the following inductive argument, and then describe the argument's structure:

> David was caught cheating on his history homework when he was in high school, and now *you* want to hire him to work the cash register in our office? Get serious. A leopard doesn't change its spots.

23. Which of the following is the one argument that relies on an induction from the past to the future? State the conclusions of all the arguments.

   a. Joey's leopard had spots in the past and it will have spots in the future. So, a leopard doesn't change its spots.

   b. Yesterday there was a full jar of jelly beans on that shelf. This morning there is a half-empty jar. Somebody took some last night, right?

   c. When you bought that goldfish, who ended up taking care of it, me or you? Now you want to buy a guinea pig, and you expect me to believe that you will take care of it. No thanks.

   d. You've got to buy either the goldfish or the guinea pig. Past experience tell us that the goldfish is cheaper to buy and to feed, although it is also a little less fun to play with. So, let's buy the guinea pig, not the goldfish.

24. The following passage describes a scientific experiment. It then makes an induction from the past to the future.

> We showed the person who claimed to be a psychic a deck of regular playing cards in which one card had been removed. The psychic was shown the backs of the cards but was not allowed to touch the cards. During the twenty times we tested the psychic, he correctly guessed which card was missing from the deck over 50 percent of the time. Therefore, he will get it right more than half of the time on the next twenty times we perform the test.

Would the above argument be improved, weakened, or unaffected if

a. The *20* is changed to *24*.

b. The phrases *missing from* and *half* are replaced by *not in* and *50 percent*, respectively.

c. The word *half* is changed to *three-quarters*.

d. The psychic was quite comfortable in the past tests but will be made uncomfortable in the future tests.

e. In the previous tests a magician trained in card tricks was present to observe the psychic and to help the experimenter discover cheating that would invalidate the experiment, but in future tests the magician will not be present.

f. In the past tests the experimenter knew which card was missing, but in the future even the experimenter won't know the answer at the time the question is asked of the psychic.

g. The past tests and results were duplicated by an independent and trustworthy research organization.

h. Instead of all twenty tests being performed on a single day in a single lab, they were spread across fourteen days in seven different labs.

■ 25. John is a part-time cotton farmer in Alabama who has tried for four years to get a decent crop on his small plot. Every year he's had so much damage from pests that he hasn't made a decent profit. You conclude that next year's results will be just as bad. Would the strength of this argument be improved, weakened, or unaffected if you were to learn that next year John will be adding alfalfa clippings as a fertilizer to his crop? Why?

● 26. Write an essay that summarizes and then evaluates the reasoning in the following article. The topic is the analogy between an aborted fetus and a disabled person.

WHEN AUNT PERRIE HAD TO MAKE A CHOICE
by Lillibeth Navarro

Lillibeth Navarro, a member of American Disabled for Attendant Programs Today, is executive director of the Southern California chapter.

Aunt Perrie lives in Australia. She married in her late thirties and in 1980, when she came here to visit, I got to see her again and meet her husband for the first time. Aunt Perrie comes from a big family, ten children. For a long while after marriage, she could not conceive. But finally, after five years of trying, she became pregnant. I remember the family being thrilled at the news that she had a healthy baby boy.

Aunt Perrie spoke often about her son. In the course of one conversation during a visit, she mentioned that soon after my little cousin was born, she became pregnant again. I mistakenly thought that she was announcing the coming of her second child.

"I had an abortion," she said. "The doctor did an amniocentesis and found that the baby was going to be handicapped." Her words fell on me like a dagger. She did not want a child similar to me.

I've always wondered exactly how my relatives viewed me and my disability, and Aunt Perrie gave me an answer. She did not think a disabled child was worth her while. She dreaded a "life of problems." No wonder she spoke to me very seldom as I was growing up.

And here I had thought that I was proving to my family, with some measure of success, that life with a disability was good, too. With great sadness, I realized that I lost to abortion the only cousin I would have had who was similar to me.

When I met the disability movement in 1985, I was immediately taken by its progressive ideas about the disability experience and its emerging ideology. I agreed with most of what I heard, except for the movement's generally pro-choice stand on abortion.

I was warned not even to touch the topic, lest we lose our financial support for ADAPT (American Disabled for Access Power Today) Southern California. I was recently called a Nazi by a fellow disabled activist for expressing my pro-life views in a speech at a National Right-to-Life conference. It is intimidating, but I want to engage in sincere dialogue. In an atmosphere of democracy and free speech, I am entitled to propose a pro-life argument compatible with the disability-rights ideology.

The cornerstone of the disability-rights philosophy is that we people with disabilities are equal to and have the same rights as people without disabilities. We enjoy the right to life, liberty, and the pursuit of happiness promised by the Constitution.

At protests and demonstrations, we chant that access to transportation, education, attendant care, housing, and employment are civil rights. When people violate those rights, when they refuse to acknowledge the inherent equality of us all, we call the violation discrimination. We protest and get arrested to decry this prejudice based on our disabilities.

And yet, when it comes to abortion, this holocaust that is also wiping out our tiny brothers and sisters with disabilities, our movement chooses to remain silent. We have bought the argument, proposed by pro-abortion activists, that we should side with the woman, who claims absolute right to do with her body as she pleases, baby or no baby. Our sentiments are supposedly with her because, like her, we suffered from years of oppression from medical doctors telling us what we can and cannot do with our bodies.

But this sentimental cry for the "choice" to kill (allegedly for the woman's benefit) is truly ideologically different from our cry to live with dignity. As a disability-rights activist, I know that when I get arrested in the fight for attendant care or transportation, I am fighting to live; I am not fighting to live at the expense of another.

The movement also has bought the argument that the "line of birth" makes a difference in the abortion debate. This dividing line has created two sets of people, the "born" and the "unborn." It is murder to kill the one, but it is a matter of "choice" to kill the other. Accepting this argument, we have agreed to the creation of yet another minority — the "unborn" — the only minority without a voice of its own. We do not realize that discrimination against them is dangerously similar to the discrimination against people with disabilities.

Disabilities are physical phenomena. Even mental and emotional disabilities may have physical origins. But isn't birth also a physical phenomenon? But discrimination based on disability is a crime, whereas discrimination based on birth is a "choice." The abortion of a disabled baby is dual discrimination — the baby is not only disabled, but also not yet "born."

Unborn babies have great similarities to many of us adults with disabilities. They cannot yet "think," "see," "hear," "speak," "walk," "taste," or "touch." They are thus dependent on and at the total mercy of those who arbitrarily decide to keep them or not.

They are an "inconvenience" for nine months and a couple of years thereafter. They intrude into the woman's lifestyle, plans, and preferences. When it comes to disabled babies, it is even deemed "socially irresponsible" to give them birth. Like us, they also are called non-persons. We are the "defectives" and "vegetables"; they are the "anomalies."

Back to Aunt Perrie. Before she left, she invited me to visit Australia. She said that her city had excellent access for people with disabilities. She assured me that living there would not be a problem. She spoke of ramps, elevators, vans, and buses with lifts.

There is another country, I thought, that is making things accessible for a future generation of people with disabilities that it does not want to be born. My own little cousin, aborted because she was disabled, was not welcome in her own country, by her own family. I wish I had been there to intercede for her.[6]

27. Criticize the following argument by analogy by using the technique of pointing out disanalogies:

> Government budgets are like personal budgets in so many ways. Since you can't last long when your own budget is in the red, you shouldn't permit deficit spending by your government.

Generalizing from a Sample

1. Evaluate the following reasoning. In answering, specify the conclusion, say whether the conclusion follows, and explain why.

> The too small and highly biased survey of major corporate executives indicates that 60 percent of those sampled believe that some American businesses often engage in price fixing. Therefore, if you were to pick, in an unbiased way, five of the surveyed major corporate executives, you could reasonably expect that three of them would believe that some American businesses often engage in price fixing.

2. If some members of the target population did not have an equal chance to be selected into the sample, then the sample must be nonrepresentative of the population.

    a. true   b. false

3. Rank the following three arguments in order of their strength, strongest first:

    (1) Our local newspaper's film reviewer liked the film; so it's a good bet that everyone else will, too.

    (2) Everyone else liked the film, so it's a good bet that our local newspaper's film reviewer will, too.

    (3) Everyone liked the film, so it's a good bet that our local newspaper's film reviewer did, too.

    a. 1 2 3   b. 3 2 1   c. 2 1 3   d. 3 1 2   e. 2 3 1

■ 4. Is a large random sample that is stratified on *all* the relevant characteristics in the population always representative of the population? Why?

■ 5. Why aren't all representative samples random? You may assume that any sample is less than the whole.

6. For the following statistical report, (a) identify the sample, (b) identify the population, and (c) discuss bias and the representativeness of the sample, mentioning sample size, stratification, and so on.

> The *State Hornet*, the State University student newspaper, conducted a survey by asking students a series of questions. The survey was conducted at noon in front of the University Union and involved 450 students out of a student body of 26,000. The interviewers were careful to get a sample with a racial, sexual, and age breakdown similar to that of the university as a whole. In the survey, 70 percent of the students interviewed said they opposed mixing sexes on the same floor of the dormitories. The newspaper presented the results of its survey in an article headlined "Majority of Student Body Opposes Mixing Sexes on Same Floor of Dorms."

Suppose that in response to this passage, Smith remarks, "There are several problems with this survey. For instance, the '70' is pseudoprecise, and just how do you tell from a distance what someone's age is?" (d) Discuss this response.

■ 7. Describe the inductive reasoning in the following article. For any generalizations from a sample, identify the (a) sample, (b) population, and (c) sources of bias.

Feeling of Inferiority Reportedly Common in Black Children

The repeating of a landmark study shows that feelings of racial inferiority among young black children are as strong now as they were forty years ago, researchers reported yesterday.

But, they said, black children can be helped to develop greater self-esteem by teachers and parents, and by changes in the ways blacks are portrayed in films and television.

The new studies involved asking children which doll they preferred, a black one or a white one. About two-thirds of the black children preferred a white doll.

Dr. Kenneth Clark, professor emeritus of psychology at the City University of New York who along with his wife, Mamie, conducted the original study, called the findings disturbing.

"What the children are telling us is that they see their color as the basis of self-rejection," he said. "We've tried to hide the damage racism does to black children, but the damage is there, and will continue as long as racism continues."

But some researchers were cautious in interpreting the findings. Judith Proter, a sociologist at Bryn Mawr, said: "I would hesitate to make any claims about black children's racial pride based on studies of younger children alone."[7]

8. For the following statistical report, (a) identify the sample, (b) identify the population, and (c) discuss how the sampling could have been improved by stratifying (but don't mention other ways to improve it).

> In an effort to determine attitudes about smog controls, the Council for Population Studies asked U.S. truck drivers whether they thought the same smog requirements that automobile drivers must meet should apply to truck drivers as well. Of the several thousand who responded to the survey, most indicated that they believed trucks should be exempt from the automobile smog regulations. The voluntary survey was taken at random times of the day at randomly selected truck stops throughout the United States.

9. Explain why there is equivocation in the following argument:

> Not all random samples are representative. This is because a sample is less than the whole. Yet the goal is for the sample to represent everyone in the population. If a sample is less than the whole, then somebody must be left out; it cannot include everyone in the population.

10. Examine the following dialogue, paying attention to the quality of the reasoning. Then answer the questions that follow.

Lesley: I think little Sam will soon be having dreams of giant needles.

Rico: What? Have you been reading the tabloids again?

Lesley: No, but his school says all elementary and pre-school kids should be vaccinated for measles.

Rico: Who is sick? Do you know anybody with measles?

Lesley: I know, but they might get sick. Evidently somebody high up thinks there's a chance. The school recommended the shots in a leaflet Sam brought home this afternoon.

Rico: What will this latest suggestion of theirs cost us?

Lesley: I don't know. That's our problem. We have to find a clinic, make the appointment, and all that. The leaflet recommended ten clinics in the county.

Rico: It may not be worth all the trouble. I don't know anybody in the last ten years who has ever gotten measles. Besides, can't you still get the disease even if you take the vaccine for protection? Do they say it's nearly perfect? Can't the vaccine itself give you the disease? Shouldn't we consider all this?

Lesley: Well, the leaflet said something about a scientific report in some medical journal. Here it is. It says, "The new vaccine uses a live form of the measles virus that is expected to be the cause of most cases of measles in the U.S. over the next few years. However, the virus is weakened so it is unlikely to cause a real case of the measles. In order to show that measles can be prevented in children, medical professors Carolyn Owen, Mary Pittman Lindemann, and Linda Bomstad gave injections last year to 1,244 children who had been admitted to Chicago hospitals for non-life-threatening problems. 622 received the vaccine; the rest of the children received an injection that looked identical but was actually a harmless placebo, just salt water. The nurses administering the injections were not told which children were getting which kind of injection. Seven months later, only one of those who received the vaccine had gotten measles, but 45 of the group whose injections contained no vaccine had been diagnosed as having the disease." How does that sound to you?

Rico: OK, the shot will help keep Sam safe, but I'd still like to know what it costs.

Lesley: Well, you go call a clinic and ask them.

Rico: You're better at dealing with bureaucracies. You call.

a. What is the main issue in this conversation?

b. The leaflet mentions an inductive generalization based on some statistics. What is the target population?

c. Describe the sample, but do not evaluate the sampling procedure itself.

d. Any problems with the sampling procedure? Comment on stratification of the sample.

e. What did this study say or show about how to cure measles in a child once the child has gotten the disease?

f. Is Rico being illogical anywhere in the conversation? If so, where and why?

■ 11. Could this be true? "I was trying to learn about the population, but my totally unbiased sampling method produced what I later learned was a nonrepresentative sample."

12. About 95 percent of the sample of 94 resistors taken from the approximately 1,500 resistors in Tuesday's output at the factory are of good enough quality to be sold. From this information about the 94 resistors, which of the following statements about the 1,500 is most likely to be true?

    a.   All of Tuesday's total output of resistors work OK.

    b.   Exactly 95 percent of Tuesday's total output of resistors work OK.

    c.   Over 90 percent of Tuesday's total output of resistors work OK.

    d.   94 to 96 percent of Tuesday's total output of resistors work OK.

13. If some members of the target population did not have an equal chance to be selected into the sample, then the sample *must* be nonrandom.

    a.   true   b.   false

14. Create an original example of an induction from the general to the specific.

15. Suppose you were interested in whether the customers who buy heavy metal music from your store would like you to carry wall posters of the musicians. You can't ask all the customers, but you can ask a few by taking a poll. You happen to know that about 60 percent of your customers who buy heavy metal music are male. You know that about 50 percent of the people in the world are female. If you were going to stratify your sample on sex, how would you do the stratification?

16. A national television producer is trying to select which of two shows to broadcast next month, Sitcom A or Sitcom B. The company decided to make its decision by running a paired comparison test of the two. Selecting a sample audience of sixty viewers, they showed half of them a videotape of Sitcom A followed by Sitcom B. The other half viewed the show in the reverse order. The viewers filled out cards indicating which show they liked best. Exactly two-thirds of the viewers preferred Sitcom A. How confident can the producer be that most of the millions of TV viewers will prefer Sitcom A? 50 percent confident? 100 percent?

17. Logical reasoners should not commit the fallacy of covering up counterevidence. In which of the following passages is the reasoner guilty of committing this fallacy, and what negative evidence is probably being suppressed either intentionally or unintentionally?

    a.   Every day of my life the night has been followed by the sun's coming up. It is reasonable, therefore, to suppose that the sun will always come up in the future.

    b.   I've tried lungfish at three different restaurants over the last few years. Every time it has tasted awful to me. So, if I order the lungfish on this menu tonight, I won't like it.

    c.   "Creation obviously occurred *before* anyone was around to witness the incident. Consequently, it is impossible to verify its occurrence by witnesses. In fact, the best evidence for evolution should appear in fossils embedded in rocks, but so many questions arise in this study (paleontology) that even many evolutionary paleontologists put little stock in the record of the rocks. Besides, all such formations can be accounted for by a universal flood, which both the Bible and modern archeology substantiate. Basing one's belief in evolution on geology or paleontology, therefore, can scarcely be considered scientific."[8]

Reasoning About Causes and Their Effects

An inductive argument can establish its conclusion with probability but not certainty. In Chapter 12 we examined several types of inductive argumentation and introduced some of the methods of statistical reasoning. In this chapter we will begin a systematic study of other methods of inductive reasoning, starting with reasoning about correlations and concluding with reasoning about causes and effects. We will investigate how to recognize, create, justify, and improve these arguments. Cause-effect reasoning often involves arguing by analogy from the past to the present, but it can also involve appealing to scientific theories and to other aspects of logical reasoning, as we shall see in this and the next chapter.

Correlations

Scientists are interested not only in statistics about a single characteristic, such as lung cancer, but also in how two characteristics are related to each other, such as how smoking is related to lung cancer. This relationship is described scientifically by saying that the values of the variable "number of smokers in a group" and the variable "number of lung cancer cases in that group" are *correlated*. The word *correlated* is a technical term meaning "associated." Finding a **correlation** in your data between two variables A and B is a clue that there may be some causal story for you to uncover, such as that A is causing B, or vice versa. That is why

> One's heart leaps up when one beholds an unexplained correlation between familiar phenomena. — W. V. Quine

Suppose that a scientific article reports that smoking is positively correlated with lung cancer. What this implies is that groups of people with a high percentage of smokers usually also have a high percentage of lung cancer cases. The two percentages tend to rise and fall together across many groups. If A = percent of smokers in any group and B = percent of lung cancer cases in the same group, then the scientific article is reporting that values of the variable A tend to go up and down as values of the variable B also go up and down.

Definition If the values of the mathematical variable A tend to increase and decrease in synchrony (parallel) with the values of the variable B, there is **positive correlation** between the values of A and the values of B.

When the values of A and the values of B are positively correlated, we also say that the variables themselves are positively correlated.

Pressure and volume of a gas are *negatively* correlated. When you increase the pressure, you usually notice a decrease in volume, and vice versa.

Definition If A tends to increase when B decreases and vice versa, there is **negative correlation** between A and B.

Definition If A changes haphazardly as B changes, there is **no correlation** between A and B.

Being correlated, either negatively or positively, means that the two variables are not independent of each other. If we were to delete the phrase *tends to* from the first two definitions, we would have **perfect correlations**. When A always increases with increases in B and always decreases with decreases in B, then A and B are perfectly positively correlated. When scientists say two variables are **directly proportional**, they mean that a perfect positive straight-line correlation exists between them. A perfect negative correlation between two variables, such as the pressure and volume of an ideal gas, is often expressed by saying they are **inversely proportional**. The accompanying graphs show some of these possible relationships between two variables A and B.[1]

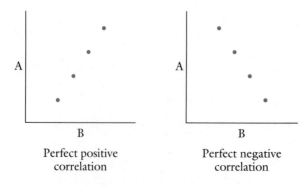

Perfect positive
correlation

Perfect negative
correlation

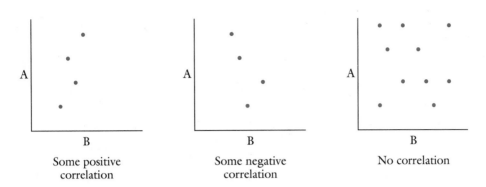

Some positive correlation

Some negative correlation

No correlation

When *A* is correlated with *B*, it follows with certainty that *B* will be correlated with *A*, and vice versa. In other words, correlation is a symmetrical relationship.

■ ············ Concept Check 1 ············ ■

Look for the correlation that is being described in the following passage.

Prompted by a lack of solid findings in previous research on physical activity and heart disease, the CDC [Centers for Disease Control] launched a two-year analysis of 43 previous studies on the topic.

When suspected flaws in some of those studies were taken into account and removed, the CDC said, researchers were left with "a consistent, statistically significant association" between a lack of exercise and coronary heart disease. . . .

"The results indicate that physical inactivity raises your risk of coronary heart disease," said Dr. Carl Caspersen, a researcher with the Atlanta-based CDC. "In general, most studies have seemed to indicate that, but no one has looked at it quite as carefully as we did."

CDC researchers also said lack of exercise may be a much more serious problem than other risk factors for heart disease, since it is so much more widespread.

Fifty-nine percent of Americans exercise less than three 20-minute sessions a week, the CDC noted. By contrast, 18 percent smoke a pack of cigarettes each day, 10 percent have high cholesterol, and 10 percent have uncontrolled high blood pressure.[2]

The correlation between amount of exercise and heart disease is

a. positive.   b. negative.

Correlations Among Characteristics

We've introduced correlations by talking about variables, but correlations can also occur among characteristics. For example, there's a correlation between the characteristics of being a Canadian and owning a warm, hooded coat. The characteristic "being a Canadian" can be thought of as a variable with two values "characteristic is present" and "characteristic is absent." In other words, the characteristic C can be thought of as a variable with the possible values of "present" and "absent" or the values C and Not-C. With this sort of variable, it doesn't make sense to talk about the values "changing in synchrony." Here are some definitions of *correlation* that apply to these kinds of characteristics:

Definition A is **positively correlated** with B in a given population whenever the percentage of A's among the B's is greater than the percentage of A's among the Non-B's.

Definition A is **negatively correlated** with B in a given population whenever the percentage of A's among the B's is less than the percentage of A's among the Non-B's.

Definition A and B are **uncorrelated** if the percentages of A's among the B's is the same as among the Non-B's.

For example, being tall is positively correlated with being a professional basketball player. You'll find a higher percentage of tall people among the players than among the nonplayers. In applying the above definition of positive correlation, we would let

   A = tall people
   B = professional basketball players
   Non-B = people who aren't professional basketball players

Is there any correlation between being Canadian and having a banana tree in one's backyard? Yes, definitely. Randomly examine groups of people. The higher the percentage of Canadians, the fewer people in the group who will have a banana tree in their backyard. There is a negative correlation.

   Correlation is a matter of degree. Some correlations are strong; some are weak. If the percentage of people with lung cancer were only slightly higher among smokers than nonsmokers, the correlation between lung cancer and smoking would be weak. In reality, however, the percentage of people with lung cancer is much higher among smokers than nonsmokers, so the correlation is strong.

Definition The **strength of the correlation** between characteristics A and B is proportional to the difference between the percentage of B's that are A and the percentage of Not-B's that are A.[3]

Concept Check 2

Are U.S. income taxes correlated with citizens' gross incomes? Positively or negatively? Strongly or weakly? Perfectly?

Some persons find correlations where others do not. Suppose that the lobbyist for the Associated Anglers of the Colorado River claims there is a correlation between the number of striped bass in the Colorado River and the amount of water taken out of the river by the State of Nevada. A housing developer in Las Vegas says he sees no correlation. At least the two don't disagree on the raw data, which consist of the following:

Water exports from the Colorado River to Nevada

Date	Water (million acre-feet)	Date	Water (million acre-feet)
1950	0.5	1975	4.5
1955	1.0	1980	5.0
1960	1.0	1985	4.5
1965	2.0	1990	5.9
1970	2.8		

Estimated Adult Striped Bass in the Colorado River

Date	Fish (millions)	Date	Fish (millions)
1969	1.6	1981	0.9
1970	1.7	1982	0.8
1971	1.6	1983	1.0
1972	1.8	1984	1.0
1973	1.6	1985	1.0
1974	1.4	1986	1.0
1975	1.8	1987	1.0
1976	1.5	1988	1.0
1977	0.9	1989	0.7
1978	1.1	1990	0.5
1979	1.1	1991	0.5
1980	1.0		

How can you look at these two sets of data and tell whether a correlation exists? If you look for trends in the data, you will notice that through time the exports of water have increased, while the number of fish have more or less decreased. As one goes up, the other comes down, which is a sign of a negative correlation. Only a statistician can tell how strong the correlation is, but you can tell from the trends that a correlation is present and that it is unlikely to be due to accidental fluctuations in the levels of water and fish.

Significant Correlations

Given an observed correlation, how can you tell whether it is significant rather than accidental? Well, the problem of telling when an association is significant is akin to the problem of telling when any statistic is significant. The point is that the correlation is significant if you can trust it in making your future predictions. Conversely, an observed correlation is not significant if there is a good chance that it is appearing by accident and thus wouldn't be a reliable sign of future events. However, you usually aren't in a position to perform this kind of calculation. If you are faced with a set of data that show a correlation, you might never be able to figure out whether the correlation is significant unless you collect more data. If the correlation is just an accident, it will disappear in the bigger pool of data when more data are collected. Significant correlations are those that continue into the future. They are the correlations that occur because some real causal activity is at work.

If you cannot collect more data, the only other way to tell whether the correlation is significant is to see whether accepted scientific theories about how the world works enable you to predict that the correlation will hold. For example, suppose you have all the data available about Napoleon Bonaparte's childhood and you discover a positive correlation between his height as a child and his age as a child. Is the correlation significant? You cannot collect any more data about Napoleon's childhood; you have all there is to have. You cannot start his life over again and collect data about his childhood during his second lifetime. Nevertheless, you know that the correlation between his height and age is no accident, because you hold a well-justified theory about human biology implying that height in childhood increases with age. If this connection holds for everybody, then it holds for French emperors, too. So the correlation in the Napoleon data is not accidental. In summary, to decide whether a correlation is accidental, you might try to collect more data, or you might look to our theoretical knowledge for an indication of whether there ought to be a correlation.

■ ············ **Concept Check 3** ············ ■

What is the story behind the correlation in the passage below?

Amid Wall Street's impenetrable jargon and stone-faced forecasts for the stock market in 1984 comes this nugget of foolishness: If the Washington

Redskins win the Super Bowl this Sunday, the market is going up. Or, conversely, if you think the market is going up this year, you ought to put your money on the Redskins.

If this method of market forecasting sounds like nonsense, you're in good company. But consider this: The results of the Super Bowl have become a . . . signal of future market activity.

In the 17 Super Bowl games that have been played since 1967, every year [in which] the National Football Conference team won, the New York Stock Exchange composite index ended the year with a gain. And in every year in which the American Football Conference team won, the market sank.[4]

a. This correlation is caused by heavy betting on the Super Bowl results.

b. There is a correlation because game results caused stock market investments by football players.

c. The correlation is a coincidence (i.e., not a significant association).

d. The correlation can be used as a reliable indicator that if the NFC won the Super Bowl last time, then the AFC will win next time.

The stronger the correlation, the more likely that some causal connection or some causal story exists behind it. Investigators are usually interested in learning the details of this causal story; that is the central topic of the next section.

Causal Claims

Magic doesn't cause food to appear on your table at dinnertime. Someone has to put some effort into getting it to the table. Effort *causes* the *effect*, we say. Similarly, houses don't just "poof" into existence along the edge of the street of a new subdivision. It takes some effort to create these effects. Although effort causes some kinds of events, other kinds of events are caused with no effort at all. For example, the moon's gravity is the cause of tides on Earth, yet the moon is not making an effort. It just happens naturally.

Cause-effect claims don't always contain the word *cause*. You are also stating a cause-effect relationship if you say that heating ice cubes *produces* liquid water, that eating chocolate *cures* most all skin rashes, that the sun's gravity *makes* the Earth travel in an ellipse, or that the pollen in the air *triggered* that allergic reaction. The terms *produces*, *cures*, *makes*, *triggered*, and so forth are **causal indicators**; they indicate that the connection is more than a mere accidental correlation. Not all causal claims are true, of course. Which one of the previous ones isn't?[5]

Concept Check 4

Here is a 1950s newspaper advertisement for cigarettes. The cause-effect claim is hidden between the lines. Identify it using the word *causes* explicitly.

More Doctors Smoke Our Cigarette

Check for yourself—smoke our cigarette and see if you don't get less throat irritation.

Concept Check 5

Some scientific reports make causal claims, and some make only associational (correlational) claims. In the following three passages, one is claiming not only that *A* and *B* are associated but also that they are causally related. In another, the scientist is more cautiously claiming only that there is an association between *A* and *B*. In the third, the scientist is being ambiguous and you cannot tell which kind of claim is intended. Which passage is which?

i.   Statistics reported by the Ugandan ministry of police establish a relationship between a person's age and whether he or she was a victim of violent crime in Uganda last year.
     a. causal   b. only association   c. ambiguous

ii. Our study has now uncovered a link between inflation and people's faith in the stability of their economy.
     a. causal   b. only association   c. ambiguous

iii. My neighbor now believes that eating too much licorice candy produces diarrhea.
     a. causal   b. only association   c. ambiguous

If you put this cup of sugar into the gas tank of your Honda this afternoon, its engine will become gummed up. This is a **specific causal claim**. More generally, if you put sugar into any engine's gas tank, the engine will get gummed up. This last causal claim is more general; it doesn't apply only this sugar to your Honda, and this date. Because it mentions kinds of objects rather than specific ones, it is a general causal claim — a **causal generalization**. So causal claims come in two flavors, general and specific. Scientists seeking knowledge of the world prefer general claims to specific ones. You can imagine why.

An event can have more than one cause. If John intentionally shoots Eduardo, then a cause of Eduardo's bleeding is a bullet penetrating his body. Another cause is John's intention to kill him. Still another is John's pulling the trigger. All three can be causes. We say they are **contributing causes** or contributing factors or partial causes.

Some contributing causes are more important to us than others. We call the most important one *the* cause. What counts as *the* cause is affected by what we are interested in. If we want to cure Eduardo, we might say the bullet's penetrating the skin is the cause. If we were interested in justice we would be more apt to say that John's actions are the cause, and we would leave all the biology in the background.

Causal claims come in two other flavors in addition to specific and general: those that speak of causes that *always* produce their effect, and those that speak of causes that only *tend to* produce their effect. Heating ice cubes in a pan on your stove will always cause them to melt, but smoking cigarettes only tends to cause lung cancer. Heating is a **determinate cause** of ice melting, but smoking is not a determinate cause of lung cancer. Rather, smoking is a **probable cause** of cancer. The heating is a determinate cause because under known proper conditions its effect will happen every time; it doesn't just make the event happen occasionally or make its occurrence more likely, as is the case with smoking causing lung cancer. If our knowledge is merely of causes that tend to make the effect happen, we usually don't know the *deep* story of what causes the effect. We understand the causal story more completely when we have found the determinate cause.[6]

We speakers are often sloppy and say that "smoking causes cancer" when such a determinate statement is false, because there are cases of smoking that do not lead to cancer. We should say that "smoking is a probable cause of cancer" or "smoking has a strong tendency to cause cancer."

Eating peanuts tends to cause cancer, too. But for purposes of good decision making about whether to stop eating peanuts, we would like to know how strong the tendency is. How probable is it that eating peanuts will be a problem for us? If there is one chance in a million, we are apt to say that the pleasure of peanut eating outweighs the danger; we will risk it. For practical decision making we would also like to overcome the imprecision in the original claim. How much cancer? How many peanuts? How does the risk go up with the amount? If we would have to eat a thousand peanuts every day for ten years in order to be in significant danger, then pass the peanuts, please.

Inference from Correlation to Causation

Unfortunately, additional problems occur with the process of justifying causal claims. If we know that *A* causes *B*, we can confidently predict that *A* is correlated with *B* because causation logically implies correlation. But we cannot be so confident about the reverse — a correlation doesn't usually provide strong evidence for causation. For example, there is an association between being fat and overeating, but we are unlikely to conclude from this that being fat causes overeating. Now consider another kind of association: the association between having a runny nose and having watery eyes. In this case, we know neither causes the other. Instead, having a cold or breathing pollen causes both. So in this case we say that the association between the runny nose and the watery eyes is **spurious**, because a third factor is at work behind the two that are associated.

In general, when events of kind *A* are associated with events of kind *B*, three types of explanation might account for the association:

1. The association is accidental and won't hold up in the future; it is just a coincidence.

2. *A* is causing *B*, or *B* is causing *A*.

3. Something else *C* is lurking in the background and is causing *A* and *B* to be significantly associated. That is, the association is spurious because of lurking factor *C*.

■ ·············   Concept Check 6   ············· ■

Why is the frequency of lightning flashes in Iowa in the summer positively correlated with popcorn production in Iowa in the summer? *Hint*: The association is spurious.

Given an observed correlation, how can you figure out how to explain it? How can you tell whether *A* is accidentally correlated with *B*? How can you determine whether *A* causes *B* or vice versa, rather than some *C* is causing both? Here is where scientific sleuthing comes in. You have to think of all the reasonable explanations and then rule out everything until the truth remains. An explanation is ruled out when you collect data inconsistent with it. This entire process of searching out the right explanation is called the *scientific method* of justifying a causal claim. Let's see it in action.

There is a strong positive correlation between being overweight and having high blood pressure. The favored explanation of this association is that being overweight puts stress on the heart and makes it pump at a higher pressure. Such an explanation is of type 2 (from the above list). One alternative explanation of the association is that a person's inability to digest salt is to blame. This inability makes the person hungry, which in turn causes overeating. Meanwhile, the inability to digest salt also makes the heart pump faster and thereby helps distribute what little salt there is in the blood. This pumping requires a high blood pressure. This explanation, which is of type 3, is saying that the association is spurious and that a lurking factor, the inability to digest salt, is producing the association.

Diagraming Causal Relationships

Diagrams can be helpful in understanding the difference between the two explanations. Here is a diagram of the first explanation (each line descends from cause to effect):

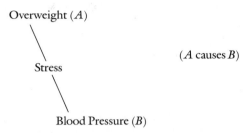

Overweight (*A*)

Stress

(*A* causes *B*)

Blood Pressure (*B*)

This diagram indicates that the correlation is not spurious.

A diagram of our second explanation shows that the association is spurious because factor *C* is causing both *A* and *B*:

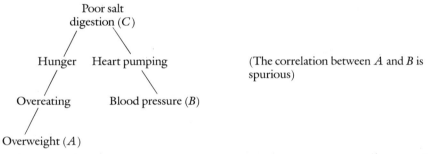

Poor salt
digestion (*C*)

Hunger   Heart pumping

(The correlation between *A* and *B* is
spurious)

Overeating   Blood pressure (*B*)

Overweight (*A*)

Here we are with two alternatives, two possible explanations of the correlation between being overweight and having high blood pressure. How do we find out whether either one is correct? We test them. To do so, we need a test that will rule out one or the other of the explanations. Let's see. How do we test whether poor salt digestion is to blame? We could look to see whether people with the problem also tend to be overweight and have high blood pressure. That is, we could see whether *C* is correlated with *A* and also with *B*. If not, we could throw out the second explanation. That would leave the first one, but it wouldn't establish that the first explanation is correct; it would only establish that the second is worse than the first. What we would then need is a second test. Perhaps we could pay people to overeat and see if their overeating increases their blood pressure. If so, we would be on the road to confirming the suggestion that overeating is the cause of high blood pressure. And this is how science works. But let's stop and look at the bigger picture.

When someone suggests a possible explanation — that is, proposes a hypothesis — it should be tested. The test should look at some prediction that can be inferred from the explanation. If the actual findings aren't what was predicted, the explanation is refuted. On the other hand, if the prediction does come out as expected, we hold onto the hypothesis. However, it is not always an easy matter to come up with a prediction that can be used to test the hypothesis. Good tests can be hard to find. Suppose, for example, my hypothesis is that the communist government of the U.S.S.R. (Russia, Ukraine, and so on) disintegrated in the early 1990s because it was fated to lose power then. How would you test that?

This process of guessing a possible explanation and then trying to refute it by testing is the dynamic that makes science succeed. The path to scientific knowledge is the path of conjecturing followed by tough testing. There is no other path.

Notice the two sources of creativity in this scientific process. First, it takes creativity to think of possible explanations that are worth testing. Second, it takes creativity to figure out a good way to test a suggested explanation.

■ ·········· Concept Check 7 ·········· ■

A third explanation of the association between high blood pressure and being overweight is that stress is to blame for the correlation. Stress leads to anxiety, which promotes overeating and consequent weight gain. This extra weight causes not only a higher body temperature but also extra blood flow. That flow in turn requires the heart to pump faster and thus to increase the blood pressure. This explanation is of which of the following three types?

1. coincidence   2. standard   3. spurious correlation

Draw the tree diagram of the causal relationships.

Criteria for Assessing Correlations

Suppose you get a lot of headaches and you are trying to figure out their cause. You note that you are unusual because you are the sort of person who often leaves the TV set on all day and night. You also note that whenever you sleep near a TV set that is on, you usually develop a headache. You suspect that being close to the TV is the cause of your headaches. If you were to immediately conclude that the closeness to the TV *does* cause the headaches, you'd be committing the **post hoc fallacy**. The fallacy lies in supposing that *A* caused *B* when the only evidence is that *A* has been followed by *B* a few times. I would commit the fallacy if I said that since my right foot itched after I had a Dr. Pepper for lunch, it must have been the Dr. Pepper that caused the itch. If you aren't going to reason so fallaciously about the cause of your headaches, then how should you proceed?

First you should ask someone with scientific experience whether there's any scientific evidence that sleeping close to a TV set that is on could cause your headaches.

Let's assume that there is no convincing evidence one way or the other, although a few statistical studies have looked for a correlation between the two. If the data in those studies show no association between sleeping near the TV and getting headaches, you can conclude that your suspicions were wrong. Let's suppose such an association has been found. If so, you are not yet justified in claiming a causal connection between the TV and the headaches. You need to do more.

Before making your main assault on the causal claim, you need to check the temporal relation, the regularity, the strength, and the coherence of the association.

1. To be justified in saying that *A* causes *B*, *A* should occur before *B*, not after it. The future never causes anything. This *temporal relation* is important because effects never precede their causes. *Fear* of sleeping near a TV in the future might cause a headache, but the future sleeping itself cannot cause it now. That is one of the major metaphysical presuppositions of all the sciences. Our claim, or hypothesis, that sleeping close to a TV causes headaches does pass this first test.

2. Suppose that three scientific studies have examined the relationship between sleeping near a TV and having headaches. In two of the studies an association has been found, but in one, none was found. Therefore, the association has not been so *regular*. Sometimes it appears; sometimes it doesn't. The greater the regularity, the more likely that the association is significant.

3. Even when an association is regular across several scientific studies, and thus is a significant one, the *strength* of the association makes a difference. The weaker the association between sleeping near a TV and getting headaches, the less justified you can be in saying that sleeping near the TV causes headaches. If, after sleeping near the TV, you get a headache 98 percent of the time, that's a much stronger association than a 50 percent rate, assuming that the rate of getting headaches at other times is comparable.

4. The *coherence* of an association must also be taken into account when assessing whether a causal claim can be inferred from an association. Coherence is how well the causal claim fits with the standard scientific ideas of what is a possible cause of what. Suppose a researcher notices an association between color chosen by painters for the Chinese government's grain silos and the frequency of headaches among Canadian schoolchildren. On years when the percentage of blue silos goes up, so do the Canadian headaches. In green years the headaches go down. Suppose the researcher then speculates that the Chinese colors are causing the Canadian headaches and provides these data about the correlation to make the case. Other scientists would write this off as a crackpot suggestion. They would use their background knowledge about what could possibly cause what in order to deny the causal claim about the colors and the headaches. This odd causal claim does not cohere with the rest of science. It is too bizarre. It is inconsistent with more strongly held beliefs. The notion of coherence is quite fascinating. We discussed it in Chapter 8 under the name *improbability*, and we will examine it in more detail in the next chapter when we discuss the paradigm of a science.

Have you ever noticed that night is associated with day? First there's the night, then there's the daytime. Again and again, the same pattern. Regular as clockwork. A consistent, strong association. This would seem to establish the causal claim that night causes day. Or would it?

Creating and Assessing Alternative Explanations

Suppose your TV-headache correlation has a proper temporal relation, regularity across several studies, strength, and coherence with background knowledge. Despite this, a factor lurking in the background could be causing both the headaches and the TV to be on. For example, maybe family quarrels cause the headaches and also cause you to turn on the TV to escape the quarrels.

Unless you had thought of this possibility, or alternative hypothesis, and unless you had also thought of ways to test it and had then ruled it out successfully, confidently asserting that sleeping next to the TV caused your headaches would be committing the post hoc fallacy.

Here is one test that would help confirm some of the hypotheses and rule out others. Suppose you were to hire several people to sleep in a laboratory near TV sets. For half the subjects in this test, the TV would be on; for the other half, the set would be off. What would you predict about the results, given each of the alternative hypotheses? The prediction from your favored hypothesis is that there would be a lot more headaches among those people whose set is on and a lot fewer among those whose set is off. However, from the hypothesis that family quarrels are to blame, you would predict that the two groups of subjects would have the same frequency of headaches. Therefore, your test can produce results that will be consistent with one hypothesis while refuting the other. That is a sign of a good scientific test.

The larger point illustrated here is that the best way to infer from a correlation between C and E to the claim that C causes E is to do a controlled experiment. In this experiment, you divide your subjects into two groups that are essentially equivalent with one major exception: the suspected cause C is present in one group but not the other. The latter group is called the **control group**. The group with the suspected cause is called the **treatment group**, or experimental group. Run the test and see whether the effect E occurs much more in the treatment group than in the control group. If you notice a big difference, then it's likely that C really does cause E.

Let's suppose that you decide it is too expensive to do this sort of testing—you don't have the lab or the TV sets or the time it would take to run the experiment.

Instead you decide to put an advertisement in a magazine asking readers to write if they have noticed headaches after sleeping near a TV set while it is on. You subsequently receive forty letters from people who have had experiences similar to yours. If you were to take these letters to be sufficient evidence that sleeping near the TV does cause headaches, you'd be jumping to conclusions. This second test isn't very good. All you've found are data consistent with your favorite hypothesis. You haven't actively tried to refute your hypothesis. So, you haven't really followed the scientific method. Your results don't qualify as a scientific proof.

This same point about experimental design can be made by considering whether it's true that every emerald is green. Let's say that, although you do suspect this hypothesis to be true, you want to test it to find out. Which would be the best test? (1) Try to find positive evidence by putting an ad in the paper asking people to let you know whether they own a green emerald. (2) Try to find negative evidence by putting an ad in the paper asking people to let you know whether they own an emerald that is not green. One response to the second ad would be much more informative than many responses to the first, wouldn't it? So strategy 2 is the best. This is the strategy of searching for inconsistent data rather than confirming data.

Probably the single greatest source of error in science is the natural human failing of trying to confirm one's own guess about the correct explanation of something while failing to pay enough attention to trying to disconfirm that explanation. That is, we all have a tendency to latch onto a hypothesis and try to find data consistent with it without also actively searching for data that would show us to be wrong. We have this tendency because we really don't want to be shown wrong, because we are lazy about using our imagination to produce alternative explanations, and because it takes a lot of effort to create tests that would show our suspicions to be wrong when it's a lot easier to find data consistent with our suspicions. In short, we have a natural tendency to look for a shortcut to the truth. Unfortunately, there is no effective substitute for the long, difficult path of conjectures and refutations. This is the path of guessing the reasonable alternative suggestions and systematically trying to refute them.

The Scientific Method for Uncovering the Truth

Let's now summarize the major points about the scientific process of finding our way to the truth. Scientific sleuths conjecture possible explanations — the so-called scientific hypotheses — then try to test them in order to rule them out. Testing is not normally a passive process of observation. Instead, it is an active attempt to create the data needed to rule out a hypothesis. When a hypothesis can stand up to many and varied attempts to rule it out, we have produced a scientific proof[7] of the hypothesis. The key idea of the scientific method is that the *true* hypothesis cannot be ruled out; the truth will survive the ruling-out process. So if A really does cause B, observing and testing will eventually produce data inconsistent with alternative suggestions. That is, we can then rule out the possibility that B causes A instead, and the possibility that some C causes both.

This whole procedure of doing science might seem easy at first, but actually scientific proofs are not easy to come by. A major problem is lack of imagination. If you cannot imagine the possible lurking C's how can you be expected to rule them out? For example, consider why lung cancer is associated with buying a copy of *The New York Times* on Tuesdays. The claim implies that the percentage of lung cancer cases is higher among those people who buy this newspaper on Tuesdays than among those people who don't buy it. Why? Although some associations are accidental, just statistical flukes, this one is not. So which causes which? Is buying the paper on Tuesday causing people to get lung cancer, or is having lung cancer causing the paper-buying behavior? Finding the answer scientifically is much like solving a mystery. Can you solve it? Here are some suggestions to pursue. What is special about the ink on Tuesday's newspaper? Could there be a cancer-causing agent in the ink? Or should we give up on showing that the buying causes the cancer and try to go the other direction? Maybe cancer victims have a good reason to buy the paper. Maybe Tuesday is the day the paper contains the most articles about cancer, so lung cancer patients are especially likely to buy the paper on that day.

Unfortunately for these suggestions, a little testing will refute them. Perhaps you spotted the error in the reasoning. You were being misled away from the real causal story behind the association between lung cancer and Tuesday *Times* buying. First, there's a significant association between lung cancer and *Times* buying on Friday, too. And Wednesday. The real story is that living in a city tends to cause *both* the lung cancer and the *Times* buying on Tuesday; it causes their association. Living in a city, any city, makes it more likely that a person will take in cancer-causing agents such as air pollution. Also, living in a city makes it more likely that a person will buy *The New York Times* on Tuesday, and Wednesday, and other days. Country folks are less likely to read big-city newspapers — on Tuesday or any other day. So, city living is the cause. By asking whether lung cancer causes the paper buying or vice versa, I was committing the false dilemma fallacy. Pointing out that something else could be the cause of both is a way of going between the horns of this dilemma.

What this story demonstrates is that proving something scientifically can be quite difficult simply because of lack of imagination. Scientific proofs can't just be "ground out" by some mechanical process. The leap from association to cause is successful to the degree that *all* the other explanations of the association can be shown to be less probable, and this can require a considerable amount of scientific imagination. This same point can be reexpressed by saying that if somebody can imagine an equally plausible explanation for the association, or a more probable one, then the original inductive leap from association to cause is weakened.

Some Case Studies and Examples

The following letter to the editor is fun to read, and analyzing it will demonstrate all the points we've made about using your creative abilities in justifying causal claims. For background: the Planned Parenthood organization, which is attacked in the letter, is the largest dispenser of birth control information in the United States.

Dear Editor:

The author of your letter to the editor last week claims we
need Planned Parenthood. We need something--but it's not
Planned Parenthood. Not if a tree is to be judged by its
fruit.

Hasn't it struck anyone a little bit strange that ever since
Planned Parenthood has been ''educating'' teenagers, teenage
pregnancy and venereal disease rates have shot through the
roof? Doesn't it seem a little awkward that legal abortions, which are supposed to eliminate all but ''wanted''
children, have coincided directly with a rise in child abuse
as well as symptoms of high stress and emotional disorders
in women?

Are we so far down the road to self-indulgence that we don't
recognize simple cause and effect?

I personally know three teenage girls who had their first
sex because of the way sex education was presented in their
high schools. They were led to think that sex was normal
for teenagers and that if they maintained their virginity
something was a little strange about them. Each episode
followed a Planned Parenthood presentation.

Planned Parenthood makes a lot of money from what it does.
Chastity would put it out of business. Are our children
only animals that we cannot expect the vast majority to control themselves?

Ashley Pence[a]

The point of Pence's letter is primarily to state her beliefs and to give a few suggestive reasons; she is not trying to provide scientific proofs for her beliefs. Nevertheless, if she expects readers to change their own beliefs and adopt hers, as she appears to want, then she has the burden of proof and should offer some good reasons. What reasons does Pence offer? In her early sentence that begins "Hasn't it struck anyone a little bit strange . . .," she suggests there are positive associations of the following sort:

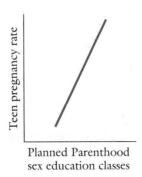

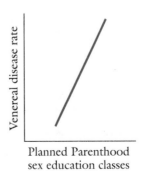

Pence implies a causal connection in these associations when she says, "Are we so far down the road to self-indulgence that we don't recognize simple cause and effect?" Assuming that the positive associations do exist, the next step for the logical reasoner is to ask whether there are plausible alternative explanations for these associations. Maybe the associations are accidental. Or maybe the causal connection goes the other direction; for example, the rise in teenage pregnancy might be causing Planned Parenthood to be invited to offer more sex education classes in order to reduce the pregnancy rate. Thus, there are serious alternative explanations that the author has not ruled out. That makes her causal claim weakly justified. However, caution is called for; an unjustified claim isn't necessarily a false one.

In the next sentence of her letter, Pence implies between the lines that legal abortions are causing three problems: child abuse, symptoms of high stress in women, and symptoms of emotional disorders in women. Can you imagine other possible causes for these effects that she hasn't ruled out? For example, what else can cause high stress?

In short, there are serious problems with the causal reasoning in this letter. As a result of our analysis, it is clear that the letter is basically stating opinion, not fact.

■ ············   Concept Check 9   ············ ■

Pence has several suggestions for what should be done about all the problems mentioned in her letter to the editor. Which one of the following is definitely not one of her direct or indirect suggestions?

a. Children should stop acting like animals.

b. Stop sex education classes.

c. Stop funding Planned Parenthood.

d. Planned Parenthood should be stopped from breaking the law by performing illegal abortions.

e. Stop permitting legal abortions.

■ ············   Concept Check 10   ············ ■

Here is part of a speech given to the County Sheriff's Association of the United States. It contains a report of a scientific study of crime.

Slowly, science is figuring out crime. A reputable, independent, Italian social research organization found that 66 percent of criminals in U.S.

jails did not have a high school degree. To me, this shows that lack of education is partly to blame for crime in our nation. Isn't it time to act on the causes, not just the symptoms of crime?

Suppose John Doe is asked to comment on the quality of the preceding argument, and he gives the following answer.

(1) The first problem with the study is that it was conducted on convicted criminals, which is not a representative sample of the U.S. (2) The study did not state the age of these criminals; maybe they were all seventeen and were not old enough to complete high school but were in the 11th grade. (3) They should also do a study on the people who had not finished high school but who were not convicted criminals. (4) They cannot say that lack of education is the cause of crime in other countries because some countries do not have the funds or desire to educate their population. (5) How do we know where this firm got its information? (6) Maybe they just got it from one prison. (7) And why should it be an Italian firm since Italians don't live in the U.S. and may not understand us Americans? (8) Lack of money causes crime, not just lack of education.

John has missed some of the key things that should have been said. There are other errors. What? Can you suggest any improvements in his answer?

Review of Major Points

In this chapter we explored the difference between a causal claim and one that is merely correlational. Causality and correlation are intimately connected in three ways. First, if A does cause B, there will always be a correlation between A and B, but the reverse isn't true. Second, if you suspect that A causes B, then finding the predicted correlation between A and B will help justify the causal claim, whereas not finding the correlation will refute it. Third, a correlation between A and B is a reason to suspect that A does cause B. Of these three connections between causality and correlation, the first is about prediction, the second is about justification, and the third is about discovery. Prediction, justification, and discovery are three major elements of the scientific process.

The "scientific method" is the method of discovering possible causes, then testing them. The key idea in justifying a claim about what causes what is to actively test alternative causal stories (hypotheses) in an attempt to rule them out. Testing is active, whereas observation alone is more passive. That is one reason that the method of inductive generalization is not as powerful a tool as the scientific method.

Glossary

causal claim A claim that asserts or denies the existence of a causal connection between two things, such as events, people, states, or between two types of things. A causal claim indicates that the connection is more than a mere accidental one. The standard form of a causal claim is: C causes E, where C is the cause and E is the effect. A causal claim is also called a cause-effect claim or a causal statement. *Example*: Ultraviolet radiation in sunlight causes sunburn.

causal generalization A generalization that makes a causal claim. Causal generalizations assert causal connections between types or kinds of things rather than between specific things. The standard form is: (All, most, many) events of kind C cause events of kind E. *Example*: Sugar gums up carburetors. That is, all cases of placing sugar into a carburetor cause cases of that carburetor becoming gummed up.

causal indicator A term that signals the presence of a causal claim. *Examples*: produces, cures, makes, triggers.

cause-effect claim A causal claim.

contributing cause One among many causes. The contributing cause that is most important for our present purposes we call *the* cause. A contributing cause is also called a contributing factor or partial cause.

control group In a controlled experiment, an experimental group that does not receive the cause that is suspected of leading to the effect of interest. For example, when caged dogs are tested for the cardiovascular effect of drug D, the dogs who don't receive any drug are the control group.

correlation An association. Finding a correlation between two variables A and B is a clue that there may be some causal story to uncover, such as that A is causing B. Characteristics A and B are correlated if the percentages of A's among the B's is not the same as among the not-B's.

determinate cause A cause that will make its effect happen every time under known proper conditions. *Example*: Heating ice cubes is a determinate cause of their melting. A five-degree temperature rise on a ninety-degree beach on Long Island is not a determinate cause of an increase in swimmers there, but it is a probable cause.

directly proportional Characteristic of a perfect positive straight-line correlation between two variables.

inversely proportional Characteristic of a perfect negative straight-line correlation between two variables.

negative correlation A relationship that exists when variable A tends to increase when B decreases, and vice versa. Characteristic A is negatively correlated with characteristic B in a given population whenever the percentage of A's among the B's is less than the percentage of A's among the not-B's.

no correlation A lack of relation between two variables —A changes haphazardly as

B changes. Characteristics *A* and *B* are uncorrelated if the percentages of *A*'s among the *B*'s is the same as among the not-*B*'s.

perfect correlation A relationship that exists when two variables always change together. That is, both may increase together or both may decrease together.

positive correlation A relationship that exists when variable *A* tends to increase when *B* increases and vice versa. Characteristic *A* is positively correlated with characteristic *B* in a given population whenever the percentage of *A*'s among the *B*'s is greater than the percentage of *A*'s among the not-*B*'s.

post hoc fallacy The mistake of supposing that *A* caused *B* when the only evidence is that *A* is followed by *B* a few times. I would commit the fallacy if I said that since I felt nauseous after eating sushi at my neighborhood Japanese restaurant, the sushi must have caused my nausea. Instead, I should say that the sushi might be the cause and that further investigation is required.

probable cause A cause that will make the effect happen occasionally. When a probable cause occurs, the effect is probable but not certain. *Example*: Smoking is a probable cause of lung cancer but not a determinate cause.

specific causal claim A causal claim that asserts a specific claim rather than a general claim. *Example*: Lightning striking that specific tree caused it to ignite.

spurious association An association between *A* and *B* that results not because *A* is causing *B* or *B* is causing *A* but instead because some lurking factor *C* is causing *A* and *B* to be significantly associated. *Example*: Two symptoms of a disease are spuriously correlated because they are both caused by the presence of the disease.

strength of the correlation A measure of how well two things are correlated. As a rule of thumb, the strength of the correlation between characteristics *A* and *B* is proportional to the difference between the percentage of *B*'s that are *A* and the percentage of not-*B*'s that are *A*.

treatment group In a controlled experiment, an experimental group that does receive the cause that is suspected of leading to the effect of interest. For example, when caged dogs are tested for the cardiovascular effect of drug D, the dogs who receive the drug are the treatment group. Also called the experimental group.

uncorrelated A lack of correlation between two variables.

Answers to Concept Checks

1. Answer (b). There is a positive correlation between *lack* of exercise and heart disease.

2. Current U.S. income taxes are positively correlated with citizens' gross incomes. The correlation is not perfect, but it is fairly strong. The correlation is weak in the highest income brackets, where those making over $200,000 a year tend to pay proportionately a fairly small percentage of their income in taxes.

3. Answer (c). The pattern will not continue in the future. It is an accident. Answer (a) is unlikely to be correct because bets are unlikely to affect the Stock Exchange so radically.

4. Smoking our cigarette causes less throat irritation than smoking other brands of cigarettes.

5. (i) b (ii) c (iii) a. The notorious word *link* is sometimes used to assert a causal connection and sometimes to assert only a correlation, so it is not a reliable causal indicator term.

6. The real causal story is that storms cause both the lightning and the rain that helps the corn grow.

7. The correlation is not spurious. The explanation is of type 2. Here is the diagram:

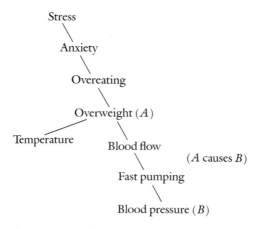

8. The correlation does support the claim somewhat, but the claim is ridiculous, as we now know. The correlation is spurious. Unlike the people of 2,000 years ago, we know what causes daylight, and it's not night. We can suggest a much better explanation of why there's an association between night and day. No doubt you are thinking about the rotation of the Earth under the sun's spotlight. If you had lived 2,000 years ago when everyone believed the world to be flat, you'd probably never have imagined the alternative suggestion that the correlation between daytime and nighttime is caused by rotation of the Earth.

9. Answer (d). The letter did not suggest that Planned Parenthood should be stopped from performing illegal abortions; the focus was on legal ones.

10. The *principal difficulty* with John Doe's response is its failure to mention the two main errors. First, the 66 percent statistic does not establish a correlation between lack of high school education and being convicted of crime in the U.S. Second, even if it did, there is no basis for jumping to the conclusion that lack of education is partly causing U.S. crime. Why doesn't the statistic make the case for the correlation? For it to do so, you'd need to know that 66 percent is unusual.

Maybe 66 percent of *all* Americans don't have high school degrees. If so, there is no correlation. Assuming for a moment that there is a significant correlation, it still isn't a basis for saying that lack of education partly causes crime, because there are other reasonable explanations that haven't been ruled out. Perhaps poverty, greed, and bad genes cause both the crime and the lack of education. Or maybe becoming a criminal causes lack of education, not the other way around.

Let's now analyze John Doe's response sentence by sentence. **Sentence 1** is wrong in saying that the sample is not representative of the U.S., as the goal is to be representative not of the U.S. but of U.S. criminals. The target population of the statistical reasoning is convicted criminals in the U.S., not everybody in the U.S.

There is also a problem with **sentence 2**. Doe is complaining that he doesn't know the ages of the criminals whose education was examined. But he mistakenly implies that his lack of information is a sign of some error in the study. He may be thinking of the correct but minor point that the reader is not given enough information to tell whether the sample is representative of U.S. criminals. If the sample were only of seventeen-year-olds, undoubtedly it would be non-random and apt to be unrepresentative of U.S. convicted criminals. However, Doe shouldn't make too much of this. His answer would be better if it showed some awareness of the fact that there is no reason to believe the sample was of seventeen-year-olds because the study was done by a "reputable . . . research organization," which presumably means a competent one. Also, Doe gives no indication that this is in fact a minor point.

The point in **sentence 3** is not made clearly. Yes, the study should also have included people who had not finished high school but who were not convicted criminals. But *why* should it have done so? The point would be to make sure that the figure of "66 percent" is unusual. A finding that significantly fewer than 66 percent of the nonconvicted people had not finished high school would demonstrate the correlation that the speaker implies does exist — namely, that there's a negative correlation between crime and education. Doe should say all this explicitly, but he doesn't. In addition, if that *is* Doe's point in sentence 3, it is a major point and should have been put first, not third.

Sentence 4 complains that some countries are too poor or are not as motivated as the U.S. to educate their citizens. That comment may be true, but it is irrelevant to whether the lack of education causes crime; it speaks only to *why* there is lack of education, which isn't the issue.

In **Sentence 5** Doe says we aren't told the source of the study's information. This would be a minor but correct statement by itself, but when 5 is accompanied by **sentence 6**, which says the study might have been done in only one prison, it makes the mistake of implying that the sample was too small. Doe's comments fail to recognize that the sample is probably large enough, simply because it is common knowledge to social researchers that the U.S. has many prisons, and a reputable research organization would not have obtained its data from just one prison. The reason that sentence 5 would be a minor point by itself is that there isn't much need for the reader to know where the organization got its information; what is more important is whether the organization is good at its research and whether it can be counted on to have made a good effort to get a representative sample of U.S. criminals. In short, is the speech maker justified in appealing to the authority of the researcher?

Sentence 7 is mistaken because there is no good reason why Italians cannot do high-quality social research on Americans.

Sentence 8 states, "Lack of money causes crime, not just lack of education." This is probably true but off the mark. The speaker said only that lack of education is *partly* a cause of crime; the speaker didn't rule out poverty as another cause. Doe's answer mistakenly implies that the argument did rule out poverty.

In summary, Doe missed or didn't adequately express the main points, and most of his other points were mistaken, too. Note how this evaluation of Doe's evaluation addresses many topics of logical reasoning: sticking to the issue, arguments from authority, vagueness, implication, identifying arguments, judging cause from correlation, and so forth.

Review and Writing Exercises

Correlations

1. Refer to the exercise at the end of Chapter 12 about Lady Theresa (page 318). Analyzing the data from the laboratory, you discover a statistically significant correlation between when Lady Theresa gets the right answer on the card tests and when she twitches her right hand. How can you determine, or what do you recommend doing to determine, whether a statistically significant correlation holds the other way around — that is, between her right hand twitching and her getting the right answer on those card tests?

2. Chapter 2 mentioned a University of Oregon study about cigarette advertising in six women's magazines (page 28). In that study, the cigarette advertising was positively or negatively correlated with what?

3. If increases in the percentage of citizens in jail is caused by decreases in income among the citizenry, among other things, what can you say about the correlation between the citizens' income and the citizens' criminal convictions.

    a. It is positive.   b. It is negative.

4. The following four questions are about this table of information:

Average Earnings for Men and Women in Various Occupations, 1981

Occupation	Men	Women	Median Weekly Earnings of	
			Men	Women
Secretary	1%	99%	n.a.	$229
Kindergarten teacher	3	97	n.a.	264
Bookkeeper	9	91	$320	222
Cashier	15	85	180	166
Waiter/Waitress	15	85	200	144
Elementary school teacher	18	82	379	311
Computer operator	37	63	342	232
Social worker	39	61	358	286
Checker or examiner	46	54	348	219
Secondary school teacher	51	49	387	321
Accountant	60	40	433	308
School administrator	68	32	520	363
Computer programmer	72	28	447	329
Manager, administrator	72	28	466	283
Lawyer	78	22	574	407
Blue-collar supervisor	89	11	409	262
Industrial engineer	97	3	549	n.a.

Adapted by permission of M. E. Sharpe, Inc.

i.   Although the median weekly earnings for men who are employed as secretaries is not available, the median earnings for women secretaries is a little less than $12,000 per year.

a. true   b. false

ii. The higher-paying jobs for men and the higher-paying jobs for women tend to be in the

a. bottom half   b. top half

of the occupation list.

iii. Which pair of concepts (variables) is negatively correlated in the table?

a. the percent of men in an occupation and their salary in that occupation

b. the percent of men and percent of women in an occupation

c. the percent of secretaries and percent of industrial engineers

iv. The most well-paying occupations in the table tend to have a high concentration of men, and the lower-paying occupations have a high concentration of women.

a. true   b. false

5. Create a nontrivial multiple-choice question, with answer, that requires an understanding of the notion of correlation of two discrete variables.

■ 6. How strong is the correlation mentioned in this passage?

> The Surgeon General has determined that breathing is dangerous to our health. This conclusion was drawn from a survey of 100 prisoners in a New York prison who have died within the past five years. All were habitual breathers. A strong correlation; take heed and watch your breathing.[9]

7. Barometers measure air pressure. When the air pressure is low, the air in the vicinity is somewhat like a vacuum, and air from farther away rushes in to restore the imbalance. This new air is likely to bring with it new weather, especially rain. So, the height of mercury in an outside barometer is

a. positively correlated

b. negatively correlated

c. not correlated

with the probability of rain (in the vicinity of the barometer).

8. State something that, in the summer in mountainous states, is positively correlated with the amount of the previous winter's snowfall.

Identifying Causal Claims

1. Which phrase below is least likely to be used to say that *A* causes *B*?

a. *A* leads to *B*.

b. *B* is caused by *A*.

c. *A* makes *B* happen.

d. *A* occurs with *B*.

e. *A* produces *B*.

f. *B* is affected by *A*.

■ 2. Rewrite the following causal claim using the word *cause* or *causes* explicitly.

> Whenever the sun sets, it gets dark.

3. In Chapter 12 exercise 10 on page 324, you are asked to analyze the conversation between Lesley and Rico about a measles vaccine. Identify the causal claim that they concluded immediately from the inductive generalization that 1 out of 622 children receiving the vaccine had gotten measles within the next seven months.

■ 4. Which of the following sentences contain causal claims, and which contain merely correlational claims?

a. Money makes you happy.

b. Sniffing ragweed pollen triggers the creation of histamine in the blood of allergy sufferers.

c. It therefore is the case that lack of education is partly to blame for crime, at least in the United States if not necessarily elsewhere.

d. Putting an infant on a feeding schedule would probably make it cry until its feeding time.

e. The data on the height of corn are associated with the amount of water the corn gets during its growing season.

f. Adding water to corn plants usually leads to taller growth.

g. There are more smokers among Japanese-born Canadians than among other Canadians.

■ 5. Identify the causal claim in the following passage by explicitly stating the cause and the effect. Be as precise as you can.

Need gas? Too bad. It costs a nickel a gallon more today — and don't blame the Persian Gulf crisis. Federal taxes on gasoline increase today, from 9 cents a gallon to 14 cents.

According to an AAA Michigan survey, the increase will take the price of gasoline in the Detroit area to an average of $1.35 a gallon for self-serve regular unleaded, $1.50 for unleaded premium.[10]

■ 6. Following are three causal claims. Which claim is least likely to be a general causal claim? Don't consider whether the claim is true or false.

a. John Jameson stabbed her with his own kitchen knife.

b. PEOPLE kill people; bullets don't.

c. Anyone who drinks a cup of gasoline will get very sick.

7. What is the general causal claim that would most likely be appealed to in defending the suggestion that the murder victim, John Jameson, died of gunshot wounds to his head?

8. Label the following passages:

i. Statistics reported by the Ugandan ministry of police establish that a person's age makes him or her susceptible to being mugged.

a. only association   b. causal   c. ambiguous

ii. Our study has now uncovered a link between people's religion and their faith in the stability of their economy.

a. only association   b. causal   c. ambiguous

iii. Medical doctors now believe that high sugar consumption is associated with weight gain in rats and mice. The previous claim is

a. only association   b. causal   c. ambiguous

iv. Medical doctors now believe that having diarrhea is associated with eating too much licorice.

a. only association   b. causal   c. ambiguous

v. Medical doctors now believe that eating too much licorice candy is associated with diarrhea.

a. only association   b. causal   c. ambiguous

9. What causal claim is Huckleberry Finn making in the following quotation (from Mark Twain's *The Adventures of Huckleberry Finn*) even though he doesn't use the word *cause*?

> "I've always reckoned that looking at the new moon over your left shoulder is one of the carelessest and foolishest things a body can do. Old Hank Bunker done it once, and bragged about it; and in less than two years he got drunk and fell off of the shot tower, and spread himself out so that he was just a kind of a layer, as you may say; and they slid him edgeways between two barn doors for a coffin, and buried him so, so they say, but I didn't see it. Pap told me. But anyway it all come of looking at the moon that way, like a fool."

a. Looking at the new moon over your left shoulder causes most cases of drunkenness.

b. Drunkenness causes looking at the new moon.

c. Carelessness or drunkenness on the shot tower was stupid.

d. Looking at the new moon over his left shoulder caused Bunker to die.

Inferring from Correlation to Cause

1. If scientific studies were to show that 80 percent of juvenile delinquents are from homes under the poverty line, someone might jump to the conclusion that being from a home under the poverty line causes juvenile delinquency. Is the person's conclusion asserting a determinate cause?

2. The passage below is from a *Chicago Tribune* report on a scientific experiment. The newspaper reporter has high hopes that the researchers have discovered a simple, painless technique for analyzing patients' breath that might be used to diagnose heart attacks.

> The breath test, in which patients exhale into a four-foot-long plastic tube, [is designed to] distinguish heart attack patients from those who suffer from other internal problems that cause similar symptoms and might also be used to monitor heart treatments, doctors said. . . .

Researchers at Loyola and the University of Illinois at Chicago analyzed the levels of pentane, a hydrocarbon gas, in the breath of twenty people who complained of chest pains. . . .

The ten patients were found through standard tests to have suffered heart attacks had pentane levels two to six times higher than the control group of the ten symptomatic patients who had not suffered heart damage, the doctors said.

Pentane is produced when cells are damaged and polyunsaturated fatty acids break off tissue in a process called lipid peroxidation. Unusual stresses such as a heart attack aggravate the peroxidation process, killing more cells and producing high pentane levels.[11]

Answer or comment on the following questions.

a. According to the scientific theory being presumed in this test, high pentane levels are supposed to be a sign of

   i. having had a heart attack.

   ii. not having had a heart attack.

   iii. going to have a heart attack in the near future.

b. What were the sizes of the two samples (namely, the sample of healthy patients with chest pains and the sample of patients with heart attacks)?

c. Were the samples taken randomly?

d. What reasons, if any, are there to believe that the statistical data produced by the experiment are significant?

3. Given that you have observed a correlation between A and B and have noticed that A doesn't occur after B, you then need to consider whether A causes B. Which one of the following would be the *worst* methodology to adopt to find out?

a. Look to see whether the causal connection between A and B can be deduced from other acceptable theories.

b. Try to eliminate alternative hypotheses about the connection between A and B by running tests on those hypotheses.

c. Consider whether some third factor C is causing A and also causing B.

d. Check to see whether the probability of A equals the probability of B.

4. The following comment was made as a joke, but if it were made seriously, what would be wrong with it?

All muskrats walk single file; at least the only one I ever saw did.

5. Explain why the correlation between monthly ice cream revenues in New York City and monthly revenues in Utah from snow ski rentals is spurious. Be specific; don't merely restate the definition of *spurious*.

6. The passage below contains a report of an inductive argument. Which statement following the passage is the least significant comment to make about it, if your purpose is to determine how accurate the causal claim is? The argument of the passage can be analyzed as an argument from analogy. However, the argument's conclusion contains a causal claim—namely, that something doesn't cause something—so the argument can also be analyzed as a causal argument—namely, an argument from lack of association to lack of causality.

No Free Lunch

Since drugs, as well as exercise, can stimulate the heart, can swallowing a pill be as good for you as sweat and strain? Probably not, according to a study by Eugene E. Wolfel of the University of Colorado Health Sciences Center in Denver.

Wolfel and his colleagues set out to study the role of heart stimulation independent of exercise in attaining cardiovascular fitness. If physical movement isn't required, people with heart disease theoretically could be spared the effort.

The researchers gave dogs a drug used in treating heart failure and compared the effects to exercise training. The exercised dogs showed various cardiovascular benefits not seen in the caged dogs given the drug and subsequently were able to exercise longer. "This is saying you can't take a drug to attain cardiovascular fitness," Wolfel says.[12]

   a. Isn't it immoral to keep dogs in cages for all those months?

   b. What are the specific cardiovascular benefits?

   c. They gave the dogs only one drug; maybe other heart drugs would have shown different results.

   d. How do we know that the way dog hearts work with heart drugs is the way human hearts would work with those drugs?

   e. How many dogs were used?

7. The "scientific method" is the method of guessing possible explanations of interesting phenomena of nature and attempting to refute them by running experiments or making observations.

   a. more or less true   b. clearly false

8. Read the following article about the assassination of Robert F. Kennedy. Certain unusual losses of evidence in the assassination led some people to suspect that these losses were part of a cover-up by the Los Angeles Police Department. It is suspected that this evidence pointed to a different assassin besides Sirhan Sirhan. But a former Los Angeles deputy district attorney offers an alternative explanation of the unusual losses of evidence. If his explanation has not been refuted or at least shown to be less likely than the cover-up explanation, logical reasoning requires us to reject the cover-up explanation, pending better proof. What is the ex-D.A.'s alternative explanation?

LONG-SECRET DATA MUDDY LA PROBE OF RFK DEATH

by Stephen G. Bloom,
James Richardson, and Nancy Weaver

Los Angeles police investigating the assassination of Robert F. Kennedy tracked conspiracy theories involving imprisoned Teamster leader Jimmy Hoffa, anti-Castro extremists, and a mysterious woman in a polka-dot dress, according to a massive collection of documents unveiled Tuesday.

After a two-decade battle to make the police records public, more than 50,000 of the documents were released in Sacramento by Secretary of State March Fong Eu.

But at the news conference, state Archivist John Burns said much of the evidence — including some 2,410 photographs and scores of key physical items — had been destroyed by the Los Angeles Police Department during its investigation.

According to the released documents, Los Angeles police spent days investigating a link between Hoffa and the Kennedy assassination. When officers asked Hoffa if he put out a contract to kill Kennedy, Hoffa told them, "That's a stupid allegation," and refused to talk further.

The documents include an interview with a Los Angeles Teamster who discussed a plot to kill Kennedy weeks before the assassination. "Forget what you heard in your father's office, or you won't live to tell about it," the daughter of the Teamster associate was told just hours after the assassination.

The Hoffa link was pursued because of Kennedy's dogged investigation, as a former U.S. attorney general, of alleged Teamster ties with organized crime.

Other conspiracy theories investigated and discarded included those involving a woman dressed in a polka-dot dress who allegedly screamed at the murder scene, "We shot him, we shot him!"

The documents also showed that police discounted another theory by proving that Sirhan had not attended a virulent anti-Kennedy rally held by anti-Castro militants a month before the assassination as initially reported.

However, the investigation paid scant attention to the only other known person in the pantry who had a gun besides Sirhan — a security guard who was carrying a .38 caliber revolver and was directly behind Kennedy when he was shot.

The release of the files represents the first time much of the material — kept secret by the Los Angeles Police Department — has been made public. Details were kept secret in the years after the shooting, which occurred hours after Kennedy won the Democratic party's California presidential primary.

Researchers at the press conference were angered to learn that so much key information had been destroyed. "I'm appalled by the missing evidence," said Gregory Stone, a University of Wisconsin political scientist who arrived in Sacramento on Monday night for the release of the documents.

"This was supposed to be a meticulous investigation, but there are many, many problems with the destruction of so much evidence," he said.

Said Burns: "There was no indication of a rationale.... What I didn't know, and I'm told others didn't know, is why so much evidence was destroyed."

Besides photographs, other items destroyed included Kennedy's coat sleeve, pierced by a bullet, as well as ceiling panels and door jambs suspected of containing bullet slugs or holes. Items not released included autopsy photographs, FBI reports, and Kennedy's bloodied clothing.

Twenty years after Sirhan Sirhan emptied eight bullets from his .22-caliber revolver inside the pantry of the Ambassador Hotel in Los Angeles, police remain convinced that the Jordanian national acted alone.

Los Angeles police have defended their investigation and what they describe as thoroughly examined evidence, which they acknowledge they destroyed. "We talked to everyone that stayed in the hotel, everyone that had access," Police Commission Secretary William Cowdin said last week. "At the time, they did everything that was established procedure."

The actual documents, copied onto microfilm and video and audio tapes, comprise 36 cubic feet. They were shipped to the state archive from the Los Angeles Police Department last August. Among the evidence were 2,500 photographs, 4,000 witness interviews, 157 items of physical evidence, 3,150 index cards, and 223 tape recordings.

Sirhan, who has always maintained that he acted alone, is serving a life sentence at the California State Correctional Institution at Soledad for first-degree murder. His attorney, Luke McKissack, said Sirhan was motivated to kill Kennedy because of the candidate's pro-Israel stance.

Kennedy, 42, was shot at 12:15 A.M. June 5, 1968. He died at 1:44 A.M. the next day following brain surgery.

The release of the evidence Tuesday raised fundamental questions that challenged the Los Angeles Police Department's version of the assassination.

Sirhan waited in the pantry area while the senator from New York gave a rousing victory speech to supporters late on the night of June 5. According to police evidence, Sirhan used an eight-shot, Iver Johnson Cadet .22-caliber revolver to shoot Kennedy.

Kennedy was shot three times. Five other people in the pantry were wounded, each shot once. Police ballistics tests and the coroner's testimony demonstrated that the fatal bullet had to have been fired one inch from the back of Kennedy's head.

But many of the 77 people who were present during the tumult told investigators that Sirhan was more than two feet from the senator — and shot him from the front.

One bullet was found in each of the wounded — Paul Schrade, Irwin Stoll, Ira Goldstein, William Weisel, and Elizabeth Evans. Two bullets were found in Kennedy's body. The eighth bullet was supposedly embedded in the ceiling panel that was later destroyed.

If additional bullet holes or slugs could be found in the physical evidence, researchers speculated they would be able to prove a second gun was used in the assassination.

Skeptics for years have said there may have been evidence of a ninth bullet overlooked by the police, which would have proved a second gunman was in the pantry, because Sirhan was subdued before he could have reloaded his weapon.

The security guard, the only other person who carried a gun in the pantry, had been hired to work that night at the Ambassador Hotel.

Ace Security guard Thane Eugene Cesar, 26, admitted to carrying—but neither drawing nor shooting—a pistol. According to police, Cesar was standing directly behind Kennedy in the pantry area.

In the files released Tuesday, police indicated they did not perform ballistics tests on Cesar's gun, they never questioned whether he used it, and they did not administer a lie detector test to the California man.

When Cesar was interviewed six years later, he said he carried a gun larger than the one that fired the .22-caliber bullet found in Kennedy's body.

Other material released Tuesday included aging films of Kennedy's victory speech at the Ambassador Hotel, supporters chanting, "Sock it to 'em, Bobby!" and Kennedy congratulating Los Angeles Dodger Don Drysdale for his sixth straight shutout that summer of 1968.

Also included was an audio tape of the police radio traffic that night, including a blasé police dispatcher's reply, "Big deal," when an Ambassador Hotel operator called for help.

The report also described an enraged Assembly Speaker Jesse Unruh, who was in the pantry at the time of the shooting. Unruh fought with police officers who attempted to take Sirhan. "This one's going to stand trial!" Unruh was quoted as yelling. "No one's going to kill him."

The officers said Unruh, a very large man, confronted the officers, telling them, "You're not taking him any place ... This is the bastard that shot Kennedy."

When the officers shoved him out of the way, he lunged back at them. Finally, the officers allowed Unruh to accompany Sirhan as they led him away.

Vincent Bugliosi, a former Los Angeles deputy district attorney who acted as counsel for one of the five people wounded with Kennedy, said in a recent interview, "I don't think there was a cover-up, but I don't think the LAPD should have destroyed evidence. The fact they did destroy evidence doesn't mean they are covering up anything. It's improper procedure or incompetence.... They could be covering up their own incompetence."[13]

- 9. Write an essay about a significant piece of scientific research that uncovers a correlation and then tries to establish a causal connection. Begin by describing the research and its results in your own words. Use a footnote to indicate the source of your information. Then show how various points made in this chapter apply to the research. The essay should contain many of the terms from the glossary on pages 346–347.

- 10. Write an essay that describes an experiment you yourself designed and ran in order to test the significance of a suspected correlation. The correlation need not have great social or scientific importance. Within your essay, argue for why your test does establish that the correlation is or is not significant.

Logical Reasoning in Science

S ince the European Enlightenment of the 1700s, most Western intellectuals have agreed that natural science produces some of the best examples of knowledge, that is, of well-established true beliefs about the world. Herbert Butterfield, a Harvard University historian of science, even makes a strong case for believing that the rise of science in the 1700s and 1800s ". . . outshines everything since the rise of Christianity and reduces the Renaissance and Reformation to the rank of mere episodes. . . . It changed the character of men's habitual mental operations even in the conduct of the nonmaterial sciences, while transforming the whole diagram of the physical universe and the very texture of human life itself."[1]

Because the contributions of modern science are our culture's best examples of advances in knowledge, it is important for everyone to have some appreciation of how scientists reason. Previous chapters discussed three main aspects of scientific reasoning: justifying a scientific claim, explaining phenomena, and making new discoveries. This chapter more deeply examines the nature of scientific reasoning, showing how to assess the scientific claims we encounter in our daily lives, how to do good scientific reasoning, and how to distinguish science from mere pseudoscience. We begin with a review of some of the principles introduced in previous chapters.

Reviewing the Principles of Scientific Reasoning

Although scientific reasoning is logical reasoning, isn't scientific reasoning somehow peculiar? Isn't it distinct from other kinds of logical reasoning? Not really. Science is not as distant from common sense as many people imagine. Scientific reasoning is what all of us normally do in coming to know about the world around us. Scientists often use more expensive tools in trying to discover things, but otherwise the discovery process is the same one that the rest of us use in our daily lives.

However, one fairly significant aspect of scientific reasoning distinguishes it from other reasoning: The justification process can be more intricate. For example, you and I might look back over our experience of gorillas, seeing them in zoos and seeing pictures of them in books, and draw the conclusion that all gorillas are black. A biological scientist interested in making a statement about gorilla color would not be so quick to draw this conclusion; he or she would contact gorilla experts and would systematically search through information from all the scientific reports about gorillas to check whether the general claim about gorilla color has even one counterexample. Only if none were found would the scientist then say, "Given all the evidence so far, all gorillas are black." The scientific community as a whole is even more cautious. It would wait to see whether any other biologists disputed the first biologist's claim. If not, only then would the community agree that all gorillas are black. This difference between scientific reasoning and ordinary reasoning can be summed up by saying that scientific reasoning has slightly higher standards of proof.

Scientists don't rummage around the world for facts just to accumulate more facts. They gather specific facts to reach general conclusions, the "laws of science." Why? Because a general conclusion encompasses a great variety of specific facts, and because a general claim is more useful for *prediction*, *understanding* and *explanation*, which are the three primary goals of science. Scientists aren't uninterested in specifics, but they usually view specific data as a stepping stone to a broader or more general overview of how the world works. This point can be expressed by saying that scientists prefer laws to facts. Although there is no sharp line between laws and facts, facts tend to be more specific; laws, more general.

A **test** is an observation or an experiment intended to provide evidence about a claim.

A **law** of science is a sufficiently well-tested general claim.

A **theory** is a proposed explanation or a comprehensive, integrated system of laws that can be used in explaining a wide variety of phenomena.

The power that generality provides is often underestimated. At the zoo, suppose you spot a cage marked "Margay" although the margay is out of sight at the moment. You have never heard the term before and have never seen a margay, yet you can effortlessly acquire a considerable amount of knowledge about the margay, just by noticing that the cage is part of your zoo's new rare-feline center. If the margay is a cat, then you know it cannot survive in an atmosphere of pure nitrogen, that it doesn't have gills, and that it was not hatched from an egg. You know this about the unseen margay because you know on scientific authority that *no* cats can survive in nitrogen, that *no* cats have gills, and that *no* cats are hatched from eggs. These last three statements are general statements, and you exploit their generality in deducing your new knowledge about margays. Of course, scientific generalizations can be wrong. The one about nitrogen probably has never been confronted with any data about margays. That is, no one has ever tested to see whether margays can live on pure nitrogen. But you are confident that if there were serious suspicions, the scientists would act quickly to run the tests. Knowing this about how scientists act, you rest comfortably with the generalizations and with your newly acquired knowledge about margays.

Testability, Accuracy, and Precision

If a proposed hypothesis (a claim) cannot be tested even indirectly, it is not scientific. This point is expressed by saying that scientists value *testability*. For example, suppose someone suggests that the current laws of chemistry will hold true only as long as the Devil continues to support them. After all, the Devil made the laws, and he can change them on a whim. Luckily he doesn't change his mind too often. Now, what is a chemist to make of this radical suggestion? Even if a chemist were interested in pursuing the suggestion further, there would be nothing to do. There is no way to test whether the Devil is or isn't the author of the laws of chemistry. Does the Devil show up on any scientific instrument, even indirectly? Therefore, the Devil theory is unscientific. Testability is a key ingredient of any truly scientific claim.

Scientists also value *accuracy* and *precision*. An *accurate* measurement is one that agrees with the true state of things. A *precise* measurement is one of a group of measurements that agree with each other and cluster tightly together near their average. However, precision is valuable to science more than in the area of measurement. Precise terminology has helped propel science forward. Words can give a helpful push. How? There are two main ways. A bird may go by one name in the Southeastern United States but by a different name in Central America and by still a different name in Africa. Yet scientists the world over have a common Latin name for it. Thus, the use of precise terminology reduces miscommunication among scientists. Second, a precise claim is easier to test than an imprecise one. How do you test the imprecise claim that "Vitamin C is good for you"? It would be easier to run an experiment to check the more precise claim "Taking 400 milligrams of vitamin C per day will reduce the probability of getting a respiratory infection." If you can test a claim, you can do more with it scientifically. Testability is a scientific virtue, and precision is one path to testability.

> Science retains and labels as "true" only those claims that have stood up to tests.

Because the claims of social science are generally vaguer than the claims of physical science, social scientists have a tougher time establishing results. When a newspaper reports on biology by saying, "Vitamin C was shown not to help prevent respiratory infections," and when the paper reports on social science by saying, "Central America is more politically unstable than South America," we readers don't worry as much about "help prevent" as we do about "politically unstable." Behind this worry is our understanding that "help prevent" can readily be given an unproblematic *operational definition*, whereas "politically unstable" is more difficult to define operationally. That is, the operation the biologist performs to decide whether something helps prevent respiratory infections can be defined more precisely, and easily, and accurately than the operation to be performed to decide whether one country is more politically stable than another.

Although precision is usually good to have, *pseudoprecision* should be avoided. Measuring a person's height to five decimal places would be ridiculous. The distance between two parallel mirrors can have that precision, but human height cannot, even though they are both lengths. Unfortunately, when newspaper and TV stories report some scientific result to us, they rarely tell us how the scientists defined their controversial terms.

How information gets from scientific laboratories to the average citizen.

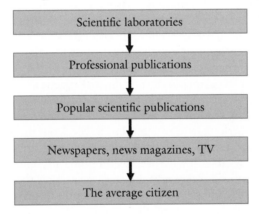

Figure from UNDERSTANDING SCIENTIFIC REASONING, Third Edition by Ronald N. Giere, copyright © 1991 by Holt, Rinehart and Winston, Inc., reprinted by permission of the publisher.

Reliability of Scientific Reporting

Almost every piece of scientific knowledge we have, we justify on the authority of what some scientist has said or is reported to have said. Because scientists are authorities on science, we usually take their word for things scientific. But chemists are not authorities on geology, and chemists who are experts in inorganic chemistry usually are not authorities on organic chemistry. Thus, when we are told that something is so because scientists believe it to be so, we should try to determine whether the proper authorities are being appealed to. Also, we know that scientists disagree on some issues but not on others, and we know that sometimes only the experts know which issues the experts disagree about. Is the reporter reporting the view of just one scientist, unaware that other scientists disagree? Scientists have the same moral failings as the rest of us, so we should also worry about whether a scientist might be biased on some issue or other. If a newspaper reporter tells us that the scientist's research on cloth diapers versus disposable diapers was not financed by the manufacturer of either diaper, we can place more confidence in the report.

Scientific journals are under greater pressure than daily newspapers to report the truth. A scientific journal will lose its reputation and its readers faster when there is a slipup than the daily newspaper will. So the stakes in reporting the truth are higher for journals. That is one reason the editors of scientific journals demand that authors provide such good evidence in their articles. If we read a report of a scientific result in a mainstream scientific journal, we can assume that the journal editor demanded good evidence. But if we read the report in a less reputable source, we have to worry that sloppy operational definitions, careless data collection, inaccurate instruments, or misunderstandings by the reporter may have colored the result.

When the stakes are high and we are asked to take an authority's word for something, we want *independent verification*. That means doing something more than merely buying a second copy of the newspaper to check whether what our first copy says is true. In medicine, it means asking for a second opinion. When the doctor says he wants to cut off your leg, you want some other doctor who is independent of the first doctor to verify that your leg really needs to be amputated. The term *independent* rules out your going to a partner in the first doctor's practice.

Ordinarily, though, we can't be bothered to take such pains to find good evidence. When we nonscientists read in the newspaper that some scientist has discovered something or other, we don't have enough time to check out the details for ourselves; we barely have enough time to read the reporter's account, let alone read his or her sources. So, we have to absorb what we can. In doing so, we are sensitive to clues. Does the report sound silly? Are any scientists protesting the result? What is the source of the report? We know that a reputable scientific journal article about some topic is more reliable than a reporter's firsthand interview with the author; we trust the science reporters for the national news magazines over those for a small, daily newspaper; and we know that daily newspapers are more reliable than grocery store tabloids. But except for this, we nonscientists have severe difficulties in discriminating among the sources of information.

Suppose you were to read the following passage in a magazine: "To ensure the safety of raw fish, it should be frozen for at least five days at minus 4 degrees Fahrenheit ($-20°C$). That temperature kills all relevant parasitic worms so far tested." Should you believe what you read? It depends. First, ask yourself, "Where was it published and who said it?" In fact, the passage appeared in *Science News*, a well-respected, popular scientific publication. The magazine in turn was reporting on an article in an authoritative scientific publication, the *New England Journal of Medicine*. The journal in turn attributed the comment to Peter M. Schantz of the Centers for Disease Control in Atlanta, a well-respected federal research laboratory. The magazine simply reported that Schantz said this. If you learned all this about the source of the passage, you should probably accept what is said.

You should accept it, but to what degree? You should still have some doubts based on the following concerns. The magazine did not say whether any other scientists disagreed with what Schantz said or even whether Schantz made this comment speculatively rather than as the result of a systematic study of the question. The occurrence of the word *tested* in the quote would suggest the latter, but you can't be sure. Nevertheless, you can reasonably suppose that the comment by Schantz was backed up by good science or the magazine wouldn't have published it the way it did — that is, with no warning that the claims by Schantz were not well supported. So, you can give Schantz's claims a high degree of belief, but you could be surer of what Schantz said if you had gotten direct answers to your concerns. Hearing from another scientific expert that Schantz's claims about fish are correct should considerably increase your degree of belief in his claims.

Descriptions, Explanations, and Arguments

Scientists and reporters of science present us with descriptions, explanations, and arguments. Scientists describe, for example, how ballistic missiles fall through the sky. In addition to description, scientists might also explain the phenomenon, saying why it occurs the way it does. The explanation will give the causes, and in doing so it will satisfy the following principle: *Explanations should be consistent with well-established results (except in extraordinary cases when the well-established results are being overthrown)*.

Scientists who publicly claim to have the correct explanation for some phenomenon have accepted a certain burden of proof. It is their obligation to back up their explanation with an argument that shows why their explanation is correct. We readers of scientific news usually are more interested in the description and the explanation than in the argument behind it, and we often assume that other scientists have adequately investigated the first scientist's claim. This is usually a good assumption. Thus, reporters rarely include the scientific proof in their report, instead sticking to describing the phenomenon, explaining it, and saying that a certain scientist has proved that the phenomenon should be explained that way.

Scientific proofs normally do not establish their conclusions as firmly as mathematical proofs do. Scientific proofs usually are inductive; mathematical proofs are always deductive. So one scientific proof can be stronger than another scientific proof even though both are proofs. In any inductive scientific proof, there is never a point at which the conclusion has been proved beyond a shadow of all possible doubt. Nevertheless, things do get settled in science. Scientists proved that the Earth is round, not flat; and even though this result is not established beyond all possible doubt, it is established well enough that the scientific community can move on to examine other issues confident that new data will not require any future revision. In fact, you haven't a prayer of getting a research grant to double-check whether the Earth is flat.

Good Evidence

Many persons view science as some vast storehouse of knowledge. That is an accurate view, but we can also view science as a way of getting to that knowledge. This latter way of looking at science is our primary concern in this chapter. In acquiring knowledge, a good scientist adopts a *skeptical attitude* that says, "I won't believe you unless you show me some good evidence." Why do scientists have this attitude? Because it is so successful. Scientists who are so trusting that they adopt any belief without demanding good evidence quickly get led astray; they soon find themselves believing what is false, which is exactly what science is trying to avoid.

But what constitutes good evidence? How do you distinguish good from bad evidence? Well, if a scientist reports that tigers won't eat vegetables, the report is about a phenomenon that is repeatable — namely, tiger meals. If the evidence is any good, and the phenomenon is repeatable, the evidence should be, too. That is, if other scientists rerun the first scientist's tests, they should obtain the same results. If not, the evidence was not any good. The moral here is that *reproducible evidence* is better than evidence that can't be reproduced. The truth is able to stand up to repeated tests, but falsehood can eventually be exposed.

A scientist who appreciates good evidence knows that having *anecdotal evidence* isn't as good as having a wide variety of evidence. For example, suppose a scientist reads an article in an engineering journal saying that tests of 300 randomly selected plastic ball bearings showed the bearings to be capable of doing the job of steel ball bearings in the electric windows of Buicks. The journal article reports on a wide variety of evidence, 300 different ball bearings. If a scientist were to hear from one auto mechanic that plastic bearings didn't hold up on the car he repaired last week, the scientist won't be a good logical reasoner if he (or she) starts believing that the plastic ball bearings don't work. He should trust the journal article over the single anecdote from the mechanic, although the mechanic's report might alert him to be on the lookout for more evidence that would undermine the findings of the journal article. One lemon does not mean that Buick windows need redesigning. If you discount evidence arrived at by systematic search, or by testing, in favor of a few firsthand stories, you've committed the **fallacy of overemphasizing anecdotal evidence**.

A Cautious Approach with an Open Mind

The scientific attitude is also a *cautious one*. If you are a good scientist, you will worry initially that perhaps your surprising new evidence shows only that something is wrong somewhere. You won't claim to have revolutionized science until you've made sure that the error isn't in the faulty operation of your own measuring apparatus. If a change of beliefs is needed, you will try to find a change with minimal repercussions; you won't recommend throwing out a cherished fundamental law when you can just as easily revise it by changing that constant from 23 to 24 so that it is consistent with all data, given the margin of error in the experiments that produced the data. The cautious scientific attitude recognizes these principles: *Don't make a broader claim than the evidence warrants, and don't reject strongly held beliefs unless the evidence is very strong. In short, don't be wildly speculative.*

Scientists are supposed to think up reasonable explanations, but what counts as a reasonable explanation? An explanation that conflicts with other fundamental beliefs that science has established is initially presumed to be unreasonable, and any scientist who proposes such an explanation accepts a heavier than usual burden of proof. A related principle of good explanation is to *not offer supernatural explanations until it is clear that more ordinary, natural explanations won't work.*

■ .... Concept Check 1 .... ■

What is the main mistake in the following reasoning?

> Yeah, I've read the health warnings on those cigarette packs, but my uncle smokes, and he says he's never been sick a day in his life, so I'm going to start smoking regularly.

a. overemphasizing anecdotal evidence

b. not having a cautious attitude about scientific revolutions

c. not appreciating the need for independent verification

d. overemphasizing unrepeatable phenomena

e. pseudoprecision

In assessing potential new beliefs, scientists actively use what they already believe. They don't come into a new situation with a mental blank. When scientists hear a report of a ghost sighting in Amityville, they will say that the report is unlikely to be true. The basis for this probability assessment is that everything else in the scientists' experience points to there being no ghosts anywhere, and so not in Amityville, either. Because of this background of prior beliefs, a scientist will say it is more probable that the reporter of the Amityville ghost story is confused or lying than that the report is correct. Better evidence, such as multiple reports or a photograph, may prompt a scientist to actually check out the report, if Amityville isn't too far away or if someone provides travel expenses.

Good scientists don't approach new data with the self-assurance that nothing will upset their current beliefs. Scientists are cautious, but they are also open to new information, and they don't suppress counterevidence, relevant evidence that weighs against their accepted beliefs. They do search for what is new; finding it is how they get to be famous. So the scientific attitude requires a delicate balance: Keep an open mind, but don't be so open that you spend most of your valuable time on wild goose chases.

Discovering Causes, Creating Explanations, and Solving Problems

Contrary to what Francis Bacon recommended in 1600, clearing your head of the B.S. and viewing nature with an open mind is not a reliable way to discover the causes behind what you see. Unfortunately, there is no error-free way. Nevertheless, the discovery process is not completely chaotic. There are rules of thumb. For example, to discover a solution to a problem, scientists can often use a simple principle: *Divide the problem into manageable components*. This principle was used by the space program in solving the problem of how to travel to the moon. The manager of the moon program parceled out the work. Some scientists and engineers concentrated on creating a more powerful rocket engine; others worked on how to jettison the heavy, empty lower stages of the rocket; others designed the communication link between the Earth and the spaceship's computer; and still others created the robot mechanisms that could carry out the computer's commands during flight and after landing on the moon. In short: Divide and conquer.

Another principle of scientific discovery says to assume that *similar effects are likely to have similar causes*. The history of medicine contains many examples of using this principle effectively. Several times before 1847, Ignaz Semmelweis of the General Hospital in Vienna, Austria had tried but failed to explain the alarming death rate of so many women who gave birth in his maternity ward. They were dying of puerperal fever, a disease with gruesome symptoms: pus discharges, inflammation throughout the body, chills, fever, delirious ravings. One day, a Dr. Kolletschka, who worked with Semmelweis, was performing an autopsy on a puerperal victim when a clumsy medical student nicked Kolletschka's arm with a scalpel. A few days later Kolletschka died with the same symptoms as the woman. Semmelweis suspected a connection. Perhaps these were similar effects due to a similar cause. Perhaps whatever entered Kolletschka via the student's scalpel was also being accidentally introduced into the women during delivery. Then Semmelweis suddenly remembered that the doctors who delivered the babies often came straight from autopsies of women who had died of puerperal fever. Semmelweis's suggestion of blaming the doctors was politically radical for his day, but he was in fact correct that this disease, which we now call blood poisoning, was caused by doctors transferring infectious matter from the dead mothers on the dissecting tables to the living mothers in the delivery rooms. Semmelweis's solution was straightforward. Doctors must be required to wash their hands in disinfectant before delivering babies. That is one reason that today doctors wash their hands between visits to patients.

A good method to use when trying to find an explanation of some phenomenon is to look for the key, relevant difference between situations in which the phenomenon occurs and situations in which it doesn't. Semmelweis used this method of discovery. You can use the same method to make discoveries about yourself. Suppose you were nauseous, then you vomited. You want to know why. The first thing to do is to check whether prior to your symptoms you ate something you'd never eaten before. If you discover something, it is likely to be the cause. Did you get those symptoms after eating raw tuna, but not after eating other foods? If so, you have a potentially correct explanation of your problem. This sort of detective work is encoded in the box below.

> To find the cause, look for the key, relevant difference between situations where the effect occurs and situations where it doesn't.

The rules of thumb we have just discussed can help guide scientific guessing about what causes what. There are a few other rules, some of which are specific to the kind of problem being worked on. Guessing is only the first stage of the discovery process. Before the guess can properly be called a discovery, it needs to be confirmed. This is the second stage, and one that is more systematic than the first, as we shall see.

Confirming by Testing

To prove your hypothesis scientifically, you would need to run some tests. One test would be to eat the tuna again and see whether it causes the symptoms again. That sort of test might be dangerous to your health. Here is a better test: acquire a sample of the tuna and examine it under a microscope for bacteria known to cause the symptoms you had.

Suppose you do not have access to the tuna. What can you do? You might ask other people who ate the tuna: "Did you get sick, too?" Yes answers would make the correlation more significant. Suppose, however, you do not know anybody to ask. Then what? The difficulty now is that even if you did eat tuna before you got your symptoms, was that the *only* relevant difference? You probably also ate something else, such as french fries with catsup. Could this have been the problem instead? You would be jumping to conclusions to blame the tuna simply on the basis of the tuna eating being followed by the symptoms; that sort of jump commits the post hoc fallacy introduced in Chapter 13. At this point you simply do not have enough evidence to determine the cause of your illness.

Let's reexamine this search for the cause, but at a more general level, one that will provide an overview of how science works in general.

When scientists think about the world in order to understand some phenomenon, they try to discover some pattern or some causal mechanism that might be behind it. They try out ideas the way the rest of us try on clothes in a department store. They don't latch onto the first idea they get, but instead are willing to try a variety of ideas and to compare them.

Suppose you, a scientist, have uncovered what appears to be a suspicious, unexplained correlation between two familiar phenomena, such as vomiting and tuna eating. Given this observed correlation, how do you go about explaining it? You have to think of all the reasonable explanations consistent with the evidence and then rule out as many as you can until the truth remains. An explanation is ruled out when you collect reliable data inconsistent with it. If you are unable to refute the serious alternative explanations, you will be unable to find the truth; knowledge of the true cause will elude you. This entire cumbersome process of searching out explanations and trying to refute them is called the *scientific method* of justifying a causal claim. There is no easier way to get to the truth. People have tried to take shortcuts by gazing into crystal balls, taking drugs, or simply contemplating how the world ought to be, but whatever they've found can't be verified as "truth."

Observation is passive; experimentation is active. Experimentation is an active attempt to create the data needed to rule out a hypothesis. Unfortunately, scientists often cannot test the objects they are most interested in. For example, experimenters interested in whether some potential drug might be harmful to humans would like to test humans but must settle for animals. Scientists get into serious disputes with each other about whether the results of testing on rats, rabbits, and dogs carry over to humans. This dispute is really a dispute about analogy; is the animal's reaction analogous to the human's reaction?

Scientists often collect data from a population in order to produce a general claim about that population. The goal is to get a *representative sample*, and this goal is more likely to be achieved if the sample size is large, random, diverse, and stratified. Nevertheless, nothing you do with your sampling procedure will guarantee that your sample will be representative. If you are interested in making some claim about the nature of polar bears, even capturing every living polar bear and sampling it will not guarantee that you know the characteristics of polar bears that roamed the Earth 2,000 years ago. Relying on background knowledge about the population's lack of diversity can reduce the sample size needed for the generalization, and it can reduce the need for a random sampling procedure. If you have well-established background knowledge that electrons are all alike, you can run your experiment with any old electron; don't bother getting Egyptian electrons as well as Japanese electrons.

Aiming to Disconfirm

In the initial stages of a scientific investigation, when a scientist has an idea or two to try out, it is more important to find evidence in favor of the idea than to spend time looking for *disconfirming evidence*. However, in the later stages, when a scientist is ready to seriously test the idea, the focus will turn to ways to shoot it down. Confirming evidence — that is, positive evidence or supporting evidence — is simply too easy to find. That is why the scientist designs an experiment to find evidence that would refute the idea if it were false. Scientists want to find the truth, but the good scientist knows that the proper way to determine the truth of some idea is to try to find negative, not positive, evidence. A scientific generalization, at least a universal one of the form "All X are Υ," will have all sorts of confirming instances (things that are both X and Υ), but it takes just one X that is not Υ to refute the whole generalization. Disconfirming evidence is more valuable than confirming evidence at this later stage of scientific investigation. Failure to find the disconfirming evidence is ultimately the confirming evidence.

> When a hypothesis can stand up to many and varied attempts to rule it out, the hypothesis is proved.

Thus, although scientific reasoning is not so different from other kinds of logical reasoning, it is special in that its claims tend to be more precise, and the evidence backing up the claims is gathered more systematically. This completes our review of what earlier chapters have said about scientific reasoning.[2] Let's now probe deeper into the mysteries of science.

Superstition

Suppose that anthropologists have discovered a remote village in the Amazon River Basin where virgins are sacrificed during every solar eclipse. The tribe doesn't know about solar eclipses as such; they blame eclipses on an angry sun god. At every eclipse, the leader of the tribe throws a teenage girl to the alligators with the intention of appeasing the sun god and making certain the god returns to shine on the tribal lands.

"Superstitious, ineffective, and immoral," you might say. However, the tribal leader is likely to say in return, "We have always sacrificed virgins, and it has worked every time before, hasn't it?" If you were to accuse the tribal leader of jumping to conclusions and if you were to tell him that if he did nothing the sun would still return, he could reasonably respond by saying, "Your suggestion of doing nothing is too dangerous to try; the village cannot risk the possibility that the sun god will never return."

Because the tribal leader has his own explanation for why the sun disappears and reappears, shouldn't we say his explanation is *true for him*, while ours is *true for us*?

No. The leader might genuinely believe what he believes, but what he believes is not true. Period. It is not "true for him." This phrase is a misuse of words. Instead we should be saying, "It's his belief." Truth in these matters is not subjective; it is not relative to whichever human subject is doing the talking. That is, truth is not a matter of human choice; it is a matter of the way things *are*, objectively out there in the world. Our culture knows why the solar eclipse occurs; it has to do with the moon casting a shadow on the Earth, not with any sun god. We have the correct explanation because we can predict when and for how long solar eclipses will occur. These predictions are made using scientific knowledge that has been successfully tested in many other ways; it can be used to predict the tides, predict the angle of the sun at noon at any place in the world, and so forth. The tribal leader cannot do any of these things. That is why we most probably are onto the truth in these matters, while the tribal leader probably is not.

What gets *called* "the truth" can be relative to one's culture, but the truth itself cannot be. Given what we know, the tribal leader is wrong and has jumped to conclusions. However, he is not being silly or irrational, because he cannot be expected to know what we know. If he had been raised in our modern civilization and yet persisted in his belief, he *would* be acting irrationally. His beliefs about the sun god are "rational relative to his culture." Nevertheless, those beliefs are not "true in his culture." The beliefs may be justifiably believed, but they are not true in his or in anyone's culture.

There are other reasons why the phrase *true for* is so dangerous. With that concept, someone can create all kinds of nonsense. If the sentence "Leonardo da Vinci was a great Italian Renaissance inventor, but he was a terrible painter" is true for you and not true for me, then it is both true and not true for *us*. Ridiculous. That is a contradiction and a telltale sign that the concept of "true for" is incoherent.

The phrase *true for* is meaningful in English when used in certain ways, but only as long as it is not taken too literally. When someone says, "Everybody should get eight hours sleep a night," it would be appropriate to respond with "Well, that may be true for you, but it's not true for me." However, more straightforwardly, what the responder means is something like "Well, you may need eight hours of sleep a night, but I don't." The straightforward response doesn't use the unfortunate phrase *true for*, and it doesn't imply that truth is relative.

A man (or woman) is **rational** provided he arrives at, accepts, and revises his beliefs according to the accepted methods. Otherwise, he is irrational. Although the tribal leader may be rational in his sacrifice of the virgin to the sun god, he is still superstitious. He is **superstitious** because he holds beliefs for reasons that are well known to us to be unacceptable and because those reasons are based on fear of the unknown, trust in magic, or an obviously false idea of what can cause what.

In our own culture superstitious people believe that Friday the 13th is an unlucky day, that they should prevent a black cat from walking across their path, and that they will be safer if they occasionally throw salt over their shoulder. They hold these beliefs in spite of ample evidence to the contrary from the experts. The proof that convinces the experts is actually a rather complicated philosophical argument that makes use of a principle called Occam's razor. According to Occam's razor, if you can have an adequate explanation without assuming some particular exotic entity (such as the hand of fate), then don't assume that this exotic entity exists. Closely related to the notion of fate are other notions that are at the root of much superstition: destiny, fortune, chance, providence, predestination, and luck. If you believe that today Lady Luck will be with you and that you have a better than one in fifty-two chance of picking your favorite card from an ordinary deck of fifty-two cards, you are being superstitious.

Not every superstitious belief is a false belief. What is important to its being superstitious is why you believe it and the conditions under which you do so. For example, it is unwise during a rainstorm to walk on a hilltop or to seek shelter there under a tree, since you become a more likely target for a lightning strike. You would be better off staying in your car, which is electrically insulated from the ground by your rubber tires. However, if you believe that it is unwise during a rainstorm to walk on a hilltop or to seek shelter there under a tree because supernatural forces might use the lightning to destroy you, you are being superstitious even though you are correct about what to do during a storm.

■ ·········· **Concept Check 2** ·········· ■

Some of these statements about superstition and irrationality are false. Which ones?

a. Australian aborigines of the twelfth century who believed that the world was flat must have been irrational for believing this.

b. If Albert Einstein had believed more accidents happen on Friday the 13th than any other day because all the statistical data available to him showed these ideas to be so, he would have been irrational.

c. A person can be both superstitious and irrational.

d. A person can be superstitious while being rational.

Because explanations need to be tailored to the audience, those that will be acceptable to superstitious people might not be acceptable to the rest of us. For example, the following story is about an unusual cult in the New Hebrides, a group of islands east of Australia. The cult is especially interested in explaining certain events that occurred during World War II when the United States was fighting Japan. How you would explain those events is quite different from how they did. Don't laugh. There but for the grace of God go you.

TANNA ISLAND, New Hebrides — The menfolk of this South Seas island gather nightly under the giant banyan trees outside their small villages, drinking kava and talking about what life will be like when John Frum comes from America.

"When John Frum comes to Tanna, he bring big white ships plenty full of cargo, full of things like you gottum in America," said Tuk, the high chief of Loanapiau, his eyes lighting up and a big smile engulfing his face.

"John Frum bring cars, jeeps, trucks, refrigerators, radios, talking pictures. He make roads for Tannese people, roads like you gottum in America.

"When John Frum he comes from America, no more work for us on Tanna. You want pig. You want cow. You want jeep. You gettum.

"No more sickness. Nobody die. Old man change skin become young man."

The 15,000 natives of Tanna, dark-skinned Melanesians, have been waiting 40 years for John Frum to come to their island, about the size of Santa Catalina, 25 miles by 8 miles, located 1,200 miles west of Samoa and 1,500 miles northeast of Sydney, Australia.

John Frum is an obsession with the Tannese, the messiah of Tanna.

There are shrines to John Frum all over the island — from simple red crosses and strange, incomprehensible mystical signs carved on tree trunks and boards, to thatched religious temples like Nima Afaki (House of Worship) in the village of Ianimaki.

Many Tannese have had little or no education because of John Frum.

"Why bother boys, girls go school," explains John Frum leader Kokari Mis,

65. "Waste time in school. John Frum bring everything you ask for. John Frum he make you smart without school."

The John Frum cargo cult started in 1939 when Kahu, a high chief of Iko-hukahuk village, had his first vision.

The whole world then, as the Tannese knew it, was their little island covered with coconut trees, bread-fruit, a variety of other fruit and nut trees, vegetable gardens, herds of wild horses, and a bush alive with wild pigs and wild chickens.

In the heart of the island the sym-metrically perfect Yasur Volcano rum-bled and erupted then throughout the day and night as it does now, above the small but stark moonscape of volcanic ash desert surrounding it. The next nearest islands, Erromango and Anei-tyum, are over the horizon and out of sight.

In the late 1930s, a white ship would appear on the horizon once every six weeks to pick up copra — dried coconut meat — and discharge a few items for the Tannese, sold by trad-ers in a couple of small stores in the main village of Lenakel, along with the gossip from other islands.

That was the extent of the Tannese contact with the outside world.

In Chief Kahu's vision he suppos-edly saw a fleet of white ships sailing to Tanna, bringing the Tannese every-thing they could imagine and many wonderful things beyond their comprehension.

Kahu said he envisioned Tannese killing their cattle and pigs, throwing into the sea all the money paid to them by the traders for their copra, destroying everything purchased from the island stores.

Then, Kahu continued, he saw the people gathered together waiting for the fleet of white ships to bring the magical cargo to them.

Kahu told them that in his vision he saw a great wise man, John from some unknown place, who told him all these things would happen in due course to the Tannese.

So the islanders gathered their few possessions and burned them. They slaughtered their cows and pigs. They went down to the sea and flung their money into the water from the cliffs. They ignored their gardens.

Then they waited and waited and waited.

And nothing happened.

Authorities from Vila, on the island of Efate 150 miles north, the capital of the New Hebrides, heard of the strange happenings on Tanna from the traders and dispatched a boat with national police to find out what was going on.

Kahu and other chiefs were taken to Vila and jailed. The Tannese were told "to stop the nonsense" and go back to living as they had before Kahu had his vision.

But it was too late. The cargo cult had taken root and could not be stopped.

In 1942 an armada of American naval ships sailed to the New Hebrides, bringing an incredible cargo to be unloaded at the staging area for the eventual invasion of Guadalcanal, Tarawa, and other islands held by the Japanese.

A U.S. liberty ship sailed to Tanna to recruit men to work on other islands for the Americans. When the Tannese

saw the fleet of U.S. ships at the nearby islands of Efate and Espiritu Santo, when they saw all the jeeps, trucks, and equipment unloaded, when they saw the roaring American planes, they knew then and there that the man named John in Kahu's vision was John from America.

The Tannese messiah became John From America or John Phrum America or John Frum America — the cult had a name: John Frum.

There was no denying the vision once the Tannese saw the cargo from the United States. But the American cargo ships never came to Tanna.

Tannese returning home to their island after working for the Americans spread the word of the wonders they had seen. They came back wearing the uniforms of U.S. servicemen — army khakis, sailor whites. They brought back cigarette lighters and other gadgets given to them by the Americans. They brought back American flags.

The people stopped caring for their crops and their livestock again, as they had done when Kahu had his vision. They knew it would not be long before the ships from America would appear at their shores.

New Hebrides government authorities asked the U.S. military leaders for advice on dealing with the Tannese.

An American Army officer was sent to Tanna to talk to the islanders. He told the Tannese that a supernatural being wasn't responsible for the cargo brought to the New Hebrides, that John Frum wasn't an American superman.

But the natives didn't buy the story.

Among themselves they agreed that

the American officer was lying, that the people on the other islands were trying to keep all the cargo John Frum had brought from America for themselves.

More leaders of the cult were jailed, as Kahu had been.

One of them, Nampus, released from jail in 1947, returned to Tanna wearing a U.S. Army medical orderly's jacket with a red cross on its sleeve. Nampus said John Frum had given him the jacket and that John Frum said red crosses should be erected all over the island. Ever since, there have been red crosses almost everywhere on Tanna.

Over the years many members of the cargo cult have told of visions of John Frum.

"John Frum tole me Tannese should stop killing and eating cats and dogs," explained Iatik, 52, who spent 32 months in jail in the 1950s because of John Frum visions. "John Frum said OK Tannese swear at cats and dogs, but not OK Tannese kill and eat um."

Cats and dogs, a favorite Tannese delicacy, thus are no longer part of the islanders' diet — at least so they say.

Only the men of the villages are supposed to talk about John Frum. Only the men have the visions.

The women are not supposed to set foot anywhere near the huge banyan trees when the men are drinking kava and talking about John Frum.

Kava, a drink prepared from the root of the kava plant, is a soporific, and after a big drinking session partakers may appear heavy-headed and dull.

If a woman should show up under one of the banyan trees, the men are supposed to whack her over the head with a club. Women have wandered

into the late afternoon gatherings of the men on rare occasions and have been dutifully whacked over the head, say the Tannese men.

A few years ago a John Frum Army was organized in Sulphur Bay. The men of Sulphur Bay village carved wooden replicas of American rifles and marched village to village, imitating the military drills they had seen the Americans doing during World War II.

A boatload of New Hebrides national police, dispatched to Tanna to "disarm" the John Frum Army, took the wooden guns from the John Frummers and destroyed them.

"John Frum show me he exist many times," insisted Tuk, who wears an American quarter around his neck and has USA tattooed on his back, a common practice with Tannese. "John Frum told me knock on big black stone by beach. John Frum say he answer. I go beach knock on stone. John Frum he say: 'Yes.'"

One day, Tuk said, John Frum told him to climb Mt. Tokusmera, the highest mountain (3,544 feet) on the island. On top of the mountain, Tuk said he saw John Frum sitting on the end of a branch in a tall tree.

He said John Frum waved his arm and a huge shed appeared on the mountain. The shed was crammed full of vehicles and other equipment from America. Then, said Tuk, John Frum waved his arm again and the shed disappeared.

This writer was invited to the village of Ianimakl to meet with three chiefs, Nilnapat, Rigiau, and Iaukalupi, and the men of the village.

Puffing on their pipes, the village men — through interpreter Nampus

Malalica—told many stories about John Frum. They wanted to know if I had ever seen John Frum in America, If I had a message from John Frum for them.

One of the men, named Iahmaga, was wearing a World War II sailor's blouse that his father, Itoga, brought back from Vila in 1947 when he was released from a prison term imposed for being a John Frum leader. Some of the village men wore American T-shirts, bought from traders on the island.

As we talked, the men insisted I join them in eating many exotic fruits and nuts that grow wild on the island, and then visit Nima Afaki, the John Frum House of Worship in Ianimakl. Inside the thatched shrine was a large red cross and behind it a large montage from an old *Life* magazine, showing Neil Armstrong in his spacesuit in the foreground with other astronauts, also in space suits, lined up in the background.

"John Frum give us many promises," said Nilnapat. "He promise us one day he give order for Americans to go to moon. Then one day long after promise made by John Frum, Neil Armstrong and America go to moon.

"John Frum he keep his promises.

"One day John Frum he come to Tanna with many ships bring Tannese people all good things John Frum always promise," Nilnapat insisted.

The people of Tanna are absolutely convinced there is a John Frum, that he is an American, and that one of these days his ships will sail in, full of incredible cargo. Without even radios, little comprehension of English, and almost total illiteracy in their own obscure island language, their naivete is almost total.

Authorities from the New Hebrides capital come here from time to time, trying to convince the islanders that their cargo cult beliefs are pipe dreams, but the John Frummers reply: "You wait 2,000 years for Jesus Christ. He no come yet. We wait for John Frum. We think he come much sooner."[3]

■ ·········· Concept Check 3 ·········· ■

Imagine that you are an American-educated intelligence agent of the New Hebrides government who is assigned to the John Frum cult case. You have gained the confidence of the average cult member to the extent that if you give him reasons, he will think seriously about what you say. Which of the following possibilities of what you could say to him would be the best *reason* to help convince him the cult's beliefs are false?

a. I will give you 50 chickens, 3 cows, and 3 goats if you will quit participating in the cult.

b. Not all Americans have waited 2,000 years for Jesus Christ; in fact, some don't believe he will ever come.

By permission of Johnny Hart and Creators Syndicate, Inc.

c. Let me give you an alternative story of where John Frum got those things he brought to Tanna. Shouldn't you check to see that my story is false?

d. I am the real John Frum. I command you to quit participating in the cult.

e. I am a descendent of Kahu, the high priest who had the first vision. He has passed on the real story of John Frum written inside this coconut shell. The shell says there is really no John Frum.

How should we react when faced with stories of the miraculous visions of the John Frum cult members or when faced with reports of clams flying over Los Angeles? We should apply the principle of logical reasoning that we need extremely good evidence before rejecting widely held beliefs. These miracles are too improbable to be believed solely on the basis of anecdotal reports, even though the reports are widespread and even though the people doing the reporting are speaking honestly. It would be a miracle if the miracle were real, so don't trust in this miracle.

The cartoon about flying clams also mentions hallucinations. All of us at one time or another imagine we see things that we later learn aren't really there. We have good imaginations; sometimes too good. Drugs can promote hallucinations. A mass hallucination, one in which everybody imagines the same thing, is rare, drugs or no drugs. Because mass hallucination is so rare, if everybody were to say they see real angels flying over the statue of the Virgin Mary but you see no angels, you would have to worry seriously that the problem is with you, not them.

Alternative Explanations

Mass hallucination is in some ways like mass hypnotism. The hypnotist can place spectacular ideas into your mind, because hypnotism is a matter of suggestion. Mass hypnotism is the key to the famous Indian rope trick, say several magicians. The trick is performed by an Indian magician, called a "fakir." After showing a rope to his audience, he throws it into the air, where it stays vertically suspended. A boy, the fakir's assistant, climbs the rope and then disappears at the top. Several magicians who have analyzed the trick claim that the Indian fakir hypnotizes all the members of the audience into believing they have seen the trick, even though they haven't. This is a fascinating but implausible explanation. Mass hypnotism is too difficult to pull off. It may not be as difficult to create as a mass hallucination, but it is right up there in implausibility.

There is, instead, a better alternative explanation. If a thin, strong wire were strung between two trees above the fakir, he could disguise a hook in the rope and toss the rope so that it hooks the wire and hangs suspended. The fakir's assistant could then climb the rope. Behind a puff of smoke, the boy could scramble along the wire and hide in the tree.

■ ·········· Concept Check 4 ·········· ■

The wire and hook explanation is better than the alternative because

a. if it were correct, the trick would be easier to do.
b. the alternatives were ruled out by testing.

c. the alternatives are self-contradictory.

d. mass hypnotism requires accepting Eastern mysticism.

To further explore the intricacies of finding the best explanation for a phenomenon when alternative explanations need to be considered, suppose you receive a letter asking you to invest your money with Grover Hallford and Associates, a new stock brokerage firm. You do have a little extra cash, so you don't immediately shut the idea out of your mind.[4] The new stock brokers charge the same rates as other major brokers who offer investment advice. GHA is unusual, though, in that it promises to dramatically increase your investment because, according to the letter, it has discovered a special analytic technique for predicting the behavior of the stock market. Normally you would have to pay for any stock advice from a broker, but to show good faith, the GHA letter offers a free prediction for you. It predicts that the price of IBM stock will close lower next Tuesday from where it closed at the end of trading on the previous day, Monday. You place the letter in file 13, the circular file. However, the following week you happen to notice that IBM stock did perform as predicted. Hmmm. What is going on?

Two days later you receive a second letter from GHA. It says that GHA is sorry you have not yet become a client, but, to once again show its good faith, the company asks you to consider its prediction that next Tuesday Standard Oil of New Jersey stock will close up from where it was at the end of Monday. Again you decline to let GHA invest your savings, but you do keep an eye on Standard Oil of New Jersey during the next week. Surprisingly, the prediction turns out to be correct. Two days later you receive a third letter suggesting that you invest with GHA, containing yet another free stock tip but warning that there is a limit to how much free advice you will receive.

Are you now ready to invest with GHA? If not, how many more letters would you have to receive before you became convinced that the brokers truly do understand the logic of the stock market? If you demand thirty letters, aren't you being foolish and passing up the chance of a lifetime? Surely GHA is on to something, isn't it? Paine Webber cannot perform this well for you. Neither can Merrill Lynch, Dean Witter, or Shearson Lehman Brothers. How often do you get a chance to make money so easily? Isn't GHA's analytic technique *causing* them to be able to make correct predictions? And even if GHA is cheating and somehow manipulating the market, you can still take advantage of this and make money, too. What would you really do if you were faced with this decision about investing?

You may not have been able to find a reasonable alternative explanation to GHA's claim that it understands the causal forces shaping the stock market. Many people cannot. That's why the swindle works so well. However, it *is* a swindle, and it is illegal. What GHA does is get a long mailing list and divide it in half. Half of the people get a letter with the prediction that IBM stock will close higher next Tuesday; the other half get a letter making the opposite prediction—that IBM will not close higher. Having no ability to predict the stock market, GHA simply waits until next Tuesday to find out who received a letter with the correct prediction. Only that half then gets a second letter. Half of the second letters say Standard Oil of New Jersey stock will go up; the other half say it won't. After two mailings, GHA will have been right two times in a row with one-fourth of the people it started with. The list of names in the lucky fourth is divided in half and GHA generates a new letter. Each new mailing cuts down by 50 percent the number of people GHA has given good advice to, but if the company starts with a long enough list, a few people will get many letters with correct predictions. You are among those few. This *explains* why you have received the letters. Along the way, many people will have sent their hard-earned money to GHA, money that will never be returned. This swindle is quite effective. Watch out for it. And don't use it yourself on anybody else.

Once again we draw a familiar moral. The degree of belief you should give to a claim that *A* causes *B* (that GHA's insight into the stock market causes its correct predictions) is improved or lessened depending on whether you can be more or less sure that reasonable alternative explanations can be ruled out. Thinking up these alternatives is crucial to logical reasoning. Without this creativity you can be more easily led away from the truth.

■ ············ **Concept Check 5** ············ ■

Back in the nineteenth century, a manuscript was discovered in a large, sealed bottle underground in London. The tightly rolled manuscript was signed "Brother Bartholomew," who was known to have been a famous prophet of the fifteenth and sixteenth centuries. The manuscript contained several remarkable statements. Unlike the vague predictions in the sixteenth-century writings of Nostradamus, this manuscript made precise predictions. It described in some detail how to build a steam engine, a repeating rifle, and a telegraph. The manuscript didn't contain the English names for these inventions, just the plans. It also said that a new country would someday be formed far to the west of London and that its first leader would be named "Woshentun." The manuscript contained the date "1523" on its cover page. A reliable chemical analysis of the ink on the cover page established it as a kind of ink commonly used during the sixteenth century, although not these days.

Assuming that this (fictitious) story is true, what is the best comment to make about whether the evidence shows Brother Bartholomew to have been a successful prophet?

a. I wouldn't put a whole lot of stock in this claim. Making a decision about Brother Bartholomew from just one source of evidence is tough; if two manuscripts were found, it would be twice as good evidence though. So, it is about 25 percent likely he was a prophet.

b. Everything Brother Bartholomew says came true, so he was foretelling the future. Also, the chemical tests that were done on the manuscript show with high probability that it was written back in 1523.

c. I can't believe this shows he is a prophet, since the manuscript doesn't predict anything that wasn't already known at the time of its discovery.

d. I can't believe in the authenticity of the document because London did not exist in 1523.

e. There is no proof that the document was *not* foretelling the future, and there is solid evidence that it was written on old paper, so the best thing to do is to believe that he is a legitimate prophet.

Creating and Testing Scientific Explanations

The power to explain is a mark of the truth. Those who can explain more know more. Hundreds of years before astronauts photographed the Earth, our civilization proved that the Earth is round, not flat. How did it do this? Not by gathering many positive reports from people declaring that the Earth is round while failing to receive any negative reports declaring it to be flat. The evidence was more indirect: the hypothesis that the Earth is round enabled so many things to be explained that otherwise were unexplainable. By assuming that the Earth is round we can explain why Magellan's ship could keep sailing west from Spain yet return to Spain. By assuming that the Earth is round we can make sense of the shape of eclipses of the moon (they are round shadows of our round Earth). By assuming that the Earth is round we can explain why, when we look away from port with our telescope at a ship sailing toward the horizon, the top of the ship disappears after the bottom. By assuming that the earth is round we don't have to worry about whether we are seeing a new sun every morning nor worry about what it was doing in the meantime. By assuming that the Earth is round we can explain why the sun can shine at midnight in the arctic. All these facts would be deep mysteries without the round-Earth assumption, and it would be nearly a miraculous coincidence if all these facts fit so well with an assumption that was false; therefore, the assumption is a fact. The moral is that science is propelled forward by its power to explain.

Probabilistic and Deterministic Explanations

The best explanations designed to explain an event or a kind of event usually give us a good reason to expect the event. Suppose you want to explain the event of a particular apple's falling onto the head of Isaac Newton while he was sitting under an apple tree. One untestable explanation would be that it was the apple's "time" to leave the tree. That explanation appeals to a supernatural notion of fate or destiny. A scientific explanation is more complicated. The apple fell because it absorbed enough water through its stem that its weight increased above a value W, the maximum downward force the brittle stem could resist. The force of the Earth's gravity that is responsible for the apple having weight pulled the apple down toward the center of the Earth. This second explanation, in addition to being testable, is so much better than the first because it tells you things that, had you known them in advance of the apple's falling, would have allowed you to predict both the time and the direction of the fall. In addition, the explanation contains information that can be used to predict the fall of other apples. All you need to know is when the apple's weight will exceed the value W for its stem.

Because explaining people's behavior is harder than explaining the behavior of apples, the current principles of psychology are less precise than the principles of physics. Psychologists depend on rules of thumb; physical scientists have *deterministic laws* that indicate what *will* happen rather than what *might* happen. For example, why did Susan decide not to go out with Wayne when he mentioned he had an extra ticket to the heavy metal concert? A psychologist might explain her action in this way after talking with her:

1. Wayne suggested that Susan spend her time doing something she believed wouldn't be interesting to her.
2. People will not usually do what they have little interest in doing, nor what they perceive to be against their self-interest.

Sentence 1 states the relevant initial facts of the situation, and sentence 2 expresses the relevant law of psychology. This law is less precise than the law of gravity. It is only probabilistic, not deterministic, because it doesn't say what will happen but only what probably will happen. Using 1 and 2 in advance, we could predict only what Susan probably would do. Psychology can't give a deterministic explanation. Such is the current state of that science.[5]

Suppose you asked why you can see through glass but not through concrete, and you were told: "Because glass is transparent." That answer is appropriate for an elementary school student, but not for a more sophisticated audience. After all, *transparent* simply means being able to be seen through. The explanation is trivial. Up until 1926, however, no one had a better explanation. Glass's being transparent was just one of the brute facts of nature. It was accepted, but no deeper explanation could show why. Then, in 1926, the theory of quantum mechanics was arrived at. From the principles of quantum mechanics, it was possible to *deduce* that anything made of glass should permit light to pass through. Similarly, quantum mechanics allowed us to find out why water is wet. These examples illustrate two main points: (1) General theories are more valuable than mere collections of specific facts, for with a general theory you can explain a large variety of individual facts. (2) If you can deduce a phenomenon from some other principles, you have a much deeper explanation of the phenomenon than if you can't carry out this deduction.

Fruitful and Unfruitful Explanations

Whereas untestable explanations are avoided by good scientists, fruitful explanations are highly valued. To appreciate this virtue of **fruitfulness**, consider the scientists' favorite explanation of what caused the demise of the dinosaurs 65 million years ago. Four explanations or specific theories have been proposed in the scientific literature: the sex theory, the drugs theory, the violence theory, and the crime theory.

According to the sex theory, 65 million years ago the world's temperature increased a few degrees. This increase warmed the male dinosaurs' testes to the point that they became infertile.

According to the drug theory, 65 million years ago the world's first psychoactive (mind-altering) plants evolved. Dinosaurs ate these plants, overdosed, and died.

According to the violence theory, 65 million years ago some violent global event — perhaps caused by an asteroid or volcano — led to the dinosaur extinctions.

According to the crime theory, 65 million years ago the first small mammals got braver and more clever. Some mammals learned to steal dinosaur eggs, which caused the dinosaur extinctions.

Of all four theories, current science favors the violence theory. Why? There are two reasons: it has been successfully tested, and it has been fruitful. The other three theories are testable in principle, but they are too hard to test in practice. The soft parts of male dinosaurs don't leave fossils, so the sex theory cannot be tested by looking for fossil remains. The drug theory is too hard to test because nothing much is known about which drugs were in which plants so long ago. There is no practical way to check whether little mammals did or didn't steal the dinosaur eggs, so the crime theory cannot be tested either. On the other hand, the violence theory can be. Suppose a violent global event threw dust into the air, darkening the Earth, leading to cold weather and the end of most plant photosynthesis. Digging down to the 65-million-year layer should reveal a thin layer of dust, no matter where in the world the scientists dig down. And indeed, scientists have discovered a layer of dust there containing a high concentration of a very rare element, iridium. Although naturally scarce on the Earth's surface, the element is relatively abundant both in asteroids and deep inside volcanos.

In addition to its having stood up to this observational test, the violence theory is favored because it is so fruitful. That is, scientists can imagine many interesting and practical ways in which the theory can be tested. They can search satellite photos looking for 65-million-year-old asteroid craters. At suspected crater sites, they can analyze rocks for signs of impact — tiny fractures in shocked quartz. Digging might reveal pieces of an asteroid. A large speeding asteroid would ionize the surrounding air, making it as acidic as the acid in a car battery, so effects of this acidity might be discovered. Imagine what that rain would do to your car's paint. Scientists can also examine known asteroids and volcanos for unusual concentrations of other chemical elements in addition to iridium. Ancient beaches can be unearthed to look for evidence of a huge tidal wave having hit them 65 million years ago. All these searches and examinations are under way today.

Thus, the violence theory is the leading contender for explaining the dinosaur extinctions not because the alternative explanations have been refuted but because of its being successfully tested (to a small extent) and its being so fruitful.

This brings us to the edge of a controversy about scientific methodology. The other alternative theories of dinosaur extinctions have not been refuted; they have not even been tested. But if they have not been refuted, and if proving the violence theory requires refuting all the alternative theories, doesn't it follow that the violence theory will never be proved, no matter how much new positive evidence is dug up by all those searches and examinations mentioned above? This question cannot be answered easily. We will end our discussion of this problem about scientific reasoning with the comment that not only is there much more to be learned about nature, but there are also unsolved problems about the nature of the scientific game itself.

■ ·········· **Concept Check 6** ·········· ■

The explanation of the dinosaur extinctions most favored by today's scientific community is the one appealing to a violent impact or explosion. One of the reasons that this explanation is favored over reasonable alternative explanations is not that the others have been tested and shown to be inconsistent with the data but that the violence theory

a. has not been falsified, unlike the alternative theories.

b. has suggested a variety of new tests.

c. is known not to be pseudoprecise.

d. has been confirmed by deducing it from previously known facts and theories.

Designing a Scientific Test

It is easy to agree that scientific generalizations should be tested before they are proclaimed as true, and it is easy to agree that the explanations based on those generalizations should also be tested. However, how do you actually go about testing them? The answer is not as straightforward as one might imagine. The way to properly test a generalization differs dramatically depending on whether the generalization is universal or nonuniversal. When attempting to confirm a universal generalization, it is always better to focus on refuting the claim than on finding more examples consistent with it. That is, look for negative evidence, not positive evidence. For example, if you are interested in whether *all* cases of malaria can be cured by drinking quinine, it would be a waste of research money to seek confirming examples. Even 20,000 such examples would be immediately shot down by finding just one person who drank quinine but was not cured. On the other hand, suppose the generalization were nonuniversal instead of universal, that is, that *most* cases of malaria can be cured by drinking quinine. Then the one case in which someone drinks quinine and is not cured would not destroy the generalization. With a nonuniversal generalization the name of the game would be the ratio of cures to failures. In this case, 20,000 examples would go a long way toward improving the ratio.

There are other difficulties with testing. For example, today's astronomers say that all other galaxies on average are speeding away from our Milky Way galaxy because of the Big Bang explosion. This explosion occurred at the beginning of time, when the universe was supposedly smaller than the size of a pea. Can this explanation be tested to see whether it is correct? You cannot test it by rerunning the birth of the universe. However, you can test it indirectly because you can test other claims that should be true if the explanation is true. One prediction that follows from the Big Bang hypothesis is that microwave radiation of a certain frequency will be bombarding Earth from all directions. This test has been run successfully, which is one important reason why today's astronomers generally accept the Big Bang as the explanation for their observations that all the galaxies on average are speeding away from us.

The lesson here is that a scientific hypothesis that cannot be tested directly can usually be tested indirectly by trying to deduce predictions from the hypothesis. Superficially, we say a hypothesis is confirmed or proved if several diverse predictions are tested and all are found to agree with the data. Similarly, a hypothesis gets refuted if any of the actual test results do not agree with the prediction. However, this summary is superficial — let's see why.

Retaining Hypotheses Despite Negative Test Results

If a scientist puts a hypothesis to the test, and if the test produces results inconsistent with the hypothesis, there is always some way or other for the researcher to hold onto the hypothesis and change something else. For example, if the meter shows "7" when your hypothesis would have predicted "5," you might rescue your hypothesis by saying that your meter wasn't working properly. However, unless you have some good evidence of meter trouble, this move to rescue your hypothesis in the face of disconfirming evidence commits the fallacy of **ad hoc rescue**. If you are going to hold onto your hypothesis no matter what, you are in the business of propaganda and dogma, not science. Psychologically, it is understandable that you would try to rescue your cherished belief from trouble. When you are faced with conflicting data, you are likely to mention how the conflict will disappear if some new assumption is taken into account. However, if you have no good reason to accept this saving assumption other than that it works to save your cherished belief, your rescue is an ad hoc rescue.

■ ·········· Concept Check 7 ·········· ■

State why this is not a successful argument:

> People such as Galileo will tell you that the Earth turns, but it really doesn't. If the Earth did turn, then when you drop a ball off the top of a tall building the Earth would turn away from the ball, and the ball would land some distance away from the building. Instead, when you try it out, the ball lands right at the base of the building. Therefore, the Earth doesn't really turn after all.

■ ·········· Concept Check 8 ·········· ■

Back in the times of ancient Greece and Rome, augurs would advise the rulers about the future. These respected priest-prophets carried a staff or wand and specialized in foretelling events by using omens, or unusual events. Because the universe is made for people, anything unusual must be a sign, a special message that people are supposed to interpret, or so the augurs believed. They would try to predict the future for their rulers by interpreting the unusual flight of a bird, the shape and markings of the guts of sacrificed animals, and the appearance of comets and eclipses. Often, when their divining with ravens, livers, and comets was obviously not working and the ruler was complaining, the augurs would blame their failure on the negative influence from nearby Christians. Their solution was to ask the ruler to order the deaths of all the Christians. Examining this story from the perspective of scientific reasoning, we see that the principal mistake of the augurs was

a. that they should have placed more reliance on the scientific use of astrology.

b. their insensitivity to pseudoprecision.

c. to use the method of ad hoc rescue.

d. to overemphasize repeatable phenomena.

In 1790 the French scientist Lavoisier devised a careful experiment in which he weighed mercury before and after it was heated in the presence of air. The remaining mercury, plus the red residue that was formed, weighed more than the original. Lavoisier had shown that heating a chemical in air can result in an increase in weight of the chemical. Today, this process is called *oxidation*. But back in Lavoisier's day, the accepted theory on these matters was that a posited substance, "phlogiston," was driven off during any heating of a chemical. If something is driven off, then you would expect the resulting substance to weigh less. Yet Lavoisier's experiments clearly showed a case in which the resulting substance weighed more. To get around this inconsistency, the chemists who supported the established phlogiston theory suggested their theory be revised by assigning phlogiston negative weight. Then, if you subtracted a negative weight during heating, you would expect an increase in the weight of the resultant substance, as Lavoisier observed.

The negative-weight hypothesis was a creative suggestion that might have rescued the phlogiston theory. It wasn't as strange then as it may seem today because the notion of mass was not well understood. Although Isaac Newton had believed that all mass is positive, the negative-weight suggestion faced a more important obstacle. There was no way to verify it independently of the phlogiston theory. So, the suggestion appeared to commit the fallacy of ad hoc rescue.

An ad hoc hypothesis can be rescued from the charge of committing the fallacy of ad hoc rescue if it can meet two conditions: (1) The hypothesis must be shown to be fruitful in successfully explaining phenomena that previously did not have an adequate explanation. (2) The hypothesis's inconsistency with previously accepted beliefs must be resolved without reducing the explanatory power of science. Because the advocates of the negative-weight hypothesis were unable to do either, it is appropriate to charge them with committing the fallacy. As a result of Lavoisier's success, and the failure of the negative-weight hypothesis, today's chemists do not believe that phlogiston exists.

Three Conditions for a Well-Designed Test

Designing a good test of a scientific claim is difficult, as we have seen, and more will be said about the difficulties later in this chapter. However, as a good rule of thumb, three definite conditions should hold in any well-designed test. First, if you use an experiment or observation to test some claim, you should be able to deduce the predicted test result from the combination of the claim plus a description of the relevant aspects of the test's initial conditions. That is, if the claim is really true, the predicted test result should be deducible. Second, the predicted test result should *not* be expected no matter what; instead, the predicted result should be unlikely if the claim is false. For example, a test that predicts water will flow downhill is a useless test because water is expected to do so no matter what. Third, it should be practical to check on whether the test did or did not come out as predicted, and this checking should not need to presume the truth of the claim being tested. It does no good to predict something that nobody can check.[6]

To summarize, ideally a good test requires a prediction that is (1) deducible, (2) improbable, and (3) verifiable. In other words, a good test of a claim will be able to produce independently verifiable data that should occur if the claim is true but shouldn't occur if the claim is false.

Concept Check 9

Which of the three conditions for a good scientific test are satisfied or violated, as far as you can tell, in the following report?

> A researcher claims that an invisible evil hand, a dark force, is at work disrupting transportation in the Bermuda Triangle. This triangle is the area of the Atlantic Ocean defined by Bermuda, Florida, and Cuba. The researcher predicted that if the hypothesis about an invisible hand were true, then there should be mysterious disappearances of planes and ships into thin air and definitely an unusual number of transportation accidents in this area. The researcher gathered data about many such cases, and then published his results claiming his testing confirmed the existence of the evil hand.

Deducing Predictions to Be Tested

Condition 1, the deducibility condition, is somewhat more complicated than a first glance might indicate. For example, suppose you suspect that one of your co-workers named Philbrick has infiltrated your organization to spy on your company's chief scientist, Oppenheimer. To test this claim, you set a trap. Philbrick is in your private office late one afternoon when you walk out declaring that you are going home. You leave a file folder labeled "Confidential: Oppenheimer's Latest Research Proposal" on your desk. You predict that Philbrick will sneak a look at the file. Unknown to him, your office is continually monitored on closed-circuit TV, so you will be able to catch him in the act.

Let's review this reasoning. Is condition 1 satisfied? It is, if the following reasoning is deductively valid:

> Philbrick has the opportunity to be alone in your office with the
>   Oppenheimer file folder. (the test's initial conditions)
> Philbrick is a spy. (the claim to be tested)
> _____
> Philbrick will read the Oppenheimer file while in your office. (the prediction)

This reasoning might or might not be valid depending on the missing premise. It would be valid if the premise were the following:

> If Philbrick is a spy, then he will read the Oppenheimer file while in your
>   office if he has the opportunity. (background assumption)

Is that premise acceptable? No. You cannot be that sure of how spies will act. The missing premise is more likely to be the following hedge:

If Philbrick is a spy, then he will *most probably* read the Oppenheimer file while in your office if he has the opportunity. (background assumption)

Although it is more plausible that this revised premise is the one actually used in the argument for the original prediction, now the argument isn't deductively valid. That is, the prediction doesn't follow with certainty, and condition 1 fails. Because the prediction follows inductively, it would be fair to say that condition 1 is "almost" satisfied. Nevertheless, it is not satisfied. Practically, though, you cannot expect any better test than this; there is nothing that a spy *must* do that would decisively reveal the spying. Practically, you can have less than ideal tests about spies or no tests at all.

In response to this difficulty with condition 1, should we alter the definition of the condition to say that the prediction should follow *either* with certainty *or* with probability? No. This revised condition would be a condition for a fairly good test, but not for an ideally good test. The reason why we cannot relax condition 1 can be appreciated by supposing that the closed-circuit TV does reveal Philbrick opening the file folder and reading its contents. Caught in the act, right? Your conclusion: Philbrick is a spy. This would be a conclusion many of us would be likely to draw, but it is not one that the test justifies completely. Concluding with total confidence that he is a spy would be drawing a hasty conclusion because there are alternative explanations of the same data. For example, if Philbrick were especially curious, he might read the file contents yet not be a spy. In other words, no matter whether the prediction comes out to be true or false, you cannot be sure the claim is true or false. In other words, the test is not **decisive** because its result doesn't settle which of the two alternatives is correct.

Yet being decisive is the mark of an ideally good test. We would not want to alter condition 1 so that this indecisive test can be called decisive. Doing so would encourage hasty conclusions. So the definition of condition 1 must stay as it is. However, we can say that if condition 1 is almost satisfied, then when the other two conditions for an ideal test are also satisfied, the test results will *tend* to show whether the claim is correct. In short, if Philbrick snoops, this tends to show he is a spy. More testing is needed if you want to be surer.

This problem about how to satisfy condition 1 in the spy situation is analogous to the problem of finding a good test for a nonuniversal generalization. If you suspect that most cases of malaria can be cured with quinine, then no single malaria case will ensure that you are right or that you are wrong. Finding one case of a person whose malaria wasn't cured by taking quinine doesn't prove your suspicion wrong. You need many cases to adequately test your suspicion.

The problem about how to design a test to detect the spy is also analogous to the problem of designing a test for a theory that is probabilistic rather than deterministic. For example, suppose your theory of inheritance says that, given the genes of a certain type of blue-eyed father and a certain type of brown-eyed mother, their children will have a 25 percent chance of being blue-eyed. Let's try to create a good test of this probabilistic theory by using it to make a specific prediction about one couple's next child. Predicting that the child will be 25 percent blue-eyed is ridiculous. On the other hand, predicting that the child has a 25 percent chance of being blue-eyed is no prediction at all. It doesn't qualify as being a specific prediction about the next child. Specific predictions about a single event can't contain probabilities. What eye color do you predict the child will have? You should predict it will not be blue-eyed. Suppose you make this prediction, and you are mistaken. Has your theory of inheritance been refuted? No. Why not? Because the test was not decisive. The child's being born blue-eyed is consistent with your theory's being true and also with its being false. The problem is that with a probabilistic theory you cannot make specific predictions about just one child. You can predict only that if there are many children then 25 percent of them will have blue eyes and 75 percent won't. A probabilistic theory can be used to make predictions only about groups, not about individuals.

The analogous problem for the spy in your office is that when you tested your claim that Philbrick is a spy you were actually testing a probabilistic theory because you were testing the combination of that specific claim about Philbrick with the general probabilistic claim that spies probably snoop. Your test with the video camera had the same problem with condition 1 as your test with the eye color. Condition 1 was almost satisfied in both tests, but strictly speaking it wasn't satisfied in either.

Our previous discussion should now have clarified why condition 1 is somewhat more complicated than a first glance might indicate. Ideally, we would like decisive tests or, as they are also called, crucial tests. Practically, we usually have to settle for tests that only tend to show whether one claim or another is true. The stronger the tendency, the better the test. If we arrive at a belief on the basis of these less than ideal tests, we are always in the mental state of not being absolutely sure. We are in the state of desiring data from more tests of the claim so that we can be surer of our belief, and we always have to worry that some day new data might appear that will require us to change our minds. Such is the human condition. Science cannot do better than this.

Detecting Pseudoscience

Whereas the word *science* has positive connotations, the word *pseudoscience* has negative connotations. Science gets the grant money; pseudoscience doesn't. Calling some statement, theory, or research program "pseudoscientific" suggests that it is silly or a waste of time. For example, it is pseudoscientific to claim that the position of the planets at the time a person is born determines the person's personality and major life experiences. It is also pseudoscientific to claim that spirits of the dead can be contacted by mediums at seances. Astrology and spiritualism may be useful social lubricants, but they aren't sciences.

Despite a few easily agreed-upon examples such as these two, adequately defining pseudoscience is difficult. One could try to define *science* and then use that to say pseudoscience is not science, or one could try to define *pseudoscience* directly. Let's take the direct approach. A great many of the scientific experts will agree that pseudoscience can be detected in the following ways:

1. Do the "scientists" have a *theory to test*?
2. Do the "scientists" have *reproducible data* that their theory is designed to explain?

You are dealing with pseudoscience if you get a "no" answer to either question. It's also a pseudoscience if you get a "yes" answer to any of these questions:

3. Do the "scientists" seem content to search around for phenomena that are hard to explain by means of current science; that is, do the scientists engage in *mystery mongering*?
4. Are the "scientists" quick to recommend *supernatural explanations* rather than natural explanations?
5. Do the "scientists" use the method of *ad hoc rescue*?

The research program that investigates paranormal phenomena is called **parapsychology**. It is pseudoscientific, although most of its practitioners call themselves scientists. Let's see why the program deserves this label. What are the paranormal phenomena we are talking about here? They include astral travel, auras, **psychokinesis** (moving something without touching it physically), plant consciousness, psychic healing, speaking with the spirits, witchcraft, and **ESP** — that is **telepathy** (mind reading), **clairvoyance** (viewing things at a distance), and **precognition** (knowing the future). Most parapsychologists believe that many of the phenomena do exist, and they also believe the phenomena cannot be explained by current science, only by a science that recognizes supernatural forces or extraordinary mental powers.

Parapsychology is a pseudoscience because of points 1, 2, and 3. First, regarding point 2, can a parapsychologist produce a person who can repeatedly cure cancer cases under test conditions established by skeptics who are competent scientists? None of the parapsychologists' claims to have found cases of cancer cures, mind reading, or foretelling the future by psychic powers have ever stood up to a good test. Parapsychologists cannot convincingly reproduce any of these phenomena on demand; they can only produce isolated instances in which something surprising happened. Parapsychologists definitely haven't produced repeatable phenomena that they can show need to be explained in some revolutionary way.

Rarely do parapsychologists engage in building up their own theories of parapsychology and testing them. Instead, nearly all are engaged in attempts to tear down current science by searching for mysterious phenomena that appear to defy explanation by current science. Perhaps this data gathering is the proper practice for the prescientific stage of some enterprise that hopes to revolutionize science, but the practice does show that the enterprise of parapsychology is not yet a science. So parapsychologists can be convicted on point 3.

Regarding point 1, scientists attack parapsychologists for not having a theory-guided research program. Even if there were repeatable paranormal phenomena, and even if parapsychologists were to quit engaging in mystery mongering, they have no even moderately detailed or precise theory of how the paranormal phenomena occur. They have only simplistic theories such as that a mysterious mind power caused the phenomenon or that the subject tapped a reserve of demonic forces or that the mind is like a radio that can send and receive signals over an undiscovered channel. Parapsychologists have no more-detailed theory that permits testable predictions. Yet, if there is no theory specific enough to make a testable prediction, there is no science.

Paradigms and Possible Causes

Your car's engine is gummed up today. This has never happened before. Could it be because at breakfast this morning you drank grapefruit juice rather than your usual orange juice? No, it couldn't be. Current science says this sort of explanation is silly. OK, forget the grapefruit juice. Maybe the engine is gummed up because today is Friday the 13th. No, that is silly, too. A scientist wouldn't even bother to check these explanations.

Let's explore this intriguing notion of what science considers "silly" versus what it takes seriously. What causes the pain relief after swallowing a pain pill? Could it be the favorite music of the inventor? No, that explanation violates medical science's basic beliefs about what *can* count as a legitimate cause of what. Nor could the pain relief be caused by the point in time when the pill is swallowed. Time alone causes nothing, says modern science. The pain relief could be caused by the chemical composition of the pill, however, or perhaps by a combination of that with the mental state of the person who swallowed the pill. The general restrictions that a science places on what can be a cause and what can't are part of what is called the "paradigm" of the science. Every science has its paradigm.

At any particular time, each science has its normal way of doing things. That is, each science has its own particular problems that it claims to have solved, and, more important, it has its own accepted ways of solving problems that then serve as a model for future scientists who will try to solve new problems. These ways of solving problems, including the methods, standards, and generalizations generally held in common by the community of those practicing the science, is, by definition, the **paradigm** of that science.

For example, the paradigm in medical science is to investigate what is wrong with sick people, not what is right with well people. For a second example, biological science is not sure what causes tigers to like meat rather than potatoes, but biologists are fairly sure the cause involves the chemical makeup of the meat, not the history of zipper manufacturing or the price of rice in China. The paradigm for biological science limits what counts as a legitimate biological explanation. When we take a science course or read a science book, we are slowly being taught the paradigm of that science and, with it, the ability to distinguish silly explanations from plausible ones. Silly explanations do not meet a basic requirement for being a likely explanation: **coherence with the paradigm**. Sensitivity to this consistency requirement was the key to understanding the earlier story about Brother Bartholomew (page 381). Scientists today say that phenomena should not be explained by supposing that Bartholomew or anybody else could see into the future; this kind of "seeing" is inconsistent with the current paradigm. It is easy to test whether people can foresee the future *if* they make specific predictions. Successfully testing a claim that someone can do so would be a truly revolutionary result, upsetting the whole scientific world-view, which explains why many people are so intrigued by tabloid reports of people successfully foretelling the future.

No scientist knows why a spider doesn't get stuck in its own web. Scientists have tried various explanations, but these explanations have always been refuted when tested. There are three possibilities for this situation: (1) an explanation exists that is consistent with today's scientific paradigm, but scientists so far have not been clever enough to find this explanation; (2) there is something wrong with the paradigm, and only a new, radically changed science with a different paradigm will be able to adequately explain spider webs, or (3) a spider's not getting stuck in its web is not the kind of phenomenon that any science could handle; it transcends the possibilities of science and will always be an ultimate mystery. Possibility 1 is the one scientists are betting on today. In fact, it is a methodological principle of all science to suppose that an unexplained phenomenon probably has an explanation within the paradigm rather than either an explanation without it or, worse yet, no explanation at all.

■ ············ Concept Check 10 ············ ■

What explanation of why spiders don't get stuck in their own webs deviates most from the paradigm?

a. The color of the web causes the spider to wrinkle its feet, which in turn causes new, wet, webbing to flow out of the spider, yet only dry webbing can stick to a spider.

b. Spiders are possessed by demons that use demonic power to keep themselves unstuck.

c. A chemical oozing out of the spider's feet won't mix with the web, much the way oil won't mix with water.

d. The hot breath of the spider sends shock waves through the web, temporarily altering its chemical structure and thereby giving the spider the power to walk freely on the web.

Suppose a scientist wants to determine whether adding solid carbon dioxide to ice water will cool the water. The scientist begins with two glasses containing equal amounts of water at the same temperature. The glasses touch each other. Solid carbon dioxide is added to the first glass, but not the second. The scientist expects the first glass to get colder but the second glass not to. This second glass of water is the control because it is just like the other glass except that the causal factor being tested — the solid carbon dioxide — is not present in it. After fifteen minutes, the scientist takes the temperature of the water in both glasses. Both are found to have cooled, and both are at the same temperature. A careless scientist might draw the conclusion that the cooling is not caused by adding the carbon dioxide, because the water in the control glass also got cooler. A more observant scientist might instead suggest that the two glasses should not touch each other. That is, the touching is **contaminating the control**. The two glasses should be kept a few inches apart during the experiment to eliminate contamination. The paradigm of the science dictates that the glasses not touch.

For a second example of the contamination of experimental controls, suppose a biologist injects some rats with a particular virus and injects control rats with a **placebo** — some obviously ineffective substance such as a small amount of salt water. The biologist observes the two groups of rats to determine whether the death rate of those receiving the virus is significantly higher than the death rate of those receiving the placebo. If the test is well run and the data show such a difference, there is a correlation between the virus injection and dying. Oh, by the way, the injected rats are kept in the same cages with the control rats. Oops. This contamination will invalidate the entire experiment, won't it?

Reputable scientists know how to eliminate contamination, and they actively try to do so. They know that temperature differences and disease transmission can be radically affected by physical closeness. This background knowledge that guides experimentation constitutes another part of the paradigm of the sciences of physics and biology. Without a paradigm helping to guide the experimenter, there would be no way of knowing whether the control group was contaminated. There would be no way to eliminate **experimenter effects**, that is, the unintentional influence of the experimenter on the outcome of the experiment. There would be no way of running a good test. That fact is one more reason that so much of a scientist's college education is spent simply learning the science's paradigm.

Review of Major Points

When scientists are trying to gain a deep understanding of how the world works, they seek general patterns rather than specific facts. The way scientists acquire these general principles about nature is usually neither by deducing them from observations nor by inductive generalization. Instead, they think about the observations, then guess at a general principle that might account for them, then check this guess by testing. When a guess is being tested, it is called a hypothesis. Testing can refute a hypothesis. If a hypothesis does not get refuted by testing, scientists retain it as a prime candidate for being a general truth of nature, a law. Hypotheses that survive systematic testing are considered to be proved, although even the proved statements of science are susceptible to future revision, unlike the proved statements of mathematics.

Scientific reasoning is not discontinuous from everyday reasoning, but it does have slightly higher standards of proof. This chapter reviewed several aspects of scientific reasoning from earlier chapters, including general versus specific claims, testing by observation, testing by experiment, accuracy, precision, operational definition, pseudoprecision, the role of scientific journals, independent verification, consistency with well-established results, reproducible evidence, anecdotal evidence, a scientist's cautious attitude and open mind, attention to relevant evidence, the scientific method of justifying claims, disconfirming evidence, and the methods of gaining a representative sample.

Deterministic explanations are preferred to probabilistic ones, and ideal explanations enable prediction of the phenomenon being explained. Explanations are preferred if they are testable and fruitful. A good test requires a prediction that is (1) deducible, (2) improbable, and (3) verifiable.

Five criteria can be used to detect pseudoscience. Science provides the antidote to superstition.

A reasonable scientific explanation is coherent with the paradigm for that science. Only by knowing the science's paradigm can a scientist design a controlled experiment that does not contaminate the controls and that eliminates effects unintentionally caused by the experimenter.

Glossary

ad hoc rescue A fallacy committed by those faced with data that appear to conflict with a claim, who try to rescue the claim by pointing out how the conflict will disappear if some new assumption is taken into account. If there is no good reason to accept this assumption other than that it successfully rescues the claim, the rescue is an ad hoc rescue.

clairvoyance Remote viewing of the world; seeing without being there.

coherence with the paradigm Logical consistency with a requirement of a science's paradigm.

contaminating the control Situation that occurs when a supposedly controlled experiment permits the control group to be affected by the suspected causal factor applied to the experimental group.

control In an experiment, applying the suspected causal factor to one group but not the other. The group that doesn't get it is called the *control group*. The group that does is called the *experimental group*, or *treatment group*. Well-designed experiments create the control group and the experimental group by random assignment.

decisive test A test between two hypotheses that will result in one of the hypotheses being refuted and the other confirmed. Ideally, we would like decisive tests or, as they are also called, crucial tests. Practically, we usually have to settle for tests that only *tend* to show whether one claim or another is false.

ESP Extrasensory perception. A person with ESP can perceive by means other than the usual sense organs. Three main kinds of ESP are telepathy, clairvoyance, and precognition.

experimenter effects Effects on the outcome of an experiment that are caused by the unintentional influence of the experimenter. Contamination of the control would be such an effect.

fallacy of overemphasizing anecdotal evidence Discounting evidence arrived at by systematic search, or by testing, in favor of a few firsthand stories.

fruitfulness The ability of a theory to inspire scientists to imagine many interesting ways in which the theory can practically be tested. A fruitful theory generates a great deal of scientific research.

hypothesis A proposed explanation or claim or theory.

law A well-tested general claim.

paradigm The ways of solving problems in a particular science, including the methods, standards, and generalizations generally held in common by the community of those practicing the science. The paradigm guides the scientific investigator by setting limits on what can be a possible cause of what.

parapsychology The field or research program that tries to scientifically study unusual (paranormal) phenomena such as ESP and psychokinesis.

placebo A substance known not to be effective for causing a phenomenon of interest. In a controlled experiment designed to test whether a drug is causally effective, the experimental group might be given a green liquid containing the drug while the control group is given a placebo, a green liquid that appears to be identical but contains only water.

precognition Sensing the future. Fortune telling is an example.

psychokinesis Giving kinetic energy to a physical object by using "mind power." Bending spoons without touching them would be an example.

rational Pertaining to those who arrive at, accept, and revise their beliefs according to the accepted methods of their culture.

superstition Beliefs based on reasons that are well known to us to be unacceptable because those reasons are based on fear of the unknown, trust in magic, or an obviously false idea of what can cause what.

telepathy Mind reading; direct mind-to-mind communication without using the normal, indirect channels such as hearing what is spoken, reading what is written, or seeing body language.

test An observation or an experiment intended to provide evidence about a claim.

theory A proposed explanation or a comprehensive integrated system of laws that can be used in explaining a wide variety of phenomena.

Answers to Concept Checks

1. Answer (a). The anecdote from the uncle should be given less weight than the warning on the pack. The warning came from statistical tests covering a wide variety of smokers.

2. Answer (a). Presumably, many aborigines believed the world is flat on the basis of the methods acceptable within their own culture. So they were rational, though superstitious. If you today believed the world is flat for those same reasons, you would be both irrational and superstitious.

3. Answer (c). Answer (a) focuses on causes, not reasons. Answer (b) is an irrelevant comment about Jesus. Answer (c) appeals to the idea that mundane alternative explanations should be more seriously considered than supernatural ones; in addition, recognizing the existence of a new alternative explanation that is reasonable should undermine one's confidence in a previously accepted explanation. Answer (c) gives a good reason to someone who is a logical reasoner. Answers (d) and (e) also appeal to causes, not reasons.

4. Answer (a). It wouldn't be too difficult for a magician to disguise a hook or create a puff of smoke in the air. It would be too difficult to hypnotize everybody in the audience. Choice (d) is a false statement. A third explanation of the trick is that the fakir uses mental energy to lift the rope and assistant. Unfortunately, it is impossible to lift things without also using ordinary physical energy.

5. Answer (c). Predicting a repeating rifle in the nineteenth century is not predicting something unexpected, because the rifle was already invented by then. Yet a good test requires predicting an unexpected event. So (c) is the right answer. Notice that there were no predictions of x-rays, lasers, genetic engineering, video games, or the AIDS epidemic. If the document had predicted something new for the twentieth century, it would be a stronger piece of evidence in favor of Bartholomew's prophetic powers. Because it did not, there is a mundane and more plausible alternative explanation that hasn't been ruled out — namely, that the document is a forgery created in the nineteenth century using a sixteenth-century cover page.

6. Answer (b). The violence theory not only is testable but can also be practically tested in many ways. The alternatives cannot be.

7. In any good scientific test, the predicted outcome of the test will follow from the hypothesis being tested. It doesn't here. A faulty prediction was made from the hypothesis that the Earth turns. The Earth does turn; however, the ball and

the building it is dropped from are both moving together at this speed, so the dropped ball should merely go straight down.

8. Answer (c). Their hypothesis was that examining omens would enable them to foretell the future. Their predictions based on this hypothesis were inconsistent with the facts. To rescue their hypothesis, they revised it to say that omens could be used to predict the future *provided* Christians didn't interfere. However, there is no basis for believing that this revision is proper; its only basis is that if it were true, then the augurs could stay in business. So their reasoning commits the fallacy of ad hoc rescue.

9. The major fault is with condition 2 (improbability). Condition 1 (deducibility) is satisfied; the researcher correctly deduced that if there were an evil hand, it would perform evil deeds. Condition 3 (verifiability) is satisfied because it is not too hard to check on whether planes and boats actually have had accidents or disappeared, and this checking doesn't depend on any assumption about whether there is or isn't an evil hand at work. Condition 2, on the other hand, hasn't been established, as far as we can tell from the information given. Condition 2 (improbability) requires that these disappearances be shown to be improbable, yet for all we know there is no higher percentage of disappearances in the Bermuda Triangle than in any other part of the world. (In fact, there have not been an unusual number of disappearances, given that this area is one of the busiest of any ocean.)

10. Answer (b). Demons are not supposed to be used in explanations that fit within the current paradigm of science. All the other possible answers are probably incorrect explanations, but at least they don't radically depart from the current paradigm.

Review and Writing Exercises

1. Suppose that for the last month and a half you've been slightly nauseous. You've had a mild headache almost every day. This illness is something new in your life. Aspirin helps with the headache but not with your stomach. Switching to other pain killers doesn't seem to make a difference. The world and your friends have lately been especially boring, and you don't want to do much of anything except watch TV. Usually you like to munch while watching the tube, but for the last few weeks you've lost your appetite. Your grades are suffering. Create several possible explanations for your illness. How would you go about testing your explanations to see whether any one is correct? [In this scenario, don't simply be passive and call the doctor; you are your own doctor.]

2. Professor William Whewell thought that the aim of science is to discover the works of God. Dr. G. Bell believed that the aim is to acquire specific facts. A more

generally acceptable answer than either of these two is that the aim of science is to

   a.   build technologically useful products.

   b.   improve our power to predict and explain phenomena.

   c.   delineate all the known facts of the world.

   d.   establish the scientific method.

■ 3. Which groups below should you examine before which others if you are trying to confirm or refute the claim that all emeralds are green? Rank them, beginning with the most important. Do not suppose that emeralds are defined to be green.

   emeralds

   green things

   nongreen things

   nonemeralds

4. If there has been a 10 percent drop in the lung cancer rate for black females over the last two years, but not for other groups such as white females, why should you not yet conclude that cigarettes are now safer for you to smoke if you are a black female? Be specific; don't simply say there could be reasons.

5. Concept Check 5 is about Brother Bartholomew's being a successful prophet. Explain why the incorrect answers to the question are incorrect. Say which answers are better than which others.

● 6. Evaluate the quality of the following reasoning and defend your evaluation. Can you suggest any improvements? (200 words)

   Inge has been a regular sun worshipper ever since she was a little girl in Denmark—summer in the pool or on a towel under the sun, spring and fall on the patio with solar reflectors focused on her exposed skin. She was a bronzed beauty, but now, after twenty-five years, two malignant skin cancers have started growing. She says it's the luck of the draw, but I say it's another case of the harmful effects of sunlight. The sun is just like an infrared lamp; if you put something under it long enough, it will fry.

■ 7. Discuss (under 50 words) the following scientific test in regard to the three conditions for a good scientific test, the deduction condition, the improbability condition, and the verifiability condition. You need not define or explain the three conditions.

   Our hypothesis is that all people have telepathic abilities that occasionally show up during their lives, even though most people don't realize it. If the hypothesis is correct, then occasionally people will be stunned by instances in which they and other persons have the same thought at the same time even though they aren't having a conversation and aren't in any other ordinary contact with each other. Our testing has documented many such instances. Some of them are truly remarkable. We have testimony from a wide variety of citizens who have no reason to lie and who in fact have passed lie detector tests. Therefore, our hypothesis is correct.

- 8. Imagine that you are an American-educated intelligence agent of the New Hebrides government who is assigned to the John Frum cult case. You have gained the confidence of the average cult member to the extent that if you give him reasons, he will think seriously about what you say. What would be the best reasons to help convince him to quit participating in the cult because its beliefs are false? Can you demonstrate that you have the *best explanation* of the appearance of the ships and of the visions? If he asked you to *confirm* your explanation of the situation, what could you do or say? Give reasons that *ought* to convince; don't give reasons that merely *would* convince, such as by your impersonating John Frum. Bear in mind that he is apt to say, "Maybe you're right, but why should I believe what *you* say when I know our leader would not agree?"

- 9. Suppose your copy of yesterday's newspaper says, "The Detroit Pistons will win their basketball game tomorrow night," and you know that this prediction came true. Prophecy by the sports writer? No, your hypothesis is that the writer is not psychic, and you don't doubt it, nor do you feel obliged to design some experiment to test it. If so, why does good scientific methodology require you to treat the Brother Bartholomew situation any differently?

- 10. Write an essay in which you critically analyze the following claims.

  > I am reincarnated. I once was a male slave who worked as a personal assistant to King Tut of ancient Egypt. I can prove it. I happen to know something that only a reincarnated person could know. I know that one of the members of Tut's harem was a dancer who wore special pearl bracelets on each wrist. I documented this fact six months ago by publishing drawings of the bracelets, yet it was only last week that archaeologists dug up the woman's tomb and found the pair of bracelets. Nowhere in Egyptian literature are the bracelets ever mentioned.

  In answering, you may assume that the last two statements have already been proved.

  11. What is the best example of the fallacy of ad hoc rescue?

  a. Newton deduced Galileo's law of falling terrestrial bodies from his own laws of motion, thereby rescuing Galileo's law from refutation.

  b. Newton adopted the particle theory of light even though Huygens's optical experiments showed definitively that light is a wave and not a group of particles.

  c. Scientists struggling to explain the odd shape of Uranus's orbit using Newton's law of gravitation suggested that God wanted the orbit to be perturbed in just the ways astronomers observed it to be.

  d. The dinosaur extinction hypothesis can be rescued by finding data that would be implied by the hypothesis.

12. Uranium becomes lead in 4.5 billion years, say the scientists. OK, but how do the scientists know this if they have never sat and watched a piece of uranium for that long?

13. What is wrong with the following reasoning?

   According to the dictionary definition of *science*, a science is a body of knowledge amassed in a systematic way. Therefore, because a telephone book and a repair manual both are systematized bodies of knowledge, it follows that they, too, are sciences. Thus, the following is a correct listing of some of the sciences: physics, botany, repair manual, chemistry, geology, telephone book, astronomy, anthropology, and so on.

14. What is wrong with this as a scientific explanation?

   Jim dropped the ball because of his carelessness.

15. The passage below was accepted by the Catholic church as a refutation of the astrological hypothesis that the stars determine every person's destiny. It is from the *Confessions* of St. Augustine, a Catholic saint who wrote in about A.D. 400. (a) Briefly explain why the refutation is a successful refutation, and then (b) alter the astrological hypothesis so that St. Augustine's remarks no longer refute the essential claims of astrology.

   Firminus had heard from his father that when his mother had been pregnant with him a slave belonging to a friend of his father's was also about to bear. . . . It happened that since the two women had their babies at the same instant, the men were forced to cast exactly the same horoscope for each newborn child down to the last detail, one for his [father's] son, the other for the little slave. . . . Yet Firminus, born to wealth in his parents' house had one of the more illustrious careers in life . . . whereas the slave had no alleviation of his life's burden.

■ 16. Gerald Aardsma has a doctorate in physics from the University of Toronto. What methodological error would the establishment scientists most likely say Aardsma is committing in the following argument? That is, what canon of good science is he violating?

   Radiocarbon dating is a principal technique used to date old objects that contain carbon. All living organisms contain carbon, and a known proportion of it is rendered radioactive by the bombardment of cosmic rays. All living organisms that breathe air have the same percentage of radioactive to nonradioactive carbon. In radiocarbon dating, the age of fossils is estimated by determining their percentage of radioactive carbon. The fossils with the smallest percentage are the oldest. This dating method works because the radioactive carbon continues to decay at a predictable rate long after the organisms die and stop taking in new radioactive carbon from the air. If an organism dies with one gram of carbon-14 in its body, then in 5,700 years there will be half a gram remaining; in 11,400 years, a quarter gram; and so forth.

Aardsma argues that scientists should not trust the radiocarbon dating instrument unless it has been calibrated against something whose age can be known without assuming the truth of the theory of either biological or geological evolution. The oldest items fitting this description are mummy wrappings from Egypt; they have been dated (independently of assuming the theory of evolution) as being made in 3000 B.C. However, Aardsma says the instrument cannot be reliable for earlier dates because of the great flood mentioned in the Bible in connection with Noah's ark, which occurred about the same time plus or minus 500 years. Before the flood, all the water that would inundate the Earth during the flood was held in a vapor canopy above the atmosphere. This vapor canopy, he says, "would have shielded the lower atmosphere from the cosmic radiation [that produces radioactive carbon] by a factor of three and thus reduced the amount of radioactive carbon found in creatures that lived before the flood."

Given that he is correct about this shielding, fossils with little radioactive carbon left may appear to be old to the physicist using radiocarbon dating but actually may not be old at all. They may simply come from this time period when the Earth was shielded from cosmic radiation. So, radiocarbon dating is unreliable.

Aardsma says it would be hard to find scientific evidence of the long-lost canopy although "it's possible that the idea of a vapor canopy above the atmosphere will be falsified" by future science that he would accept. However, if the canopy theory had to be rejected, he would not also reject the flood story, because doing so would be to say the Bible is wrong. What should be rejected instead, he says, is his own interpretation of the flood story or some other part of the Bible. "I must be misunderstanding what's written in Genesis. I've not made the plain sense interpretation of Scripture. So I'll forsake that path [of appealing to a vapor canopy to show why evolution is wrong.]"[7]

17. A science's paradigm is

    a. that part of the science's methodology that has not changed throughout the history of science.

    b. the normal way to solve problems in the science.

    c. a nonstandard way of constructing explanations within the science.

    d. the accepted way of revolutionizing the science.

■ 18. Occasionally in disputes about creationism and evolution, someone will say that the theory of evolution is both a theory and a fact, and the opponent will say that evolution is a theory and so should not also be called a fact. This could be an example of a semantic disagreement. Explain.

19. The International Testing Service, which tests third- and sixth-grade students throughout the world, recently reported that students at the Shalom Day School, a private school, have been doing significantly better each year for the last five years. Knowing that the tests do give an accurate report of the students' basic skills in reading, writing, and arithmetic, Dr. Julius Moravcsik of the Nashville

School System commented that the report evidently shows that teachers at Shalom Day School are doing a better job each year. Justify why this comment could be an example of committing the post hoc fallacy. Do so by giving a specific alternative explanation of the improved scores, not by simply stating the definition of the fallacy.

20. Susan Manring says that her psychic friend has extraordinary mental power. When asked why she believes this about him, Susan said, "Because once he offered to tell me what I was thinking. He said I had been thinking about having sex with my boyfriend but had decided not to, and he was right." Explain why Susan is jumping to conclusions about her psychic friend. More specifically, what condition for a good test most obviously fails to hold and thus makes Susan's test not a good test of the psychic's power?

a. Deducibility. b. Improbability. c. Verifiability.

21. I'm going to test my precognitive powers. I predict that my mother will be calling me the next time my phone rings. Oh, there it goes now. "Hello? Mom! Hey, I knew you were going to call!"

    Discuss whether all three conditions for a good scientific test apply to this test. That is, is the predicted outcome of the test (a) deducible, (b) improbable, and (c) verifiable?

22. Suppose competent archaeologists have extensively looked for, but no one has ever discovered, a trace of an ancient city on a particular island. Suppose some person points out their failure to find the ancient city, mentions the fact that other archaeologists don't dispute their results, and from this concludes that there was no ancient city there. Is the person's conclusion probably correct? Why?

• 23. Write an essay about astrology. Describe astrology and explain how its practitioners believe it works and what evidence they might offer in defense of its success. Use footnotes to indicate the source of your information. By applying some of the five criteria mentioned on page 392, create an argument for why astrology is a pseudoscience.

• 24. Write an essay that responds to the following remark. "Evolutionary theory is both a science and a religion and cannot be conclusively proved. Creation science is no different."

25. Why can't scientists give poorly supported hypotheses the benefit of the doubt, and simply accept them? Why the obsessional preoccupation with matters of validation?

26. Francis Bacon said that the way to do science is to clear your mind of all the garbage you've previously been taught, then collect data with an open mind, and after the data is collected the correct interpretation of the data will come to you. Today's philosophers of science say science doesn't work that way. What do they say?

• 27. Create a four-page essay in which you explain to a high school audience how science works. Use this textbook as your primary source of information, but express everything in your own words; don't quote from the text.

APPENDIX

A List of Fallacies with Examples

I f the term *fallacy* included all sources of error in reasoning rather than kinds of error, the following list could be a lot longer. For example, excessive loyalty to one's group is a source of error in reasoning, and some authors of critical thinking textbooks have identified this as a fallacy. Ill health is another source of error, but to my knowledge no author has advocated this one. Being a bigot, being hungry, and having a poor sense of proportion are also sources of error in reasoning, but they do not qualify as fallacies. Nevertheless, there is no sharp line between a source and a kind of error, so there is a certain arbitrariness to what appears in lists such as this.

Ad Hoc Rescue Psychologically, it is understandable that you would try to rescue a cherished belief from trouble. When faced with conflicting data, you are likely to mention how the conflict will disappear if some new assumption is taken into account. However, if there is no good reason to accept this saving assumption other than that it works to save your cherished belief, your rescue is an ad hoc rescue. Example:

> **Yolanda:** If you take four of these tablets of vitamin C every day, you'll never get a cold.
>
> **Juanita:** I tried that last year for several months, and still got a cold.
>
> **Yolanda:** Did you take the tablets every day?
>
> **Juanita:** Yes.
>
> **Yolanda:** Well, I'll bet you bought some bad tablets.

The burden of proof is definitely on Yolanda's shoulders to prove that Juanita's vitamin C tablets were probably "bad" — that is, not really vitamin C. If Yolanda can't do so, her attempt to rescue her hypothesis (that vitamin C prevents colds) is simply a dogmatic refusal to face up to the possibility of being wrong.

Ad Hominem You commit this fallacy if you make an irrelevant attack on the arguer and suggest that this attack undermines the argument itself. Example:

> What she says about Johannes Kepler's astronomy of the 1600s must be just so much garbage. Do you realize she's only sixteen years old?

This attack may undermine the arguer's credibility as a scientific authority, but it does not undermine her reasoning. That reasoning should stand or fall on the scientific evidence, not on the arguer's age or anything else about her personally.

Affirming the Consequent If you have enough evidence to affirm the consequent of a conditional and then suppose that as a result you have sufficient reason for affirming the antecedent, you commit the fallacy of affirming the consequent. Example:

> If she's Brazilian, then she speaks Portuguese. She does speak Portuguese.
> So, she is Brazilian.

The two premises of this argument do make it likely that the person is Brazilian. However, if the arguer believes that the premises establish with certainty that she is Brazilian, the arguer is committing the fallacy.

Anecdotal Evidence If you discount evidence arrived at by systematic search or by testing in favor of a few firsthand stories, you are committing the fallacy of overemphasizing anecdotal evidence. Example:

> Yeah, I've read the health warnings on those cigarette packs, but my brother smokes, and he says he's never been sick a day in his life, so I'm going to start smoking regularly.

Appeal to Authority You appeal to authority if you back up your reasoning by saying that it is supported by what some authority says on the subject. Most reasoning of this kind is not fallacious. However, it *is* fallacious whenever the authority appealed to is not really an authority in this subject, when the authority cannot be trusted to tell the truth, when authorities disagree on this subject (except for the occasional lone wolf), or when the reasoner misquotes the authority. Example:

> You can believe the moon is covered with dust because the president of our country said so, and he should know.

This is a fallacious appeal to authority because, although the president is an authority on many matters, he is no authority on the composition of the moon. It would be better to appeal to some astronomer or geologist, not the president.

Appeal to Emotions You commit the fallacy of appeal to emotions when you use reasons designed to arouse your listener's feelings of anger, grief, sexuality, pride, fear, and so on, thereby encouraging the listener not to reason logically. Example (the speaker knows he is talking to a person whose house is worth much more than $100,000):

You had a great job and didn't deserve to lose it. I wish I could help somehow. I do have one idea. Now you need financial security even more. Your family needs cash. I can help you. Why don't you sell me your house now for $100,000? We can skip the realtors and all the headaches they create.

Appeal to Ignorance The fallacy of appeal to ignorance comes in two forms. (1) Your not knowing whether a certain statement is true is taken by you to be a proof that it's false. Example:

Nobody has ever proved to me there's a God, so there is no God.

(2) Your not knowing whether a statement is false is taken by you to be a proof that it's true. Example:

Nobody's ever shown me it's false that psychic surgery cures cancer, so I believe Dorothy when she says psychic surgery cured her cancer.

The fallacy occurs in cases where absence of evidence for something is clearly an insufficient reason to declare this to be evidence of the thing's absence.

Avoiding the Issue A reasoner who is supposed to address an issue but instead goes off on a tangent has committed the fallacy of avoiding the issue. However, the fallacy *isn't* committed by a reasoner who says that some other issue must first be settled provided the reasoner is correct about this. Example:

A city official is charged with corruption for awarding contracts to his wife's consulting firm. In speaking on this issue, the government official talks only about his wife's conservative wardrobe, the family's lovable dog, and his own accomplishments in supporting Little League baseball.

Avoiding the Question The fallacy of avoiding the question is a type of fallacy of avoiding the issue that occurs when the issue is how to answer some question. The fallacy is committed when someone's answer doesn't really respond to the question asked. Example:

Would the Oakland A's be in first place if they were to win tomorrow's baseball game? Answer: What makes you think they'll ever win tomorrow's game?

Biased Statistics This fallacy is committed whenever we use biased statistics as if they are not biased. Example:

We talked to a random sample of people in our corporation, and they say they are voting Republican. We predict a Republican landslide in the national election.

A random sample within one corporation is unlikely to be a representative sample of the nation's voters.

Black-White The black-white fallacy is a false dilemma fallacy that limits you to only two choices. Example:

> Well, it's time for a decision. Will you contribute $10 to our environmental fund, or are you on the side of environmental destruction?

A proper challenge to this fallacy would be to say, "I want to prevent the destruction of our environment, but I don't want to do it by giving $10 to your fund."

Circular Reasoning (Begging the Question) Circular reasoning occurs when the reasoner begins with what he or she is trying to end up with. It is a fallacy because the point of good reasoning is to start out at one place and end up somewhere new. The point is to make progress, but in circular reasoning there is no progress. Example:

> "Women have rights," said the Bullfight Association president. "But women shouldn't fight bulls because a bullfighter is and should be a man."[1]

The president is saying that women shouldn't fight bulls because women shouldn't fight bulls. Circular arguing is also called "begging the question" because it tries to achieve its conclusion for free (and thus by begging) when instead it ought to achieve it by real work, namely by offering a good reason.

Composition The composition fallacy occurs when someone mistakenly assumes that the properties held by members of a group are also held by the group itself. Example:

> It really doesn't cost that much for the government to pay social security benefits to a retiree. It's just a few thousand dollars a year. So social security payments to retirees can't be a big factor in the national budget.

The group is the retirees. The property is "not costing the government much to pay social security benefits to."

Denying the Antecedent You are committing a fallacy if you deny the antecedent of a conditional and then suppose that doing so is a sufficient reason for denying the consequent. Example:

> If she were Brazilian, then she would know that Brazil's official language is Portuguese. She isn't Brazilian. So it follows that she doesn't know this about Brazil's language.

Division Just because a group as a whole has a characteristic, it doesn't follow that individuals in the group have that characteristic. If you suppose that it does follow, you commit the fallacy of division. Example:

> Joshua's soccer team is one of the best because it had an undefeated season and shared the division title, so Joshua must be one of the best players in the division.

Double Standard There are many situations in which you should judge two things or people by the same standard. If you use different standards for the two, you commit the fallacy of using a double standard. Example:

> I know we will hire men if they get over a 70 percentile on the SAT test, but women need an 80 to do well in these jobs.

Equivocation Equivocation is the illegitimate switching of the meaning of a term during the reasoning. Example:

> Those noisy people object to racism because they believe it is discrimination. Yet even *they* agree that it's OK to choose carefully which tomatoes to buy in the supermarket. They discriminate between the overripe, the underripe, and the just right. They discriminate between the TV shows they don't want to watch and those they do. So, what's all this fuss about racism?

The word *discrimination* changes its meaning without warning in the passage.

False Dilemma A reasoner who unfairly presents too few choices and then implies that a choice must be made only among the offered choices commits the false dilemma fallacy. Example (question in a poll):

> On average each week, your present employer (or your previous employer if you are not now employed) is drunk on the job
>
> a. occasionally
> b. usually
> c. always

You can "go between the horns" of this fallacy (the horns being the three choices) by saying, "You didn't give me the choice of 'never.'"

Faulty Comparison If you try to make a point about something by comparison, and if you do so by comparing it with the wrong thing, you commit the fallacy of faulty comparison. Example:

> We gave half the members of the hiking club Durell hiking boots and the other half good-quality tennis shoes. After three months of hiking, you can see for yourself that Durell lasted longer. You, too, should use Durell when you need hiking boots.

Shouldn't Durell hiking boots be compared with other hiking boots, not with tennis shoes?

Genetic Fallacy A critic commits the genetic fallacy if he or she attempts to discredit a claim because of its origin (genesis) when such a criticism is irrelevant to the claim. Example:

> Your reasons why we should buy that tape must be mistaken, because you said you got the idea for buying the tape from last night's fortune cookie.

Fortune cookies are not reliable experts on tape purchases, but the reasons the person is willing to give are likely to be quite relevant and should be listened to. The speaker is committing the genetic fallacy by paying too much attention to the genesis of the idea rather than to the reasons offered for it.

Guilt by Association   Guilt by association is a version of the ad hominem fallacy in which a person is said to be guilty of error because of the groups he or she associates with. Example:

> Kepler said that planets move in ellipses around the sun because of magnetic attraction between them and the sun. They do move in ellipses, but he gave a ridiculous reason why, as you can tell by remembering that Kepler was allied with the alchemists. As we all know, alchemy has been wholly discredited by the advance of modern science.

Alchemy may not be good science today, but the quality of Kepler's idea about the cause of elliptical orbits should be assessed on its own merits, not on whether Kepler associated with alchemists.

Inconsistency   We reason inconsistently when we make claims or hold beliefs that logically conflict with each other. Example:

> I'm not racist. Some of my best friends are white. But I just don't think that white women love their babies as much as our women do.

The last sentence implies the speaker *is* a racist.

Jumping to Conclusions (Hasty Conclusion)   When we draw a hasty conclusion without taking the trouble to acquire all the relevant evidence, we commit the fallacy of jumping to conclusions. Example:

> Hey, this car is really cheap. I'll buy it.

Before concluding that you should buy it, you ought to have a mechanic check its condition.

Non Sequitur   When a conclusion is supported only by weak reasons or by irrelevant reasons, the argument is fallacious and is said to be a non sequitur. Any fallacious argument is one whose conclusion doesn't follow from its supporting reasons, so any fallacious argument is appropriately called a non sequitur. However, we usually apply the term only when we cannot think of how to label the argument with a more specific fallacy name and when it is fairly easy to show that the reasons are weak. Example:

> Nuclear disarmament is a risk, but everything in life involves a risk. Every time you drive in a car you are taking a risk. If you're willing to drive in a car, you should be willing to have disarmament.

Sometimes the term *non sequitur* is defined more broadly to include a nonargument that is mistakenly put forward as an argument.

Oversimplifying   You oversimplify when you cover up relevant complexities or make a complicated problem appear to be too much simpler than it really is. Example:

> President Flores wants our country to trade with Fidel Castro's Communist Cuba. I say there should be a trade embargo against Cuba. The issue in this election is Cuban trade. If you are against it, then vote for me.

Whom to vote for should be decided by considering quite a number of issues in addition to Cuban trade.

Post Hoc (Confusing Succession with Causation)   If, in noticing that an event of kind B follows an event of kind A, we leap to the conclusion that A caused B, we commit the post hoc fallacy. It's a form of hasty generalization. The Latin expression of the fallacy is *post hoc, ergo propter hoc*. Example:

> I got a flu shot last week and now I've got the flu, so the flu shot must have caused the flu.

Although flu shots could possibly cause the flu, you'd need to rule out many other possibilities, such as the flu shot's being ineffective or your having caught the flu bug prior to the shot, before you may use the strong word *must*.

> Here I am in Dwayne's Restaurant again. I've only eaten here twice for dinner, and I now remember when. I've been fired twice in my life, and both times it was on the day after I had dinner here. Let's go to another restaurant, or this place will screw up my life tomorrow.

Quibbling   We quibble when we complain about a minor point and falsely believe that this complaint somehow undermines the main point. To avoid this fallacy the logical reasoner will not make a mountain out of a mole hill or take people too literally. Example:

> I've found typographical errors in your poem, so the poem is neither inspired nor perceptive.

Rationalizing   We rationalize when we inauthentically offer reasons to support our claim. We are rationalizing when we give someone a reason to justify our action even though we know this reason is not really our own reason for doing it. Example:

> "I bought the matzo bread from Kroger's Supermarket because it is the cheapest brand," says Alex, who knows that he bought the bread from Kroger's because his girlfriend works there.

Red Herring   A red herring is a smelly fish that would distract even a bloodhound. In reasoning a red herring is a digression that leads the reasoner off relevant considerations regarding the topic and onto some irrelevant consideration. Example:

> Will the new tax in Senate Bill 47 unfairly hurt business? One of the provisions of the bill is that the tax is higher for large employers (fifty or

more employees) as opposed to small employers (six to forty-nine employees). To decide on the fairness of the bill, we must first determine whether employees who work for large employers have better working conditions than employees who work for small employers.

The issue of working conditions is the red herring.

Scare Tactic If you suppose that terrorizing your opponent is giving him a reason for believing that you are correct, you're using a scare tactic and reasoning fallaciously. Example:

> **David:** My father owns the department store that gives your newspaper 15 percent of all its advertising revenue, so I'm sure you won't find anything newsworthy in this report of my arrest for spray painting the college.
>
> **Newspaper editor:** Yes, David, I see your point. The story really isn't worth publishing.

David has given the editor a good reason not to publish, but he has not given a relevant reason why the story is not newsworthy. See also the related fallacy of appeal to emotions.

Slippery Slope Suppose someone claims that a first step (in a chain of causes and effects, or a chain of reasoning) will probably lead to a second step that in turn will probably lead to another step and so on until a final step ends in big trouble. If the likelihood of the trouble occurring is exaggerated, the slippery slope fallacy is committed. Example:

> **Mom:** Those look like bags under your eyes. Are you getting enough sleep?
>
> **Jeff:** I had a test and stayed up late studying.
>
> **Mom:** You didn't take any pills did you?
>
> **Jeff:** Just caffeine, like I always do.
>
> **Mom:** Jeff! You know what happens when people take drugs! Pretty soon the caffeine won't be strong enough. Then you will take something stronger. Then, something even stronger. Eventually, you will be doing cocaine. Then you'll be a crack addict!

The form of a slippery slope fallacy looks like this:

> *A* leads to *B*.
> *B* leads to *C*.
> *C* leads to *D*.
> *D* leads to . . .
> . . . which leads to HELL.
> <u>We don't want to go to HELL.</u>
> Don't take that first step *A*.

A slippery slope argument usually employs a scare tactic. It often implies that if you do this first thing, something else will happen; if that happens, then again something further will happen; and so forth until finally some scary thing will happen. You don't want the scary thing to happen, so don't do the first thing. The reasoning is fallacious if it exaggerates the consequences of taking that first step. If A leads to B with a probability of 80 percent, and B leads to C with a probability of 80 percent, and C leads to D with a probability of 80 percent, is it likely that A will eventually lead to D? No, not at all; there is about a 50-50 chance. The proper examination of a slippery slope argument depends on sensitivity to such probabilistic calculations.

Straw Man You commit the straw man fallacy whenever you falsely attribute an easily refuted position to your opponent that the opponent wouldn't have proposed himself and then proceed to attack the easily refuted position. Example (a debate before the city council):

> **Opponent:** Because of the killing and suffering of Indians that followed Columbus's discovery of America, the City of Berkeley should declare that Columbus Day will no longer be observed in our city.
>
> **Speaker:** This is ridiculous, fellow members of the city council. It's not true that everybody who ever came to America from another country somehow oppressed the Indians. I say we should continue to observe Columbus Day, and vote down this resolution that will make the City of Berkeley the laughing stock of the nation.

The speaker has twisted what his opponent said; the opponent never said, nor even indirectly suggested, that everybody who ever came to America from another country somehow oppressed the Indians.

Superstitious Thinking Beliefs deserve to be called *superstition* if they are based on reasons that are well known to be unacceptable. A superstitious belief usually arises from fear of the unknown, from trust in magic, or from an obviously false idea of what can cause what. Example:

> I never walk under ladders; it's bad luck.

It may be a good idea not to walk under ladders, but a proper reason to believe this is that workers on ladders occasionally drop things, or that ladders might have wet paint that could damage your clothes. An improper reason for not walking under ladders is that it's bad luck to do so.

Suppressed Evidence The fallacy of suppressed evidence involves intentionally failing to use information suspected of being relevant and significant. This fallacy usually occurs when the information counts against one's own conclusion. Example:

> Buying the Cray Mac II computer for our company was the right thing to do. It meets our company's needs; it runs the programs we want it to run; it will be delivered quickly; and it cost much less than what we had budgeted.

This appears to be a good argument, but you'd change your assessment of the argument if you learned the speaker has intentionally not mentioned that the company's Cray Mac II was purchased from his brother-in-law at a 30 percent higher price than it could have been purchased elsewhere. This fallacy usually occurs when the information counts against a favorite explanation of the evidence suppressed; the fallacy is then called the fallacy of suppressing the counterevidence.

Traditional Wisdom (Past Practice)   If you say or imply that a practice must be OK today simply because it has been the practice in the past, you commit the fallacy of traditional wisdom. Procedures that are being practiced and that have a tradition of being practiced may be able to be given a good justification, but merely saying that they have been practiced in the past is not good enough. Example:

> Of course we should buy IBM's computer whenever we need new computers. We have been buying IBM as far back as anyone can remember.

Tu Quoque (You Too)   The fallacy of tu quoque is committed if we conclude that a speaker's argument not to do something is no good because he himself does it. Example:

> You say I shouldn't become an alcoholic because it will hurt me and my family, yet you're an alcoholic, so your argument can't be worth listening to.

Discovering that a speaker is a hypocrite is a reason to be suspicious of the speaker's testimony, but it is not a sufficient reason to discount it.

Two Wrongs Make a Right   When you defend your wrong action as being right because someone previous has acted wrongly, you commit the fallacy called "two wrongs make a right." Example:

> I've seen people sneak newspapers from in front of other apartments in the complex, so I can do it, too, and you shouldn't complain.

Wishful Thinking (Positive Thinking)   A reasoner who suggests that a claim is true merely because he or she strongly hopes it is, is committing the fallacy of wishful thinking. Wishing something is true is not a relevant reason for its actually being true. Example:

> It would be outrageous if we soldiers were fighting for the wrong side in this war. So, it's OK to fight on.

APPENDIX

Creating Helpful Definitions

The definition of a word can serve a variety of purposes other than simply stating how everybody uses the word. In addition, people use a wide variety of techniques in creating definitions. Because errors in creating definitions can be an obstacle to communication, this appendix is designed to improve your skill at avoiding these faults.

Different Definitions for Different Purposes

Definitions should be distinguished from descriptions. We define words, not objects, although most people aren't very careful about this. Saying that a neurotic person is an emotionally unstable person is describing a neurotic and not defining *neurotic*, strictly speaking. However, ordinary speakers will usually permit a good description to serve as a definition because the description can be turned into a definition, such as that *neurotic* means "emotionally unstable."

"*Neurotic* means he is not as sensible as I am, and *psychotic* means he's even worse than my brother-in-law." As you can tell from the two "definitions" in this well-known joke, definitions aren't always like the things you find in dictionaries. Definitions are used for a variety of purposes. For example, people sometimes define a word to make it be more precise. Every time a high court judge makes a decision in a case of assault, it sets a precedent that makes the legal term *assault* more precise.

Definitions serve other purposes. Powerful political institutions often exert their power by defining terms their own way. For example, an ordinance was once proposed to the city of Cambridge, Massachusetts, to outlaw "all animal experimentation involving pain with inadequate anesthesia." It required adequate anesthesia for all experimentation on animals. However, it permitted inadequate anesthesia for rats and mice. Lest you think there is an inconsistency here, the ordinance noted that rats and mice are not animals, at least not according to the U.S. Department of Agriculture's definition of *animals*, to which the ordinance referred. Evidently, the Department of Agriculture has the power to define animals not to be animals. Such is the power of government, the power of the word, the power to control definitions.

Not only do people create definitions for a variety of purposes other than simply to describe how everybody has been using the word, but they also use a variety of definitional techniques. Let's consider some of them. If you do not know what a labrador retriever is, I might be able to define the term by pointing to a specific dog and saying, "This is what I mean." A definition by pointing is an **ostensive definition**. Ostensive definitions are a kind of **definition by example**. If I define *physical science* as "something like geology, chemistry, astronomy, or physics," I'm giving a definition by example. Dictionaries cannot use ostensive definitions, but occasionally they do use definitions by example. A dictionary definition is called a **lexical definition** because dictionaries are called *lexicons*. Here is an example of a lexical definition that is not a definition by example:

> By definition, *vixen* means "female fox."

The definition is correct, so the definition's sentence is a true sentence.

A **stipulative definition** stipulates how a new term is to be used from now on. If I define the term *boke* to be a broken coke bottle, I have coined a new term for our language, although there isn't much chance my definition will be adopted by other speakers. In 1840, in his introduction to *The Philosophy of the Inductive Sciences*, William Whewell wrote: "We very much need a name to describe a cultivator of science in general. I propose to call him a 'scientist.'" Whewell's stipulative definition caught on. It became a lexical definition.

Persuasive definitions are another category of definitions. Take the definition of *atheist* proposed by William, an acquaintance of mine: "a non-Christian pervert who will rot in hell." Well, the definition is not especially accurate because it doesn't reveal the way most other people use the term *atheist*. Even though his definition will never find its way into a proper dictionary, that won't bother William; he was creating a persuasive definition, not a lexical one.

Sometimes a definition of a term will offer some operation or procedure to tell whether something should be called by that term. The procedure of asking a woman whether she is pregnant and taking a "yes" answer to indicate pregnancy would be an **operational definition** of *pregnant* that a social science researcher might use when studying whether pregnant women have a better diet than other women. This operational definition isn't what most of us would give if we were asked to explain what *pregnant* means, but it could succeed at identifying who is and who isn't pregnant and so deserves to be called a definition of *pregnant*.

■ ············ Concept Check 1 ············ ■

Create an operational definition of *popular TV show*.

How to Avoid Errors in Creating Definitions

Let's turn now from examining the purposes and kinds of definitions to the more important topic of avoiding errors in definitions. For example, here is a faulty lexical definition:

By definition, a *square* is a four-sided, plane, closed geometrical figure in which all angles are 90 degrees.

Did you notice the problem? The definition permits too many things to be called squares. It lets in rectangles. So we say it is *too* **broad**. The same kind of error is made when a vegetable is defined as a food that is not a fruit.

Here is the opposite kind of error:

By definition, a *triangle* is a three-sided, plane, closed geometrical figure with equal sides.

This definition rules out triangles that don't have equal sides, so it is *too* **narrow**. Both of the above kinds of errors would be committed at the same time if someone were to define a *vixen* as a young fox. The definition is too broad because it permits young male foxes to be vixens. It is too narrow because it rules out old female foxes.

■ .... Concept Check 2 .... ■

Is the following proposed definition too broad, too narrow, or both? Why?

Science: The study of geology, biology, chemistry, or physics.

Ambiguous definitions and **overly vague definitions** are two other faults in constructing definitions. Suppose you did not know the meaning of the slang term *put down* and I defined it this way:

By definition, a *put down* is a shot intended to harm.

If you didn't know that a put down is something done verbally, you might be misled into thinking that it is something that can be done with a pistol. So, the definition suffers from ambiguity.

A definition of *dog* as "a thing like Lassie" would be of little help to a biologist. Definitions by example are always vague. Defining *dog* in terms of a dog's genetic makeup would be less vague and better biology. Figurative language in a definition always produces an overly vague definition. That would be the problem if we defined *dog* as "man's best friend" or defined *president of a country* as "pilot of the ship of state." Science and mathematics have progressed in part by carefully avoiding imprecise definitions whenever possible.

Scientific definitions are usually overly complex for the nonscientist. Hoping to learn how to distinguish a spider from other bugs, the nonscientist might ask a biologist to define *spider*. If the biologist gave a definition that referred to the spider's genetic code, the definition would fail to elucidate. That is, it wouldn't get the point across. If a definition is *too complex*, it will be *inappropriate for the intended audience*. Defining *dog* for a third grader by giving several examples would be vague, but appropriate. After all, we give definitions in order to achieve the purpose of getting the meaning across to others. If we achieve our purpose, that is all that counts, vagueness or no vagueness.

Failure to convey the grammatical category is also a source of error. If the audience doesn't know the grammatical category of the term *lassitude*, then defining it as "when you feel very tired" could mislead an unwary member of the audience into supposing that the definition could be substituted this way:

> Monroe's lassitude got him fired.
>
> Monroe's when you feel very tired got him fired. .

Suppose someone had never heard the word *nigger* and you defined it as "black person." By covering up the negative connotation, you would have been offering a faulty definition that could get the user in trouble. So, *failure to convey the term's connotation* is the type of error here. It could be corrected by defining *nigger* as "offensive or derogatory term for persons with black skin."

Another way that a definition can fail is by being *circular*. The author of a **circular definition** makes the mistake of improperly using the term that is supposed to be defined. For example, the person who defines an *apprentice* as "someone who is an apprentice to a laborer" is not informing anybody of anything other than the grammatical category of *apprentice*. Here is another example:

> By definition, the bialystok fallacy occurs when there is an instance of either circular reasoning or a bialystok fallacy. Because the bialystok fallacy is the most significant of all the fallacies, you can be sure that it is a fallacy of the highest significance.

Circularity can also be a problem with a chain of definitions, even if no single definition in the chain is itself circular. Here is an example:

> *Effect* is that which is produced by a cause.
> *Cause* is that which produces an effect.

Another kind of error in the definition process occurs in the following pair of definitions:

> An airline stewardess is a woman who provides service to airline passengers during flight.
>
> An airline steward is a male airline stewardess.

This is an **inconsistent definition** because it implies that a steward is both male and female. To remove the gender identification from *steward* and *stewardess*, airlines recommend using the genderless term *flight attendant*. Usually it is not important, and is even sexist, to identify the sex of a worker or occupation. That's the main reason that the term *mailman* is dying out, to be replaced by *postal carrier*.

■ ‥‥‥‥‥   Concept Check 3   ‥‥‥‥‥ ■

When someone gives the lexical definition of *atheist* as "non-Christian," the error is to give a definition that

a. commits an attack on the arguer, not the argument.

b. is too broad.

c. is too narrow.

d. is circular.

Errors in operational definitions are hard to avoid. The problem is really to minimize the degree to which the class of things identified by the operational definition deviates from the class identified by the lexical definition. For instance, suppose some scientists report that

American homes are neater now than they were in 1900.

Before you accept the scientists' claim, ask yourself how the term *neater* was operationalized. A good reporter would provide the reader with the actual operational definition. A reader not given this information would have to worry that the term was operationally defined by counting the number of objects in the house; the fewer objects, the neater the house. This definition is both too narrow and too broad and thus isn't true to the lexical definition of *neat* that you use. Readers should put less faith in this scientific report if they can't be satisfied that the term was adequately operationalized.

■ .... Concept Check 4 .... ■

What is the main flaw in this set of definitions?

Vague means "suffering from vagueness." *Vagueness* means "the result when vague words are used."

Review of Major Points

Clear, precise definitions are an aid to communication. Definitions are used not only to inform people of the meanings of words but also to make jokes, remove vagueness, and push a political agenda. Definitions come in various flavors: ostensive, lexical, stipulative, operational, by example. Helpful definitions are often difficult to create. Definitions can be faulty because they are too broad, too narrow, ambiguous, vague, inappropriate for the audience, misleading as to grammatical category or connotation, circular, or inconsistent.

Glossary

ambiguous definition   A definition that expresses the meaning ambiguously.

broad definition   A term's definition that would permit too many things to be called by that term.

circular definition   Using the term to be defined as part of the term's own definition.

definition by example   Defining a term by indicating examples of things appropriately named by that term.

inconsistent definition   A definition that expresses the meaning inconsistently.

lexical definition   A dictionary definition.

narrow definition   A term's definition that would permit too few things to be called by that term.

operational definition   A term defined by stating an operation or method to follow in deciding whether the term applies.

ostensive definition   A definition by example offered by a speaker who indicates the example by pointing.

overly vague definition   A definition that expresses the meaning too vaguely.

persuasive definition   A definition that could be used to persuade the hearer to take a particular stand on an otherwise controversial issue. A definition that is not objective.

stipulative definition   Stipulating how a term will be used from now on. Coining a term.

Answers to Concept Checks

1. "A TV show is popular if it has a Nielsen rating of at least 17." Note that the point of the answer is to give an operation or recipe or procedure for a researcher to follow to know how to label a given TV show as "popular" or "not popular."

2. Too narrow; it leaves out sociology, astronomy, linguistics, and psychology, for example.

3. Answer (b). This definition would lead to calling all Moslems and Jews "atheists." It is too broad because it lets too much into the category of atheists.

4. They are circular.

Review and Writing Exercises

- 1. Operationalize the concept of acid. Make it sufficient for a junior high school science text.

■ 2. Describe what is wrong with this lexical definition:

> By definition, a vixen is a kind of fox.

3. Create a nonoperational definition of *acid* that would be appropriate for third graders.

■ 4. Which kind of definition is this?

> "I defined 'Republican,'" the pollster said, "to mean anybody who checked the Republican box on the enclosed form."

5. Suppose you define *water* to a five-year-old in the following way:

> The wet stuff that comes out of your faucet when you wash your hands is water. It is also the stuff in rivers and lakes and oceans.

This definition
a. commits the fallacy of failure to elucidate.
b. is circular.
c. is a definition by example.
d. is stipulative and lexical.
e. is an operational definition.

6. Suppose you define *water* to a five-year-old as "the wet stuff." The definition is
a. too narrow.
b. circular.
c. too broad.
d. autonomous.
e. an operational definition.

7. In an ordinary conversation, if you were to define *steam* as the white stuff given off in the air when water is boiled, your definition would probably be acceptable. However, to a scientist, this definition would be incorrect. Find out why, then write an explanation of why your first definition was unacceptable. Hint: Steam is not white.

■ 8. Analyze the errors in the following reasoning:

> According to the dictionary definition of *science*, a science is a body of knowledge amassed in a systematic way. Because a telephone book and a repair manual both are systematized bodies of knowledge, it follows that they, too, are sciences. Thus, the following is a correct listing of some of the sciences: physics, botany, repair manual, chemistry, geology, psychology, telephone book, astronomy, anthropology.

Is the definition too broad, too narrow, or both? How would you improve on the dictionary definition?

9. Construct a definition of *bat* that is too broad but not too narrow.

10. Construct definitions of the terms *ballistic missile* and *cruise missile* that make it clear whether a cruise missile is a ballistic missile. Do not use the term *cruise missile* in your definition of *ballistic missile*. In the U.S. military, a Tomahawk missile is a cruise missile. This exercise requires additional research.

11. Consider this argument: "Either it rains or we are going to San Francisco, but not both. It does rain. So we're not going to San Francisco after all." Here is an analysis of it in sentential logic (see Appendix C):

> R is the sentence "It rains."
>
> S is the sentence "We are going to San Francisco."

Then the pattern of the above argument is

> R or S, but not both R and S.
> R.
> _____
> Not-S.

and that is the form of a valid argument in sentential logic.
  In this analysis of the argument, the definitions are

a.   lexical.

b.   stipulative.

c.   circular.

d.   inconsistent.

e.   vague.

Explain why your answer is correct. One major part of this question is to *find* the definitions.

- 12. Define the phrase *right to privacy*, then create an argument defending your definition. You may use outside legal research to enrich your answer.

13. Give an operational definition of *water* for an adult audience.

14. Describe any flaws you notice in the following definitions.

a.   By a *tall woman* I mean "a woman over 5′9″."

■ b.   "History is an account, mostly false, of unimportant events which are brought about by rulers, mostly knaves, and soldiers, mostly fools." (Ambrose Bierce)

c.   An apple pie is a pastry with apple filling.

d.   The definition of *likes better* that I used in my report on whether rich women like sex better than poor women was to count the number of "yes" answers from women who answered my question "Do you like sex?"

e.   The definition of *likes better* that I used to establish that rich women like sex 1.25 times better than poor women was to count the number of "yes" answers from women who answered my question "Do you like sex?"

15. By definition, *busybody* means "curious person."

Logical Form and Sentential Logic

Abstracting from the content of an argument reveals the logical form of the argument. The initial sections of this appendix show that logical form is the key to the validity of deductively valid arguments. The appendix then explores sentential logic, the logic of sentences. Finally, the appendix investigates the tricky terms *only*, *only if*, and *unless*. To understand reasoning that uses these terms, many persons are forced to hire a lawyer. Consequently, once you have mastered this appendix, you can proceed directly to opening your own law practice and can skip going to law school.

Logical Equivalence

If you were told "John stepped on the camera by accident," you wouldn't have learned anything different from having been told "The camera was accidentally stepped on by John." These sentences say the same thing — they make the same statements — even though they are grammatically different. Because the two say the same thing logically, they are said to be *logically equivalent*. Logical equivalence is somewhat like synonymy except that it is for sentences (or statements), not words. The phrase *say the same thing* is a bit imprecise, so here is a definition using more precise terminology:

Definition Statement P is **logically equivalent** to statement Q provided P follows from Q with certainty and Q also follows from P with certainty.

The certainty mentioned here is not a psychological notion; it is a logical notion. That is, the certainty is not about feeling sure but instead about the solidity of the logical relationship of support among statements.

Alternative Definition Statement P is **logically equivalent** to statement Q provided P logically implies Q and also Q logically implies P.

Here is a pair of logically equivalent statements:

> Tiffany is so sincere, you can't doubt her.
> The sincerity of Tiffany cannot be doubted.

Yet these two are not logically equivalent:

> Tiffany got married and got pregnant.
> Tiffany got pregnant and got married.

Time order is the problem.

Suppose *P* is the sentence "Not all mammals are land dwellers" and *Q* is the sentence "Some mammals are not creatures that live on land." Does *Q* follow from *P* with certainty? Yes. How about vice versa? Yes. So *P* and *Q* are logically equivalent. This relationship between the two sentences would hold even if the word *mammal* were replaced by the phrase *fish in the Indian Ocean*. Consequently, logical equivalence between two sentences can be a matter of the form of the two sentences, not just what they are about.

■ ············ Concept Check 1 ············ ■

Does the definition of logical equivalence permit a true sentence and a false sentence to be logically equivalent to each other?

Deciding whether two phrases are logically equivalent can be critical in assessing the quality of an argument. Here is an example (note that the conclusion does follow from the premises with certainty):

1. If the attraction that baseball has will persist in America over the next decade, then our income from concessions will also remain steady over the next decade.
2. The attraction that baseball has will in fact persist in America over the next decade.

3. Our income from concessions will remain steady over the next decade.

Would the conclusion still follow if premise 2 were replaced with the following statement?

2'. Baseball will continue to flourish in America over the next ten years.

It depends. If statement 2' is logically equivalent to statement 2, then the conclusion would still follow with certainty. However, if you cannot be sure they are equivalent, you cannot be sure the conclusion follows with certainty. To decide whether 2 and 2' are equivalent, you should be sensitive to context and use the principle of charity. If, after doing all this, you still cannot tell whether 2 and 2′ are equivalent, and if you need to be sure, you will have to ask the speaker or author to be clearer.

> ■ .... Concept Check 2 .... ■

Does the conclusion follow with certainty from the premises in this argument? Explain why a simple "yes" or "no" answer is unacceptable.

> If the latest version of the word processing program WordPerfect is warmly received on presentation, its owners and programmers are going to be happy about what they created. All reports indicate WordPerfect did hit the market with a splash and got many good reviews. So we can conclude that WordPerfect's creators felt a sense of accomplishment.

The concept of logical equivalence is useful in other ways. This usefulness arises from the fact that the deductive validity or invalidity of an argument usually depends on the logical forms of its sentences, as we will see later in this appendix. In turn, the ability to identify the logical form of a sentence requires the ability to paraphrase the sentence in a certain way, such as the ability to translate the sentence into a logically equivalent one of sentential logic or of class logic. The first of these two topics will be introduced in this appendix; the second will be introduced in the next.

Logical Forms of Statements and Arguments

The logical form of an argument is composed from the logical forms of its component statements. These logical forms are helpful for assessing the validity of deductive arguments. For instance, consider the following argument, which is in standard form:

> If all crystals are hard, then diamond crystals are hard.
> Diamond crystals are hard.
> _____
> All crystals are hard.

This is a deductively invalid argument, but it can be difficult to see that this is the case. The difficulty arises from the fact that the conclusion is true and all the argument's premises are true. One way to detect the invalidity is to abstract away from the content of the argument and to focus at a more general level on the form of the argument. The argument has this logical form:

> If Cryst, then Diam.
> Diam.
> _____
> Cryst.

The term *Cryst* abbreviates the clause "All crystals are hard." The term *Diam* abbreviates the clause "Diamond crystals are hard." It is easier to see that the form is invalid than it is to see that the original argument is invalid. The form is invalid because other invalid arguments have the same form. For example, suppose *Cryst* were to abbreviate "You are a Nazi" and *Diam* were to abbreviate "You breathe air." The resulting argument would have the same form as the one about diamonds:

> If you are a Nazi, then you breathe air.
> You do breathe air.
> _____
> You are a Nazi.

Nobody would accept this argument. Yet it is just like the argument about diamonds, as far as logic is concerned. That is, the two are **logically analogous**. So if one is bad, both are bad. The two arguments are logically analogous because both have the following logical form:

> If *P*, then *Q*.
> *Q*.
> _____
> *P*.

It is really the logical form of the diamond argument that makes it be invalid. If someone were to say of the argument about diamonds, "Hey, I can't tell whether the argument is valid or not; I'm no expert on diamonds," you could point out that the person doesn't have to be an expert. All that is needed is to pay some attention to pattern.

Just as valid patterns are a sign of valid arguments, so invalid arguments have invalid patterns. All arguments have patterns. The first person to notice that arguments can be deductively valid or invalid because of their pattern was the ancient Greek philosopher Aristotle. He described several patterns of good reasoning in his book *Organon*, in about 350 B.C. As a result, he is called "the father of logic." He started the whole subject with this first and yet deep insight into the nature of argumentation.

In our example, the terms *Diam* and *Cryst* served as logical symbols that abbreviated sentences. We will be introducing more and more logical symbolism as this appendix progresses. The reason for paying attention to logical symbols is that when arguments get complicated, a look at the symbolic logical form can show the important heart of the problem. The reason is much like that for translating mathematics word problems into mathematical symbols: the translation makes the mathematics within the statements more visible for those who have a feeling for the symbols. The purpose of introducing symbols and logical forms is to aid in evaluating reasoning that is too complicated to handle directly in the original English.

However, this appendix hasn't yet spelled out how to determine the logical form of a sentence. Unfortunately, determining the logical form of a sentence is tricky because the same sentence can have more than one logical form depending on how one treats it. It can have a *sentential* form in an area of logic called sentential logic, a *class logic* form in class logic, or even other forms. This difficulty will be clearer after the following introduction to sentential form and sentential logic.

The argument about diamonds was analyzed using sentential logic. **Sentential logic** is the branch of logic that focuses on how the logical forms of complex sentences and arguments are composed from the logical forms of their subsentences or clauses. The clauses must be connected by one of the following sentence connectors or their synonyms: *and, or, not, if-then, implies.*

Strictly speaking, sentential logic is about statements, but this appendix won't be careful about this. Also, it is arguments, not forms, that are invalid. However, that distinction will not be observed in this appendix either. Nor will the distinction between a statement constant and a statement variable; that is, sometimes the letter *P* will stand for a specific statement, and at other times it will stand for any particular statement.

The Logic of *Not*

In sentential logic, an inconsistent group of sentences is defined via their logical form. Be definition, a sentence group is inconsistent if it implies some complex statement whose logical form is "*P* and not-*P*." This complex statement is composed of two substatements, the statement *P* and its opposite, not-*P*. The two substatements are joined by the connector *and*. The statement form "*P* and not-*P*" is said to be the **logical form of a contradiction**. Note that the statement form "not-*P*" does not stand simply for any statement that isn't *P*; rather, it stands for any statement that *negates P* — that says something that must be false when *P* is true and that must be true when *P* is false. Not-*P* is thus called the **negation** of *P*. This information about negation can be summarized in the following truth table for negation:

P	not-*P*
T	F
F	T

Here the letter T represents the possibility of the sentence above it being true, and F represents the possibility of being false.

In sentential logic, there are two ways a pair of sentences can be inconsistent. They are **contradictory** if they are inconsistent and if, in addition, one sentence must be true while the other must be false. However, two sentences are **contrary** if they are inconsistent yet could both be false.

Sentences A and B below are contradictory, whereas sentences A and C are contrary. Sentences B and C are consistent.

A. The house is red.

B. The house is not red.

C. The house is green.

■ ·········· Concept Check 3 ·········· ■

Create a sentence that is contrary to the claim that it's 5 P.M. but that does not contradict that claim.

■ ·········· Concept Check 4 ·········· ■

Which statement below serves best as the negation of the statement that Lloyd Connelly is an assemblyman who lives in the capital?

a. Lloyd Connelly lives in the capital and also is an assemblyman.
b. No one from Lloyd Connelly's capital fails to be an assemblyman.
c. It isn't true that Lloyd Connelly is an assemblyman who lives in the capital.
d. Lloyd Connelly doesn't live in the capital.
e. Lloyd Connelly is not an assemblyman.

If you were to learn that $x = 8$, would it be reasonable to believe that it isn't true that x is unequal to 8? Yes. The valid form of your reasoning is

$$\frac{P}{\text{not-not-}P} \quad \text{[deductively valid]}$$

One could infer the other way, too, because any statement is logically equivalent to its double negation.

The Logic of *And*

Sentential logic explores not only the patterns of sentences but also the patterns of arguments. In this section we will explore arguments whose validity or invalidity turns crucially on the use of the word *and*. The truth table for *and*, or *conjunction* as it is called by logicians, has four rows for all the possibilities:

P	Q	P and Q
T	T	T
T	F	F
F	T	F
F	F	F

If you were to learn that $x = 5$ and that $y < 7$, would it be valid for you to infer that $y < 7$? Yes. It would also be trivial. The general point of this example is that the following is a deductively valid form:

$$\frac{P \text{ and } Q}{Q} \quad \text{[deductively valid]}$$

If you were to learn that $x = 105$, would it be valid for you to infer both that $x = 105$ and that $y = 14$? No The general point is this:

$$\frac{P}{P \text{ and } Q} \quad \text{[deductively invalid]}$$

The truth table for conjunction can be used to demonstrate that in the previous argument form there are possibilities in which the premise is true while the conclusion is false. There are no such possibilities for deductively valid forms. In this way, the tables provide a general method of assessing the validity of arguments in sentential logic.

The Logic of *Or*

In a complex *or statement* of the form "P or Q," the statement P is called "the left disjunct," and the Q is called "the right disjunct." Consider the statement "$x = 5$ or $y < 19$." If you were told that either the left or the right disjunct is true, but not which is true, could you be sure that the right one is true? No. The moral is the following:

$$\frac{P \text{ or } Q}{Q} \quad \text{[deductively invalid]}$$

However, if you knew that either the left or the right disjunct is true and you were to learn that the left is *not* true, you could infer that the right one is true. The general form is

$$\frac{\begin{array}{c} P \text{ or } Q \\ \text{not-}P \end{array}}{Q} \quad \text{[deductively valid]}$$

■ ·········· Concept Check 5 ·········· ■

State whether the main argument below is a deductively valid inference, then describe the logical form of the inference.

Assuming $x = 4$ and $y < 7$, as you have said, then it is not the case that x is unequal to 4.

■ ·········· **Concept Check 6** ·········· ■

Consider the following deductive argument:

> Your information establishes that President Abraham Lincoln was assassinated by Ulysses Grant. Now we can be sure that John was right when he said, "Abraham Lincoln was assassinated either by Grant or else by Booth."

In trying to assess whether the argument is deductively valid, you can abstract the main argument to produce the following form:

P
___
$P \text{ or } Q$

P = President Abraham Lincoln was assassinated by Ulysses Grant.

Q = Abraham Lincoln was assassinated either by Grant or else by Booth.

The first premise happens to be false, yet the conclusion is true. The problem, however, is to decide whether the logical form is deductively valid.

The truth (and falsehood) possibilities for *or* can be summarized in this truth table:

P	Q	$P \text{ or } Q$
T	T	T
T	F	T
F	T	T
F	F	F

The Logic of *If-Then*

Some argument patterns are so common that they have been given names. The most common of all is called **modus ponens**.

If P then Q
P
___ [deductively valid]
Q

The validity of this form can be checked by using the truth table for implication (that is, the conditional) and noticing that "If *P* then *Q*" is false only when *P* is true and *Q* is false. The ancient Greek logician Chrysippus discovered the modus ponens form in 200 B.C. Here is an example of an argument whose sentential logical form is modus ponens:

> If they bought that much aluminum stock right before Chile had its general strike, then they will be wiped out.
> They bought that much aluminum stock just before Chile had its general strike.
> _____
> They will be wiped out.

To show that this argument does have the modus ponens logical form, we would use this dictionary of abbreviations:

> *P* = They bought that much aluminum stock right before Chile had its general strike.
> *Q* = They will be wiped out.

In addition to modus ponens, there are other forms of deductively valid reasoning in sentential logic. **Modus tollens** is another common one, and it has this form:

> If *A* then *B*
> $\underline{\text{not-}B}$ [deductively valid]
> not-*A*

Examples of this form of faulty reasoning were examined in earlier chapters without mentioning the Latin term for it. Here is an example of an argument of that form:

> If he is a lawyer, then he knows what the word *tort* means. Surprisingly, he doesn't know what the word *tort* means. So, he's not a lawyer.

In this example of modus tollens, the letters *A* and *B* represent the following:

> *A* = He is a lawyer.
> *B* = He knows what the word *tort* means.

In daily life, you wouldn't be apt to detect the modus tollens form so clearly. The above argument might instead be embedded in the following passage:

> If he were really a lawyer as he claims, he'd know the word *tort*. So, he's some sort of imposter.

This passage contains the same modus tollens argument that was in the previous passage. However, the premise *not-B* is now implicit. The conclusion of the modus tollens is also implicit. In addition, a second conclusion has been drawn — namely, that he's an imposter.

Although the modus tollens form is valid—that is, any argument with that form is a valid argument—there are apparently similar arguments that are invalid yet are often mistaken for valid ones. Here is an example of a common one:

> If she's Brazilian, then she speaks Portuguese. She's no Brazilian, so she doesn't speak the language.

The reasoning is fallacious if the arguer is intending to create a deductively valid argument. In standard form it might be written this way:

> If she's Brazilian, then she speaks Portuguese.
> She is not Brazilian.
> _____
> She does not speak Portuguese.

The conclusion does not follow with certainty. To suppose it does is to commit the **fallacy of denying the antecedent**. The fallacy also occurs more transparently in this argument: "If you are a Nazi, then you breathe air, but you obviously are not a Nazi, so you don't breathe air." This invalid argument is logically analogous to the one about speaking Portuguese.

In sentential logic, the logical form of the fallacy is

> If P then Q
> Not-P [deductively invalid]
> _____
> Not-Q

The form is what defines the fallacy. The *if* part of a conditional is called its **antecedent**. The second premise, "not-P," denies—that is, negates—the antecedent P of the argument's conditional premise, which is "If P then Q." The arguer asserts the conditional, denies the antecedent, then draws an invalid inference. That is why the fallacy has the name it does.

There is an argument that uses the same conditional as in the previous one. It commits a different fallacy but is often mistaken for the deductively valid reasoning we have called modus ponens.

> If she's Brazilian, then she speaks Portuguese. She does speak Portuguese.
> So she is Brazilian.

The premises of this argument do give a reason to believe the woman is Brazilian. However, if the arguer believes that the premises establish with certainty that she is Brazilian, then the arguer is committing the **fallacy of affirming the consequent**. Rewriting the argument in standard form yields

> If she's Brazilian, then she speaks Portuguese.
> She does speak Portuguese.
> _____
> She is Brazilian.

The logical form, in sentential logic, of the fallacy is

If P then Q

$\dfrac{Q}{P}$ [deductively invalid]

The fallacy has its name because then *then* part of any conditional is called its **consequent** and because affirming the second premise Q affirms the consequent of the conditional.

■ ············ **Concept Check 7** ············ ■

Which passage commits the fallacy of denying the antecedent?

a. If pork prices continued to drop in Japan from 1789 to 1889, then pork would have been eaten regularly by the average citizen of Tokyo in 1890. Pork prices continued to drop in Japan during that time. Consequently, the average citizen of Tokyo in 1890 did eat pork regularly.

b. If pork prices continued to drop in Japan from 1789 to 1889, then pork would have been eaten regularly by the average citizen of Tokyo in 1890. The average citizen of Tokyo in 1890 did not eat pork regularly. So pork prices did not continue to drop in Japan from 1789 to 1889.

c. If pork prices continued to drop in Japan from 1789 to 1889, then pork would have been eaten regularly by the average citizen of Tokyo in 1890. So the average citizen of Tokyo in 1890 did not eat pork regularly, because pork prices did not continue to drop in Japan from 1789 to 1889.

d. If pork prices continued to drop in Japan from 1789 to 1889, then pork would have been eaten regularly by the average citizen of Tokyo in 1890. The average citizen of Tokyo in 1890 did not eat pork regularly. So pork prices did continue to drop in Japan from 1789 to 1889.

e. If pork prices continued to drop in Japan from 1789 to 1889, then pork would have been eaten regularly by the average citizen of Tokyo in 1890. The average citizen of Tokyo in 1890 did eat pork regularly. So pork prices did continue to drop in Japan from 1789 to 1889.

■ ············ **Concept Check 8** ············ ■

In Concept Check 7, which passage commits the fallacy of affirming the consequent?

■ .... Concept Check 9 .... ■

In Concept Check 7, which passage is an example of modus ponens?

Logicians working in sentential logic have discovered many other deductively valid and invalid argument forms. For example:

> A conditional statement of the form "If P, then Q" implies with certainty the statement whose form is "If not-Q then not-P."

In other words, the following argument form is deductively valid:

$$\frac{P \text{ implies } Q}{\text{not-}Q \text{ implies not-}P} \quad \text{[deductively valid]}$$

If someone says to you, "If it snows today, you should seek shelter at David's cabin," is the person implying that it is snowing today? No, and the point behind why the person is not is captured by the following invalid argument form:

$$\frac{\text{If } P \text{ then } Q}{P} \quad \text{[deductively invalid]}$$

The following inference is also deductively invalid:

$$\frac{\text{If } P \text{ then } Q}{Q} \quad \text{[deductively invalid]}$$

The last three argument forms represent points about logical reasoning that were made informally in Chapter 11 when the notion of a conditional was first introduced. With the tools of logical symbolism, the points can be made more briefly, as we've just seen.

The techniques of sentential logic can often be helpful in analyzing deductive argumentation, but there are many deductive arguments for which sentential methods do not apply. Although no single method works for all deductive arguments, the method of class logic is often applicable. This method is developed in Appendix D.

Necessary and Sufficient Conditions

Some conditions must hold in order for other conditions to hold. For example, oxygen must be present for a match to light when it is struck. We say the presence of oxygen is a *necessary condition* for the lighting. However, the presence of oxygen isn't the only condition that must hold. The oxygen must be in its gaseous form, and the temperature must be high enough—the match won't light at 300 degrees below zero. So, the presence of oxygen isn't a *sufficient condition* for getting the match to light. Its presence is not sufficient, but it is necessary.

More generally, if a conditional such as "If *A*, then *B*" is true, where the letters stand for certain conditions, we can tell that *B* is a necessary condition for *A*. We can also tell that *A* is a sufficient condition for *B*. If in addition we also knew "*A* if and only if *B*," then *B* would be both a necessary and a sufficient condition for *B*. If *A* = "John is a bachelor," a necessary condition for John's being a bachelor is that John be a male. Yet John's being a male isn't by itself sufficient to make him a bachelor. Other conditions must also hold; he must also be an unmarried adult. The three necessary and sufficient conditions for John's being a bachelor are thus that he be an unmarried adult male. Each of the three conditions alone is necessary, but only together are they sufficient.

Here are more formal definitions of the terms *necessary* and *sufficient*. In the two definitions, the letters *A* and *B* can stand either for a single condition or a set of conditions.

Definition   *A* is a **sufficient condition** for *B* if *A* logically implies *B*.

Definition   *A* is a **necessary condition** for *B* if *B* logically implies *A*.

■ .... Concept Check 10 .... ■

What is a necessary condition for a rock's being a diamond rather than some other mineral?

■ .... Concept Check 11 .... ■

What is a sufficient outside thermometer reading to make it be a hot summer day in New York City?

The Logic of *Only, Only If,* and *Unless*

The word *only* is an important one for logical purposes. To explore its intricacies, suppose that to get an A grade in Math 101 you need to do two things: get an A − or better average on the homework, and get an A average on the tests. It would then be correct to say, "You get an A grade in Math 101 only if you get an A − or better average on all the homework." Now drop *only* from the sentence. Does it make a difference? Yes, because now you are left with the false statement "You get an A grade in Math 101 if you get an A − or better average on the homework." Speaking more generally, dropping the *only* from *only if* usually makes a significant difference to the logic of what is said. Let's display the logical forms of the two in sentential logic, using these abbreviations:

A = You get an A in Math 101.

B = You get an A − or better average on all the homework.

The logical forms with and without *only* are

A only if B.

A if B.

The first is true, while the second is false. So "A only if B" and "A if B" are not equivalent; they must be saying something different. They have a different "logic."

Here is a summary of the different logical behavior of *if* as opposed to *only if*. The following three statement patterns are logically equivalent:

(1) P only if Q.

(2) P implies Q.

(3) If P, then Q.

But none of the above three is equivalent to any of the following three:

(4) P if Q.

(5) Q implies P.

(6) If Q, then P.

Yet (4), (5), and (6) are all logically equivalent to each other.

The phrase *if and only if* is a combination of *if* plus *only if*. For example, saying, "You're getting in here if and only if you get the manager's OK" means "You're getting in here if you get the manager's OK, and you're getting in here only if you get the manager's OK."

■ ············ Concept Check 12 ············ ■

Which of the following are true?

For all x, $x = 4$ only if x is even.
For all x, x is even only if $x = 4$.
For all x, x is even if and only if $x = 4$.

■ ············ Concept Check 13 ············ ■

Are all three of these sentences logically equivalent to each other? If not, which two
are equivalent to each other?

a. If you're from the USA, then you're from North Dakota.
b. You're from the USA only if you're from North Dakota.
c. You're from North Dakota if you're from the USA.

   The logical form of sentences containing the word *unless* is important to examine
because so many errors and tricks occur with the word. It means the same as *or*,
although many people, on first hearing this definition, swear it is wrong. You're going
to go to jail unless you pay your taxes, right? So, either you pay your taxes or you go
to jail. This is an example where *unless* and *or* say the same thing.
   Let's now consider a more complicated situation. Suppose you will not get an A
in this course unless you are registered. Does it follow with certainty that if you are
registered, you will get an A? No. Does it follow that you will *not* get an A? No, that
doesn't follow either. Does it follow instead that if you do not get an A, you are not
registered? No. What would, instead, be valid is this:

   You will not get an A in this course unless you are registered.

   If you get an A, then you are registered.

The logical form is

   Not-A unless REG.

   If A, then REG.

Review of Major Points

This appendix introduced the concept of logical equivalence between sentences and the concept of a sentence's logical form. Arguments have logical forms because their component sentences have logical forms. Logical form in turn is the key to assessing whether a deductive argument is valid. Once you've identified the logical form of a deductive argument, the hardest part of assessing validity or invalidity is over, because with the form you can spot logical analogies, determine whether the argument has a counterexample, or demonstrate the validity if it is valid. In this appendix we concentrated on logical forms in sentential logic. We also examined three terms that cause logical confusion: *only*, *only if*, and *unless*. You have now developed an arsenal of powerful logical tools to use in attacking cases of complex reasoning.

Glossary

antecedent The *if* part of a conditional.

conditional An if-then statement.

consequent The *then* part of a conditional.

contradictory A logical inconsistency between two statements in which one must be true while the other is false.

contrary A logical inconsistency between two statements when both could be simultaneously false.

fallacy of affirming the consequent A deductive argument of the form "If P then Q; Q; so P."

fallacy of denying the antecedent A deductive argument of the form "If P then Q; not-P; so not-Q."

logical form of a contradiction The statement form "P and not-P."

logically analogous Having the same logical form.

logically equivalent Logically implying each other.

modus ponens A deductive argument of the form "If P then Q; P; so Q."

modus tollens A deductive argument of the form "If P then Q; not-Q; so not-P."

necessary condition Q is a necessary condition for P if Q must hold whenever P does.

negation A statement of the form "not-P" that is true when P is false and that is false when P is true.

sentential logic The branch of logic that focuses on how the logical forms of complex sentences and arguments are composed from the logical forms of their subsentences or clauses. The clauses must be connected by one of the following sentence connectors or their synonyms: *and, or, not, if-then, implies*.

sufficient condition Q is a sufficient condition for P if P must hold whenever Q does.

Answers to Concept Checks

1. No, if one is true and the other is false in the same circumstances, they must be saying something different from each other and thus cannot be logically equivalent.

2. The argument's conclusion follows with certainty from its premises if the principle of charity permits us to say that "warmly received on presentation" means the same as "hit the market with a splash," and if it permits us to say "happiness" here is the same as "feeling a sense of accomplishment" and if the "owners and programmers" include the "creators." It is likely that these equivalences hold, but you cannot be sure and therefore cannot definitely say, "Yes, the conclusion follows with certainty." If you needed to be sure, you should ask the author to be clearer about all this.

3. "It is noon." Being noon implies it is not 5 P.M. Both sentences could be false if it is, say, 2 P.M., but both cannot be true (in the same sense at the same place).

4. Answer (c). Answer (d) is incorrect because both the original statement and (d) could be false together. A statement and its negation cannot both be false; one of them must be true.

5. Yes, it is valid.

$$\frac{P \text{ and } Q}{\text{not-not-}P} \quad \text{[deductively valid]}$$

P is $x = 4$
Q is $y < 7$

6. It is valid.   7. Answer (c).   8. Answer (e).   9. Answer (a).

10. There are many necessary conditions: being hard, being clear or almost clear, and being able to scratch glass but not vice versa.

11. A reading of 97 would be sufficient to make it a hot day. Most any number above 90 would convince almost everybody. However, *hot* is a vague term, so the lower boundary of thermometer readings will also be vague. Some people will say 88 degrees is hot, but others might say, "Oh, it's not really so hot." And you must keep in mind that hot is also a function of humidity, not just temperature.

12. Just the first one.

13. All three are equivalent to each other. All three are also false.

Review Exercises

Logical Equivalence

1. Is every statement logically equivalent to itself?
2. Does the definition of logical equivalence ever permit false sentences to be logically equivalent to each other?

3. Let A = "x is 4," let B = "x is an even number," and let C = "x is 8/2." Then

    i. A and B are logically equivalent.   ii. A and C are logically equivalent.

        a. true b. false   a. true b. false

4. If no items from column C are nondeductible, can we infer with certainty that *all* items for column C are deductible? How about vice versa?

The Logic of *Not, And, Or,* and *If-Then*

■ 1. Show, by appeal to its logical form in sentential logic, why the following argument is valid or invalid.

> If politicians are corrupt, their friends are also corrupt. Thus, if politicians are not corrupt, they don't have peculiar friends because they have peculiar friends if their friends are corrupt.

2. The following argument is

    a. deductively valid   b. deductively invalid.

> I don't know whether polyvinyls are corrosive or not, but I do know that if they are corrosive, then ferrophenyls are also corrosive. Therefore, if polyvinyls are not corrosive, they don't have picoferrous properties because they have picoferrous properties if ferrophenyls are corrosive.

Defend your answer by appeal to logical form.

3. The following argument is

    a. deductively valid   b. deductively invalid

> I don't know whether polyvinyls are corrosive or not, but I do know that if they are corrosive, then ferrophenyls are also corrosive. Isn't it reasonable, then, to suppose that, if polyvinyls are corrosive, they have picoferrous properties because, as you've already said, they have picoferrous properties if ferrophenyls are corrosive?

Defend your answer by appeal to logical form.

4. Consider this amusing argument: "If God had wanted people to fly, He would not have given us bicycles. But He *has* given them to us; so it's clear what God wants."

    a. State the implicit conclusion.

    b. State the logical form of the argument in sentential logic.

    c. Is the argument deductively valid? Why or why not?

    d. Is the arguer assuming that God is not evil?

5. The following passage contains one or more deductive subarguments, all of whose premises are stated explicitly. For each one, (a) identify the subargument

by rewriting it in standard form, (b) give its logical form, and (c) say whether it is valid.

> You've got to give up this sort of behavior. God frowns on homosexuality. Besides, all the community standards oppose it, and this is hurting your father's business. He has to serve the public, remember. Also, if your homosexuality is illegal, you should give it up, and your homosexuality *is* illegal, as you well know. You say it's OK because it feels right, but there is more to this world than your feelings. I love you, but you must quit this nonsense.

■ 6. Valid or invalid?

> If *A*, then *B*
> *A*
> ———————
> *A* and *B*

■ 7. Is this a deductively valid argument pattern?

> *P* or not-*P*
> If *P*, then *R*
> not-*R*
> ———————
> not-*P*

8. Is the following argument form deductively valid in sentential logic?

> *A*
> If *A*, then *B*
> ———————
> *B*

9. Here is the logical form of an argument in sentential logic. Is it valid or invalid?

> If *A*, then *B*
> *A*
> ———————
> *A* or *B*

10. Which statement patterns below would be inconsistent with the pattern "*P* or *Q*"?

   a. not-*P*   b. not-*Q*

   c. not-*P* and not-*Q*   d. not-*P* or not-*Q*

   e. If *P*, then not-*Q*

11. Which of the following statement forms has the logical form "If *A*, then *B*"?

   a. *A*, from which it follows that *B*.   b. *A*, which follows from *B*.

12. Is this argument deductively valid?

> The report writing was not difficult. Since report writing is either difficult or pleasant, the report writing must have been pleasant.

13. Identify the lowercase letter preceding any passage below that contains an argument or a subargument that has the following logical form:

> not-*B*
> *A* implies *B*
> ———————
> not-*A*

a. *X* is the family of all open-closed intervals together with the null set. If *X* is the family of all open-closed intervals together with the null set, then *X* is closed under the operation of intersection. Consequently, *X* is not closed under the operation of intersection.

b. *X* is not the family of all open-closed intervals together with the null set. If *X* is the family of all open-closed intervals together with the null set, then *X* is closed under the operation of intersection. Consequently, *X* is not closed under the operation of intersection.

c. *X* is not the family of all open-closed intervals together with the null set. *X* is the family of all open-closed intervals together with the null set if *X* is closed under the operation of intersection. Consequently, *X* is not closed under the operation of intersection.

d. If *X* is the family of all open-closed intervals together with the null set, then *X* is closed under the operation of intersection. *X* is the family of all open-closed intervals together with the null set. Consequently, *X* is closed under the operation of intersection.

e. *X* is the family of all open-closed intervals together with the null set. If *X* is the family of all open-closed intervals together with the null set, then *X* is closed under the operation of intersection. Consequently, *X* is closed under the operation of intersection.

f. If *X* is closed under the operation of intersection, then *X* is the family of all open-closed intervals together with the null set. *X* is not the family of all open-closed intervals together with the null set. Consequently, *X* is not closed under the operation of intersection.

14. In regard to question 13, identify the labels of the passages that are deductively invalid.

15. Is this argument deductively valid? Defend your answer by appeal to sentential logic.

> If state senators are corrupt, their staff members are corrupt. The staff members of state senators are indeed corrupt, so state senators are corrupt.

■ 16. Is this argument deductively valid? Defend your answer by appeal to sentential logic.

> If Einstein were alive today, the physics at Princeton University in New Jersey would be affected by his presence. So, he's one dead duck.

17. Rewrite the following argument in standard form, give its logical form in sentential logic, and say whether it is deductively valid.

You're fat, so you are at least six months' pregnant, because if you're at least six months' pregnant, then you're fat.

Necessary and Sufficient Conditions

1. What is a necessary condition for being the president of the United States at some time in your life?
2. What is a sufficient condition for passing the course for which you use this textbook?
3. The chapter introduction contains a joke about proceeding directly to opening your own law practice and skipping law school. Explain why it is a joke by showing the confusion in logic that is made in telling it. (*Hint*: Is understanding the logic of this chapter a sufficient condition for knowing what you need to know from law school?)
4. If A implies either C or D, and A implies either E or not-D, but E is false, then C is
   a. a necessary condition for A.
   b. a sufficient condition for A.
   c. neither a necessary nor a sufficient condition for A.

The Logic of *Only*, *Only If*, and *Unless*

1. You can usually get from the bottom to the top of a building that has a working elevator _____ you walk up the stairs.
   a. only if   b. if and only if
   c. just when   d. unless
   e. none of the above
2. You are president of the United States _____ you are a U.S. citizen.
   a. only if   b. if and only if
   c. provided that   d. if
   e. unless
3. You are president of the United States _____ you are not president of the Unites States.
   a. only if   b. if and only if
   c. just when   d. if
   e. unless

4. For any whole number x, x is even _____ x is odd. (Which ones cannot be used to fill in the blank and still leave a true statement?)

    a. only if   b. if and only if

    c. provided that   d. if

    e. unless

■ 5. For any whole number x, x is even _____ x is not odd. (Which one cannot be used to fill in the blank and still leave a true statement?)

    a. only if   b. if and only if

    c. provided that   d. if

    e. unless

6. If it were the case that only people favoring cost-cutting techniques in the administration are advocates of decreasing the number of administrative positions, would it follow that you have got to be an advocate of decreasing the number of administrative positions to be a person favoring cost-cutting techniques in the administration?

7. A sign says, "Only adults may view this film." Does it follow with certainty that if you're an adult, you may view this film?

8. Joseph will not graduate in cosmetology unless he passes either developmental cosmetology or experimental design. So if Joseph passes experimental design, he will graduate in cosmetology.

    a. deductively valid   b. not deductively valid

9. Carlucci calls us only if the war room is in condition orange, but the war room *is* in condition orange. So, Carlucci will call.

    In analyzing this argument, let the word *Orange* stand for the statement "The war room is in condition orange," and let the word *Call* stand for "Carlucci calls us." Rewriting the first premise as a conditional and then generalizing to the argument pattern yields which one of the following?

    a. If Orange, then Call.   b. If Call, then Orange.
       Orange.   Orange.
       ――――――――――   ――――――――――
       Call.   Call.

    c. Call only if Orange.
       Orange.
       ――――――――――
       Call.

10. The argument in question 9 commits the fallacy of denying the antecedent when the first premise is rewritten as a logically equivalent conditional statement and then the argument is translated into its form in sentential logic.

    a. true   b. false

11. Consider this memo from an employer:

> Employees must be given the opportunity to give or withhold their consent before the private aspects of their lives are investigated. The firm

is justified in inquiring into the employee's life only if the employee has a clear understanding that the inquiry is being made. The means used to gain this information are also important; extraordinary methods would include hidden microphones, lie detector tests, spies, and personality inventory tests.

- i. If the quotation is correct, then if the employee has a clear understanding that the inquiry is being made, the firm is justified in inquiring into the employee's life.
  a. true   b. false

  ii. If the quotation is correct, the firm is justified in inquiring into the employee's life if the employee has a clear understanding that the inquiry is being made.
  a. true   b. false

  iii. If the quotation is correct, then if the firm is justified in inquiring into the employee's life, the employee has a clear understanding that the inquiry is being made.
  a. true   b. false

12. Suppose $x = 4$ if and only if $y < 22$. From this fact, which of these follow with certainty?
   a. $x = 4$ provided that $y < 22$.
   b. $x = 4$ unless $y < 22$.
   c. $y < 22$ if $x = 4$.
   d. $x = 4$ or $y < 22$.
   e. $(y = 22$ or $y > 22)$ just when $x \neq 4$.

13. Are these two arguments logically analogous? Is either of them deductively valid?

   Carlucci will call us only if the war room is in condition orange, but the war room *is* in condition orange. So Carlucci will call.

   Carlucci will call us only if he is alive. Carlucci is alive, so he will call.

- 14. Are these two sentence forms logically equivalent?

   Not-*A* unless *B*.
   A only if *B*.

APPENDIX

Aristotelian Logic and Venn Diagrams

A lthough there is no system of logic that can be used on all deductive arguments to successfully determine whether they are valid, the system of Aristotelian logic and its method of Venn diagrams can be used on the arguments of class logic. Class logic, which was created by Aristotle in ancient Greece, talks about classes, collections, or sets.

Aristotle's Logic of Classes

A *class* is any collection, group, or set. **Class logic** focuses on the classes that are mentioned in subjects and predicates of sentences and on the occurrence of words such as *all*, *some*, and *none*. For example, the word *Greek* refers to the class of Greeks, and the sentence "All Greeks are Europeans" can be interpreted as saying that the class of Greeks is included within the class of Europeans. The sentence "Socrates was an ancient Greek" can be interpreted as saying that one object (namely, Socrates) is a member of a class (namely, the class of ancient Greeks). In class logic, the sentence "No Americans are Europeans" would be interpreted as saying that the class of Americans doesn't overlap with the class of Europeans. The focus in class logic is on class membership and on classes being included within other classes.

Sentences about classes have logical forms in class logic. For example, the sentence "Some Europeans are Greek" has the form "Some *E* are *G*" where the letter *E* stands for the class of Europeans and the letter *G* for Greeks. The statement form "All *N* are *B*" is a briefer version of "All members of the class *N* are members of the class *B*."

Just as sentences have logical forms, so do arguments. The form of an argument is the form of its component premises and conclusion. For example, here is an argument that can be paraphrased in English to reveal its class structure:

> Nazis are bad.
> Nazis like to beat up Catholics.
> So, liking to beat up Catholics is bad.

Paraphrase:

> All Nazis are bad persons.
> All Nazis are persons who like to beat up Catholics.
> So, all persons who like to beat up Catholics are bad persons.

In creating a paraphrase for use in class logic, we search for *logically equivalent sentences* in which the main verb is some form of *to be* and in which the subject and predicate can be read as being about classes. Using some obvious abbreviations of the classes, we can display the logical form of the above argument as follows:

All *N* are *B*.
All *N* are *L*.
All *L* are *B*.

where

N = (the class of) Nazis

B = (the class of) bad persons

L = (the class of) all persons who like to beat up Catholics

The test of whether we have actually found the logical form of the argument is whether we can reproduce the argument, or one that is logically equivalent to it, by substituting the words back in for the letters.

If the letter *L* were to stand for the class of persons who like to breathe air, then on substituting words for letters, we would get the analogous argument about Nazis liking to breathe air.

Nazis are bad.
Nazis like to breathe air.
So, liking to breathe air is bad.

The two arguments rise and fall together because they are logically analogous — that is, they have the same form or pattern. This particular form is deductively invalid.

■ ·············   Concept Check 1   ············· ■

Which one of the choices below has the logical form of the following argument about whales? (*Hint*: The order in which the premises are presented in an argument is not essential to an argument's validity.)

Whales are mammals, but the biggest fish in our sea is definitely not a mammal, so it's not a whale either.

a. Potatoes are produce. Not all fattening foods are potatoes, so not all fattening foods are produce either.

b. That squirming thing has no backbone, but fish are the kind of things that have backbones. So it's not a fish.

c. Fat fish are swimmers. No house cat is a fat fish, so no house cats are swimmers.

■ ············ Concept Check 2 ············ ■

Choose the correct class logic pattern for the following biological argument:

> All insects have exactly six legs. So no spider is an insect because all spiders have exactly eight legs.

Instead of using single letters, the classes are named with groups of letters. Here are four choices for the pattern. SIX stands for the class of things that have six legs.

a. All INS are SIX.
    No SPID are INS.
    No SIX are EIGHT.
    _____
    All SPID are EIGHT.

b. All INS are SIX.
    No SPID are INS.
    No SIX are EIGHT.
    _____
    No SPID are INS.

c. All INS are SIX.
    No SPID are INS.
    No INS are SPID.
    _____
    All SPID are EIGHT.

d. All INS are SIX.
    All SPID are EIGHT.
    No SIX are EIGHT.
    _____
    No SPID are INS.

The two arguments below have different forms. Any argument with the form on the right is valid:

All *N* are *B*.
All *N* are *L*.   (invalid)
_____
All *L* are *B*.

All *N* are *B*.
All *B* are *L*.   (valid)
_____
All *N* are *L*.

> Any argument of the logical form "All *F* are *G*, so all *G* are *F*" is deductively invalid.

■ ············ Concept Check 3 ············ ■

If some *A* are *C* and all *C* are *R*, must some *R* be *A*?

■ .... Concept Check 4 .... ■

Is this a deductively valid argument form?

No *A* are *B*.
Some *B* are *C*.
No *A* are *C*.

■ .... Concept Check 5 .... ■

Is this argument form deductively valid?

No *A* are *B*.
All *B* are *C*.
No *A* are *C*.

Using Venn Diagrams to Test for Invalidity

Previously, in speaking of negation, we have meant the negation of a statement. For example, the statement "Cuba isn't in Southeast Asia" is the negation of the statement "Cuba is in Southeast Asia." This negation happens to be true. In addition to whole statements, it is also possible to negate terms. For example, non-Jews are those people who are not Jews, such as Palestinian Arabs and Indian Hindus. The *non* serves to negate the term *Jews* and thereby to direct our attention to the class of all those who are not Jews. In mathematics and logic, we call this kind of negation *complementation*. The **complement** of the class *A* is the class of everything that is not in *A*.

Assuming that nobody can be both a Jew and a Christian, it would be true to say that all Jews are non-Christians and true to say that some non-Jews are non-Christians, but it would be false to say that all non-Christians are Jews and false to say all non-Christians are non-Jews. Whew! Congratulations and compliments if you could comprehend the complexities of that complementation.

■ .... Concept Check 6 .... ■

John is not a white male if John is

a. a white non-male.   b. a non-white male.

c. a non-white non-male.   d. all of the above.

■ ·········· Concept Check 7 ·········· ■

If it is not the case that the person is a white male, then the person is definitely

a. a white non-male.   b. a non-white male.

c. a non-white non-male.   d. none of the above.

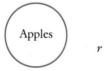

Skill at negating terms is needed for constructing **Venn diagrams**. This diagraming method is a helpful way to quickly assess the deductive validity of arguments in class logic. It can guide you to the correct assessment when the argument is too intricate to analyze in your head. In presenting this method, we shall first introduce the diagrams for classes, then generalize the method so that it can be used to display whether sentences about classes are true or false, and then generalize the method again so that it can be used to show whether arguments using such sentences are deductively valid.

The circle below is a diagram of the class of apples.

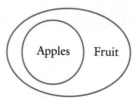

Any point in the circle represents an apple. A point outside the circle represents a non-apple. The small letter *r* labels the point to the right of the circle that represents a specific non-apple, namely Thomas Edison, the American inventor and founder of the General Electric Corporation. There is nothing important about the shape of the area. An ellipse or a rectangle would be fine, just as long as it is clear what is in the area and what is out. The size of the circle isn't important either. Nor do we pay attention to moving the diagram to the left or right or up or down. All those changes would produce the same diagram, logically.

Following is a diagram that represents both the class of apples and the class of fruit. In the real world, the class of apples is included wholly within the larger class of fruit. The diagram provides a picture of this relationship:

Any label for a circle can be inside or outside it, provided there is no ambiguity about which label goes with which circle. Sometimes we will call ovals "circles."

Consider the points *x*, *y*, and *z* in the following diagram. The classes *A* and *B* intersect — that is, they have members in common. One of those members is *y*.

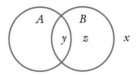

Point *x* is neither in *A* nor in *B*. Point *y* is in both *A* and *B*. Point *z* is in *B* but not in *A*. By viewing the diagram you can see that some members of *B* are in *A* and some aren't. However you cannot tell whether *A* has more members than *B*. If region *A* is larger than *B* in a diagram, you can't tell whether *A* has more members than *B*. For that matter, you can't even tell whether the class has any members at all. However, in all diagrams from now on, we will assume that we are starting with classes that are not empty.

Here is a diagram representing the relationship among apples, fruits, oranges, apples in Paris, apples in restaurants in Paris, and fruit owned by our friend Juan:

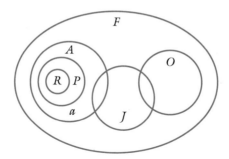

A = things that are apples

F = things that are fruit

O = things that are oranges

P = things that are apples in Paris

R = things that are apples in restaurants in Paris

J = things that are fruit owned by our friend Juan

To be clear, we shall always use capital letters or capitalized words for classes of things. If we want to add the information that some specific object is a member of one of the classes, we will use a lowercase letter to represent the member. In the previous diagram the lowercase *a* represents the one apple in my refrigerator. You can see that the letter *a* is outside the *P* circle; this shows that the apple in my refrigerator is not in Paris. Notice that Juan himself is not a member of any of the classes in the above diagram; the information about Juan is embedded in the definition of *J*. By inspecting the diagram you can tell that Juan doesn't own any Parisian apples, but he does own apples, oranges, and some other unspecified fruit.

Find some classes in the real world that have the relationships indicated in the following diagram:

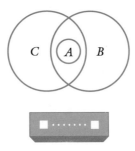

The diagram method can be used to represent what the world would look like if a sentence were true. Consider this sentence:

All apples are fruit (but not vice versa).

It is logically equivalent to this sentence:

The class of apples is included in the class of fruit (but not vice versa).

The diagram is

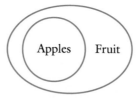

Notice that the notion of logical equivalence was used to discover the proper class logic diagram.

Here is a diagram in which statements of the form "No *A* are *B*" are true:

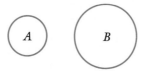

What is important about this diagram is that the two circles do not intersect (overlap). The circles shouldn't be tangent either, because that would make it hard to tell whether the two classes have a common member.

Concept Check 9

Create a diagram in which statements of the form "No *B* are *A*" are true.

How would you draw a diagram in which the statement that some apples are from Canada and some aren't is true? This will do the trick:

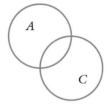

C = the class of things from Canada

A = the class of apples

The sentence pattern "All *A* are non-*B*" is true in the following diagram:

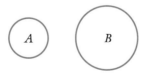

Notice that it is the same as the diagram for "No *A* are *B*." Logically equivalent sentence patterns have the same diagrams. The above diagram would represent the false sentence "No Texans are Americans" if the following dictionary were used:

A = Texans

B = Americans

Although the sentence is false in the real world, the diagram shows how the world would be if the sentence were true. The same point is made by saying that the diagram is a picture of what is true in a certain "possible world" that isn't the actual world.

■ ············ Concept Check 10 ············ ■

Make the statement "All Texans are non-Americans" be true in a diagram, using the above dictionary with *A* and *B*.

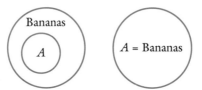

In the following two diagrams, the sentence "All apples are bananas" is true, where *A* is the class of apples:

In the second diagram, the class of apples and the class of bananas are the same class. A diagram of the real-world relationships between apples and bananas would instead look like this:

■ ············ Concept Check 11 ············ ■

Draw a diagram for apples and fruit in which the following sentence isn't true in the diagram: " All apples are fruit." The sentence is true in the real world, but it won't be in the possible world represented by your diagram.

With a sentence such as "All apples are fruit," the analyst has the option of treating it in class logic or in sentential logic. In class logic, it is logically equivalent to "All things in the class of apples are also things in the class of fruit." This states a relationship between two classes. In sentential logic, the sentence is logically equivalent to "If it's an apple, then it's a fruit." This states a conditional relationship between two sentences.

We can now generalize the diagram method to a technique for assessing the deductive validity of arguments, provided that the sentences constituting the argument describe how classes of objects are related to each other. The Venn diagram method works only for deductive arguments in class logic. It shows an argument to be valid if there is no diagram of a counterexample to the argument. By definition, the **counterexample to an argument** is an argument with the same form but with true premises and a false conclusion. More specifically, here is how to apply the **method of Venn diagrams**:

> Translate the premises and conclusion of the argument into logically equivalent sentences of class logic. Try to diagram these sentences in class logic so that the premises come out true in the diagram and the conclusion comes out false in the diagram. If there is a diagram that does so, this diagram shows that the argument is deductively invalid. However, if all possible diagrams fail to do so, then the argument is declared to be deductively valid.

To see the technique in action, we will try it out on this argument pattern:

No *A* are *B*.
No *C* are *B*.
———————
No *A* are *C*.

Here is a diagram that makes all the premises be true:

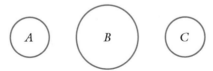

None of the circles intersect or are contained within another. In this diagram the conclusion is true. Can we conclude that the argument pattern is valid? No, not from this information. We should instead have been searching to make sure that there is no diagram that makes the premises true but the conclusion false. In fact, there is such a diagram:

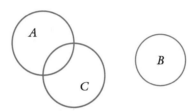

Here the conclusion is false when the premises are true, a telltale sign of invalidity. Therefore, the diagram method declares the argument pattern to be invalid.

■ ············ Concept Check 12 ············ ■

Use the diagram method to show the validity of this argument pattern:

All *A* are *B*.
All *B* are *C*.

All *A* are *C*.

■ ············ Concept Check 13 ············ ■

Use the diagram technique to assess the validity or invalidity of this argument. Interpret *some* as meaning "at least one but not all."

Some cats are felines.
Some animals are felines.

Some animals are cats.

Diagrams can be useful for demonstrating the logic of the word *only*. These two sentences are not equivalent:

Only Americans are Texans.

Only Texans are Americans.

Their difference can be shown with a diagram. Let *TX* be the set or class of Texans, and let *USA* be the set of Americans. Then "Only Americans are Texans" has this diagram:

"Only Texans are Americans" has this diagram:

Now it is clear that the two sentences are not saying the same thing.

Concept Check 14

Use the diagram technique to show the validity or invalidity of the following argument:

> Only living things can have children.
> A computer does not have children.
> So, a computer is not a living thing.

When trying to find the logical form of an argument, it is not always possible to tell whether you should look for its form in class logic or in sentential logic. Experiment to see what will work. Some arguments have logical forms that cannot be expressed adequately either way. Here is one.

> Tom and Dick are brothers (of each other).
> Dick and Harry are brothers.
> _____
> Tom and Harry are brothers.

What is needed to show the validity is a more powerful logical apparatus that includes *predicate logic*, *quantification theory*, or *first-order logic*. Advanced symbolic logic courses study these more powerful tools, which were developed at the beginning of the twentieth century by Gottlob Frege, Bertrand Russell, and Alfred North Whitehead.

Some arguments are deductively valid although their validity is not a matter of logical form at all. Here is an example:

> John is a bachelor.
> So, he is not married.

The validity is due not just to form, but to content — in particular, to the fact that the definition of bachelor implies that all bachelors are not married. Valid arguments that are valid just because of their form are called **formally valid**. All formally valid arguments are deductively valid, but the reverse doesn't hold.

The Logic of *Only* in Class Logic

Consider whether these two sentences are logically equivalent:

> Only Americans are Texans.
>
> Only Texans are Americans.

They aren't equivalent; one is true and one is false. Logically equivalent sentences are true together or false together. The first sentence is saying, "If you are a Texan, then you are an American." The second sentence is saying, "If you are an American, then you are a Texan." It should be clear why the first is true and the second is false.

To abstract from these examples, the main points about the logic of the word *only* are that the class logic statement

> Only *A*'s are *B*'s

is equivalent to the class logic statement

> All *B*'s are *A*'s.

Both of these are equivalent to the condition statement

> If anything is an *A*, then it's a *B*.

■ ············ Concept Check 15 ············ ■

Create a counterexample to the following argument by producing a logically analogous argument that is more obviously invalid:

> Only Simbidians are Greek. So only Greeks are Simbidians.

Now let's examine some difficult arguments that depend crucially on the word *only*. Is the following argument deductively valid?

> Only living things can have feelings.
>
> A computer is not a living thing.
>
> So, a computer cannot have feelings.

How about this argument?

> Only living things can have feelings.
> A computer does not have feelings.
> So, a computer is not a living thing.

Both of these arguments appear to be valid to many people who hold certain views about artificial intelligence — namely, the views stated in the arguments' conclusions. Yet these people are being illogical.

■ ············· Concept Check 16 ············· ■

Are either of the previous two arguments about computers deductively valid?

Review of Major Points

This chapter focused on the logical forms of arguments in Aristotle's class logic. For deductive arguments involving class relationships, Venn diagraming is a useful picture method for assessing validity or invalidity. The method is applied to an argument in an attempt to discover a counterexample to the argument. If one is found, the argument is deductively invalid. If none is found, the argument might or might not be valid. But if none *can* be found, then the argument is valid.

Glossary

class logic The logic developed by Aristotle that turns on the relationships among classes of things, especially the classes referred to by the subjects and predicates of sentences whose verb is a form of "to be."

complement The class composed of all the things not in a particular class.

counterexample to an argument Another argument of the same logical form that has all true premises and a false conclusion.

formally valid Deductively valid because of its logical form.

Venn diagram Diagram representing the class inclusion and class membership relationships among classes of things.

Venn diagram method A method of determining the validity of arguments in class logic by using Venn diagrams.

Answers to Concept Checks

1. Answer (b). To get the correct answer, you need to make use of the fact that the order of the premises is not important.

2. Answer (d). Only (b) and (d) have the correct conclusion below the line.

3. Yes, this is deductively valid reasoning in class logic.

4. No, it is deductively invalid.

5. No, it is deductively invalid.

6. Answer (d). He cannot be a white male if he is non-white. He cannot be a white male if he is non-male.

7. Answer (d). You cannot tell whether the person is a white non-male or a non-white male or instead a non-white non-male. The person might be any one of the three, as far as you can determine from the information in the antecedent of the conditional.

8. A = U.S. citizens who live in New York City, B = city dwellers, C = Americans.

9. Use the same diagram as the one used for "No A are B." Logically equivalent sentences have the same diagrams.

10. Notice that every Texan A is outside America B and thus is a non-American.

11. There are many diagrams that will work.

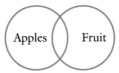

12. Here is a way to draw a diagram of both the premises being true:

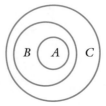

Other diagrams of the premises would permit circle A to equal circle B, or for B to equal C. However, in all the possible diagrams of the premises, the conclusion

comes out true in the diagram. So, no counterexample can be produced. Therefore, the technique declares this argument pattern to be valid.

13. The argument is invalid; the following diagram serves as a counterexample:

Some *C* are *F*.
Some *A* are *F*.
_____
Some *A* are *C*.

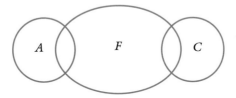

14. The argument is invalid because in the following diagram the premises come out
true but the conclusion doesn't:

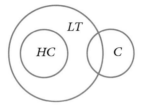

    HC = the class of things that have children
    LT = the living things
    C = computers

15. Consider the situation in which a "Simbidian" is a European. In this situation,
the argument has a true premise and a false conclusion. I made up the word
Simbidian; you won't find it in the dictionary.

16. The first argument is valid. Change *children* to *feelings* in 14 above.

Review Exercises

1. Find three classes in the real world that have the relationships indicated in the
following diagram:

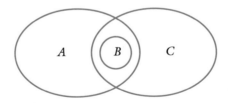

2. Draw a diagram in which the following statement is true, and draw one in which it is false: "Only non-handheld things are returnable." Be sure to define your labels.

3. Draw a diagram in which it is true that although no Americans are voters, some of them are free and some aren't, yet all of them are rich. In your diagram, are all the voters rich?

4. If all *A* are *C* but no *C* are *B*, then are some *A C*?

5. Finding something that has both properties *W* and *Y* tends to confirm the statement "All *W* are *Y*"; for example, finding a black raven tends to confirm the statement "All ravens are black."

   a.   true   b.   false

6. If all non-black things are non-ravens, then you can be sure there are no albino ravens.

   a.   true   b.   false

7. Assuming that all non-black things are non-ravitious, it follows with certainty that all non-ravitious things are non-black.

   a.   true   b.   false

8. Even if all ravens are black, it would not necessarily be the case that everything that is not black fails to be a raven.

   a.   true   b.   false

9. The sentence below is an invalid argument. Turn it into a deductively valid argument by rewriting it and adding exactly one word. Underline the word you add. Make no changes in word order, no deletions, and no other additions to the sentence.

   Children pay no taxes at all, because children are not adults and because adults pay taxes.

10. Give the logical form of the following argument in class logic. Define your new symbols, but let *M* = the class of modern works of art. Draw the relevant diagrams for assessing the deductive validity of the argument. Assess its validity by referring to your diagram(s): that is, say, "These diagrams show that the argument is valid (or invalid) because . . ."

    Since all modern works of art are profound works of art, but not all profound works of art are modern works of art, and because some religious works of art are modern works of art, even though some aren't, it follows that *some* religious works of art fail to be profound.

11. The diagram technique is a way of testing whether something is wrong (invalid) with the pattern of arguments that are about classes of things.

    a.   true   b.   false

12. Given a class logic argument that is deductively valid but unsound, the diagram technique can show why it is unsound.

    a.   true   b.   false

13. Use the method of diagrams to determine the validity or invalidity of the following argument:

   There are doctors who aren't rich, because all doctors are professionals yet some professionals are not rich.

14. If no items from column C are nondeductible, and if column C is not empty of items, then can we infer with certainty that at least one item from column C is deductible?

■ 15. Is this argument deductively valid?

   Some anthropoids are surreptitious and some aren't; hence there are brazen things that aren't anthropoids because all surreptitious beings are brazen.

■ 16. Is this argument deductively valid? Use the method of diagrams, and show your work.

   There are prize winners who aren't avaricious, because every early entrant is a prize winner and because one or more avaricious beings did enter early, though some didn't.

17. Is this argument deductively valid? Use the method of diagrams, and show your work.

   There are prize winners who aren't avaricious, because all early entrants are prize winners and some avaricious persons entered early and some early entrants aren't avaricious.

18. Is the statement "Some Arabs are Dravidians" true in the following diagram?

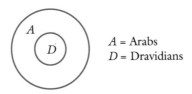

   A = Arabs
   D = Dravidians

   a. yes   b. no   c. depends on the meaning of *some*

19. Is this argument deductively valid? First, consider whether the argument is best handled with sentential logic or class logic.

   The moon maidens don't like Miller Lite. If the Beast controls planet Gorp, then Xenon is in power on that moon. If Xenon is in power on that moon, then the moon maidens like Miller Lite. So the Beast doesn't control planet Gorp.

   Give the logical form of the argument. Define your terms.

20. One of the following two arguments is deductively valid, and the other is not. Identify the invalid one, and use the method of diagraming to defend your answer.

a. There are biopical persons who aren't devious because some devious persons are not surreptitious, and some are, and because a person is surreptitious only if he or she is biopical.

b. There are biopical persons who aren't devious because some surreptitious persons are not devious, and some are, and because any person is biopical if he or she is surreptitious.

21. Use the technique of diagrams to assess the validity of the following arguments:

a. If some *A* are *C* and all *C* are *R*, some *R* must be *A*.

b. No *A* are *B*.
    Some *B* are *C*.
    ───────────
    No *A* are *C*.

c. No *A* are *B*.
    All *B* are *C*.
    ───────────
    No *A* are *C*.

22. Which diagram demonstrates the deductive invalidity of the following argument?

No apes are bears.
No bears are cats.
So, no apes are cats.

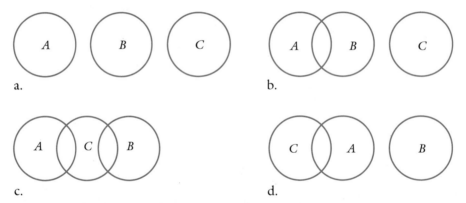

a.   b.

c.   d.

23. Draw a diagram that will demonstrate the deductive invalidity of the following argument that might be given by a political liberal:

No conservatives in Congress are for helping humanity, because all supporters of legislation to increase welfare programs want to help humanity, yet none of the conservatives support legislation to increase welfare programs.

24. Are the following statements logically consistent with each other? Use diagrams to defend your answer.

Not only are no bluejays arachnids, but no dialyds are either. Still, some bluejays are catalytic, but not all are. Anything catalytic is a dialyd.

25. To say that all the people who go to this restaurant are kids is to say something logically equivalent to

    a.   Only the people who go to this restaurant are kids.

    b.   Only kids (are the people who) go to this restaurant.

    c.   Neither a nor b.

    d.   Both a and b.

■ 26. Which pairs of statement forms from the following list are logically equivalent to each other? In answering, use only the lowercase letters, not the statement forms themselves.

    a.   No *A* are *B*.   b.   No *B* are *A*.

    c.   All *A* are not-*B*.   d.   All not-*B* are *A*.

    e.   Only not-*A* are *B*.

27. Which pairs of statements from the following list are logically equivalent to each other? In answering, use only the letters, not the statements. *Hint*: Use Aristotelian logic.

    a.   Every hand-held thing is nonreturnable.

    b.   No returnable thing is hand-held.

    c.   All nonreturnable things are hand-held.

    d.   Only non-hand-held things are returnable.

    e.   No hand-held thing is returnable.

■ 28. Are these logically equivalent? If not, why not?

    a.   Not all profound works of art are modern.

    b.   Not all profound works of art are modern works of art.

29. During Ronald Reagan's presidency, the United States Attorney General Edwin Meese III criticized the Supreme Court's Miranda decision that spelled out the legal rights of accused persons that the police must respect. Meese said, "The thing is, you don't have many suspects who are innocent of a crime. . . . If a person is innocent of a crime, then he is not a suspect." One of the following statements is logically equivalent to what Meese said in his last sentence. That is, Meese said

    a.   If a person is not innocent of a crime, he is not a suspect.

    b.   No suspects in a crime are innocent.

    c.   No persons who are not innocent of a crime are suspects.

    d.   All suspects in crimes are innocent.

    e.   If a person is innocent of a crime, then he is not guilty of the crime.

30. Let's try out some more terminology from everybody's friend, the Internal Revenue Service. If no items from column C are deductible, then can we infer with certainty that no deductible items are from column C? How about vice versa? What can you conclude about whether the two statements are logically equivalent?

31. *Sofa* and *couch* are equivalent terms — that is, they are synonymous. Now consider the term *weird*. Is the term closer to being equivalent to *unusual* or instead to *very unusual*? If someone disagreed with you about this, what could you do to prove the person wrong?

32. To say that only the people who go to this restaurant are kids is to say something logically equivalent to

    a. All the people who go to this restaurant are kids.

    b. All kids go to this restaurant.

    c. Neither a nor b.

    d. Both a and b.

33. Suppose someone says, "Only kids go to Chuck E. Cheese restaurants."

    i.   Would the following sentence, if true, be a counterexample?

    Some kids in Russia don't go to Chuck E. Cheese restaurants.

    ii. How about this as a counterexample instead?

    I'm an adult, not a kid, and I go to Chuck E. Cheese restaurants.

34. Consider this argument:

    All cylinders contain petroleum, since each one has a blue top and only petroleum containers have blue tops.

    Does it follow from the second premise that some things can have blue tops but not be petroleum containers?

Answers to
Selected Exercises

Chapter 2

General Exercises

5. Here are two answers:

> How could you not use Mycene Shampoo? It's here. It's now. It's Mycene, and it's for you.

> If you want him to be more of a man, you need to be more of a woman. Bushwhack Perfume. For the man in your life.

Creating a commercial of the form "Famous people use it, so you should, too" is giving a reason and thus is an inappropriate answer.

Loaded Language

1. The loaded language is capitalized:

> The spokeswoman for the PRO-ABORTION group BLATANTLY ADMITTED today that the mother of the UNBORN CHILD can MURDER the CHILD if she "chooses."

Calling the fetus a "child" loads the description because a central point of disagreement is whether the fetus is or is not morally equivalent to a child. The label *pro-abortion* is a term with negative connotations. Members of the group would not agree that they are pro-abortion; they say they are pro-choice, not pro-abortion. A more objective (that is, fair) way of reporting would be:

> The spokeswoman for the group said today that the woman who carries a fetus should have the option of an abortion if she chooses.

2. The loaded terms are capitalized:

> The "female" leader of the ANTI-CHOICE group said today that a pregnant woman is "guilty of murder" if she EXERCISES HER RIGHT TO CONTROL HER OWN BODY by aborting the fetus.

Here is a better edited version:

> The spokeswoman for the group said today that a pregnant woman is "guilty of murder" if she aborts her fetus.

Replacing *anti-choice* with *anti-abortion* is acceptable, as is giving the explicit name of the group; but choosing *pro-life* would just replace a negatively loaded term with a positively loaded term.

Exaggeration

1. Here is one answer: (a) "Safari [perfume] by Ralph Lauren. A world without boundaries. A world of romance and elegance. A personal adventure and a way of life." (b) They are overstating what this perfume will do for you. It's just a chemical that smells good. You cannot reasonably expect to use it as a principal path to romance, elegance, adventure, and a way of life. (c) Source: *Glamour Magazine*, May 1991, p. 79.

   An exaggeration is an overstatement that contains a kernel of truth. An exaggerated claim is false, but not all false claims are exaggerations. For example, a headline that says, "World War II bomber found intact on moon" is false; it is not exaggerated.

Chapter 3

1. The headline makes a trivially true claim; it conveys essentially no new information to the reader. However, you can imagine the intention of the creator of the headline. He or she probably wanted to make the point that, unlike Christmas with its commercialism, Easter is a less commercialized and more religiously oriented holiday.

5. "Passing water is a natural bodily act." Other euphemisms are "relieving" oneself, "using the facilities," going to the "little girl's room," and so on. *Pissing* is a synonym but not a euphemism.

7. The connotation of the nickname *Hell* is too negative.

15. He is the very *pinnacle* of politeness or the *epitome* of politeness. This paradigm example is why a funny misuse of words is called a *malapropism*.

Chapter 4

2. "Honduran Military Chief Quits, Saying He Is Fatigued." In other words, what he said when he quit was, "I'm tired." The silly interpretation that the comma helps remove is "Honduran military chief has been saying he is tired, but now he has stopped saying this." The disambiguation could also be performed by starting a second line with the word *saying*.

4. You cannot be sure. Maybe Mario ate two grapes, found seeds in both, didn't examine any others, and then made a cautious statement about what he knew for sure at that point.

11. Answer (d).

12. Answer (b). Since the dispute is merely verbal, answer (a) is not correct.

15. In rewriting the sentence, you will have to add information that was not specifically contained in it. For example:

   You have to decide which of your interests are more important than others. Rank them. Then change your life so that you try hardest to satisfy the highest ranking ones.

16. Get a life. (This answer was suggested by Carlo C. Rose.)

22. There are many ways to make it less precise. Here is one:

   Patrick McEnroe was defeated by Jimmy Connors in a tennis tournament.

24. You might have rewritten it as follows: "It is raining now." This reduces the information conveyed by the sentence and thereby makes it less precise.

30. Answer (c). The sentence expresses a generalization about women volleyball players.

33. A universal generalization uses *all* or its equivalent; a nonuniversal generalization uses a term that is less universal, such as *many* or *most* or *some*. For example, here is a universal generalization:

   All (healthy) fish can swim.

   Here is a nonuniversal generalization:

   Many fish are smaller than the typical house cat.

   Both generalizations are true.

37. Answer (a). The dispute is merely verbal. The disputed term is *dead*. If the two would just agree on what *dead* means, they would resolve their conflict, because there are no other facts in dispute. Samantha believes that *dead* means there is no heartbeat or breath, but David believes that *dead* means there is no brain activity.

38. Answer (b).

39. Answer (a).

44. The first person could mean *theory* in the sense of a set of general principles, but the second person could mean *theory* in the sense of an uncertain statement, one not backed up by evidence. Both persons would be correct with their own usage of the term.

   A Texas law that was on the books from 1974 to 1984 required that all state-supported school textbooks clearly distinguish scientific fact from mere theory. In particular, the Texas law required the theory of evolution to be taught as a hypothesis on an equal par with the creationist "theory."

   This law perpetuated an error in the philosophy of science that turns on the ambiguity of the word *theory*. When a detective says, "My theory is that the butler committed the crime," the word *theory* means the same as "hypothesis" or "educated guess." The word *theory* can also mean something less specific, such as "a general explanation or general system of laws." In addition, the term can also mean "unjustified opinion or mere hypothesis." The theory of evolution is a theory in the sense of a general explanation, but *the theory of evolution is not a theory in the sense of being a mere hypothesis*; the following comments will try to explain why.

When we distinguish fact from opinion, we mean that a factual claim is an opinion backed up with a solid justification. If a claim is a fact, then it is not just somebody's opinion—it is a true opinion, as far as the experts can tell. It is important here that the vast majority of experts agree; if they disagree with each other, it would be jumping to conclusions to call a theory a "fact." The theory of evolution is sufficiently well justified scientifically that it deserves to be called a "fact." Creationist theory, on the other hand, is without a solid scientific justification, despite the loud objections of a few of its advocates. It has many religious supporters but no significant scientific support.

The theory of evolution is a fact and not just somebody's opinion. It is a fact in the sense in which we say that anything we have good reason to call "true" we also call a "fact." But the theory of evolution is not a *specific fact* as is "This water boiled at about 212 degrees." The theory of evolution is, however, a *general fact* because it is so wide-ranging. It is general because it is a comprehensive system of principles that is used for explaining a wide range of specific facts, such as the fact that dinosaur bones are buried more deeply than human bones, the fact that DNA proteins in human cells are more like those in monkeys than those in tomatoes, and hundreds of other specific facts. Creationism is also a theory in the sense of being general and not specific. It is general, but it is not a general fact.

So, what is the answer to the question, Is evolution a theory or a fact? The answer is that it all depends on how the terms are being defined. It could be both; it might also be neither; or it could be one but not the other. The *theory of evolution is a fact* in the sense of being true. Yet the *theory of evolution is not a fact* because it's a general truth and not a specific truth. The *theory of evolution is a theory* because it's an integrated set of principles. Yet the *theory of evolution is not a theory* in the sense of being a mere opinion without a solid scientific justification.

47b. Not too vague. There is no need for more precision in such a situation. Turning around and saying, "How far up do you mean?" would be likely to be answered with a bullet.

   c. The answer depends on the nurse's background knowledge. The phrase would be too vague if the nurse has no access to more precise directions as to the kind and exact amount of the painkiller that the doctor expects to be administered. The phrase would not be too vague if the doctor could presume that the nurse already had access to such directions, say, on the patient's chart. A simple answer to part (c) such as "Not too vague" or "Too vague" would not adequately demonstrate depth of insight into the exercise.

Chapter 5

1. Yes, you still have a burden of proof. A proof doesn't have to be 100 percent; that standard is required only in mathematics. Informally, a proof is what it takes to be convincing. So, if you want to be convincing, you have the burden of proving your case.

5. "I believe that there can be time travel back to the time of the Egyptian pyramids and the pharaohs because nobody has ever proved that there can't be." Here, the speaker does not realize that, because of the oddity of the claim that there can be time travel, he or she has the burden of proof. It is not sufficient to say the claim has never been disproved; it must instead be proved.

6. The issue is *whether* you should break your promise to Emilio, not *that* you should break your promise to Emilio.

11. The issue is *whether* it would be better for the daughter to have tried and also failed rather than not to have tried at all. In stating what the issue is, be clear what the two (or more) sides could be. For example, it would have been unclear to have answered the question as follows: "The issue is that the friend believes it wouldn't have been better for the daughter to have tried and yet failed." This is true, but it would have been an incorrect answer. It would also have been incorrect simply to make the true statement, "The mother does not really listen to what the friend is saying."

20. Haypole says that the issue is whether Kunsinger is an honest person, but the real issue is whether Haypole changed his position on the death penalty to advance his career or instead changed it because of a good-faith reassessment of the evidence. Haypole doesn't answer Kunsinger's charges that Haypole switched positions to advance his career. Instead, he avoids the issue by launching an attack on Kunsinger himself.

Chapter 6

1. This is a black-white fallacy. An innocent person would have a tough time finding an answer if the question were taken literally. The defendant could escape the two unpleasant choices by saying, "Hey, I never bought any gun, and I never shot the clerk." This defense via pointing out a third possibility

besides the two unpleasant ones is called "escaping between the horns of the dilemma." The D.A. should not have required a simple yes or no answer.

To remove the fallacy, you could make a variety of changes; the easiest is to say, "Did you shoot the clerk?" followed by "Did you buy a gun?" An OK question would be "Just a simple yes or no: did you buy the gun used to shoot the liquor store clerk?" It is not really sufficient to rewrite the question as: "Will you tell us where you bought your gun?" Assuming this is still a yes-no question, the question does not permit the option of "I never bought any gun." However, the questioner might say that no yes-no answer was required, so there was no fallacy; still, the question does set a trap, because if that question receives a "no" for an answer, the D.A. can pounce on the answer, turn to the judge and jury and say, "Now that the defendant has admitted his guilt, I have no further questions."

2. The point of a fallacious ad hominem argument is to attack someone else's reasoning by attacking that person personally. In this example, the person argues against having Columbus Day as a holiday. You could commit the fallacy if you attack this person by saying, "Hey, you are wrong about Columbus Day; you're some sort of bleeding heart liberal, so your word cannot be trusted." The personal attack alone isn't enough to make the fallacy; you must also suggest that this attack somehow shows that the person's reasoning is unreliable. Here is a different sort of ad hominem fallacy: "What do you know about Columbus Day? You and everyone else in your radical organization are out to smear the good name of white people." This latter kind of ad hominem fallacy is called the "fallacy of guilt by association," because the reasoner is said to be guilty of error because of groups he or she associates with.

5. Answer (b). It is often appropriate to appeal to an authority. However, sometimes the appeal is fallacious, as when the wrong authority is quoted or when the authority is apt to lie.

9. Here is one of many ways to create the straw man fallacy:

   The arguer is asking you to join in holding up our lawyers and judges to public ridicule. This is a simple witch hunt, like that in Puritan New England hundreds of years ago. Do you really want to engage in this sort of disgraceful behavior? Hasn't our society lifted itself above the narrow intolerance of the past?

13. Answer (a). The two horns of this dilemma are stated in choice (d). Choice (a) expresses just one horn of that dilemma.

16. Appeal to inappropriate authority. In this argument, *so* is a conclusion indicator term, and the conclusion is preceded by two almost irrelevant reasons.

20. First, notice that Russell is making a joke. He is not committing the ad hominem fallacy, nor is he making a point about conjugation. The serious point behind the joke is that we don't judge others by the same standards that we judge ourselves. The more distant the actor is from us, the more likely we are to see the fault in the action. Therefore, this passage offers another example of how reasoners often do not treat the issue fairly.

21. The conclusion, which is signaled by the conclusion indicator term *therefore*, is just a restatement of the reason for the conclusion. The conclusion does not "go anywhere." Logicians call this kind of error *circular reasoning*.

24. You are not justified in saying she committed a fallacy. Although she used loaded language by calling the suggestion absurd, her letter contains several reasons to back up her charge. Only an expert on economics would be in a position to tell whether her reasons make her case. In short, even if she committed a fallacy, only an expert could tell.

27. The error was made by the mother. She did not respond to her friend's question about whether it would be worse for the daughter to try yet get an F than not to try at all. Therefore, the mother committed the fallacy of avoiding the question, regardless of whether she avoided it on purpose or simply didn't get the point of the question.

Chapter 7

1. a. Description of a quartz crystal oscillator. Not an explanation.

   b. This is an explanation of how a quartz crystal oscillator works in a clock. The passage also provides some additional description of the inside of a clock that uses the oscillator.

   c. Like passage (b), this one describes the inner workings of a certain kind of clock. Compared to (b), it is harder to tell whether any explanation is present. To tell whether an explanation is present, the reader must look at what is said, then try to reconstruct the intentions in the mind of the speaker. If the intentions were to say (1) what causes what, (2) what motivates an action, (3) what purpose something has, or (4) what origin something has, then an explanation is present. Otherwise, there is only description.

5. Betsy Ross is describing but might or might not be explaining, depending on the context. If she just makes this statement out of the blue, she is not offering a cause for some event, nor offering a motivation for what happened. She is simply describing the state of her body or mind. However, if the context were that she has just been asked to explain why she ripped her new flag to pieces, her response would count as an explanation of this action.

6. Answer (a). The passage is describing the constituents of sea water; it is not giving reasons for some conclusion or asking anything of the reader.

Chapter 8

The Principles of Fidelity and Charity

1. The criminal trial of Amy Boycott began yesterday *on the border of* Illinois and Indiana, making headlines in both states.

    This interpretation applies charity by removing the inconsistency, and it applies fidelity by not interpreting the sentence in a way that could not have been intended (as far as you can tell from the evidence available), e.g., by saying there were two trials.

4. If you commit the straw man fallacy, you misinterpret someone's remarks and thus violate the principle of fidelity. However, you can violate the principle without committing that particular fallacy; in fact, you can violate the principle without creating any argument whatsoever.

Improbability

2. Answer (a). The better evidence is required to overcome the initial obstacle of the claim's being so improbable.

5. Answer (d). The article by the priest promises to provide solid information, unlike the sensational book about terrorizing someone's baby. There is no reason to believe that being a priest would unduly influence the author's opinions on this topic. The source of the priest's article, a reputable scientific journal, adds credibility to the priest's comments on this topic. Regarding (b), West Virginia is a big state, so your uncle is not likely to be able to put your neighbor in contact with the right farmers. Even if your uncle could, the information would be valuable only if the farmers said the whole story was false; but if the farmers said the story was true, your neighbor shouldn't accept the story so easily. Such extraordinary claims require extraordinarily good evidence — better evidence than a few stories from the farmers. If their story were backed up by independent investigators from the military and the universities, the story would be much more likely to be true. Regarding (c), the U.S. Army radar operator is likely to have heard stories about other radar operators encountering unidentified objects on their radar screens, but he or she is likely to have unreliable information about those objects; besides, nobody can look at a blip on a radar screen and tell whether it is coming from E.T. So, the best bet is the priest.

7. You can keep your body of beliefs from getting penetrated by a lot of false ideas if you are skeptical and demand decent evidence before embracing an idea.

Chapter 9

Inconsistency

1. Answer (b). Perhaps the person means that it is raining in some place but not raining in some other place. That could be true. Using the principle of charity, you would assume that the person intends to say something true; logically inconsistent statements cannot all be true.

3. Answer (a). This contradicts her statement.

12. The three could all be true, so they are consistent.

13. Answer (a).

14. Answer (a).

15. Answer (b). We have been using the term to mean *logical* consistency.

19. Yes, because the statement that spirit and matter cannot interact means that no spiritual thing can interact with any material thing.

21. No inconsistency nor improbability. However, it is likely that either the guerrillas were lying or they were cheated by the representative.

25. Yes; (a) presupposes what (b) denies.

26. Answer (b). All that is required is that they *could* be true.

28. Answer (a).

32. No. If *exist* can have different senses, then hell might not exist literally as a place you can go to after you die, but it might exist here on Earth in people's minds. However, if *exist* cannot have this latter sense, then the second statement is simply false, but still not inconsistent with the first.

33. Answer (b).

36. It follows that one of them said something false. It doesn't follow that anyone was *intending* to say something false — i.e., lying.

41. Yes, they are inconsistent. From the first three statements, it follows that we will all die. From the fourth, it follows that we won't. This is an inconsistency. If you know something, then it is true; that idea is applied to the fourth statement.

Counterexamples

2. (a) All (present or past) basketball players are HIV positive. (b) Magic Johnson (a basketball player for the Los Angeles Lakers) is HIV positive. (c) Johnny Dawkins (a basketball player for the Philadelphia 76ers) is not HIV positive.

3. All even numbers are integers.

6. Consider the example of a promise you made to your friend to return the knife you borrowed. In the situation in which he rushes up to you raving mad and saying he wants his knife back so he can kill his mother, you should break your promise.

   Saying "You should not keep promises that might hurt someone" is a relevant answer. It is in the ballpark, but it is inadequate because it provides no specific *example* of a promise. A counterexample is always a specific example from the category that the generalization is about.

Chapter 10

Following From and Implication

1. Answer (a). If *all* ice melts, then the president's ice melts, too.

2. The correct answer is "Yes and no." No, it doesn't follow with certainty, but yes, it does follow with significant probability. The mere fact that the person is arrested is some reason to increase your degree of belief in the person's guilt. Usually the police arrest the correct persons. However, police do make mistakes, so even if it does follow, from the person's being arrested, that the person is guilty, it doesn't follow with sufficient probability that a member of the jury should vote for conviction on this evidence alone.

4. It follows from what Jeremy Irons says but it doesn't follow from his saying it. The two need to be distinguished. The reasoning in the paragraph doesn't distinguish them. There may also be a second error. It may misinterpret what *follows from* means. In this context, "B follows from A" simply means that B is forced to be true if A is true. The reasoner may have supposed it meant instead that A is the most important reason to believe B. The requirements in the U.S. Constitution are in fact the most important reasons to believe that the U.S. president is a citizen, but the president's being a citizen follows from all sorts of statements. It even follows from the false statement that all two-legged beings are citizens.

10. Answer (a). This is the correct answer because, if you own it, you certainly have it, and if it's a pig, it's certainly an animal.

12. Answer (b). Given when the song was created, and your background knowledge that in those times most farms were family owned, it is probable that he actually owns the farm rather than is a tenant farmer or leases the land, though you cannot be *sure* that he owns it.

19. Answer (a). It is deductively valid because the conclusion is forced to be true whenever the premises are. Of course, we have no way of knowing whether the premises are actually true, so we cannot judge the argument's soundness.

22. Answer (a).

26. Yes, they all are.

27. Yes, they all are.

36. Answer (a). It's a matter of what *asexual* means.

Drawing Implications from Charts and Graphs

5. Answer (b), lettuce, according to the second chart.

Chapter 11

Detecting Single, Explicit Arguments

1. Answer (a). The conclusion is:

> Dynamic random access memory (DRAM) chips are the popular choice for memory storage on personal computers.

One clue is the premise indicator term *since*.

4. *Suppose that*.

5. *Thus*.

6. Yes, the word *since* is used *twice* as a premise indicator.

12. Answer (d).

14. Not an argument. Could it be interpreted as an argument for the conclusion that Snow White is the fairest of them all? Couldn't the reasons for this conclusion be that the mirror said so? No, what is happening in the passage is not an argument trying to convince the reader or the queen of this conclusion. Instead, the queen asked a question about who is the fairest, and the mirror answered that it is Snow White and proceeded to *describe* Snow White. The passage is a narrative, a story. The passage does give sufficient information to draw the conclusion that Snow White is the fairest for the reason that the mirror said so, yet the reader is not expected to do this kind of reasoning. The reader can tell from the rest of the passage that the writer's intent is merely to provide the information that Snow White is fairest and then to elaborate on the point by providing the information about the mirror.

19. The conclusion of her argument is not clear. It could be either "The percentage of American homes containing personal computers is more like 80 percent," or it could be "There is a personal computer in nearly every American home." The two conclusions are almost equivalent. Here is the standard form if you selected the first one:

> We have two computers at home.
> All of my friends have at least one computer.
> _____
> The percentage of American homes containing personal computers is more like 80 percent.

To assess the argument's strength, ask yourself these questions: Is it a proof of its conclusion? Is it deductively valid? Is it inductively strong? In fact, the argument is inductively weak.

20. It is not an argument. The passage is just a description of scientific change though history.

Conditionals

2. Yes. A statement that expresses a deductively valid argument is true.

Implicit Elements of Arguments

1. Answer (a). If all the premises were left unstated, there would be no arguing and instead merely the making of a claim.

3. Your mother, too, will be killed by AIDS. The argument is deductively valid.

5. *All* zebras have stripes.
   That animal is a zebra. [implicit]
   _____
   That animal has stripes.

The conclusion "That animal is going to have stripes" is logically equivalent to "That animal has stripes," by the principle of charity. If it weren't, the argument wouldn't be deductively valid.

10. None contain arguments.

13. Answer (a).

17. Her capitalism argument was described this way:

> Stories critical of the free enterprise system offend her, she said, because "capitalism is ordained by God."

Rewriting this argument in standard form makes it clearer:

> The free enterprise system is a form of capitalism.
> Capitalism is ordained by God.
> Anything critical of something ordained by God is offensive.
> _____
>
> Stories critical of the free enterprise system are offensive.

Multiple Arguments

1. The subargument in standard form is:

> Galileo said good science uses mathematics.
> _____
>
> Good science uses mathematics.

The subargument is an argument from authority. Here is the tree diagram for the entire argumentation:

A = Galileo said good science uses mathematics.

B = Good science uses mathematics.

C = Charles Darwin's work on evolution contains no mathematics.

D = Charles Darwin's work on evolution is not good science.

The subargument in this argument is the following:

9.

Cynthia   Not-Like

Not-David   Not-Michael   Kings-Tickets   Not-Steve   Candidates

Not-Yolanda–Saturday Night

Other-Class

Cynthia = David is living with Cynthia.

Not-Like = David doesn't really like Yolanda.

Not-David = David can't be convinced to go out with Yolanda Saturday night.

Kings-Tickets = Michael and Yolanda haven't said much to each other ever since she got stuck holding the extra Kings tickets that she couldn't resell.

Not-Michael = Michael can't be convinced to go out with Yolanda Saturday night.

Not-Steve = Steve can't be convinced to go out with Yolanda Saturday night.

Candidates = David, Michael, and Steve are the only possible candidates for finding someone to go out with Yolanda on Saturday night.

Not-Yolanda–Saturday Night = There's no way that Yolanda is going out Saturday night with anyone from our class.

Other-Class = If Yolanda goes out Saturday night, it will be with someone not in our class.

Chapter 12
Analogies, Typical Examples and Inductions from the Past
to the Future

1. Conclusion: Winning an election depends on a great crime. A = amassing a fortune; B = winning an election; C = depends on a great crime.

2. An abortion clinic is like a nest of wasps in that both harm innocent persons.
    A nest of wasps deserves to be bombed (with pesticides).
    _____

    Abortion clinics deserve to be bombed.

6. This argument is weak. Here is a better argument:

    All liquids seek their own level when not confined.

    Mercury is a liquid.

    So, Mercury will seek its own level, too, when not confined.

    The first premise follows from a scientific theory of liquids. The reason that the original argument is weak as it stands is that it is quite similar to the following inductively weak argument:

    Mercury is like water in that they are both liquids. Water is a thirst-quenching liquid, so the mercury in that thermometer is, too.

    Mercury is actually poisonous, as are all metals.

13. Defeating Princeton in baseball would be like taking candy from a baby.

16. Answer (a). This will make it more believable because it will make it more difficult for her to cheat. In short, you will have a better-designed experiment.

    (b) The answer is 25 percent, which is one queen out of four.

    (c) It probably wasn't significant, because so few tests were run. Maybe she guessed twice and was correct one of the two times. Do more tests.

22. Conclusion: David will continue to cheat if he is hired to work the cash register in our office. It's an argument from the past to the future. The past pattern of cheating will continue in the future. The comment about leopards is a common expression used to make the point that old patterns will continue to hold in the future.
    This passage could be analyzed as containing two arguments. First comes the argument mentioned in the preceding paragraph. The second argument has more implicit elements: its conclusion is that we shouldn't hire David. The argument contains implicit premises about it being unwise to hire people who cheat, especially if the job is to work a cash register. It is unclear, however, whether the second argument actually occurs; perhaps it doesn't and we are just guessing that the second argument is likely to be created or accepted by the arguer.

25. The argument probably will be weaker, because there is now less similarity between the past and the future in regard to a causally relevant characteristic. In particular, the fertilizer might make the crop more hardy and thus more resistant to the pest. Only if you knew that adding this fertilizer would tend to hurt the crop — say, by promoting pest growth — could you say that the argument would be strengthened. If you didn't know whether adding the fertilizer would help or hurt the crop, just the fact that you know that adding it would be likely to *affect* the crop is reason enough to say the argument is weaker.

Generalizing from a Sample

4. No. Such a sampling procedure won't *guarantee* a correct conclusion. Only a deductive argument will do that. Generalizing from sampling less than 100 percent of the population is always risky.

5. For example, your sample of blueberries (which you discover to be 10 percent fuzzy) might be representative of all the blueberries in your carton (which are also 10 percent fuzzy), even though you picked your samples only off the top row. A sample might be representative of a population even if obtained in a biased way. Getting a random sample is one of several methods that will help get a representative sample, but a representative sample can also be obtained by luck.

7. (a) The sample consisted of an unspecified number of black children. (b) The population was all black children (presumably now rather than 40 years ago). The conclusion of the induction was that two-thirds of the black children in the population prefer a white doll. (c) Proter said that the sample was biased by the fact that the children in the sample were too young. We have little information to go on regarding the sample. A further generalization was inferred from that generalization—namely, that black children have more feelings of racial inferiority than white children, although this induction is not an induction by sampling.

11. This could well be true. Being unbiased only promotes the production of a representative sample; it won't guarantee it.

Chapter 13

Correlations

1. You need to do nothing. If *A* is correlated with *B*, then *B* must be correlated with *A*.

3. Answer (b).

4. iv. Answer (a).

6. Would you find less death if you looked at nonbreathers? There is no significant correlation.

Identifying Causal Claims

2. The setting of the sun causes darkness.

4. a. causal

   b. causal

   c. causal

   d. causal

   e. correlational

   f. causal

   g. correlational

5. *Effect*: The nickel rise in gasoline prices. *Cause*: The increase today of federal taxes on gasoline from 9 cents a gallon to 14 cents.

6. Claim (a). It makes a specific causal claim rather than a general one.

Inferring from Correlation to Cause

4. First, by making a universal generalization from just one example, the speaker is committing the fallacy of hasty generalization. In addition, there is no file at all if there is just one member of the file. If you noticed that one muskrat cannot walk single file, then you realized that the generalization is an inconsistent remark. By the principle of charity, you might consider assuming that the one muskrat was walking single file with other nonmuskrats; however, this assumption probably violates the principle of fidelity because it lessens the impact of the original joke and because there is no other indication that any other animals were observed. (This joke was told to the author by Robert Garmston.)

7. Answer (a). This description of the scientific method as being the method of conjectures and refutations was first clearly stated by Karl Popper.

Chapter 14

3. Ranking of groups: (1) emeralds, (2) non-green things, (3) green things and non-emeralds. The most useful group to examine would be the emeralds. Check to see that they are all green. If you can't do that, then check the non-green things making sure you don't discover an emerald in there.

7. Doesn't satisfy the improbability condition for a good test. The test result would be likely to occur either way.

9. The sports writer wasn't claiming prophetic powers; he or she was merely using the evidence at hand to guess what the future might bring. What the sports writer did is ordinary; the Bartholomew prediction is extraordinary, and extraordinary claims require extraordinarily good evidence. If the story about the Detroit Pistons is true, nothing much turns on that fact, compared with the story about Brother Bartholomew—at least nothing much as far as our worldview is concerned. If the prophecy part of the Bartholomew story is correct, then science's fundamental beliefs about precognition (seeing into the future) will need to be revolutionized.

16. Aardsma is treating the flood story as being unfalsifiable. Doing so is methodologically suspect, the establishment scientists would say.

18. The two are using the words *theory* and *fact* differently. The first person means by *theory* a general system of laws, and means by *fact* that these laws are true. The opponent could be doing one of two things: (i) he or she could mean by *theory* something that is general and mean by *fact* something that is not general; and in these senses a theory cannot be a fact. (ii) The opponent could mean by *theory* something that is poorly supported by the evidence and mean by *fact* something that is well supported by the evidence; and in these senses a theory cannot be a fact. If the opponent is using the terms in sense (i), then the two people are merely having a semantic disagreement; each could easily agree with the other once they straightened out how they are using their terms. But if the opponent is using the terms in sense (ii), then not only are the two persons disagreeing about the meaning of the terms, they are also disagreeing about whether the theory of evolution is well supported by the evidence. See p. A-65.

Appendix B

1. Perform the litmus test. Take a strip of purple litmus paper and dip it into the liquid. If, when removed, the paper is red, the liquid is an acid.

2. The definition is too broad. It is imprecise because it does not say what kind of fox, and it should say what kind because not all foxes are vixens.

4. An operational definition.

8. The definition of *science* in the dictionary is too broad because it includes too many things among the sciences. Being systematic is only one of the requirements for science. The definition of *science* could be improved to prevent phone books and repair manuals from being included by noting that science is a systematic way of *explaining and predicting* events. Science is not merely a systematic collection of facts.

14(b). Too figurative, and thus too imprecise for seriously conveying the meaning of *history*.

Appendix C

Logical Equivalence
1. Yes.

The Logic of *Not*, *And*, *Or*, and *If-Then*
1. The argument can be treated in sentential logic using the following definitions of the sentences (clauses):

> PC = politicians are corrupt
>
> FRIENDS = the friends of politicians are corrupt
>
> PECULIAR = politicians have peculiar friends

Here is the logical form:

> If PC, then FRIENDS.
> If FRIENDS, then PECULIAR.
> _____
> If not-PC, Then not-PECULIAR.

This form is invalid. It commits a fallacy that is related to the fallacy of denying the antecedent. Maybe the invalidity is easier to see by using a logical analogy. Here is an analogous argument that is also invalid:

> If it's a house cat, then it's a feline.
> If it's a feline, then it's a mammal.
> _____
> If it's not a house cat, then it's not a mammal.

This argument has true premises and a false conclusion.

6. Valid.

7. Yes.

16. Valid because its sentential form is modus tollens. The argument is superficially invalid but is actually valid when the principle of charity is used in these two ways: (1) to say that the conclusion is logically equivalent to "Einstein is not alive," and (2) to add the implicit premise that the physics at Princeton University in New Jersey is not affected by the presence of Einstein.

Necessary and Sufficient Conditions

2. That will depend on some formula that was agreed on the first day of class. Perhaps your getting an average of 70 percent for the course as a whole is sufficient to pass the course.

The Logic of *Only, Only If,* and *Unless*

5. Answer (e). It would be true to say "*x* is even unless *x* is odd." Adding the *not* makes (e) not fit in the blank.

11. (i) Answer (b). The phrase *only if* works like *if-then* in the sense that "Inquiry is justified only if employee has understanding" is logically equivalent to "If inquiry is justified, then employee has understanding." Note that statement (i) is the converse of this—namely, "If employee has understanding, then inquiry is justified." Consequently, (i) does not follow from the statement containing the *only if*, which is why the answer is (b).

14. Yes. The first is equivalent to "not-*A* or *B*." The second is equivalent to "*A* implies *B*." These two are equivalent to each other.

Appendix D

1. *A* = fruit, *B* = oranges, *C* = things that grow on trees.

3. There are many acceptable diagrams. The relationship between voters and rich people is not fixed by the sentence. Consequently, you have leeway about where the voters' area can go. It can go outside the rich area, it can intersect it, or it can be wholly within it—provided that the voter area is wholly separate from the American area. In the following diagram all the voters are rich, but this need not be true in other acceptable diagrams.

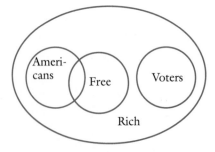

5. Answer (a).

10. Although you weren't asked for the standard form, here it is:

> All modern works of art are profound works of art.
> Not all profound works of art are modern works of art.
> Some religious works of art are modern works of art.
> Some religious works of art are not modern works of art.
> _____
> Some religious works of art fail to be profound.

The logical form of the argument is:

All *M* are *P*.
Not all *P* are *M*.
Some *R* are *M*.
Some *R* are not *M*.
_____

Some *R* are not *P*.

where we used these definitions:

M = (the class of) modern works of art

P = the profound works of art

R = religious works of art

"Not all *P* are *M*" means that not all members of *P* are members of *M*.

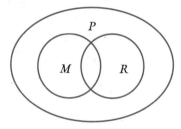

This diagram shows that the argument is deductively invalid because the diagram makes the premises (of the logical form) true while the conclusion is false.

11. Answer (a).

15. It is invalid because of the possibility of the situation shown in the following diagram:

16. To find the answer, translate it into the kind of English that more obviously talks about classes and that uses the terms *all*, *some*, and *none* in place of their equivalents.

All early entrants are prize winners.
Some avaricious beings are early entrants.
Some avaricious beings are not early entrants.
_____

Some prize winners aren't avaricious.

The logical form of the above is:

All *EE* are *PW*.
Some *AB* are *EE*.
Some *AB* are not *EE*.
_____

Some *PW* are not *AB*.

where

    EE = (the class of) early entrants

    PW = (the class of) prize winners

    AB = (the class of) avaricious beings

Goal: To draw a diagram showing that the argument can have true premises while having a false conclusion — the sure sign of deductive invalidity. The diagram below achieves this goal:

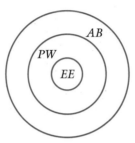

26. All pairs from the group {a, b, c, d} are logically equivalent.

28. Yes, they say the same thing, using the principle of charity. They are different grammatically but not logically. It is possible to interpret the two sentences as saying different things in the sense that the first might mean modern in time and the second might mean modern in style. However, if you make the latter point, you should also notice that the two *could be* (better yet, are *likely to be*) logically equivalent; it is wrong to say they definitely are not equivalent. In fact, if the two sentences were used in a piece of reasoning and they did have different meanings, and if the context didn't make this clear, the reasoner would be accused of committing the fallacy of equivocation.

Endnotes

Chapter 1

1. Here is some more information about *Giardia* from Cindy Ross, a columnist for *Backpacker* magazine, as reported by Kerry Drager in *The Sacramento Bee*, June 5, 1991, p. D11. Boiling is safer than using most water purification tablets, especially iodine tablets, because the tablets often don't completely sterilize the water. According to Drager, "Heating water to a full boil for at least one minute kills *Giardia*. 'Boiling will also destroy other organisms causing waterborne disease,' the National Park Service points out, 'although at high altitudes you should maintain the boil three to five minutes for an additional margin of safety.' . . . Chemical disinfectants, such as iodine tablets, are inexpensive, lightweight and easy to use, but they are not always effective in killing *Giardia*. And, says Ross, 'There's a waiting time of 5 to 20 minutes, depending on water temperature. Iodine also leaves a foul taste in your mouth.'"

2. Appendix C shows that contrary sentences are inconsistent but not contradictory. See page A-23.

Chapter 2

1. The word *claim* here refers to some statement or other. A statement is what people make when they use a declarative sentence. Normally, you don't make a statement when you ask a question or give an instruction.

2. Adapted from Laurel Pallock, "Consumer Check List" *San Francisco Chronicle*, February 1, 1989.

3. Adapted from a remark in *Consumer Reports* magazine.

4. From *Los Angeles Times*, reprinted in *The Sacramento Bee*, September 27, 1987, p. A18.

5. This claim is from a column "prepared as a public service by the American Psychiatric Association" which quotes Dr. Linda Teplin, of the Department of Psychiatry and Behavioral Sciences, Northwestern University Medical School, as saying that "the mentally ill [in her study] did not commit . . . crimes at a rate disproportionate to their numbers. . . . Thus it is particularly unfortunate that the mentally ill continue to be portrayed by the news and entertainment industry as crazed and violent people." Reprinted in the *Newsletter of the Alliance for the Mentally Ill of Napa State Hospital*, March 1991. In a letter to *Science News* of January 18, 1992, Teplin says, "The current thinking on this issue is that the severely ill are *no more* — or at worst only *slightly more* — violent than the non-severely ill." The less severely ill are significantly less violent.

6. From the University of California, Berkeley *Wellness Letter* (The Newsletter of Nutrition, Fitness, and Stress Management), December 1990, p. 7.

7. PDM, Inc. Westbury, New York, from an advertisement in *Weekly World News*, vol. 7, issue 4, November 5, 1985.

8. Adapted from a complaint made in *Consumer Reports* magazine.

9. So says Harry Snyder, West Coast director of Consumers Union, according to Rick Kushman in "Do What It Takes, Political Pros Told," *The Sacramento Bee*, April 24, 1989, pp. A1, A11.

10. "The Packaging of Reagan — 1984" by Leo Rennert, *The Sacramento Bee*, September 20, 1988, p. A12.

11. Adapted from Dave Cassafer, "Media Watch" in *Psientific American*, August 1990, p. 2.

Chapter 3

1. From a list of signs reported on by Jon Carroll in the *San Francisco Chronicle*, July 30, 1990.

2. Ibid.

3. From *The Sacramento Bee*, February 24, 1988.

4. "Dear Abby," *The Sacramento Bee*, July 27, 1987.

5. "Death Prayers: A New Extremist Tactic," *Forum*, Fall 1986, p. 12, People For the American Way, Washington, D.C.

6. From *CT Flea Market*, Spring 1988, vol. 2, no. 1, Mayfield Publishing Co., p. 2.

7. *The Sacramento Bee*, February 24, 1988.

8. How about "hexagonally cross-sectioned, graphite cored, inscription device"?

9. These examples were collected by James Hollinseed at California State University, Sacramento.

Chapter 4

1. From *Red Tape Holds Up New Bridge and More Flubs from the Nation's Press*, edited by Gloria Cooper, collected by the *Columbia Journalism Review*, Putnam Publishing Group, copyright by Columbia University of New York, 1987.

2. Syntax is grammar. Semantics deals with meaning and reference, that is, with certain relations between expressions in a language and the objects or states of affairs referred to by those expressions.

3. The two meanings seem to be quite distinct. Actually they arose from the same prior word *bank*, which meant what we now mean by "shelf." People used to think of moneykeepers as storing their wealth on shelves, and the side of the river was thought of as a shelf that held dirt above the water.

4. This joke by Woody Allen is logically inconsistent because it literally says the author doesn't believe in life after death, yet the fact of his taking along a change of underwear when he dies implies that he really does believe there is life after death. The joke implies the author holds logically inconsistent beliefs.

5. This statement appeared in the *Allentown Morning Call*, as quoted in *The New Yorker*, August 17, 1987, p. 72.

6. Much of the material on machine processing of natural language is adapted from "Computer Software for Working with Language" by Terry Winograd in *Scientific American*, vol. 251, no. 3, September 1984, pp. 131–145.

7. The real Professor Weddle is a distinguished researcher in the field of critical thinking and logical reasoning and is not at all confused about these matters.

8. Is the word *tree* in "He purchased a tree at the nursery" ambiguous or vague or general? In answer to this question, consider the fact that the word *tree* could refer to apple tree or maple tree, but that's not ambiguity, because there are not multiple meanings involved, only multiple references. If there were a problem about whether the tree is a phone tree, then there would be ambiguity, but the context here rules out the phone tree. However, the term *tree* refers to a class — the class of trees of which apple and maple are members. So, *tree* is general even if not ambiguous. Is it also vague? It is vague only insofar as you have trouble with borderline cases. Because we do have trouble telling whether tall shrubs are trees, to that extent the word is vague. Consequently, the answer to our original question is that the term *tree* is not ambiguous, yet it is both vague and general. However, it is not important for most persons (e.g., the readers of this book) to be skilled at classifying a term this way. That is a skill for philosophers and linguists.

9. "Astrologers Make Their Predictions for 1991" by Pat Christensen, *The Independent*, January 1, 1991.

10. This sentence uses the word *imply* in the sense of "require." The word *imply* also can be used in the sense of "suggest," although it usually will not be used that way in this text.

11. From *The Sacramento Bee*, June 6, 1987, p. E10.

12. From *Red Tape Holds Up New Bridge and More Flubs from the Nation's Press* edited by Gloria Cooper, collected by the *Columbia Journalism Review*, Putnam Publishing Group, copyright by Columbia University of New York, 1987.

13. Ibid.

14. From *Suttertown News*, March 9, 1987.

15. From David Macaulay, *The Way Things Work* (Boston: Houghton Mifflin, 1988), p. 160.

Chapter 5

1. Adapted from remarks made in program 20 of the syndicated TV series *Against All Odds: Inside Statistics*, copyright by The Consortium of Mathematics and its Applications, Inc., 1988.

2. Liberally adapted from an article by Eric Mattson in *The Sacramento Bee*, September 17, 1990.

3. From *Interview*, July 1987. p. 46.

4. From "Surgeon General Rebukes Tobacco Industry over Combative Ads," by Irvin Molotsky, *The New York Times*, national edition, January 12, 1989, p. A7.

5. From *The Sacramento Bee*, May 22, 1987.

6. Adapted from a letter to the editor by Edward Peizer, *The New York Times*, national edition, June 6, 1989, p. A18.

7. From "Cutting Edge" by Sally Roesch Wagner, *Suttertown News*, August 20–27, 1987.

8. Extracted from her remarks in "Unequal Partners," *The Washington Post Magazine*, June 28, 1987, pp. 46–47.

Chapter 6

1. From "Justice O'Connor Regrets 'Christian Nation' Letter," James H. Rubin, *The Sacramento Bee*, March 16, 1989, p. A28.

2. From *Psientific American*, June 1987, p. 4.

3. From *The New York Times*, June 14, 1988.

Chapter 7

1. From Cheri Smith, *Suttertown News*, March 19, 1987.

2. From *The Detroit News and Free Press*, December 1, 1990, p. 1.

3. From *Science News*, August 16, 1986, p. 105.

4. From John Steinbeck, *The Grapes of Wrath* (New York: Bantam Books, 1972), p. 7.

5. Ibid., p. 13.

6. Ibid., pp. 14–16.

7. From William Faulkner, "A Bear Hunt," *Collected Stories of William Faulkner*, (New York: Vintage Books, 1977), p. 65.

8. These first sentences of the paragraph are from comments by the American philosopher Morris R. Cohen, but they are taken out of context; they were not originally given as a criticism of William James's views.

9. The question in this passage is from A. L. Lehninger's *Principles of Biochemistry*, according to Ed Regis in *Great Mambo Chicken & The Transhuman Condition*, Chapter 6 (Addison-Wesley). Some statements in this passage are adapted from remarks by Regis in his Chapter 6.

10. Steinbeck, p. 235.

Chapter 8

1. Eddie Clontz, Reuters dispatch, reprinted in *The Sacramento Bee*, November 26, 1988, p. A2.

2. Adapted, with changes, from classified advertisements that appeared in *Discover* magazine, June 1987, p. 106.

3. As reported by Rick Kushman, "TV Radically Changes Our View of Politics," *The Sacramento Bee*, February 4, 1992, pp. A1, A8.

4. From Jerry Mander, *Four Arguments for the Elimination of Television*, pp. 292–293, copyright 1977, 1978 by Jerry Mander, William Morrow and Company, Inc., 105 Madison Ave., New York, NY 10016. Morrow Quill Paperback Edition.

5. *Kauai Beach Press*, July 29–August 4, 1991, p. A-14.

6. From *Weekly World News*, February 9, 1988, p. 25.

Chapter 9

1. We cannot imagine it unless we allow words to change their meanings — which we do *not* allow for purposes of assessing possibility. If we were to permit language to go on holiday this way, there would never be any inconsistency.

2. From *Newsweek*, September 26, 1988, p. 15.

3. Gandhi was a Hindu leader who advocated nonviolence as a means of expelling the British from India. India did become a republic in 1950, although Gandhi was assassinated in 1948 by an anti-Hindu Muslim.

4. The first explanation is supported but not totally confirmed. Not all reasonable explanations have been considered, such as the bulb not being screwed in properly, or the power having been off temporarily.

5. United Feature Syndicate, Inc., 1956.

6. From "Moneylist" by Bremdon Boyd, *The Sacramento Bee*, April 10, 1988.

7. From *The Sacramento Bee*, September 9, 1987, p. B6.

8. From "Books: Goody Sergeant, The Powerful Katrinka; K.S.W." by John Updike, *The New Yorker*, August 10, 1987, p. 75.

Chapter 10

1. From *The Sacramento Bee*, September 14, 1987, p. B11.

2. Andrew Johnson was Abraham Lincoln's vice-president. He was president after Lincoln and before Grant.

3. Note to instructors: This text intentionally does not draw the fine distinction between a syntactic and a semantic definition of implication. Similarly, no distinction is made between a syntactic definition of inconsistency and a semantic one.

4. Using this technical terminology, *valid inductive argument* and *sound inductive argument* would be nonsense phrases (technically speaking).

5. From *The Sacramento Bee*, June 2, 1989, p. B2.

6. San Francisco Chronicle Research, California Department of Water Resources, California Department of Food and Agriculture. Adapted from the *San Francisco Chronicle*, March 4, 1991, p. C1.

7. Water Education Foundation, Sacramento, California. Adapted from the *San Francisco Chronicle*, March 4, 1991, p. C1.

8. The figures are for 1985, but for the purposes of this exercise, assume that the figures hold today.

Chapter 11

1. From *The Sacramento Bee*, February 6, 1988, p. 1, by Maria Newman, Mexico City Bureau.

2. From Mike Dunne, "Relaxed Elegance at Village Choice," *The Sacramento Bee*, August 23, 1987, p. Encore 24.

3. Ellen Robinson-Haynes, "Cronkite Gives Us the Bad News About Medicine," *The Sacramento Bee*, December 17, 1990, p. A21.

4. From *Newsweek*, July 28, 1986. Copyright 1986, Newsweek, Inc. All rights reserved. Reprinted by permission.

5. Note to instructors: The method of displaying the support relationship between premises and conclusions is called *tree diagraming* because the structure is like a tree in mathematical graph theory. However, because a premise may directly support more than one conclusion, the diagram is mathematically a lattice rather than a tree. It's only because the term *tree* is more familiar than *lattice*, that I've chosen the name *tree diagram*.

6. From Isabel Wilkerson, "Illinois Top Court Rejects Chicago School Reform Law," *Detroit Free Press*, December 1, 1990, p. 4A.

7. Mark D. Grossman and Connie Matthiessen, "Why Meat and Poultry May No Longer Be Safe," *The Sacramento Bee*, September 21, 1986.

8. From *The New Yorker*, June 9, 1986.

9. From *Personal Computing*, June 1987, p. 293.

10. Stefi Weisburd, "Celebrating Newton," *Science News*, July 4, 1987, p. 11. Reprinted with permission from SCIENCE NEWS, the weekly newsmagazine of science, copyright 1987 by Science Service, Inc.

11. From *Suttertown News*, March 9, 1987.

12. *Science News*, vol. 139, January 26, 1991, p. 139, from an advertisement for *A Forest of Kings*.

13. Mitch Albom, "The Picks," *Detroit Free Press*, December 1, 1990, p. 3B.

14. From *Discover*, September 1990, p. 14.

Chapter 12

1. The first and third paragraphs of this passage are from Robin Evelegh, *Peace-Keeping in a Democratic Society: The Lessons of Northern Ireland* (London: C. Hurst & Co., 1978), pp. 133–136.

2. In a later chapter we'll see that this testimonial commits the post hoc fallacy.

3. This example was suggested by Angela Scripa.

4. The information in this paragraph is from Gina Kolata, "Are U.S. Students the Worst? Comparisons Seen as Flawed," *The New York Times*, national edition, December 24, 1991, p. B6.

5. Art Nauman, "The Ombudsman," *The Sacramento Bee*, June 21, 1987, pp. B1, B5.

6. Reprinted by permission of Lillibeth Navarro.

7. By Daniel Goleman, *The New York Times*, August 31, 1987, p. 1.

8. From Tim LaHaye, *The Battle for the Mind* (Old Tappan, N.J.: Fleming H. Renell, 1980), p. 110.

Chapter 13

1. These are discrete, not continuous variables; that is, the points on the graphs are disconnected. Many other variables are continuous — e.g., time, altitude, degree of satisfaction with a politician. Continuous variables can always be turned into discrete variables by dividing the continuum into separate categories; for example, one could use the discrete variable of time-to-the-nearest-minute.

Correlation between two variables can actually be quantified. That is, a number can be assigned to the correlation. The number, called the *correlation coefficient*, can range from minus one for a negative correlation to plus one for a positive correlation. In this chapter, we will not investigate how to calculate these coefficients. The correlation coefficient is a measure of how well a straight line graph will represent the data. Consider a graph that looks like this:

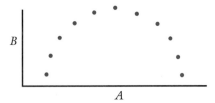

This graph has a small correlation coefficient, so a straight line does not do a good job of representing this graph. Nevertheless, there is clearly some sort of correlation between A and B, a *nonlinear correlation*.

2. From *The Sacramento Bee*, July 10, 1987, p. A22.

3. Statisticians prefer to use a somewhat more complicated measure of strength for correlations, but this definition can be quite helpful as a rule of thumb.

4. R. Foster Winans, "Wall Street Ponders If Bull Market in '84 Hinges on Redskins," *The Wall Street Journal*, January 18, 1984, p. 49.

5. The claim about chocolate is false. The claim about pollen might or might not be true, depending on the circumstances. Because you don't know the circumstances, you are not in a position to call it false.

6. In some systems, there are *no* determinate causes to be found. So-called "stochastic systems" behave this way. Quantum mechanics is a theory of nature that treats natural systems as being stochastic in the sense that the state of the system at one time merely makes other states probable; it does not determine which state will occur. Systems described by quantum mechanics are stochastic systems. So are the systems of inheritance of genes, which the Austrian monk Gregor Mendel first described in the nineteenth century.

7. Unlike a mathematical proof, which is a deductively sound argument, a scientific proof establishes

its conclusion only with high probability. A scientific proof is simply a strong inductive argument.

8. Reprinted by permission of *West County Times*. Author's name has been changed.

9. This is a variation on a joke by Howard Kahane, *Logic and Contemporary Rhetoric: The Use of Reason in Everyday Life*, 4th ed. (Wadsworth, 1984), p. 111.

10. From *The Detroit News and Free Press*, December 1, 1990, p. 1.

11. From the *Chicago Tribune* as reported in *The Sacramento Bee*, August 9, 1991, p. A13.

12. Joanne Silberner, "No Free Lunch," *Science News*, vol. 130, December 6, 1986, p. 360. Reprinted with permission from SCIENCE NEWS, the weekly newsmagazine of science, copyright 1986 by Science Service, Inc.

13. From *The Sacramento Bee*, April 20, 1988, pp. A1, A15.

Chapter 14

1. From Herbert Butterfield, *The Origins of Modern Science 1300–1800*, rev. ed. New York: Free Press, 1957), pp. 7–8.

2. Although the review has not introduced any new scientific concepts, it has developed a few concepts in somewhat more depth.

3. Charles Hillinger, "Island Cult Waiting for John Frum," the *Los Angeles Times*, August 10, 1978, pp. 1, 6, 7.

4. Some textbook authors sure do make some fantastic assumptions, don't they?

5. Whether future psychology will ever be able to do any better is one of the major issues in an area of philosophy called the philosophy of psychology.

6. These criteria for a good test are well described by Ronald Giere in his *Understanding Scientific Reasoning* (New York: Holt, Rinehart and Winston, 1979), pp. 101–105.

7. Adapted from S. Boxer, "Will Creationism Rise Again?" *Discover*, vol. 8, October 1987, pp. 80–85.

Appendix A

1. From the *San Francisco Chronicle*, March 28, 1972, p. 21. This example was suggested by Jamil Nammour.

Index

A

Accuracy, 362–363
Ad hoc rescue. *See* Fallacy, ad hoc rescue
Ad hominem, 107–108, 123, 125, A-2
Advertising, 14, 47, 289, 341
   cigarettes and, 28, 93
   political campaigns and, 181–184
   techniques of deception in, 22–36, 113–115, 180–181, 227, 301, 334
AI. *See* Artificial intelligence
Alternative explanation, 340, 379–381
Alternative hypothesis, 340, 379–381
Ambiguity
   and artificial intelligence, 59–61
   definition of, 55–64, 73, 76–77
   in definitions, A-13, A-16
   and multiple reference, A-78
Ambiguous. *See* Ambiguity
Analogy. *See* Faulty analogy; Induction, by analogy
Anecdotal evidence (fallacy of), A-2
Anecdote, 177, 190, 366
Antecedent of a conditional, A-28, A-34
Appeal to a typical example, 286, 291–292, 311, 313
Appeal to authority. *See* Fallacy, appeal to authority; Induction, argument from authority
Argument
   complex and atomic, 15
   definition of, 4, 13, 16, 151, 162, 222

and description and explanation, 135–140, 154–155, 162
   diagram of, 260–265
   independence of, 263
   main, 259
   mathematical and scientific, 151
   structure of, 15, 258–266. *See also* Logical form
   structure of argument chain, 258–259
   structure of multiple arguments, 258–266
   structure of subargument, 258–266
Argumentative essay, 135–162, 165–179
Artificial intelligence (AI), 59–61, 77, 160–162, 202
Association. *See* Correlation
Assumption: *See* Premise
Astrology, 67, 79, 221
Authority. *See* Credibility of sources and experts; Induction, argument from authority; Science, reporting of
Average, ambiguity of, 75
Avoiding the issue, 89, 96, 123, A-3
Avoiding the question, 89, 96, A-3

B

Background knowledge, 57, A-65, A-68
Bacon, Francis, 368, 404
Begging the question. *See* Fallacy, circular reasoning
Bias and fairness, 120–122
Biased sample, 297, 311, 408

Black-white fallacy, 111, 125, A-4
Burden of proof, 85–86, 93, 95–96, 365

C

Categorical generalization, 66
Causal claim. *See* Claim, causal
Causal generalization. *See* Generalization
Causal indicator, 333, 346
Cause, 135
   and correlation, 345
   See also Claim, causal; Contributing cause; Correlation, spurious; Determinate cause; Probable cause
Cause-effect claim. *See* Claim, causal
Chain letter, 39–40
Charity, principle of, 44, 51, 173–174
Circular definition, A-14, A-16
Circular explanation, 186
Circular reasoning, 186, A-4, A-66
Claim
   causal, definition of, 135, 333, 346
   causal, specific and general, 334, 347
   definition of, 17
   general. *See* Generalization
   statistical, 296, 312
Clairvoyance, 392, 396
Clarity in writing, 55–84
Class logic, A-42, A-55. *See also* Logical form, class logic
Coherence
   of correlation, 339
   with a paradigm, 394, 396
Coincidental pattern, 307, 311

Complement of a class, A-45,
A-55
Complementation, A-45
Composition, fallacy of, A-4
Con, 22
Conclusion, 4
implicit, 251–252, 255–257
indicator term for, 14, 16,
245–247, 249, 266
See also Argument, definition
of
Conditional statement,
249–250, 266, A-27,
A-34
Confidence level, 302,
308–309, 311
Confirmation, 341, 369–371,
385
Conjecture, 207. *See also*
Hypothesis
Conjunction, A-24
Connotation, 33, 36, 46–47,
52
Consequent, A-28, A-34
Consistent. *See* Inconsistent
Consistent data. *See*
Confirmation
Consistent explanation, 187
Contaminating the control,
395–396
Context, 56, 64, 73, 79
Contradiction
definition of, 11, 17, 198,
A-34. *See also*
Inconsistent, definition
of logically
logical form of, A-23, A-34
Contradiction in terms, 202,
211–212
Contradictory and contrary, 11,
A-23, A-24, A-34, A-77
Contributing cause, 335, 346
Control group
contaminating the, 395–396
definition of, 340, 346,
395–396
Correlation
versus causation, 345
coefficient, A-80
coherence of, 339
criteria for assessing,
338–339
definition of, 327, 330, 346
lack of, 328, 330, 346–347
negative, 328, 330, 346

nonlinear, A-80
perfect, 328, 347
positive, 328, 330, 347
regularity of, 339
significant, 332–333, 369
spurious, 336–337, 347
strength of, 330, 339, 347
temporal relation of, 339
Counterargument, 92, 96,
154–162
Counterevidence, 211
Counterexample
to an argument, A-51, A-55
to a claim, 205, 211
Creation science, 404
Credibility of sources and
experts, 116–122,
177–185. *See also* Science,
reporting of
Critical thinking, 1, 62

D

Damning with faint praise, 48
Decisive test, 390, 397
Deduce, 225. *See also*
Deductively sound
Deducible prediction, 388–391
Deduction and induction,
227–234, 286
Deductive argument, 228, 234
Deductively sound, 228, 231,
234
Deductively valid, 228, 234,
A-53, A-54
Definition
ambiguous, A-13, A-16
broad, A-13, A-16
circular, A-14, A-16
by example, A-12, A-16
inconsistent, A-14, A-16
kinds of, A-12–A-14
lexical, A-12
narrow, A-13, A-16
operational, 70–74, 82, 363,
A-12, A-16
ostensive, A-12, A-16
persuasive, A-12, A-16
purpose of, A-11–A-12
stipulative, A-12, A-16
vague, A-13, A-16
Degree of belief, 381
Description. *See* Argument,
and description and
explanation

Design of a test. *See* Science,
design of a test
Determinate cause, 335, 346
Deterministic explanation,
382–383
Deterministic law, 383
Digression, 144–149
Dilemma, true and false, 111.
See also Fallacy, false
dilemma
Directly proportional, 328, 346
Disambiguate, 56–57, 73
Disanalogy, 289, 312
Disconfirming evidence. *See*
Confirmation
Disjunction, A-25, A-26
Diversity of factors. *See* Sample,
diversity
Double standard, A-5
Doubletalk, 47, 53

E

Entail, 225
Enumeration, induction by,
286, 312
Equivalent, logically, A-21,
A-22, A-24, A-34
Equivocation, 62–63, 73, A-5
Escape between the horns, 111,
113, 125, A-66
ESP, 392, 397
Essay writing, 141–162
Euler diagram (Venn diagram),
A-45–A-55
Euphemism, 46–47, 51–53
Evaluative term, 75–76
Evidence
in science, 366–367
suppressed, A-10
Evolution, theory of, 83,
402–404, A-65
Exaggeration, 21–22, 40
Experimental group, 340, 347,
396
Experimenter effects, 395, 397
Explanation
alternative hypothesis, 340,
379–381
circular, 186
criteria of good, 185–189
definition of, 135–140,
154–155, 162
fruitful, 384–385, 397

probabilistic, and
    deterministic, 382–383
Extend the analogy, 289, 312

F

Fact
    ambiguity of the term, A-73
    and opinion, 85, A-65
    and value, 34, 156
Fallacious appeal to authority.
    See Fallacy, appeal to
    authority
Fallacy
    ad hoc rescue, 386–388,
        396, A-1
    ad hominem, 107–108, 123,
        125, A-2
    affirming the consequent,
        A-2, A-28, A-29
    anecdotal evidence, A-2
    appeal to authority, 115–122,
        125, 175–185,
        285–286, A-2
    appeal to emotions, 290, A-2
    appeal to ignorance, A-3
    avoiding the issue, 89, 96,
        123, A-3
    avoiding the question, 89,
        96, A-3
    begging the question, A-4
    biased statistics, A-3
    black-white, 111, 125, A-4
    circular reasoning, 186, A-4,
        A-66
    composition, A-4
    definition of, 87, 96, 107,
        123
    denying the antecedent, A-4,
        A-28, A-34
    division, A-4
    double standard, A-5
    equivocation. *See*
        Equivocation
    false dilemma, 107, 110–113,
        125, A-5
    faulty comparison, 113–115,
        125, A-5
    genetic, 122–123, 125, A-5
    guilt by association, A-6
    hasty generalization, 297,
        312
    inconsistency, A-6. *See also*
        Inconsistent

irrelevance, 87, 123
    jumping to conclusions,
        284–285, 312, A-6
    non sequitur, 123–125, A-6
    overemphasizing anecdotal
        evidence, 366, 397, A-2
    oversimplifying, A-7
    past practice, A-10
    positive thinking, A-10
    post hoc, 338, 347, 369,
        A-7, A-80
    quibbling, A-7
    rationalizing, A-7
    red herring, A-7
    scare tactic, A-8
    slippery slope, A-8
    straw man, 107–110, 125,
        A-9
    superstitious thinking, A-9
    suppressed evidence, A-9
    traditional wisdom, A-10
    tu quoque, A-10
    two wrongs make a right,
        A-10
    wishful thinking, A-10
    you too, A-10
False dilemma, 107, 110–113,
    125, A-5
Faulty analogy, 288, 312
Faulty comparison, 113–115,
    125, A-5
Fidelity, principle of, 173–175,
    190
Figurative, A-73
Final argument, 262
Final conclusion, 259, 266
First-order logic, A-53
Follow
    with certainty, 225, 234
    logically, 225
    necessarily, 225
    with probability, 225, 234
Form. *See* Logical form
Formally valid, A-54, A-55
Fruitful explanation, 384–385,
    397

G

General claim. *See*
    Generalization
General fact. *See* Generalization
General term, 65, 73

Generalization, 65–66, 74, 81,
    84, 291, A-64
    categorical, 66
    from a sample, 295–312
    statistical, 66, 74, 298–299
    universal and nonuniversal,
        65–66, 74, 81–82, 206,
        386, 390
Genetic fallacy, 122–123, 125,
    A-5
Grammar, abusing rules of, 43,
    53, A-14
Guilt by association, A-6

H

Half-truth. *See* Selective
    representation
Hasty conclusion, 284–285,
    312, A-6
Hasty generalization, 297, 312
Hedge, 27, 37
Heterogeneous group, 303,
    312
Homogeneous group, 303, 312
Horns of the dilemma, 111,
    113, 125, A-66
Hypothesis
    alternative, 240, 379–381
    definition of, 207, 337, 397,
        A-64

I

Ideology, 112, 183
Implication, A-26–A-30, A-78,
    A-79
    with certainty and with
        probability, 222–234
    See also Conditional
        statement
Implicit argument, 255–258
Implicit conclusion, 251–252,
    255–257
Implicit premise, 252–254,
    255–257, 266
Imply. *See* Implication
Imprecision. *See* Precision
Improbability, 175–181,
    192–196, 339
Improbable prediction, 388
Inconsistent
    and ambiguous, 57–58

Inconsistent (*continued*)
    definition, A-14, A-16
    definition of implication and,
        224, 230
    definition of logically, 10, 16,
        198–199, 211
    fallacy, A-6
    and false, 201
    with presupposition,
        203–205
Independent verification, 364
Indicator, causal, 333, 346
Indicator term, 14, 16,
    245–247, 249, 266
Induction
    by analogy, 286–295
    appeal to a typical example,
        286, 291–292, 311, 313
    argument from authority,
        285–286
    argument to the best
        explanation, 287,
        340–345, 360–396
    from correlation to cause,
        287, 335–346
    and deduction, 227–234,
        286
    by enumeration, 286, 312
    from general to specific, 286,
        310–311
    generalizing from a sample,
        286, 312
    mathematical, 318
    from past to future, 286,
        292–295
Inductive
    argument, 228, 234
    generalization, 286, 312
    strength, 228, 234
    See also Induction
Inference. *See* Argument
Information content, 31, 67
Innuendo, 48–49, 51
Inversely proportional, 328,
    346
IQ test, 72
Irony, 212
Irrational, 372
Issue, 87–88, 96

J

Jumping to conclusions,
    284–285, 312, A-6

K

Knowledge, definition of, 96,
    115–116

L

Law
    deterministic, 383
    scientific, 397
Lexical definition, A-12, A-16
Lie, telling a, 21–22, 37, 75
Loaded language, 33–35, 37,
    40
Logical form
    in class logic, A-42–A-55
    in sentential logic, A-21–A-34
Logical reasoning, 1
Logically analogous, A-22,
    A-34
Logically equivalent, A-21,
    A-22, A-24, A-34

M

Main argument, 259, 266
Main conclusion, 259
Malapropism, 54, A-64
Margin of error, 302,
    308–309, 312
Mathematical induction, 318
Meaning and reference, 59
Method of Venn diagraming,
    A-45–A-55
Mill's methods, 368–370
Miracles, 379
Modus ponens, A-26, A-34
Modus tollens, A-27, A-34
Multiple argument, 258–266
Mutually exclusive, 287

N

Natural language, 60, 77
Necessary condition, A-31,
    A-34
Necessitates, 225
Negation, A-23, A-34
Negative evidence. *See*
    Confirmation
Non sequitur, 123–125, A-6
Nonuniversal generalization,
    65–66, 74, 81–82, 206,
    386, 390

O

Objective description, 33
Objectivity, 184
Occam's Razor, 373
Operational definition, 70–74,
    82, 363, A-12, A-16
Operationalization, 70–74, 82,
    363, A-12, A-16
Opinion and fact, 85, A-64
Ostensive definition, A-12,
    A-16
Overgenerality, 65
Oxymoron. *See* Contradiction
    in terms

P

Paired comparison test, 308
Paradigm, 339, 393–397
Parameter, 306, 312
Paranormal, 392
Parapsychology, 392, 397
Past practice (fallacy), A-10
Pattern. *See* Logical form
Persuasive definition, A-12,
    A-16
Placebo, 395, 397
Polls, 72
Population, 295–296, 312
Position on an issue, 87, 92, 96,
    108–109
Positive evidence. *See*
    Confirmation
Post hoc fallacy, 338, 347, 369,
    A-7, A-80
Precedent (in law), 64, 255,
    A-11
Precision
    and accuracy, 362–363
    definition of, 55–84
    See also Pseudoprecise
Precognition, 381–382, 392,
    397
Predicate logic, A-53
Premise, 223, 234
    implicit, 252–254,
        255–257, 266
    indicator term, 14, 16,
        245–247, 249, 266
    unstated, 252–254,
        255–257, 266
Presupposition, 203–205, 212
Principle of charity, 44, 51,
    173–174

Probabilistic explanation, 382–383
Probable cause, 335, 347
Proof
  definition of, 85, 96, 151, 163, 164, 231, 234, A-65
  mathematical and scientific, 151–154, 234, 365–366, A-80
Propaganda, 36, 386
Pros and cons, 5, 165
Pseudoprecise, 66–71, 74, 363
Pseudoscience, 391–393
Psychokinesis, 397

Q

Quantification theory, A-53
Quantify, 69, 74
Quantity term, 65, 74
Quantum mechanics, 383, A-80
Question-begging. *See* Fallacy, circular reasoning
Quibbling, A-7

R

Random sample, 297–301, 312
Random sampling method, 298, 312
Rational, 372, 397
Rationalizing, A-7
Reason indicator term, 14, 16, 245–247, 249, 266
Rebuttal, 156
Red herring, A-7
Reference and meaning, 59
Refutation, 108, 125, 205–208, 212
Regularity of correlation, 339
Representative sample, 297, 300, 309, 311–312, 370
Reproducible evidence, 366
Rules of discourse, 50

S

Sample
  biased, 297, 311, 408
  biased sampling method, 297, 311
  definition of, 295–296, 312

diversity, 294, 302, 310, 312
generalizing from, 286, 312
random, 297–301, 312
random sampling method, 298, 312
representative, 297, 300, 309, 311–312, 370
size, 301–305
stratified, 303–305, 313
Sarcasm, 51
Satire, 267
Scam, 22, 37
Scare tactic, 24, 37, A-8
Science
  confirmation, 341, 369–371, 385
  control groups, 340
  definition of, 64, 67, 71, 152–154, 207, 286, 338, 360–396, 402
  design of a test in, 307–310, 342, 369, 382–391, 395
  evidence in, 366–367
  paired comparison test, 308
  paradigm of, 339, 393–397
  proof, 151–154, 234, 365–366, A-80
  reporting of, 363–365
  scientific method, 341–342, 356, 370–371
  skepticism in, 153, 366–367
  supernatural and, 175–176, 208, 262–263, 366–367
  superstition and, 371–379, 397, A-9
  theory, 393, 399, A-64, A-65, A-73
Selective representation, 25–28, 36–37
  emphasizing the trivial, 27, 37
  hedge, 27, 37
  stereotype, 26, 37
Self-contradiction, 200–201, 212. *See also* Contradiction in terms
Semantic disagreement, 61, 74, 78, 82–83
Semantics, A-78
  abusing rules of, 43
Sentence and statement, 57, 74
Sentential logic, A-34. *See also* Logical form, sentential

Shift the burden of proof, 85–86, 93, 95–96, 365
Significance of statistics, 305–310, 313
Significant correlation, 332–333, 369
Simple statistical claim, 296–312
Slanting, 33–34
Slippery slope, A-8
Smear tactic, 107
Some, ambiguity of, 58
Sound. *See* Deductively sound
Specific term, 65, 74
Spurious cause. *See* Correlation, spurious
Standard form of an argument, 248, 266
Statement and sentence, 57, 74
Statistic, 306, 308, 312
Statistical claim, 296, 312
Statistical generalization, 66, 74, 298–299
Statistical significance, 305–310, 313
Stereotype, 26, 37
Stipulative definition, A-12, A-16
Stochastic system, A-80
Stratified sample, 303–305, 313
Straw man fallacy, 107–110, 125, A-9
Strength of correlation, 330, 339, 347
Subargument, 285–286
Subconclusion, 259, 266
Substantial disagreement, 61
Sufficient condition, A-31, A-34
Supernatural. *See* Science, supernatural and
Superstition. *See* Science, superstition and
Suppressed evidence, A-9, A-10
Syntax, A-78

T

Telepathy, 118, 152, 392, 397
Temporal relation of a correlation, 339
Test, 397

Test design in science,
307–310, 342, 369,
382–391, 395
Testable claim, 67, 188
Theory, 393, 399, A-64, A-65,
A-73
Traditional wisdom (fallacy),
A-10
Treatment group, 340, 347,
396
Tree diagram, 260–266, A-80
Truth table
conjunction (and), A-24
disjunction (or), A-26
implication (if-then), A-27
negation (not), A-23
Tu quoque, A-10
Typical example. *See* Induction,
appeal to a typical example

U

Uncorrelated. *See* Correlation,
lack of
Universal generalization,
65–66, 74, 81–82, 206,
386, 390
Untestable claim, 67, 188
Utilitarianism, 156–159

V

Vague term, 63–65, 74,
78–79, 84
Vague definition, A-13, A-16
Vague explanation, 188
Value of the variable, 304, 313
Values and facts, 34, 156
Variable
and constant, 304, 313

discrete and continuous,
A-80
value of, 304, 313
Venn diagram, A-45–A-55
Verbal dispute. *See* Semantic
disagreement
Verifiable prediction, 388
Verification, independent, 179,
364

W

Weighing the pros and cons, 5,
165
Wishful thinking, A-10
Writing, essay, 141–162

Credits